D1288164

THE LIFE OF

SIR WILLIAM OSLER

Emery Walker ph. sc.

Father and Son
Oxford, June 1905

THE LIFE OF
SIR WILLIAM OSLER

BY

HARVEY CUSHING

VOL. II

'Let me recall to your minds an incident related of that best of men and wisest of rulers, Antoninus Pius, who, as he lay dying in his home at Lorium in Etruria, summed up the philosophy of life in the watchword, *Aequanimitas*. As for him, about to pass *flammantia moenia mundi* (the flaming ramparts of the world), so for you, fresh from Clotho's spindle, a calm equanimity is the desirable attitude.'

Aequanimitas.

Second Impression

OXFORD

AT THE CLARENDON PRESS

1925

Oxford University Press
London Edinburgh Glasgow Copenhagen
New York Toronto Melbourne Cape Town
Bombay Calcutta Madras Shanghai
Humphrey Milford Publisher to the University

Printed in England

CONTENTS OF VOLUME II

PART III

THE OXFORD PERIOD, 1905–1919

ILLUSTRATIONS IN VOLUME II

LIST OF ABBREVIATIONS IN VOL. II

A.E.F.	American Expeditionary Force.
A.M.A.	,, Medical Association.
A.M.S.	Army Medical Service.
B.A.A.S.	British Association for the Advancement of Science.
B.E.F.	,, Expeditionary Force.
B.M.	,, Museum.
B.M.A.	,, Medical Association.
B.M.J.	,, ,, Journal.
B.O.	Bibliotheca Osleriana.
B.Q.R.	Bodleian Quarterly Record.
C.A.M.C.	Canadian Army Medical Corps.
C.C.S.	Casualty Clearing Station.
C.M.A.	Canadian Medical Association.
C.O.	Commanding Officer.
D.G.M.S.	Director-General of Medical Service.
D.N.B.	Dictionary of National Biography.
E.Y.D.	Egerton Yorrick Davis.
F.A.	Field Ambulance.
F.R.C.P.	Fellow of the Royal College of Physicians.
G.H.Q.	General Head-quarters.
G.S.W.	Gunshot wound.
J.H.H.	Johns Hopkins Hospital.
J.H.U.	,, ,, University.
M.O.	Medical officer.
M.R.C.	,, Research Committee.
M.R.C.P.	Member of Royal College of Physicians.
O.C.	Officer commanding.
O.T.C.	Officers' Training Corps.
P.-G.	Post-graduate.
Q.J.M.	Quarterly Journal of Medicine (London).
R.C.P.	Royal College of Physicians.
R.C.S.	,, ,, ,, Surgeons.
R.F.A.	,, Field Artillery.
R.P.M.	Regius Professor of Medicine.
R.S.M.	Royal Society of Medicine.
R.V.H.	,, Victoria Hospital (Montreal).
S.G.L.	Surgeon-General's Library (Washington).
S.G.O.	,, ,, Office.
T.B.	Tubercle bacillus. Tuberculosis.
V.A.D.	Voluntary Aid Detachment.
V.-C.	Vice-Chancellor.

PART III

THE OXFORD PERIOD

To no member of its body to-day does the profession of medicine owe so great a debt—not that humanity is not also deeply in his debt. Jenner or Pasteur has his first mortgage on mankind, his second on men of medicine. With Osler the order is reversed. He has made no profound or fundamental discovery ; but no one of our day has, in his life, teaching, and example, so radiated, far and near, an inspiration to his fellow physicians. Wide and accurate learning ; enthusiasm in the pursuit of truth ; a character in which elevation and charm are singularly marked and rarely blended ; a personality which wins perforce the love, admiration, and respect of all who come within his influence ; a kindly eye which sees the good in every man and thus stimulates him to better it—these are the main threads woven into the fabric of his beautiful life. Who that meets him, who that reads his essays and addresses, in particular, does not come forth or rise with renewed strength and hope to the service of his fellow man, a better soldier in the medical corps of the Divine army ?

From F. C. Shattuck's 'A vigorous Medical Septuagenarian' (1919).

CHAPTER XXV

1905

LEARNING THE ROPES

No transition could have been greater. From a noisy Baltimore corner and the hurly-burly of the preceding month, to the quiet of an Oxford suburb where they were kept awake by the wood-pigeons which sat on the chimney and cooed; from sweltering Maryland to an English May so cold and raw that it penetrated to one's bones. They promptly built a fire in the dining-room, which greatly shocked the warmly dressed Oxonians who first dropped in on them.

We have had our first Sunday [Mrs. Osler soon writes to her mother] and are feeling very happy and not so strange as you might imagine. We have been wonderfully favoured. . . . We found everything ready—butler at the door, maids in the hall, rooms ready and a delicious dinner. Mrs. Max Müller has been most kind in every way. The house is comfortable. There is a little lawn with broad flower-beds and shrubs and lovely trees. It looks into the Parks, and nothing could be more wonderful than the lilacs, laburnum and hawthorn. It is one huge mass—up and down every street and in every garden, hanging from the roofs. It is really wonderful. We were up early this morning [May 28] and all four attended service at 10 o'clock at Christ Church. . . .

She does not mention that on that first Sunday W. O. took *two* of his late steamer companions to dine in Hall at Christ Church—thereby for the first time breaking a rule of the House he never seemed able to remember. And, after the usual dinner and the formalities of toast-water, taking their napkins the Dons and Osler's guests adjourned to the common-room for fruit and nuts, port, coffee, and snuff; and then for their tobacco to another. And about the time Great Tom tolled they repaired to Osler's rooms, barren except for many boxes which they began to unpack, sitting meanwhile on the floor—a memorable evening: with a full moon outside, the distant sound of chimes, and of undergraduates singing in their rooms.

Two days later the Regius sends this to W. S. Thayer:

. . . Everything is new and strange of course, and it will take months to shake down & feel at home. Evidently the Bodleian will have to be my chief workshop. The clinical facilities are good as far as they go, but there has not been any attempt made to foster practical work. A good deal is going on of interest in the physiological laboratory. I went to London on Monday to the College Club dinner, an old & unique organization among the Fellows of the College going back two hundred years. Very select (only 22 members) & most interesting. . . . The birds are wonderful—such choruses at 4 a.m.—but the doves are a nuisance when they perch on the sill at 3.30 & bill and coo until 5.30.

And the next Friday to another of the deserted 'latchkeyers':

We had a splendid crossing—sun—even sea & skies. We had not a very good set of Doctors aboard—except Klebs, but it was not like the N. A. M. Soc.[1] of last year. We were horribly homesick for two days—the quiet was rather oppressive. Tom said do let us go out & shout. Evidently I shall have to settle down into a quiet academic life but in time I shall like it very much. Thomson the Anat. Prof. is a trump & has been guide & friend. The Radcliffe Inf. is very nice & I shall be able to have a group of the junior students to introduce to the art. I enclose you the notice to the Bodleian meeting, my first official act & I have to appear in cap & gown. The Radcliffe Lib. has some treasures. I have been browsing several afternoons. . . .

His Regius Professorship[2] made him automatically a Curator of Bodley, and the summons from the Vice-Chancellor to this 'first official act', dated from Lincoln College, May 30, 1905, was responded to eagerly. 'A special meeting of the Curators of the Bodleian Library will be holden in the Delegates' room on Friday next the 2nd day of June at 5 o'clock.' 'Will be holden' delighted

[1] North Atlantic Medical Society (cf. Vol. I, p. 647).

[2] Osler's Chair was one of the five Regius Professorships (Divinity, Civil Law, Medicine, Hebrew, and Greek) founded in Oxford by Henry VIII in 1546, to each of which a yearly stipend of £40 was assigned—a large item in Tudor times. James I augmented this income in the case of the 'R.P.M.' by annexing to the Chair in 1617 the Mastership of the alms-house at Ewelme in Oxfordshire. Later (1858) the Aldrichian Professorship of the Practice of Medicine, with a stipend of about £130, was also annexed. His position made him an official Examiner in all examinations for degrees in medicine given by the university.

him always. The same day he wrote to C. P. Howard in a way that did not bode well for 'a quiet academic life':

We are now getting into pretty good shape but it will take months to settle down. You did find out the figures of the abdominal tumours did you not? I would like copies of them all. I am preparing a lecture on the subject, & have an article for Keen's New System of Surgery. I wish you would ask 'Buch' to look over the figures in their [J. W. Williams's] department and let me have anything that is especially striking or useful. Ask Bloodgood if you could not look over his list. . . . Tommy has the sweetest looking tutor about his own age & size. Love to the boys.

It was 'eights' week, Oxford was filled with people, and they were amused and delighted with the Englishness of everything—even to the 'tweeny' among their domestics—and soon 'there are many callers every afternoon, and last evening we had our first Rhodes student'. There was an early beginning, too, of the succession of guests in a home which for the next fifteen years was rarely without one or two at least. Among them were his late colleagues Halsted, Welch, and Kelly; and all four on the 9th had their first sitting with Sargent, who remarked on seeing Osler that he had never before painted a man with an olive-green complexion. 'They all met me at lunch at the Carlton', wrote Mrs. Osler, 'and reported it as intensely interesting. Sargent was worried over posing them and evidently did not think them beauties. W. O. tried to make Dr. Kelly drink a whisky-and-soda, but he said he was just starting on a tour of temperance lectures.' The tempter may have had in mind that Kelly and Halsted were soon to go north of the Tweed to receive honorary fellowships at the quater-centenary celebration of the Royal College of Surgeons of Edinburgh.

On the 13th of June in the beautiful old Divinity School he was duly matriculated as a student. *Quo die comparuit coram me ex Æde Christi Willelmus Osler Gen: Fil. et admonitus est de observandis Statutis hujus Universitatis et in Matriculam Universitatis relatus est.* Then by special decree in Convocation the Oxford degree of M.D. was conferred upon him, for which, like any other student, he paid the customary £30. On the 'testamur' of matriculation he has written: 'I was matriculated to-day before the Vice-Chancellor and was an undergraduate for about half an hour, while the Dean of Ch. Ch. and I waited outside for the convocation to pass on my incorporation as D.M. Then I was taken in and given a seat with the Dons.' But he can be more easily followed by his wife's letters. She wrote on June 19th:

Saturday Willie and I paid a visit to the much-talked-of Almshouse, at Ewelme. It is a most interesting place—fourteen miles from here, two miles back from the Thames. In 1437 the Countess of Suffolk, who was I believe a granddaughter of Chaucer the Poet, gave three manors, the incomes from the farms to support the alms-house and thirteen men occupants—and built a chapel adjoining. We have not discovered when the Regius Professor was made Master, but he has been so a long time. There are rooms for the Master but they have been altered and look painfully modern. The building nearly 500 years old is very picturesque and looks its age. The men have two rooms each and if married can have a wife there or a daughter to care for them. The surgeon who looks after them met us & we visited each member—it was most amusing. We carried tobacco and illustrated papers for each, and they were enchanted. I am sure Willie will make them all fond of him and be good to them. It is a long drive, and we had luncheon at the Inn and tea in our own sitting-room; and got back in time to go out to dine at New College with the Warden and Mrs. Spooner—the name seemed familiar.

There was a garden-party at Blenheim; a dinner for them in town by Mr. Parkin, an old friend and at this time Secretary of the Rhodes Trust; the wedding of Mr. Phipps's daughter and Captain Guest; a reception at Lord Strathcona's on Dominion Day. 'There is hardly a mail without a dinner invitation', she wrote. 'I have now 113 visits to return. Revere and his Dad went off early fishing but they got nothing, not knowing the best place.'

To his niece from W. O. 22 Clarges St., Mayfair, W., Saturday [June 24th].

Dearest Gwen, I am delighted to hear that you have parted with that useless bit of a girl's machinery—the heart. I am sure you have picked a nice good laddie & hope with *Ma*'s approval. Give him my love & blessings & ask him to write me about his prospects &c. Have you known him for long? has he blue eyes? has

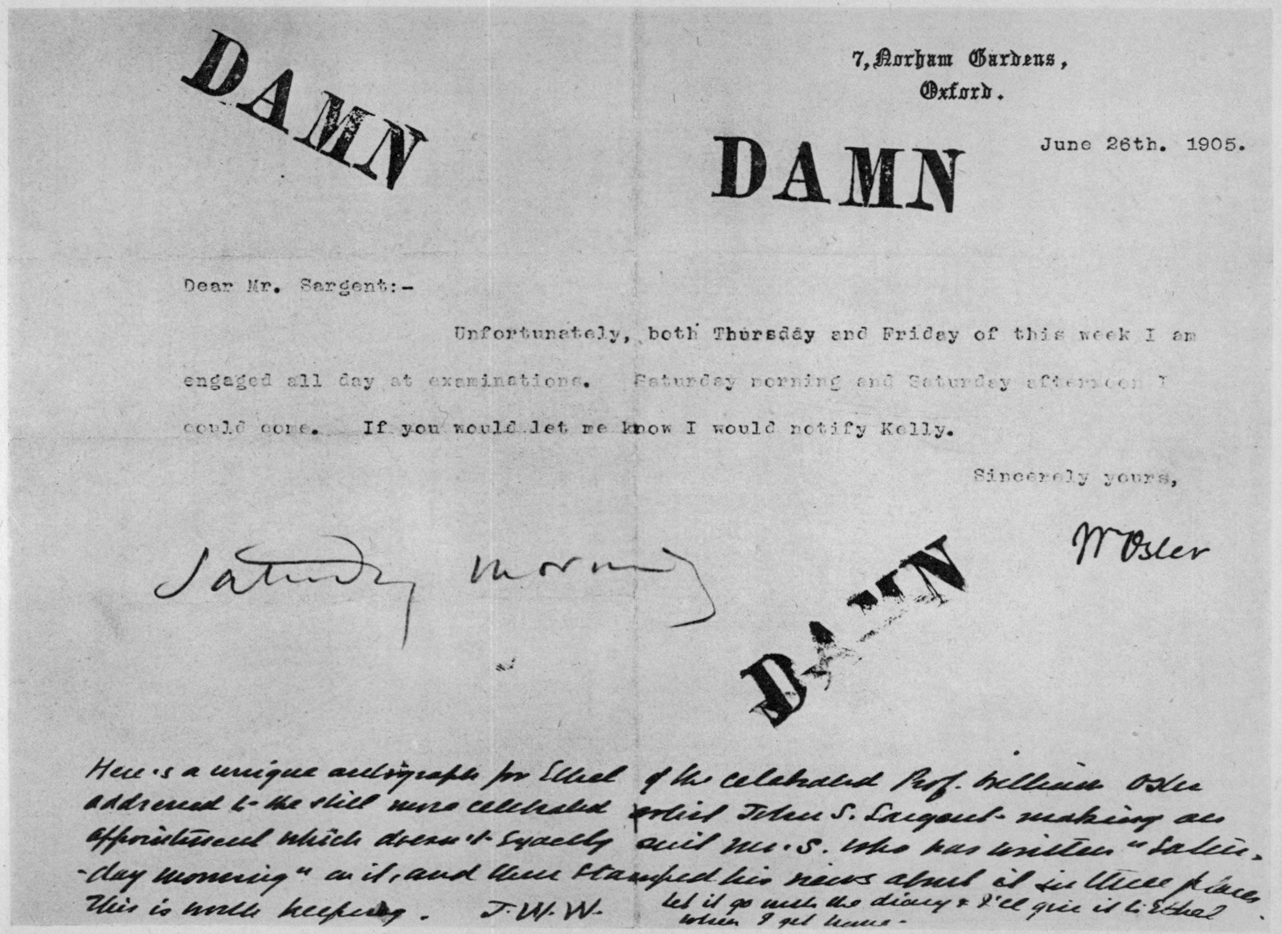

7, Norham Gardens,
Oxford.

DAMN

DAMN

June 26th. 1905.

Dear Mr. Sargent:-

Unfortunately, both Thursday and Friday of this week I am engaged all day at examinations. Saturday morning and Saturday afternoon I could come. If you would let me know I would notify Kelly.

Sincerely yours,

W Osler

Saturday morning

DAMN

Here's a unique autograph for Ethel of the celebrated Prof. William Osler addressed to the still more celebrated artist John S. Sargent—making an appointment which doesn't exactly suit Mr. S. who has written "Saturday morning" on it, and then stamped his views about it in three places. This is worth keeping. J. W. W.

Let it go with the diary & I'll give it to Ethel when I get home.

A MEMENTO OF THREE CELEBRATED MEN

he a mother? there are a thousand questions to be asked. How excited B. will be & Bill. . . . We are very comfortably settled. Tommy likes the life here so much. Rachel & Amy are with us at present & Marjorie Howard. I have just come up to town for the Whitelaw Reid dinner & have no stylo. so excuse pencil. I hope you got some things at Murray's. Ask them to send the bill to Professor Osler, 7 Norham Gardens Oxford. I will send your July allowance next week. Tell me all about your laddie's prospects. Many blessings on you dear. Your affec.

Old Doctor.

Oxford, too, gave dinners galore; one for example with the Vice-Chancellor. 'There were twenty guests', wrote Mrs. Osler, 'and the old dining-room was really enchanting—all the College Heads can use the tankards or bowls belonging to their college and they are wonderfully handsome. Paul Revere would have to take a back seat.' By this time there were two nieces staying with them from Canada, and Revere's little friend Doris from Baltimore, the gift-girl Osler had named in September of 1895, she also of the Guy Fawkes conspiracies, with whom, now, 'Revere has just returned with five good fish and much joy, naturally.' And on the 27th she wrote:

Yesterday afternoon we had a real 1 West Franklin Street time. I was entertaining the president of one of the colleges when in walked Mr. Camac and his wife—Dr. C.'s brother. I have not seen him or her for years. In a moment W. O. came in with five doctors, Examiners for the Medical School—they come from other colleges to examine at Oxford; then some people to call on the Gwyns, through some Canadian friends. I think William the butler thinks we are quite mad. I have already had to pay all the servants extra, as Mrs. M-M is a family of *one*.

The examinations had caused him to break an appointment in town, where a man, whose profanity in all likelihood is entirely confined to a rubber stamp, emphatically cancelled the note announcing this fact; and, shortly after, J. William White of Philadelphia, who dropped into the studio, pilfered the thrice-damned missive from the artist's desk and forwarded it to his wife as a memento of two celebrated men.[1]

[1] Dr. White, according to his biographer Agnes Repplier, had sailed for England June 16th, to consult W. O., who regarded his ill-health as a cardiac

There were many interesting stories told of the painting of this, one of the greatest of modern portrait groups:[1] of the trouble Sargent had at the outset with the grouping; how Welch's head and his 'blue beard' was painted-in practically at the first sitting; how the book he is supposed to be reading is a seventeenth-century edition of Petrarch; how Osler's likeness gave him the greatest trouble and was once scraped out and done again; how Sargent became discouraged over his composition and finally brought from another studio the old Venetian globe, which could not be got through the door until part of the casing was chipped away. Welch had asked Sargent if he might wear his Yale robe, and the painter acquiesced, but when Osler spoke of wearing his red robe of Oxford, Sargent said:

'No, I can't paint you in that. It won't do. I know all about that red. You know, they gave me a degree down there, and I've got one of those robes.' Musingly he went on: 'I've left it on the roof in the rain. I've buried it in the garden. It 's no use. The red is as red as ever. The stuff is too good. It won't fade. Now, if you could get a Dublin degree? The red robes are made of different stuff, and if you wash them they come down to a beautiful pink. Do you think you could get a Dublin degree?—No, I couldn't paint you in that Oxford red! Why, do you know they say that the women who work on the red coats worn by the British soldiers have all sorts of trouble with their eyes,' etc., etc.

Osler paid an early visit to Cambridge, and as Professor Nuttall writes: 'He dropped in upon us like a breeze, made a bee-line for the nursery, and within five minutes by the clock had my daughter Carmelita, aged three, on his back with her arms around his neck, and one boy—aged nine and ten—on each knee. The four were uproarious.' Nuttall, of course, had been one of the early

neurosis. In this fascinating biography she says: 'Never in his correspondence with Dr. White did Sargent consent to sully his pen by writing the word 'damn'. He always stencilled it in large letters, red or black as the fancy seized him. When red, it took on a lurid significance. When black, it had an impressive solemnity, reminding the reader of that clergyman commended by Thomas Fuller, who "could pronounce the word damn with such emphasis as left a doleful echo in the hearer's mind a long time after".'

[1] Cf. *Johns Hopkins University Circular*, 1907.

Johns Hopkins group, with whom intimacy was natural enough; but with Osler intimacy spread rapidly, and among his Cambridge friends, whom he numbered by the score, for none had he a greater attachment than for Sir Clifford Allbutt. Allbutt subsequently wrote of him:[1]

> A quality that made him so fascinating a companion, his teaching so vivid and telling, and his parts in debate so lively, was his wit and humour; the sharpness of the wit tempered by the sweetness of the humour. Indeed, much of his playfulness and whimsical mystification were, in naturalist's phrase, 'a protective colouring' that covered deep sensibilities. In its finesse his conversation resembled that of Henry Sidgwick, not a more or less laboured deliverance of epigrams but a light and nimble play of insight and fun. Much of its piquancy lay in the half concealment of the treasures of the mind.

So it was not merely the skilful doctor, the great scholar, the research student, or often the wise and tactful reformer, but far more the sympathetic friend which made him what he was to others—and as a brother to the Regius of Cambridge. There is a story told, indeed, of their arriving at a reception somewhere in London, and proceeding up the broad stairs arm in arm; they entered the room together, whereupon the irrepressible Osler murmured a word into the ear of the usher, who in a stentorian voice announced 'The Brothers Regii!' who advanced together and made a low, stage bow.

Osler's recovered letters for the time are few and laconic. Thus, a postcard on July 7th from Oxford says: 'See very good lecture on purpura by Bramwell in his "Clinical Studies" July 1st 1905. All well with us. I am getting rested. Outlook for a peaceful life most attractive. Yours W. O.' Yet that same night his wife wrote from London:

> Willie came up early for a sitting—he 's delighted with Sargent's likeness of himself; does not care much for Drs. Kelly or Halsted. He delights in Sargent—finds him most interesting to talk to. . . . We are spending the night at Dr. Pye-Smith's—he 's an old friend of Willie's. They are giving us a dinner, and we sleep here—at least I do. W. O. goes down on the midnight train as he has a university engagement at ten o'clock.

It was hardly an attractive outlook for a peaceful life.

[1] *Nature*, Lond., Jan. 8, 1920, p. 472.

I really have so much to tell you [she writes to her mother on the 18th] I hardly know where to begin. I must tell you about a dinner we went to Friday night. Mr. Boyd, the Principal of Hertford College, is the son of an old friend of Willie's father. He was a rich old man with many sisters—Edmund was named for him—*E. B. O.* The Oslers always stayed with these Boyds [the senders of the missionary boxes to Bond Head] when they came home, and at Chattie's there are pictures of the family. Of course Mr. Boyd found us out, and is most friendly. He is delightful—is a parson, but the merriest kind; paints delightfully and travels everywhere; knows America by heart. He invited us to dine Friday, and Rachel and Amy. He has one of the charming college houses, but not very old. An antique sister (he is not married) came from Birmingham to meet us, and Miss Gaviller of Hamilton (Canada) whom we knew. There was no one else and we had such a delightful time. The college chef carved the dinner—standing behind the table in the corner arrayed in white, with cuffs up to his elbow and a white cap on—it was enchanting. Such fruits and flowers from the college greenhouses, and such port wine. I haven't touched a bit yet but it looks so good. After dinner, Mr. Boyd showed us his treasures and paintings. The maiden sister looked as though her dress had been kept in lavender since 1850. The Gwyns were fascinated by the quaintness of it all. Saturday was boiling hot. We got a good train to Cambridge across country and reached there at four o'clock. The Allbutts are the people who stayed at 1 West Franklin Street when W. O. was ill, and we left them there while we went to the Conynghams'—you remember.

And she adds in a postscript: 'When you get this, W. O. will be at Leicester for the British Medical Association.' The visit to the Allbutts was one of many to his 'brother Regius' of Cambridge, and one may assume that they talked 'medical education in London' which was to be the topic of an important address soon to be given by Allbutt in which he dwelt on education versus instruction; on the functions of a university; on the examination question; and much else, in a manner after Osler's own beliefs. However, he tucked this away in a foot-note:

It is some thirty years since I read a paper to the Leeds Philosophical Society to illustrate what I believe to be the truth—namely, that the greatest achievements of the human mind have nearly always found their consummation not in the earliest but in the riper decades of life. Thus Regius Professors may supplement each other's researches.

By this time Osler had begun to get at some of his unfinished papers: the spirit of work was again stirring, and his brief letters were mostly to his young friends in Baltimore asking for photographs of some old cases to illustrate a paper on aneurysm which he appears to have been finishing.[1] He accepted, too, the post of Thomas Young Lecturer in Medicine at St. George's Hospital, London; this carried the obligation of a series of lectures, and he had decided to talk upon abdominal tumours, which necessitated getting at some of his old Johns Hopkins records. He no longer had a secretary who could take shorthand with facility, and his missives had become more laconic than usual. The British Medical Association met at Leicester the week of July 24th, and in company with C. N. B. Camac, who had been in Oxford for some time engaged in making a book,[2] he attended the meeting, took part in some discussions, read a paper as part of a symposium on meningitis, and presided at the annual luncheon of the Continental Anglo-American Medical Society, a body organized for the purpose of fostering international amities.

To H. V. Ogden from W. O. 7 Norham Gardens, July 28.

How are you getting on? How is Mrs. Ogden? I hope she has had no recurrence of the trouble. We are comfortably settled here in the Max Müller house for a year, & I am beginning to learn the ropes. Fortunately, we have had satisfactory weather, & Mrs. Osler and the small boy have enjoyed it very much. How is our ochronotic friend? I was reminded of him at Leicester yesterday by finding at the hospital some coloured drawings of a most remarkable case in

---

[1] *Lancet*, Lond., Oct. 14, 1905, ii, 1089–96.

[2] 'Counsels and Ideals from the Writings of William Osler.' Boston and N.Y., Houghton, Mifflin & Co., 1905. Before leaving Baltimore, Osler had had considerable difficulty in forestalling the publication of a collection of his medical aphorisms—clinical *obiter dicta* which had fallen from his lips during ward rounds and had been jotted down by his students. This volume of excerpts from his writings which he permitted Camac to publish was something of quite a different order and has doubtless saved from the oblivion of medical journals many of his picturesque turns of thought. He wrote to Camac saying: 'In the teacher I have always valued the message of the life above the message of the pen, but if you think a mosaic of scraps from my addresses &c. would be of any service to young men please do what you wish about it.' A second edition appeared in 1921.

which the pigmentation of the face had been wide-spread & the diagnosis of Addison's disease had been made.

He evidently had visited the local hospital, leaving new-made friends behind him; and as an aftermath of this visit there appeared ere long in the *Lancet* (January 6, 1906) the report by Dr. Frank M. Pope, of the Leicester Infirmary, of 'A Case of Ochronosis', accompanied by a coloured supplement, the author stating that Professor Osler had drawn his attention to the true nature of the condition. There are traces, too, of another characteristic visit he made at this time, in company with Dr. A. G. Gibson, one of his new-found young colleagues at Oxford —a visit to the town of Burnley near Manchester. Of this, Sir James Mackenzie writes: 'One of Osler's great charms was the kindly interest he took in obscure workers in any field of medicine; and in 1905 when I was a general practitioner in a remote town in Lancashire he paid me a visit; and though my work was not that in which he was directly interested, yet his appreciation was in itself a very great encouragement.' Of this visit Osler's companion adds two incidents, non-professional in character: '*one*, that Osler drew up an examination-paper in English for Mackenzie's two little daughters; and, *two*, that he and they made me an "apple-pie bed" that night and put lumps of sugar in my pyjamas.'

To Sir John W. Moore from W. O. July 28.

I have such a press of work already for October that it would be quite impossible to . . . give the opening address at the Meath Hospital [Dublin]. I shall certainly be present on St. Luke's Day. I was afraid too that that might be prevented, as I thought the unveiling of the monument of Sir Thomas Browne had been fixed for that date. I am glad to hear to-day that it is on the 24th. It is really a great regret to me to feel that I could not comply with your request, as both Graves and Stokes are among my special professional 'friends'. Of course I shall be only too delighted to stay with you.

Needless to say, Graves and Stokes (Bovell's teacher) were the two great physicians who had brought the Irish school into prominence sixty years earlier; but the letter shows that Osler was becoming involved, for when possible he always responded favourably to such invitations. Though Sir John persisted, Osler finally begged off on the ground of his other engagements, adding: 'Mentally, too, I am rather desiccated, having had a most trying year'—which was probably the real reason, and which may account for his few recovered letters. Those from his wife, therefore, must continue the story. She wrote on July 31st:

Willie met Mr. Abbey the artist at Sargent's in London, and the other day I had a note from Mrs. Abbey asking us to come to Fairford about twenty miles from here for a cricket match and tea at their place, and to bring friends. We started out at 12.30; took Mrs. Eckstein and Mrs. Taft, Drs. Parsons and Camac; lunched at an inn; went to see a lovely old church; and reached the Abbeys' at 3.30. . . . We had a most enchanting afternoon and only reached home for dinner at 8.30. The Abbeys have a dear old place, and he an enormous studio. They lived there all the time he was doing the Grail pictures for the Boston Library. You know he is an American—born in Philadelphia, and Mrs. A. in New York. We saw the huge studies he is doing for the dome of the State House at Harrisburg. The cricket was between the Artist Club and some Fairford men. The eleven Artists stay all the week at the Abbeys'.

Other outings followed. Under most favourable auspices, on a palatial yacht, they attended the Cowes regatta—a particularly gala week, with sixty battleships, French and British, in line—a sight which must have given comfort to those who may have listened a few days before, at the Mansion House, to Lord Roberts's speech of warning against the lethargy of England and her unpreparedness for war. But of all this he makes scant mention in the following letter to Weir Mitchell:

We are here for a week with Mr. W. Johnston on his yacht. — S. Y. *Kethailes*, R. M. Y. C., Cowes, Aug. 6th.

Dear Dr Mitchell, We have not been two months in Oxford & I send you my impressions. We have had a very cordial welcome, and the round of dinners & teas became rather irksome, but in it all there was a heartiness & sincerity very pleasing to strangers. . . . The weather has been glorious & we have enjoyed the birds & flowers in our little garden. Early in June there were thirty different birds in song in the park near us. At 4 a m the chorus hymeneal began. I had forgotten how wonderful they were in the spring. By the middle of June, most of them had ceased to sing & now the blackbirds, robins & thrushes are quiet. We are taking much pleasure in the river & go out nearly every afternoon usually with the tea basket. The boy has a tutor who gives him lessons in the morning & is teaching him the river in the afternoon. He is a crazy fisherman & thinks of nothing but his rod & reels and lines. He has caught about eight of the fish Izaak Walton describes—roach, tench, &c.[1] It is a very good life for him and he is very happy with one or two young friends. Mrs. Osler seems happy also which delights me of course. She will miss many things & the life will not be too quiet. We have had a succession of visitors and many chance callers.

I have been resting as much as possible & trying to pick up the medical threads—not an easy task, as they are all twisted and knotted. The Departments of Physiology, Anatomy & Pathology make up the Medical School—separate Laboratories, all fairly active. There is also a small Pharmacological laboratory. The men go to London for the 4th & 5th years. The Radcliffe Infirmary has 150 beds and I have arranged with the Staff & Committee to do what teaching I like—a junior class of 15 or 20 men for elementary work. The Radcliffe Library is very good—chiefly medical and scientific. I am one of the curators of the Bodleian, and am beginning to search out its treasures. I hope to take great pleasure in my connection with Christ Church of which I have been elected 'a Student', or Fellow. . . . Thanks for your letter from the woods. What a remarkable dream! The memories of your great kindness linger sweetly, and I shall always feel that it was the most fortunate day of my life when I met you & Mrs. Mitchell in London. How much it has meant to me! . . .

August 15th found them at Inverness about to leave by motor for Beaufort Castle for a week with the Phipps'—'Revere very much excited over the Highlands, brilliant with heather, but still more over promising streams.' They visited Glendae, Lord Lovat's shooting-lodge—an incomparable spot—where Revere and his Dad fished with ill luck, while the others shot grouse with far better. Among the guests were Mr. and Mrs. Yates Thompson—she a 'Smith-Elder'—with whom the Oslers struck up an enduring friendship, which is the reason why the *Dictionary of National Biography* finally came to the Clarendon Press; but this is another story.[2] On the day of departure, word went to Dr. Camac from Mrs. Osler:

We are leaving here this afternoon for Skye. Dr. Osler will write

[1] This, it may be mentioned, was Osler's method of inoculating his son with a taste for literature. Revere's collection of books began with Waltoniana.

[2] The 'D.N.B.', begun by the munificence of George Smith, launched

you from there. We have had a most glorious week—only occasional showers. Revere has fished to his heart's content but with not much luck. Dr. Osler is looking so brown and robust; it has been a splendid outing for him. We had one day on Loch Ness with wonderful views. We have motored in all directions—there have only been a few guests in the house and we have had much independence, which you know I consider real hospitality.

Later in the day Revere finally caught a record pike with which he triumphantly returned, saying: 'Really Muz, I thought I should die of nervous perspiration.' Then to Loch Alsh through the glorious scenery of the Highland Railway which ten years later came to be transported to France at a time when rails were more needed there than in North Britain.

To F. C. Shattuck from W. O. The Highland Railway Station Hotel, Kyle of Loch Alsh, 21st.

Thank you so much for your kind letter. I have not yet seen my lay sermon ['Unity, Peace and Concord'] in print. It was written rather hurriedly but from the heart as I have always felt deeply the miserable misunderstandings which are so common in the profession. I suppose a good hater has his joys but he must have a good many uneasy moments which a man of my temperament escapes. The migration so far has been a success. . . . I shall certainly try and be at the A M A in June if the date does not clash with our examinations, which seems to be the most important part of the work of the Regius Professors. Everything must come thro their hands—a most antique arrangement. Greet George Cheyne with my congratulations. How satisfactory that he did so well. We are touring the land of lakes—Izaak Walton Jr (Revere) is learning the gentle art & has had good sport at pike & trout. Ever yours W. O. Love to the G. C's & greetings to Mrs Shattuck & the girls.

Finding the hotel uncomfortable and the fishing bad

in 1882, was completed in 1901. In the set presented to Osler by his friends in Baltimore two years later (cf. I, p. 609) is inserted a letter of April 24, 1917, from Mrs. Thompson to Sir William, stating that her sister had satisfactorily concluded the arrangements for transferring the business of Smith, Elder & Co. to Mr. John Murray, so that the family was now able to consider the fate of the 'D.N.B.' It goes on to say: 'You have always taken so kindly an interest in the matter that I should like to tell you we are all agreed to offer the Dictionary to the University of Oxford. . . . My brothers and sisters share the feeling that this course would have satisfied my father's wishes for his latest and most cherished undertaking. . . . I thought I should like to let you know first of all.'

except for conger eels, they finally crossed with their trunks in a rowboat to Kyleakin, Skye, a quiet little place with houses clustered about a green, where a week was passed at the King's Arms, an old-fashioned whitewashed hotel. There the three played, fished, and walked on the moors, where one morning they encountered a young man botanizing, for whom this was a memorable day. He proved to be the son of the schoolmaster at Kyleakin, and when Osler found that he was an Edinburgh medical student he promptly gathered him in. Dr. Gunn, now a distinguished ophthalmologist, recalls :

I had not then begun the study of clinical medicine, but the eminence of Osler in medicine was not lost on me. I had read some of his addresses and they had served greatly to exalt, in my eyes, my profession and its great ones. I readily conceded that position to Osler, and if further explanation be needed as to why I succumbed so completely to his undoubted charm, it should be remembered that the lumen siccum of science may become almost an object of adoration, some share of which falls to the priesthood, and that I was of a race that does not consider itself superior to a wholesome hero-worship.

The following week I regard as a remarkable period of my life. I saw Osler daily. He was a Celt (Cornish) and I was a Celt (Scottish) and we were in a land where ancient customs die hard and where Gaelic is still the mother tongue. A common theme of conversation was the Celtic character. Osler loved to hear stories of the intense love of learning of the Gael, his natural aptitude for speculation and for poetic expression. But there was hardly anything, I think, that we did not speak of—Mendelism, Herbert Spencer, antiquities, religion, literature, are a few of the things I can recall. I am confounded now when I think of the marvellous patience with which he listened to my ideas—crude and often extreme—but I suppose he recognized the enthusiasm inseparable from youth in process of education and his wise and kindly tolerance served as a corrective and a guide. Needless to say, we talked much of medicine and I received much sage advice and wise information, all the more impressive in that it was so little academic. Afterwards, we corresponded frequently, and I have now no doubt he suffered a great deal from being made my unprotesting confidant in several successive enthusiasms. He never forgot me : he was always kindly and humorous ; always interested, always wise, and also always great.

The last week of August found them with the Howards

on the lonely Island of Colonsay in the Lesser Hebrides at the entrance to the Firth of Lorne. To reach there they had left Kyleakin and taken the picturesque passage through the Sounds of Sleat and Mull to Oban, where they were met by Strathcona's yacht and taken to the island. Palmer Howard's eldest son Jared, the elder half-brother of Osler's three particular wards, and in whose company in 1884 he had passed one of his brain-dusting summers among the continental clinics, had long before married Strathcona's only daughter. The island, a unique possession, had recently come into Strathcona's hands, and, as Mrs. Osler wrote to her mother—

If you look at the map you will see how far west it is, and the broad sweep of the Atlantic before us. Such an interesting place; the late owner was Sir John McNeill whose people had owned the island for generations. He was equerry to the Queen for twenty-five years and went to Canada with the Lornes and was a great friend of Lord Strathcona. I fancy Lord S. has helped him financially for years, for when he died last year the Island fell to Lord S. It is about eight miles long and three wide, and all rocks and heather except a few acres of fine trees in which the quaint old house is nestled. It looks like a Virginian house, with wings on either side. The Gulf Stream flows on either side of the island so that vegetation is like the south of England—high hedges of fuchsia, climbing roses, and lemon-verbena trees above the window-tops; figs, peaches and plums ripening on walls in the open. Everything in the house came to Lord S., even the silver. He gave the family all presents that were here from Royalty, and all the portraits, but everything else is left the same; so all the Howards did was to walk in—even cook and housekeeper here. Lord Strathcona has his big castle at Glencoe in the Highlands, and as much of the responsibility falls on Mrs. Howard she is enjoying the freedom here tremendously.

At Colonsay there was more fishing; the partly fossilized prow of an old Viking ship was discovered; and an excursion was made to see an early Christian cross and the ruins of an ancient monastery on the adjacent island of Oronsay which looked three thousand miles across an open ocean to where Baron Komura and M. Witte were struggling over the final terms of a treaty of peace. From Colonsay House, Osler wrote to Dr. Thayer:

I have had a quiet summer, getting rested. I was very much used up after arriving—just squeezed dry—but I am now feeling in good form. Things look hopeful at the Radcliffe—there are several nice young fellows who are willing and anxious to work & I think there will be material enough to keep us going. Camac was with us off & on for several weeks. Ike has fished all the good pools on the Cher & at Beaufort caught his first big fish—a huge pike. Welch we hope to see again on his way from the Continent. The picture bids fair to be a success. Welch is very good. I do not like Halsted or Kelly, & H. says mine is awful. I think that when hung & looked at from a distance it will be a good representation. We sail about Dec. 10th—to spend Xmas in Boston & I hope to spend Jan with you all at the Hopkins. Do set to work at the heart material, so as to have it all ready for the articles. I forget in which volume you come, 3rd I think.

They were back in Oxford on September 8th, and a few days later Mrs. Osler wrote:

We have been in London all day, and are back with Doris Reid to stay until Friday. After writing yesterday I went to Christ Church with Willie to arrange about his rooms. It is the custom for a student or fellow to have rooms in the college he is associated with. W. O. has a sitting-room and wee bedroom; he can put up any man friend there any time he wants. . . . He can have some of his books there, and has wonderful plans of what he will do down there. He also has rooms in the Museum, where other books are to be stowed, so he will gradually get all his books here. As we were driving home we discovered Dr. and Mrs. Sinkler and the two girls from Philadelphia. They came in the afternoon and had tea. Each day since we came home some Americans have been here. . . .

To L. F. Barker from W. O. 7 Norham Gardens, 15th.

Just a line to welcome you to the J. H. H.! What a happy life you will have there! It is a unique position. You will be very much at home with the young fellows & the students. Keep an eye on the societies and begin to report & show cases early—even the simpler ones. Do not feel over-modest about your clinical knowledge,—'tis much greater than you appreciate. I hope to spend the month of Jan. *quietly* at the Hospital with you all. I wish to look over some of the typhoid material. I know you will find Thayer congenial. 'Tis a rather hard place for him, so encourage him. Cole & Boggs, Howard & Emerson are jewels. Love to your wife & to Johnnie (2nd). We have had a very nice holiday in Scotland. I am well rested & am beginning to feel at home here. There will be enough clinical material to keep the rust away. Yours ever,

W. O.

To J. William White (at Fairford, Glouc.) Saturday.

Dear White, Please tell Mrs. Abbey that I had a most interesting visit to Witney. I found mine host of the Fleece a very good fellow, who told me all the gossip of the town & showed me the way to Coggs Church. I attended Vespers—ask Mrs. White what that word means—and made one Theophilus among six Dorcases—one of whom, dear soul! near whom I sat discreetly skipped from verse 5 to verse 19 of the CIX Psalm—from which you got your favourite execrations! I met my nephew at 6^{19} full of enthusiasm over his visit. Do thank Abbey for his kindness to him. I will see you tomorrow evening.

To James R. Chadwick. Sept. 22.

Thank you so much for the memoir of your father & for the address on Cremation. Did I ever get for the Library a copy of Ward's Diary? I have rather an idea that I did. It is a wonderful old book. If you have not a copy, please send me word at once and I will send it to you. It is a book which has become exceedingly rare because of the Shakespeare references. Sincerely yours, &c.

This letter never reached his old friend, who two days later met his death from an accident; and on hearing of this Osler not only sent off the touching obituary which appeared (unsigned) in the *Lancet*, but wrote to F. C. Shattuck: 'How sad about Jim Chadwick's death! Why did we not have the portrait done last winter? Not too late now. His friend Lockwood would do a good one. Let us arrange it. It should be in the Library to which he devoted so much time and which he loved so dearly.'

Meanwhile, Mrs. Revere of Canton, Mass., is told by her daughter that she would laugh could she see her grandson established in an English school, where he particularly enjoys football. 'I hope he does well with his books but can't expect too much—he is so good and obedient and such a happy soul that I shall try to keep from worrying about his lack of interest in books and pray that it may come'—and it did. Also that people were at work getting 'the Master's rooms in order at Ewelme so we can stay there when we want to'; that the Christ Church rooms were being furnished as well as those at the Museum, 'where he attends to all university matters—no idleness about here, I assure you.' And on September 26th she writes: 'W. O. and Willie F[rancis] are at Fairford for lunch with the Abbeys to meet the J. William Whites of Philadelphia, and I've had a great time clearing out the rooms at the Museum, which were packed full of things belonging to the Regius Professors for years back—old bottles and old rags galore.' On the following day the Regius himself sends a postcard to Dr. Thayer, which, though brief, tells the essentials :

27th.

Delighted with your Cotton Mather—just received to-day. I hope you have had a good summer. We had a splendid month in Scotland. We are just off to Paris for the T. B. [Tuberculosis] Congress. Yours W. O.

The congress was a great success. Paris always stages these things well. The congressists were welcomed at the Hôtel de Ville, that incomparable municipal building ; the meetings were held in the Grand Palais ; there was a banquet and reception at the Élysée by Émile Loubet ; also a gala performance at the Châtelet Theatre, where among other items, *Le Médecin malgré lui* was presented ; and much else.

These international congresses seemed fated to be the occasion of some startling announcement by an eminent bacteriologist, as was true of the preceding Congress of 1901, when Koch proclaimed the non-transmissibility of bovine tuberculosis. This one was no exception, for Emil von Behring, the discoverer of the antitoxin treatment of diphtheria, announced that he had discovered a new remedy for tuberculosis : 'buvovaccine', which was both prophylactic and curative. He made the curious statement that it was long before his antidiphtherin had been fully accepted, and this new remedy might take a still longer time to receive general recognition. It has.

But there was another and pleasanter incident of this congress worth remembering—one which also was the source of editorials in the press, though not until after it had happened. Some twenty of the American members had gathered together on Thursday, October 5th, for a luncheon, and, acting on an inspiration, Osler suggested that they make a pilgrimage to Louis's grave and place a wreath upon it. But as no one, not even the French physicians who were consulted, had any idea where Louis was buried, it was some time before the site of the forgotten tomb of the *famille Louis*, in which Louis, his wife, and son rest, in the cemetery of Montparnasse, was disclosed. There the band of sixteen Americans repaired, by one of whom, subsequently, the story was most feelingly told.[1] Crowded in the narrow room of the door-keeper's house, they waited for an autumnal downpour to cease, while a few rain-soaked *gendarmes* peeped through the window wondering what these foreign-looking gentlemen could intend. The shower ceased, and as the band of intimate friends, bound together by a great common interest, stopped at the door of the mausoleum which held Louis's remains, Osler placed a wreath of autumn leaves on the steps and told in a few words the simple story of Louis's life which has no parallel in the profession; of the sad death of his son at the age of eighteen from tuberculosis; of his own death from the same disease at the age of eighty-five; of his special claims to remembrance—not so much his attempt to introduce mathematical accuracy into the study of disease, as his higher claim to have created the American school of clinical medicine through his pupils. After paying this tribute of deep solemnity and meaning to the great French master, back they went silently to their work at the congress. No possible act could have touched French sentiment more deeply.

'Willie has so many things going on. The new edition of the Text-book is just out and No. 100,000 has been given to Revere.[2] Isn't that a splendid sale.' So wrote Mrs. Osler from Oxford on October 9th; and three days later: 'W. O. has gone to town to-day to lecture and have a dinner given him.' As he had written to Sir John Moore, October was to be a full month, and two of 'the things that were going on' related to that *amplissimus vir*, his beloved Sir Thomas Browne, the tercentenary of whose birth fell on the 19th.

Osler had been asked by the students of Guy's Hospital to speak before their society—the same society indeed, which according to tradition had been the first, a century before, to ask Jenner to give a public pronouncement

[1] A. C. Klebs, 'Osler at the Tomb of Louis.' *Journal of the American Medical Association*, 1906, xlvi. 1716.

[2] This volume is in the E. R. Osler Collection of the Tudor and Stuart Club of Johns Hopkins University.

regarding vaccination. Originally a faculty society, it now bore the unusual name of Guy's Hospital Pupils' Physical Society, and as a matter of fact its foundation in 1772 made it the oldest London medical society of continuous existence. Accordingly, on the evening of October 12th in the Physiological Theatre of the famous old hospital across London Bridge, Osler opened the winter session with the address which first brought him prominently before the British public, and which showed them the kind of professor Oxford had secured.[1] There was a certain fitness, he said, in his introduction to London there, seeing that he professed himself a Guy's man, if not by birth at least by adoption and grace, as, while yet in his pupilage he had sat at the feet of a Guy's man [Bovell] and had received unto himself the traditions of the school.

The 'Religio Medici' was of course his title, and some fragments of the address, of a biographical character, have previously been quoted. He gave an interesting account of 'the man', who in his wanderings 'pierced beneath the shell of nationalism into the hearts of the people, feeling at home everywhere and in every clime'; of his home life in Norwich, his children and grandchildren. He passed on to 'the book', his own collection of the fifty-five editions being nearly complete. With them before him on a table he gave in his usual manner a bio-bibliography, repeating, for example, the story of the 'Observations' of Digby, 'who holds the record for reading in bed', adding: 'This little booklet of Sir Kenelm has floated down the stream of literature, reappearing at intervals attached to the editions of the "Religio", while his weightier tomes are deep in the ooze at the bottom.' His third section of the address was an 'appreciation' of the man, whom Lowell called 'our most imaginative mind since Shakespeare', and who was at the same time naturalist, philosopher, scholar, physician, and moralist. And he closed with this counsel—born of his own experience—to his young hearers:

For the student of medicine the writings of Sir Thomas Browne

---

[1] 'Professor Osler and the "Physical Pupils".' Cf. *Pall Mall Gazette*, Oct. 13, 1905, p. 8.

have a very positive value. The charm of high thoughts clad in beautiful language may win some readers to a love of good literature; but beyond this there is a still greater advantage. Like the 'Thoughts of Marcus Aurelius' and the 'Enchiridion' of Epictetus, the 'Religio' is full of counsels of perfection which appeal to the mind of youth, still plastic and unhardened by contact with the world. Carefully studied, from such books come subtle influences which give stability to character and help to give a man a sane outlook on the complex problems of life. Sealed early of this tribe of authors, a student takes with him, as *compagnons de voyage*, lifelong friends whose thoughts become his thoughts and whose ways become his ways. Mastery of self, conscientious devotion to duty, deep human interest in human beings—these best of all lessons you must learn now or never—and these are some of the lessons which may be gleaned from the life and from the writings of Sir Thomas Browne.

Osler had come to have a no less 'sane outlook on the complex problems of life' than his famous seventeenth-century prototype, and it is not surprising to find him the next day distributing prizes to the students of a school of an altogether different sort—of the Royal Dental Hospital of London: a school which had only 33 entering students, whereas the country needed thousands. There can be no doubt of Osler's willingness to comply with the invitation. One of the sessions of the recent Leicester meeting of the British Medical Association had been given over to a discussion by Victor Horsley and others on maladies supposedly of dental origin—neuralgias for the most part. But there were more important things than this relating to the teeth. He had always been distressed and shocked by the habitual neglect of their teeth by the English people as a nation, and though a new-comer, at the risk of giving offence, he told some plain truths to the young men before him whose duty it was 'to convert the enormous percentage of bolters and make chewers of them'; and to 'preach the gospel of cleanliness—cleanliness of the mouth, of the teeth, of the throat' for reasons of personal hygiene as well as comeliness. And there were sensible remarks about the routine inspection of the mouth and teeth of school-children, all of which later on was made the subject of a lengthy editorial by the *Lancet*, which admitted that 'in the land upon which he has so recently turned his back, the individual citizen pays more attention to the teeth than in this country. The question, as Professor Osler remarks, is a national one, and he made the remarkable statement that if he were asked to say whether more physical deterioration was produced by alcohol or by defective teeth he should unhesitatingly say "defective teeth".' These were days, be it said, long before arthritis and a score of other maladies were even under suspicion of being due to dental disorders.

Dr. Osler is just off to Norwich for the unveiling of Sir Thomas Browne's statue [writes Mrs. Osler on the 17th to Thomas McCrae]. I am sending the Pall Mall Gazette with the account of his lecture at Guy's. Your friend Dr. Shadwell 'of Tortoise Fame' has been elected Provost at Oriel. We thought we could get his house which is fascinating inside and was once the priory of St. Mary's, and Dr. Shadwell claims that Erasmus lived there; but he declines to leave until they build him a decent house at Oriel.

The ceremonies at Norwich [1] opened with a meeting on the 19th in the museum of the local hospital 'to express to Professor Osler the thanks of the institution for the handsome casket and pedestal for the reception of the skull of Sir Thomas Browne'.[2] Later on, the statue was unveiled by Lord Avebury, and there were appropriate addresses followed by a luncheon at Blackfriars' Hall, Sir Peter Eade presiding, when there were many toasts, to one of which Osler's reply is thus in part recorded:

There are three lessons to be gathered from the life of Sir Thomas Browne, all of them of value to us to-day. First, we see in him a man who had an ideal education. He was thoroughly versed in the classics; he lived abroad for two years, and thereby learned the hardest lesson in life, for he became denationalized as far as his intellect and his human sympathies were concerned. All places made for him but one country, and he was in England everywhere.

---

[1] Fully reported in the *British Medical Journal* for October 28th. There was published for the occasion a souvenir volume by Charles Williams of Norwich, who also prepared a complete bibliography of the 'Religio'.

[2] To Osler, who appreciated no less than did Thomas Browne himself 'the tragical abominations escaped in burning burials', nothing would have given greater satisfaction than the knowledge that the skull which 'had been knaved out of its grave' was one day to be re-interred. The re-burial, with every mark of reverence, took place at St. Peter Mancroft, on July 4th, 1922. Cf. 'Sir Thomas Browne: His Skull, Portraits and Ancestry,' by M. S. Tildesley, *Biometrika*, vol. xv, and privately reprinted, Camb., 1923.

The second important lesson we may gain is that he presents a remarkable example in the medical profession of a man who mingled the waters of science with the oil of faith. I know of no one in history who believed so implicitly and so simply in the Christian religion, and yet it is evident from his writings that he had moments of ardent scepticism. One might have wished he had been a little less credulous, and I was glad to hear Lord Avebury defend him so warmly from the charge brought against him in regard to the trial of the witches; but it must be remembered that a man must be judged by his day, by his generation, and by his contemporaries. The third lesson to be drawn is that the perfect life may be led in a very simple, quiet way. Norwich in those days was provincial and small, and yet here is a man who lived perfectly, and who lived his life successfully, not only doing good, but also being able through his industry to carry out those extensive literary works which are now our pride and our joy. . . .

And he went on, as would be expected of him, to call to his hearers' minds the work of Mr. S. Wilkins, a Norwich man, who re-introduced Sir Thomas Browne to this generation; and that also of Dr. Greenhill. Then, in the evening there were services in the ancient church of St. Peter Mancroft—St. Peter in the Pasture, *Magna Crofta castelli*—with a sermon by the Master of Pembroke, representing Sir Thomas's old college, who at the close read, as his blessing, Browne's 'Evening Hymn'.

To W. S. Thayer from W. O. 7 Norham Gardens, Oct. 26.

I was just going to write to you this week when your nice long letter came. Rolleston is stirring us up about the revision of the malaria in Allbutt's 'System'. It is an awful nuisance, but it has got to be attacked. I am so glad to hear that you will have it ready by the first of January. . . . The time is getting close for us to sail, December 16th. I am looking forward to a month spent quietly in the hospital, with the greatest pleasure. I wish you could have seen me yesterday—my first official duties, a group of fifteen at the Radcliffe, beginning on the old lines. I think there will be material enough to make a satisfactory clinical class. Mrs. Osler and Tommy are very well. . . .

He was indeed 'beginning on the old lines'. Some one else had to say that the Sunday before 'we had an invasion of callers—about thirty young men—among them several Rhodes scholars—quite like Baltimore'. His letter to Thayer fails to say that two days before he had read a paper before the Leamington Medical Society on a topic [1] not often discussed by the physician; nor did he say that he was just leaving for Bristol, where that same afternoon at University College as guest of the medical faculty he distributed prizes and certificates and made an address—a good one, be it said—on the dual aspects of the student's life; and stayed for their dinner afterwards, to the students' great gratification. But his footsteps must not be dogged too faithfully. By this time his rooms in 'the House' had been fitted up, as the following double note to C. P. Howard written from there the next evening indicates—the first from his wife:

Christ Church, Sunday, Oct. 29.

Dear Campbell, Doccie O's new old desk is being used for the first time to send a line to you. Marjorie is with me. We have just come from the service in the Cathedral and 'Reggie' [2] has gone into his own stall arrayed in surplice and hood and winking at M. and me as he came down the aisle. I wish you could see the rooms—they are really charming and it has been great fun getting them in order. We are now looking forward to showing you all the pleasures of Oxford and particularly your godson—who is rapidly becoming an English boy with an accent. . . .

Dear Campbell, These old fools have put me in a surplice & I had to go to chapel, but I wished I had been in the pulpit instead of the Regius Prof. of Divinity—who is a dry old stick. Yours, W. O.

Perhaps this dryness accounts in a measure for the fact that he soon gave up the Cathedral for the Infirmary on Sunday mornings, and gave there each week his regular weekly consultation-clinic for visiting physicians from the countryside who preferred practice to prayer as a method of doing good in the world. He had a pleasant surprise the following day, the nature of which is explained in a letter promptly sent to his 'dear students':

Last evening I was told that a box had arrived from America, and in a few minutes there was brought in a handsome quarto volume with an inscription on the back—'Collected Papers of the Graduates of the Johns Hopkins Medical School.' Naturally, I was delighted, and in a few minutes was deep in the contents of the volume, filled

[1] 'Medical Aspects of Carcinoma of the Breast.' *British Medical Journal*, 1906, i. 1–4.

[2] This flippant nickname had been given the Regius by one of his young friends.

with gratitude that you had so kindly remembered me. When, a few moments later, the man came in and asked if he should bring the others, I looked more carefully at the back and found that I was reading only one of a series of twelve superbly bound quarto volumes . . . a striking testimony to the success of an undertaking, which we all feel has already passed the experimental stage. . . .

And he went on to give them, the students, the chief credit for what had been accomplished in Baltimore and what could be reduplicated in other places animated with a similar spirit of scientific research, reminding them at the same time to 'maintain an incessant watchfulness lest complacency beget indifference, or lest local interests should be permitted to narrow the influence of a trust which exists for the good of the whole country'. These thoughts must have led him to write a few days later to the man who had most to do with the undertaking before it passed from its experimental stage:

To Daniel C. Gilman from W. O. Nov. 5th.

I am settling into my new life very comfortably. We are in Mrs. Max Müller's house for the winter & have not yet found a permanent home. Houses are very scarce. I have very nice official rooms at the Museum, with two laboratory rooms attached, but I shall do all my work at the Radcliffe Infirmary. I have a class of 15 men and I am drilling them in the elementary work. There are 150 beds & a large out-patient department. I have been appointed an active consultant with a free range of all cases for teaching purposes—this at the request of the staff. So that I have ample material, & shall hold a weekly consultation for outside physicians. The local Doctors are very pleasant & friendly. I have rooms at Christ Church of which I am a 'student' & a member of the governing body with a special stall in the Cathedral &c with the privilege of reading the lessons, if I like! The men at 'The House' (as Ch. Ch. is called) are very nice & I shall enjoy my connection with it greatly. My quarters are in the old [Library] building & I picture to myself that Burton or Locke may have inhabited them. I have been elected on the Hebdomadal Council, the governing body, 21 in number, of the University. I have only been at two meetings—most interesting & I shall get an insight into the workings of the complicated academical machinery. Officially I am a Curator of the Bodleian & have free range of the place. I have scarcely begun my excursions into highways & by-ways. Mrs Osler and the boy enjoy the life here so much. He is at school & is very happy. We sail Dec. 16th. I hope to spend four weeks at the Hospital playing about with the boys & keeping in touch with the work. Give Mrs Gilman my love. Greet Remsen & Gildersleeve & Ames. Welch I have written to several times.

It was a mistaken notion on the part of his new colleagues that it would take Osler a long time to shake down among them. He adapted himself from the first, as though born an Oxonian, and took the keenest interest in every detail of the new life, even to the work of the small committees. The Hebdomadal board, when originally instituted in 1631 by Charles I, consisted of the Heads of Houses and Proctors; but by Act of Parliament, some two centuries later, changes had been made, with the transfer of its 'powers, privileges and functions' to a new body, a Hebdomadal Council consisting of some official and some elected members, chosen for terms of six years by the Congregation of the university. This council meets every Monday for twenty weeks in the year, 'to deliberate on all matters relating to the maintenance of the privileges and liberties of the university, etc.', and thus has the initiative in all legislation. Osler had felt it his duty to accept the election to this council as the best way of learning something of the complicated workings of the university, though it was not a position for which his mind, given to generalization rather than to legislative details, particularly fitted him; and before his resignation [1] three years later on going abroad for the winter, he spent many long hours during which James Bovell's name was often scribbled on the agenda of the tiresome meetings. But there were other things to atone for the tedium he may have experienced in his attendance on these official occasions:

Revere had a half-term holiday Saturday and Monday [writes Mrs. Osler to her mother]. When I got home from town I found that he and his Dad had gone down the river in the morning as far as Sandford—trolling for pike. They were back to meet me at 3.00 p.m.—no fish but much pleasure. Yesterday the boys celebrated Guy Fawkes' Day with fireworks and a huge bonfire in the evening, so the holiday was a great success. . . . We are occupied all the time and each day seems full, with dinner invitations ahead until December 10th. They all send them out a month beforehand as people entertain tremendously in term. We must begin the next term

[1] October 19, 1908.

ourselves; I shall have much to learn, as the etiquette is quite severe and the Heads of Colleges very particular about precedence. . . . The American undergraduates here are having a Thanksgiving dinner and have asked W. O. to preside and me to be present. Isn't that amusing?

And a few days later she wrote:

Last evening we had a most delightful dinner in the common room of Corpus Christi College, the common room being a small dining-room where the Tutors and Dons lunch and have their dessert. There were some very interesting men, who told me lots about the older colleges. It was so mysterious and queer there. There was a dense fog and our coachman could hardly find his way. When we came out, Willie and I walked about among the college buildings in the fog, with the moon shining through. Willie's delight in the college life is a joy to see. . . .

He had been elected during the month to a select dinner club, the Tutors' Club, of which he has left this brief note:

In Oct. 1905 a few months after coming to Oxford I was asked to join this Club which was started about 1820. The first meeting was at Wadham, and Wells the Secretary before dinner announced to the members that he had an interesting communication to make. He had received that morning from Dr. Bright the Master of Univ. College, a note stating that he had come upon a MS. book belonging to the Club which had been mislaid by Bradley his predecessor in the Mastership and this, Wells said, was the long-lost book in which all the members of the Club had entered their names. It had been missing, much to their grief, for 25 years. The first name in the book was James Jackson Lowe of Brasenose: each man had entered a sort of biography. Among the notable men were both the Arnolds, Benjamin Jowett, Archibald Tait, George Moberly and others. Goldwin Smith, Rait, and Robinson Ellis were the only men whose names were in the book among existing members. When I joined the other members were Raper, Goudy, Dicey, Oman, Phelps, Anson, Heberden and Wells.

In the winter of '05–'06 we had six dinners, Nov. 6, '06, 1st dinner of club at Robinson Ellis' at Trinity—delightful evening, sat next Dicey who was full of stories. Told one of Whately: a student had come to him with an essay on some aspects of truth. W. said at our time of life we find so many who think truth is on their side, but precious few who are 'on the side of truth'.

Again and again to his friends of earlier days he reiterated in his brief notes that he had settled down and liked it very much; that 'the life of course is very different but very restful after the sort of racket I have had for some years'. On November 11th he wrote to one of the 'latch-keyers':

> I wish you could have been at the Annual Visitation of Bodley's Library on Wednesday. It was a quaint ceremony. The curators first meet in the old Chapter House, where a Latin address of praise to Bodley is given by an M.A. of Christ Church. Then we proceed to seclude the librarian, that is, he retires to his room—and the curators hold a meeting at which the affairs are discussed, & then certain portions of the library are formally visited. It was really great fun. I am beginning to know some of the books, but it is an awful problem to know where to begin. . . . You should see my rooms at Christ Church! I hope, when you come over, that you will stay there. They are in the old part—the Old Library building—and I feel quite convinced, though I have no evidence for it! that they are the same as were occupied by John Locke, & I think Burton had them for a few years. I am beginning to know the men and get shaken down professionally. My work at the Radcliffe is very interesting, & there is enough to keep my hand in. . . .

By no means, however, did he look upon his connexion with Bodley as *merely* 'fun'. One needs but recall his relation to the Maryland 'Faculty' Library; and it is not surprising to find him writing as follows to Whitelaw Reid, the American Ambassador, a few days after this his first 'visitation':

> Many thanks for your letter of the 14th. The Bodleian is used so extensively by Americans and they are so well treated and so warmly welcomed, that this would be an appropriate occasion for some of them to express their appreciation in a practical manner. . . .

Some of his activities (they were by no means confined to Oxford) can be easily traced—others less easily. On November 14th he was at the University of Cardiff, Wales, giving one of his stimulating and characteristic addresses, partly intended for the faculty, partly for the community, but chiefly for the medical students with whom he dined that night, making himself one of them: there is a reminder of this occasion in one of his books which contains a letter from one of his dinner companions saying:

> You may perhaps remember my mentioning at our dinner on the 14th the book 'Church and King' by your grandfather [uncle] I think. I have hunted up my copy, dated 1837, with Edward

Osler's signature dated 1841—by 'Edward Osler, formerly one of the Surgeons to the Swansea Infirmary'. Have you got this book? If not, and if you would like to have it, I shall be very pleased to transfer it from my keeping to yours. I picked it up at a bookstall for 6d., being attracted by the 'Surgeon to the Swansea Infirmary', and by the name 'Osler'.

But it is less easy to keep on his track when, as was so often the case, he played an influential and helpful rôle behind the scenes while others occupied the stage. His method of helping to get things done when he saw the need, was an admirable, indeed an enviable one. Few have the primary imagination, the knowledge of the right people whose interests at the outset should be enlisted, the ability to give the initial impulse, and the unselfishness to withdraw and let others take the credit of the *fait accompli.* This is of course the great secret of getting things done in the world, as many know; but he practised it, as many do not.

For several years sporadic and futile efforts had been made to amalgamate under a single organization—an Academy of Medicine—the twenty or more medical societies of London. Of these there were two of chief importance: one was the Medical Society of London, founded by Lettsom in 1773 as a protest against the Royal College of Physicians, then at a low ebb. In protest against this society in turn, there had split off in 1805 a group of the more influential physicians and surgeons of the time (Matthew Baillie, John Abernethy, Astley Cooper, and others), who founded the Medical and Chirurgical Society, which had subsequently received a royal charter, and of which Mr. (now Sir) John Y. W. MacAlister was at this time the active Secretary. Both these societies had accumulated large libraries and held other properties, the one at 11 Chandos Street, the other at 20 Hanover Square, where their respective meetings were held. They were noble rivals, these century-old societies, which divided between them the allegiance of Harley Street—to such an extent, indeed, that even its nursery-rhymes were affected:

Hush little baby, Mother is nigh;
Father has gone to the Medico-Chi.

The medical journals of this year 1905 contain repeated references to a new proposal of consolidation, though neither the name of the man who had the idea nor of the man who gave him encouragement is mentioned. Doubtless those who played the more prominent rôles in the organization of the Royal Society of Medicine, finally consummated in 1907, had little knowledge of how it came about that so many of the individuals who had stood in opposition to this highly desirable movement finally came around to their way of thinking. Osler often referred to Sir John MacAlister as 'the man who pokes the embers'. Sir John in this case had also laid the fire, though it was given to Osler to light it, and periodically to add fuel at the right moment which gave the quondam Secretary of the Royal Medical and Chirurgical Society something to poke. Sir John gives this account of an early moment of discouragement:

It was probably some time in 1904, but as I think I told you, the only date I remember is the Battle of Waterloo, 1066. Anyhow, it was shortly after a disappointing conference I had had with some of our leaders on my pet subject of amalgamation which I had told W. O. all about, and he was keenly interested. Since Andrew Clark's death I had never found a single one of the leading men keen enough to take it up or even to encourage it. And perhaps to this was added a little hepatic congestion. Anyhow, he burst in on me in his dear breezy way, with: 'How goes the Amalger?' and I replied: 'Cut it out; it will probably come after I am gone, and so the sooner I quit the better!'

He sat down beside me with his old affectionate trick of embracing the shoulder, and got me to tell him all about it, and after a little thought he said: 'It has got to come, and you are the man to do it, but you will have to get at the young men. Drop the old fossils and try to inspire the young men who have to look at the future.' So we smoked and chatted, and whether the hepatic congestion was subsiding, or whether I was absorbing his faith and enthusiasm, I don't know, but the next day I sat down and wrote the first sketch of my new scheme, which as an official necessity—and, as I thought, a mere formality—I sent to Douglas Powell, who was then our President.

He was so interested that he suggested I should take a fortnight's leave to enable me to work out details, financial and otherwise, and I went away to Hastings, where I knew I should not be disturbed, and slogged at the job for a fortnight, and then sent him the detailed scheme, which at his request was printed and circulated; and from that we marched right on, till success was reached within two years, after, of course, numerous meetings of all the various societies concerned.

That he was much on the wing, in town and elsewhere, and that others no less than MacAlister 'absorbed his faith and enthusiasm', is apparent from an abundance of similar episodes which have been supplied. But even in his absence 7 Norham Gardens went on as usual—already a lure for the young, just as 1 West Franklin Street had been:

We had a lovely Sunday [writes his wife] though W. O. was in Cambridge. Our Sunday afternoons are astonishing—the men come pouring in from 3.30, and then again at 8.30 after church for supper which is always informal and all on the table—the chafing-dish being a great amusement and surprise to the Englishmen. I met W. O. in town and tried to carry him off to see L——, but he had two consultations in the other direction and could not take the time. He is dining in London tonight [Nov. 27th] and returns early for Sir John Burdon Sanderson's funeral; and many men for luncheon who come to the funeral.

To judge from the 'University Acts' the funeral of a former Regius Professor, however, did not interfere with a scheduled university function, for: 'In a Convocation holden on Tuesday, November 28th, the following business was submitted to the House':

1. *Nomination of Delegate of the University Press.* William Osler, D.M., Hon. D.Sc., Student of Christ Church, Regius Professor of Medicine, was nominated by the Vice-Chancellor and Proctors to be a Delegate of the University Press, in place of William Sanday, D.D., Canon of Christ Church, who has been constituted a Perpetual Delegate thereof, [etc., etc.].[1]

---

[1] The present Oxford Press occupies a building resembling more closely a college than a book factory, for it is built around an enclosed garden on the quadrangular plan of the Oxford colleges. It moved into these quarters 100 years ago from the old Clarendon Building where the Delegates continue to hold their stated meetings. This accounts for the fact, confusing to many, that a 'Clarendon Press imprint' signifies that the Delegates themselves, *auctoritate universitatis*, have passed favourably upon a manuscript, whereas an imprint of the 'Oxford University Press' (of which there are many types) indicates that the responsibility of publication has unofficially been accepted by the Publisher to the University, whose

This added another to his stated weekly meetings, for the delegates of the Press, ten in all, meet on Fridays at 2 p.m. for what is apt to be a long session. What he accomplished for the Press, to which he became devoted no less than to the Bodleian, can be gathered from the 'minute' upon the delegates' records, of the date '6 February, 1920', which says in part:

When Dr. Osler became a Delegate in 1905 the medical books published by the Press were insignificant in number; to-day in virtue of the *Quarterly Journal of Medicine* and of the *Oxford Medical Publications* issued in co-operation with Messrs. Hodder & Stoughton, and including Osler's 'System of Medicine', the Press stands in the front rank of medical publishers both at home and in America. The Delegates owe their present position in great part to Sir William Osler's initiative and supervision, and to his unique influence in the medical world.

On December 8th, at the Oxford Town Hall, Osler made what seems to have been his first and last appearance at a political rally. The meeting had been arranged by the Oxford University Tariff Reform League and Joseph Chamberlain was to speak. The President of Magdalen, a strong tariff reformer, had written to Osler a month before, begging him to speak, and he had replied: 'Yes, if you think it will be all right. I should be very glad to say a few words, certainly not too many.' Here the story may be taken up by Mrs. Osler, who wrote:

A lovely mild morning and the thrushes singing outside; evidently they think spring has come. E. B. O. [Osler's brother] came last evening and we all went to hear Mr. Chamberlain. It was tremendously exciting. The huge Town Hall was packed. Mary C. was there and she and Mrs. Warren, with whom they are staying, sat on the platform. W. O. offered the resolution of thanks for the Colonies. I met Mrs. C. afterwards and had a nice chat. She is as attractive as always; just as Peabody-ish and Salem-y and refined as ever. What an interesting life she leads. His address was fine,

---

office was long at Amen Corner—now in new quarters at Amen House, Warwick Square—in London.

The Delegacy consists of ten members, five of whom, to ensure continuity of service, are 'perpetual delegates'. On the death of William Sanday (1919), Osler was 'subrogated' *ad supplendum numerum quinque Perpetuorum Delegatorum*.

and particularly interesting at the moment, owing to the excitement in the change of government. Only one more letter to you after this!! I can hardly realize it.

Sir Herbert Warren says that on this particular occasion in Oxford Town Hall Osler 'successfully and gracefully avoided the public issues in a few well-chosen words'; he adds that in politics W. O. was a strong Imperialist, and, like himself, a tariff reformer, but became in time an ordinary Liberal, so that in 1919 they endeavoured without avail to get him to stand as the Coalition candidate for Oxford to support the Lloyd George Liberals and the Unionists. But it is too soon to talk of Lloyd George and a Coalition Government. Indeed a mass meeting, with Lord Avebury in the chair, was being held that very month at Westminster for the promotion of better relations with Germany.

Their first term in Oxford was near its end—a happy time, yet they were eager to return to what for so many years had been home. The ties that bind are not cut so easily, and England was still a little strange. Shortly after Osler had been elected to the Press, two elderly Dons strolling by the river one evening were heard to say: *1st Don*—'How do you feel about this new Regius getting so many appointments?' *2nd Don*—'Oh, a good thing. New blood.' *1st Don*—'Too untried: terrible risk, terrible risk.' And they passed on.

During this early period of his transplantation, Osler may well enough have shared the feeling so well expressed by Clifford Allbutt on his being called thirteen years before to the corresponding position in Cambridge. At the close of his inaugural address, Allbutt had turned to the representatives of the university to express his gratification in returning to the scenes he had known so well as an undergraduate:

> If to you [he said] who have never left this home the roaring of the great loom of the labouring and sweating world without has become at times even inaudible; if at times you have been tempted to become a little too fine for common things, a little too high for low things, it is well that some of us, who have fought hard in the ranks of the Philistines, and learned to love them also, should return

to you with hands perhaps somewhat rougher, opinions somewhat ruder than your own.[1]

Of the two, Osler's transplantation had been the more trying; yet neither the Cambridge nor the Oxford Regius Professor of Medicine ever showed, so far as is apparent, any roughness of hand or rudeness of opinion, to grate upon his highly refined surroundings. One who was at this time a Fellow and Tutor of New College [2] has written:

> Though Oxford is proverbially hospitable and generous, she does not easily capitulate to strangers, especially if their claim to distinction rests upon scientific rather than on literary grounds, but Osler left Oxford no choice, and from the first the surrender of the university was absolute and immediate. Of course his great reputation as a physician and medical writer had preceded him, but we immediately discovered that finished competence in his own art and science was but a small part of the man, that the new Regius Professor was the least professional of doctors and the least academic of professors, that he was amazingly devoid of vanity and pedantic inhibitions, that his spirit was free, alert, vivacious, and that there was apparently no end to the span of his interests or to the vivid life-giving energy which he was prepared to throw into any task which fell to him to discharge. Old and young alike acknowledged his mastery and never left his presence without feeling the magnetism of the man and that insatiable, but unobtrusive appetite for helpfulness which made him the prince of friends and benefactors.

---

[1] 'The Standards and Methods of Medical Teaching.' *British Medical Journal*, May 14, 1892, i. 1007.

[2] The Rt. Hon. Herbert Fisher, ex-President of the Board of Education.

CHAPTER XXVI

1905–6

THE HARVEIAN ORATION AND OTHER THINGS

It had not been an idle statement, made to ease the parting, that they would return to America every year. It was doubtless their intention, for no two people could have been more tenacious of friendships. Both of them had aged mothers as well as large family connexions in New England and in Canada, not all of whom could be gathered at one time in Oxford, though it sometimes appeared that they made the endeavour. Nor was the repeated statement that he was to have a good month's rest with the 'boys' in the hospital entirely idle, for to work and play with them for a month savoured at least of recreation. But such a hullabaloo was made over him on this and his succeeding visits, and he returned each time so exhausted, that these sojourns in America came to be looked upon with not a little apprehension. 'They pulled too severely on his heart-strings', as Mrs. Osler expressed it in one of her letters.

For this their first visit they sailed on Saturday, December 16th, and reached Canton, Mass., at 9 p.m. on the 24th in time to hang up their stockings in company with numerous Revere children. And the following day, despite its many festivities, he found time to send off a number of letters, which give his itinerary if nothing else:

To F. J. Shepherd from W. O. Canton, Xmas Day.

Can you give me a bed on Friday night? I leave here on Thursday eve & should reach you by breakfast time. If you are full turn me over to Gardner. I shall spend Friday & Saturday with you and go on to Toronto in the Eve. I hope to spend some hours in the Museum. Dr. Abbott's catalogue grows apace—it will be one of the best pieces of work ever done at the School, & we should encourage her to take up the other systems in order. She evidently has a genius for this sort of thing. The sections I have just finished (Endocardium) are really remarkable. I do not believe there is a museum in Gt. Britain with a better collection—there is nothing like it on this side. We had a good crossing tho several rough days. The Caronia is a big Ocean Club House. Love to Cecil & Dorothy.

And to Dr. Maude Abbott on this same Christmas Day he sent but one of a succession of encouraging letters : 'What are museums for but to educate? A good catalogue such as you have prepared acts as the showman. I will meet you in the museum Friday at 11.' Thus he began pouring himself out for others. From 125 College Street, Toronto, he wrote on January 3rd that he was 'off in the morning to Baltimore', where it appears his promised month's rest with the boys proved a discontinuous visit, for a letter on the 15th says : 'I have been away in Philadelphia and New York. I am having such a festive time—too much so—too many dinners &c but it is very nice to see my old friends.' One of the dinners was at the Maison Rauscher in Washington on January 11th in honour of Dr. Robert Fletcher ; and there a group of men (John S. Billings, Walter D. McCaw, G. T. Vaughan, H. W. Wiley, W. S. Thayer, Osler, and others, who deeply appreciated this modest and courtly old gentleman) gathered to give him a loving-cup and to tell him in prose and verse what they thought of him and his remarkable career which, beginning in anthropology, craniology, and medico-military statistics, had been crowned by his work on the 'Index Catalogue' and *Index Medicus*.

Revere and his mother were obliged to return the middle of the month because of the boy's school, and Osler subsequently took up his abode as of old in the hospital, where it was easier to dodge consultations, and where he might apply himself with McCrae to the task which for a year had consumed far too much of his time. A note scribbled to Thayer on Sunday the 28th indicates what it was :

Sunday.

Dear T. We have been going over the System work—so as to notify the contributors. We shall begin to print at once & Vol. I & II should be ready by Oct. 1st. The MSS. of Vol. III & IV should be in hand by Oct. 1st. Get some of your boys at the material so as to have it well in hand for you. Yours, Wm Osler.

This was not all, however, for he allowed himself to be

worked both at bedside[1] and in lecture-room by his old staff; nor did he fail to attend the monthly meeting of the Baltimore profession at the 'Faculty' building, and of course dropped in on his protégées, the Librarians there, on many occasions. Above all, the students at the Hopkins were beyond words thrilled. They followed on his heels in the wards and amphitheatre, and on one of their regular Monday evening meetings he took part in a symposium on the six holders of 'The Gold-headed Cane'. John Radcliffe naturally was apportioned to Osler, and he said in part:

His fortune, by his will, he left wisely and generously. His Yorkshire estate he left to the Masters and Fellows of University College for ever, in trust, for the foundation of two travelling fellowships which still exist. They are conferred upon men who have taken certain degrees at Oxford, the conditions being that six months of the three years during which the fellowship is held must be spent abroad, and any surplus must be turned in and used by University College. In addition, his will provided £5,000 for the enlargement of the buildings of University College, where he himself had been educated; £40,000 for the building of a library, and instructions regarding the purchase of books on medical and natural history. Some years ago this building became so full that the library was moved, and at the cost of the Drapers Company of London, £60,000 being spent and a new Radcliffe library built. Then in the fourth place he left £500 annually towards mending the diet at St. Bartholomew's Hospital, the balance of his property being handed to his trustees to do with as they saw fit. They built the large Radcliffe Observatory, and pay all its expenses, and in 1770 built the Radcliffe Infirmary, paying the major part of its cost.

So there are at least four special foundations connected with his name, all are associated with scientific work, and certainly there is no modern physician with so many large and important monuments. Yet he put no line to paper, but saved with a special object in view. One lesson learned from his life is that if you do not write, make money; and, after you finish, leave it to the Johns Hopkins Trust.

Osler himself in his make-up was a sort of twentieth-century edition of these six men rolled into one—though with less

[1] That he profited by it is evident if one traces him through his publications. In an article in the *J. H. H. Bulletin* for Oct. 1907 he says: 'On January 21, 1906, while I was taking Dr. Barker's ward classes, I found a patient whose case is here described, and I saw immediately that it was a form of generalized telangiectasis which I had never met with before, [&c.]'

of Radcliffe perhaps than of the others; and of Richard Mead more. Samuel Johnson once said of Mead that he lived more in the broad sunshine of life than any man he knew; Osler's nature, likewise, had a southern exposure. He shared, too, with Mead and Askew their love of rare books, and like them also was the kind of collector who made his books accessible to others—qualities not always possessed by bibliophiles. What Austin Dobson said of Mead, that 'neither the princely Grolier nor the unparalleled Peiresc could have made a more unselfish use of their possessions', might equally well be said of William Osler.

On the morning of his departure this friendly appeal was sent to his old colleague of McGill days:

To F. J. Shepherd from W. O. [Johns Hopkins Hospital]
Jan. 30.

How stupid of the railway people, considering the number of parcels we get. Thanks all the same for the apples. Perhaps they will be there on our return. It is too bad that the M. G. H. should be depleted at intervals, but I cannot but feel that the persistency of a hostile feeling, latent or manifest, between the two great institutions is very detrimental, & it is having a very bad influence among the younger men. I hear it talked about outside Montreal. I think that the seniors among you should put a stop to it and make the school a rallying point, & reach a mental attitude that makes no difference whether a man is at the R. V. H. or the M. G. H. so long as he is a good McGill man & working earnestly at the school. After all, the hospitals are only clinical laboratories for the school, & what the deuce difference does it make at which one of them a man works? Do get the older men to take a more rational view of the situation. . . .

The last few days were passed in Toronto, to say good-bye to his mother; and at eight o'clock on Saturday morning from the University Club of New York, two hours before sailing with his protégé Dr. Campbell Howard on the *Campania*, there issued many bread-and-butter notes, like the following to his successor:

Saturday.

Dear Barker, It has been a great pleasure to be with you all again & particularly to see how well you have settled in the new work. I had no fear about it whatever, so I only saw what I expected —all the same it is delightful to hear on all sides such good accounts.

It will be so nice to have Cole with you—he is such a trump. Keep your eye on Boggs too—he has possibilities. With love to Mrs Barker & Jack Ever yours Wm OSLER. Get at the local societies—anything in the way of good practical cases—they need your stimulation.

And in one of his steamer letters he says: 'I had a rushing visit—too much so—Montreal, Toronto (twice), Boston, Baltimore, N. Y. & Phila. I did not get much work done but it was nice to see the many old friends again.' Small wonder that on his reaching home his wife should write: 'Dr. Osler nearly killed himself when he was over, and I shall never let him go again for a month in the winter. He came back a wreck.' One of his periodic bronchial attacks, indeed, had followed the fatigue and exposure incidental to his 'quiet month with the boys'. Even so, his spirits were unsinkable, and that he was reading as usual with pen in hand and pad on knee, an abundance of notes to his old pupils testifies:

To Dr. Louis M. Warfield. [7 Norham Gardens], Feb. 16.

I am very glad to see your work in the *St. Louis Medical Review.* Keep it up and go slowly. You have plenty of time, and do not forget how much room there is at the top. Is the Miss Green I met at the Fischels still without cardio-vascular attachments? If so, please tell her from me—no, I had better not say, but you will understand the message I would like to send her. Sincerely yours, Wm OSLER. Love to the Fischels.

And a postcard of February 26th, notifying Thayer that he is being sent the *Biographie Médicale* of Bayle, states: 'I had a good trip back, but caught a heavy cold on landing which has rather knocked me out. Fine weather here & all well.' Many engagements for the year had already been made, the Harveian Oration among them, to be given in October. Of this he must have told Weir Mitchell, who wrote: 'There is room for an essay *on* the Harveian Oration. The older ones might be interesting. Many were missing when I looked them up at the College. Why not do this?' But there were things more pressing than this, one of them a meeting to be held in Manchester, for which he planned to review certain aspects of his angina pectoris material; and detailed letters went to T. R. Boggs and others in Baltimore asking for minutiae about many old patients of whom his notes were incomplete. Then, too, plans were already under way for the August meeting in Toronto of the British Medical Association which he expected to attend, and for which in an unofficial capacity he was soliciting papers. Meanwhile his projected 'System of Medicine' was on his hands, and he was adding to McCrae's troubles:

March 2.

Dear Mac,—I have not yet got my introduction ready. They must go on with the printing and not wait. I will cable on Monday. There is nothing in it which deals with disease *specifically* as the first articles do, so that there is no impropriety in having the general introduction in Roman type and in front. It is so in all the other Systems. In the new Allbutt the introduction precedes a group of wordy articles—not as in our System a consideration at once of the special diseases. I must insist on this. So let them go ahead with the printing and that will give plenty of time.

Things move on here quietly [he wrote later in the month to one of his former 3 West Franklin Street neighbours]. We are still houseless but hopeful. I am feeling all right again. I was rather knocked out by the racket in America. I am evidently reaching a state of pre-senile enfeeblement. Have you a copy of Gui Patin's letters? I am reading them at night now with the greatest interest. He was a unique old rascal but devoted to books. You will be glad to hear that I was elected to the Athenaeum Club the other day. The committee is allowed to elect nine every year among men who have a certain measure of respectability. Otherwise you have to wait your turn on a waiting-list of four or five hundred. I have been elected a member of the Bibliographical Society, which is most interesting. I attended the first meeting last Monday and heard a very good paper on the old Chapter House at Canterbury. . . .

'A certain measure of respectability.' The seriousness with which that eminently respectable institution, the Athenaeum Club, is taken by Englishmen, often stirred the E. Y. D.-ish streak in Osler in ways which reacted differently upon the members of this 'synthesis of national intellect and responsibility'. One of them writes: 'The way he would slap you on the back, and pick your tail pockets while you were reading the telegrams was delightful. Everyone, I think, looked upon him as a personal friend, almost as a special friend of his own.' Another, less under-

Tower of the Five Orders and Schools quadrangle

Duke Humphrey's Library, looking towards the Selden End

THE BODLEIAN LIBRARY

standing, felt that it was 'undignified of Osler to secretly insert bulky objects in one's coat-tail pocket while leaning over the umbrella-stand harmlessly deciding upon one's own property'—an episode reminiscent of what Lord Salisbury said about the fallibility of bishops at the Athenaeum umbrella-stand—the recreation-ground of their weaknesses.

But more important than the Athenaeum Club was his reference in the last letter to his election to the Bibliographical Society of which he had been made a 'candidate member' on March 19th. The society at that time, according to its Secretary, A. W. Pollard, was passing through the rather difficult period of its 'teens, and was as yet not sufficiently established for many book-lovers to wish to join it. The society, indeed, needed new inspiration, and this Osler brought to it; and his first attendance is vividly recalled by its Secretary, who says: 'A meeting had begun, when the entrance of a stranger with an attractively mobile face, alert figure, and notably light tread, caused a whispered secretarial inquiry as to who he was. The answer came back that it was Professor Osler, and the Secretary had an instinctive conviction that his coming meant much for the society.'

The active interest which Osler had shown while in Philadelphia in the Library of the College of Physicians, and while in Baltimore with that of the Maryland Faculty, had been whole-heartedly transferred, on his reaching Oxford, to the Bodleian, to which he makes constant reference in his brief letters. His Regius chair made him *ex officio* one of the Curators, who meet only twice a term, but he was soon made a member of and re-elected each year to the Standing Committee, a far more important body that meets every Friday noon. But it was not his official duties alone that drew him to Bodley. Indeed, scarcely a day passed when the Tower of the Five Orders dominating the Old Schools quadrangle did not see him pop in at the unpretentious entrance to the library, to skip two steps at a time up the winding and worn flight of stairs to Duke Humphrey's Library, where there was a cheerful greeting to all, from Nicholson the Librarian to the boy lowest on the pay list. This was what is chiefly remembered, and so when one asks of Bodleian officials what he did for the library they look about and say: 'Why, he gave the new clock, and guaranteed the cost of the "*B.Q.R.*", but the chief reason of our grateful and affectionate feeling for him is of a more general kind.'

It was not merely [writes Falconer Madan, E. W. B. Nicholson's successor] that he was always cheery and breezy. As an *ex-officio* Curator he might have performed his duties perfunctorily, and as a medical specialist he might have taken little interest in literary matters. But he was always enthusiastic about anything that could be done for the good of the library or to increase its efficiency. If he bought a remarkable book he would bring it to us to see—if he heard of a new publication or a collection of manuscripts he would come and tell us—if he had a distinguished visitor he would bring him to the library and introduce him—if any of the staff were ill he would go and visit them. He was frequently in the library, interested in all its details, always ready to sympathize in one's difficulties, full of encouragement for our efforts and very jealous for the prestige of the place. We miss him, not because he promoted this or that piece of work, but because of his living influence, which helped and stimulated us all.

A character, in short, sloping towards the sunny side. But Osler's real work was done, as must again be pointed out, most often behind the scenes, whence the spotlight was turned on other actors. There is given out to readers at the Bodleian a small manual, in the back of which, in chronological order, are listed some of the more important happenings since—

1598 [when] Sir Thomas Bodley a statesman and diplomat high in the favour of Queen Elizabeth, being weary of state-craft, determined 'to set up' his 'staffe at the Librarie-dore in Oxon', and once again furnished Duke Humphrey's room with bookcases, and became, to his eternal glory, the founder of the Bodleian Library.

A perusal of this leaflet shows that from 1860, except for the Shelley relics, there had been little to note in the history of the library till 1906, when things for some unapparent reason began to happen—things which required imagination, initiative, and energetic action, all of which a newly appointed Curator possessed. The first entry follows:

1906 The original copy of the First Folio of Shakespeare which came to the library in 1623 under the agreement with the Stationers' Company . . . and which had been parted with after the Restoration as superseded, was bought by public subscription from W. G. Turbutt, Esq., of Ogston Hall, Derbyshire, for £3,000.

At the risk of telling the story backwards, a letter of later date, which between the lines tells much of it, may be given:

From Lord Strathcona to W. O. 29th March, 1906.

Your letter of the 27th I received somewhat late yesterday, and in the evening I telegraphed you that it would afford me pleasure to send you to-day my cheque for five hundred pounds to help to secure the First Folio of Shakespeare for the Bodleian Library. Your telegram I am also glad to have this morning, and it gives me much gratification to send you this my cheque No. X10184, of even date, on the Bank of Montreal, to your order, for the sum mentioned, say five hundred pounds. It would indeed have been a misfortune had you not been able to secure the book, and I congratulate you and Library on the success of their efforts.

But to go back to the beginning, there had been issued by Bodley's Librarian, three months before, an appeal, marked 'private', to Oxford graduates, which began as follows:

In 1623 or 1624 the Company of Stationers sent to the Bodleian in sheets a copy of the newly published first collected edition of Shakespeare's works. They did so under an agreement made with them by Sir Thomas Bodley in 1610–11. In those days there was no Copyright-act, so that the copy sent by the Company to the Bodleian may be said to be the one most authentic copy existing. 'It is the only one which can be regarded as a standard exemplar. It was the copy selected by the publisher for permanent preservation.'

The Bodleian sent the sheets on Feb. 17, 1623/4, to the Oxford binder, William Wildgoose, and on its return the book was duly chained on the shelves, where it remained till 1664. But in 1674 it had disappeared from the catalogue.

The Bodleian Statute then in force contained a most unhappy clause allowing the Curators, if unanimous, to consign books to be changed for others of a better edition, or to be removed as superfluous and of little use. And there is no reasonable doubt that the First Folio was got rid of between Sept. 1663 and Sept. 1664, among a number of 'superfluous Library Books sold by order of the Curators' for which an Oxford bookseller, Richard Davis, paid the Library £24. . . . The subsequent history of the First Folio thus thrown out as 'superfluous' is unknown till the middle of the eighteenth century. Apparently at some time before 1759 it was acquired by Mr. Richard Turbutt of Ogston Hall, Derbyshire, and now belongs to his great-great-grandson, Mr. W. G. Turbutt, an old Christ Church man.

On January 23, 1905, Mr. Turbutt's son, Mr. G. M. R. Turbutt, B.A., of Magdalen, brought the book, which had suffered some damage, to Mr. F. Madan, senior sub-Librarian of the Bodleian, to ask his advice about it. As it was in ancient binding, Mr. Madan showed it to Mr. Strickland Gibson, also of the Bodleian staff, who has rapidly made a reputation as one of the chief British authorities on the history of binding. Mr. Gibson at once saw that it was Oxford binding, and in a few minutes had found the proofs that it was the old Bodleian copy.

I lost no time in writing to Mr. Turbutt to ask whether he would consent to allow the volume to be re-purchased for the Bodleian by subscriptions from past and present members of the university, and offered to submit to him proposals for valuation. He was unable to reply definitely then, but near the end of October he informed us that he had received an offer of £3,000 from a purchaser who was represented by a certain well-known London firm, and that he had suspended his answer for a month in the hope that the Bodleian might be able to give the same price. *He has since most generously extended the time for doing so till March* 31. . . .

And the frantic Librarian went on to say that it was practically certain that the offer had been made from the United States, and 'for the Bodleian to pay £3,000 for any printed book is simply impossible. . . . It dares not even *borrow* the sum required for the recovery of its Shakespeare: to do so would be to cripple itself for an indefinite number of years.' Osler, too, was much exercised, and not only subscribed generously to the fund himself, but secured still larger contributions from Lord Mount Stephen and from Mr. Henry Phipps; but the weeks went on until the end of March drew near with the total amount far short of the purchase price, in spite of a second letter of appeal to Oxford men, published in *The Times*. To every one's despair it looked as though the volume would be lost, and with only three days remaining, Mr. Nicholson sent a note to Osler, saying, 'Paid or promised £2,598: 13s: 3d.' Some time before this Osler had endeavoured, without avail, to enlist Strathcona's interest in the matter, and knowing the ways of his old friend, he must have written again at this crucial moment. So it happened that early on the morning of the 29th a welcome telegram was handed in at 7 Norham Gardens; this, promptly transmitted to Mr. Nicholson, who lived near by, brought the following answer:

2 Canterbury Road.
29 March, 1906.

My dear Osler,—You deserve a statue in the Bodleian quadrangle. I have wired Turbutt. I'll take my chance of seeing you later in the day. I shall write to the papers and send out a circular to the subscribers. Yours most sincerely,

E. W. B. Nicholson.

That Bodley's Librarian, when they did meet later on, in his excitement sat on the floor and wept perhaps lies beyond this story. 'Mr. Nicholson told me to-day a curious sequel [wrote Osler two weeks later]: he had a telegram from Sotheran that the man who offered £3,000 now wished to offer the Bodleian £1,500 if he could have the Turbutt folio *for his lifetime*.' Evidently Bodley was unwilling to take any such chances.

Still under the expectation that the autumn would see him again in America, he wrote on April 13th to one of the 'latch-keyers':

Sorry to hear there is not much chance of seeing you over here this summer. You will of course be in Toronto. I shall come out early in August. We have bought a house in Norham Gardens, which will I think be very satisfactory. We will have to add to it. There is a very nice garden of about an acre. We cannot get possession until August the 1st. I forget whether I told you about the seventeenth & eighteenth-century medical library I am trying to secure for the Johns Hopkins University. I am having the books catalogued before making a final statement as I found there were a great many blanks. Isaac has bought a boat. He is very well & wonderfully happy here—a different child.

This library to which he refers was 'the Warrington collection', now housed in the Johns Hopkins Medical School—an interesting lot of books, abounding in rather rare English pamphlets gathered in the heyday of the old Warrington Dispensary, when John Aikin and his coterie flourished there. 'Everything is moving very quietly', he wrote a few days later. 'We are having a very extraordinary spring—bright sunshine every day. I am off to Munich next week for the Congress of Innere Medezin

[April 23–26], where I hope to get some inspiration.' He went in company with one of the Oxford practitioners, who perhaps also needed a 'brain-dusting'; and though Osler himself had to hurry back to hold examinations on the first few days of May at Cambridge, his companion was introduced to the European clinics from Munich to Groningen. They stopped first at Marburg to see Professor Aschoff, in whose laboratory Adami, at Osler's suggestion, had gone to finish off his text-book on pathology. At Munich, when not at the sessions of the congress, they spent most of their time with Friedrich v. Müller, under whom Campbell Howard was at work; and later they went to Frankfort to see Ehrlich, who unfortunately was ill, 'but his assistant took us all over the menagerie.'

While at Marburg they must have first seen the news of the devastation by earthquake and fire of four square miles of San Francisco; and though, as will be recalled, outside assistance was politely declined, there were other than official ways of holding out a helping hand. One who had been through the Baltimore fire must show his sympathy in some way, particularly for the doctors, who had been hard hit; so on his return Osler promptly wrote to J. H. Musser and John S. Billings urging that a committee be organized to collect books for the San Francisco Library, adding: 'I am sure we could gather a great many interesting volumes here, particularly the sets of journals and Transactions.' Meanwhile plans were on foot for the meeting of the British Medical Association to be held in Toronto in the late summer. He writes on May 18th that he has already booked his passage and is arranging with 'MacKenzie to billet a group of you *respectable* young fellows in one of the college halls'.

> Have you a copy [he adds] of Gui Patin's letters? I think I asked you before. I am just finishing them and am perfectly enchanted with the old rascal. Everybody is raving about the picture, with which there is nothing else in the Academy to compare.[1] I am very busy doing nothing. The days seem very full, but I am gradually developing the proper brand of Oxonian mental inertia. . . .

[1] Mr. E. A. Abbey is reported as having said that the Osler portrait in the group was the most interesting one Sargent had ever done.

The days were indeed very full of his sort of doing nothing, and Mrs. Osler was similarly idle. 'Apparently this is the promoting agency for the B. M. A. in Toronto', she writes. 'About six men a week come for advice—what to speak about and what to wear. I say linen or pongee every time. Fancy a visit to America for the first time in August.'

There was a movement on foot, about the time of Osler's transfer to England, fostered chiefly by Drs. Wilmot Herringham, A. E. Garrod (now Osler's successor), William Hale-White, H. D. Rolleston, J. Rose Bradford, and Robert Hutchison, to start a new medical journal of a type rather different to any then being published in England; and, recognizing how great would be the value of his support, Osler was approached on the subject. To judge from contemporary letters, he had another project in mind and saw the chance of fusing his scheme with this other one. Accordingly, at the preliminary meeting held on May 23rd at Herringham's house, in the course of the discussion he casually remarked: 'Why not form a National Association of Physicians first, and let the journal come to be its official organ?'—adding that the Oxford Press might be prevailed upon to undertake the publication, though it was somewhat out of their line. The suggestion was warmly welcomed, and as an outcome of this informal gathering the Association of Physicians of Great Britain and Ireland, with the *Quarterly Journal of Medicine* as its official mouthpiece, came into being, and the Oxford University Press made its first venture into the field of medical publications. Though Osler never held an official position in the association he served for the following twelve years, until the time of his death, as one of the editors of the journal, and is said to have been 'indefatigable in encouraging its growth, shaping its policies and smoothing out its difficulties'. He had had abundant experience not only with the editing of medical journals but with the founding of medical societies, and knew full well that they both require at the outset much careful steering. In this instance it was particularly important, if the good-will of the Scotch and Irish physicians was to be gained, that the London group should not be too much to the fore. Consequently, emissaries were sent to the provincial medical centres, as well as to Edinburgh and Dublin, to explain the project—Osler agreeing to go himself to Dublin.

To Mrs. Henry M. Thomas from W. O. 7 Norham Gardens, Oxford, May 25.

Dear Mrs Harry T. How is it with thee & the dear family? Do drop me a line now and then to say how you all are. It is just a year since we landed. On the whole I think the move has been a success—certainly it has been so for Revere, and Grace & I have borne the transplantation wonderfully—considering our years and the wrench to our hearts caused by leaving. It was pretty hard at first but there are many compensations & this is a wonderful spot. I am getting into my niche gradually. I have never had so idle a year but it has been good for me. We have bought a house not far from this, not what we wanted particularly as it will need many changes, but there is an acre of garden & it is on the parks. Mrs. Revere, Mrs. Chapin & Will Revere came last week so we have the house full.

The picture is an astounding success. The critics are extravagantly enthusiastic. 'No such group since Rembrandt' &c. I cannot feel that he has done justice to Halsted & Kelly. Welch is wonderfully good. You can see his strength as a halo. He has caught my eyes and the ochrous hue of my dour face, but he evidently has no surgical leanings as there is a hidden want in the other two. . . .

Early in June, from the 6th to the 12th, he gave the Thomas Young Lectures at St. George's Hospital, six of them in all; the first devoted to the life and works of that amazing person after whom the lectureship was named, and the others to the general subject of abdominal tumours and the patterns they make on the abdominal walls—a subject, as his students well remember, which always interested him. The lectures were never published; indeed, he did not even finish his sketch of Thomas Young, though there are fragments of the address among his posthumous papers.

During this first year Revere's former governess, with scant training for the task, had taken some lessons and done the best she could in the position of secretary: such a thing as a trained medical stenographer was a rare bird in Oxford at this time, and Osler's correspondence and papers had been written for the most part in longhand.

W. H. Welch, W. S. Halsted William Osler, H. A. Kelly

THE SARGENT PORTRAIT

However, an amanuensis was finally engaged; for, at the top of a letter penned to L. F. Barker late in the month of June, the following message was added for the benefit of his former secretary, whom Dr. Barker had inherited: 'Dear Miss H. Please forward. All well here. Mrs. Revere sails to-day. I have a new sec. coming this eve and am scared to death Tom will shoot her at sight.' 'Tom' was, of course, Revere, to whom his father's letters, at least to old friends, never failed to allude—'Tommy is a new boy [he writes], full of energy at school and at games —he's beginning to bowl a very good ball at cricket.' But other children occupied his attention no less, even though less likely to be mentioned in his correspondence. One of them has submitted the following:

He first came under my immediate notice in the summer of 1906 when I was five years old, and it was a case of love at first sight. My mother and father had gone to America and left me with my nurse at the King's Arms. This meant that I went to Norham Gardens to luncheon every Sunday, and I dare say fairly often in the week as well, but the Sunday luncheons form the backbone of my recollections. The love at first sight was so violent on my part that I immediately announced my matrimonial intentions, and 'Uncle Willie' entered into the game with a wonderful mock seriousness that almost made one believe he was in deadly earnest. Twenty-three was fixed upon as a suitable age for the bride, and he evolved a series of plots for ridding the earth of 'Aunt Grace', the only obstacle to our happy union. Poison was the method in which we had the greatest confidence, and I remember so well one Sunday luncheon at which he produced a box which he said contained poisonous pills to be concealed in 'Aunt Grace's' food. Accordingly when the fingerbowls came round we concocted a fearful and wonderful soup out of the remnants of everything on the table; the fatal pill was dropped in with the utmost care and circumspection, and 'Aunt Grace' inveigled into drinking it, after which the conspirators retired into a corner and danced with joy. When finally the victim succumbed on the library hearthrug, the chief conspirator, smitten with agonies of remorse, administered coffee as an antidote, with instantaneous effect. For a long time after my family returned and removed me from the scene of action, we corresponded at length, signing ourselves 'your loving husband' and 'your devoted wife'. He kept the game up wonderfully, and his letters consisted chiefly of this sort of thing: 'Aunt Grace very robust to-day, alas!' and 'Aunt Grace very pale: I think she is waning. Be quick and catch up to 23!' And when he went to

France he sent me an enormous old flint-lock pistol which I still have, with this ferocious inscription: 'Babs Chapin from The Wicked One. *To shoot Aunt Grace.*' It was a marvellous game.

The Toronto meeting of the B. M. A. was still engaging his attention, to judge from the following letter, which shows, too, that overtures were being made to him suggesting a change of abode:

To Dr. A. B. Macallum from W. O. June 12.

I am sorry you have had trouble about the subsidies. I think an erroneous impression got abroad through the B. A. A. S. experiences. I am so glad to hear from Adami this week that Aschoff has taken his passage. He is a very strong card, and the best of the younger men in Germany. I wrote to MacKenzie the other day, asking who was to look after Aschoff. He speaks English perfectly. I think it would be nice to pay his travelling expenses all the way. He has not, of course, a large salary, and he is just moving to Freiburg. I am making arrangements in New York to have him met and taken care of, so that he will have no expenses there. I do not think there is any chance for Gotch. I will attack him again. Horsley was operated upon for appendicitis last week. It has been an old trouble and I do not think it will interfere with his trip, though Lady Horsley said their plans were somewhat uncertain.

I have had some communication with Whitney [Sir James, the Provincial Prime Minister] on the subject of the presidency, but I am not a suitable man for such a position at all, not having special executive ability. Why should they not take you? If they cannot settle upon a Canadian, there is a man here called Gerrans who practically runs the university. He married a Canadian woman, and is a man of very wide sympathies. I sail August 4th on the *Campania*.

Evidently he was not going to be tempted from Oxford. What he meant by not having special executive ability was probably that he detested the detail of executive work; and he knew well enough that his were not the qualities needed by a modern college president. From this, a second refusal, of a position of this kind, it is a little pathetic to contemplate him—a man who a short year before had countless satellites at his beck and call, the strongest university backing, and superb laboratories—now engaged almost single-handed in the onerous task of putting some life into the much-neglected Oxford School of Medicine. No contrast could have been greater than that between the vigorous school he had left in Baltimore in its short-clothes, and the venerable one of which he was now the titular head—so venerable in fact it could claim as a graduate John of Gaddesden, one-time Fellow of Merton and supposedly the original of Chaucer's 'Doctour of Physick'. Even as late as the seventeenth century little had been required of the Regius Professor of Medicine. He was expected to read a lecture, to whoever cared to listen, twice a week, on the text of Hippocrates or Galen, in addition to which there was one dissection a year conducted during Lent by the Reader in Anatomy 'if the execution of a criminal happened opportunely'. At best, little was offered, and before the time of Radcliffe's benefactions the student sought his medical training abroad. Science lay under suspicion of heterodoxy, and her votaries were few until H. W. Acland's advent as Reader in Anatomy; indeed, there is a story of the Regius Professor even of Acland's early days, who, being shown a delicate preparation under the microscope, declared, first, that he did not believe it, and, secondly, that if it were true he did not think God meant us to know it! But, in time, a scientific renaissance came to Oxford through Acland, 'a man of enlightened mind and a strenuous fighter against the academic powers of darkness'. And just now had been imported another champion as fearless as he was picturesque in speech—as wise as he was fearless; one, moreover, who could hobnob over Aristotelian philosophy with the Dons at the high table, no less absorbingly than he could talk arm in arm with the youths below over the new science.

There appeared in the *British Medical Journal* for June 3rd a long, anonymous article written to dispel 'the misconception even now too prevalent among public and profession that there is no medical school at Oxford'.[1] The article gave full details of the course of study and examinations, of the teaching and the teachers, of the museum which John Ruskin and Acland had planned together, and of the laboratories associated with it in which physiology,

[1] It is not entirely clear who composed the major part of this article. If it was not Osler himself he must have given copious notes to the scribe furnished by the *B. M. J.*, who obviously wrote the last part of it.

anatomy, and pathology were properly housed and admirably presented; of still another department, however, it said:

> Pharmacology is excellently taught at Oxford, but it is only right to say that the credit for this belongs not to the university but to the lecturer. Dr. Smith-Jerome, in his teaching capacity, presents the picture, said by the ancients to be pleasing to the gods, of a good man struggling with adversity. He is an enthusiast who devotes himself to teaching as a labour of love. He lectures, prepares solutions, makes the arrangements for experiments and directs the practical work of his students in a sort of out-house in the Museum ground which is little better than a shed. For nine years he has done all this for a pittance which does not cover the expenses of his department. His only assistant is a boy who does little more than sweep out the rooms. All the mechanical work is done by the lecturer. . . . It is surely a disgrace that a great university like Oxford should be without a properly equipped department of pharmacology. . . .

This was plain talk for a new-comer; but there were pleasanter things to say of the Radcliffe Infirmary and Library; and here the article suddenly breaks off from what sounds a good deal like Osler to what is obviously 'representative' of the *B. M. J.*, for there follows a pen picture of the method of teaching by the Regius Professor of Medicine—'the most remarkable thing to be seen in Oxford to-day.' This was *gauche*, and probably the inevitable reaction of journalism, but the article served at least to call attention to the fact that Oxford had a medical school to be reckoned with.

The end of the month found him at St. Thomas's Hospital distributing the annual prizes to the medical students, a privilege which carries with it the need of giving an address, partly to the students, partly to their teachers. In the course of his remarks he dwelt at some length upon that thorny subject, not yet solved by London hospitals—the paying wards—wards for the 'poor rich' as contrasted with the 'rich poor'. He was in Dublin for the first four days in July, though it could not have taken all of that time to acquaint the Irish physicians, as he had agreed to do, with the purposes of the new association; consequently there must have been other engagements of which there is no record—some of them rather upsetting engagements, to judge from the second of the following notes. These were written to A. Salusbury MacNalty, now of the Ministry of Health, who at this particular time, having left Oxford to enter University College Hospital, was spokesman for the students who had asked Osler to give a post-prandial talk to their medical society.

Dear MacNalty, Kind boys! Yes of course I will dine with you—Trocadéro—anywhere! Send me word. Sincerely yours, Wm Osler. PS. Any hints about the Society?

Tuesday.

Dear MacNalty, Find out for me like a good fellow the date of the foundation of the Med. Society at U. C. & who were the chief men of the early days. What time do we dine at the Trocadéro? Do not order much dinner—at least not for me—I have been on the 'bread of affliction' for a week with a gastro-duodeno-jejuno-ileo-colic catarrh of Irish extraction. Sincerely yours, Wm Osler.

From all accounts they 'had a most enjoyable dinner, and a delightful lecture afterwards on the advantages of a medical society'. But it is difficult, indeed unnecessary, to dog the 'R. P. M.' too faithfully on his frequent peregrinations away from Oxford, where he should be 'having such a peaceful time'. In a letter of July 17th he wrote:

. . . Such a busy summer so far! Glorious weather & plenty of company. Mrs. Revere's visit was a great success. We have a house at last—very good situation 13 Norham Gardens, on the Parks. We get possession Aug. 1st & Grace will spend the month in getting the workmen into New England methods. You would not know Isaac Walton. Such changes in a year—an independent schoolboy. We have to give up Mrs M M's house for this month & he has gone to school to board. I have been flitting between Ch Ch & London. The Marburg [Warrington] collection will be a great addition—all sorts of good books and I have been adding some very good ones, a fine old Burton—a Basle Galen &c. The Ewelme rooms are in order & Grace & Miss N have been there with Bill for four days. I spent my first night there yesterday. . . . There is a new Royal Commission on vivisection—I have just been asked to be a member. I do not want to get tied up with these outside things. Already they have been piling up & they take the leisure I need for all sorts of work. I have just come from Manchester—meeting of the New Path. Society of Gt. Britain, very encouraging. Give my love to all the boys & kiss the bairns. . . .

To begin at the end: with the 'new' Pathological

Society of Great Britain and Ireland which was 'so encouraging'. Though by no means a new project it needed influential backing, and the one-time Pathologist to the Montreal General Hospital played much the same rôle behind the scenes that he had played with the Association of Physicians. Both he and Allbutt lent their presence to this first meeting, held on July 14th at Victoria University, Manchester, where Professor J. Lorrain Smith, who must be considered the actual founder of the society, was chief host. Osler's colleague, James Ritchie, says that it has always been a feature of the society that it should be a common meeting-ground for the physician and the professional pathologist, and consequently Osler's interest and regularity of attendance was a never-failing source of encouragement. However, there appear to have been other things in Manchester even more appealing than pathology, for later on he wrote to one of his American protégés: 'I am sending you this week a description of the Rylands Library which I saw this summer. It would be nice if we could spend a week there together. The place is ideal.'

But a far more engrossing place for a sojourn is Ewelme, and there, during the last two weeks of July, for the first time in man's memory the Master's rooms were actually occupied by their rightful owner. That the thirteen aged almsmen were thrilled needs no saying, even though they must be punctilious about attending prayers while the Master was in residence, for he had once before chided them in regard to what he considered a serious neglect, in view of all they owed to Alice of Suffolk. Heretofore, with the possible exception of Acland, the connexion of the Regius with this ancient house of benevolence, confined to a few hasty visits, had been of the most formal and perfunctory character. But the 21st Regius in sequence was a man of a new order: he was fascinated with the serene beauty of the place, knew the pains and aches of the old inmates and was generally adored by the villagers, among whom he played the part of antiquarian, physician, country gentleman, and lover of nature; enjoying everything and enjoyed by all. One day a picnic was given for the old men, with all the children of the village invited. In breaks they were taken to a place with the prickly name of Nettlebed, about five miles down the Henley Road, where in an open field booths had been set up, tables spread, an ample tea and its accessories provided. Other people from the neighbourhood who had children were also invited, among them some folks who had a big estate at Swyncombe on the hills above Ewelme; and late in the afternoon a child of ten who had been missed by her mother was found wandering around hand in hand with an unknown man she was calling 'William'. He had been devoting himself to her, and she was carrying a new doll.

But the great event of the week is still to be recorded. Ewelme church, with its low squat tower, stands on the edge of a hill overlooking a valley scooped out of the lower slopes of the Chilterns. Below lies the wee thatched village of some four hundred people, through which runs a brook lined by a watercress farm. To the visitor who may gain access to the Master's apartments adjoining the church and overlooking the picturesque and cloistered court of 'God's House' where the thirteen almsmen abide, there are many things of interest besides the architecture of a venerable building. For example, on the walls is an old engraving whose legend reads:

> This Palace derives its name from the Number of Elmes that grew here and formerly was call'd New Elm. Wm de la Pole duke of Suffolk marrying Alice only daughter of Thos Chaucer had by her large Possessions hereabouts and built this house with Brick—the Estate became Crown Land. K. H. VIII made this House an Honour by bestowing on it certain Manours.

The story of the Duke of Suffolk is given in Shakespeare's 'Henry VI', and his palace, like the de la Poles themselves, has long since disappeared; but the church, together with the cloistered court into which the Master's rooms look down, remains intact and unchanged after nearly five centuries. In one of these rooms stood an old safe which had last been opened no one knew when. In this room to-day is an elephantine folio entitled 'Ewelme Muniments', on the fly-leaf of which, under a kodak print, is written in Osler's hand:

> This photograph was taken on the day [July 28] we opened the

Safe in 1906. The Safe had rusted & we had tried in every way to open it & at last had to get Chubb's man from London. The interior was coated uniformly with mould & the documents were reeking with damp. We took them into the graveyard & the photograph shows my nephew Dr. W. W. Francis of Montreal spreading them to dry in the sun. I then took them to the Bodleian where Maltby [1] put them in order & bound them.

WILLIAM OSLER Master.

One can imagine Osler's delight at the discovery of this amazing collection of documents of the fourteenth to sixteenth centuries. One of the earliest is dated 1359—a grant of various manors in England to Thomas de la Pole, Knt., by the Abbot and Monks of the Convent of Grestens in Normandy. Ancient title-deeds, indentures, audit accounts, conveyances, court rolls—some of them, of the fourteenth century, in Norman French; as well as the original charter with the great seal of Henry VI attached, endowing the alms-house at Ewelme with the manors of Marsh, Connock, and Ramridge. Undated, but earliest of all, is a parchment roll of receipts, with directions for making what has since been called gunpowder: 'Cape Salepetr—pondus xvjd, de sulfure [&c.].' It was then unknown to warfare, but was useful for making a *'orrible* noise [*oribilem sonum*]. One might almost think Roger Bacon had been at Ewelme. And there are letters written on bits of parchment by Alice to her house-steward:

> My good Cok of Bylton, I grete you wele, and wol and pray you that ye take my litell Cofre of Golde, and wrappe it sure and fast in some cloth, and seele it wele, and send it heder to me by some sure felyship that cometh betwix, and in any wise that it be surely sent. And God have you in his merciful keping. Written in London in myne Inne the xiiii day of Marche. ALYCE.

This was all very exciting, and naturally enough when the muniments, having been restored by Maltby, were returned to their proper quarters there were many visitors to see them; indeed it is recorded that 'the Master of the Hospital' once invited the Oxford Architectural and Historical Society to hold a meeting at Ewelme, when he

[1] The University binder.

EWELME CHURCH AND MASTER'S ROOMS

RESCUING THE MUNIMENTS

'learnedly discoursed on the foundation, respecting which he exhibited interesting munimentary information'.

On August 1st they got possession of their new house at 13 Norham Gardens. Much was required in the way of reconstruction, and a few days later Osler wrote:

I have had to give up my sailing to-day. I am in a mess with the contractor for the changes in a new house & as we have to give up this one Nov. 1st I must have the papers signed before I leave. I have transferred my passage to the 11th in the hope of having everything settled but as we only got possession of the place on the 1st it may not be possible, in which case I cannot leave.

Many amusing stories are told of their getting into this their permanent abode—of an architect unacquainted with any but the huge bathtubs of English extraction, built into a room; of the scandal among Oxford plumbers when the Regius Professor's wife appeared in the shop to inspect an imported porcelain tub and, while backs were discreetly turned, actually climbed into it to see if it was long enough; but still more when they learned that four of these objects, without zinc trays underneath, were to be put into 13 Norham Gardens for a professor and his family, who with their guests apparently needed considerable washing; of the Oslers' efforts to get a tree cut down in order to let in more sunlight, an unheard-of request, which almost required an Act of Parliament. There were delays seemingly without end, Osler's antidote to which appears to have been Miss Haldane's 'Life of Descartes', to judge from the extracts therefrom entered during the month of August in his commonplace book. From all this they escaped to Scotland for a fortnight early in September—at Colonsay House again with Strathcona and the Howards; and possibly with Mr. Phipps, who at least had sent this characteristic and cordial invitation:

. . . and so [he says] we have taken Glenquoich. It is the place Lord Burton had for 23 years. We do not let the entire acreage, but what we have is ample for shooting and fishing. A character in Shakespeare says, 'A library, dukedom large enough for me,' so I suppose 34,000 acres will be a dukedom large enough for us. The fishing I understand is very good, and this will come in well for Isaac Walton Jr. We do not expect to have many visitors, but we hope that you and Mrs. Osler and Revere can come to us.

To Lewellys F. Barker from W. O. 7 Norham Gardens, Oxford, September 17, 1906.

I am glad to see that you gave a talk at Toronto on Hospital Organization, a topic on which they need enlightenment, and not only in Toronto, I fear. I hope you are returning in good form for the autumn's work. The meeting seems to have been an unusual success. I had most enthusiastic letters from some of the Englishmen. We have just returned from Scotland, and we go back next week to the Aberdeen celebration. The summer here has been delightful. I am at present struggling with the Harveian Oration—an awful task. It seems hopeless to make anything decent of it, but I am getting some information on the way about these sixteenth-century fellows. I am sorry that I had not an option, as I should have liked to have been prosector to Fabricius. Emerson's book is excellent—is it not? I have had several very enthusiastic letters from men to whom I sent it here. We hope to sail about the 1st of December. Sincerely yours, Wm Osler. Greetings to the family and the staff.

The quater-centenary of the University of Aberdeen—there is something enduring as granite in the very phrase—was held from September 25th to 29th with 'due pomp and circumstance'. The four Scottish universities have a stamp peculiar to themselves, the influence of Bologna and Paris still apparent in their constitutions. Especially at Aberdeen the spirit of simplicity, austerity, and earnestness had overcome the hindrances of poverty, meagre equipment, and adversity. But by now the benefactions of Andrew Carnegie had made the university education, which Bishop Elphinstone intended to put in the hands of every ambitious youth, even more accessible than it had been before; and, by an equally strange turn of fortune, another who nearly seventy years before had trudged all the way from Forres to Aberdeen, where he took ship for Canada, was now Chancellor of the university. Strathcona, indeed, had been one of the chief contributors to the new and beautiful building for Mareschal College which the King was about to dedicate.

Town, Gown, and weather all co-operated to make the occasion most auspicious. On the opening day there was a service in the Founder's chapel, and in the afternoon a parade in brilliant robes all the way from the new college through the town to the Gallowgate, where Strathcona had caused to be erected a temporary hall to hold 5,000 persons, a long procession of graduates, friends, and delegates from all over the academic world. The next day 150 of them were given degrees and duly capped by the Chancellor; but Thursday was the crowning day, when the King and Queen were present to declare the new building open; and that evening the great Strathcona banquet, about which so much was written at the time, was given to 2,400 guests; and there were fireworks afterwards and the usual students' torchlight parade. But Osler had slipped away from the banks of the Dee and this gay company, to read a paper on pneumonia, on the evening of the 28th, at Cupar-Fife before the local medical society—an act which probably pleased the profession of Scotland more, and was better for his health, than if he had stayed to the end in Aberdeen.

Not only was the Harveian Oration, of which he had written to Barker, giving him trouble at this time, but he was constantly being prodded by McCrae for his introduction to the forthcoming 'System of Medicine'; and as appears from another letter to his successor in Baltimore, he was planning for an address eight months ahead of time:

To L. F. Barker from W. O. 7 Norham Gardens, Sept. 21, 1906.

. . . It is by no means easy to settle the distribution of our subjects for our symposium [Washington, May 7, 1907]. Under our title, the question of functional diagnosis could come in very well, but it is impossible to say how far such a subject would appeal to Krehl. I think I had better write to him, but I hear, through a student, that he does not return to Strasburg until October 1st. Any change you, Stengel and Cabot care to make in the sub-division suggestion would, of course, be agreeable to me. The part I have selected, namely, the evolution of the idea of experiment in the study of nature, would form an interesting historical introduction. I will send Krehl's answer at once. I have sent a copy of this letter to Stengel and Cabot. . . .

The 18th of October came round and with it the Harveian Oration—that 'awful task' with which he had long been struggling; and as he subsequently wrote to Adami: 'I have had good fun reading all summer for it, but as usual put it off until the last moment and only finished the evening before.' This oration, it may be said, is the blue-ribbon event of British Medicine, and almost without interruption an annual lecture has been given since 1651, when William Harvey 'gave to the College of Physicians during his lifetime his patrimonial estate at Burmarsh in Kent, then valued at £56 a year'. Among other things, Harvey directed that—

> . . . once every year there shall be a general Feast kept within the said College for all the Fellows that shall please to come; and on a day when such feast shall be kept some one member of the College . . . shall make an oration in Latin publicly in the said College wherein shall be a commemoration of all the Benefactors of the said College by name . . . with an exhortation to imitate these Benefactors . . . and to the Fellows and Members to search and study out the secrets of Nature by way of experiment; and also for the honour of the profession to continue in mutual love and affection amongst themselves without which neither the dignity of the College can be preserved, nor yet particular men receive that benefit by their admission into the College which else they might expect, ever remembering that *Concordiâ res parvae crescunt, discordiâ magnae dilabuntur.*

These then are the terms of the gift left by the immortal discoverer of the circulation of the blood, to the college of which he was justly proud—terms, it may be added, not entirely lived up to except for the Feast. This is always good, and the Oration (in English since 1865) often is.

The Royal College of Physicians, as can be gathered, is a venerable institution,[1] in its way as conservative and respectable as the Athenaeum Club its neighbour. It occupies a handsome building at the Trafalgar-Square end of Pall Mall, containing, in addition to a most precious collection of portraits and medical memorabilia, a magnificent though little-used library. It has been seen that Osler was made a Fellow in his Montreal days and subsequently gave the Goulstonian Lectures; and if the College did not receive him twenty years later with open arms, doubtless it was because enthusiasm over a new-comer would be foreign to its dignity. Moreover, no

[1] Henry VIII in the tenth year of his reign (1518) founded the College at the solicitation of Thomas Linacre, the 'restorer of learning' in England, and by the advice of Cardinal Wolsey.

practising physician or surgeon can be transplanted to another community without provoking some misgivings on the part of those who dislike new ideas or who picture him as a possible rival. But Osler never heeded pin-pricks. He had lived for five years in Philadelphia with Pepper and kept on the friendliest terms, and would not have recognized Jealousy had he met her, green eyes and all. She and Gossip were almost the only people who never sat at his table or sojourned under his roof. 'He that repeateth a matter separateth many friends.'

Osler's unconventional ways were unquestionably caviare to the 'old brigade' in the College who were in control of its affairs, the younger men remaining inactive in the background. The old college of Linacre speaks for the consulting physicians, but is no longer the mouthpiece of the profession at large, and the growth of other and more democratic societies has robbed the R. C. P. of its function of presiding over medical progress. In consequence it has become largely an administrative body, concerned in the main with the medical education and the conduct of its licentiates and members. Osler took little interest in administration as such, regarded the system of examinations as not only antiquated but opposed to the best interests of the profession, and fell into no comfortable position in an institution that had lost close touch with progressive medicine. He was too generous and kind to let such things as these generate any antipathy in his mind, but he did not feel drawn to take an active part in its work. Had he been forced to do so by an election to the presidency, there is little doubt that his progressive instincts, his efficiency, his wide following, particularly among the younger men, his ability to activate dormant institutions like the Maryland 'Faculty' into renewed vigour—that these qualities might have combined to make an ideal presiding officer who could, if any one, pull the old College out of its doldrums. But the presidency is practically restricted to Fellows resident in London, and, despite his keen appreciation for its long and honourable history, it would appear that the only feature of the College which he found after his own heart was its library. This he used constantly, and on it, as on all libraries he used, he showered gifts. Indeed he went through the library so thoroughly in search of unused Harveiana that, finding the Royal Charter granted to William Harvey, his pension, diplomas, and so on, to be sorely in need of proper care, he, in characteristic fashion, gave the honorarium paid for his Oration for the purpose of having them properly bound.[1]

For the oration Osler did not follow Weir Mitchell's advice given earlier in the year, but chose as his title 'The Growth of Truth as illustrated in the Discovery of the Circulation of the Blood'. He took his hearers back in spirit three centuries, to days when 'the dead hand of the great Pergamite still lay heavy on all thought, and Descartes had not yet changed the beginning of philosophy from wonder to doubt'. No summary could do justice to his review of the state of knowledge and the mental attitude of men towards scientific truth at the time when Harvey broke the bonds holding their minds in slavish submission to authority. Perhaps his vivid description of Harvey's Lumleian Lecture in the middle section of the address may best serve to give an idea of the text. He had spoken of the fact that the really notable years in the annals of Medicine were few, and that with many of the greatest names and events we cannot associate any fixed dates. He said, however :

> There is one *dies mirabilis* in the history of the College—in the history, indeed, of the medical profession of this country, and the circumstances which made it memorable are well known to us. At ten o'clock on a bright spring morning, April 17, 1616, an unusually large company was attracted to the New Anatomical Theatre of the Physicians' College, Amen Street. The second Lumleian Lecture of the annual course, given that year by a new man, had drawn a larger gathering than usual, due in part to the brilliancy of the demonstration on the previous day, but also it may be because rumours had spread abroad about strange views to be propounded by the lecturer. I do not know if at the College the same stringent rules as to compulsory attendance prevailed as at the Barber Surgeons' Hall. Doubtless not ; but the President, and Censors, and Fellows would be there in due array ; and with the help of the picture of

[1] An interesting note made by Osler on the Harveian Orations will be found in 'Bibliotheca Osleriana', p. 83 (in press).

'The Anatomy Lecture by Banister', which is in the Hunterian collection, Glasgow, and a photograph of which Dr. Payne has recently put in our library, we can bring to mind this memorable occasion. We see the 'Anatomy', one of the six annually handed over to the College, on the table, the prosector standing by the skeleton near at hand, and very probably on the wall the very *Tabulae* of dissection of the arteries, veins and nerves that hang above us to-day. But the centre of attention is the lecturer—a small, dark man, wand in hand, with black piercing eyes, a quick vivacious manner, and with an ease and grace in demonstrating which bespeaks the mastery of a subject studied for twenty years with a devotion that we can describe as Hunterian. A Fellow of nine years' standing, there was still the salt of youth in William Harvey when, not, as we may suppose, without some trepidation, he faced his auditors on this second day—a not uncritical audience, including many men well versed in the knowledge of the time and many who had heard all the best lecturers of Europe.... And we may be sure that Harvey's old fellow-students at Padua—Fortescue, Fox, Willoughby, Mounsell and Darcy—would honour their friend and colleague with their presence; and Edward Lister, also a fellow-Paduan, the first of his name in a family which has given three other members to our profession—two distinguished and one immortal. It was not a large gathering, as the Fellows, members, licentiates, and candidates numbered only about forty; but as the lecture was a great event in the community, there would be present many interested and intelligent laymen of the type of Digby, and Ashmole, and Pepys—the 'curious', as they were called, for whom throughout the seventeenth century the anatomy lecture equalled in attraction the play. Delivered in Latin and interspersed here and there with English words and illustrations, there were probably more who saw than comprehended, as Sir Thomas Browne indicated to his son Edward when he lectured at Chirurgeons' Hall.

He went on to describe the opposition aroused by Harvey's revolutionary views, the publication of which was delayed for another twelve years, even then to be tardily accepted, so well illustrating Locke's dictum that 'Truth scarce ever carried it by vote anywhere at its first appearance'.

It was subsequently said by one who was present, that the delivery of the annual panegyric on William Harvey has become so great a tax on human ingenuity that many go to hear the oration much as people fond of sensation go to see a performance on a tight-rope, for it is as difficult to say anything original in a Harveian Oration as in a Bampton Lecture. Osler, however, had no need to stoop to the usual artifices, for, as poor Stella said of Swift, he could write beautifully on a broomstick, and with no display of learning hastily borrowed or 'conveyed' for the occasion. Even his method of handling his obligation to the Founder's admonitions, in his closing paragraphs, is of interest in showing something of his reverence for tradition :

But the moving hand reminds your orator, Mr. President, of a bounden duty laid upon him by our great Dictator to commemorate on this occasion by name all of our benefactors ; to urge others to follow their example ; to exhort the Fellows and Members to study out the secrets of Nature by way of experiment ; and lastly, for the honour of the profession, to continue in love and affection among ourselves. No greater tribute to Harvey exists than in these simple sentences in which he established this lectureship, breathing as they do the very spirit of the man, and revealing to us his heart of hearts. Doubtless, no one more than he rejoices that our benefactors have now become so numerous as to nullify the first injunction; and the best one can do is to give a general expression of our thanks, and to mention here and there, as I have done, the more notable among them. But this is not enough. While we are praising famous men, honoured in their day and still the glory of this College, the touching words of the son of Sirach remind us : 'Some there be that have no memory, who are perished as though they had never been, and are become as though they had never been born.' Such renown as they had, time has blotted out ; and on them the iniquity of oblivion has blindly scattered her poppy. A few are embalmed in the biographical dictionaries ; a few are dragged to light every year at Sotheby's, or the memory is stirred to reminiscences as one takes down an old volume from our shelves. But for the immense majority on the long roll of our Fellows—names ! names ! names ! —nothing more ; a catalogue as dry and meaningless as that of the ships, or as the genealogy of David in the Book of Chronicles. Even the dignity of the presidential chair does not suffice to float a man down the few centuries that have passed since the foundation of the College. Who was Richard Forster ? Who was Henry Atkins ? Perhaps two or three among us could tell at once. And yet by these men the continuity and organic life of the College has been carried on, and in maintaining its honour, and furthering its welfare, each one in his day was a benefactor, whose memory it is our duty, as well as our pleasure, to recall. Much of the nobility of the profession depends upon this great cloud of witnesses, who pass into the silent land—pass and leave no sign, becoming as though they had never been born. And it was the pathos of this fate, not less pathetic because common to all but a few, that wrung from the poet that sadly true comparison of the race of man to the race of leaves !

The story of Harvey's life, and a knowledge of the method of his work, should be the best stimulus to the Fellows and Members to carry out the second and third of his commands; and the final one, to continue in love and affection among ourselves, should not be difficult to realize. Sorely tried as he must have been, and naturally testy, only once in his writings, so far as I have read, does the old Adam break out. With his temperament, and with such provocation, this is an unexampled record, and one can appreciate how much was resisted in those days when tongue and pen were free. Over and over again he must have restrained himself as he did in the controversy with Riolan, of whom, for the sake of old friendship, he could not find it in his heart to say anything severe. To-day his commands are easier to follow, when the deepened courtesies of life have made us all more tolerant of those small weaknesses, inherent in our nature, which give diversity to character without necessarily marring it. To no man does the right spirit in these matters come by nature, and I would urge upon our younger Fellows and Members, weighing well these winged words, to emulate our great exemplar, whose work shed such lustre upon British Medicine, and whom we honour in this College not less for the scientific method which he inculcated than for the admirable virtues of his character.

An interesting function occurred at the close of the oration which permitted Osler to turn congratulations upon another—an unusual ceremony, in which a member of the College of Surgeons for the first time was presented with the Moxon Medal of the College of Physicians, 'for his long and valuable services to clinical medicine'. This was his old and greatly valued friend, Mr. Jonathan Hutchinson, who had written to say that he was aware the award had been made through Osler's instigation. Then there followed the Feast, to which Osler had invited two guests, one of them Mr. Henry Phipps of New York, the other a shaggy-browed old gentleman of eighty-six, one-time factor of the Hudson Bay Company, now Lord Strathcona and Mount Royal, Chancellor of the universities at Montreal and Aberdeen.

Needless to say, the oration was widely commented upon in medical circles, even the 'Thunderer' devoted a full column to it; but Osler had disappeared and was evidently paying dearly for the experience, for in his account-book opposite October 21st is written: 'Heavy cold—housed.' He recovered, however, and is found in Reading on the

24th buying at an old book shop, 'Horace in London', 1813, by the author of the 'Rejected Addresses'; and two days later from Oxford he writes: 'We have a fine exhibit of Vesal this eve at the Junior Scientific—nearly everything! I got a curious *Fabrica* the other day, Ingolstadt, 18th century. You will see my Harveian Oration in the Lancet & B. M. J. this week—a hard job over. It seems to have pleased the boys.' That he was looking forward to his annual visit to America for his mother's birthday now appears in a letter of November 1st to L. F. Barker:

So glad to have your letter this eve & to hear that you are better. You were most wise to have the tonsils attacked. What a source of endless mischief they are! I am much impressed here with the extraordinary frequence of tonsilar enlargements in the children & no doubt the great prevalence of acute rheumatism among them is connected with this. I am so glad that Norton is taking Hurd's place as it will put him in the line for work of this sort. Thanks for the offer for quarters but I have promised to stay with Jacobs & I shall put up for a few days at the Hospital so as to see as much as possible of the boys. . . . The Harveian went off very well. I could not get in all I wished to say & could not touch two interesting points illustrated in all discoveries of the first rank—the law of anticipation & the law of residuals—very well shown in Harvey's work. I have a nice little clinical class, & the school seems gaining, but the antique collegiate system is very obstructive and it is hard to do much in short terms of 8 weeks—& only three of them. With love to the family all—Yours ever W. O.

The San Francisco earthquake had served to dislodge one of his former assistants, George Blumer, into a new position as Professor of Medicine at Yale, to whom he wrote on the 13th and told what would be a good thing for Yale, but what took Yale some time to learn:

I am very glad indeed to have your letter with the interesting memorandum of Glisson who was, as you say, really a great observer and a great clinician. I am glad to hear that you like your work at Yale. I wish they could give you a proper University Hospital. It would be a very good thing for Yale to undertake some good scheme exactly on the same lines as they would undertake a scientific laboratory. Organized by the university, equipped by it, paid for by it, and managed by it without any outside help or interference, separate clinics and good laboratories, it would be an encouraging example to scores of other places, and I am convinced that there is no one greater need in the medical profession in the United States than the establishment of these clinics on Teutonic lines. I will send you my Harveian Oration very soon. With love to Amaryllis, Sincerely yours.

Some time during the autumn, it may be assumed, Osler must have been prevailed upon by Albert Venn Dicey, Professor of English Law, and Fellow of All Souls, to lend himself for a lecture in Camden Town before the Working Men's College, of which Professor Dicey was President. Accordingly on Saturday evening, the 17th of November, before these working-people, he drew a picturesque and understandable parallel between the human body and the steam-engine, using terms in regard to personal hygiene which the people before him could grasp—about fuel and food, about small repairs and large repairs, regularity of work and play, and finally about tobacco and alcohol. Man's chief foes are those of his own making. 'Throw all the beer and spirits into the Irish Channel, the English Channel and the North Sea for a year', the *Abingdon Herald* quotes him as saying, 'and people in England would be infinitely better. It would certainly solve all the problems with which the philanthropists, the physicians, and the politicians have to deal. Do you suppose you need tobacco? On the day after you had dumped all the tobacco into the sea you would find that it was very good for you and hard on the fishes.' Never mind if Benjamin Franklin had made a similar remark long before, it deserved repeating.

To whatever soil he was transplanted, the same Osler grew and flourished, modifying his environment more than it modified him. It is interesting to see how consistently he began anew in Oxford with precisely the same projects as those which had engaged him in Montreal, Philadelphia, and Baltimore. A consuming interest in libraries and librarians; the revivifying of an old medical society or the organization of new ones; the establishment of a medical journal, the bringing together of discordant elements in the profession, and the raising of money when money was needed. Lavish in his own name when it came to giving, he must have been a hard man to refuse when in an offhand way he asked for help, as he had occasionally asked Mr. Gates, Strathcona, and others. Oxford was in great need of funds, for, however rich some of the colleges might be, the university had scant funds to expend on general projects. The Bodleian, for example, was bursting with books which lined every staircase and landing; the accommodation for readers was far from sufficient; and the older portion of the catalogue was sadly in need of revision. The ageing Nicholson had these needs well in mind, but the poor man knew not where to turn. Some one to raise money was needed.

Though in his letter to Whitelaw Reid twelve months before this, Osler had broadly hinted that gifts from Americans would be acceptable, the part he played in starting the Oxford University Endowment Fund is not in the official record, which states that 'the Fund arose out of an appeal made on the suggestion of the late Lord Brassey, by the Chancellor of the University—Lord Curzon of Kedleston—in 1907', but Osler at least had certainly started to work before the official appeal, as the following letter, among others, indicates:

To Mr. Henry Phipps. Friday [Nov. 23rd]

I am sure you will like the suggestiveness & pleasant style of Crozier's books. How delighted you must be to see the family growing. We sail on Wednesday, 28th, to be present at my mother's birthday. It is a shame to bother you about outside matters, but the Hon. C. T. [*sic*] Brassey & a few of us have a scheme afoot for meeting the needs of this old University. I have been assigned the superintendence of the collections for the Medical School Laboratories. We need about £40,000. I am especially interested in a small laboratory & clinical department for the out-patient work at the Radcliffe Infirmary which would cost about £5,000. Would you care to help me in this matter? I will have the general circular sent you. I will send you my Harveian Oration in a few days. With kind remembrances to Mrs. Phipps.

The whole project so strongly savours of Osler's methods that one is impelled to believe he must have been, though not the prime mover, at least an activating influence. Probably, however, were he living, nothing would induce him to admit it. The original trustees included the Archbishop of York, the Hon. T. A. Brassey, Henry Miers, Sir William

Anson, and Osler. The fund finally became vested in a body of twelve trustees, of whom four were resident members of the university, and in this capacity Osler served during the remainder of his life. The sum of about £150,000 was collected during 1907 and subsequent years, and largely through Osler's influence the trustees spent considerable sums in the interest of science, particularly in endowing the School of Engineering and in contributing largely to the new clinical laboratory. Then, too, both he and Sir William Anson were curators of the Bodleian, and the construction of the underground storage chamber, with Osler's enthusiastic support, was thus undertaken. But some of these things happen later on, and it must suffice here to pursue Mr. Phipps, who wrote from New York, December 13th: 'I hope you will be able to raise a sum sufficient to carry out your plan for a medical school laboratory for Oxford. When you have got in your large subscriptions I shall be pleased to help you with a small one.' And the following June Osler wrote:

Thank you so much for your kind letter and for your generous contribution. It is extremely good of you to help us in this way. Oxford may not seem to have any special claims on America, yet if you could have seen the gathering we had the other night of the 160 Rhodes scholars, the great majority of whom are from the United States, you would have realized how much of American life goes on here. It is remarkable, too, the number of people who come over to study different subjects, particularly to work at the Bodleian. I will write to Lord Curzon & tell him of your kind subscription, which can go into the general fund, but ear-marked for my new clinical laboratory.

On Sunday the 25th he wrote to H. B. Jacobs in regard to the death of an old Baltimore friend; and as usual he fended off any too great show of sentiment—a feeling which he once said, 'brought all his mother into his eyes'—and turned quickly to other things:

Sunday.

Dear Jacobs, So sad to hear of poor Atkinson's death—it was so good of you to cable. I have cabled Mrs A. to-day. He was one of my best friends & I shall miss him sadly in my visits. He told me that pneumonia was the one disease he dreaded as he had an old heart lesion. I do hope he has left his family comfortable. . . .

I am glad you liked the Harveian. We sail by the Celtic on Wednesday 28th & shall come down from New York. I hope to be in time for the presentation of the Marburg collection. I am bringing a very special treasure for it. The book market is very active just now & I have been getting a few beauties at auction. The other eve at the Academy Club dinner young Sieveking said incidentally that he had the sale catalogue of Sir Thomas Browne's books! I whistled as there is but one copy known & that in the B. M. The next day like an angel he sent it to me! We have had splendid weather until a few days ago. All well.

It was to be another home-coming trip like the one of a year before—even more exhausting, if anything. They landed in New York on December 6th, went immediately to Baltimore, and submitted to dinners and receptions for a week; then to Canada, stopping in Hamilton for a day to see his old friends, among them the Mallochs and Mullins. The following day was his mother's one-hundredth birthday, which excited other people more than the hale and hearty recipient of their attentions in the Wellesley Street house, for she had had considerable experience with birthdays. But it was not solely a family affair. There were countless messages, letters, and telegrams of congratulation: from the Archbishop of Canterbury, from the Governor-General, Earl Grey, the Canadian House of Commons, the Johns Hopkins staff, and so on. She was rather inclined to see the humour of it, as she did of most things in life. But the day unloosed her recollections, and she told of having walked all the way from Hampstead to Bushy Park to carry the news of the Battle of Waterloo; and how she had been 'delicate, frail and indulged' as a child, but this all changed, and before they 'came out' she took lessons in how to patch leather boots. The marvellous birthday cake with 100 candles was brought up to her room, which she was not permitted to leave—a cake representing the five rulers she had lived under: two Georges, William, Victoria, and Edward—and it took two men to carry it. She had had some spoons made, with a Cornish cross for a handle—three sizes of them, for the three generations of descendants, 6 living children, 26 grandchildren, 21 great-grandchildren; and there were souvenir plates given to the cousins and others who were equally numerous. As a final touch, the Cornish Society in Toronto gave her a serenade and sang some old Cornish songs she loved. Needless to say, the occasion roused the newspapers and an effort was made to revive a discussion on the chloroform theory. But a *World* reporter who got access to the one of her distinguished sons 'whose views on the age limit readily admit of such perversion that no amount of explaining could now correct false impressions of them', got little satisfaction beyond the reply: 'That 's an old chestnut.'

They stayed on for several days at the home of his brother, Edmund, where he spent a Sunday morning raining notes upon his old friends—to 'Ned' Milburn, his Barrie schoolmate, and others he had been unable to see. One of them, for example, went to the wife of his former pupil, who was making a gallant fight in Gravenhurst against an infection contracted while in charge of the tuberculosis clinic at the Hopkins:

To Mrs. C. D. Parfitt. Craigleigh, Rosedale [no date].

I cannot tell you how distressed I am to leave Toronto without seeing Charles. It was quite my intention to visit him but so many matters of the greatest importance came up about the new Hospital & the University that I could not escape, either yesterday or Monday. I got here on Friday to find my mother wonderfully well. She enjoyed the day so much. I had a long talk with C about Charles, whom he had just seen. I am glad to hear that he thinks him better and should gradually pick up. I do hope he may gain strength as the acute process subsides. Let me have a line to the J. H. H. next week. We go to Montreal tonight & then on to Boston, N. Y., Phila, and Baltimore—sailing Jan. 8th. I am sending Charles my Harveian Oration. With best love to you both.

While at 'Craigleigh' he was waited upon by representatives who formally offered him the presidency of the University of Toronto. To an outsider it would seem to have been a vain proposal, though there appears to have been no thought of this in the minds of the Toronto people. However this may be, he gave no definite reply until two weeks later. Among other things of which there is record, was his unveiling, before the Toronto Library Association, of the portrait of his old friend, James E. Graham; and it was no less characteristic that he should take the trouble to write the leading article to help boost a new medical journal just being started at Winnipeg for the benefit of the profession of the Canadian North West.[1] From Toronto they went to Montreal for a few days, and thence to Boston to spend Christmas at Mrs. Revere's, with whom Mrs. Osler and Revere remained while he returned to Baltimore to stay for a brief sojourn with Dr. Jacobs. From there on the last day of the year he wrote to the chairman of the Toronto committee saying:

I have given the most careful consideration to the proposal made by the Governors of the University, and regret exceedingly to say that I cannot see my way to accept the position. While realizing fully the importance and the extraordinary possibilities of the situation I am confident that neither by training nor disposition am I adapted to it. . . .

---

[1] 'Note on the Use of a Medical Journal.' *Western Canada Medical Journal*, Jan. 1907, i, 1–2.

CHAPTER XXVII

1907

THE 'OPEN ARMS'

THE new year began characteristically with a gift to a library, an obituary tribute to a physician, and a re-crossing of the Atlantic—it had become a saying in Oxford that the Oslers often spent their week-ends in America. The Warrington collection, which Mr. W. A. Marburg had purchased for the Johns Hopkins Medical School, was formally presented on January 2nd, when Osler, Welch, and the university librarian, Mr. Raney, all made interesting addresses.[1] Osler told the story of the acquisition of the books and of their previous habitat in the old Warrington Academy, the educational centre of the Unitarians in England; of the Rev. John Aikin, of his son the doctor, and his granddaughter Lucy; of Joseph Priestley, and of Thomas Percival, whose work on 'Medical Ethics' was the basis of the code of the American Medical Association. He spoke of what a library should represent in the future development of the school; how it should co-operate rather than compete with the other local libraries; and how collections of the sort to be presented enhanced its usefulness, particularly on the historical side. 'When a man devotes his life', he said, 'to some particular branch of study, and accumulates, year by year, a more or less complete literature, it is very sad after his death to have such a library come under the hammer—almost the inevitable fate.' The intrinsic value of that portion of the Warrington Library which had been purchased was not especially great, and, to atone for this, Osler had secured a few rare duplicates from the library of the Royal College of Physicians, and had added himself the volume of chief value:

> In practical illustration of my remarks [he said], I beg to present to the Marburg collection an original edition of the 'De Motu

---

[1] Cf. *Johns Hopkins Hospital Bulletin*, April 1907.

Cordis', 1628, perhaps the greatest single contribution to medicine ever made, and which did as much for physiology as the 'Fabrica' of Vesalius did for anatomy. The 'De Motu Cordis' has become an excessively rare book. I had been on the lookout for a copy for nearly ten years. It had not appeared in an auction catalogue since 1895. Then in August of last year a very much cut, stained, and unbound copy was offered to me at a very high figure. It had come from the library of Dr. Pettigrew, the author of a work on 'Medical Biography'. I had been waiting a long time for a copy, but this looked so shabby and dirty that I decided not to take it. Some months later the booksellers sent it back nicely cleansed and beautifully bound, and this time I succumbed. Within forty-eight hours the same dealers sent me another copy from the library of the late Professor Milne Edwards, of Paris, uncut and very nicely bound, which they offered at the same price. Naturally, I took the larger copy, and the other went to a friend in this country. The copy I here present to the library has been a little too energetically cleansed, so that the leaves are very tender and in places have had to be repaired. It came from the library of a physician in London and the bibliographical data are found attached.

The tribute to a physician was paid two days later, shortly before his sailing, when with many others he attended a meeting held in New York in memory of Dr. Mary Putnam Jacobi, the wife of his old friend. In his brief address, he said:

For years I have been waiting the advent of the modern Trotula, a woman in the profession with an intellect so commanding that she will rank with the Harveys, the Hunters, and Pasteurs; the Virchows, and the Listers. That she has not yet arisen is no reflection on the small band of women physicians who have joined our ranks in the last fifty years. Stars of the first magnitude are rare, but that such a one will arise among women physicians I have not the slightest doubt. And let us be thankful that when she comes she will not have to waste her precious energies in the worry of a struggle for recognition. She will be of the type of mind and training of Mary Putnam Jacobi; her victory will be not on the practical but on the scientific side in which many new avenues are open to women, much more attractive and suitable than in general or special practice to which heretofore they have been restricted. . . .

They sailed from New York on the 8th; and a week later a postcard to McCrae reads:

Wonderful trip: 5 days, 11 hours & a few seconds! No bad weather. Everything here in such confusion—workmen still in the house, but it looks very well & we live in hope. I am greatly pleased with the prospects of the System. By the way, do you like the name Modern Medicine? I do not—who selected it? I would prefer a System. Send you titles very soon. Love to Welch & all. Yours, W. O.

For six months they had been struggling with the necessary alterations to their new house. They had returned to find one side of it open to the world, necessitating a sojourn of ten days at the King's Arms Hotel; and it was months after they moved in before the last of the workmen vanished. Little wonder that when they finally took up their abode his account-book records: '*Jan.* 27. In bed—schnupfen. *Jan.* 31. Out.' And betweenwhiles he writes: 'I am enjoying two days in bed with a cold. Such a mess here! Workmen everywhere but when they get out we will have a very comfortable house. We have had a cold spell just in time to test our new furnace & the water-heater.'

There may have been reasons for all this delay. There was encountered in later years at 13 Norham Gardens a person on his back, tinkering with some water-pipes, who, to atone for some mildly disparaging remarks he had uttered on the subject of American plumbing, said: 'We loves to work 'ere for 'er Ladyship ever since we was first on the job in the 'ouse. There was 120 of us, all told, many now dead with the Hoxford and Bucks in France, plumbers and painters and paper-'angers and carpenters and masons—especially plumbers when Sir William an' 'er Ladyship was in America. When we was through, sometime in the hautumn, we found Dr. Osler—'e wasn't Sir William then—'ad left money for us to 'ave a big dinner, and we 'ad it in the garden, foremen and all, and drank their 'ealths and 'ad our photograph taken and it 'angs in the hoffice to-day. There 's always a good tip comes when we works 'ere.'

To J. William White from W. O. 13 Norham Gardens, Feb. 1st.

Dear J. W. W. I hope by this time you are back and in harness & happy. We had a very nice trip—rather too short and hurried. It was nice to find Mitchell in such good form & the Trust Co is all the better—apparently—for the acute 'bust-up'. We got back two weeks ago & have been trying to get settled in our new house, but it seems hopeless. We are living in two rooms & trying to drive the workmen out. It will be very nice when finished. The Phila. rooms [there were also Baltimore, Boston and Montreal rooms] are at your disposal when you come over next year. I hear from Mrs. Abbey that E. A. is much better & has finished the reredos. Also from Baltimore that Sargent's picture, which has just reached there, has captured the town. I wish there was a decent place to hang it. I come out in April—for the Congress. If I spend a night in Phila. it will be at 1810 [Dr. White's]. Love to your *patient saviour*.

Another letter shows that he continued to take an interest in the subject with which he began his career :

To Professor J. W. Robertson, Montreal. Feb. 3, 1907.

When in Montreal a few weeks ago, I had a chat with Sir William [Macdonald] and Mr. Peterson on the possibility of organizing, in connection with the Agricultural College, an extensive Department of Medical Zoology in which the whole subject of parasitism should be considered. Sir William was anxious that I should see you, but I had only part of two days in Montreal. I promised him to get a schema from Stiles of Washington, who is certainly the leading expert on parasites in the English-speaking world. The department could be made a most important one and it has such close affiliations with disease that the same man could very well lecture on parasites in the medical school. There would be no lack of candidates for such a place, and there are one or two very good men available, particularly Todd who has done so much good work on the ticks. I should not be surprised, however, if such a position were thrown open, that Stiles himself might be a candidate. I have asked him to prepare a memorandum which I will forward to you.

On February 7th he was in Edinburgh as the guest of the Royal Medical Society, and at their annual dinner made a most effective speech, subsequently published,[1] in which he dwelt particularly on the relations of this, the oldest medical society in the English-speaking world, to the profession of the United States and Canada. 'Looking over the list of members since 1737', he said, 'I was prepared, of course, to find the names of many of the great men of the profession, but I did not expect to find a list of such extraordinary distinction. I doubt if there is any

[1] *Scottish Medical and Surgical Journal*, March 1907.

other society in the world, except perhaps the Royal Society of London, with such a roll of honour.' And he went on to mention in picturesque phraseology some of the more notable Scotchmen who had been members, particularly those who had so markedly influenced American medicine, in which connexion he naturally referred to the Edinburgh theses purchased five years before.

> And let me in conclusion [he said], call to remembrance the memory of a man to whom we all owe a great debt. I hold in my hand a volume of the MS. Notes of the Lectures of John Rutherford, who introduced clinical teaching into Edinburgh in 1747–8. It was my intention to leave this precious volume here, but to my joy I found this afternoon, in the Library of the Royal College of Physicians, the lectures of 1749–50, and in the same handwriting, curiously enough. . . . They are of great value as a record of the initiation of clinical teaching in the English-speaking schools; and what has been called the Edinburgh method dates from the introduction by Rutherford of practical classes in the Royal Infirmary. But we owe the method to the Dutch, who are our masters in this as in nearly all the advances in modern civilization. Rutherford and his colleagues, Plimmer, Sinclair and Innes, were pupils of Boerhaave, the Dutch Hippocrates, under whom the objective method of Sydenham reached its highest development, and out of which, when united to the 'anatomical thinking' of Morgagni, and the new methods of physical diagnosis, modern clinical medicine has evolved.

The following day was devoted to the students, before whom he spoke on cerebrospinal fever—a timely subject, for there had been an outbreak of the disease in epidemic form in Glasgow, Edinburgh, and elsewhere in Scotland. The lecture was to have been given in the largest theatre in the Infirmary, but this proving inadequate for the crowd demanding admission, an adjournment was made to McEwan Hall which was filled to overflowing, even to the platform. He had a great reception, according to all reports, particularly from the students, who had him to dine that evening as their particular guest, and as likely as not, in view of what happened the next year, some of them, then and there, said to themselves: 'That 's the kind of human being we should elect Lord Rector.'

To Thomas McCrae from W. O. Feb. 16.

Dear Mac, I am still a delinquent. I am struggling with that introduction [for the 'System of Medicine'[1]] and hope to get it off next week. I have the bulk of it done. They could go ahead as I have always urged & print my introduction with roman pagination as is the case with von Ziemssen and Nothnagel. It will not take a week to print my part & it need not come back. I have written to Poynton. I have not heard from Billings or perhaps he has written to you direct. I suppose we must accept the name Modern Medicine. I will write about the title page in which of course your name must come. I doubt if they will allow it on the back. What have you settled about the mental section?

I have been knocked out with a cold but am better. My secretary's mother has been ill & is dead and she has been laid up with the grip —dry & wet. The house is still in possession of workmen but one by one we are ousting them. I had a most festive visit last week in Edinburgh. I was half dead with a cold but I lectured to the students & had a great evening at the Royal Medical Society, at which they asked Rush, Shippen, Wistar, Bard, Hosack, Sam L. Mitchill, the Moultries (Charleston) David Ramsay, Upton Scott (1st President, Medical & Chirurgical Faculty of Maryland) & a number of old Colonial members to meet me. I wish Welch had been there. Yours, W. O.

The same day, on a postcard from Oxford, he wrote: 'I am sending Vivisection Commission, 1st report. Starling's evidence is A.1. He 's a cracker-jack.' This note refers to the hearings before a Royal Commission on the subject of vivisection; and as Huxley in 1876 had been the chief exponent of animal experimentation, so now Professor E. H. Starling was the most active agent in organizing the profession in its defence—and, it may be added, with much greater success. He had written to Osler on October 16, 1906, asking him to give evidence and suggesting the outline of his précis, which the witness was expected to submit before being questioned. But although the hearings began on October 31st of 1906, a full year elapsed before it became Osler's turn to be called upon.[2]

[1] Vol. I was issued by the publishers for distribution on April 24, 1907.

[2] The testimony, which was not completed until March 25, 1908, is contained in the five successive folio reports of the Royal Commission, giving the minutes of evidence comprised in nearly 22,000 questions which, with

Among the many unfinished articles and scraps of memoranda found among Osler's papers after his death there is one entitled 'The College of the Book', to which the following extract of a letter of February 19th, to Mr. Gilman, in all probability refers:

> Thanks for returning the manuscript and for your criticisms. I think the name would have to be carefully considered. I doubt if the word 'College' could be used. I will bring out more clearly the distinction you refer to between the requirements of a cataloguer or attendant and those of the men who wish to take up administration work. A big scheme might, of course, appeal to Mr. Carnegie, and the question is, who would be the best person to present it if put together in an attractive form. I suppose, in this country, John Morley is as close, or closer, to him than any one—what do you think?

His idea, apparently, was that there should be established at Oxford in connexion with the Clarendon Press and the Bodleian a training-ground for the large army of library workers throughout Great Britain, whose experience ordinarily is acquired in a most haphazard way as apprentices, without any actual preliminary training other than that given by a general education:

> There should be [he says] a college where men could learn everything relating to the Book, from the preparation of manuscript & the whole mystery of authorship, to the art of binding; everything from the manufacture of paper to the type with which the book is printed; everything relating to the press & to the mart; everything about the history of printing from Gutenberg to Hoe; everything about the precursors of the printed book: the papyrus, the rolls, the parchment & the vellum, even about the old writing on the burnt bricks of Nineveh; everything about the care of books, the Library lore, how to stack & store books; how to catalogue, how to distribute them; how to make them vital living units in a community; everything that the student should know about the use of books, his skilled tools in the building of his mind. That there should be such a College & that it should be at Oxford is evident to any one who knows the Bodleian Library & the Clarendon Press. Here is a unique opportunity—let us see how it can be utilized.

And he proceeds, on separate sheets, to speak of the four great departments of the College: (1) the School of Library Economics, (2) the School of Bibliography, and

their answers, will serve as a mine of information on the subject of vivisection, and its opponents, for all time (see below, p. 108).

apparently a School of Publication, and of Printing; but he gets lost in notes on the history of libraries. There is a lecture-list to cover four prospective courses on libraries ancient and modern; another on 'the book' itself, and its make-up; still another to cover copyrighting, publication, reviewing, selling, auctions, &c. 'To carry out a scheme of this extent', he says, 'would require a rearrangement of existing conditions at the Bodleian and the Press—changes which are urgently called for in both places—a separate fireproof building, in underground communication with the present ones and which should be devoted to administration, reading-rooms, department-rooms, and teaching-rooms. . . .' No wonder he suggested that they might have to call upon Mr. Carnegie, for such a project would be far beyond the reach of the University Endowment Fund.[1]

During this Hilary term he was due for a four-day examination of candidates for the Radcliffe Travelling Fellowship commencing February 26th, but in the midst of it he is found at Bath, where he became much interested in 'Bath Olivers',[2] and where, incidentally, he read a paper before the Bristol and Bath branch of the British Medical Association, on the Early Diagnosis of Cancer of the Stomach. In the course of this paper he said some unpalatable things about the training of English surgeons, and had no hesitancy in urging early exploratory operations. Those were days, needless to say, before the X-ray had become the chief aid to early diagnosis. In a letter to Mrs. Robert Brewster, written on his return, he said:

. . . Mrs Osler has been driven crazy (almost) by the workmen here. Such a set of duffers! . . . But we are getting settled gradually, & the garden will be such a pleasure. I have not yet got my books out as my library is unfinished. I have been seeing a good deal of the country since I got back—a delightful visit to Edinburgh with the

---

[1] Nothing came of this project, so far as Oxford is concerned, though ten years later in an address (July 31, 1917) at Aberystwyth, Wales, on the occasion of the opening of the Summer School of Library Science, he came back to the same subject, and there his plan found a more favourable soil.

[2] A biscuit 'invented' by Dr. Wm Oliver (1695–1764) of Bath. The secret receipt was confided to his coachman, who opened a shop and acquired a large fortune by their sale.

students. I gave a talk to 1000 of them, & then we had a big dinner. Wonderful city! but I am glad I did not go there eight years ago when offered the Chair of Medicine. I have just come back from Bath. I wish you could see the old furniture shops there. Why should not you and R. B. come over in June on a house furnishing expedition? . . .

He was still causing McCrae uneasiness, and on March 1st wrote: 'I hope to have that introduction off in a few days. 'Tis most mortifying to have been so slow about it but I have a sort of mental paresis about some things. What a job you must have found the index!' And the next day to J. William White who, since getting his degree at Aberdeen, had been racketing about Europe and Africa with his accustomed vigour, which rebelled at repose:

I am delighted to have the letter announcing your safe return. A letter from Stengel states that you are in blooming health. It is delightful to hear of your reception. Do not *rush* it too much, please, & be careful not to overtax your bread-basket. Remember you have not the ostrich-like digestion of twenty-five years ago. The farm, I dare say, will be your salvation.[1] We have got into our house & I think it will be very comfortable. At present we are trying to drive the workmen out. We have been having wonderful weather—such sunshine! I wish you could have seen the boat-races here last week. They would have steadied your old pump as well as rejoiced it. One of the most satisfactory things in Oxford is the way they have settled the athletic problem. All the men are at exercise in some form, every day, rain or shine, as a part of their regular routine . . .

Though already deeper in official business than he could have wished, he accepted at this time an appointment as consulting physician on the staff of the new King Edward Sanatorium for tuberculosis at Midhurst, Surrey, and soon after his first visit wrote to his American friends asking that they send on papers and reprints to help in building up a proper library. Meanwhile he was doing his duty by his university posts, though sometimes they might be irksome. He had been re-elected, that is 'returned without opposition' as professorial representative on the Hebdomadal Council, in the course of which time-consuming

[1] This was the 'Oh Hell' Farm, which Agnes Repplier describes in her biography of Dr. White.

job he occasionally scribbled notes to his friends, such as the following:

Hebdomadal Council,
March 18.

What do you think of geography in the civil service examinations? That is the question we are debating at present in this august body. Not always interesting but a very interesting body of men. I am sandwiched in between the Warden of New (Spooner) & the Warden of Keble. Spooner has not made any slips yet but some of his spoonerisms are delicious. We are 21 including the V.C. [Vice-Chancellor] and the two Proctors. We meet from 2–? every Monday. 'Tis 5 or 5.30 sometimes before we rise. All sorts of business. I am getting an education.

The house is still chaotic—painters everywhere but it is for the last coat. My library will be very nice in oak—panelled. My treasures are still in boxes. A few at Ch Ch & at the Museum. It will be a great comfort to have them all together again. I am not doing much in the auction room, but I think I told you that I bought a fine 17th century very early Religio Medici MS—I pick up an occasional book—Yesterday Coste's lecture in Latin 1782 at Williamsburg Va on the Ancient learning adapted to the new world. C was a remarkable man—surgeon to the French forces—see Bayle— By the way have you a Bayle? A mine, a storehouse & treasury. I sail April 20th, rather a hurried visit but it will be nice to see you all again. Ike is well. A. G. with a cough—but not bad. The garden will be delightful. Yours, W. O.

But he sometimes found pleasanter things to do than sit at council meetings, and on March 22–23 did one of them. Wherever Osler went, whether by train, tram, or car, he usually carried with him a bundle of journals, interspersed with book catalogues or auction lists, and the number of these things that he could go through in a short time with the unerring scent of the true collector was amazing. He had a rare nose for books, and could track to its lair anything that lurked in them.

Somewhere in his commonplace-book he has jotted down a number of quotations from the sayings of Sylvestre Bonnard, the character depicted by Anatole France—thus: 'I do not know any reading more easy, more fascinating, more delightful than that of a catalogue'; and 'My old books are Me—I am just as old and thumbworn as they are.' He notes too, that it is a good scene where Bonnard bids at Hotel Bullion, Sale No. 4, for § 42, 'The Golden

Legend', an old Alexandrian manuscript. So it is not surprising to find, on the fly-leaf of the sale catalogue of the William C. Van Antwerp portion of the Rowfant Library just then under the hammer, that he has scribbled in pencil the account of 'A record Day at Sotheby's'.[1] It is reminiscent of the 'Burrowings of a Book-worm' written by 'E. Y. D.' some time before, in which 'the final stage of the malady sung of so sweetly by John Ferriar' was graphically described. But things must have grown too lively for him to continue far with this scribble, and ere long among treasures too numerous to mention—'Mr. Tom Hodgson could not conceal his excitement'—a first folio Shakespeare was knocked down at £3,600, 'with much applause', and a Compleat Angler, 'one of the finest if not *the* finest copy known', at £1,290 to Mr. Quaritch.

Osler's mother had survived her one-hundredth birthday scarcely three months; and in the following letter to Dr. White he speaks of her death, and abruptly dismissing the subject turns to chide White—doubtless 'to keep his mother out of his eyes'. Those who knew him best realized that his pose of imperturbability was, in terms of psychology, merely a defensive mechanism.

Sunday.

Dear White, Thanks for your kind note of sympathy. The cable was very unexpected as we had had only a day or two before a letter saying that she was keeping so well. A brother had been at death's door with acute gout & as he lives with her she had insisted upon going to his room very often & it worried her greatly. She had a fine outlook on life—ohne Hast, ohne Rast—and even the vagaries of her sons did not disturb her tranquillity. I hope you have killed your cook & settled down to a Chittenden diet—eating nothing you do not grow yourself & avoiding all roots, red meats, sweets, whiskey, champagne & tobacco. It is only in this way you can keep your purin-bases quiet & check the shaking of your glandulae epiploicae. Love to your suffering companion. Sincerely yours,

Wm Osler.

He wrote early in April: 'We have had a most extraordinary spring, weeks of sunshine and so mild. Our garden

[1] The Introduction to 'Bibliotheca Osleriana' contains a description of the Van Antwerp sale, evidently worked up from these notes made at the time.

begins to look so bright with the crocuses and daffodils. The house is still unsettled but we are driving the workmen out by degrees—room by room.' Apparently, during this time he had been going through the Christ Church Library in his quest for the books which had belonged to Burton, and he appears to have come upon a duplicate which found its way to his own shelves. The source of many of his books has been carefully noted, and the provenance of this particular volume, though not an exceptionally rare one, may be given in illustration. It contains a postcard on which is written:

Gotch tells me to tell you that we have found in our library a duplicate copy of John Mayow, *Tractatus quinque medico-physici*, Oxon. MDCLXXIV—without the portrait-frontispiece which some (I dare say all complete) copies have. I think the Library ought to present it you out of gratitude. I shall be back in Oxford tomorrow and arranging about clearing some duplicates out of the Library. Yrs, F. HAVERFIELD.

The following letter of April 6th to Dr. Barker tells something of his plans, and indicates that the triennial revision of his Text-book is getting on his conscience:

I hope everything is going well with you and the family. I hope to see you all before long, as I sail on the 20th. I shall go to Boston first and then round by Montreal and Toronto. I shall have rather a hurried visit, as I have to get back before the 20th of May. We have some rather important business coming up in connection with the medical school here. They have agreed at last to put the Anatomical and Pathological Departments on a sound financial basis, and we have also to get a new Professor of Pathology. I want an hour's chat with you about the Text-book. This new edition [the VIIth] due October 1908, will not be a very serious revision, as they will not break up the plates, but in the next edition we can do as we like. It would be very nice if you and Thayer came in with me as joint authors. It would be possible, I think, to arrange to have the work kept up as a Johns Hopkins Hospital Text-book of Medicine. I think some arrangement could be made with the publishers and some plan devised by which the head of the Medical Department would have *ex-officio* rights in it. In the IXth edition I would probably go out altogether and the book would appear from you and Thayer—perhaps, I retaining a small financial interest. I am just finishing the little paper on hereditary telangiectasis. You remember Crum's case, and I have a remarkable family in New York supposed to be hemophiliacs. I saw that remarkable man, High, at

ELLEN PICKTON OSLER IN HER 101st YEAR

your clinic in January 1906. I had intended just to refer to him in the paper as an extraordinary case, but I think, if you will allow me, I will report it separately in the *Bulletin*, as Emerson has got me some very remarkable photographs. Sincerely yours.

On the 12th he wrote to Mrs. Brewster, giving some picture of their life:

I have just been putting Revere to bed with a good romp. He has a tutor during this vacation as he is not quite up to the English boys in the Latin. They begin so early. He is having cricket lessons too & taking great interest in it. This is a splendid place for boys—such a wholesome life and so healthy. The stream of visitors on their way from the south has begun. We have had someone at luncheon every day this week, on their way to Liverpool. It makes the life very pleasant to see so much of our friends and we are beginning to get settled. We had tea outside every day last week and the garden begins to look so attractive. I wish you could see the place in June. Perhaps you & R. B. may come back with me & Uncle Ned on the 11th of May. I have to take the Etruria much to my sorrow. I have been in town to-day inspecting Lord Amherst's Library. Poor man! his solicitors invested nearly all his money in South African mines & it has gone so he has to sell his Library. Wonderful collection, 17 Caxtons! 11 of them perfect. I never saw such treasures. I wish Mr. Rockefeller or Carnegie would buy it for some American University. I am taking great interest in the Bodleian, and am beginning to know my way about; but dear me! they need so much rearrangement & a new catalogue is to be prepared but it will cost £50,000. . . . Thanks so much for your kind sympathy about Mother's death. I knew you would be thinking of us. We have had most touching letters from my sister—an ideal, peaceful ending. I must send you from Toronto one of her photographs taken in her armchair only a month before. . . .

The next morning *The Times* published the news of the burning of the McGill Medical School, with the museum which contained his old specimens—he seems to have been pursued by fires—but he wrote cheerfully to Dr. Abbott: 'Sad news this morning about the burning of the school. I am afraid the loss in the museum is serious, but I hope it is not quite as bad as the newspapers state. In any case, a few years will put the museum in a much better condition than we could have hoped to see it in the old quarters, so please take courage.' He sailed, as he had planned, on April 20th, with no more luggage than his Oxford friends would have taken for a week-end visit. No wonder they thought he was crazy to run off to America in this fashion; but could they have seen a quiet man on the deck of the *Lucania* reading Pacton's 'Life of Lady Mary Montague' and making notes from it, thoroughly enjoying a week's rest, they would have fully understood. However, other things were in his mind, as the following indicates:

To Frederick T. Gates from W. O. R.M.S. *Lucania*, April 26, 1907.

You have of course noticed the hard whacks which my old alma mater McGill has had in these two big fires. No doubt Sir William Macdonald, who built the engineering Department, will restore it, but I am afraid from what I hear that the Medical Faculty has been very hard hit by the loss of their fine buildings. Do you think it would be possible to interest Mr. Rockefeller to the extent of a couple of hundred thousand dollars? It would mean everything to them & would really encourage a group of men who have been doing splendid work for the community. I shall be in the country for a couple of weeks, in Montreal on Tuesday & Wednesday, at Dr. Shepherd's, 135 Mansfield St. After that my address will be Johns Hopkins Hospital, Baltimore. With kind regards, [etc.].

New York, Boston, Montreal, Toronto, Baltimore, Washington, and Philadelphia—at least—and all in two weeks. He must have been relieved to find that his own specimens at McGill had not suffered greatly nor had the library. Nevertheless they needed help, and from his brother Edmund's house in Toronto he wrote a second letter in their behalf on May 2nd:

Dear Mr Gates, Thanks for your letter, which I received last evening, just before leaving Montreal. I have asked the Dean of the Faculty to prepare a statement of the research work which has been carried on lately at McGill in medicine. I think you will be surprised at its extent & variety. An endowment of $500,000 would enable them to further extend and carry on this work. To rebuild a thoroughly modern fireproof building will take all the moneys available & leave them hampered sadly for this advanced work, which they are really prepared to do, so far as the personnel of the faculty is concerned. I am sending you a couple of books which may interest you to look over, and Vol. I of my new system of medicine. With kind regards, Sincerely yours, Wm Osler. I shall be at the Johns Hopkins Hospital all next week—I sail May 11th on the New York.

He did not let the matter rest with Mr. Gates alone, but

pushed it in other directions, too, and it was not until three months later that he confesses in a letter to Adami : 'I hear from Welch privately that the Rockefellers will not do anything for McGill at present towards the buildings, but that after everything is settled they may be prepared to make some endowment for research.'

Osler had crossed for the special purpose of attending the triennial Congress of American Physicians and Surgeons which assembled in Washington during the week of May 6th. One of the many affiliated societies which met at the time was the National Association for the Study and Prevention of Tuberculosis, of which Osler seems to have been a permanent Vice-President—an honour he shared with Theodore Roosevelt and Grover Cleveland. In the two short years since his departure the association had grown apace, to 1,200 members, including many laymen ; and through its agency the crusade against the disease had received an impetus such as to warm Osler's heart. The enthusiastic greeting accorded him was enough to show that his part in all this was not forgotten.

It is customary at these triennial congresses to devote certain sessions, when all the constituent societies participate, to some subject of general interest which is presented from different angles by a number of speakers. As indicated in one of Osler's letters of the preceding September (cf. p. 61) such a symposium had been arranged, possibly at the suggestion of R. H. Fitz, the President of the congress for the year, in which Osler, Barker, Richard Cabot, and Alfred Stengel were to take part. The subject agreed upon was, in general terms, 'the historical development and relative value of laboratory and clinical methods of diagnosis'. Osler chose as his title, 'The Evolution of the Idea of Experiment in Medicine'—a subject which must have been born of his Harveian Oration. 'That man can interrogate', he began, 'as well as observe nature, was a lesson slowly learned in his evolution'; and he went on to say that 'had the Greeks added to their genius for brilliant generalization and ample observation the capacity to design and carry out experiments, the history of European thought would have been very different, but neither Plato nor Aristotle had any conception of the value of experiment as an instrument in the progress of knowledge'. 'One man alone', he said, 'among the ancients (Claudius Galen) could walk into the physiological laboratories of to-day and feel at home.' And from this he went on to show by what stages and under what influences we had come in the last half of the nineteenth century, into the real era of experimental medicine:

> . . . No longer [he said] do physiologists, like Hunter, Bowman and Lister, become surgeons; chemists like Prout and Bence-Jones, clinicians; and saddest of all, the chair of pathology is no longer a stepping-stone to the chair of medicine. The new conditions must be met if progress is to be maintained. In every country there will be found strong men like Weir Mitchell, Mackenzie of Burnley, and Meltzer and Christian Herter, who find it possible to combine experimental work with practice; but we must recognize the pressing need of organization if internal medicine is to keep in close touch with the rapid advancement of the sciences. A glance at the programme of the Association of American Physicians' meeting indicates the dominance of experiment at the present day. . . .

The 'American Physicians', indeed, were holding their twenty-second annual meeting, and Osler's remarks lead one to look over their programme—an altogether admirable one, to be sure, in which the new opsonic blood phenomenon was the chief matter for discussion. But perhaps, of all the papers, the only one which aroused no discussion was by Francis Hodder-Williams on the detection by the X-ray of early pulmonary tuberculosis. It has taken nearly two decades for physicians to lay aside the stethoscope in favour of this more exact method of diagnosis which may well enough be regarded as a laboratory procedure.

Another meeting he had promised to attend was held on May 10th and 11th in Philadelphia, in celebration of the semi-centennial of the founding of the Pathological Society, of which for five years he had been such an active member. He is said to have given an address, though there is no printed record of it. Perhaps it was given at the dinner when Weir Mitchell, the only surviving member of the original group who started the society in 1857, gave some personal reminiscences—reminiscences chiefly of the 'bloody '60's', in which conflict most of the founders had participated. He ended in much lighter vein with some verses of 'pathologic nonsense about "Killing Time"', but this was an occupation in which Osler rarely engaged, and he escaped to take a train for New York. Late on the night of the 10th, at the University Club, he posted a brief note to Henry Phipps, saying:

> We had a rousing meeting in Washington this week—most enthusiastic & encouraging. The best men were there from all over the country. I have just got in—we sail in the morning, at 6. So sorry not to have seen you. The [Tuberculosis] Dispensary is doing so well—180 patients in the past six weeks. . . .

It had been a hurried visit; and though two years were to elapse before his return, this could not have been his expectation, for jotted down in the back of his day-book there is written, possibly during this crossing: '*Lectures for Baltimore*, 1908. (1) The Ewelme Hospital and Chapel. (2) The Bodleian. (3) Christ Church, Oxford. (4) Gabriel Naudaeus. (5) Thomas Fuller. (6) Ulrich von Hutten. (7) The Anatomy of Melancholy.'

During his brief absence some important things had been happening. On May 2nd an announcement of the proposed Oxford University Appeal Fund, signed by the Chancellor and Vice-Chancellor, was published in the newspapers; and on May 16th, two days before he landed, a public meeting had been held at Burlington Gardens at which Lord Curzon, the Chancellor, presided. In his introductory remarks he said:

> . . . I dare say that the ordinary university man, whose memories and affections are for the most part centred in the college of which he was once a member, hardly realizes what is the university as distinct from the college to which he formerly belonged. And yet it is the university—its governing body, its statutes, its institutions and buildings, its examinations and degrees, its professors and lecturers, its noble library and its liberal Press—it is the university, even more than the colleges, which is the real air and spirit, the real guardian of the traditions of Oxford.

And in regard to the origin of the present movement he went on:

> . . . Five years ago the authorities of the university conducted a careful scrutiny into the educational requirements of Oxford at that time, and the results of that scrutiny can be seen in a printed report,

which is accessible to those who desire to see it; but scrutiny is a very different thing from solution, and solution is not possible without funds. Then it was that, in a fortunate moment, Mr. Brassey, who had already shown himself a most liberal benefactor to Balliol, appeared on the scene and turned his active mind and his generous disposition to the relief of the larger needs of the parent university. The Vice-Chancellor of Oxford, Sir William Anson, Professor Miers, and Professor Osler joined hands with him. Together they sifted and collaborated the most urgent among the requirements of Oxford, of which I have spoken; and they drew up a scheme framed for the satisfaction of the principal among those needs for what I think may be considered a not unreasonable sum of money—a quarter of a million sterling.

There was more of this, three columns in fact.[1] A resolution offered by Lord Curzon was seconded by Mr. Asquith; the Archbishop of Canterbury made a proposal regarding the composition of the body of trustees, which Lord Milner seconded; whereupon the Vice-Chancellor offered a final resolution regarding the appointment of a committee of twenty-three, Osler's name among them, to consider ways and means of raising the suggested £250,000; finally the (then) Hon. T. A. Brassey proposed a vote of thanks which the Chairman duly acknowledged. All thoroughly prearranged; all very formal; none of it what might be called inspiring, nor the sort of talk that would stir people to empty their pocket-books. However, a preliminary announcement was made of the donations so far promised, the list being headed with £10,000 from 'Mr. Brassey who started the scheme', and an equal sum from 'that most generous American gentleman, Mr. W. W. Astor'—a donation, it is safe to say, that was promised through the personal influence of a person not at the meeting.

Osler was a man of action rather than words, and had he been present, listening to those addresses, he would probably have held his impatience in check by his habit of scribbling while he listened. At least this is what he did a few days later when forced to sit through a Saturday afternoon with the Bodleian Curators when 'a draft case for the opinion of Counsel, received from the Hebdomadal Council', was con-

[1] *The Times* for Friday, May 17, 1907, p. 12: 'The Needs of Oxford University—Important Meeting.'

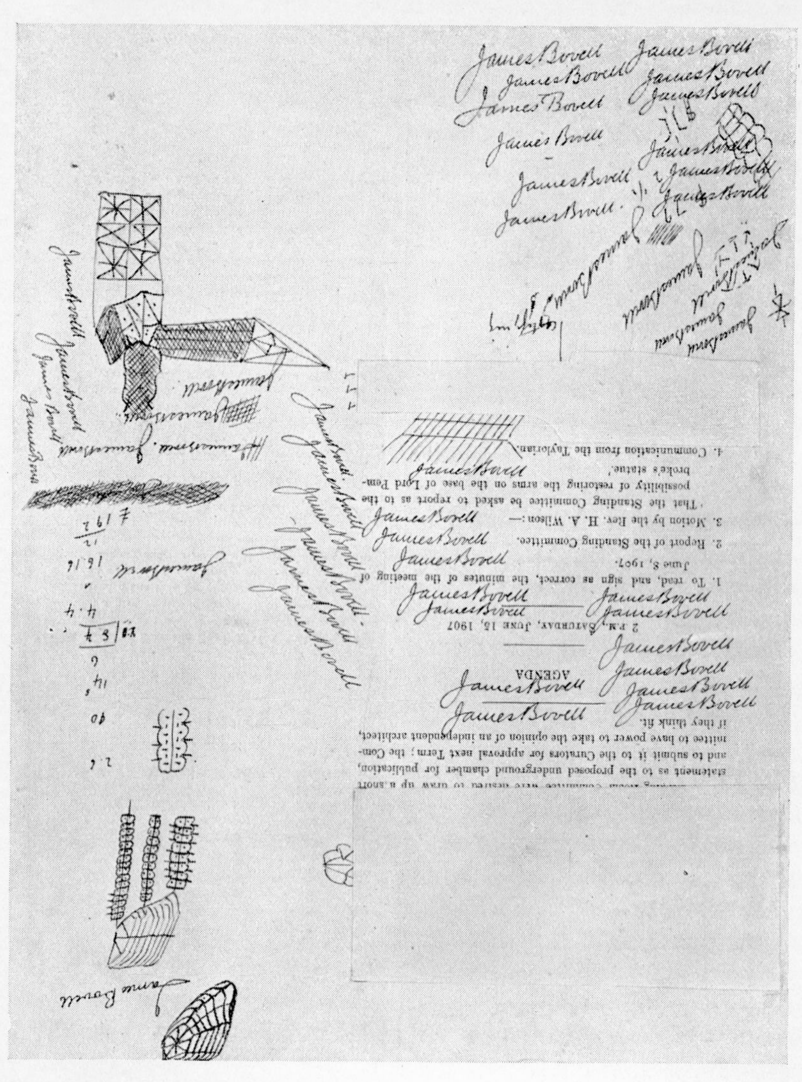

... Committee were desired to draw up a short statement as to the proposed underground chamber for publication, and to submit it to the Curators for approval next Term; the Committee to have power to take the opinion of an independent architect, if they think fit.

AGENDA

2 P.M., SATURDAY, JUNE 15, 1907

1. To read, and sign as correct, the minutes of the meeting of June 8, 1907.
2. Report of the Standing Committee.
3. Motion by the Rev. H. A. Wilson:—
   That the Standing Committee be asked to report as to the possibility of restoring the arms on the base of Lord Pembroke's statue.
4. Communication from the Taylorian.

A cobwebbed page of Agenda

sidered and amended; and when 'a letter from the solicitor of the Radcliffe Trustees' was read, regarding 'a lease for the construction of an underground chamber between the Library and the Radcliffe Camera', and it was decided to request him to obtain the views of the Trustees [of whom Osler was one] as to the length of the term, and the amount of rent—and much more. Possibly a long discussion thus aroused, possibly memories of his recent visit to Toronto, possibly a new pen, may have made him cover the back of the printed 'Acta' with cobwebs and 'James Bovell'.

Though Osler had missed the Burlington Gardens gathering, he was in time for the first annual meeting of the new Association of Physicians of Great Britain and Ireland—to become the counterpart of the society which had just met in Washington for its 22nd successive year, and of which he had also been a founder. The meeting, which proved an unqualified success, was held in London in the rooms of the Royal Medical and Chirurgical Society on May 23rd and 24th. The question of the journal was discussed before the Executive Committee, and it was agreed that the proposal of the Clarendon Press was satisfactory, whereupon an editorial board with Osler as chief was appointed, together with a body of collaborators. The scientific session was fully attended; the programme was an excellent one, and many of the papers presented, Osler's included, found their way subsequently into print in the first number [1] of the new *Quarterly Journal of Medicine*, the name of which was not decided upon until June 6th, when at a dinner in London he gathered together the collaborators.

On the heels of this came another meeting, of which later on he wrote: 'We baptized the Royal Medical Society the other afternoon and had a most satisfactory initial meeting.' Something has already been told of the proposed amalgamation of the London societies, and of how Osler had dropped

[1] This appeared on Oct. 1st, Osler's paper on multiple hereditary telangiectases, illustrated with two coloured plates, being the leading article. It was the second of his papers on this particular malady, which deserves to be styled 'Osler's Disease'. (See above, Vol. I, p. 595.)

in at the right moment to re-inspire the greatly discouraged 'Amalgar'. By this time, through the activities of the Amalgamation Committee, with Sir William Church as Chairman, the movement was well under way, and the first general meeting of the new society, whose charter permitted it to be called the Royal Society of Medicine, was held on June 14th at 20 Hanover Square. Though the old London Medical Society held aloof, seventeen of the possible twenty societies were brought into effective co-ordination on this occasion, and, under the chairmanship of Sir R. Douglas Powell, by-laws were adopted and officers elected. The name of Sir William Church was proposed for President by Sir Thomas Smith, and in seconding the nomination Osler took the opportunity to remind the society that money would have to be raised both for a new building and for the development of the library, and he wished to add that 'he who asketh much getteth much'.

He subsequently threw himself whole-heartedly into the work of this new society; almost invariably dropped in when in town; wrote countless letters to MacAlister and others regarding the library, arranging for speakers, giving dinners for guests before the meetings which he frequently attended; and was active in the movement for the new building at 1 Wimpole Street, which was to come three years later. Though offered high positions, indeed the presidency on one occasion, he refused to have his name submitted. However, he remained a member of the Council for the first three years, was on the Library Committee from that time until his death, and also, as will appear, founded in 1912 a new section, on the History of Medicine, a branch not represented by any pre-existing society, and of which he was the first president. Having Osler in the chair was certain to draw a gathering.

Thus he was back and forth from London several times a week, and yet there was much to be done in Oxford, particularly at this very time, for a pathologist had to be chosen to succeed James Ritchie, who had accepted a call elsewhere. What is more, examinations were in progress and the responsibilities relating thereto weighed upon him far more heavily than the examinees realized, if one may judge from the recollections sent by A. S. MacNalty, who was one of them :

In 1907 when up for my final M.B. examination at Oxford—the examination lasts a fortnight and is always a time of anxiety for the victims—Sir William's (then Dr. Osler) innate kindness cheered us through the wastes of written papers, practicals and orals. Every one of the candidates felt that he was as anxious for each one of us to do well as if he had been a personal relative. The smile, the jest and the inquiry as to how we had got on helped us greatly. Bending over a heart case on which a full clinical report was asked for, unexpectedly the candidate would find the Regius Professor at his elbow and a hand laid on the patient's praecordia—' A good thrill that—that 's a nice case to have ', would be the comment, and he passed on. British examinations too often are rigid and formal. Sir William lightened them to the candidates by the ' human touch '.

No wonder that a man who habitually thus put himself on the students' level was eagerly consulted for his advice as to their careers by ambitious young men in many places, most of whom would have been glad to work in his environment :

To Dr. G. L. Rowntree. May 31, 1907.

The place for you to go to is the Hopkins. If you could arrange to work for six years and wish really to get at the roots of things, attach yourself to Dr. Barker's clinic and gradually work into line. The clinical advantages here are slight and you could not begin to do the sort of work with me that you could with Dr. Barker. Of course it means a great sacrifice [of time] for you, but you have youth, and probably brains, and if, attached to these, you have the necessary perseverance with enough cash to keep you floating, six years of hard clinical work should put you in a first-class position in the profession. With kind regards and best wishes, Sincerely yours,

Wm OSLER.

For some months Oxford had been bestirring herself with preparations for a great celebration on a large scale. ' I wish you could be here for the next week's festivities ', said Osler in one of his letters of the middle of June. ' There is going to be a great circus. The pageant is wonderful. I sent a programme last week.' Held in Christ Church meadows, with literally thousands of participants, both town and gown, it was perhaps the most notable of many notable pageants ; and much has been written of it. The ' Book of Words ' which enumerates the scenes, from the eighth century of St. Frideswide to the visit of 'farmer George' in the eighteenth, ends with an effort by Quiller-Couch to explain 'the secret of Oxford'—a secret which looks easy but grows harder as one begins to understand it, and which is really the secret of youth despite her disguise that consists in looking old:

> Tower tall, city wall,
> A river running past;
> Youth played when each was made,
> And shall them all outlast.

On the 26th, the day before the pageant opened, was held Lord Curzon's first Encaenia, and there was an unprecedented turn-out of the Oxford populace to see the academic procession, perhaps because Kipling, and another popular author disguised as Samuel Langhorne Clemens, made part of it; and later the old Sheldonian Theatre presented an unusually brilliant scene. To quell the usual boisterousness of the undergraduates, they were scattered about in small groups, but even this did not make them spare the Regius Professor of Greek, who was seen but not heard presenting his thirty-four candidates for degrees, and he was told from the gallery 'not to wake the baby', and that 'it was bad manners to whisper in public'. It is recorded, too, that the receptions were all cordial, 'some strikingly warm'—those of the Lord Chancellor, the Prime Minister, the American Ambassador, Sir Evelyn Wood, Auguste Rodin, Sir William Perkin, &c.; but those of 'General' Booth, the venerable Archbishop of Armagh, Kipling, and 'Mark Twain' were 'most vociferous of all'.

The pageant itself, which lasted a week, from June 27th to July 3rd, is said to have been finely carried through, and one can almost believe Mark Twain's account of it, in which he relates that he met that greatest of all widowers, Henry VIII, in the streets, and found him a much more pleasant personage to talk to than he had expected. But all this is past and gone, though the whole literature, down to the picture-postcards, is in Bodley available for reference for all time. It needs no saying that 13 Norham Gardens, meanwhile, was dispensing its usual hospitality and that the customary pursuits of the household were pleasantly interrupted—even those of Revere, for to go on afternoon rambles with so understanding a person as the author of 'Puck of Pook's Hill' was far more exciting than the mounting of butterflies and the stuffing of moths, just now his main occupation in life.

> Land of our Birth, our Faith and Pride,
> For whose dear sake our fathers died;
> O Motherland, we pledge to thee
> Head, heart, and hand through the years to be!

But this ended abruptly, and the day after the pageant found Osler in town distributing prizes at the London School of Medicine for Women. There he gave an address on the avenues open to women in the profession and advised them to hold, as their philosophy of life, that they were in the world not to get what they could out of it, but to do what they could for the happiness of others—advice he was accustomed to give to all graduates in medicine. At about this time, too, pressure was brought to bear upon him to accept the Chair of Medicine at Manchester University to succeed Professor Dreschfeld, the chief inducement being that its clinical opportunities excelled those at Oxford, but he could hardly have considered the matter seriously. On July 19th he wrote to Mrs. Brewster:

> We have had such a busy summer, so many people coming & going. I sent you a paper with an account of the Encaenia & the reception to Mark Twain and Kipling. The latter stopped with us —such a jolly fellow, so full of fun and with an extraordinary interest in everything. Mrs. K. is very bright, & we fell in love with them both. Mark Twain was most enthusiastic about Kipling. It was delightful to hear them joking together. Our garden is thriving. Mrs. Osler has just come in with a huge armful of sweet peas, & our roses are—for the first year—splendid. After months of winter we have had a week of bright sunshine. Revere's school is over to-day. He lives such a happy life & is becoming an A.1. cricketer. We go to Scotland for a month—to Colonsay I hope & for ten days to Glenquoitch with Mr. Phipps. I am sending to-day Jowett's introduction to Plato—much of which will interest you.

Osler, however, was not doing what in 1905 he threatened to do—enjoying his garden, his friends, and his family, and making a sinecure of his position. This is evident from a letter to *The Times* of July 24th, on the 'Need of Reform at Oxford', signed by himself and fifteen others, to the effect that the constitution and machinery of Oxford, both legislative and executive, needed revision; that the relation between the university and its colleges, both constitutional and financial, required modification; and:

> . . . that the studies of the universities are themselves too narrow in scope and that fresh endowments of various branches of study are necessary; and especially that a greater encouragement should be given to research, which at Oxford is probably to a larger extent divorced from teaching than in any other great university.

With H. A. L. Fisher and others he was prominent in the reform party which protested that the only practical way of carrying out the necessary changes would be through a Royal Commission and legislation by the King in Council. This was opposed by a more moderate party, who felt that much risk attended this course. A turn had been given to affairs by the unexpected death of Lord Goschen and the succession to the Chancellorship of Lord Curzon, who avowedly belonged to the party in favour of only moderate reforms. The others, headed by Bishop Gore, forced matters to a conclusion by a definite demand in the House of Lords for the appointment of a commission. Mr. Asquith, a moderate reformer, after some consideration replied that the fairer course would be to allow the new Chancellor to try his own hand at reforms from within. These efforts occupied the next few years, and though the results were not startling, several important statutes were passed.[1]

To leave this matter, Osler writes on July 25th to J. William White:

> Only the other day I said to Mrs. Osler, 'I suppose the Whites will be over if they can leave the chickens'. I am so glad to have your

[1] Cf. p. 253. What would have happened had there been no war is difficult to say. This with its sequel of high prices brought about a different situation, and both Oxford and Cambridge found themselves compelled to apply for state assistance. The war had entirely revolutionized the attitude of the country and the legislature towards the universities which played such a heroic and satisfactory part in the struggle. A Royal Commission under the chairmanship of Mr. Asquith in 1922 recommended many of the changes which the reformers of 1907 had in view, and the Commission is now engaged in getting statutory authority for these recommendations.

letter & wish we could have you here for Sunday, but the house is full. Miss Woolley, two nieces, one with a husband, & Drs. McCrae and Boggs of the Johns Hopkins Hospital are here. I am going to Exeter on Monday to the B. M. A. I shall be in London on my way there & shall be delighted to lunch with you and Mrs. White. I have not heard anything of the Abbeys this summer. We must see you here. I shall be at the Exeter meeting until Friday.

Presumably his former Hopkins assistants accompanied him to the British Medical Association meeting. Moreover, as both of them had bibliophilic tendencies they were probably introduced by ‘ the Chief ’, between the scientific sessions of the meeting, to the old book shops of Exeter. At all events, the dates of purchase in two or three interesting volumes in Osler's library bear evidence in this direction. This Exeter meeting over, the week of August 5th was given up to the sessions of the second (the first was in Nüremberg) International Congress of School Hygiene, held under royal patronage at the University of London. Sir Lauder Brunton was President of the Congress, and Osler President of that one of its eleven subdivisions which dealt with medical and hygienic inspection of schools. In these days of an organized and highly endowed movement towards preventive medicine with richly endowed schools for the education of public health officers, one is apt to forget that the physicians of a few decades ago were earnestly attacking many of these same problems. There were delegates, lay and medical, to this meeting, 2,000 in all, from many countries ; and the subjects for discussion covered every aspect of school sanitation, provision for defective children, the maintenance of the health of the others by medical inspection—even the question of military drill.

The congress was opened by the Earl of Crewe, and many other notables participated. Osler in his presidential address stated that Great Britain, so far as systematic methods of school inspection were concerned, was far behind most of the continental nations. Though the question, he said, bristled with difficulties, sociological and economic, nevertheless the ideal conditions were easily defined, and he recommended a separate department at the Board of Education, to supervise and co-ordinate the work throughout the country. He proposed that there should be a trained nurse for each school, who should carry out observations at intervals and should assist a visiting doctor in all matters relating to school hygiene ; also that a school dentist should make a quarterly inspection of the children's teeth.[1] England had more reasons than she could have realized for taking every possible step to prevent the deterioration of the health of her young people. To be sure, a Peace Congress at this very time was in session at The Hague ; but war or no war, in campaigns of this kind which concerned public hygiene Osler was quick to enlist.

Meanwhile, there were other things in abundance to attend to. He was busy not only with his own section (written in collaboration with John W. Churchman) for the third volume of his 'System of Medicine', but at the same time with the revision of manuscripts submitted by others. These were giving him trouble, as is indicated by the following admonition to one of the contributors :

> I am sorry about the condition of plethora in your article. I am afraid we must agree to the Leas' request and cut it down to as near as possible the space they assign. I know how hard it is to do this, but it is surprising how much may be done by cutting out redundant words and sentences. For example, I cut out nearly four lines to the printed page from one edition of my Text-book simply by condensation. It is, of course, a great aggravation and it is often harder to boil down than to write.

The first two volumes of this important work had already appeared,[2] and preceding letters have shown that he had agonized a good deal over his Introduction to the first volume. To illustrate how quickly these great 'Systems of Medicine' became antiquated, Osler had called attention in his introductory pages to the fact that many of the chapters to follow were on subjects that could hardly have been touched upon twenty years before when Pepper's

[1] The full account of this most important meeting, which aroused the sanitary conscience of the people, is given in the successive numbers of the *British Medical Journal* for 1907. Sir Victor Horsley proposed a resolution which was finally passed in this form : 'That the principles and practice of hygiene should form a part of the education of every citizen.' And as an outcome of the meeting a Bill for the medical inspection of schools was promptly introduced in the House of Commons.

[2] Vol. II was issued by the publishers on June 20, 1907.

'System' was published. And one only needs to turn the pages of the volume, in which, to take a single example, appears Chittenden's important article on metabolism, to realize how soon these encyclopaedic publications become out of date. For to-day many a physician has even a calorimeter in his office; a knowledge of vitamines has revolutionized the question of rickets and scurvy; the discovery of insulin that of diabetes; and the X-ray in its relation to medicine, dismissed with three or four pages, to-day would require a volume in itself.

There were many other things to engage him besides the 'System of Medicine'. Some of them he mentions in an undated letter addressed to C. N. B. Camac, at Caribou Cottage, Pointe-à-Pic, where they had passed previous summers together. Camac was just preparing to issue a volume entitled 'Epoch-making Contributions to Medicine' to which the opening paragraph refers:

13 Norham Gardens.

Dear Camac, I am so glad to hear that you have made final arrangements with Saunders. Would it not be helpful to have the title-pages of some of the books reproduced—just as in my Browne article—by the new process—it is not expensive. The De Motu Cordis, Laennec 1st edition &c would add greatly to the interest of the work. You will have hard work to keep within the limits of 400 pages. I am sorry in a way that you did not come over & try the Press. Let me know if I can be of any help in getting pictures &c What title? all important, consult Welch. I knew you would like the Charaka men—Dana is a trump & it is a good group. I wish we had a club like it over here.

The Press is issuing for us a new Quarterly Jr. of Med. in connection with our new assoc. of British Physicians, both hobbies of mine which I hope may stir up clinical study. I will send you a copy next month. I am delighted to hear about Harding & will write him at once. He deserves his success. We have had a very busy summer. T. McCrae, Futcher, Barker, Boggs & others have been with us. McCrae has lost his heart to one of my nieces Miss Amy Gwyn. We are all delighted. Counsels & Ideals seems to keep up a good sale here. I do not think a photo would help. . . . I am trying to get my biographical essays together in a companion vol to Aequanimitas—under the title 'An Alabama Student & others' &c. The Press will take it.

I have given two lectures this summer in the Extension Course one on Early Medical Work in Oxford dealing with the scholastic

& renaissance periods the other An Introduction to the Study of the 'Anatomy of Melancholy'. The former I must still work on as part of a study of the whole subject of Oxford Med. (in 4 periods —Scholastic, Renaissance, Caroline & Victorian) the latter I have nearly ready. We have got out the Burton books at Ch. Ch. I am having them all put together & am collecting all the editions to put under a copy of the Brasenose picture which will be an insert among the books. Love to Mrs Camac & the bairns, to the McCaggs, the Bowditches—tap your rt. ventricle when you meet Margie B. for me & your left when you meet Lois S. Mrs Osler sends love.

In seeking 'a few weeks of seclusion', after this delightfully busy summer, they settled upon a cottage at Bude, on the picturesque and iron-bound north coast of Cornwall, which he describes in a letter of August 29th: 'It is something like Bar Harbour in its superb freshness & greenness, but the rocks are bolder and the headlands very striking. We were at Morwenstow yesterday where there is a cliff almost perpendicular—500 feet in height. The bathing & the golf are excellent, but my young friend Isaac Walton hasn't caught any fish.' There were walks on the cliffs, and excursions to Tintagel, Clovelly, and Bideford; indeed, on one occasion he and Revere went still farther afield, as the following scribble sent on a picture-postcard indicates: 'Isaac & I went off together for a trip—to see the Roman remains at Bath & Glastonbury. The ruins are magnificent and we met King Arthur & Guinevere late in the eve at Joseph of Arimathea's. Love to the darlings.' On this expedition, too, they paid a visit to Mrs. Neville, whose son it was, so many years before in Montreal days, who had died of smallpox under Osler's care. And on still another expedition they must have gone across the Bristol Channel to Swansea, where the 'Uncle Edward' had lived, of whose writings and hymns the parsonage at Bond Head used to be so proud. While there he of course visited the local hospital, for Edward Osler had been house surgeon there in 1819; and a Dr. Florence Price (she of subsequent letters) took him into the wards, where he discovered the case of ochronosis afterwards shown at a meeting of the Royal Society of Medicine. On September 4th he wrote to H. B. Jacobs:

We miss Colonsay and I am sorry not to have ten days with

Mr. Phipps but this is a delightful spot, the bathing excellent & the golf links very good. I have put Revere into the hands of the Pro & we are now playing nine holes every afternoon. The fishing is very good, Isaac says, but the fish do not bite! Tom McCrae's lapse is sad, but he has got a good girl and they seem very happy. I am sweating at articles for the system—the first two volumes look very well. The Oxford Press is issuing the work here & I have T. McC's name on the outside and have called it ‘ A System of Medicine ’. We must stir up the brethren about the [International Tuberculosis] Congress next year. I hope Fulton will come over. I could arrange a series of meetings for him & if Magnin did the same in Paris, & [Prof.] His Jr. or [Prof.] Leyden in Berlin, it would stir up interest. . . .

‘ We have had a good holiday and are back to glorious weather ’, he wrote from Oxford later in the month. ‘ The garden is a great delight. We have had tea on the terrace every afternoon for the past fortnight. The “ hotel ” is opened and we have had a succession of old friends.’ But despite the goings-on at the ‘ hotel ’, coming to be known as the ‘ Open Arms ’, he confessed in a letter of October 7th : ‘ Everything here is still in the peaceful inter-term state—the University seniors never think of returning until the last moment. Not a soul dining at Ch. Ch. last eve! I am sending you No. 1 of the new Journal which Garrod, Rolleston, & Co. are editing.’ It was a good time for work—this inter-term period; his own books were being put on their shelves; those which had once belonged to Burton he was reassembling at Christ Church, where permission had been given him to have them installed in one of the rooms off the picture gallery; there were probably trips to Ewelme, which was now accessible because of a motor-car; altogether there was plenty to do.

He had been, meanwhile, in Glasgow, for a meeting of the Library Association; and on October 3rd was at St. Mary's Hospital in London to open the winter session with an address to the students. He is reported to have advised them to stop their ears ‘ against the wiles of that Celtic siren Sir Almroth Wright, who would abolish Harley Street and all that it represented, though there is still much virtue left in that long, unlovely street ’. And it may be mentioned that the two had an amusing and friendly tilt at the dinner subsequently, when in all certainty the 'Celtic siren' got the better even of Osler.

As a result of the growing interest in all countries in public health measures, this year of 1907 saw formed in Ireland a Women's National Health Association, of which the Countess of Aberdeen was President, and it was apparent that some effort to stay the appalling ravages of tuberculosis among the Irish would be one of its foremost duties. The success in the United States of the itinerant tuberculosis 'exhibition' as an educational measure had become known; and, with the object of organizing something similar, advantage was taken of the international exhibition being held in Dublin, to open, in the Home Industries subsection of this exhibition, a tuberculosis exhibit, subsequently to be taken about the country. A special committee was formed, a course of lectures arranged, and Osler consented to give the inaugural address planned for Friday evening, October 12th, in the lecture-hall of the Royal Dublin Society. There had been several excellent papers read earlier in the meeting, the salient features of which Osler assembled into a brief, hard-hitting and effective speech—a 'trumpet call' as the Lord-Lieutenant subsequently described it.[1] It ended with this prophetic paragraph:

In this crusade against tuberculosis there are two indispensable factors, *enthusiasm for the work*, which should not be hard to main-

[1] This speech bears internal evidence of having been largely extemporaneous—the more effective for that reason; but it had a curious aftermath. Together with the other addresses it was published in Dublin in 1908 in a booklet entitled 'Ireland's Crusade against Tuberculosis', edited by the Countess of Aberdeen.

Mr. Edward Bok, of *The Ladies' Home Journal*, waited upon Osler during his visit to the States in 1909, with the proposal that he write an article on 'The American Woman's Health' for the Curtis Publishing Company. Osler seeing nothing wrong in this, and believing that to educate the public was a professional duty, accepted the proposal and wrote the article while crossing on the steamer. He subsequently withdrew from his agreement, on the grounds that such a paper written for a lay magazine, especially by a Regius Professor, might be misunderstood in England and be regarded as bad form.

There exists what is known as a literary broker—a person who collects unprotected articles and sells them to journals. Lady Aberdeen's volume was not copyrighted, and Osler's address appears to have been pilfered there-

tain, since we are everywhere fighting a winning battle; and the second essential factor is *perseverance*. It is not a year's work, not five years' work; a decade will make a great difference; a generation should see a reduction in the mortality of 50%; and your children and grandchildren should be able to point to a victory over tuberculosis as memorable as that which our fathers have won against typhus and typhoid fevers.

On the following day the exhibit was formally opened. Lord Aberdeen presided, read a message of commendation from the King, called on Augustine Birrell, the Chief Secretary for Ireland, who spoke, and then on the chief guest. Osler began his impromptu remarks by saying:

It may not be known to many, or to any of you, that it was in this city that a strong public health movement was first inaugurated by that remarkable man, Sir William Petty, whose studies on the public health of Dublin I commend to all who are interested in the question or in antiquarian research. I was particularly pleased to see in your little pamphlet the motto of his friend, and I think possibly his instructor in public health matters, John Locke. There is a manuscript book of Locke's in the Bodleian Library which shows that he was interested in the public health of Dublin, and there are letters from Sir Patrick Dun and the Molyneuxs, and from other friends, relating to the investigations which Dun and Petty had instituted in this city as far back as 1683 dealing with the very same issue which we have been discussing here to-day—namely, the proper notification of disease. . . .

And he went on to say that it was not a Government battle but a people's battle, and that the most serious obstacle to the eradication of the disease was public apathy. Lady Aberdeen had asked him to comment on the Irish climate—'a very sensitive subject'. This he did as follows:

People say sometimes that on this side of the Atlantic we have only weather and no climate. But peripatetic as I have been, living in many places, I have always regarded climate and weather as two of the non-essentials, and I think the people who take that view of both climate and weather are the only happy ones in life. But there is no reason whatever for you here in Ireland to growl about the weather. It is quite good enough for you. And it is a first-rate

from, sold to, and reprinted as an original article in, *The Woman's Home Companion*. There Mr. Bok saw it, and wrote a letter of warm expostulation to Osler, who up to that moment was apparently unaware even that Lady Aberdeen had published the address.

climate for consumptives. It is not a bit more moist in any part of Ireland than it is in that tail-end of England—Cornwall. Yet in no climate do consumptives do better. I do not know where this idea that Ireland is a bad climate for consumptives comes from; certainly I do not think it comes from the profession. It is one of those fads that possibly women have encouraged. . . . Sunshine is not an essential for the cure of the disease. The things that are essential are fresh air, good food, good houses, and hope.

Though his presence was doubtless much needed to launch this crusade in Ireland, it was needed none the less the following Sunday afternoon at Oxford, where occurred the usual influx of visitors. This may account for the following in a note sent from 13 Norham Gardens that evening: 'W. O. is momentarily expected from Dublin, where he and Lady Aberdeen have been fussing over tuberculosis.' Unquestionably there was a good deal of time spent over it which might have been devoted to pleasanter things. But, as he had said, there were two indispensable factors: *enthusiasm for the work*, and *perseverance*; and very shortly he wrote to Mr. Phipps:

I was very sorry to miss you in London as I hoped we might make one or two little excursions together to the new tuberculosis hospitals. How gratified you must feel that the work at the Phipps Hospital has been so successful. Flick and his staff really deserve the greatest possible credit for the way in which they have worked. I only heard this week of your last donation to the Phipps Dispensary at the Johns Hopkins Hospital. Thank you so much. I sent you last week a newspaper clipping about tuberculosis in Ireland. I found the conditions there shocking beyond description, but I think Lady Aberdeen's crusade should bear good fruit.

On October 16th he was again addressing medical students in London on matters of their education, this time at University College Hospital with Sir Thomas Barlow in the chair, and while in town must as usual have called on the 'Amalgar', to whom he soon wrote:

Oct. 23, 1907.

Dear MacAlister, I would like to have a talk with you when I get the details I have asked for about the other medical library buildings. I thought it would be useful to present to the Council a brief statement, with lantern slides, illustrating what has been done elsewhere. Of course the Hanover Square building represents a large amount of good solid effort, but it is quite evident that it is not adapted to so large & important a society, and it will be wholly inadequate as the library grows. A plan of campaign should be carried out—first, in the profession: a committee in each section of the society actively taking up the work; secondly, the families of notable old members, who might not only subscribe, but would help fit up certain rooms in the building; thirdly, the public at large; & lastly, I feel quite certain that if we go to Mr. Carnegie with a statement of what *has been done* & show the position the library holds, he will put down a lump sum just as he has done for the new building at Philadelphia.

The last day of the month found him once more in town, giving an address this time at St. Thomas's Hospital,[1] when he spoke on 'The Medical Student's Library'. He without doubt, no less than the students themselves, greatly enjoyed these meetings, for the daily contact with a large student group was the one thing above all others which he missed in the life at Oxford.

The middle of November saw the well-remembered visit of the German Emperor and Empress to England as the guests of King Edward and Queen Alexandra. Though 'not political', there was much flurry excited thereby on both sides of the Channel lest the *Entente cordiale*—the fancied anti-German combination engineered by the King—be thereby affected. They were most graciously received by both press and public, even though the new German naval programme was announced almost on the same day that the Kaiser made his famous speech in the Guildhall; but this made no difference, and 'Deutschland über Alles' and 'God save the King' were cordially commingled. On November 15th Oxford honoured him with her highest degree, and of this function, held at Windsor, Osler has left a pencilled note which reads as follows:

The deputation consisted of the Chancellor, the V-C., the Proctors, the Regius Professors, Sir William Anson & the Registrar. We had a special carriage & a room was arranged at the White Hart for robing. At 4.45 carriages were sent from the Castle & we drove to the state

[1] Cf. *St. Thomas's Hospital Gazette*, 1907, xvii, 195, which not only contains an account of the amusing 'Examination Paper on Osler' first published in the *Gazette* in 1902, but adds a new type of parody, a tale built up of lines taken from the Text-book and pieced together: 'The notorious Duchess of Cleveland met | my good friend Evans | in a farmhouse so constructed as to shut out the sunlight | ' &c.

entrance. The Master of Ceremonies took us up to one of the reception rooms which was hung with pictures by Van Dyke, chiefly of Charles II. Lord Curzon came in with the faithful Moon [the university bedell] holding up his train. We were arranged in a semicircle in order of precedence, the Chancellor in the middle & a little in front of us. The Emperor came in with a staff of 11, among whom were the German Ambassador & Lord Roberts. He looked a little nervous & did not know just how far away from the Chancellor he should stand. At first he did not look at all happy—as if bored or tired—and he seemed fagged and worried. Lord C. made a singularly felicitous speech, extempore. Only he said it was the Degree of Common, instead of Civil Law. And he made a cold shiver pass round the semi-circle when he said, 'and you remember Sir, the telegram you sent'. Everyone felt that it might be an awful break but was relieved when the Ch. added, 'about the aquatic contests on the Thames', referring to some incident in the races years ago.

One interesting reminiscence of this occasion was subsequently mentioned. When the deputation was returning to Oxford after the brief ceremony a discussion arose. That under his red gown of an Oxford D.C.L. the Kaiser had worn the uniform of a British Field Marshal all agreed; but whether in turning the pages of the address which he had read he had thumbed them over or had turned them with his left hand could not be clearly remembered—an example of the defectiveness of observation and the fallibility of witnesses.

On November 20th Osler gave his testimony before the Royal Commission on Vivisection,[1] to which reference has already been made. It was not his first experience, for he has already been seen giving somewhat heated testimony before a U.S. Senator, when a similar inquiry was being held, though on that occasion ignorance and prejudice presided, whereas a British Parliamentary hearing is of a different calibre. In his précis he had chosen to dwell upon three

[1] This may be found in the Appendix to the *Fourth Report of the Commissioners; Minutes of Evidence*; Oct. to Dec. 1907, pp. 157–67. It was also given in full in the *British Medical Journal* for Nov. 7, 1908 *et seq.*, and was subsequently reprinted, as was Lord Justice Moulton's testimony, in pamphlet form for distribution by the Research Defence Society. This society, with Lord Cromer as its President and Stephen Paget its Secretary, held its first meeting in June of 1908, with the object of disseminating information to offset antivivisection propaganda.

things which had not previously been considered in the evidence. The first was the story of yellow fever and the experiments which Walter Reed had conducted on human volunteers—experiments which had extensively influenced the commercial relations of nations, revolutionized life in the tropics, and had saved thousands of lives and millions of pounds annually. Secondly, he took up the story of cretinism and myxoedema ; and lastly, he defended the use of animals, such as was being practised in the Hunterian Laboratory of the Johns Hopkins Hospital, for the training of young men in surgical technique. Some of the 272 questions and answers, recorded in the course of his testimony, may be given :

16607. You think that we might trust implicitly to the humanity of the physiologists ?—Absolutely. I know these men ; they are just as humane as any other men ; and to place these vexatious restrictions upon them is an insult.

16608. Referring to the special cases which you have brought under our knowledge, I understood that in the case of yellow fever the recent experiments have been on man ?—Yes, definitely, with the specific consent of these individuals, who went into this camp voluntarily. They were volunteers, just like 'forlorn hope' volunteers.

16609. We were told by a witness yesterday that, in his opinion, to experiment upon man with possible ill-result was immoral. Would that be your view ?—It is always immoral, without a definite, specific statement from the individual himself, with a full knowledge of the circumstances. Under these circumstances any man, I think, is at liberty to submit himself to experiments.

16610. Given a voluntary consent, you think that entirely changes the question of morality or otherwise ?—Entirely.

Many other questions were asked and answered, but this is enough to register his small though effective part in what historically is an important episode in the history of experimental medicine. One is glad to turn to the Radcliffe Infirmary, where a week later he is found giving his regular Tuesday afternoon clinic so largely attended by the country doctors of Oxfordshire. On this occasion he showed a patient [1] with a rare disease which had come to be asso-

[1] 'A Clinical Lecture on Erythraemia (Polycythaemia with Cyanosis, Maladie de Vaquez'). *Lancet*, Jan. 18, 1908.

ciated with his name, a distinction which he disclaims in the following paragraph :

A word about the name, always a difficulty in connection with a new disease. The choice lies between an eponymic, an anatomical, or a symptomatic name. The one suggested by Parkes Weber—splenomegalic polycythaemia—has been adopted in this country. In France it has been called maladie de Vaquez, or Vaquez-Osler, and in the United States some of my friends have been kind enough to associate my name with it. But the priority of description rests with Vaquez and if a name is to be associated with the disease it should be that of our distinguished French colleague.

And one may be sure that at the close of the clinic most of the visiting doctors were carried off to 13 Norham Gardens for tea, at which Mrs. Osler again presided after a month's absence for a visit to her mother in Canton, Mass. In like fashion December passed. He opened a discussion on pneumonic infections on the 9th before the Medical Society of London ; on the 13th at the new Royal Society of Medicine he talked again on Vaquez's disease ; and from the 16th to the 18th was 'examining' in Cambridge, a function he seems to have enjoyed, from the following note to McCrae :

Dear Mac, Cable this week from the Leas !! We are hurrying. Gibson has had a hard term & not many spare minutes, but he is working hard & we hope to have the whole MS. ready within a fortnight. I have been examining in Cambridge & having a very jolly time. I found yours of the 8th on my return. 1. Yes, I think Lymphatics might come in with circulation. It would be a short section. The only difficulty would be separating the glands which would sometimes be involved. What does Galen tertius think? 2. Certainly the thymus should go in with the ductless [glands] in Volume VI. Is everything in for Volume IV? [1] I see the proofs are coming fast. Yours ever, W. O.

[1] Volume III of the 'System' had been issued by the publishers on Dec. 9th, and this next volume to which he refers appeared June 13, 1908. Osler had written the chapters on Acute Endocarditis ; on Diseases of the Arteries ; on Aneurysm ; and, in collaboration with Dr. A. G. Gibson, on Diseases of the Valves of the Heart, the chapter for which the publishers had been pressing him. 'Galen tertius' doubtless meant Professor William H. Welch, with whom, at 807 St. Paul Street, McCrae was living at that time in Baltimore.

And near the close of the year he sent the following letter which tells something more of his doings:

To Daniel C. Gilman from W. O. 13 Norham Gardens,
Friday 28th.

I am so distressed to hear that you have not been well. Do ask Mrs. Gilman to send me a line if even a postal card. Someone mentioned it in a letter to Mrs. Osler, but we have heard nothing first hand, & it would be such a satisfaction. I sent you a little Xmas reminder—which I hope reached you in time. We have had a very busy Xmas—the first we have spent in our own home. We had a party of 16 to dinner, chiefly waifs & wanderers, among them four Rhodes scholars. We are very comfortable in our house. I have at last got my books about me. I am seeing a great deal of the Bodleian & am chairman of the Committee for the proposed alterations. But such difficulties to overcome! I wish you were 50 and here as President—how we would make this old place hum! There are such possibilities, & it is such a delightful spot, that it seems hard to have essential changes blocked by antiquated machinery. . . . You will have read of Lord Kelvin's death and funeral. I went to the Abbey—a most impressive ceremony & a remarkable gathering. Give my (our) love to Mrs Gilman & to all old friends. The boy keeps well—not a student but interested in butterflies & fish. Most sincerely yours, Wm Osler.

CHAPTER XXVIII

1908

A CONTINENTAL BRAIN-DUSTING

MENTION has been made of Osler's habit of jotting down in his engagement-book brief notes of the successive colds and bronchial attacks to which he was so susceptible; and the frigid rooms of the old university buildings where so many meetings were held were his anathema. So in this winter: '*Jan. 28.* Slight cold and housed. *Feb. 7.* In bed heavy cold no fever no cough. *Feb. 9.* Better. *Feb. 10.* Up. *Feb. 16.* Drove to Burford in motor fresh cold. *Mar. 7.* Slight cold chilled to bone.' Draughty rooms in an Oxford winter were poor places for one so disposed, and though it may not have been the sole reason, this may at least have influenced them in their decision to spend the next winter in France.

I am just contemplating with terror the Queen's Letters which it has pleased Lord Grey to send me as a present [writes Weir Mitchell at about this time]. My own opinion about letters is that *selected* letters tell you very little about the character of the person, but that if you had all the letters and all the notes and moreover all the *checks* a person ever wrote, you might then have an opinion.

In Osler's case, however, even without 'all the letters and all the notes', his character may easily be gauged; the fact that he never found in England an amanuensis to whom he could dictate rapidly may account in a measure for the extreme brevity of his typewritten letters. Even so, they almost always contain a postscript or something added in his own hand at the time they were signed: a message to some one's children, whose names he always remembered; a friendly greeting to the L L (meaning 'light of your life'), or a humorous quip of some sort. But the letters in longhand, often undated, scantily punctuated, continue to be more enlightening than anything he dictated. So to various people:

3rd [January]

You may like to have the enclosed letter from Lister. We went to Windsor & gave the Kaiser an honorary degree & he asked me

VIEW OF CHRIST CHURCH FROM ST. ALDATE'S

BURTON BOOKS AND PORTRAIT

particularly about Lister & sent him a message. This is his reply. We have had a very jolly time—A. G. [Mrs. Osler] doing all sorts of kind acts as usual. It is very hard to live up to these Boston women. Did I tell you we are issuing a 2 or 3 Vol edition of all Lister's writings from the Press. 'Tis very hard to get the old man to shell out the MSS. I have just been in town at the meeting of the Path. Soc. of Gt. Britain—very good men & good papers. I am trying to get on the track of Wren's Anatomical Drawings—Did you know that he was one of the first to do microscopical drawings! Wonderful man! Love to all those darlings—

5th [January]

We have had a very jolly Xmas—Isaac Walton had a couple of boys with him & we got a number of the Rhodes scholars to join us at dinner. The house is most comfortable & it is a delight to have my books at hand. I have been picking up a few treasures here & there. The most interesting bibliographical item is the collection of all Burton's books at Christ Church, about 500 (which were scattered indiscriminately). I have had a copy made of the Burton picture at Brasenose and have had it inserted among the books with the 17th cent. editions above & the 19th cent. below.[1] The Bodleian continues to be a delight. We are hoping for a big grant from the Curzon [Oxford Endowment] Fund which will enable us to get a new stack.

28th

. . . I have not got anything very good lately. I have picked up a job lot among which some good anatomical & surgical items—one or two will do for you. I got some Bartholins particularly his account of an epidemic sore throat in Sicily—& a good Naudaeus. I am glad to hear that the Historical Society keeps up so well. I hope to have some good things for October next. I should like to get a peaceful (?) month at the Hospital. I knew you would be pleased with the Fuller. I hope to have a lecture ready on him—'08 is the centenary of his birth. Do you know anything of Mareschal the founder of the Academy of Surgery Paris & the organizer of the French school of surgery. I have just finished reading his life by a descendant. He cut a great figure at the court of Louis XIV. I am having great fun at the Bodleian. The new reading room is ready but the T. is only 42° in these cold days so we have had a deuce of a time. The All Souls people wish to get rid of their Scientific & Medical books—about 3000. Some beauties—not to sell! I am hoping to divert them to the Museum. We are beginning to print the Lister Vols

---

[1] This idea of having the man's portrait framed by his books was subsequently utilized by the Bodleian when it came into possession of Ingram Bywater's library. It was an expression of Osler's feeling that the man himself and his books should not and could not be divorced.

at the Press. I have my Biographical Essays (An Alabama Student &c) in the same hands.

And on February 7th, the day of the 'in bed heavy cold' entry, he wrote to Thayer about the new *Archives of Internal Medicine*, still under the impression he would see America in the autumn:

I like the new journal so much—No. 1 came last eve. It should be a great stimulus and to have it issued by the A. M. A. indicates the revolution which has quietly been progressing in the profession. Stewart's paper is A.1. but surely the peripheral view of the cause of collapsing pulse has been advanced before! It is a most interesting and suggestive article. I hope you are planning to come over this summer. I shall not be out until September for the Congress. We have had a good winter so far. Tommy keeps well. Mrs O & I have been down with heavy colds & the whole country is in the grip of influenza. I am settling down to the life of a pre-senile Don—only I am quite unable to do justice to Port!—Councils & committees. 'Tis often a bore but it is interesting from an educational standpoint. I am afraid nothing short of a French Revolution will modernize Oxford & Cambridge. Have you seen the new Edition of Gui Patin's letters? Vol. I just out. . . .

At about this time the physicians of Vancouver, British Columbia, had organized a medical society, and some one, perhaps one of his old McGill pupils, had acquainted him of the fact, which called forth this reply of February 11th:

I am so glad to hear that you have started a library. There is no better index of the intellectual status of the profession in any town than the condition of its medical library. It will do you all so much good to work at it, particularly in connection with the medical society. I would urge you to join the Association of Medical Librarians. Write to Mr. Huntington at the Brooklyn Medical Library for information. Let me indicate briefly the lines along which I think you should develop:

(1) The current journals, general and special, taking particularly those not likely to be subscribed for by the individual members; (2) as soon as possible fill up one or two sets of first-class journals: the *Lancet*, the *British Medical Journal*, the *American Journal of the Medical Sciences*, the *Annals of Surgery* and journals of that type; (3) of books get the good systems and special works in each department rather than the ordinary school text-books.

It would be a great matter if you could get a few thousand dollars from some of your fellow-citizens with which to make a good start. Every citizen has a direct personal interest in the development of the profession. I hope that every physician in the place will feel that he should help as much as he possibly can, not only by his individual subscription, but, when he feels he can afford it, by an occasional donation. Tell some of the members from me, please, that money invested in a library gives much better returns than mining stock.

In conclusion, as precept is not nearly so satisfactory as example, I enclose you a small subscription as practical evidence of my good-will and good wishes.

Also on the same day, possibly as an aftermath of his cold, he wrote: 'We are having a peaceful winter. I have rather a protracted attack of mental inertia & poor McCrae and the System are having a hard time. I think he has done uncommonly well to get out three volumes in one year.' And towards the end of February a letter from Mrs. Osler, written from the 'Open Arms', states that:

Revere is up to his father's ear and only twelve; evidently he will be tall like my brothers. I am hoping to go abroad with him for the Easter Vac and let him have a month in a French family. Dr. Osler is going to Vienna for a meeting. We have been in the agonies of a series of formal dinner-parties, and have had eighty-four people in three dinners. My strength has given out, and no more till spring. We are having March-y weather but the bulbs are courageous and many things are in bloom already.

Some worrying things were taking place at this time, which promised to impair the welfare of the struggling medical school. It is a rather long story, which concerns the action of the English schoolmasters in bringing influence to bear on Oxford and Cambridge to restrict the season of scholarship examinations to a fixed period in the year, so that these examinations should not involve such frequent breaks in the school year. In bidding for science-candidates the Oxford School could not compete with Trinity College, Cambridge, and had always held her examinations a month earlier. The small group of Oxford scientists, Osler among them, opposed a change which would be, as he expressed it, a 'suicidal policy'. But they were overruled by the majority of college representatives, and as a consequence time saw a great falling-off, for example, in the number of men reading for honours in physiology, with the result that there has tended to be a shortage of competent young teachers at Oxford in this as in other pre-clinical subjects. But Osler took what came with equanimity, and that he found Oxford to his liking, despite its paradoxes, is shown by the following letter of March 3rd to Weir Mitchell—a letter of unusual length, since Mitchell had been chiding him about the brevity of his notes:

It was a great pleasure to have your nice long letter & to hear of your good health at 78. What a fortunate man you are to have had such an innings! How few score in the eighth decade! Your hand keeps its cunning, & the Red City, which we are reading with great interest, promises to be one of your best. It is interesting to note how many people here have read your stories. One doctor was greatly interested to learn that the author of Hugh Wynne & of the Weir Mitchell treatment were one & the same! By the way, will you remind J. K. [Mitchell's son] of his promise to send a list of your writings. You gave me one, but it has been mislaid. I wish it for a purpose.[1]

We are very comfortable in our new house—or rather rearranged house—& the life here is very interesting. I am beginning to get to the heart of the mystery of this old place. It is a bundle of paradoxes. For example this afternoon at one of the important Delegacies (committees which manage certain departments) a proposal to extend the geography school along German lines was declined but £100 a year for three years was voted to a Flemish priest (one of the most distinguished 13th century scholars) to enable him to come to Oxford to complete a bit of work! He had not a single claim on the university but the good work he has done & the friendship of a couple of scholars who are working on the same lines. I have become deeply interested in the University Press of which I am one of the managers. The meetings form a sort of literary seminar, & we really have great sport, particularly with the expert opinions sent in upon works which are offered. It is an immense business. We employ 700 people. The Bodleian too is a great pleasure & I am beginning to know my way about the shelves. We are in hopeless arrears in cataloguing & could spend £500,000 in rearrangement, stacks &c. I am in town a good deal. I am on the Council of the Royal College of Physicians & on the Library Committee & the same on the new Royal Medical Society & the British Medical Association. Last week I was elected one of the Radcliffe Trustees, the body in charge of the old Doctor's Estate—a most select group of eight comprising the Chancellor, the Archbishop of Canterbury, the Duke of Bedford & Sir William Anson. The Trustees support the Radcliffe Library, the Camera, which is part

[1] He was elected a Foreign Member of the Royal Society in the following May. Cf. p. 128.

of the Bodleian, the Observatory, & three Radcliffe Travelling Fellows who get £300 a year each for three years. Altogether I have got rather deeper than I could have wished into official business.

We are beginning to see something of very nice county people. Did you see a life of Lord Wantage? an old Crimean hero? Lady W. has a wonderful estate near here—the largest single farm in Gt Britain—12,000 acres under one management. She has been most kind & we have met some charming people there. Baden-Powell is a man after your own heart—such a keen fellow & as ready with pencil & pen as with sword & rifle. His Mafeking sketches are wonderful. He had tea with us this week before his Scouting lecture. We have a succession of people—scarcely a day passes without some-one of interest turning up. Old Dr. Windsor, who looked up Sanctorius for you & Billings, spent last night—an encyclopaedia of Bibliography. We had a great evening together & I picked up a good deal from him. I buy a few good things now and again. I had a find last week, 140 original letters to Baglivi, 17th century—from Redi, Malpighi, Pitcairn, Bellini & the famous old Anatomists & physicians of the day. B's answers are with them. I got the collection at the Duc d'Altemps Sale at Rome. I am glad Keen did not see the catalogue! I give the new Linacre Lecture (recently organized at Cambridge) in May. Instead of the old lectureship which L. founded they have established a [single] lecture, and I have been asked to speak upon the Life & Works of Linacre.

I do hope you will come over this summer. It would be nice if you took a house for a few weeks in some good district—servants & all. It can be done easily. The difficulty is about the weather & the locality. Do you wish the sea or the mountains? There are lovely spots on the south coast. Dorset is splendid. Shall I make inquiries? You will be interested to know that we are having Harvey's Padua diploma reproduced for the Fellows of the College. I shall certainly get a copy for you. With the fee from my Harveian Oration I had all the Harvey documents at the College put in order & bound. I have had no word yet from Scotland about licences to practise. Give my love to Mrs Mitchell & Jack. Mrs Osler is very well, Revere thriving—waiting anxiously for the opening of the fishing season.

Apparently a defeat at the hands of the Classicists was not worrying him unnecessarily and meanwhile pleasant things were happening, even in the thin ranks of science. At a meeting of the Junior Scientific Club, Sylvanus P. Thompson gave an informal address on 'Petrus Peregrinus and the Mariner's Compass in the Thirteenth Century'. 'One of the best lectures I have ever heard', Osler subsequently wrote. Thompson had spoken of the mythical properties formerly ascribed to the loadstone; of the early references in the literature to means of directing a ship's course; of Peregrinus and John Peckham, afterwards Archbishop of Canterbury, who are described by Roger Bacon as the only two perfect mathematicians; of the first mention by Peregrinus of the pivotal magnet; and much else. All of which is touched upon merely to give association to the copies of Professor Thompson's privately printed historical essays to be found in Osler's library, that on Gilbert the Physician containing a presentation note bearing the date of March 7th which says: 'To the privilege of making your acquaintance last evening [at Balliol] was added the pleasure of discovering that you are a good Gilbertian, etc.' In connexion with this lecture the entry 'Mar. 7. Slight cold chilled to bone' may be recalled. Sylvanus Thompson, it is to be hoped, was more immune.

In describing the formation of the Royal Society of Medicine, mention has been made of the oldest and most famous of the London societies, that founded by Lettsom and Fothergill in 1773, which had held aloof from the amalgamation, preferring to retain its own individuality. Of the principles for which this old society was founded, one was the promotion of pleasant social relations among medical men; therefore among other customs there is held annually a festival dinner. On March 11th Osler was present as a guest on this occasion, and reports of the after-dinner speeches relate that he who had favoured amalgamation, and Mr. Edmund Owen, who had been one of its strong opponents, 'were both particularly happy in their combination of wit and wisdom.' Osler evidently made an appeal to his hearers as individuals not only to join the Royal Society of Medicine, but spoke of their duty towards the British Medical Association as well—a body which stands in much the same relation to the general profession in Great Britain as does the American Medical Association in the country he had left, the two sharing similar failings and virtues. But, as in his American days, Osler chose to work with rather than against the machine, and he had accepted a position as member of the Central Council of the B. M. A., which accounts for his saying: 'It may do things which you do not like, or do them in ways of which you do not approve, but that is no reason for keeping out of it; you should join it and help to have them altered. Those of you here who are consultants and on the medical and surgical staffs of the London hospitals, but do not belong to this association, do justice neither to yourselves nor to the profession to which you belong.'

The antivivisection hearings by this time had been completed, and the reports of the commissioners containing Lord Justice Moulton's remarkable summing up of the rights and wrongs of experimentation had been published; but meanwhile in America the Rockefeller Institute had become the target of the antivivisectionists, as this note of March 24th to Flexner indicates:

> Deuce take these women! why do you have them at the Institute at all? You are too soft hearted. It would be well to have Mr. Justice Moulton's evidence before the Vivisection Committee (just issued) published in the United States as a separate campaign pamphlet. It is too bad you should be having so much trouble. Here the anti-people seem to have got into ill odour—at last!

Meanwhile at Oxford 'people were coming and going'. It had become a familiar phrase in Osler's letters. Those coming to England were as certain to hear from him as those leaving for America, though, as in the case of William James, they occasionally side-stepped his offer of hospitality.[1] In Osler's copy of 'Pragmatism' this letter has been inserted:

From William James to W. O. 95 Irving St., Cambridge, Mass., April 3, 1908.

My dear Osler,—I thank you for your letter of March 24th, but listen to how it is with me! I find myself in a state of as bad nervous fatigue as I have ever been in my life, and that says a good deal. (To-day, e. g., awake since 2.30, and had to stop work on my 5th lecture—out of eight—after two hours because of flushed head). Three-hour-long dinner-parties tire me badly; and if I succeed in

[1] Professor James was to deliver the eight Hibbert Lectures at Manchester College. At the time he was far from well, and was suffering from 'the infernal nervous condition' that, he confessed, always accompanied literary production. His impressions of Oxford appear in 'The Letters of William James', Boston, Atlantic Monthly Press, 1920, vol. ii, p. 307.

getting through my lectures themselves, I shall be lucky. This is not to *com-* but only to *ex*-plain why the notion of being 'lionized' in any way whatever at Oxford strikes terror into my rabbit-like heart. So *don't* invite your London M.D.'s to meet me! All that I am good for under present conditions is a few more intimate talks with old (and new) Oxford friends. Don't consider me churlish, for I *ain't*!...

The letter is quoted for the opportunity it gives of contrast between two intellectual men who shared a certain kind of gaiety of spirit. Osler practising his own philosophy and largely unconscious of self, could submit with imperturbability to the 'lionizing' which unavoidably forms a part of such things as foreign lectureships; whereas the very thought put the mind of a philosopher-in-precept in a panic.

His old friend, E. A. Schäfer, of University College days, was planning a trip to America at this time, the Herter Lectureship at the Johns Hopkins being a part of his programme; and Osler writes:

What a grand tour! Do see poor Bowditch—I am afraid he has failed very rapidly, paralysis agitans. Dock at Ann Arbor is a special friend. I will write and tell him to look out for you. Stir them up a bit in Montreal—I fear the bad times have prevented them re-building. You will see great changes in the country. Where do you stay in Toronto? Either of my brothers would be only too glad to put you up. I shall miss your lecture at the College as I am going to Vienna on the 4th. I had a letter from Jack the other day. Poor fellow! it is hard lines to be sent off so soon. Is Ruth with you? With love to all at home...

The trip to Vienna which he mentions was taken in company with his former Johns Hopkins pupil, Joseph H. Pratt, with the purpose of attending the annual German *Kongress für Innere Medizin*, of which his friend von Müller of Munich was President for the year. He presented no paper and went merely as an everyday onlooker, though he could hardly escape being dragged out of the audience from time to time to take a seat on the platform. They went to Vienna without stop, and Dr. Pratt's recollection is that he was immersed most of the way in the very dull poems of Thomas Lovell Beddoes (1803–49), in whom he had become interested and whose trail they expected subsequently to follow to Basle in search of his grave. What had awakened his interest in the professional aspects of T. L. Beddoes's life rather than in those of his father's (a much more distinguished person) is not apparent, though during the preceding month he had been in correspondence regarding him not only with Edmund Gosse, who had republished Beddoes's poems and letters, but also with the Basle authorities.

In an earlier chapter a quotation has already been given from the long letter concerning this Vienna visit which he subsequently wrote for publication,[1] resuming thereby his early habit of so doing when paying a visit to foreign clinics. In this letter he mentions the sessions of the congress, the social functions, the old hospital which he revisited ; and Dr. Pratt recalls that on entering the time-worn wards, at that time constituting von Neusser's clinic, he exclaimed : 'Shades of Hippocrates ! the same old place. Even the nurses haven't changed.' Nevertheless there were plenty of contrasts to former days. He had what he calls a 'Queen-of-Sheba sensation' on visiting the first group of the new buildings of the *Allgemeines Krankenhaus*, erected at Government expense, the most perfect of their kind in the world, well worthy of the founder of the Vienna school—buildings to make one despair of private institutions. The letter makes clear that he chiefly foregathered with the younger men—Pick, Brauer, and Wenckebach ; also that Max Neuburger the historian took him through the Vienna libraries :

The *Hofbibliothek* [he wrote] is unusually rich in manuscripts and early printed books. I was anxious to see the copy of 'Christianismi Restitutio' of Michael Servetus, 1553, in which for the first time the lesser circulation is described. This is one of the only two known copies in existence. The entire edition was confiscated, and the author at the time a practitioner in the little town of Vienne, near Lyons, fled for his life to Geneva. Here his heterodoxy was quite as obnoxious to Calvin, into whose hands he fell, and he was burnt at the stake in the same year. The 'Restitutio' is one of the rare books of the world. Only two of the 1,000 copies known to have been printed have survived. The one in the *Bibliothèque Nationale*

1 'Vienna After Thirty-four Years.' *Journal of the American Medical Association*, May 9, 1908, i. 1523.

originally belonged to Dr. Mead, and the history is fully given in an appendix in Willis's work, 'Servetus and Calvin'. The Vienna copy is in excellent preservation, beautifully bound, and states on the title-page that it came from the library of a Transylvanian gentleman living in London. It fell into the hands of Count de Izek, who presented it to the Emperor of Austria. It is a thick small octavo of about 700 pages. The first one to give credit to Servetus for the discovery of the lesser circulation was Wotton, whose 'Reflections upon Learning, Ancient and Modern', 1694, is a most interesting book, for an introduction to which I have long been grateful to my friend, Dr. Norman Moore. The other work that I was most anxious to see was the famous manuscript of Dioscorides, prepared at the end of the fifth century for Julia, daughter of the Emperor Flavius. It is one of the great treasures of the library. Now to us in the West only a name, Dioscorides, an army surgeon of the time of Nero, fills a great place in the history of medicine, and is still an oracle in the Orient. He was not only a great botanist, but he was one of the first scientific students of pharmacology. Scores of fine editions of his work, with commentaries, were issued in the fifteenth and sixteenth centuries. Two years ago this Vienna manuscript was reproduced in facsimile at Leyden. Though very expensive, the two volumes costing $150, it is a work which all the larger libraries should get, and it is just the sort of present that librarians should make our wealthy consultants feel it a privilege to give.[1]

Mrs. Osler was to have joined him on the Continent, but this was frustrated by Revere's having an attack of measles; and apparently he gave up his search for T. L. Beddoes's remains and was back by April 10th, when he wrote to McCrae:

Dear Mac. I have had a bully visit to Vienna—great town! (1) I have returned figures with legends. (2) Shirres has written giving up section. Ask Russel who could do it easily—but he will have to hustle. I have written—will you also write giving details? (3) I return heart proofs with corrections—not many. What splendid proofs they send! What a fine programme of the Interurban. I hope we may have a good meeting at Edinboro. It is hard to stir the men up to much enthusiasm. Ike is well again. Love to the boys. Yours, W. O. You have never sent word as to the date. I am trying to settle sailing.

And soon he writes to J. H. Pratt, his recent *compagnon de*

[1] Of the important pages in the 'Christianismi Restitutio' he had photographs made which were subsequently used in his essay on Servetus, and also printed with pictures on a folio sheet at the Clarendon Press and distributed as a Christmas gift to many friends.

voyage, showing that after all he had not completely abandoned T. L. Beddoes; also, by the postscript, that the *Dictionary of National Biography* his pupils long before had given him, was once more in reach:

What a good visit we had. I found Tommy all right on my return. Let me hear how you are getting along. I shall expect you before the B. M. A. I quite expected to hear that you had gone to Charlottenburg! I wish you would look in the library for Transactions of any Medical or Scientific Society of Göttingen for the years 1825–50. If so, will you look through the Index for any communications by Thomas Lovell Beddoes? Sincerely yours, Wm Osler. In 1832 he took his degree at Würzburg—could you find if there is a list of W. theses of that date? 1836, Schönlein of Zurich proposed him as Prof. of Comp Anatomy.

Though he continually used his young friends in this way, he lost no opportunity to do them good turns. O. H. Perry Pepper, one of the sons of his former Philadelphia colleague, had published in an obscure local journal an article which came to his attention, and he promptly wrote:

Dear Perry, Delighted to see your name—and associated with such a good bit of work. Send me a reprint. It is so nice to see the name kept up so worthily in the 3rd generation. My sincere regards to your mother & to Will.

This missive, though one to delight a young man's heart, is less noteworthy than the fact that in its next issue the London *Lancet*[1] printed a long 'annotation' calling especial attention to Dr. Pepper's article. Unexpected acts of kindness of this sort, the possibility of which so many people recognize but rarely pursue, represented his normal reaction—done quickly and on impulse. Countless illustrations could be cited. Mention has been made of his visit to the Swansea Hospital in August of 1907 and of his having made some new acquaintances while there: a Miss Price, the house physician, and Dr. Frank G. Thomas, her chief. Among the many brief notes these two subsequently received from him and still treasure—encouraging and helpful letters on subjects in which they were separately interested—

[1] 'A case of Hodgkin's Disease with General Eosinophilia.' *Lancet*, Lond., Apr. 25, 1908, i. 1226 (unsigned).

there came one of kindly banter on learning of their engagement:

24th [April]

Dear Miss Price, Cruel girl! deliberately to divert an innocent young man from the Minervan path! And think of your wasted life! & of the loss to the profession! & the bad example you set to female medical students! & the worse example to young female graduates! & the distrust you have engendered in Hospital Committees! & the suspicion & apprehension such lapses arouse in the minds of the staff! Altogether your conduct seems most reprehensible, & yet! how natural! Wishing you every happiness, Sincerely yours,

Wm Osler.

He writes, April 27th, that: 'We are in the depths of winter—a furious storm and yesterday about a foot of snow.' The man 'uninfluenced by weather' meanwhile must have been putting the finishing touches on his Linacre Lecture,[1] delivered May 6th at St. John's College, Cambridge. It will be remembered that there looked down on him from the panel over his mantel the triumvirate of Linacre, Harvey, and Sydenham, in each of whom he had an unflagging interest. That he should choose Linacre as his subject was inevitable. In the lecture Osler dealt with him first as a medical humanist, and then as a grammarian, recalling Fuller's comment: 'It is questionable whether he was a better grammarian or physician'; and in this connexion he mentioned why, since boyhood, he had been anathematizing some one who proved to be Protagoras:

Fed to inanition on the dry husks of grammar and with bitter schoolboy memories of 'Farrar on the Greek Verb', I can never pick up a text-book on the subject without a regret that the quickening

---

[1] The Linacre Lectureship was instituted by Thomas Linacre, physician to King Henry VIII, a founder and first President of the Royal College of Physicians. By a deed dated Aug. 19, 1524, to which Linacre, Sir Thomas More, and others, were parties, the 'Maister and Fellowes' of St. John's College covenanted to found a 'lecture of physicke'. Linacre stated that by his will he had bequeathed to them a house called the Belle and Lanthorne in Adlyng Street (now Addle Hill) in London; he also gave the sum of £221 13*s*. 4*d*. for the purchase of land. Originally the lectureship extended over a four-year period. Osler's appointment was a new departure in that for the first time it was decided 'to invite annually a man of mark to give a single lecture on the same general plan as the Rede Lectureship'—likewise on an old foundation going back to Linacre's time.

spirit of Greece and Rome should have been for generations killed by the letter with which alone these works are concerned. It has been a great comfort to know that neither 'Pindar nor Aeschylus had the faintest conception of these matters and that neither knew what was meant by an adverb or preposition, or the rules of the moods and tenses' (Gomperz). And to find out who invented parts of speech and to be able to curse Protagoras by his Gods has been a source of inexpressible relief. But even with these feelings of hostility I find it impossible to pick up this larger work of Linacre without the thrill that stirs one at the recognition of successful effort—of years of persistent application. No teacher had had such distinguished pupils—Prince Arthur, the Princess Mary, Sir Thomas More, and Erasmus the greatest scholar of the age.

He went on to quote what Erasmus had said of Linacre,—a description which probably inspired Browning's poem, 'The Grammarian's Funeral'. From this he proceeded to speak of the Linacre Foundations whereby provision was made for two lectureships at Oxford and one at Cambridge, 'dutifully his respect to his mother double above his aunt', as Fuller says; 'the act of a wise old man to encourage the study and teaching of medicine' in Osler's words.

'The Lady Margaret' [he said], whose glorious monument is your college, had already established her Divinity professorships, but with these exceptions Linacre's bequests are memorable as the first attempts to endow university teaching. Centuries had to pass before the fulfilment of the wish which his practical mind had in this way indicated. Meanwhile through the centuries the collegiate tail continued to wag the University dog, and to this day in Oxford at least the higher faculties remain to a great extent unorganized and under the control of the Masters of Arts. The system has worked well for the squire but badly for learning, admirably for the schoolmaster and the parson, but badly for the nation since it permitted the old Universities to sleep on for years after science had cried her message from the housetops—awake! awake! for the light has come!

A sentiment not at all in accord with what William James at the moment was writing to Charles Eliot Norton: 'Let other places of learning go in for the improvements! The world can afford to keep her one Oxford unreformed. If I were an Oxonian, in spite of my radicalism generally, I might vote against all change there.' The month of May might have this effect on any visitor to Oxford; and Osler on his return from Cambridge soon writes: 'The invasion is in full swing. We shall have a roaring term from this on. We are getting settled by degrees. The garden is lovely and the bare walls of the new part of the house are gradually being covered. Grace has managed so well, she 's really wasted in a house and should run a summer hotel. Revere is well and happy—interested in cricket, not much of a student. Kiss the darlings for me.'

During all that time, as his correspondence testifies, Osler was deeply engaged with the furtherance of the Oxford medical publications which had been inaugurated by the first issue of the *Quarterly Journal of Medicine*. A good beginning was made with a series of manuals, Burghard's 'System of Operative Surgery', a 'System of Syphilis' in six volumes, and some monographs, and soon the opportunity was seized of purchasing Mr. Young J. Pentland's business, comprising, among other important books, Cunningham's 'Text-book of Anatomy', his 'Manual of Anatomy', Muir and Ritchie's 'Manual of Bacteriology', and Thomson and Miles's 'Surgery'. This business brought Osler into close relations with the publishers to the Press in London—Henry Frowde and his successor, Humphrey Milford—and with their colleagues, Mr. (now Sir Ernest) Hodder Williams, and Mr. J. Keogh Murphy, who subsequently died on active service as a naval surgeon in the war. It was unusual for him to be in town without dropping in at Amen Corner, or for them in turn to miss seeing him in Oxford; and, as Mr. Milford writes: 'We never came away without having received valuable advice and fruitful suggestions.'

At the time of his visit in Cardiff three years before, he had made his usual provocative appeal to the well-to-do members of the community to come to the support of the local hospital—an appeal which seems to have borne fruit. In any event, money had subsequently been raised to build a model out-patient department for the local Infirmary, and naturally enough he was invited to give the dedicatory address, at which time he was presented with a suitably inscribed key to commemorate the occasion. He spoke[1] on

[1] An account of his remarks appeared in a special number of the *British Medical Journal*, June 20, 1908, devoted to a variety of hospital questions.

'The Functions of an Out-patient Department', saying that he had haunted these departments for years, having a special interest in them from the standpoint of a teacher. He dwelt particularly on what should be their relation to the busy general practitioner who might regard an out-patient department as a rival, but for whom it should really play the part of consultant when dealing with his poorer patients, should they be in need of a second opinion. And in his concluding paragraph he emphasized that the hospital should become an integral part of the university system. 'After all,' he said, 'it is a great laboratory in which we collect for rectification the experiments which Nature makes upon us. The study of disease is just as much a part of university work as is the study of mathematics, and a close affiliation of the two institutions is the best guarantee of that combination of science with practice which it is the right of people at the present day to demand.' This sentiment was picked up by Principal Griffiths when his turn came to thank the speaker, and the statement was made that the Infirmary had been under a cloud, and that out of a community of half a million there were only four hundred on its subscription list. Whereupon Osler replied: 'If all this has been done with the Infirmary under a cloud, what are you going to do when you come out into the sunshine? Four hundred out of half a million! Well, Abraham would have thought that a pretty high percentage!'

To J. Y. W. MacAlister from W. O. May 21.

I am just back from Cardiff and find your telegram and letter. I was depending upon a mutual friend who said he would let me know at once when Mr. Morgan returned. Instead of the ordinary type-written letter I thought it would be much better to send him a statement in print and I enclose you a proof in which you will see there are a number of lacunae. Please look over it and return at your earliest convenience. I will write at once and ask for an appointment for [Sir William] Church and myself. I have had a long letter from Kinnicutt, a warm personal friend of J. P. M., who had already written to him. I am afraid it will be hard to push matters. From what his friend says, he is not a man to be hurried in these matters. He brooded some months over the Harvard bequest. . . .

Thus he spared no pains to gain the support for worthy

causes of people with funds at their disposal. There was a frequent exchange of letters at this time with Henry Phipps, whose interest was becoming aroused in the establishment of a psychiatric clinic at the Johns Hopkins; in one of these letters Mr. Phipps prodded him by enclosing an article on a tabooed subject. This Osler acknowledged, saying: 'Thanks so much for the article, but it gives only one side. An equally striking one could be written on what the world would have gained if certain distinguished men had stopped writing at 40. It would perhaps have been much better for the reputation of some of us—for example of myself!' Meanwhile he was by no means forgetful of his old American friends, one of whom, in his 80th year, had by no means stopped writing. Some months before this Osler had put Weir Mitchell in train to secure the 'Edward Jenner' inkstand, into which for another six years he dipped his inspired pen; and now he wrote to him, on 'Saturday 23rd', of something else:

I cabled you on Friday that you had been elected a Foreign Fellow of the Royal Society. I am delighted. Brunton suggested it two years ago but your name was not brought forward. Ferrier is on the Council this year & with his support & Rose Bradford's you went thro. swimmingly. It was between you & Ehrlich, I believe. There are only four or five Americans on the list,—Agassiz, Geo. Hill, Michelson, Newcomb & Pickering. It will be most gratifying to all your friends, and is a most welcome recognition in this country of your great services to science. You will get of course official notification, but as the formal election has to be made by the Fellows at a meeting I added in my cable not to make any announcement before you hear. I was greatly pleased as at the last meeting a few weeks ago the general impression was that Ehrlich would have the nomination. Drop a line to Ferrier, who has been most kind in the matter. Much love to Mrs Mitchell & Jack.

Nor had he forgotten the Maryland Faculty, at this time struggling to raise money for a new building, which was to have an auditorium bearing his name, and where his portrait was to be hung. On June 2nd he wrote to the Librarian:

Dear Miss Noyes, What an aggravation to have the appropriation cut one half! Isn't it distressing! Still, the greater the discouragement the greater should be the effort, & after all when one thinks what the library was when your feminine feebleness took hold of it and what it is now, we have a great deal to be thankful for. I am so sorry to hear that your sister is worse again. It must be a terrible trial to you. I wondered why I should be feeling & looking so much better lately, but it is no doubt the telepathic influence of the improvement which Corner has made in the portrait. I hope to spend a couple of weeks in Baltimore in October. Give your sister my kindest regards.

On June 19th the second meeting of the Association of Physicians of Great Britain and Ireland opened its sessions in Edinburgh. As usual, Osler was on the programme for a paper,[1] but something less commonplace, so far as he is concerned, happened at the time of this meeting. The Rectorial Representation Committee, consisting of some forty students of the various faculties of the University, had appointed a delegation to call upon him; of this the following letter gave warning:

From Dr. Norman Walker to W. O. 7 Manor Place, Edinburgh, June 11th.

Dear Osler,—I understand that you are to be waited upon to-morrow by a deputation of students who will ask you to permit your name to be put forward as a candidate for the Lord Rectorship of the University [to succeed Lord Haldane]. They tell me they are confident that they have enough backing to ensure your election. Though I would rather have had you in the university in another capacity I shall be glad to see you in any, and I am sure you would be very warmly welcomed by the medical profession here. Aberdeen and St. Andrews have elected their Rectors on non-political lines and though it grieves me to reflect that your views on the Tariff differ from mine it is not on political grounds that you are approached. . . .

In the long history of these triennial contests, dating back to 1859, such a thing had only happened two or three times before, that a non-party candidate should stand for the Lord Rectorship—John Ruskin in 1862 had done so and come within 183 votes of election, while in 1871 Thomas Carlyle won by a large majority over Lord Beaconsfield. Though these rectorial elections lie entirely in the hands of the undergraduates, politicians have come to regard them as a significant weathervane, and the contests are supported

[1] 'Chronic Infectious Endocarditis.' *Quarterly Journal of Medicine*, Oxford, Jan. 1909, pp. 219–30.

by funds from the party organizations. Osler's entry into the field was a gamble, but the medical vote was strong and it all depended upon how high the party feeling should run between the two other candidates already in the field, neither of whom was over-popular—the Rt. Hon. George Wyndham, supported by the Conservatives, and the Rt. Hon. Winston Churchill, by the Liberals. Only once before had a triangular contest been held. Party feeling did run high, and Osler was defeated, but it was by no means a one-sided election, as will be seen. He made a good run for his money —or for his brother's money, for, as it was an expensive business, Sir Edmund footed the campaign bills; and he may at least have had the satisfaction of knowing that painted on the walls of the house in Lindsay Place, where were the Conservative (Wyndham's) head-quarters at this election, there is still plainly to be seen, indelible to this day despite much scrubbing, VOTE FOR OSLER, and DOWN WITH WYNDHAM—an indication that the Oslerites during the 'rag' had successfully stormed the premises of their chief opponents. But this is anticipating. It is evident from contemporary letters that he looked into the matter fully with the help of G. A. Gibson and others in Edinburgh before his candidature was made public. Meanwhile there were examinations to hold in Oxford, which as usual laid him low with a cold and gave him the opportunity he always grasped to catch up on his reading and to write many letters, while propped on pillows, his pad on his knee. Thus to H. B. Jacobs:

23rd [June].

Many thanks for the Walt Whitman which came to-day & looks most interesting. Did you read Bliss Perry? He seems to have put the old man's case before the world as the old man himself would have liked—in the nothing-extenuate style. We are having a glorious summer—such days! and the country is at its best. Our garden begins to look so well & we are dining on the terrace, living there in fact. These are busy days—such an invasion for the Encaenia & Commemoration week! We must have had 75 people on Sunday afternoon—all sorts & conditions. The Torrey-Linzee-Weld combination arrived last week—partly here & in part at the King's Arms. Raymond came this afternoon. He gets an honorary degree to-morrow. I could not go to his *entente cordiale* lecture yesterday as the examiners were here. Dick Cabot spent four days with us

& I took him to Edinboro to the Ass. of Phy. of Gt. Britain. He is seeing London under the best of auspices & is enjoying it so much. The prospects for visitors from this side to Washington [for the Tuberculosis Congress] is brightening. Woodhead is going & he mentioned a half-dozen good men. Ireland & Scotland are to send separate representatives. Is it not splendid about Mr. Phipps's gift of a Psychopathic clinic? Welch cabled—I see in the paper £200,000 is mentioned, but I can hardly hope it is so large a sum. He arrived in London yesterday. He dines with me on the 1st at the Darwin-Wallace Commemoration—50th anniversary of the reading of the abstract of the Origin of Species. Love to Mrs. Jacobs.

In all probability the conferring of the D.Sc. at this Encaenia upon Professor J. Raymond of the Salpêtrière was at his instigation. There was good reason to foster the *entente cordiale*,[1] and it may be noted that at this same time the then Chancellor of the Exchequer, David Lloyd George, received a D.C.L. and was considerably heckled by the light-hearted students in the Sheldonian galleries: 'Hello, David, what about Pudsey?' 'When am I to expect my pension?' &c. July was no less crowded with meetings than May and June had been. As foretold in the last letter to Jacobs, he took Mr. Phipps to the Darwin-Wallace Commemoration at the Linnean Society, of which occasion he has left the following reminder in a copy of the Proceedings of the society (1858, vol. iii, no. 9), which after a long search was finally added to his library on February 28, 1915:

I owe this number to the kindness of my colleague Prof. Poulton. For years I have been on the lookout for it, but could never find a separate copy & I did not care to buy a whole series. I had again written to Sotheran on Feb. 26th asking him to search once more, but I met P. that day, & remembering his close association with the Linnean Society I asked him to see if there were extra copies in

[1] Just at this time there had been a deputation of 200 French physicians sent over to London. The sixth edition of Osler's Text-book had just appeared in a French translation with a preface by Pierre Marie. It was his first real introduction to the French profession. As was then said, 'his exceptional knowledge of pure English and ability to say exactly what he meant in plain and well-balanced phrases made possible its almost exact transposition into French.' In Oxford, as in Baltimore and Montreal, Osler was continually drubbing into the students the necessity of acquiring a working knowledge of French and German, which became so noised about that a long editorial in the *British Medical Journal*, Sept. 26, 1908, deals with his position on the subject.

the library. The next day he sent me the numbers for 1858 & the memorial volume. I have had this number bound separately as containing the two most fruitful contributions to science made in the 19th century, contributions which have revolutionized modern thought.

The memorial meeting in 1908 was intensely interesting, particularly to see and to hear such veterans as Hooker and Wallace. It was a memorable occasion. I remember how Sir John Lubbock (Lord Avebury) recalled 'the astonishment and indignation with which the principles promulgated in the Joint Memoir, & in the "Origin of Species" by which it was succeeded, were received'.

I only saw Darwin once. During the winter of 1872–3 his son Francis worked at the table next to me in Burdon Sanderson's laboratory at University College. Several times in the spring he talked of taking me to Down for the week-end, but his father was ailing. It was, I think, the next spring, I mean in '74, that I saw him at the Royal Society reception. . . . He was a most kindly old man, of large frame, with great bushy beard and eyebrows. W. O.

On July 2nd came the meeting of the National Tuberculosis Association, where he likewise planned to take Mr. Phipps, to whom he wrote: 'I will call for you at 3.10 sharp unless I have a line from you at the Athenaeum Club that you are engaged. You will be interested in Lady Aberdeen's account of the struggle in Ireland.' Mr. Phipps apparently *was* engaged, for on the 4th Osler wrote again to the effect that 'she said in her remarks that among the things which had stimulated them to take up the work were the Reports from the Phipps Institute. I have sent the cheque to her. I am sure she will appreciate highly your practical support.' But these were side remarks. The exchange of letters chiefly dealt with Osler's endeavour to get Mr. Phipps in touch with Kraepelin in Munich and with other continental psychiatrists, from whom he might get first-hand information in regard to his projected psychiatric clinic.

Meanwhile much has been going on at 13 Norham Gardens, and even the Regius, in a letter of July 10th to Mrs. Brewster, admits that:

We have been very busy—all sorts & conditions of people have been here, but it has been very good fun and fortunately Mrs. Osler likes the racket. It sometimes is a little too much for me. I am now torn in twain—America in September or a break for the winter, a real holiday in Italy? I have not had a year off—ever, & I feel it is about time, but it cannot be settled for a few weeks. If I decide to take a long holiday I shall not come out until the spring. It will be a great disappointment as I have been looking forward to a peaceful visit, & an introduction to Sylvia. Please do not mention my possible change of plans as I am *slated* for Washington & the Tuberculosis Congress at the end of September. I wish you could see our garden —such a joy & the weather has been superb. Day after day we have dined on the terrace. Revere is so well & very happy—butterflies & moths, fish & cricket, not too much study, fill out his days. You will be amused at the enclosed. I was in Edinburgh a few weeks ago and was surprised to have a deputation from all the faculties asking me to stand for the Lord Rectorship. The students elect. 'Tis a purely honorary office, only a few rectorial addresses. Send the slip on to Uncle Ned. . . .

Mrs. Osler's letters, rather than his, make it clear that July saw no let-up in the invasion at the 'Open Arms', where 'the tennis court draws young men every afternoon, which makes it nice for the Weld girls'. On a postcard of August 2nd Osler wrote:

I send my Linacre lecture to-day.[1] We are having the most wonderful summer—such sunshine. The garden is splendid. The hotel is in full swing. We have had such a nice set of old friends. Roddick and his wife left yesterday. We are off to Scotland in the motor on the 5th. I have just got back from the British Med.

[1] A note should be made about Osler's reprints, which of course accumulated in enormous numbers. Many of these papers, like this Linacre address, were privately reprinted and he distributed them freely. He took the trouble, moreover, to set aside ten more or less complete sets which were indexed, bound as 'Collected Reprints', and all but one set, which he retained, given to special libraries—the Hopkins', the Faculty's, the Surgeon-General's, the Boston Medical, &c. The following note on the subject of reprints is written in a copy of H. I. Bowditch's translation of Louis's monograph on typhoid:

'V. Y. Bowditch sent me these volumes in May '08. I asked him for a book from his father's collection with his name in it to put in the best of company on my shelves. H. I. Bowditch impressed me as one of the best of men. When I went to Boston in 1875 to look up the subject of haemorrhagic small-pox I took a letter of introduction from Dr. Howard, and I spent a memorable evening with him. He was full of enthusiasm for his old teacher Louis, whose biography he had recently written. When giving me a bundle of reprints and saying good-bye at the door he remarked, "You are a young fellow just coming on the slate, I am going off. Take my advice and have a reprint of everything you write and collect them. I would give $1,000 for a set of all my papers." This made a great impression on me and I have followed his advice. Through him I became friends with his nephew H. P. and his son V. Y.'

Assoc. at Sheffield. Isaac is off fishing for a couple of days with some boys.

The automobile, though not a form of progression in which Mrs. Osler took unalloyed pleasure, made it easy to reach otherwise inaccessible places like Ewelme; and occasionally, as now, it was used for longer trips.

To Mrs. Brewster from W. O. Logan's Low Wood Hotel, Windermere. 21st [August]

Dear Mabel, A week in this glorious country—& no rain—has made me feel that I should like to stay here for ever. We have had such a happy time—our first long motor trip. We went up the great north road to Scotland. Revere had been promised trout fishing in the Fleet in Kirkcudbright which took us into the Guy Mannering & Crockett country It was most interesting. I did not know that the Highlands came so low in Scotland—i. e. (to explain an Irishism) so far south. We had glorious weather—not a drop of rain for weeks. The river was so low & clear that the trout winked at Revere & passed the time of day with his flies. We made excursions all about the country—& saw all that is left of Ellangowan & peeped into Dirk's cave—I have got him (R) interested in Scott & it was most instructive to visit the places mentioned in the novels. We have been for a week at the English Lakes. I sent you a p.c. of Wordsworth's cottage at Grasmere and a sprig of heather from the mound in the garden of his house at Rydal Mount. His granddaughter most kindly showed us all the treasures of the house and allowed us to roam about the garden & enjoy the wonderful views. I am not surprised that he & nature were akin. Such surroundings! We have seen them under most favourable circumstances—beautiful clear skies and everything so fresh & green. Yesterday we saw the great Northern Olympia at Grasmere where the Westmoreland & Cumberland men have their famous wrestling matches. It is held in a natural amphitheatre amid the hills & one famous feature is the guides' race up one of the mountains—the 25 men could be seen scrambling up the rocks. We return via North Wales. . . .

Their plans to spend the ensuing winter abroad were apparently decided upon during this trip, and soon after his return he must have interviewed the Vice-Chancellor, Prof. Herbert Warren, and asked his colleague, Arthur Thomson, to act as his deputy:

13 Norham Gardens, August 27th.

Dear Thomson, Will you play D. R. P. M. [Deputy Regius Prof. of Medicine] again this year? After 34 years with the harness on

I am going to steal a winter, & the V.-C. consents. Everything is going on smoothly—and you 'know the ropes' better than I do. Of course you would take the Stipend—minus the Ewelme. It would be nice if you could arrange to present the men—could you not have an *ad eundem*. It looks very awkward to have the presentations made by a man who is not a member of the faculty. I hope to spend the winter in France and Italy—playing diabolo & studying medicine. Love to the three girls.

Dead as Oxford might be at the end of the summer, one 'hotel' at least kept full while its proprietor laboured over the seventh edition of his Text-book. This is apparent from the following to H. B. Jacobs:

16th [September]

I am really desolated not to be at the Congress. I know I shall miss a great deal and there will be so much of interest. Keep an eye on Dr. Charles Williams who is a good old soul; also Stafford of Dublin; Newsholme, too, is a very good fellow. I am so sorry Bulstrode could not come as he is one of the best. I have been very busy trying to get the revision of my text-book ready by Oct. 1st, & finishing an article for Allbutt's system.[1] We have had an interesting relay of visitors. Coll Warren & his boy John were here for five days; Anders & his wife; J. William White; Keen comes tomorrow. You will have my Alabama Student very soon. The University Press has published it. I am sending it from the New York House. Mac is settled to-day—he is getting a good wife. I wish we could have been with them. . . . I am off Oct. 1st. Brown, Shipley, Paris, will be my address. Mrs Osler will join me in about a fortnight after she gets Revere settled at the School. He has had a very good summer & adds every week to his collection of butterflies and moths. . . . I am glad the Faculty Building is in sight. The reading room should certainly be called after Charles Frick & a nice tablet should state how much W. Frick did for the Library. Love to you both.

That he was 'desolated' at missing the International Congress on Tuberculosis which opened in Washington, September 21st, is no exaggeration. The part he had played in 1904, making it possible, has already been told.[2] At this

[1] He had two chapters in Allbutt and Rolleston's 'System of Medicine', Vol. VI, 1909: the chapter on Aneurysm; and with Arthur Keith, that on Stokes-Adams disease. He was also preparing his three chapters for Vol. VI of his own 'System' ('Modern Medicine'), published with McCrae. These were attacked while in Paris, later on.

[2] The congress, under Lawrence F. Flick's direction as Chairman of the

time, Dr. Adolphus Knopf of New York, one of the active participants in the crusade against tuberculosis, had been victimized by a yellow journal, which, garbling an address he had given, accused him of recommending that consumptives be killed off with morphine, and that he himself followed this practice. Knopf asked for a retraction of the statement, which was ignored, and a suit followed. Osler's reaction to this is indicated in the two following letters—the first to Dr. Joseph Walsh of the Phipps Institute:

Sept. 22nd.

I have been much interested in your papers in the last *Phipps Institute Report*. What good work you are doing there! I know it is a great satisfaction to Mr. Phipps. I have recently had all the papers sent to me about the Knopf suit against the *North American* newspaper. I had no idea that he had been so outrageously slandered. I do hope that, if the suit comes on, the profession of Philadelphia will support him loyally, and particularly all of you at the Phipps Institute, who are more directly interested in the disease. Your brother keeps us busy reading his interesting books. What a genius he has for this sort of work! His 'Thirteenth Century' is delightful reading. . .

And a few days later one of a succession of letters—in some of which he uses profanity, an unusual thing for him—sent to encourage the victim of the slander, reads as follows:

Dear Knopf, That is an admirable letter. I do hope they will accept your terms but I doubt it. Really the irresponsibility of the press is disgraceful & the only way to rouse a sense of decency is to touch their pockets. It must have been a most prejudicial thing for you and all the worry & annoyance must have been most distressing. Do not let him bull-doze you. This is a matter for the profession—we are all personally interested. I should be glad to start a subscription with $100 to help pay your expenses to fight it. I am sure we could get a substantial sum. I am not coming out in Sept. I am starting a sabbatical year for study &c on the continent and I must make all my arrangements before I leave. With best wishes—Do let me hear how you get on.

And again, he said: 'No compromise! Fight it out and

Committee on Arrangements, was held under most favourable auspices and with strong governmental backing. Mr. Roosevelt consented to be honorary President, with Trudeau the President; and many of Osler's friends, William H. Welch, A. Jacobi, V. Y. Bowditch, the Surgeon-General and others as Chairmen of the several sections.

we will try and arouse the profession to pay your expenses. I will write a strong letter to the Journal of the Association urging the active co-operation of all interested in fair play. You have been outrageously treated and any decent judge would give you large damages. After all you have done to stimulate public interest in the tuberculosis campaign it's a damned shame that such a worry should come to interfere with your work.'

By the end of the month, having nearly finished the Text-book revision, it was characteristic that he should unceremoniously walk out of the house on October 1st with nothing but a bag in his hand, as though prepared for a week-end sojourn rather than the long absence necessary to secure a 'thorough brain-dusting'. Reaching Paris, he rummaged about for an apartment, staying meanwhile at an hotel where he was nearly devoured by mosquitoes during a very hot spell. Then came a windfall—a furnished apartment at 44 Avenue d'Iéna belonging to the niece of one of their friends, who chanced to be in America for the winter. Knowledge of this he concealed from Mrs. Osler, who had joined him on October 13th. He told her, in fact, that it was impossible to get anything at all, so that he had taken rooms at an hotel. Not suspecting any mischief, in spite of his cheerfulness, the keys of the place where he had been staying were given up and they drove off 'lickety-cut' to their new abode; and when she remarked that it did not resemble an hotel, he said that it was only a private entrance, took her up in the lift, and ushered her into the place with its beautiful library, servants and all else provided, before she knew that she had been fooled.

It was to be a well-earned winter of actual freedom—the first he had had in which to pursue his own inclinations since his appointment to the Institutes of Medicine at McGill in 1874; but, however free, he was by no means idle, as his letters indicate.

44 Avenue d'Iéna, Paris,
15th [Oct.]

To Lawrason Brown:

Congratulations on the Tb. No. of the Out-Door Life—excellent, & Trudeau's introduction is fine. Give him my love. I am sorry not to have been with you all, but as I dare say you have heard, I am off for a long holiday, first here for three months & then on to Italy.

When are you coming over—do not delay. You need a good rest & you deserve it. I hope to be out in May. Nothing here has begun, so I am devoting myself to the Libraries. How is your collection getting on? It is nice to see that the Journal has been so successful. You must often be hard put for contributors. I feel a pig to have failed you but I have been over head & ears in work—chapters for Allbutt's System, my text-book & my own System.[1] I hear very nice things said of your articles over here. Love to all my old friends.

And on the same day to Jacobs:

I have been thinking a great deal of 'you all' & the Congress. I knew it would be a great success and you have had a splendid foreign representation. The meetings were fairly well reported & the Koch episode very fully. It is strange that he still clings to his views in spite of all the overwhelming evidence against him. In the Figaro there was a growl from one of the Frenchmen about the bad arrangements for the meetings, but there must always be malcontents ... I have an *élève* of the École des Chartes who comes to me for three hours each afternoon to talk French and to go about. We have been doing the Library [Sorbonne] very thoroughly & I have been looking into some things at the Bibliothèque Nationale. Boulanger says you have cleaned him out of all the good old books. I shall make a systematic inspection of the shops. We have been fortunate enough to get Marguerite Chapin's apartment for 3 months—delightfully situated and so cosy & with two splendid servants. Wonderful weather—not a cloud for weeks. I hope you have had the Alabama Student;[2] ... The Times & Spectator have given very good reviews. The latter is greatly taken with Bassett who must have been a remarkable man. The Edinburgh election is very doubtful; the political organizations are very powerful and they can get plenty of money from the liberal and conservative clubs, but the medical men write encouragingly. They had a regular riot the other evening ... Very good word from Isaac Walton who is with Mr. Merry & having a very good time. An old chap 80, once Surgeon to the Infirmary has left us £80,000 so that we shall get a good lecture room & amphitheatre ...

To Mrs. Daniel C. Gilman. 16th [Oct.]

Dear Mrs Gilman, I have just seen in the Times the announcement of the death of my dear friend—or rather, Mrs. Osler read it

---

[1] Vol. V of the series was issued by the publishers on Dec. 5, 1908.

[2] Compared with 'Aequanimitas', 'An Alabama Student' had a very small sale. Osler distributed copies widely among his friends, and in acknowledging his copy Weir Mitchell wrote: 'You kept me up late last night with your confounded biographies. As if anybody could be biographed. Why not write undisguised fiction. However, I ended with Pepper and went to bed, as a Jap said to me, "much thankful".'

out and I exclaimed from my heart—My father! My father! The chariots of Israel & the horsemen thereof! My next feeling was of gratitude that he should have been able to do so much, for higher education in America and for medical education. A splendid life & a splendid work. We of the medical profession owe him an everlasting debt of gratitude. Not of us he was always with us, heart and soul, and it was always a great satisfaction to me to feel that he knew we appreciated his efforts on behalf of the medical school. The start on our own lines which he gave the Hospital was one of the best things he ever did. What memories of those happy days come up! Little did we think that so much would be accomplished & in so short a time. We had hoped to see you this summer. I do hope you got home safely. I was a little worried (after what I heard last winter) that you had gone abroad. Do not trouble to answer this. I know how busy you will be. Mrs. Osler joins me in love and deepest sympathy.

On the 18th he wrote to H. M. Thomas in Baltimore:

You and your friend François Pourfour Petit gave me a very pleasant half hour at the library this afternoon. Who he was I have not been able to find out. The 'Lettres' is a small quarto without the author's name, but his initials are at the end of a brief preface or note. The first letter is really a remarkable production. He first deals with the question, much discussed, as to the paralysis on the side opposite to the cerebral lesion, & refers to many old cases from Aretaeus down . . . I will look him up; he is not in Bayle but I dare say I can find him. I do not suppose anyone had given before a clearer description or he would have mentioned it, as he seems to have an accurate knowledge of contemporary literature.

Wonderful weather here—just like Baltimore. I have been here since the first—only two days of rain. I am finishing the revision of my text-book—only a partial this time, as the plates are not broken up. I have been reading Marie's articles. I have slipped in a long note on his views. M. is Prof. of Pathology now & lectures on general pathology three times a week. He is a delightful fellow. Love to your girls. Yours ever, W. O.

To F. C. Shattuck from W. O. 44 Avenue d'Iéna, 18th.

I am off for a brain-dusting. I have not had a winter free for 34 years & have long wished to see more of Paris & French medicine so I am here for 3 mos and then on to Italy & perhaps America in time for the spring meetings. We have left the boy at school. My work at Oxford is arranged for very easily & we have left the house in order. . . . Nothing here has begun yet—not until Nov 1st. Meanwhile I am browsing in the Bib. Nationale & on the quais. You must come and see us at Oxford while term is on—dinner at Ch Ch with the old dons on Sunday, as Cheyne will tell you, is great fun. The snuff has been taken (& is taken) in the Oxford common rooms from the middle of the 17th century. I always insist that it shall be passed—'tis too good a custom to be allowed to lapse. My good friend Harvey—a don of 80 summers—carries three snuff boxes. I am glad to hear that the boys are doing well. I am sure you will have great comfort with G. C. tertius or is it quartus. My love to Henry Bowditch when you see him. I am glad you like the volume—I was a bit doubtful about putting those essays ['An Alabama Student', etc.] together but these are lives pour encourager les autres. Yours Wm Osler. Love to G. B.

His pocket note-books give abundant evidence of his 'browsing in the Bib. Nationale', the 'Bib. de l'École de Méd.', and elsewhere, for from the very first he spent many hours delving in the libraries. There are pages of notes in his minute script, now largely illegible, on Servetus, Champier, Riolan, Vesal, Guinterius and others; likewise detailed transcripts from the Gui Patin MSS.,[1] from the letters left by Laennec, and from the Bichat papers out of which he copied in full one or two remarkable case reports on pneumonia. But this pastime in which he delighted was not so absorbing that the interests of other people were forgotten. The Baltimore profession was urging him to come to the opening of the new Faculty Hall, and as Dr. Cordell promptly came to mind he sent off a card on October 24th, saying:

Did Jacobs ever speak to you about Cordell's portrait for the Faculty. We should have it—& the good old man deserves the recognition. Put me down for $25. It would be nice to present it when the new building is opened. I am having such a good time here—sight seeing—reading in the libraries &c. Love to the family. Election to-day—not much chance! W. O.

And on the same day to his former pupil, Dr. Albert Chatard of Baltimore:

I have written the Committee asking if possible to postpone the meeting until the middle of May. I had arranged to spend the month

[1] 'I have been spelling out Gui Patin's letters', he said in a contemporary letter. This must have led to his article 'Gui Patin's "Jugement" on the "Religio Medici"', published in the *Athenaeum* for March 20, 1909, for he wrote: 'The other day, in looking through a collection of Patin letters in the Bibliothèque Nationale, I found at the end of Vol. I and unconnected with any letters a much fuller criticism which is worth reproducing.'

of April at the Italian Lakes with Mrs. Osler & Revere, whose holidays do not begin until the 1st of April. It would be such a pleasure to be with you all & I feel that *I should be*. Perhaps a fortnight's postponement under the exceptional circumstances of the new building would be a convenience rather than otherwise. I have asked Ruhräh to cable. It will be a memorable occasion for the old Faculty. I wish your good father could have lived to see it. The Lord Rectorship contest took place to-day. The politicians were too strong. Wyndham was elected. An Independent has not been elected since Carlyle defeated Dizzy. I am not a Carlyle. I did not expect it. We are very happy & are enjoying Paris immensely. My kindest regards to your mother & to the Avicennians. . .

The preceding notes were evidently written the morning and evening of Saturday, the day of the election. Though neither of them shared his popularity nor magnetic personality, the politicians had been too strong and the poll stood for Wyndham 826, for Churchill 727, and for Osler 614 votes. However, there were consolations. Professor G. A. Gibson wrote on the 25th:

I was away yesterday and therefore could not get a letter written to you upon the result of the Rectorial Election. Your supporters made a splendid fight against the political odds, and came within 200 of victory. A very little transference from Wyndham to yours would have made all the difference. I would like to congratulate you on the magic influence of your name, as I do not believe any other human being standing as an independent candidate could have shown anything like the same result. I have been wondering whether you would allow yourself to be put up next time as an independent conservative. If you did you would romp in. . .

Curiously enough, there had also been a triangular contest at Glasgow, where the Unionist candidate was also returned, and in a long editorial the Glasgow *Herald* of the following Monday said:

. . . No doubt the result of the two polls is satisfactory, in so far as a Rectorial contest can be held to distil any political significance. But the universities are inherently Conservative. That is one reason for the contempt in which they are held by many Socialist orators; and one can hardly be surprised if Mr. Keir Hardie's opinion of the academic intelligence now stands lower than ever. Our chief seats of learning have merely followed precedent in preferring Lord Curzon to Mr. Lloyd George, and Mr. Wyndham to Mr. Churchill, and both of the latter to an Independent academic candidate. But aspects of peculiar interest in these contests are the extreme narrowness of Lord Curzon's majority, the existence of triangular contests in both universities at the same term, and the fact that a purely academic candidate should at last have challenged two politicians so stoutly as did Professor Osler at Edinburgh. Twenty years ago the supporters of so distinguished a savant as the late Max Müller, after entering him for the Rectorial Stakes, and publishing a good deal of 'literature' too deep for the ordinary undergraduate, prudently withdrew him from an unequal contest with Lord Rosebery and Lord Lytton. Professor Osler has achieved a measure of success never approached by any non-political candidate. . .

On the day after the election there had been started a long letter to Osler from the still enthusiastic student who was leader of the Independent forces. This the recipient forwarded to McCrae with the following comment appended: 'How is this for mediaeval students' life. Read it to Welch & *Mc*Jacobs & *Mc*Futcher & *then return.* All well—writing hard at article. Love to Amy. W. O.' The letter said in part:

. . . We all got a surprise yesterday when the poll was closed. Practically every one of us reckoned that it lay between you and Mr. Churchill, and that Mr. Wyndham was out of the running as we had captured so many Conservative votes. . . I am resuming the writing of this on Wednesday the 28th, as I felt that I had undertaken an awkward task. Your wire and letter have made this much easier for me and have cheered us all up. I feel convinced now that you have not underestimated the difficulties we have had to contend with. The stone wall of political prejudice we had to face was practically invulnerable. . . We could not get motor cabs in Edinburgh to bring men up to the polling, so we had to fall back on the horse cab, a wretched substitute. On the other hand, a host of Conservatives and Liberals in the city put their private motors at the service of the political candidates.

This is the dark side of the picture but there is a bright side too. One of the traditions of a Rectorial here is that each party must struggle to raid and wreck if possible the committee rooms of their opponents. That our party would destroy this tradition, by not taking rooms and fighting like the political parties, was one of the first and most strongly pushed objections against us. We did not hesitate to make capital out of this allegation. Within about a week from the start of the campaign we had entirely wrecked the Liberal rooms and left them uninhabitable. We unscrewed all their doors and took them down to the Osler fort and made barricades of them so that when the Liberals came to attack us they had to batter down their own doors. We had no furniture when we started the campaign, but we had too much by the end of the war. We had a lot of difficulty with the Conservative rooms as the police would not allow any fighting about them, owing to the value of the neighbouring property. . . . At two o'clock, twenty of us stripped for fighting, left the Osler garrison and crept through the streets with ladders, axes and crowbars, etc., towards the Conservative rooms. We found that one of the shutters of their windows appeared to be unfastened. Our ladders were too short to reach it, but we crept on to an adjoining house-roof and from there clambered along a narrow ornamental ledge which ran beneath their windows. Ten of the men remained in the street below with overcoats stretched out to catch any of our men if they fell. We managed to put nine men into their rooms before the night guard awoke. Terror and the fierceness of our onslaught overcame them, and they capitulated. Just as our men were entering the window an Inspector arrived with about thirty or forty policemen. He wanted to stop us, but I promised that if we made any disturbance or did anything which he disapproved of I would call off our men at once. As I had kept my word to him in a former fight about a similar matter, he consented to allow us to go on.

During the next half hour, our men wrought their will. Every room was completely wrecked; chairs, tables, piano, etc., etc., were reduced to matchwood. The whole of the place, inside and out, was painted over with the legend, VOTE FOR OSLER. We then came away bearing some of the spoils of war which we deposited in the Osler fort. Day and night since the campaign started we have had a guard in our rooms. We did not have beds, in case our men should be overpowered by sleep as our opponents were. Our roof was our weak point, and many a night have we sat on the roofs all night watching by turns. We have had several small attempts to catch us napping and three great organized attacks. In each of these, our opponents were beaten off with many casualties. Luckily the Infirmary was close at hand, and during each engagement a host of minor wounds had to be dressed. The motto of the Oslerites before a battle was 'Get hurt'. Fortunately none of us were detained long in bed, the severest case being ten days. We gained great prestige by the fact that not a single man had entered the Oslerite rooms without the consent of the Oslerites, and that we had utterly wiped out both of the opposing forces and swept their rooms. Now I rather suspect that you will think all this physical fighting in your behalf rather puerile, and you will also fail to see how it could beneficially affect your candidature . . . Personally I can never hope to be associated with a more virile and self-sacrificing body of men and women than those who have borne the brunt of an unsuccessful battle in your behalf. They believed that you were their ideal Lord Rector and I was touched by the many ways they showed it. Classes, clothes, time, convenience were sacrificed; and even health, life and limb were endangered for 'the cause' . . . This letter I am afraid is getting long and tedious, therefore I shall try and bring it to a close. We are trying now to get the business side of things attended to. The balance is certainly going to be on the wrong side of the ledger, but we are going to try everything we can to cut down the tradesmen's accounts. I expect that we will have an exact statement of how we stand in about a week. Making up the reckoning is very dry work, but we are proud to have wrought things more economically than our opponents . . .

To those in other lands, where the ebullition of undergraduates has been subject to repression, the last paragraph of a newspaper editorial on the outcome of the election and the methods of conducting it may be interesting :

Apparently no new methods of making a noise have been invented. The old ways are still sufficient. But we have said enough to show that the Rectorial spirit is far from being decadent. *O-quid-est-esse-juvenum !* as a student once, to the agony of the professor, declaimed in the Latin Prose section of the class of Junior Humanity. It is a good thing to be young—even to be very young—once at least in a collegiate lifetime.

From this episode it is well to return to the victim of it, whose evenings were passed in delight over the well-filled shelves in the Paris apartment, as shown in the postscript to the next letter to H. B. Jacobs :

3rd [November]

We are having a delightful time—such weather since Oct. 1st & there have been only two and a half days of rain. We are doing Paris thoroughly—I work in the morning and about two p.m. we start out for an excursion. To-day we have seen the old houses on the Ile St. Louis & the old church. Such a quaint bit of old Paris. The street where Budaeus, Erasmus & Linacre's friend, lived still bears his name. The monument to Barye on the Quai is very good. Then we took the boat all the way to the Pont d'Iéna, just at the foot of this avenue. Magnificent views of the city. It is a wonderful place. . . . We have enjoyed seeing the devotion of the Parisians to their dead on All Saints' Day & the day after, the Jour des Morts. I laid a wreath on Louis's tomb on Saturday afternoon for the sake of James Jackson Jr., Bowditch & Holmes. . . . The town is full of Americans—it is astonishing how many are living here permanently. . . . PS. I sent you the other day some dastardly extracts from that old rascal Montaigne. I wish you could see the books in the Apt. I am deep in Voltaire.

And not only was he deep in Montaigne and Voltaire, but

to judge from his note-book he seems to have found a set of Swinburne which he read through discovering for the first time, in Vol. V, the Children's Poems, 'among the most beautiful in the language'; and from them he took many excerpts, as: 'Men perish, but man shall endure; lives die, but the life is not dead.'

On the 8th he wrote: 'Lectures have just begun—they are very late in starting & as yet very irregular. I begin with Raymond to-morrow morning & I wish you were here.' And on the 20th he says, on a card to Jacobs:

In full swing—such busy days—hospital every morning—Raymond, Marie, Dieulafoy, Vaquez, have been most kind. Moutier, Marie's second interne, has given me a splendid demonstration of the aphasia work. I go to the Académie with Chauffard every week, & to the Société des Hôpitaux with Rist who is a most delightful fellow. Magnin & Schulman are well. We are beginning to have very interrupted evenings, dinners—which Mrs Osler dislikes. Our apartment is most sumptuous—we are in clover. Love to Mrs. Jacobs & the boys. W. O.

So his days passed, and, occupied though he was, they were interspersed with many kindly acts. A young physician in far-off Indiana tells how he had purchased a copy of 'Aequanimitas' and was distressed because of the many literary allusions he could not identify: 'shrill-toned Fulvia'; 'Epicharmus'; 'Numa'; 'Astral wine', &c.—and so wrote apologetically for help, scarce daring to hope for a reply. Not only, to his extreme delight, did he get a full reply to his questions, but Osler adds:

I am glad you have taken to Montaigne—dear old man! so full of good sense. He is rather hard on the Doctors, but I dare say he had good reason in those days. I am sending you a book just out with the extracts from Montaigne relating to medicine. If you do not read French easily you can get the references, & the book will give you the pictures of the castle, &c. Greet the brethren for me in Indiana. I have many old friends & pupils among them.

By December he wrote: 'I am up to my eyes in work—too much to see. Such nice men; but Dieulafoy embarrasses me by making me sit at his right hand in his clinic, and Raymond insists that I have an armchair on his platform.' On the 18th he wrote again to Dr. Jacobs:

We are very busy—something fresh every day. I have just come in from the Tropical Disease Society at the Pasteur with Laveran. A young fellow read a most interesting account of the treatment of sleeping sickness by the French Commission—some 500 cases & good results so far as arrest goes, but recurrences seem the rule. 'Twas rather sad as in the room was one of the young fellows who went out, who has the disease, tho. he looks remarkably well. Magnin had a good laugh with me the other night about your letter in which you thought he, M, had had overtures from the Johns Hopkins. It was, as no doubt he has written, about v. Pirquet, Escherich's 1st assistant. I do not know whether or not you met in Washington. I saw him here four or five times, and heard him read a paper at the Société des Hôpitaux & at the Paediatric. He talks French like a native & his English is wonderful. If they have any thought of importing, he is the man. Sunday eve, Landouzy [Dean of the Faculty] gave a great dinner—really a beautiful affair, 30 at table & he made a really remarkable speech—he must have been posted by someone. He had read several of my books & he referred to my Tub. article in the text-book in gallic terms. I was warned by Marie—dear soul! that there was to be a little speech so I got off a phrase or two in French & then laid on the butter in English. Mrs Osler has sent the menu to Mrs. Revere & has asked her to send it to you The arms of the Faculty are most interesting. After dinner there was a big reception—about 300. All the young agrégés, their wives, &c, music & at 11.30 a supper! Landouzy married the widow of the Revue des Deux Mondes & a superb old Empire hotel—beautiful rooms. Chauffard gave us a lovely dinner on Tuesday & on Friday Raymond, so we are *very full.* Mrs. O. goes on Saturday to Oxford & brings Isaac. I have been getting a few good things, a first ed. of Avenbrugger wh. I have been after for some years, & a Gilbert's Magnet; the first great scientific book published in England. I got it at the Amherst sale last week. Did you get a catalogue? Morgan bought the Caxtons, 17 of them, 11 perfect! Weather has broken—four days of London fog!

They evidently had got in very deep. He had been given a special work-room in the Library; was elected a member of the Société des Hôpitaux; read a paper at one of the meetings; and in one of his letters said: 'It is really delightful meeting these men and staying here long enough to get to know them.' During all this time, too, he was getting even better acquainted with a sixteenth-century physician, Michael Servetus or Villanovanus. He examined in the Bibliothèque Nationale one of the two known copies of that rarest of books the 'Christianismi Restitutio'—the copy that Richard Mead had traded for some coins, and which now reposed in what had once been Cardinal Mazarin's library; he searched high and low for von Murr's 1790 reprint;[1] corresponded extensively with an American Servetian then studying in Jena; was deeply involved with the 'Comité du Monument Michel Servet'; and was evidently reading in and around the times of Servetus to get a background for the historical sketch he published the next year, after it had done 'double duty' as an address.

Always one of those who send their Christmas remembrances early and easily, he had sent to some of his medical friends the facsimile copy of Harvey's diploma which had been published by the Royal College of Physicians; to others a photograph of the statue made for the proposed monument to be unveiled at Annemasse in Savoy, showing Servetus in his prison rags.[2] On December 23rd he wrote to Leonard Mackall in Jena:

Kind Man! Yes I got the Post—excellent review! Ask your Bkseller to send Linde. I have the translation—very good. I have been going over the Servet *procès* (in the Faculty records) this after-

---

[1] Dr. J. F. Payne subsequently bequeathed his copy of this rare reprint to W. O.'s library.

[2] This needs some explanation. The monument at Annemasse (Osler spells the word incorrectly in his address) was placed there because the Geneva authorities had already erected an expiatory monument at Champel in 1903. Another monument was to be erected at Vienne, and Osler had evidently offered to help the *Comité* to raise funds for the purpose, on learning that no one else in England had answered their appeal. He was made a *Membre du Comité de Patronage*; wrote letters to the *Lancet* and *British Medical Journal* (July 11, 1908, p. 104); and apparently had agreed to participate on the occasion of the unveiling to take place in August of 1909. It dragged on, and W. O. was expected to shoulder the whole movement. The Secretary wrote to him from Vienne on June 4, 1909: '. . . Veuillez excuser notre insistance. Mais votre lettre de Septembre 1908 nous laissait espérer que vous trouveriez beaucoup d'argent en Angleterre et en Amérique. Et, comptant sur votre concours, nous avons permis au sculpteur d'augmenter les proportions de son œuvre, ce qui a augmenté proportionellement les frais d'exécution. Sans cela, si nous n'avions pas mis notre espoir en vous, nous aurions réduit la dépense au strict nécessaire; et maintenant, si les concours attendus nous font défaut, nous serons fort embarrassés . . .' And by August nothing had happened, to judge from the following:
'Il n'y a pas—il n'y a pas encore—de statue de Servet à Vienne. L'année dernière, au mois d'Août, on a inauguré solennellement *le socle* qui doit porter la statue future. Pour le moment, c'est tout. La statue est commandée, l'artiste y travaille—mais l'argent manque . . .'

noon. Most interesting. His lectures on Judicial Astrology scandalized all the Faculties & they had to make it a Parlement (de Paris) matter. His pamphlet is in the Bib. Nationale. Tollin reprinted it. I had a letter from Billy F. today; he is seeing Ed VII of my text-book thro. the press. The German Edition is just out—A French one appeared last year, & a Spanish & Chinese (!) [1] are in preparation. I wish you were coming thro. England later. I am sending you my Counsels & Ideals for New Year—a bit medicated but you can stand it. Yours ever, Wm OSLER.

Revere had been brought over by his mother for Christmas, and had his first glimpse of the land where he was destined in the end to lie.[2] His father got a microscope and they were to go and look for algae together in the Trocadéro ponds, but he was not a 'Father' Johnson to Revere in this pursuit. Fathers are not apt to be to their sons. Meanwhile, exciting things were going on at the École de Médecine which led him the day after Christmas to send a letter of explanation to *The Times*. Though no lover of student rows he could see the students' point of view—even in a Rectorial 'rag'—and, what is more, felt towards the French *concours* much as he did towards the formal British system of examinations—extreme disapproval. His letter, published in the issue of Dec. 29th, reads in part:

Sir,—As the only 'stranger within the gates' on Monday, the 21st, it may interest your readers to have the account of an eye-witness. There have been three 'rows' in the Latin Quarter this semester . . . the virus of disorder has been on both sides of the Boulevard St. Michel. [But] . . . the affair of Monday the 21st, was of a very different character. The participants were not students

[1] Translated by Dr. P. B. Cousland, President of the China Medical Missionary Association, Shanghai.

[2] Peace-loving as he was, Osler was no pacifist nor fool. The ferment of the European crisis was already at work. The perennial 'Balkan crisis' was even more annoying than usual. Austria-Hungary had annexed Bosnia and Herzegovina, and the Serbians were clamouring for war. The King of Portugal had been murdered early in the year. Army and Navy estimates were rising by leaps and bounds, 'though all danger of an Anglo-German rupture is artificial'. Roosevelt had sent an American battle-fleet around the world and through the Panama Canal. Asquith had become Prime Minister and the Women's Enfranchisement Bill was up. Orville Wright in America and his brother in Paris during these very months had demonstrated the practical possibility of sustained flight. It was enough to cause the earthquake at Messina with which the year ended.

but a group of men comparable in years and repute with the assistant physicians of the London hospitals or with the young Oxford tutors—men of from thirty to thirty-five years of age, many of them with European reputations. The examination was the *concours* for *agrégation*—i. e., for the *agrégé* professorships for twenty places in all the branches in all the medical schools of France. There were 128 candidates. A new regulation had come into force by which this was to be a preliminary *concours* of admissibility, an examination in elementary subjects—anatomy and physiology. This has been most unpopular, and the candidates protest that these are subjects with which they have finished, and that it is absurd to ask men actively engaged in practical work in the hospitals, and even distinguished investigators, to take up these elementary branches again.

As there were rumors of a terrible *chahut* I was early at the Medical School, and with a letter from a member of the jury of the *concours* I was admitted. By 11.30 the police were in full force in the Rue de l'École de Médecine, and the gates of the court were guarded by *agents* who only allowed the candidates to pass. The crowd increased rapidly, and about 12 o'clock the main gate was forced and about 250 got into the court. The senior men collected in groups and protested energetically against the invasion of the school precincts by the police, some of whom were not in uniform. A good deal of jostling and a few serious scuffles occurred, but, as a rule, it was a good-natured crowd, though boisterous and excited. About 1 o'clock an attempt was made to force the doors leading to the small amphitheatre, where the *concours* was to take place, and the glass panels were broken. M. Lepine then called out the soldiers (Republican Guard) [1] who took possession of the court and began to clear out all but the candidates. Meanwhile two members of the jury came out, and after a conference with several of the leading candidates induced a majority of them to come into the amphitheatre. I brought up the rear of a pretty orderly set of men as they filed upstairs, but once inside there was a great row, everyone talking or shouting, and in the midst of it the jury walked in headed by Professor Bouchard. A storm of protests greeted them as they took their seats, and one candidate, who acted as spokesman, declared that the *concours* was a farce, in which they would take no part. The hubbub continuing, Professor Bouchard sent for the soldiers, who lined up along one side of the room. As this only increased

[1] There was an aftermath of this act which the letter does not mention. It was Bouchard, the Dean, who had the Guard (police) called out. He was an arbitrary person who had made himself most unpopular; and the Premier, M. Clemenceau, himself a medical graduate, subsequently ordered the Prefect of Police in the future not to obey any such requisition which was likely to be a provocative rather than a preventive measure.

the row the jury left the room. Most of the men followed them, and after a brief conference it was decided to adjourn the *concours*.

It seems a pity that the police and the soldiers were called in, as most of the candidates and the members of the jury seemed to be on the most friendly terms, and if left alone could have settled the matter between themselves. But I suppose there was an outside element to be considered, and the student body has been in an excited state.

On Thursday at 7.30, the *concours* was held in the Medical School, but only twenty-eight candidates took part; the others refused to write on the papers. By 9 a.m. the school was in a state of siege, every avenue to it guarded by soldiers and police, and throughout the day there were numerous attacks by the students. A good many arrests were made, and there were a few serious injuries. The streets were cleared by the mounted guards. Yesterday and to-day have been quiet, and notices are posted of the closure of the Medical School until March 1 and the adjournment *sine die* of the *concours*.

While such disturbances are most regrettable, the good record of the past fifty years does not bear out your statement that the larval medical man is more prone to rowdyism than his fellow-students of other faculties. In London you have no cause for complaint, and the only disturbance of late years was a very just protest against a disgraceful insult to a great teaching body and to the whole profession.[1] As I have seen him during the past three months at work in the hospitals, the Paris medical student is a very hard-working fellow, keenly alive to the importance of scientific and practical medicine, and with a charming touch of human sympathy with the patients entrusted to his care.

The following New Year's Eve letter to Mrs. Brewster introduces a new playmate, a child of eight:

Happy New Year to you & Sylvia & R. B.! I hope my Xmas greetings reached you in time—I was a little late I am afraid. Time has slipped away so quickly I have been here three months & it does not seem a month. We have been so happy & comfortable. I have seen a great deal of my colleagues & we have had several ordeals of enormous dinners (enormous in every sense of the word!) but it has been great fun. I have had a regular routine—8[30] off to the Hospital where they make the visit at 9 sharp. Lunch at

[1] This reference undoubtedly is to the memorial fountain to 'The Brown Dog done to Death in the Laboratories of University College', erected in 1906 in the Latchmere Recreation Ground, Battersea, as a protest against vivisection. This fountain was finally removed March 10, 1910, by the action of the Battersea Borough Council. The memorial had been continuously protected by the police since its establishment, and frequent attempts to destroy it had been made by medical students.

12^{30} & then at 2^{30} we go somewhere or I slip away to one of the Libraries. They have given me a special room at the École de Médecine Library & I am browsing in some interesting 16th century books. We have avoided the American Colony as much as possible—everybody in fact, as I wished to be in seclusion as much as possible & Mrs Osler has had such a busy year that she needed rest. A few days before Xmas she went to Oxford for Revere, who is spending his holidays with us—very happy & big & good. But he is no student—books will skip his generation. We have been interested in your miniature a perfect angel of a child, Susan Revere Baker from Boston who is your living image, so we call her Mabel. She is aged 8 & called after Mrs. Revere. What a charm and delight a child is! Do let me know of your plans for the summer. I hope to be out in May. I am due in Baltimore on the 14th for the opening address of the New Building, the Hall of which is to be called after my name—& to which R. B. so generously subscribed. We leave here Jan. 12. This apartment has been delightful. I wish you could drop in & see us this eve.—all three deep in books (all two!) and such a lovely library. Mrs. Osler tells me there is a book at Oxford from Uncle Ned. Send me his address when you write next. . . . A friend of mine has insisted on having a portrait of me—so Seymour Thomas, an American artist, is doing it—very good so far. Not quite so mediaeval as Sargent's. Affectionately yours,

Wm OSLER.

CHAPTER XXIX

1909

OLD WORLD AND NEW

THEY had evidently enjoyed their Parisian sojourn to the full. Osler had had a thorough 'brain-dusting', and, as the time for their departure drew near, the reaction of his younger days led him to send off an open letter[1] for the 'consumption of the brethren' in America. This lies buried in the files of a medical journal, from which its opening paragraphs at least may be rescued because of their biographical interest. They deal with French reverence, which struck in him a sympathetic chord, for he was not cold-blooded Anglo-Saxon:

After a stay of three and a half months, I am leaving Paris with many regrets. I am sorry not to be a member of the Faculty of Medicine: I should be glad to put after my name *Médecin des Hôpitaux*; the position of *chef de clinique* at the Hôtel-Dieu with Professor Dieulafoy would suit me admirably; I could be quite happy as an interne with Professor Raymond at the Salpêtrière, or as an externe with Professor Pierre Marie at the Bicêtre or even as a *stagiaire* at the Cochin with Dr. Chauffard! Best of all, I should like to be a P. C. N. at the Jardin des Plantes, a student who is working at physics, chemistry and natural history in the year preliminary to medicine. I should like to do the *vice versa* trick of Anstey's story, and change places with the young P. C. N. in this year's class who will go through the grades of my regrets just mentioned and who about the year 1940 will become Dean of this ancient and remarkable medical school.

It would be pleasant to see the superstructure which the next two generations will build on the scientific foundations of the nineteenth century—but these are fancies, not impressions, and it is the latter which I wish to give to my brethren on the other side of the Atlantic, impressions of a long-desired medical holiday among some of the older universities of Europe. Asked the strongest single impression made on me here, I should reply: 'The extraordinary reverence of the French.' The streets, the squares, the churches, the public

[1] Dated Jan. 15th, the day of their departure; it was probably finished at Cannes. See the issues of the *Journal of the American Medical Association* for Feb. 27th and Mar. 6th. He had evidently intended to send a series of such letters.

buildings, the schools, all tell the same story; the books repeat it, the newspapers echo it, and with it the lecture-rooms resound—reverence for the great men of the past. The Panthéon, with its inscription, '*Aux Grands Hommes la Patrie reconnaissante*,' is but a great expression in stone of this universal sentiment. The history of science is writ large in the city; in monuments, in buildings dedicated to the illustrious dead, and in streets called by their names. There are more statues to medical men in Paris than in Great Britain and the United States put together; many of the hospitals are called after the men who have shed glory on France—Bichat, Laennec, Broussais, and Claude Bernard—and in the hospitals themselves each ward is dedicated to the memory of some distinguished man. Every Frenchman is a hero-worshipper, and has a master, dead or alive, whom he adores. Among the men of this generation you can tell very quickly who have been under Claude Bernard or Trousseau or Charcot or Potain. The lecture, the clinic, the casual conversation, is almost certain to bring in a reference to 'my honoured master'; and this delightful feature is seen in all circles. Even in the salon-catalogues, after the name of the painter of a picture is put the name of his master.

But to realize what the sentiment means to Frenchmen, one must be in Paris on All Saints Day—*Toussaint*—the fête of the eternal absent, which is kept in a way that appeals with extraordinary sympathy to the heart of one who believes in the immanence of the mighty dead 'who live again in minds made better by their presence'. During the last week of October the streets begin to tell of the great festival. In stalls along the boulevards, in temporary markets, in the ordinary flower-shops, there is a rich display of decorations—crowns, crosses, stars in fresh flowers, or leaves, with which to decorate the graves. November 1st fell on a Sunday. . . . I had a little pilgrimage of my own to make on Saturday afternoon to the cemetery of Montparnasse. The main avenue leading to it was an open flower-market, and for three or four hundred yards the cemetery wall was lined with booths for the sale of every sort of emblem, and fresh and dried flowers. Through the 'Gates of Grief' a steady stream of people poured, each one bearing some tribute to the memory of a loved one. I stood for several minutes just inside, watching the procession. A group of young schoolgirls passed, each one bearing a bunch of chrysanthemums to lay on the tomb of a fellow pupil or of a loved teacher; close at hand were two Sisters of Mercy arranging wreaths on a vault that looked one of the oldest in the cemetery—perhaps the annual devotion of the guild to a loved member. A little laddie of eight hurried by with a bunch of violets in his hand, running with the ease of one who knew his road. A young mother in deep mourning with a baby in her arms, an aged couple arm in arm, each with a little basket of flowers; two young students; a little old lady with her daughter followed by a footman carrying large wreaths; workmen in rough clothes; soldiers; sailors—a motley group, a touching sight, but on the whole not a sad one. Here and there we could see the stricken heart in the pale, set features, but the general impression was one of cheerful festival; and the glorious sunshine, the bright flowers and the merry voices of the children helped to dispel the gloom of the city of the dead.

Then I turned and sought the tomb of a man whom my teachers taught me to honour. . . . In Odessa a young Frenchman met with an experience which has happened to every thoughtful physician. An epidemic of diphtheria with its awful mortality struck the terror of helplessness and hopelessness into his heart, and he decided to return to Paris, again to take up the student life and to endeavour to know more of disease before he undertook its treatment. An old friend at the Charité Hospital gave him the opportunity he sought, and for years he worked quietly at the problems of disease. With the publication of his books on typhoid fever and on tuberculosis, Louis found himself famous, and he ranks to-day with the great French physicians who laid the foundation of modern clinical medicine.

My old teacher, Palmer Howard, a man of the same type, taught me to reverence his memory, but my pilgrimage had another inspiration—gratitude to the devoted teacher and friend of the veterans whom I loved in the profession in the United States—W. W. Gerhard, Oliver Wendell Holmes, Henry I. Bowditch, George C. Shattuck and Alfred Stillé. But as I laid my wreath in front of the grille of the tomb it was not of these men I thought, but of young James Jackson whom Louis loved as a son and who was stricken at the very outset of a brilliant career, and whose memoir by his father should be in all medical libraries, as the story of his life is an inspiration to all young men. And to Louis himself came a similar tragedy. Inside the tomb is a slab of marble to the memory of his only son, a medical student who died of tuberculosis in his eighteenth year. At dinner one evening Dr. Bucquoy, President of the Academy of Medicine, who was Louis's last interne, told me the story of the illness—a sudden hemoptysis and then a long lingering progress to the grave!

To the famous cemetery of Père Lachaise all Paris flocks on Toussaint and the following day. Hundreds of thousands visit the tombs of the great men who lie there, and the place is literally strewn with flowers. We went on both days, as it takes time to see the tombs and to find those of interest. Here I had a special mission, to see the tomb of that rare genius, Bichat, who started a revolution in medicine before he was thirty, and who died at thirty-two, leaving a name which is reverenced throughout the world. It was good to see that his simple grave was not neglected—a wreath, fresh flowers, and several plants showed that his memory was still cherished, and I added a bunch of pansies 'for thoughts'.

Toussaint gives an indication of the spirit which makes France great. Present in the daily life and everywhere in evidence it breaks out into this magnificent demonstration of loyalty to the family and of reverence to the *men* who have helped the nation and the race. To the cold-blooded Anglo-Saxon this festival of the dead is a revelation, which he cannot witness without profound emotion and without a regret that England and America miss in great part the moral and intellectual inspiration associated with such celebrations. France sings one song: 'Glory to Man in the highest! for Man is the Master of things', with which words Swinburne (who has been of all modern Englishmen the most sympathetic interpreter of the French) ends his famous 'Hymn of Man'.

In the medical world of Paris at a first glance the men only are recognizable; everything else is different, and so very different! But here is the charm; and it does one good to get into an atmosphere charged with novelty, where the burning questions are for a time unintelligible. There are four factors of the first importance—the medical school, the hospitals, the medical societies, and the Pasteur Institute. [These he went on to describe.]

But before allowing them to depart from Paris, a few letters of the preceding two weeks will serve to tell something of their pleasant though frustrated plans:

To Dr. Albert Chatard, Baltimore. 44 Avenue d'Iéna, Paris, 2nd [Jan.]

Yours of the 10th came last eve. I am delighted that the meeting has been postponed as I should have been greatly disappointed not to have been able to give the Oration [before the Maryland 'Faculty']. I shall sail from Genoa about the end of April, giving myself time, I hope, to be at the Assoc. of Amer. Physicians. You will I am sure have a great deal to do before you can get the inside of the building in order, & the question of entertainment is a serious one. Make a special point of the other 18th century Associations—the College of Phy. Phila, the N. Y. & one of the N. E. societies, there are only four or five. Their Presidents should have places of honour. I should think the Committee could go to prominent citizens & ask for subscriptions for entertainment. . . .

To Mr. Edward Milburn, Belleville, Ontario. Paris, 4th Jan.

Dear Ned, It was nice to have the Xmas reminder from you. Did you get my volume of essays—The Alabama Student? . . . I hope to be out in Canada in June. I must arrange to see you. It would be such a pleasure. I hope you are all keeping well. Do you ever hear from Jemmy Morgan? I have heard nothing from him for years. I often think of the happy days we had as boys. Are any of the Checkleys alive? What a good time we had that winter. How far you could throw stones on the ice! I suppose you still have muscles like iron. I keep pretty well—not quite the energy of some years ago but I have much to interest me in my new life at Oxford. How I wish I could go with you for a row on the Thames. My boy at 13 (now with us for Xmas) pulls an excellent oar. Dear me your heart must ache for your boy. . . . Your affec' friend.

To Prof. H. P. Bowditch, Boston. Jan. 8th.

I am sending you the Berthelot address at the Académie Française in which you will be interested. It was a famous occasion, I had never seen the reception of a new member & the ceremony was interesting—first a post-mortem & then a vivisection of the new immortal by the President. I have had a delightful three months here—Hospitals chiefly but taking in a few lectures at the Sorbonne, a course by Bergson on Berkeley & one on Rabelais by Lefranc. Bergson paid a remarkable tribute to William James whom he called the most distinguished & stimulating of living thinkers in Philosophy. I have been working at my System of Medicine—wretched thing! five vols of which are out & two to follow—and at some other back articles. You never were the same soft hearted fool & accepted everybody's invitation to write. . . . I hope to sail for G. O. C. May 1st. Love to Mrs Bowditch & the girls. I hope the young Doctor is progressing. Yours ever, Wm Osler. Richet by the way is in Brazil—back next month.

To Dr. H. B. Jacobs, Baltimore. 11th [January]

. . . Mrs. O. and Tom have gone back to Oxford. T. had a great time here. The aeroplane show was a great treat. The Wrights have captured the town. Wilbur is the hero of the country. I have been very busy—every afternoon at the Library—so much to see & to read. I have got to know Hahn & his two associates quite well. I show the Harvey diploma at the Historical Club tomorrow. I am so sorry to leave—everyone has been most kind. 'Tis a great town—lacks only trained nurses!

And on this same day to William H. Welch he wrote:

We are off on the 13th—to Lyons first to see Symphorien Champier & Rabelais. I understand their cliniques are the best in France. We shall stop at Vienne to call on Servetus & Apollos Rivoire,[1] the father of the late Paul Revere. (I have just been going through the

[1] Mrs. Osler's direct ancestor, born at Vienne, exiled by the revocation of the Edict of Nantes.

Servetus trial for Astrology, 1537. 'Tis given in full in du Boulay's History of the University of Paris.) Then on to Montpellier to see Rondeletius, from whom I shall take a course in ichthyology. We shall take in Nîmes & Avignon on the way. I have had a very good time here and have got beneath the shell in some places, but it is very difficult. Bouchard rules the roost, & there is an active revolt and a great row. It is too long a story—I shall write it out. B. has been most kind & as President of the Institute has sent us tickets for all the ceremonies. . . . I have had great fun at the Library & have looked over a great many papers and books of interest. Bichat's lecture notes & the MS. of the Genl. Path., Laennec's lecture notes, private letters of Broussais, & the whole story of the surgical war of 500 years are to be seen in the papers. The most extraordinary are the well known Faculty *Commentaires* the annual reports of the Dean, 1395, to the Revolution—an uninterrupted series. . . . We go to Naples about the 28th from Genoa; then Rome, Florence & the North Italian towns. I shall sail about the end of April to get out in time for the Maryland Faculty meeting. Greetings to the Major & Halsted. Sincerely yours, Wm OSLER. Dr. & Mrs. Rush are just coming to dine. I wish you could see this library. I have wasted hours browsing. I have read through six volumes of Swinburne. I did not know before of his Children's Poems. . . .

Before dismissing Swinburne's Vol. V and the Children's Poems, a *carte postale* which also went off this Monday morning of January 11th may be recorded, though its interpretation must wait for Rome:

Dear Mrs. Baker, Grace will not be back till Tuesday eve late. She tells me that you and Susan & Marguerite & the darling of my heart were coming to lunch. Alas! I have accepted an invitation. So sorry. I hope you will come in for tea on Wednesday. We leave Thursday a.m. Yours sincerely, Wm OSLER.

Servetus, his friend and patron Symphorien Champier, and Calvin who burned him at the stake, live together in rare editions in handsome covers in a section of Osler's library, but he was not destined to visit them on this trip in spite of his letter to Dr. Welch. The explanation lies in the following note in his account-book: 'Left Paris for Cannes on the 15th. I had a tonsilitis on and off and felt very seedy. Just redness, swelling and soreness. It persisted at Cannes. We stayed at the Mont Fleury Hotel—excellent place.' Though his letters from Cannes were enthusiastic—'a glorious spot—such sunshine and I had no idea the vegetation was semi-tropical'—yet he continued to be very 'seedy' for the next two weeks. The local physician is reported to have said he had a 'Cannes sore throat' and must take some calomel—that every one coming to Cannes had to begin that way; and he went on to dilate upon medical practice in Cannes, which divided itself into two parts—(1) practice for the American ladies, (2) practice for the English ladies—though since every American lady travelled with Osler's 'Practice of Medicine' in her trunk one had to be very cautious in prescribing; but in any event it was safe to begin with calomel. Accordingly he left a large pill for the Regius. The pill was found unaltered in the patient's bed the next morning and when the fact was called to his attention he scrutinized it and remarked: 'That was a peculiar pill.' The Regius had his own way of treating, or not treating, his personal indispositions.

A long letter of the 31st to McCrae indicates that Vol. VI of the 'System' was about to receive the manuscript for its last chapters:[1]

> . . . I hope you got the angio-neurotic-oedema. I am finishing the erythromelalgia & scleroderma—and the whole should go the end of this week. I have considered the multiple neurotic gangrene & the obliterative endarteritis forms in the diagnosis of Raynaud's disease. I hope I shall not have caused delay; if only 200 pp. are printed I hope you may not have reached my section. I do not think I shall be more than the 50 pp. I could not go to Lyons and to Montpellier. I had a sore throat, tonsils & larynx and it hung on here in this heavenly climate for ten days—just raw & sore and a huskiness. The Doctor here says it is gouty—possibly. I have been better for the past three days. . . .

On a picture-postcard showing the Pont du Loup, post-marked February 8th, he repeated:

> This is a great coast. Such sunshine. We have been here 2 1/2 weeks—delighted with everything. This is a gorgeous spot; where I put the x is a little town of Gourdron. They had to get high up on account of the Moors. I am thinking of settling at Monte Carlo

[1] Osler had taken upon himself the task of writing upon a difficult group of vasomotor and trophic disorders whose pathology is so obscure that they constitute a group of 'eponymic' maladies, in which he was always interested—Raynaud's disease, Weir Mitchell's erythromelalgia, Milroy's hereditary oedema, Friedländer's endarteritis, Quincke's oedema, Morvan's disease, &c.

—they say there is a good opening. I lost $25 in five minutes & then stopped We go on to Rome on the 7th. So far as women are concerned this is the Remnant Counter of Europe. Love to the darlings for me.

Though in his letters he constantly referred to the Riviera as an 'earthly paradise' he has noted in his account-book: '*Feb.* 9. Rome—Hotel Royal. Sore throat & hoarseness kept up nearly all the time I was in Cannes, not a good place for a cold—winds high and a hot sun.' And two days later one of his postcards reads:

Feby 11.

Rome at last! Wonderful What pigmies we are in comparison with these old fellows. So much to see & everything intensely interesting. I have not yet been to the Vatican Library. Splendid book shops here. I have already got some treasures. Redi and Vallisneri—splendid editions. So glad of your letter to-day (11th). Love to the darlings. Yours, W. O.

He began promptly with books, as can be seen. Indeed, the 'Opera di Francesco Redi' which had come from the library of Duke Massimo was on the mantel at the hotel when they arrived; and in the volume Osler has written: 'When in Rome Feby 1909 I heard a great deal of "talk" about this Duke who is known as the wicked Duke and is believed to have the evil eye. Many people will not mention his name. Once at a big reception, just as he came into the room the chandelier fell & killed 3 people. A prominent lady said to me that they were "poor as mice" and lived like pigs.'

We are settled here for a month [writes Mrs. Osler] and if we continue to have good news from Revere I shall be very content. We have come into midwinter, which is rather a trial after Cannes but the sunshine is delicious, and for sight-seeing I much prefer it to hot weather. One's breath is really taken away by the wonders of Rome—and by the horrors of modern Rome: fancy a hotel just being finished called 'The Select Hotel'—a large sign in English in gilt letters—it makes one shudder. Of course one meets Americans everywhere. . . . Mother's friends the Bakers are here.

With this reminder of the Bakers, and in explanation of a letter of January 11th, it is appropriate to return to the little girl of eight who had been left in Paris, and to forget for a moment Servetus, Francesco Redi, the 'System of

Medicine', and the wonders of Rome. She is now grown up and has real instead of play-children, but this is what she recalls. It has something to do with Rosalie, a pudding-faced and dishevelled doll of early vintage, and her daughter Wilhelmina; with Marguerite, a gorgeous and talkative creature from a Christmas window—as likely as not the *Paradis des Enfants*; with their maternal 'parent' and their 'grandparents'—and with Osler's 'M'Connachie':

Dr. Osler first became acquainted with Rosalie and her 'mother' in Paris in December, where he entertained them both very often and loved so to feed the latter (aged eight) on her heart's desire, chocolate éclairs, that she nearly always returned to her mother in not very good health, but happy nevertheless. On Christmas of that year S. B. acquired a new doll, Marguerite, who was a real Parisienne with beautiful clothes and real hair, and Dr. Osler felt that she was altogether too dressy and too spick-and-span. He used to say her face was too clean and she had no spots on her apron and that she was really unbearable. As for Rosalie, she was more than ever before the darling of his heart, and would be always.

Later, that winter, Rosalie and Marguerite, with their 'mother' and 'grandparents', stayed in Rome at the Hotel Royal where Dr. and Mrs. Osler were for a too-short while. Dr. Osler used to write notes to the dolls, or if Rosalie were passing the night with him, as she did frequently, he would write news of her to her mother. Mrs. Osler was afraid the chambermaid would think Dr. Osler had lost his mind when she discovered a doll in his room, carefully put to bed according to instructions from its mamma. . . .

'Its mamma' still treasures these messages from the Hotel Royal, Rome:

Miss Rosalie sends her love to her Grandmother & is very sorry to say that she is not very well this morning. As she had not her night-clothes she had to sleep in her day-clothes, & in consequence has a headache. She has sent for the Doctor and is staying in bed, & would like to see you.

From Rosalie to her 'mother'. 13th.

My dear Muz, Your letter came this morning. I am very well but the baby was upset this evening. Her little breadbasket turned upside down on the floor—spilt everything there was in it. The wet-nurse is still very wet & good. We hope you will like the name I have given to the baby—Wilhelmina. Dr. Osler was not very good to-day—he laughed when Wilhelmina upset herself on the carpet, and tickled me at the dinner-table & I choked when I had a mouthful of soup. Give my love to grandmother and grandfather

Baker. Your affectionate daughter ROSALIE. Thank you for the new hat. I want new pantilettes very very badly.

Rosalie's 'mother' continues, to say: 'He would give up an important engagement, to have five o'clock supper with a little girl and her dolls, and no little girl could ever forget the joy of his presence, for he entered into the make-believe so genuinely.' Rosalie's 'grandmother', too, recalls that one of the most amusing incidents she ever witnessed was when a member of the Archaeological Society, which was meeting in Rome, came to the hotel one afternoon to request the Regius Professor to participate in one of their sessions. He was shown into the nursery, where he found the object of his visit with Susan on one knee, Rosalie on the other, and Marguerite in disgrace on the floor; and when it was made clear in nursery language that some one had come to Rome to play with his granddaughter Rosalie, and that he could not be induced to write any papers, the expression on the archaeologist's face was to be remembered. Then, too, while this story was being elicited many years later, Rosalie's 'grandfather' grunted from behind his newspaper, and said: 'That man Osler sent me to a doctor in Rome because I was complaining of rheumatism in my arm. The doctor used to bake it and I was compelled to go every afternoon, with great loss of time and unheard-of expense. After this had gone on at some length, I overheard Mrs. Osler ask her husband if he thought that young doctor was doing me any good, and he said: "Not in the least, but the poor man has a child five years old and needs to get her some toys." And the strange thing is, that I continued to go to the doctor after listening-in at this conversation.' Unlike Cannes, practice in Rome evidently did not begin with calomel.

Osler could not entirely escape from consultations even on this well-earned holiday. In the *Lancet* for May 15th there is a brief report [1] of a remarkable case he had seen at this time with Dr. G. Sandison Brock, an occurrence which makes it possible to introduce another little girl variously named Muriel, Marjorie, or Maude, who was found in

[1] 'The Relation of the Capillary Blood-vessels in Purpura'. *Lancet*, Lond., 1909, i. 1385.

Dr. Brock's nursery and whose table-manners were corrupted ; but though introduced she may wait until later on, lest Rosalie and her ' mother ' become jealous.

He must have looked up an Oxonian, the Rev. H. M. Bannister, the authority on the palaeography of music, who was accustomed to pass his winters in the Vatican and his summers in Bodley, poring over ancient liturgies. Osler once said that he was the only amphibian Catholic he knew—Roman one half the year and Anglican the other (which may not be the reason he bequeathed his silver snuff-box to Osler), but Bannister, being on intimate terms with Monsignor Achille Ratti, then the Vatican Librarian—now Pope Pius XI—had keys to the shelves and could therefore introduce his friend to the innumerable treasures of the library.[1] In Osler's note-book is this fragmentary sketch of the reading-room, dated February 17th :

> It was opened under the auspices of Leo XIII in 1885 and is used only for MSS. It is a room about 70 by 80 ft. with four windows opening on to one of the courts. At one side between the central windows Padre Erhle has his desk. At a special desk at the end of the room are places for members of the Vatican with easy-chairs. There are only four readers' tables, with space for about ten readers. The walls are covered with pictures of the old Cardinal Librarians. The MSS. are very accessible. There are full catalogues and it takes only 15–20 mins. to get any special vol. The rooms are only open from 8.30–12 daily. There are more ecclesiastic than lay readers. Next to me was an ancient Padre with a long grey beard & flowing hair which reached to his shoulders. He was working at great MSS. and about every 5 mins. stimulated his grey cortex with a big pinch of snuff. Opposite sat a monk in brown and a young Englishman. The room is warm but had also the odour of unwashed humanity to a marked degree. Even at 9.45 on entering the room it was evident, & it became intensified as the morning wore on.

A pity he did not continue, but in a letter to McCrae shortly after, he said : ' He had out for me their oldest Hippocrates and Galen MSS.—to my surprise none antedating the 11th century. It is interesting to see so modern a place—the reference library for workers is most complete

[1] The late summer, it may be added, saw the Rev. Dr. Bannister with his friend Mgr. Ratti at work in the Bodleian—also in Osler's library and guests at his table.

but the Index does not touch it, curiously enough—perhaps all the prohibited books go there for inspection. The Museum treasures are wonderful and so well arranged.'

. . . I am delighted [he writes on Feb. 24th to H. B. Jacobs] to hear of Wm Marburg's gift—how good of him! He is a generous soul. That will help a great deal. Did my brother, E. B. Osler, give anything or was he asked? He might like to do a little, & a letter from the Committee stating the case would be no harm. He has rather a big job on hand at present—building and endowing a home for aged women in memory of my mother in our old home, Dundas. We are working hard here but there is so much to see. I have just begun to get involved with the doctors—Marchiafava, Celli & the Bastianellis. The Hospital is A.1. but they need new buildings for the school. I am to see the malaria work with Celli next week—the Campagna is gradually getting healthy. Enormous reduction in deaths from the disease in 20 years. . . . The weather has been fine but the days are cold & Rome is the dirtiest place I have ever seen—dust everywhere. It must be awful in summer. We had a great day yesterday at Frascati & the Alban Mountains. Countess Andreozzi took us into her old villa—nephews of the 17th century popes, the builders! Wonderful views. Cicero had a choice spot here for a country seat. We have seen something of the Garretts. Mrs. John is an old friend & patient. She is very attractive & is already a favourite & it is nice that she knows Rome. We are going together on Saturday to the Island to say our prayers to Æsculapius—whose serpent in stone, at one end, is all that remains of this famous temple. . . . I have found a few good books, but the shops are not first class with the exception of Lang Bros. I hoped to find incunabula at every corner.

His reference to Professor Celli and to the Roman Campagna—that hotbed of malaria which probably had more to do with 'the Fall' than Gibbon could even have surmised—recalls his own active rôle in the studies of the disease, begun at Blockley Hospital in 1886. He became so impressed by the results the Italians had obtained that before leaving Rome he sent a long account of this 'lesson in practical hygiene' to *The Times*:[1]

We owe much [he wrote] to the Italians for their contributions to our knowledge of the cause of malaria. . . . As an old student of the disease, and deeply interested in the practical problems of its prevention, one of my first visits in Rome was to the Laboratories

[1] 'Malaria in Italy: a Lesson in Practical Hygiene', *The Times*, Lond., March 15, 1909.

of Physiology and Hygiene, to find out from the Directors, Marchiafava and Celli, the progress of the battle. It was not enough to know the cause; we had to know how it worked before effective measures could be taken, and the demonstration by Ross of the transmission of the disease by the mosquito at once put malaria on the list of easily preventible infections. Just ten years ago the Italian Society for the Study of Malaria was founded, and I was able to get a full report of the work. . . . In Professor Celli's lecture-room hangs the mortality chart of Italy for the past twenty years. In 1887 malaria ranked with tuberculosis, pneumonia, and the intestinal disorders of children as one of the great infections, killing in that year 21,033 persons. The chart shows a gradual reduction in death-rate, and in 1906 only 4,871 persons died of the disease, and in 1907 4,160. This remarkable result has been very largely due to the sanitary measures introduced by the society. It has long been known that malaria disappears 'spontaneously'. The Fen country is now healthy; parts of Canada, about Lakes Ontario and Erie, which were formerly hotbeds of the disease, are now free. This cannot be attributed altogether to cultivation and drainage. I know places on the shores of the lakes just mentioned in which the conditions to-day are identical with those which I remember as a boy. The Desjardin Canal Marsh at the extreme western end of Lake Ontario was a well-known focus of the disease. The marsh remains, the mosquitoes are there, but a case of malaria is almost as rare as in England. The settlers early recognized the important fact that malaria was a disease liable to recur, and it became a common practice to take Peruvian bark every spring and autumn for a year or two after an attack. This is a point in prophylaxis which the work of the Italian Society has brought into prominence. . . .

Malaria illustrates the stages through which so many of the great discoveries in medicine have had to pass. At first a period of doubt—that the actual germ had been discovered seemed too good news to be true, and for ten years or more there was much, and perhaps justifiable, scepticism. Except for the great help in diagnosis, we did not get much further until 1898, when the experiments of Ross demonstrated the truth of the old suggestion of Lancisi (revived by King and Manson), that the disease was transmitted by the mosquito. And now we are in the stage of prevention—the practical application of the knowledge of the cause and the method of its action. It would be hard to name any single event of the nineteenth century of greater practical importance to the race than the discovery of Laveran. In the words of Colonel Gorgas, it has made the tropics habitable by white men. The Panama Canal Zone is an astounding witness to the success of modern sanitary measures against malaria. The monthly reports of Colonel Gorgas give a death-rate (among nearly 50,000 workpeople) lower than that of any large city—it has been as low as 12 per 1,000! And let us not forget that Holland dates this triumph to the men who introduced experiment into medicine, to the Harveys, the Hunters, the Magendies, and the Claude Bernards—the arch-vivisectors whom it has become fashionable to abuse!—and who have thus enabled us to wring from nature what Harvey calls 'her closet-secrets'.

On another morning with G. Bastianelli he visited the Biblioteca Lancisiana, went over the Lancisi MSS. and made many fragmentary notes, such as: '7 books published before 1480: there is no copy of the De Motu Cordis 1628; one of 1652 Religio Medici; none of Caius; one only of Linacre; there are only two old portraits—one of Lancisi and one of John Howard, who probably visited the hospital—look it up!' &c.

To W. G. MacCallum of the Johns Hopkins. Hotel Royal, Rome, Feb. 28th.

Dear Mac, I have only just heard of your appointment at Columbia—hearty congratulations! It was not unexpected as Butler had written some months ago. It will be a great wrench to leave Baltimore, but you are wise. You should have your own position—you have earned it. What ever will Welch do without you! I hope you do not leave before the summer. I should not like to see the J.H.H. without you—the last of the old guard in the house. This is a fascinating place. Marchiafava, Celli, Bignami & the Bastianellis are charming. The pathologists are in practice—and the laboratories tell the tale. . . . Do give your father my kindest regards.

(*In his pocket note-book*). March 1st, 1909.

Went to the Sant Agostino, Rome, and saw the 'Madonna del Porto', the famous Madonna which helps the pregnant women. It is a large gaudily bedecked figure—like a fashionably dressed queen with a crown on her head & an infant in her arms. The figure and the whole wall of the end of the choir were covered with votive offerings: pictures dealing with circumstances in which the Madonna had been helpful—a man falling off a broken ladder & who had time to pray and so fell easy, & was not hurt—ships—pictures of raised [illegible], models of eyes, hands, feet, chiefly in metal—of gaudy gilt or silvered—crutches on the side of the stand, braces, trusses, &c., watches, chains, &c, in the greatest profusion. Two pregnant women were praying before her and several men and boys. The toes of her left foot are worn away by the kisses of the faithful & are now coated with silver. In the same church over the High Altar is the picture painted by St. Luke & in a chapel to the left is the tomb of St. Monica.

To Dr. J. William White of Philadelphia. 2nd [March]

I enclose you a little prayer to St. C. & St. D. [Cosmas and Damian] our patron Saints which may be useful. I have made a pilgrimage to their mother church and have burnt a candle—a small one—for my surgical colleagues. The instruments with which they cut off a leg which had a cancer & transplanted the sound leg of a just dead man are carefully preserved in the church—with an arm of each saint and a bottle of the milk of the Virgin Mary. We are having a delightful visit. . . . I hope to see you in May or June. I sail about April 22nd. I hope you are in good form & still appreciating the fact that you would have been a wretched Adullamite had it not been for the fostering care of that long-suffering saint to whom greetings and love from us both. . . .

To Leonard L. Mackall, at Jena. [March 3]

I have put your note in the hands of a man who says he can (possibly) be of help—a Mr. Bannister who knows Italy thoroughly. He leaves for England for 3 weeks but returns April 1st. There should be no difficulty in tracing the descendants of so notable a man as Medwin [the friend of Byron and Shelley]. There are probably genealogical journals in which a note could be inserted. Schiff the Librarian at Florence may be able to help. We leave for Florence tomorrow (via Perugia & Assisi Hotel du Nord) for two weeks. Rome has been delightful. I have enjoyed everything. Several of the Book-shops are A.1. I got a splendid Aristotle (Venice) 1476—de animalium partibus, and several good sets relating to Medical History—de Renzi's School of Salernum &c. I got a fine Gesner—Dictionary Greek & Latin. Wonderful man! well called the German Pliny—Bibliography, Philology, Medicine, Chemistry, Natural History—& above all a most lovable soul. When in Oxford in Aug. remind me to show you a touching tribute which I found to his character.[1] He died at 45. I have a very good collection of his works. I look forward to seeing you in Oxford. I shall be back from America July 1st. Oxford always finds me—letters are forwarded twice weekly.

'This place looks hopeful', he writes from Florence on a p.c., March 4th, 'I go to Grocco's clinique tomorrow and to Banti on Monday.' A few days later, however, he was dragged back to the capital, where all by himself and with no one to check him, except perhaps 'Rosalie', he evidently had an orgy in the book shops.

. . . I was recalled to Rome (stranded American) and I sanctified

[1] See below, p. 183.

my fee by buying 3 copies of Vesal, 2nd edition, fine one for myself, a 1st for McGill (300 fr. was stiff, but it goes for 500 !) & another for the Frick library. I was sorry to miss the Rhazes, the Brussels Library secured it. I have two copies also of the Venice edition of the Vesal. Have you one? I bought one Imperialis for the sake of the Vesal picture—they have another which I will ask them to send. . . . I have a set of votives for the [Maryland] Faculty—terra cotta arms, legs, breasts, eyes, ears, fingers—which the votaries hung in the Æsculapian temples in gratitude to the god—the modern R.C. ones are wretched (tin) imitations. . . .

Thus he 'sanctified his fee' largely in donations to other than his own library, and in the copy of the 'Fabrica' of 1543 forwarded to McGill through F. J. Shepherd is a note of presentation dated from Rome, March 9th, 'to the library of my old school in which anatomy has always been studied in the Vesalian spirit—with accuracy and thoroughness.' Evidently he had forgotten that six years before he had already given them a copy. And once more in Florence, at the Hotel Paoli, he writes:

This place is of overwhelming interest—libraries, pictures &c. The Laurentian Library is just too splendid for words *7000 chained MSS.* All in the putei or cases designed by Michael Angelo. I have a photo of an end of one for you. The book-shops are good. Olschki one of the best in Europe. He has 500 incunabula on the shelves, a Silvaticus a *cuss* of no moment—of 1476—a superb folio, one of the first printed in Bologna—fresh and clean as if printed yesterday & such a page! but he asks 1500 francs ! ! His things are wonderful but really auction sale is the only economical way to get old books. . . . I am in a state of mental indigestion from plethora—it 's really bewildering—so much to see & to do. . . .

Some time during this month he must have written for the Yale undergraduates' daily paper [1] at the request of the editors a letter of advice to prospective candidates regarding Rhodes Scholarships—he being, unofficially and in the introductory words of the Editor, a 'friend and adviser of all the American Rhodes Scholars.' In this letter, tinged though it possibly may be by his own recent brain-dusting, he emphasized that 'the more a man brings to Oxford the more he will take away', and he went on to outline 'the academic life of a young fellow who means

[1] Yale *Daily News* for March 31, 1909.

business' and comes 'prepared between the short Oxford terms to get an education neither Oxonian nor Anglican, but European.'

He [the Rhodes Scholar] gets settled in Oxford by the middle of October and his first term is one of bewilderment, sometimes of discouragement. He has settled on his course—history, classics, law, literature, medicine, etc.—and then about November 20 he should hold that great inquisition which Descartes says every man should make for himself once in his lifetime. If a sensible fellow the main result of this will be a determination to get the best Europe has to offer in his subject. With this object in view, the day after term closes sees him in a 'pension' in Paris and alone—no other student with him, or he will not learn to speak French. As there is practically no Christmas vacation at the Sorbonne he will have six weeks during which he can hear three or four lectures on any study he may have selected, and he can begin to get interested in its French literature. After the Winter term in Oxford, April 14th sees him again in Paris for a second period of six weeks. The note-books begin to show that he understands the lectures and he has completed the analysis of a couple of French monographs in his special subject. Living in the Latin Quarter he will soon appreciate its delightful life; but he will be wise and careful as he will have left his affections at home, either in the safe-keeping of some Neaera—or in cold storage. The Summer term in Oxford will open his eyes to the possibilities of English college life, but early in June he is back again in Paris with two clear months ahead in which he should get a good reading and speaking knowledge of French and hear the lectures of the best men on his specialty. From the middle of August to the 10th of October is spent at the seaside in a French family, looking after his health and studying four or five hours a day. Returning to Oxford for the second year he begins to feel that he understands a little of English and French life. The short eight weeks' term passes and December 7 sees our scholar with a ticket to Berlin or Leipzig prepared to spend his vacation in mastering the German language and getting in touch with the German side of his work. He will go back to the same place in April for another period of six weeks, and in these two visits he should have a fair knowledge of the language—enough at any rate to be able to understand lectures. Back to Oxford for the delightful Summer term during which there is so much to do that no one can do any work. The middle of June, Leipzig or Berlin again for the long Summer semester. From the middle of August to the middle of September he will join some of his fellow students in a walking tour in Switzerland.

At the beginning of his third year our young Rhodian should

have his eyes opened. It may be urged that so rapid a change of diet would bring him 'to death's door of a mental dyspepsy' and, also in Lowell's phrase, without power of combining, arranging, discerning, he could not digest the masses he learned into learning. I am speaking of a man who is following a post-graduate course for a research degree and who is working a very limited field; but men reading for the ordinary degrees could follow the same plan. The last Christmas vacation? Yes, Paris again, a few more lectures at the Sorbonne and two or three hours a day at the Bibliothèque Nationale working at the literature of his thesis. The Easter vacation will puzzle him—where? Let him find the man who is making the greatest stir in his subject in Europe, and put in the last continental visit with him. Then for the saddest of all the Oxford terms—the one before graduation; but the Western light will be in his eyes and the longing for the home which (if he is sensible) he has not seen for two years and nine months. Of this period he will have spent about seventy-two weeks in England and about sixty-four abroad. Perhaps if there is any money left he should see Scotland before he sails. Oxford offers a delightful life for the Rhodes scholar—a more carefully selected group of his countrymen than he will meet in any American college, a fine body of colonial students, and the pick of young Englishmen will be his associates. Many things are different—the men, the studies, the methods, the sports—all will test his adaptability or, in other words, his capacity to meet new conditions, wherein lies the secret of success in life. He will have these powers still further tested under the more novel environments of France and Germany. Carrying out this programme—and it is a possible one—the man will return knowing the best England has to offer, the best France has to offer, the best Germany has to offer. If after this he does not turn out 'a truly good man, four-square and without flaw', to use Aristotle's expression, he must be a 'dull and muddy mettled rascal', who should have chosen other parents and a different career.

All this may have made him a little homesick, for in a letter of the 15th he said: 'We have been here [Florence] for two weeks—seeing the galleries under trying circumstances of cold & rain. We go to Bologna, Venice & Padua, and my plans are to sail from Naples on the 21st. I have not seen the boy since Xmas and now my heart begins to fail, and I may go to England and sail from Southampton April 14th.' Evidently he had longings for a sight of Revere, and so far as Naples was concerned his heart did fail, as is evident in a letter sent a week later to his old Gower

Street room-mate of the London days of 1870, who had suffered a stroke:

To Dr. Arthur Browne of Montreal. Hotel Paoli, Florence, 22nd [March]

I was so glad to hear from Francis this week that you were better & able to be up. What a sad trial this illness has been. It must be some consolation to you to feel that your many friends have been so full of sympathy with you & Mrs. Browne. I am sailing for New York next month & hope to be in Montreal early in June. We have had a very good winter in Italy—everything delightful but the weather. I had a month in Rome & saw nearly everything but the Pope. I spared him. The Vatican Library is wonderful; though for old Manuscripts it is not so rich as the Medici Library here. To-day I saw the MS. of Celsus which had been lost for so many centuries. . . . We go back to England for Easter to see the boy who is preparing for Winchester. He is not much at books—prefers butterflies & fish. I never saw such a devoted Waltonian, & the Compleat Angler is one of his favourite books—complete conversation book he calls it. With much love to you both Ever yours.

A few days in Bologna were enough to let him scour the University Library and the Museo Civico to which the card of a Curator of the Bodleian gave him ready access; then Venice, whence he wrote:

To Dr. Albert Chatard of Baltimore. Grand Hotel Britannia, 30th [March]

I shall be out earlier than I had anticipated, but I do not suppose now the committee would wish to make any change in the date. I have to go to England next week unexpectedly, so that I shall sail from Southampton & not from Naples. I wish I had known of this before, but the business is quite unexpected. I have provisionally taken passage for April 14th, which is a week earlier than I had intended. I sent you the other day a reproduction of an Avicenna MS. page. I saw the original at Bologna wonderfully coloured—the text is in Hebrew, XI century I think. I am bringing a set of the old Votive offerings of the Æsculapian temple which will be of interest. I can get a suitable show case. It would be well to get out some of the special editions for the meeting. I am sending the 1st edition of Vesalius, De humani corporis fabrica to the Frick Library. Those Edinboro theses would make a good show. Coming earlier, I shall be able to spend a longer time in Baltimore. I must meet your Avicenna Club. We have had a splendid visit in Italy. Rome was wonderful, Florence enchanting. I have seen

Bologna thoroughly and shall see Padua, Venice and Pavia. I am glad you like the Paris letters, there are more to follow. My greetings to your mother & uncle.

There is little record of Venice except that his pocket note-book is filled with jottings from the 'Bib. San Marco. Dr. Frati Librarian'; and the same is true of Padua, where on March 30th he notes:

Library of Univ, very old building—Ducal palace, good catalogue. No MS. of Mundinus' anatomy. Two fragments of XV cent MSS. of his—not important. . . . Montagnanus edition 1498, with his two plates. Vesal—no letters, no MS. No autograph copies of works. The 1543 [ed.] of the De humani corp. fab. is well worn. At lower right hand margin is 'Fabricius sibi & suis'. Probably the copy belonged to F. . . . Harvey De motu cordis orig. ed. not there. . . . Univ. Court. Not so fine as the loggia of the Archiginnasio of Bologna. Same style. The stemmas are chiefly in stone and not coloured. The aula is splendid, the walls brilliant with coloured stemmas. A good many old portraits. Could not find Harvey's stemma—went twice round (bitterly cold & had to give it up). Lecture room given by Fabricius in 1595—the one in which Harvey heard his (F's) dem. of the valves of the veins—is very remarkable—6 tiers of places, very steep—standing-room only—curious open woodwork of the places. The well is very narrow, no entrance, except a communication with the cellar by which the body could be lifted up on the table. The lecture room very small, accom. 75–100. No old book shop.

Probably owing to the inclement weather, the stay in Venice was cut short, and April 1st found them in Milan; whence to a former Radcliffe Travelling Fellow, now a physician in Nairobi:

To Dr. A. J. Jex-Blake at Oxford. Gd. Hotel de la Ville, Milan, April 1st.

On May 20th I hope to be in Boston! I sail about the middle of the month. My leave is for the annus medi[c]us so I don't return until the end of June. I am sure you will have a very pleasant dinner—I hope Curzon will come. Do express my regrets. I saw Malpighi & Morgagni at Padua the other day—wonderful aula—over the doorway *Ichabod! Ichabod!*—in large letters—I could see them. Yours sincerely Wm Osler. Congratulations on your election.

Truly the glory had departed from Padua; but there were

compensations. On the following day a postcard to L. L. Mackall in Jena, says:

I have the Gesner. I will look up the Johnston when I get to Oxford. He was a most prolific poet I believe. I got the 3 vol. Historia animalium of Gesner for 5 fr. at Bologna. I have a fine copy so I shall send this one to the Coll of Phy—who have not one. I have had great luck in Florence & Venice—several gems—an Aristotle De animalium partibus 1476, a Pietro d'Abano 1474, Arnold of Villanova Sch. of Salernum 1480 [1500]. Olschki of Florence has the finest collection of old books I have seen, 600 incunabula—Prices sky-high—Martelli of Bologna very good. Hoepli here very disappointing. I was told he had a large stock but he has very little & is really not an antiquariat. I sail April 14th, back about July 1st. Yours, W. O.

. . . I have changed my plans [he writes to H. B. Jacobs, April 2nd]. Some matters came up about our proposed new laboratories & clinique & rooms at the Radcliffe, which it is important for me to try to settle before the end of next term. . . . We had a splendid month in Florence. Wonderful city. . . . Altogether I have had some fine hauls—particularly of the good old Italians. Bologna & Padua were not quite up to my expectations. Padua is perhaps a bit disappointing—the Aula is wonderful. We had nearly a week in Venice and three glorious days. I saw the unique 1538 six plates of Vesal—very interesting in comparison with his 1543 work as the drawings, though done by Calcar, are much inferior. Many years ago, Sir William Stirling-Maxwell had them reproduced, but his copy is very rare. I shall get an estimate from the Press—they would be worth reproducing. The Italians are very up to date in Library work—the catalogues are excellent. We spent the day at Verona—not much there except the amphitheatre. They had not even a copy of Fracastorius' poems in the Library. I saw the Spedale Maggiore here this a.m. greatly changed internally since John Morgan's description in 1759. It is one of the largest in Europe. I am going to see Golgi at Pavia tomorrow. . . . We leave here [Milan] Sunday night & will be at the Grand Hotel Trafalgar Square Monday night.

On April 9th, from 13 Norham Gardens, he wrote to Mrs. Brewster:

Here I am, at home again, and very glad indeed to see my boy, & my books. Revere has had such a good winter & has grown so big—butterflies, fish & sketching are his special fancies. He will never do much with his books, but he is a dear good lad. We enjoyed Venice so much. I saw Verona & Padua & Pavia and we stayed a few days at Milan. After all there is nothing so superb as a fine

Gothic cathedral, & we came to the conclusion that about the best thing we saw in Italy was the last—Milan cathedral. I have picked up a great many treasures in the way of old books—a few fine incunabula, but they are getting scarce & usually fetch prices beyond my purse. . . . I sail by the Adriatic (White Star) next Wednesday. . . .

There is an entry in his account-book opposite this day which reads: 'I took a heavy cold, was in bed 10th 11th 12th & 13th fever & schnupfen. No cough. Was to have sailed on 14th gave up passage.' This entry accounts for a note dated the 12th, sent to the S.S. *Adriatic*, in which her 'loving grandfather' tells his 'sweet Rosalie' he will not, alas, be on the steamer with her, and adds: 'Do not wash your face on the voyage, & if you are seasick make that horrid Marguerite wait on you.' As usual during these times, many notes were scribbled on his knee. In one of them he spoke of his Paris letters to the *Journal of the American Medical Association*, saying: 'I have been so busy that I have not had time to finish the others—I hope to do so on the steamer,'—optimist that he was, with three addresses to prepare! He wrote to Mrs. Brewster on the 13th:

I am not sailing until the 21st (Majestic). At present I am enjoying the luxury of a few days in bed after a sharp attack of grippe. We have had a wonderful Easter—such sunshine. I wish you could see the garden—everything bursting into bud or bloom. I am sending you the Times notice of Swinburne—so good! I did write to you about the children's Poems—did I not? They are exquisite. I am sure he describes Sylvia's toes to the life!

To Dr. J. George Adami, Montreal. On board R.M.S. *Majestic*, Wednesday [April 28]

Your nice bundle of reprints came the other day & I beguiled several bed hours with them. A lot of good work! I was laid up for ten days with influenza and could not sail on the 14th. I hope to meet you perhaps in Washington. In any case, I shall be in Montreal about the 12th of June and hope to have the best part of a week with you. I am anxious to see the new buildings, and all the changes in two years. You will be sorry to hear that [J. Wesley] Mills has not been doing well. I saw him last Wednesday, 21st, just before sailing—he was better—no fever but the operation was, I fear, not very successful. He looks well & has borne the suffering most heroically. It will be nice to see you all again. Love to L. M. C. and the chicks.

He must have gone promptly to Baltimore, possibly in time to hear the last of Professor Schäfer's series of Herter Lectures, and was put up by the McCraes in what he termed 'the prophet's chamber', whence issued letters in regard to further contributions for 'that awful System', as Mrs. Osler called it.[1] On Monday evening of May 10th he spoke on Servetus before the Hopkins Historical Club. The paper was evidently incomplete, for he gave most of it impromptu, reading only the opening section, which follows:

The year 1553 saw Europe full of tragedies, and to the earnest student of the Bible it must have seemed as if the day had come for the opening of the second seal spoken of in the Book of Revelation, when peace should be taken from the earth and men should kill one another. One of these tragedies has a mournful interest this year, the four hundredth anniversary of the birth of its chief actor; yet it was but one of thousands of similar cases with which the history of the sixteenth century is stained. On October 27th, shortly after twelve o'clock, a procession started from the town hall of Geneva—the chief magistrates of the city, the clergy in their robes, the Lieutenant Criminel and other officers on horseback, a guard of mounted archers, the citizens with a motley crowd of followers, and in their midst, with arms bound, in shabby, dirty clothes, walked a man of middle age, whose intellectual face bore the marks of long suffering. Passing along the rue St. Antoine through the gate of the same name, the cortège took its way towards the Golgotha of the city. Once outside the walls, a superb sight broke on their view: in the distance the blue waters and enchanting shores of the Lake of Geneva, to the west and north the immense amphitheatre of the Jura, with its snow-capped mountains, and to the south and west the lovely valley of the Rhone; but we may well think that few eyes were turned away from the central figure of that sad procession. By his side, in earnest entreaty, walked the aged pastor, Farel, who had devoted a long and useful life to the service of his fellow citizens. Mounting the hill, the field of Champel was reached, and here on a slight eminence was the fateful stake, with the dangling chains and heaping bundles of faggots. At this sight the poor victim prostrated himself on the ground in prayer. In reply to the exhortation of the clergyman for a specific confession of faith, there was the cry, 'Misericordia, misericordia! Jesu, thou Son of the Eternal God, have compassion upon me!' Bound to the stake by the iron chains, with a chaplet of straw and green twigs covered with sulphur on his head, with his long dark face, it is said that he looked like the Christ in whose name he was bound. Around his

[1] Vol. VI of the series was issued on May 27, 1909.

waist were tied a large bundle of manuscript and a thick octavo printed book. The torch was applied, and as the flames spread to the straw and sulphur and flashed in his eyes, there was a piercing cry that struck terror into the hearts of the bystanders. The faggots were green, the burning was slow, and it was long before in a last agony he cried again, 'Jesu, thou Son of the Eternal God, have mercy upon me!' Thus died, in his forty-fourth year, Michael Servetus Villanovanus, physician, physiologist, and heretic. Strange, is it not, that could he have cried, 'Jesu, thou Eternal Son of God!' even at this last moment, the chains would have been unwound, the chaplet removed, and the faggots scattered; but he remained faithful unto death to what he believed was the *Truth* as revealed in the Bible. The story of his life is the subject of my address. . . .

This was all serious enough, but during those Baltimore days Osler, debonair, in a grey frock-coat, top hat, and the inevitable nosegay in his buttonhole, passed no familiar spot without a visit and the leaving of a touching or humorous recollection in some one's mind. He must also have been in Washington to see an old doctor-friend who was ill—'very much "gone at the top", so distressing, for he bursts into tears when he sees his old friends; but the young doctor is doing well and is evidently a very fine fellow' [W. O. had started him on his career]; and he added: 'I saw Lois who has got as far as the 2nd coat of paint on the President—Mrs. Taft spoke very hopefully about the picture—I did not see the President, who was golfing.'

On the morning of Thursday the 13th came the dedication of the new building of the Maryland Medical and Chirurgical Faculty held in connexion with the annual spring meeting—'the greatest day', as was said, 'in the history of medicine in Maryland'; and Osler's fifteen years in Baltimore had had much to do—indeed nearly everything to do—with making it possible. The Governor of Maryland, the Mayor, General Leonard Wood, commanding the Department of the East, and other notables, were present, in addition to those representing the N. Y. Academy, the Boston Medical Library, the College of Physicians of Philadelphia, and the Surgeon-General's Library. At the exercises of the afternoon, Cardinal Gibbons, Osler's friend and former neighbour, gave the invocation; Weir Mitchell the principal address; and in the evening were held the ceremonies to dedicate 'Osler Hall'. The President, Dr. Brice W. Goldsborough, in due course called on Osler for his oration; this, entitled 'Old and New',[1] began as follows:

In the collegiate churches and cathedrals of England before the sermon, the preacher, in what is known as the 'bidding prayer', asks the people, often in very quaint phraseology, to pray, among other things for the estates of the realm, and then he offers a special prayer of thanks for the liberality of founders and benefactors, 'men in their generation famous and in ours never to be forgotten.' At Oxford in the University church every Sunday in term it is interesting to hear recalled the memory of the Duke Humphrey, the Lady Margaret and other worthies. And whoever the preacher may be, he finally mentions the founders and famous men of his particular college. Following this happy custom I would ask you in the first place to be profoundly thankful to the men of 1799 who gave this Faculty to the country and who made this day possible. . . . It does not often happen that a man is called upon to participate in the dedication of a Hall to himself. More often it is a posthumous honour for which the thanks are tendered by relatives or friends. It is difficult for me to express the deep gratitude I feel for this singular mark of affection on your part. The distinction is not a little enhanced by the association with corresponding halls in other cities of the names of some of the most distinguished of American physicians: Oliver Wendell Holmes in Boston, David Hosack in New York, and S. Weir Mitchell in Philadelphia. If by any process from the large lump of your gracious kindness the grains of merit on my part could be extracted, they would be found to consist of that all-precious material faith—the pure gold of faith which I always had in the future of the Faculty. Just twenty years ago I joined this society and began my professional life here by giving the Annual Oration. Its history and tradition appealed to me strongly and I soon began to find my way to the old quarters under the Historical Society's Hall. . . . As a boy, some of my happiest recollections in the early '60's are of school days in a small Canadian town, where in the summer evenings we paraded the streets, company formation, with a bonnie blue flag bearing a single star, and singing 'Maryland, My Maryland'. Little then—or later—did I dream that my affiliation would be so close with this State, and that with it, through your gracious act to-day, my name may find its most enduring remembrance. These festivals illustrate how quickly the memory of a name perishes. In how many minds did the mention of David Hosack arouse a thrill of remembrance? His works—and they were good ones—have

[1] *Journal of the American Medical Association*, 1909, liii. 4–8.

perished, and his more enduring association is with the Hall of the Academy of Medicine which bears his name—and this is likely to be my fate. We can imagine a conversation in a library—A.D. 2009—between two assistants wearily sorting a pile of second-hand books just sent in. 'What are we to do with all this old rubbish by a man named Osler? He must have had very little to do to spoil so much paper. Where did he live anyway?' 'Oh, I don't know. Baltimore, I think. Anyhow they have a Hall there that bears his name.'

And now that you see fulfilled the desire of your eyes in the possession of the beautiful new building, what is the special message of such an occasion? A double one—to the profession at large, and to ourselves in particular. . . . The secret of success in an institution of this kind is to blend the old with the new, the past with the present in due proportion, and it is not difficult if we follow Emerson's counsel: 'We cannot overstate', he says, 'our debt to the past, but the moment has the supreme claim; the sole terms on which the past can become ours are its subordination to the present.' Let me indicate very briefly how the old and the new may be interwoven in the life of this Faculty. . . . In one of his Hibbert Lectures last year at Oxford, William James made a remark that clung—'We live forward, we understand backwards. The philosophers tell us that there is no present, no now—the fleeting moment *was* as we try to catch it.' In the opening of this new building we have to-day made a happy addition to a happy past. Towards this day we have all lived forward, and the future should still be in our thoughts. This old Faculty must continue to be our rallying-ground—once inside its portals, schools, colleges, hospitals, societies, all other affiliations are absorbed in something vastly greater, which includes all and claims from all devoted service, *the united profession of the state*. . . .

There followed a large public reception and other attentions, from which he finally escaped, though it was from the frying-pan into the fire. Four weeks later, on the 11th of June, from the University Club, Montreal, he wrote as follows to H. B. Jacobs, who was still abroad, and to whom he had apparently sent an account of the Baltimore festival:

Since my last letter I have had a strenuous time—Boston, Philadelphia, New York, Buffalo, & Toronto. I had a great day at Harvard Med. School, and in the eve. sat between the out and the in President. Both spoke charmingly. I had a good talk next day with Lowell, who is most sanguine about the School & the Brigham Hospital. I talked quite plainly about the absolute necessity of a close affiliation and a joint appointing board. The M. G. H.

and the B. C. H. men are not very anxious for a new large general Hospital and there is a bit of a hitch. I spent a Sunday with the Brewsters at Mt. Kisco where they are building a summer home. Starr is nearby and it is a lovely country. They come to E. this summer. Cole and the new plans of the Rockefeller appear to fit each other. Flexner is in very good form. Mitchell is wonderfully well. The new Coll. Phy. building is splendid, but not any more convenient than the Medical & Chirurgical. I went over a good many things with Miss Noyes. Really when one thinks of 10 or 12 years ago and present conditions, we cannot but be thankful. Bill and Margery Howard come over with me. B. [W. W. Francis] has just brought out my new edition which you will find on your return. The new buildings here are splendid—a fine library & a superb anatomical dept. What an age of growth everywhere! I do hope we may see you in England. I sail Empress of Great Britain on the 18th and should be in Oxford on the 26th. Mrs Revere & Mrs Chapin are [in Oxford] with Mrs Osler.

The 'great day at the Harvard Medical School' refers to an alumni gathering which the new Dean of the school, Henry A. Christian, one of his old pupils, had invited him to attend.[1] He must have spent some time with the 'in President' the next day in looking at the treasures in the Harvard Library [2] to which two years later he made a gift; and there exists one touching reminder of this Boston visit—a photograph of his old friend H. P. Bowditch, become a victim of Parkinson's disease, standing on his front steps supported on either side by Osler and J. Collins Warren. There followed a brief sojourn with Weir Mitchell in Philadelphia, and from there he went to Toronto, stopping *en route* in Buffalo in all probability to spend a few hours with his bibliophilic friend and former patient, R. B. Adam. While in Toronto visiting his relatives, he attended the annual gathering of the Ontario profession, before whom on June 3rd, as their invited guest, he gave another carefully prepared address, choosing 'The Treatment of Disease' as his topic.[3]

[1] It would appear from contemporary letters that pressure had been brought to bear on him to act as Medical Adviser of the new hospital which was soon to be erected adjacent to the Medical School on the Peter Bent Brigham Foundation.

[2] Cf. letter of April 17, 1911.

[3] *British Medical Journal*, 1909, ii. 185–9, and elsewhere.

WILLIAM OSLER, AET. 59

Photograph by Notman, Montreal

How he had found time for its preparation is difficult to see, but it proved to be a most inspiriting address, and like most of the things he wrote in his later days on general topics it called forth much editorial comment. 'As is our pathology so is our practice' was his theme, and after speaking of the earlier conceptions of the nature of disease, beginning with the view of 'sin and sickness' against which even the wisdom of Solomon could not prevail and which to-day sends more people to the shrine of Ste. Anne de Beaupré than to all the hospitals of the Dominion, he passed on to the views of modern times: 'These are glorious days for the race; nothing has been seen like it since the destroying angel stayed his hand on the threshing-floor of Araunah the Jebusite.' And he proceeded to point out the directions in which our modern conception of disease had radically altered our practice: how in a disease like tuberculosis we had substituted 'the open air and dietetic treatment for the nauseous mixtures with which our patients were formerly drenched'; how the study of morbid anatomy combined with careful clinical observation (so true in his own case) had taught us to recognize our therapeutic limitations.

> To accept [he said] a great group of maladies, against which we have never had and can scarcely ever hope to have curative measures, makes some men as sensitive as though we were ourselves responsible for their existence. These very cases are 'rocks of offence' to many good fellows whose moral decline dates from the rash promise to cure. We work by wit and not by witchcraft, and while these patients have our tenderest care, and we must do what is best for the relief of their sufferings, we should not bring the art of medicine into disrepute by quack-like promises to heal, or by wire-drawn attempts at cure in what old Burton calls 'continuate and inexorable maladies'.

He went on to speak of the newer organotherapy, which 'illustrates at once one of the great triumphs of science and the very apotheosis of charlatanry'; and here, nevertheless, he made a prophecy, saying: 'As our knowledge of the pancreatic function and carbohydrate metabolism becomes more accurate we shall probably be able to place the treatment of diabetes on a sure foundation.' It would be pleasant to imagine a young man named Banting, preparing to enter the Toronto Medical School, who, aware that his parents had been neighbours of the Oslers in the frontier days at Bond Head, had dropped in to the lecture in time to hear these words which rested uneasy in his mind until *insulin* was discovered—too late, alas! for Osler to applaud. But the speaker continued in a retrospective vein:

> Upon us, whose work lay in the last quarter of the nineteenth century, fell the great struggle with that many-headed monster, Polypharmacy—not the true polypharmacy which is the skilful combination of remedies, but the giving of many—the practice of at once discharging a heavily-loaded prescription at every malady, or at every symptom of it. Much has been done and an extraordinary change has come over the profession, but it has not been a fight to the finish. Many were lukewarm; others found it difficult to speak without giving offence in quarters where on other grounds respect and esteem were due. As an enemy to indiscriminate drugging, I have often been branded as a therapeutic nihilist. . . . I bore this reproach cheerfully, coming, as I knew it did, from men who did not appreciate the difference between the giving of medicine and the treatment of disease; moreover, it was for the galled jade to wince, my withers were unwrung. The heavy hands of the great Arabians grow lighter in each generation. Though dead, Avicenna and Averroes still speak, not only in the Arabian signs which we use, but in the combinations and multiplicity of the constituents of too many of our prescriptions. We are fortunately getting rid of routine practice in the use of drugs. How many of us now prescribe an emetic? . . .[1]

With his characteristic frankness he went on to discuss two other matters, one of them 'the specious and seductive pamphlets issued by pharmaceutical houses' which indicate 'a thraldom not less dangerous than the polypharmacy from which we are escaping'; the other 'the outbreak of faith-healing which seems to have the public of the American

[1] Lest an impression of Osler's so-called 'therapeutic nihilism' lead to the impression that practical instruction in therapeutics had been neglected in his Johns Hopkins clinic, reference may be made to his discussion of the subject on October 5th of this year before the Therapeutics Section of the Royal Society of Medicine. He gave an account of the system which had been in operation and of the exercises conducted by H. B. Jacobs and Thomas McCrae—a system to which another speaker at the time referred as one that filled him with 'admiration tinged with envy', for it was an impossible system to introduce in London. (Cf. *Proceedings, Royal Society of Medicine*, 1910, vol. iii, Therapeutics Section, p. 7).

continent in its grip'. 'The less the clergy have to do', he said, 'with the bodily complaints of neurasthenic and hysterical persons the better for their peace of mind and for the reputation of the cloth.' And, with the memory of Rome in mind, he continued:

Credulity in matters relating to disease remains a permanent fact in our history, uninfluenced by education. But let us not be too hard on poor human nature. Even Pericles, most sensible of men, when on his deathbed, allowed the women to put an amulet about his neck. And which one of us, brought up from childhood to invoke the aid of saints and to seek their help—which one of us under these circumstances, living to-day in or near Rome, if a dear child were sick unto death, would not send for the Santo Bambino, the Holy Doll of the Church of Ara Coeli? Has it not been working miracles these four hundred years? The votive offerings of gold and of gems from the happy parents cover it completely, and about it are grateful letters from its patients in all parts of the world. No doll is so famous, no doll so precious! No wonder it goes upon its ministry of healing in a carriage and pair, and with two priests as its companions! Precious perquisite of the race, as it has been called, with all its dark and terrible record, credulity has perhaps the credit balance on its side in the consolation afforded the pious souls of all ages and of all climes, who have let down anchors of faith into the vast sea of superstition. We drink it in with our mother's milk, and that is indeed an even-balanced soul without some tincture. We must acknowledge its potency to-day as effective among the most civilized people, the people with whom education is the most widely spread, yet who absorb with wholesale credulity delusions as childish as any that have ever enslaved the mind of man.

He said further: 'Having recently had to look over a large literature on the subject of mental healing, ancient and modern, for a new edition of my Text-book just issued, I have tried to put the matter as succinctly as possible' and the address, from which many more paragraphs clamour to be quoted, may be left, to take up the 7th edition of the Text-book which W. W. Francis had just seen through the press. It contains for the first time in his discussion of functional diseases this statement regarding 'faith-healing' which puts the matter in a nutshell:

In all ages, and in all lands, the prayer of faith, to use the words of St. James, has healed the sick; and we must remember that amid the Æsculapian cult, the most elaborate and beautiful system of faith-healing the world has seen, scientific medicine took its rise.

As a profession, consciously or unconsciously, more often the latter, *faith* has been one of our most valuable assets, and Galen expressed a great truth when he said, 'He cures most successfully in whom the people have the greatest confidence.' It is in these cases of neurasthenia and psychasthenia, the weak brothers and the weak sisters, that the personal character of the physician comes into play, and once let him gain the confidence of the patient, he can work just the same sort of miracles as Our Lady of Lourdes or Ste. Anne de Beaupré. Three elements are necessary: first, a strong personality in whom the individual has faith—Christ, Buddha, Æsculapius (in the days of Greece), one of the saints, or, what has served the turn of common humanity very well, a physician. Secondly, certain accessories—a shrine, a sanctuary, the service of a temple, or for us a hospital or its equivalent, with a skilful nurse. Thirdly, suggestion, either of the 'only believe', 'feel it', 'will it' attitude of mind, which is the essence of every cult and creed, or of the active belief in the assurance of the physician that the precious boon of health is within reach.

One can easily get so lost in the things Osler said and wrote[1] as to forget the things he was doing; and it is pleasant to picture a sojourn with 'Ned' Milburn in Belleville; and a visit in Montreal with Shepherd, whose daughter gets married at the time, and from whose house he writes on June 17th:

I am off tomorrow from Quebec. Many thanks for the books which I shall enjoy on the steamer. I have had such a busy visit here—scores of old friends to see, & all sorts of meetings, about the University & the medical school. I am glad these strenuous days are over, but it has been a great pleasure to get back to my old home. I had ten very happy years here & owe everything to the dear old men who gave me such opportunities for work. . . .

The 18th found him, in company with his nephew and one of the Howard children, on the *Empress of Britain*, reading and making notes from Shorter's 'Life and Letters of the Brontës' (1907), from which he took excerpts possibly intended for the article he was preparing for Mr. Bok on 'The Nervousness of American Women'—an article never published.[2]

[1] In a long editorial on this last address, the *Lancet* of Oct. 2nd said: 'By his words of counsel and encouragement to the young practitioners, and of sympathy and understanding with the older, which have on many former occasions fallen from his lips, Professor Osler has well earned the title of the Nestor of British Medicine.'

[2] Cf. foot-note, p. 104.

The three reached Oxford on June 26th, the 'Open Arms' being already filled with family guests. It had been practically a nine months' absence, and his library and consulting room can be imagined : desks piled with unanswered letters ; floors, by now, knee-deep in unopened book parcels. Both were in due course attacked. Thus, on June 30th, to a former pupil :

Dee-lighted ! I am so glad. This will give you what you deserve. I am writing to R. and congratulating *her*. When is the happy event ? Why not this summer ? and go to Ewelme for a post-endocarditic honeymoon ? What a curious infection it is ! I do not know of any proper psychological study of the mental state of man a few weeks after acceptance. Plato hits it off—I wish James would study the condition. Of course you feel like a new being—never felt the same ! Love to you both & many blessings.

Soon the contents of the book parcels began to find their proper owners. In Conrad Gesner's 'Historia Animalium' forwarded to George Dock, Osler copied out under the date of July 1st the following lines—all unconscious, in his admiration for the author, of how appropriate they were to himself.[1]

Oxford, July 1st, 1909.

'Conrad Gesner who kept open house for all learned men who came into his neighbourhood was not only the best naturalist among the scholars of his day but of all men of that century he was the pattern man of letters. He was faultless in private life, assiduous in study, diligent in maintaining correspondence and good will with learned men in all countries, hospitable—though his means were small—to every scholar that came into Zurich. Prompt to serve all, he was an editor of other men's volumes, a writer of prefaces for friends, a suggestor to young writers of books in which they might engage themselves, and a great helper to them in the progress of their work. But still, while finding time for services to other men, he could produce as much out of his own study as though he had no part in the life beyond its walls.'

Thus many of his holiday purchases were distributed, and

[1] When questioned subsequently by Dr. Dock, Osler had forgotten where he got the quotation. He used it again in his address at Aberystwyth in 1917 on 'The Library School and the College', and asked in a foot-note if any reader knew the source to let him know. He also used it in the Silliman Lectures without even then having traced it to Henry Morley's 'Life of Jerome Cardan', Vol. II, p. 152, whence it had been transcribed many years before (cf. above, Vol. I, p. 549).

meanwhile he dropped back into the old groove. 'I knew you would be pleased with Midhurst—it was very nice to have the day with you', he wrote to Mr. Phipps on the 10th; and to his old pupil, T. R. Boggs, two days later: 'I wish you could have been with us yesterday at Ewelme.' And on the 23rd this to the son of his old friend in Hamilton, Archibald Malloch, showing that he kept track of the next generation:

> Dear Archie, When you go back to McGill keep an eye on a freshman called Harry Wright from Ottawa son of the late Dr. H. P. Wright whom your father knew well. Perhaps he could get rooms with you, in any case be kind to him and make him work. I am sending you a German-English medical dictionary & the new Neurology section of Quain's Anatomy which will stretch your pia mater. . . .

A further illustration of the working of Osler's ferment (though it did not have as enduring an effect in England as it had in America) was the foundation of a Medical Library Association. Under his presidency twenty-seven librarians met this year, for the first time, on July 28th, in unofficial connexion with the B. M. A. at Belfast, just as the loyal group of librarians in the States were accustomed to meet in connexion with the A. M. A., as at Saratoga in June of 1902. An account of the meeting says:

> Professor Osler gave one of his characteristic addresses.[1] He began by referring to the honourable record of English physicians as book-lovers and collectors since the thirteenth century, and said his experience had been that there were more medical libraries in this country than in any other. He emphasized the importance of reading as a part of post-graduate study. There had been men whose only book was nature, but they were the exceptions. The average non-reading doctor might play a good game of golf or of bridge, but professionally he was a lost soul. The driven and tired practitioner might plead that he could not find time to read. He could not unless he had formed the practice in less busy days; then the habit of reading, like any other habit, became his master. He should get away from the notion that it was necessary to read much. One or two journals and a few books every year were enough, if read properly. Journals should be kept and filed for reference, and all reading should be done with that mental concentration which

[1] 'The Medical Library in Post-graduate Work.' *British Medical Journal*, Oct. 2, 1909, ii. 925–8.

made reading profitable. It was easier to buy books than to read them, and easier to read them than to absorb them. He urged on the meeting the collection of books on a definite system as the best of hobbies for the medical man.

There had been arranged, too, an exhibit of medical MSS., incunabula, &c., to which he had added a collection of books relating to Servetus, this year (or 1911) being his quater-centenary; also books by Ulrich von Hutten, the scholar-knight, and a series of volumes relating to consumption, beginning with Celsus and ending with the Countess of Aberdeen's 'Ireland's Crusade against Tuberculosis'. But this is all very dry; one despairs of properly abstracting Osler's papers. 'One of the best features', he said, 'I find in my "Old Country" colleagues is the frequency with which they have hobbies. No man is really happy or safe without one, and it makes precious little difference what the outside interest may be—botany, beetles or butterflies, roses, tulips or irises; fishing, mountaineering or antiquities—anything will do so long as he straddles a hobby and rides it hard.' Naturally he made a plea for 'the pleasant paths of bibliography', and for the habit of reading; but the address may be left after quoting a further paragraph, another reminder of his recent months in Italy:

Were there time I should like to say a few words on the subject of *how* to read, but the essence of the whole matter I found the other day in the Biblioteca Lancisiana, Rome. . . . In the opening address, 1714, *De recto usu Bibliothecae*, the Abbé Carsughi discusses the subject in three sections, and gives some good rules. The first section, *Librorum scilicet delectum*, need not detain us, but in the second, *Legendi methodum*, he urges two important points—to read in a certain order and with a definite object, and *lente festinans*, 'unhasting but unresting'. In the third section, *Adnotandi modum*, he urges the necessity of careful note-taking, quoting the praise of Clement of Alexandria, 'Oblivionis medicamentum, monumentum senectutis et adjumentum memoriae.' He dwells upon the importance of study in the morning, which was all very well in those days, but is not one hour after six in the evening worth now two before eight in the morning? (I am sure it is to me!) With half an hour's reading in bed every night as a steady practice, the busiest man can get a fair education before the plasma sets in the periganglionic spaces of his grey cortex.

All of which, from its length, forbids reference to the

rest of the Belfast meeting, except to mention Osler's discussion of the paper by his 'brother Regius' of Cambridge, on the subject of Angina, the varied pronunciation of which word was mirth-provoking.[1]

There followed three weeks of comparative quiet, or of as much quiet as 13 Norham Gardens, well filled even in the summer session, afforded. A breakfast guest brought good news of McGill and a note was promptly scribbled to F. J. Shepherd, with 'If Dr. Shepherd away Mr. E. Shepherd to open' on the envelope:

Dear Shepherd, [Principal] Peterson has been here to bkfast to tell me the good news of the ½ million bequest [from Strathcona] for the completion of the building—This is magnificent! Congratulations! This should clear all difficulties Yours ever Wm Osler. Tell Ernest's wife to tell Rita to tell my godson to keep an eye on her.

A photograph came from a little girl in New Hampshire, with this result:

2nd [August]

Dear Susan, Your picture with the pidgeons came to-day and I am delighted with it. You are an angel to have sent it. I never saw a sweeter picture. I do wish you were here that I might give you a hug & a kiss. How is my sweet Rosalie? Do be very kind to her & please do not wash her face too often—once a month is enough. You must come over next year—perhaps your mother will allow you to stay with us. Bring the dear Rosalie too—the other horrid girl can stay at home! unless she promises to be awful kind to Rosalie.

The usual visits were made to the Sanatorium at Mid-

[1] 'I wish I could say more on the point of W. O's generous and modest reticence on his own work and published opinions [writes Sir Clifford Allbutt of this episode]. Although I noticed it many times, yet they were fugitive instances hard to pin down. One small point does remain in my mind because it put me to a little shame. I once on some public occasion declaimed against angina pectoris, that it was no uncommon disease if one included mild degrees of it, and I described a mild form, and so on. W. O. was there and spoke also in agreement, never mentioning any work of his own; and some weeks later I turned up A. P. in W. O.'s last edition, and to my dismay found that he had formally divided A. P. into (four?) divisions (I write away from books), of which No. 1 was 'angineuritis' (!). I say to my dismay because I might have seemed to him to be a poacher; or was I overawed by his magnanimity? A little of both, but such minor points as these cannot be formally recorded—they are too evanescent or unsubstantial.

OSLER AND THE 'TABULAE SEX'

From a snapshot taken in the Selden End, July 1912

hurst; the Servetus paper was finished and read before the University extension-course students, some 1,600 in number, most of whom it would appear subsequently came to tea; a rare incunabulum or two was added to the library; a succession of visitors were taken for trips on the river, and to Ewelme of course, as well as to the old college libraries and gardens; Sir John Stirling-Maxwell loaned his original copy of Vesalius's 'Tabulae Sex' that had belonged to his father, Sir William Stirling-Maxwell, in care of the Bodleian for Osler and one of the visitors to see—an incident which led to the disclosure that a number of the reprints of these rare plates which were in existence had never been distributed; whereupon Sir John kindly sent copies to several libraries that Osler named.[1]

There had been, indeed, such an invasion of people that they finally escaped for two weeks as far away as they could get on the Cornish coast. So on August 28th Osler writes from Sennen Cove to H. B. Jacobs:

We have had a long summer—people coming and going all the time. . . . We came here a few days ago—such a lovely spot. We have a house for a couple of weeks & are enjoying the bathing. It is a mile from Land's End—such rocks & sea and so far glorious weather. The motor will meet us at Exeter & we shall take a week in Devon & Somerset on our way home. . . . I have my Servetus lecture ready for the Bulletin. I wish I could have gone to the Vienne celebration. Love to Mrs. Jacobs from us both & from Isaac Walton Jr. who took us out fishing yesterday & we were both seasick.

Back in Oxford, there were many things to engage him—one of them the needed preparation for the Schorstein Lecture he was to deliver. Accordingly on September 10th he writes to Dr. Maude Abbott of Montreal:

I have just returned from a holiday in Cornwall. I wrote you I think about the Strathcona gift, was it not splendid? I do hope that you will now be able to get the Museum in as short a time as possible. . . . Have you got that old specimen of mine of perfora-

[1] Osler had intended that the Press should reprint these anatomical tables in connexion with the quater-centenary of Vesalius's birth, to be celebrated in Brussels, December 1914—a celebration never held, for reasons which the date explains. An edition was subsequently issued by Professor Sudhoff of Leipzig in 1920.

tion of the aorta, formation of aneurysm, and perforation into the oesophagus? If so, you could get Klotz or someone else to make a section of the edge and of the aorta in the neighbourhood, to determine the histological lesion. Then you speak of two other cases of the same character—have they been studied histologically? I am giving a lecture on the 19th of October on aneurysm, and I would like very much to have the references early in the month.... Dr. Peterson will be here next week, and I shall have a talk with him too, on the museum question. Gardner also comes on the 15th. I think everything will go smoothly.

A shadow passed over him early in September in the death of Sir Stephen Mackenzie, whom he had first come to know in 1873 when studying in Berlin, and with whom he had since been fast friends. In an obituary note he said: 'The true gold of the man was shown in the heroism with which for years he fought an ever-strengthening foe—always cheerful, always facing his fate with unbowed head.' But from such a shadow Osler always quickly passed to sunlight. He usually sought diversion in children, and just now it was the little girl named Muriel Brock, who was introduced in Rome in the February past:

13 Norham Gardens, Sept. 11, 1909.

Dear Muriel, So glad to hear that you are coming to see me on Wednesday next. It was very nice to get your letter. I am sending this typewritten as on Saturdays I always write a very bad hand. I see you wrote yours on Wednesday which accounts for its goodness. Of course I have not forgotten you three saintly children; never did I meet such angelic, sweet, amiable, well-behaved, polite, neat, tidy well-mannered creatures. Please when you come bring your very best manners, because I have a boy whom I should not like to see you eat with your fingers and suck your thumbs at tea! Affectionately yours, Wm OSLER.

Sept. 20 [script]

Dear Muriel, Wicked girl! I was very glad you left your klyyyyydoscope [kaleidoscope]. I have been playing with it ever since. I am so sorry for your poor Auntie Margaret, she tells me that your behaviour there was even worse than at the Oslers'. I have not yet got leave from the Lord Chancellor to send that letter about children's behaviour at tea. He is a horrid old pig & perhaps it would be best if you wrote directly to him. Give my love to your Father & Mother.

Sept. 24 [script]

The Secretary of the High Cockolorum Lord Chancellor presents his compliments to Miss Muriel Brock & begs to inform her that the Lord Chancellor himself is at present engaged upon a handy manual dealing with the whole subject of table-manners for children. He asked me to say in addition, that being once at the Gaudy dinner at Christ Church, he sat next to Professor Osler, & was made painfully aware of the horribly teutonic character of that gentleman's table-manners, and he has instructed the Solicitor-General to bring an action against Dr. Osler should he dare to bring out his proposed tea-table manners for children.

Signed Obadiah Tweedledum,
General Secretary.

An explanation of these messages by their recipient follows :

The first time he came to tea with me and a few of my friends he behaved in a manner such as we had never before come across, and which delighted us immensely. For instance, he insisted upon cutting the cake from the *inside*, in squares ; and gave us cups filled with sugar, in which there were only two or three drops of tea. He also assured us (contrary to all previous teachings !) that it was absolutely the correct thing to lick all one's fingers one after the other after eating anything sticky ; and that the only enjoyable way of having bread and jam was a pile of jam on the plate with a few crumbs of bread in it, the whole of which one ate with a spoon ! He also said that the way to eat chocolates was to open your mouth and shut your eyes and have them thrown in by someone at the other side of the table. Every time he came he would invent some new amusement, and we found these things so pleasant that we asked him to write a treatise on 'Table-manners for Children' as he said our manners were atrocious and he felt we ought to have some sort of manual to guide us. He managed after some years' correspondence, to evade it by making up the letter of the Lord High Cockolorum. That is how it all came about, as far as I can remember.

The only satisfactory explanation of Osler's unforgetting memory for all the pet- and play-names he concocted on first acquaintance with the innumerable 'darlings' who came to know him—and not only the names but the incidents—lies in the reality of his play ; and his carryings-on for years with 'Susan' and Rosalie, with 'Muriel' and her table-manners, are merely examples chosen from many similar episodes, which had their origin in as many nurseries. They deserve a volume to themselves, could one be written out of 'thistledown and moonbeams', for of such elements, according to one of his playmates, the episodes largely consisted.

To Thomas McCrae from W. O. October 11, 1909.

Dear Mac, How goes the System? So glad to have the proofs coming so rapidly, which means I suppose that you will finish very soon. I suggested to the Leas a sort of summing up which would give an opportunity of adding certain recent additions. Did they ever speak to you on the subject? Arthur Lea I think was not very favourable. It would not do of course to make it too long. All well here. I am busy with the Schorstein Lecture on Syphilis & Aneurysm, & a Tropical School Introductory Lecture. Comfort T. B. F. Marriage is not such a hopeless state as many suppose. The 'Open Arms' has had a good season. I wish we could see you both here before long.

The first of the two lectures he mentions was delivered at the London Hospital four days later, an event which was immediately preceded by the formal opening of the new laboratories for physics, chemistry, and physiology at the London Hospital Medical College. The occasion gave him an opportunity to express in no uncertain terms what were his feelings in regard to the neglect of laboratory studies in most of the British medical schools; and subsequent comments upon his remarks say that 'they were divided between an appeal for research, and an impeachment of the University of London for not having found a way to provide a readily accessible M.D. degree for the industrious London student'. Of research, he said every student should cultivate it without thought of examinations; of the other subject, that there was 'something rotten in the State', and he advised the students present to organize and agitate in some constitutional manner, and insist upon their just deserts. Prof. M. J. M. Hill, the Vice-Chancellor of that mysterious body, the University of London, which had been reconstituted nine years before, supported Osler in this, saying that he had had occasion to look up the archives of the University, which consisted of a room full of documents all labelled 'Medical Grievances', and in this room was written 'All hope abandon ye who enter here'; adding that during the nine years no definite proposal had ever been put before the Senate by the Medical Faculty—all of which referred to a matter which was soon to be thrashed out at the hands of a commission appointed by Lord Haldane. The Schorstein Lecture[1] followed—an important and scholarly address on an 'ugly subject'—one dealt with, almost for the first time, in an incunabulum recently added to Osler's library, written by one Nicolaus Leonicenus:

> There are those [Osler said] who see only dark clouds lowering on the horizon of the newly opened twentieth century; but already within its first decade we may boast of three achievements of the very first rank, each illustrating in its special way the spirit with which humanity is tackling its eternal problems. The dream—no, the carefully thought-out plan—of Leonardo da Vinci has been realized in the conquest of the air; the final tribute to the enterprise and endurance of man has been paid at the North Pole; and a Sphinx has been forced to break the silence of four centuries.
>
> Syphilis has been one of the great riddles of the race. For generations it shared with malaria the peculiarity that we knew the cure without knowing the exact cause. As prevalent to-day as a century ago, problems of its origin and prevention have remained insoluble. In one direction our knowledge has widened greatly: it added terror to an already terrible disorder to know that such implacable and cruel foes as locomotor ataxia and general paralysis of the insane, to say nothing of a host of less important affections of the nervous system, were of syphilitic origin. And now after long years of patient research, the riddle of its origin has been read, and the brilliant work of the much-lamented Schaudinn has opened a new and hopeful chapter in the history of one of the greatest of human scourges. . . .

Mention of the 'Libellus de Epidemia' of Leonicenus (Aldus, 1497) as a recent accession to his library gives occasion to speak again of the provenance of the volumes in his collection, which of themselves furnish a profitable subject of biographical study. One of them has an association with an aged Don whose death occurred on the 23rd of this October. He had long been a Student of 'the House', incidentally an Alpine climber of note as well as Vicar of Binsey, a small Christ Church living, near Oxford. Osler had formed a particular attachment for this old gentleman, 'who could be as excited as any youngster when the House went the head of the river'; and whose death left a sad gap at the high table where Osler so regularly took his Sunday evening dinner. In the copy of Lachmann's

[1] *British Medical Journal*, Nov. 27, 1909, ii. 1509–14.

Lucretius, Berlin, 1850, is written 'T. J. Prout, Ch. Ch. Oxford, 1852', and below, in Osler's hand:

When I joined Ch. Ch. in 1905 Prout was one of the senior Students & had lived in the House since 1842. Shortly after my election he called, and when he found that I knew of his father the well-known physician ('Prout on the Stomach'), there was at once a bond of sympathy. He sent me the engraving of his father, now in my rooms at Ch. Ch. He was stone deaf so that it was very difficult to make oneself intelligible, & he kept very much to himself. He died in his 87th year. His sister asked each one of his fellow Students to choose a book from his library & I took this one to-day, Dec. 1st, 1909. There is a good notice of him in the Oxford Magazine. Wm Osler.

The 'Tropical School Introductory Lecture' was given October 26th under the auspices of the Seamen's Hospital Society, and in connexion with the opening of the winter session of the London School of Tropical Medicine. The American Ambassador, Whitelaw Reid, presided and introduced the chief speaker as a very excellent example of what the States could do with a Canadian when caught young. Osler's address, entitled 'The Nation and the Tropics',[1] as some one subsequently said, well illustrates the delightful manner in which he could present important and sometimes unpalatable facts:

It is no light burden [he said] for the white man to administer this vast trust. It is, indeed, a heavy task, but the responsibility of Empire has been the making of the race. In dealing with subject nations there are only two problems of the first rank—order and health. The first of these may be said to be a specialty of the Anglo-Saxon. Scarlet sins may be laid at his door—there are many pages in the story of his world-exodus which we would fain blot out; too often he has gone forth in the spirit of the Old Testament crying 'The sword of the Lord, and of Gideon'. But heap in one pan of the balance all the grievous tragedies of America and Australasia, the wholesale destruction of native races, all the bloodshed of India, and the calamities of South Africa, and in the other pan put just the one little word 'order', which has everywhere followed the flag, and it alone makes the other kick the beam. . . . There may be a doubt as to the grafting of our manners, and still greater doubt as to the possibility of inculcating our morals; a doubt also as to the wisdom of trying everywhere to force upon them our religion;

[1] *Lancet*, Lond., 1909, ii. 1401–6.

but you will, I think, agree that the second great function of the nation is to give to the inhabitants of the dependencies, Europeans or natives, good health—a freedom from plague, pestilence and famine. And this brings me to the main subject of my address, the control of the tropics by sanitation.

He went on to describe what he termed 'the new crusade':

Quietly but surely [he said] this great work has been accomplished by a group of patient investigators, many of whom have sacrificed health and life in their endeavours. Let us pause a moment to pay a tribute of gratitude to these saviours of humanity who have made the new mission possible—to Pasteur, to Koch, to Laveran, to Reed and his fellows, to Ross, Manson and Bruce. And let us not forget that they built upon foundations laid by thousands of silent workers whose names we have forgotten. A great literature exists in the contributions published during the past century by the members of the medical department of the old East India Company service, and of the army in both the East and West Indies. I should like to awaken in your memories the names of Lind, Annesley, Moorehead, Pringle, Ballingall, MacGregor, Hillary, Waring, Cheevers, Parkes, Malcolmson, and Fayrer. Many did work of the very first quality with very little recognition at home or abroad. I sometimes think of the pathetic letters received from that splendid investigator Vandyke Carter of Bombay, the first in India to confirm the modern studies upon malaria in the early days when we were both working on the subject; how he spoke of his isolation, the difficulties under which he struggled, the impossibility of rousing the apathy of the officials, and the scepticism as to the utility of science.

No one has expressed more deeply this sentiment of lonely isolation in the tropics than Ronald Ross in his poem 'In Exile':

Long, long the barren years;
Long, long, O God, hast Thou
Appointed for our tears
This term of exile.

Few have been able to sing with him the paean of victory, when he discovered the mode of dissemination of malaria through the mosquito—

Seeking His secret deeds
With tears and toiling breath,
I find thy cunning seeds
O million-murdering death.

And the pathway of victory is strewn with the bodies of men who have cheerfully laid down their lives in the search for the secrets of these deadly diseases—true martyrs of science, such as were

Myers, my friend and former assistant Lazear (both of whom died from yellow fever), Dutton and young Manson. Of them may fitly be sung in words from the noblest of all American poems, that in which Lowell pays a tribute to the young Harvard men who fell in the war of secession :

> Many in sad faith sought for her,
> Many with crossed hands sighed for her ;
> But these, our brothers, fought for her,
> At life's dear peril wrought for her,
> So loved her that they died for her.

With equally picturesque phrases he told the story of the Panama Canal, and though expressing some doubt as to whether the nations would ever find an outlet for their increasing populations by settlement in the tropics, he nevertheless outlined a wise plan of campaign and ended with this paragraph :

> When Isaiah was discussing the burden of Babylon, the burden of Tyre, and the burden of Egypt, I wonder what he would have said could his prophetic eye have glanced at the map on which is depicted the burden of the British Empire. Surely no nation in history has ever had such a load of responsibility. But fit as it has been in the past, it will ever be fit so long as *salus populi* remains *suprema lex.* It only behoves us to see that we are well equipped for the second great task—the task of the future, to give to the teeming millions of our great dependencies that greatest of all blessings in life, good health.

Osler was, of course, addressing those who were experts on ' the health side of the Empire ', but nevertheless handled his important subject in its broad aspects with an intimacy no less than their own ; and his words must have heartened those self-sacrificing people who with scant recognition from their Government were engaged in the warfare against the plagues of the tropics. He made an appeal for an Imperial Institute ' to represent the general staff of an army of sanitation, the expeditionary force of which could concentrate at any place and be used for education, investigation and supervision '. ' For church missions alone [he said] millions are contributed annually. It is not too much to ask for rich endowments for the missions of science.'

Sir Ronald (then Major) Ross, in seconding the vote of thanks for Osler's ' eloquent address ', said he had known the speaker for a long time, that he had a lot of grudges against him which he would not work off at the moment, for he had 'come to praise Caesar not to bury him'. It is possible that he had in mind an episode of No. 1 West Franklin Street. It must have been in the autumn of 1904 when Ross was on his way to see what was being accomplished by Gorgas towards the sanitation of the Canal Zone, and stopped *en route* for a few days' visit with Osler in Baltimore. Early in the morning the neighbouring household was aroused by shouts of delight, and saw from their windows overlooking Osler's back yard an Englishman engaged in an investigation of the various empty but water-holding window-boxes, flower-pots, and so on; and on being questioned as to his occupation, said with glee: 'I have found more mosquito-larvae in the garden of the Professor of Medicine of the Johns Hopkins than I expect to find in the entire Canal Zone.'

But 'the sword of the Lord and of Gideon!' Despite the King's visit to Berlin, where Bethmann-Hollweg had succeeded Prince Bülow as Imperial Secretary of State, the year had seen no abatement of the popular apprehension almost amounting to hysteria of the designs of a nation that felt she had 'no place in the sun'. There had been a play—'An Englishman's Home'—produced at Wyndham's Theatre; there were disquieting rumours about the 'two-power standard', and a party in the Cabinet was demanding large reductions in the navy estimates—four 'Dreadnoughts' instead of eight or more; the War Minister, Mr. Haldane, was advocating an Imperial Army, to include the Dominions, and was booming a Territorial Force; the suffragettes were making politicians exceedingly uncomfortable; Zeppelins were being built in Germany; Blériot, a Frenchman, had actually flown in an aeroplane across the protecting Channel; and the Balkan volcano was in its perennial state of threatened activity. The country greatly needed some wise psychotherapy for its state of nervousness, but governments had as yet provided no cabinet portfolio for this particular task. 'Order' is necessary for the sanitation of the tropics, and all these elements were threatening to disrupt a state of order. The only quieting thing was the fact that a young man, ‘ devout and serious in character,’ had succeeded to the throne of Belgium.

Barely a week after his Tropical School address he is found delivering the ‘ annual inaugural oration ’, as it is called, before the York Medical Society.[1] He spoke on ‘ The Beginning of Medicine ’—perhaps better ‘ Medicine’s debt to Greece ’—and evidently, to judge from the tenor of the customary vote of thanks and its rejoinders, had mistaken his audience ; for, expecting a purely medical one, he found the Dean of York and other divines, with many laymen, not to say laywomen, in the hall before him. At the time of his recent address in London he did not escape from an allusion to the ‘ Fixed Period ’, and so here the gentleman who proposed the vote of thanks was ‘ glad to see that the speaker had not yet reached the age when he should be chloroformed out of existence [laughter and applause] ’. Osler in reply simply said that he owed the major part of his audience an apology, and, having forgotten that he was expected to give a popular address, feared they had suffered from a very dull lecture ; still, they could have the satisfaction of not having understood him. For, when attending lectures beyond his own understanding, he always felt that the lecturer must be a man of considerable attainments (again laughter and applause). But one had to know Osler exceedingly well to know when he was bored. A banquet followed, with much afterwards by the Dean of York concerning the Church and doctors ; and Osler in his turn picked out some notable Yorkshire physicians for special comment : Martin Lister, James Atkinson, Dr. Burton, the original of Dr. Slop, together with Laurence Sterne himself, ‘ who should have been a doctor ’ ; and as Sterne’s bicentenary was coming so soon he needed a monument, which he (Osler) would like to design. So much trouble was he willing to take for others ; it was a red-letter day for the York Medical Society. But in these ways he came to know at first hand the profession of ‘ the Old Country ’ better, it has been said, than any other physician in it. Some weeks

[1] Quoted *in extenso* in the *Yorkshire Herald* for November 3rd, p. 8. The MS. of this address (unpublished) is among Osler’s papers. He used it again on May 29, 1910, as a lecture in Professor Gilbert Murray’s course.

previous to this, he had written to Mr. Phipps an undated letter from Oxford, saying:

> So sorry I did not know you were in town as I passed through this afternoon from Midhurst. I cannot possibly come to-morrow as I have returned for a Bodleian meeting about the extension & as I am Chairman of the sub-committee in charge I must be present. I hope you have enjoyed your Switzerland trip. The young men at the Sanatorium spoke very appreciatively of your visit. I am just stirring up an antituberculosis fight here. We are to have a big exhibit in November under the auspices of the university (I hope).

Ever since the brief holiday in Cornwall he had been deep in preparation for this exhibit. He had joined—indeed had been responsible for—the organization of an antituberculosis society for Oxfordshire,[1] at whose meetings he usually presided and of which he remained till his death the most active member. In scale, the activities of this small society were a marked contrast with the great national movement in the United States with which he had been identified; but he would never have stopped to make such a comparison himself. At the same time he was encouraging the work elsewhere; and on learning that the Irish association was meeting with opposition in regard to compulsory notification of the disease, even among the profession, he had written a widely published letter on the subject, meeting the arguments of the opponents in an emphatic but friendly way.

These long-planned 'tuberculosis exhibitions and conferences' were held in Oxford, November 8th to 13th. It was the beginning of the local campaign in which he took so prominent a part and of which there will be more to say later on. The only trace of this particular meeting is a page of memoranda, evidently the basis of his spoken address, divided into seven headings: the first a *General View of the Tuberculosis Campaign*, and the last, *Miss Price*—from which it is evident that Miss Mabel F. M. Price received some well-deserved compliments for her share in the work. Of all this he soon wrote to Mr. Phipps, saying: 'We have had a great meeting here. We are trying to stir up interest and

[1] A branch of the National Association for the Prevention of Tuberculosis.

get a dispensary started on proper lines. The exhibition was a great success.' Indeed, it was of more than local significance, for out of it grew the proposal by Dr. Robert Philip to hold an annual meeting of the national association, to be conducted on similar lines, Edinburgh rather than London being suggested as the next place of meeting.

A collection of books by or concerning Etienne Dolet, the martyr of the Renaissance, came under the hammer at about this time, a fact which accounts for the following letter of November 9th to H. B. Jacobs and its allusion again to Servetus—not a person to be easily dropped:

> We have not yet got the Dolet catalogue from Sotheby's. The American copies are sent out several weeks in advance of the English. I will bid for you in any items that I think would be of interest and likely to go at a reasonable rate. The Vienne celebration did not come off at all though advertised for August. The sculptor failed them, and there appears to have been a pretty mess. I was anxious to have a photograph of the new statue for my article, and wrote twice about it to the Mayor, and to Wolf the Paris photographer. I only heard about ten days ago from Maiot of Vienne that the celebration had been postponed for a year. I wish you would ask Miss Noyes to get for me the height of the Osler Room and the entrance hall. I am going to order a reproduction of the Æsculapius now at Naples, which formerly stood in the Temple on the Island in the Tiber. I suppose it would have to go upon a pedestal. If it is much more than a life-sized figure it might be like the Vicar of Wakefield's portrait. Sincerely yours, Wm OSLER. Glorious weather—after a shockingly wet season.

It was a sad day when he went to the Dolet sale three weeks later, for, as he wrote, 'the books all went in one lot to Quaritch, whether for single purchase or for sale I did not find out. The other items I wanted also went far above my bids. The two books of Champier (a man whom I collect) went for very high figures.' So, in spite of the many meetings and professional engagements which called Osler hither and yon, there runs an ever-strengthening under-current of bibliophilic interests through all this period. But these interests were by no means limited to accessions to his own growing collection. He was equally interested in book-making. At the Press the great Dictionary was in progress—indeed had been in progress the better part of

THE OXFORD UNIVERSITY PRESS

Inset, the Controller, Horace Hart, and Osler, a Delegate of the Press

twenty years;[1] and the workers, from James Murray down through the thirty sub-editors and their helpers, were kept cheered and amused in their stupendous task by the frequent visits of the Regius Professor of Medicine, whose pranks, as one of them recalls, made him the life of the place. With Horace Hart, the Controller of the Press at this time, no less than with Henry Frowde, the Publisher to the University, and his people at Amen Corner in town, he was on most intimate terms; and during this autumn there was issued 'at the Clarendon Press' a new edition of the 'Religio Medici' with Digby's 'Observations', 'printed from copies lent by Professor William Osler, the text following that of the first authentic edition of 1643, page for page and line for line.' Osler distributed many copies of this beautifully printed book, explaining in the note accompanying them that 'it is printed with perhaps the oldest font of type in use in England, that designed by Bishop Fell about 1660'. Then, too, the Burton books had by this time been got together at Christ Church, and on November 15th, the Monday after the close of the tuberculosis meeting, he read a paper on 'The Library of Robert Burton' before the Bibliographical Society, which holds its monthly meetings in London, at 20 Hanover Square.[2] A summary of this paper,[3] subsequently published in the *Transactions* of the Society (Vol. XI, p. 4) and lost there to general readers, deserves

[1] Projected in 1857, the first volume of this 'New English Dictionary on Historical Principles' (familiarly known as the N. E. D.) did not appear until 1888. On observing Dr. Murray one day as he emerged from the Old Ashmolean where the work was in progress, Osler remarked: 'The University pays me my salary to keep that old man alive till his eightieth birthday in 1917 when the Dictionary will be finished'. Sir James Murray, alas, died two years before that limit, and the colossal task he had before him is not yet fully completed.

[2] This society was founded by Walter Copinger, then Professor of Law at the Victoria University, Manchester, and apparently was the outgrowth of a paper which he read before the Library Association at its annual meeting in Reading, September 1891. Osler was elected to membership March 19, 1906; served on the Council after January 1910; was made Vice-President in December 1911, and President January 20, 1913, in succession to H. B. Wheatley; he held this office for the next seven years, until his death, when he was succeeded by Falconer Madan, Bodley's Librarian.

[3] The MS. of the paper, together with the lists of Burton's books, is in the Osler Library, and will probably be published.

to be rescued, as it explains the results of his browsings in the old college libraries, more particularly at Christ Church, in search of Burton's books:

Migrating from Brasenose College to Christ Church, Robert Burton lived, as he says, 'a silent, sedentary, solitary, private life' in the university, dying in 1639. Having Saturn as lord of his geniture, and 'fatally driven' (to use his own expression) upon the rock of melancholy, to ease his mind, and out of a fellow feeling for others, he composed his immortal work, 'The Anatomy of Melancholy'. He calls it a cento, a patchwork, laboriously collected out of divers writers, but *sine injuria.* He says with Macrobius '*Omne meum nihil meum*'—'It is all mine and none mine'.

'The Anatomy of Melancholy' has not always been understood, it is much more than—

> A mire, ankle deep of deliberate confusion,
> Made up of old jumbles of classic allusion.

It is a great medical treatise (the greatest ever written by a layman), orderly in arrangement, intensely serious in purpose, and weighty beyond belief with authorities. The sources are to be found in sacred and profane literature, to the time of Burton. There is probably no English author who quotes from so many writers on so many subjects.

As he says, he had access to good libraries in the Bodleian and Christ Church. His own library as disposed in his will, went in part to friends, in part to the Bodleian, and in part to Christ Church. His books are readily identified, as the name 'Robertus Burton' or 'R. B.' is written on the title-page of each, usually across the middle. Photographs were shown of some of the title-pages, and particular attention was called to Burton's curious cipher, usually at the bottom of the page, which looks as though it were made up of three *r*'s. The Bodleian books have been picked out and number 580. The Christ Church books, 429, have been collected together and now surround a portrait of Burton, copied from the original in Brasenose College.

Only a few of the books are annotated. There is a memorial verse for the tomb of King James, numerous astrological memoranda, a horoscope of Queen Elizabeth, and Burton's own horoscope, practically the same as that on his tomb in Christ Church. The most important part of the collection at the Bodleian is composed of seventeenth-century plays and pamphlets, the 'baggage books' which Bodley thought might bring scandal were the library stuffed with them.

Though by profession a divine, by inclination Burton was a physician, and there is no English medical author of the seventeenth century whose writings have anything like the same encyclopaedic character. The first two partitions form a great treatise on mental aberrations, preceded by a remarkable introduction, and diversified with digressions, as he calls them, one of which on 'Air rectified' is a treatise on climate in relation to health. There are about 86 medical works among the Burton books, none of which are of very great importance. Part III of the 'Anatomy' examines all the kinds of love, its nature, difference, objects, etc., and forms the most elaborate treatise ever written on the subject. Reference to all the love stories of sacred and profane literature are to be found in these pages. Among the Bodley books are scores of contemporary plays and an interesting 1602 edition of the 'Venus and Adonis'. Burton's favourite poets were Chaucer, Spenser, Daniel, Buchanan, Sydney, Ben Jonson, Toftes, and Challoner.

In many places Burton apologises that he should have been carried away by a bye-stream 'which as a rillet is deduced from the main channel of my studies'. He had ever been desirous to suppress his studies in Divinity. More than one half of the books are theological. From some of these he gets a few details for his remarkable section on Religious Melancholy, in many respects the most original in the work.

A complete set of the seventeenth-century editions, eight in number, was exhibited.

Of this meeting Osler makes brief mention in a letter written a few days later to one of the 'latch-keyers' in Baltimore, to whom he was evidently sending gifts:

Your books will leave next week—Morley has been so slow in repairing &c I will send direct to B. by a London steamer. Too big for the Smithsonian. Very busy—all sorts of things on hand—Tb., books &c. I had a great meeting at the Bibliographical Society. I had a good set of slides. My new Fraülein has gone over the 1080 Burton books looking for MS notes—only a few—his own very interesting—all the leading Bibliographs of London. I was their guest & as a member I took W. Buckler. We had a great eve.

And shortly after, to the same, on learning that a small surgical society was contemplating, as a body, a tour of the British clinics the following summer:

I think it would be great fun for the Wanderers to visit England next year, particularly in June, and you must give me a date for a dinner, wives &c included, at Christ Church; and we could have a medical séance in the amphitheatre of the Infirmary, & Thomson could demonstrate some of his anatomical treasures in the afternoon. I could get out a fine set of Bodley books so that they could have a profitable meeting, & we could finish up with a picnic on the

River, and a late supper at the 'Open Arms'! It will be a great spree. Give me the dates & I could arrange with the men in the different places with a minimum of friction. You would get a great reception everywhere, and the London men would be delighted.

All well here, in midst of exams, but not hard work. I have been going over some of the Ch Ch drawings of Raphael, L. da V. and Michael A. I forgot in my haste when you were here to show them. Marvellous collection & with them many anatomical sketches. The Windsor L da V drawings must have been made from first class dissections—whether done by L da V himself or Torre. You have seen them of course in the fasciculus at the Peabody. I got it the other day in Paris. They are the first modern dissections of the muscles—just compare them with all the early 16th century ones until Vesal. L da V was quite as capable of doing good dissections as he was of doing everything else & we know that he did plenty of dissections for his work on flight. . . . Yours sincerely, W. O.

PS. Deuce of a time at the Bodleian over fixed vs movable cases for the new storage rooms. All sorts of complications.

On December 8th the Oxford and Reading Branch of the B. M. A. met at Oxford, Osler giving the main address, on Arteriosclerosis. And as usual the entertainment he provided for the members of this small society was not only intellectual, but one hesitates to offer this explanation for the fact that such meetings were particularly well attended during these years. In an undated letter to H. B. Jacobs of about this time, he says:

Everything here is in full swing—so many meetings &c. Bodleian, Tb. [tuberculosis], Royal Med Soc. so that we have had a very long term. The weather has been splendid until recently. I have been keeping the examiners in good form this week. Did you see in Sotheby's catalogue the Jesse Foot 'Hunter', grangerized to three folio volumes. I lost it yesterday by 10s—worse luck! They might have had the sense to extend my bid a pound or two. I hope it has gone for one of the libraries. I could not find out. I have had the 1643 Religio reprinted at the Press & am sending copies as Xmas presents. You will have one next week. Ike is very well & beginning to work hard. We have a French girl living with us this winter—a great success. I am so glad you are arranging a suitable celebration for Welch. He deserves all he gets & more. Yours ever.

The examiners whom he had been 'keeping in good form' were those who during the Oxford examination week were always put up at 13 Norham Gardens, and had a very enjoyable time. However, they did not one and all

Physiology Paper
Conjoint Oxford & Cambridge
From the Regius Professor of Medicine, Oxford.
Boards Hilary Term 1660

1 A study of the hormonics of the body.

2 If you cut the depressor nerve and stimulate the central end, explain the effect on the dilators of the pupils

3 The relation of the parathyroid glands to the Islands of Langerhans.

4 Give a diagram of the centres in the Valve of Vieussens – what relation do the anterior pair bear to the Olivary bodies?

5 State the evidence in favour of an internal secretion of tauro-cholate of lithium by Küpffer cells.

6 If the filum terminale is cut, draw a diagram of the ascending degeneration as it affects the columns of Clarke & of Gowers at different levels.

Thomas Willis

Ex Aede Christi
1660

P.S. Where necessary, explain anachronisms

A FICTITIOUS EXAMINATION-PAPER

approve of their host's behaviour towards the candidates, whom he treated with no less informality than he did their examiners, as many of them—'Trotula' for example—will testify:

I was at that time [she says] working for the second M.B. and had been introduced through two mutual friends, the one a medical student, the other an aspiring lawyer who had recently left Oxford. To them Dr. and Mrs. Osler stood for the ideal man and woman, to them No. 13 Norham Gardens was a place of rest and delight known as the 'Open Arms'. Race, nationality, profession, creed, mattered little, so wide and catholic was the warm-hearted hospitality there, but to those who belonged even as students to his own profession, Sir William was always especially kind. I am speaking from my own experience. In every stage of my medical life, from the day of my first meeting, Sir William stood by me, a very present help in all days of need. The rare week-ends I spent with them stand out as the most delicious moments of rest in strenuous student days. The charm of the house, the daintiness of the room in which I slept, the inspiration of the wonderful library; but all dependent for their magic on the personality of the host and hostess. When I became engaged, my home being far away in Canada, my fiancé and I were both invited to spend a few days at the 'Open Arms', and we were urged to have our wedding from the house and to be married at Christ Church. Of course Sir William chaffed us very much, insisting that my career was ruined, that I no longer needed my head, having allowed it to give way to heart, and was mortally offended that my choice should have been a surgeon instead of a physician.

The amusing examination paper was written just before I went up for the physiology examination. It was to discourage me in my hopes of being able to pass. He gave me the name of 'Trotula' at my first meeting and never called me anything else. His delight was great at the general mystification of all my friends, including my medical friends, as to who or what Trotula was, and it was months before a friend managed to unearth her history for me. It turned out that she was a female surgeon of Salerno who lived about the middle of the eleventh century, was suspended for quackery, but later emerged triumphant and wrote several books.

The 'amusing examination paper' was a fictitious test in physiology for 'The Hilary Term, 1660,' signed 'Thomas Willis ex Aede Christi'. Later on, he writes:

December 20.

Dear Trotula, I am delighted to hear from you. I thought you were dead, and for months have had your memory enclosed in a melanotic border. What are you doing for Christmas? We should be delighted to have you here, & you could work hard, and I would guard your heart!

And still later, to the same:

Dear Trotula, I am so glad to hear—though not surprised—that the examiners were deceived. Considering how little you know of the higher physiology, as illustrated by my paper, you must have had shocking duffers as examiners on that subject. I still have hopes that you may be rejected at the University examination. Mr. Fenwick wrote the other day not very encouragingly, speaking of the London Hospital as the stone wall, but that is not much of an obstacle nowadays to women. I will come in and see you before long. Sincerely yours, Wm Osler.

From this he turns to write to Dr. Jacobs regarding a recently published catalogue of 'Rara Arithmetica' and to ask if he has ever seen Plimpton's collection of the old arithmetics. But Christmas draws near, and a card from her 'affectionate friend' goes to his 'dear Rosalie'. Also another to a variously named Muriel Brock:

Dear Marjorie, I thought your photograph so good and saucy. You looked just as if you had landed a piece of soft mushy cake in the middle of your forehead. I have been behaving so much better since I saw you, & Mrs. Osler often says how good your influence has been. No wonder your father and mother are such sweet people. I wish I could get away to Rome this winter but it is impossible. If I get my lectures ready on *Table Manners* I shall certainly come in the spring. Your affectionate friend Wm Osler. My love to those other dear sweet-behaved angels.

CHAPTER XXX

1910

THE LUMLEIAN AND OTHER LECTURES

'WE have had a very strenuous New Year—seven in the house over Sunday—such a jolly party', he wrote the next day. The party, of which he was probably not the least gay, had apparently gone to his head, for in a letter to H. A. Kelly the same morning he said: 'I dreamt of you last night—a very curious circumstance, you were plenipotentiary of England and America, dealing with two Chinese who were arranging terms after a successful overflow of the Chinese into Europe. How does the Biography progress?'[1] And also to H. V. Ogden: 'It was nice to get your letter and to hear that you are having disturbed nights with the children, which is a good deal better than having peaceful nights without them. How many chicks are there? Do you not think you could steal a week or ten days from work and come here? There is so much that would interest you. Give my greetings to our ochronotic friend.' The same day to the 'mother' of Rosalie:

> Dear Susan, It was so sweet and kind of you to send that nice photograph, I have got it in my room next the great big one which shows you feeding the pigeons; only I do feel a bit sad that you have not on your lap my darling Rosalie, instead of that stuck-up, overdressed, disagreeable, plain Marguerite! I do hope you have washed Rosalie's face for the year, & given her a clean petticoat & some new gloves! I am sending you a photo. Revere is at home, but is just going back to school. Give my love to your mother and father & the boys. I hope to see you in the summer, & then I shall bring back Rosalie to live with me. Please tell her & give her a kiss. Yours affectionately, Wm OSLER. o o o o for you o o o for Rosalie · for Marguerite.

With the beginning of the year had come a new steno-

[1] Howard A. Kelly was engaged in writing his two-volume 'Cyclopaedia of American Medical Biography, 1610–1910', published in 1912 and dedicated to Osler. On their appearance, Osler wrote a review of these volumes for his 'Men and Books' series (*Canadian Medical Association Journal*, Oct. 1912, ii, 938).

grapher, to whom he evidently dictated one paragraph of the following letter and found the process laborious :

To H. M. Thomas from W. O. Jan. 4, 1910.

[Dictated] Dear Harry T.—I will have the 'Petit' title-page and plate photographed for you ; the book could be sent here. I have asked also about Mistichelli, and if his Trattato is in London I will have it also photographed.

[W. O.'s script]. What a very superior secretary you have—such beautiful typography ! I have a fluffy-haird daughter of Heth who can read Middle English & Monkish cartularies, but is an awful dufferine as yet, but she is green & will I trust dry into something helpful. We have had a fine Christmas & New Year. You should see Ike dancing ! He is off to Winchester on the 19th—to a very good house—Mr. Little's. He has grown so much—up to my ear top. I am glad to hear good news of the boys. My love to them. Tell Hal there are some angels here whom I will try to keep at about his age till he comes as a Rhodesian. I am so glad you have got through your section. I have not got it yet. I have no doubt Mrs. Harry T's touches are the best part of it. . . .

Evidently H. M. Thomas's section for the 'System' (a long task now reaching its last and seventh volume) was on its way. But there were new tasks in sight, as he indicates in a letter to J. H. Pratt of Boston : 'I could not possibly come next spring', he says. 'I did not think the Congress was so near. I have got to work up my Angina Pectoris material for the Lumleian Lectures at the Royal College of Physicians in the spring.' One of Osler's excuses in going to Oxford, as may be recalled, was that he might have an opportunity to work over in quiet the immense mass of clinical observations of which he had notes—an idle dream for a man who was still in the current and was not likely to pull up and sit on the bank. There were, however, many other things to occupy him, and despite his youthful appearance—and behaviour, at times—he had reached the philosophical age which inclined him in his writings towards the broader aspects of medicine rather than the elucidation of specific disorders. This has been expressed in an appreciation by the Rt. Hon. H. A. L. Fisher, who says :

How well his friends remember the alert carriage and elastic tread, the soft, grave, playful manner, the ready quip, the fine deep-set eyes so dark, subtle and tender, the lofty well-moulded brow, and the air of decision and command which marked his bearing.

He never appeared to be busy or fussed, or to find a situation intractable. He did not, to all appearance, allow small things to worry him, but moved smoothly forward, enjoying all the blessings of life, always resolute to take human nature at its best and to seize every occasion for kindness which the day might offer.

How far he was able in later years to keep abreast of the march of science in the sphere of medicine is a matter on which I am incompetent to speak; but his activities were so many and various, and his exercise of hospitality so lavish and unceasing (for he and Lady Osler kept open house in Norham Gardens) that it is difficult to imagine that he can have found as much time for study as he could have desired. I have always, however, imagined that he had come to the conclusion that after the creative period of early manhood had been passed, the most valuable employment for his energies lay in the direction of giving elevation and breadth to medical studies, of illustrating the unity and interdependence of fields of experience and inquiry which are too often cultivated apart from one another, and of infusing a spirit of fresh and vital interest into every region of the great domain which was committed to his charge. If this were indeed his aim he succeeded in achieving it; if it were not, then like many other great men 'he builded better than he knew'...

The week of January 17th found him laid up with the recurrence of an acute and painful malady from which he had suffered once before in his Baltimore days; and his account-book contains a daily entry regarding his paroxysms. But as on the previous occasion when he had sent a pebble from his garden for the Professor of Chemistry to analyse, pretending it was the stone he had passed, so now he assumed a playful attitude towards his ills—a complaining one would have been foreign to him. Thus on a postcard to H. M. Thomas, after four days of it:

Your section is AA.1 and no mistake! It is one of the best things I have read & you have taken the whole subject so sensibly and on quite new lines. I do not know of any system in which the question is considered so thoroughly and so clearly. Congratulate Mrs. H. T. & your secretary. You really have a very happy way of putting things. Very few mistakes. I sent a few galley proofs back to T. McCrae. I am in bed with another attack of renal calculus—rt. side. You remember the one 8 years ago in which I passed the unique quartz stone. This has lasted longer & I have enjoyed the luxury of two hypodermics. I am writing flat on my back which improves my hand-writing! Love to Z., M. & the boys. Yours, W. O.

With Osler laid up and unable to attend the various committee meetings of this week, of which otherwise there would be no record, it becomes possible to get a glimpse of one at least of these sessions through the following exchange of notes:

From Professor Arthur Thomson. University Museum, Oxford. Jan. 21, 1910.

Dear Osler,—The Standing Medical Committee of Council meets Tuesday, Jan. 25th at 3.30 to consider the question of Pharmacology. Enclosed is a copy of the memorandum I propose to submit to them. I hope you approve. Will you support this appeal by a strong letter which I could read? Hudson Bays are up again I see; isn't Strathcona now in a position to help towards the endowment of the Chair?

Osler's undated reply follows: it was probably sent immediately:

Dear Thomson, I approve most heartily of your memorandum. The four lines of progress for our school are Pharmacology, Hygiene, the History of Medicine, & a clinico-pathological laboratory in connection with the Infirmary. Of them, the first is a pressing need. Everywhere, I am sorry to say except in this country the science of Pharmacology is making rapid strides, & the subject is universally recognized as of the first importance in university work. Moreover, it is one of the hopeful progressive departments of medicine, with great possibilities for public service. I can testify in the strongest possible way to the work of Prof. Abel and his department in connection with the Johns Hopkins Medical School. There are no classes more popular & the researches that have been carried on have been very valuable.

We should ask for the endowment of a full professorship—if done, let us do it thoroughly. Lord Strathcona promised a bequest for the purpose but when the financial crisis came withdrew. Since then he has given a large bequest to the Medical School at Montreal & I have hesitated to go to him again. I will do so, however, within the next few weeks, with success I hope. Yours W. O.

Four days later, he says on a postcard to Jacobs:

T. B. F. will have told you of my rocky experience. Got rid of it yesterday (Uric acid). It took a week of squirming. Gout, I suppose. I shall live on aq. destil. & hominy grits. I am feeling a bit shaken, but very well. Very good haul of old books at Hodgson's last week. Do you get their catalogues? Tommy writes very content from Winchester. He has had a good winter so far. I do hope we may arrange to meet on the Continent. I am going to Congress of Internal Med., Wiesbaden, end of April.

During this sharp illness, which looked for a time as though recourse would have to be taken to surgery, he must have been cogitating over the ultimate disposition of his 'Practice of Medicine'. So in a long letter to L. F. Barker on the 25th, in which he speaks of himself as 'no longer in active work, rather in the rear guard than in the van', and with the intent of having the volume kept up in some way in connexion with the medical department of the Hopkins, he proposes that his successor reconstitute and rearrange the Text-book on new lines so that the 1912 edition would be a really new work, the publishers to issue a circular to the teachers. In short 'the business heretofore conducted by Osler (Humpton) [1] & Co. would be for the future conducted by Barker (Humpton) & Co. at the old stand'. 'Naturally,' he continued, 'I have a strong sentiment about the book, but I know quite well that the life and success of a work depends upon the life of the man, and it is quite to the interests of the publishers as well as my own, to make provision for a gradual or immediate transfer of editorial control.' [2]

As in his actions, so there are constant reminders in his letters of Osler's unforgetting memory of his old boyhood companions, his teachers, his colleagues, his friends, his pupils, and of the children of all of them—across the sea. His successive migrations—Toronto, Montreal, Philadelphia, Baltimore and Oxford—might have been expected to lessen his hold, but this he never permitted. So it is not surprising to find him at this time engaged in erecting a memorial window to Dr. Wright, one-time Professor of Materia Medica at McGill, over whom the students had had such a rumpus in 1883, and who subsequently became ordained and joined the staff of clergy in 'the little church around the corner', St. John the Evangelist. And though Osler hinted that the suggestion came from Father Wood, the Rev. Arthur French has already (Vol. I, p. 75) explained it otherwise.

[1] Miss B. O. Humpton, Dr. Osler's secretary during his entire Baltimore period, had become Dr. Barker's secretary in turn.

[2] For various reasons this proposal was withdrawn in a letter of April 25th.

To F. J. Shepherd. 13 Norham Gardens, Jan. 26, 1910.

When in Montreal in June, Father Wood spoke to me of a memorial window to Dr. Wright, & I told him that I would be very glad indeed to subscribe to it. I forget whether I mentioned the matter to you; I did to Roddick and Gardner. French has written saying that the window has come! Of course there are not many left in the Faculty who remember the old man. Let me know if there is anybody left to whom I could write. I hope the Mills pension scheme will go through, it would be a great matter to have a new man starting the laboratory, & Mills is evidently not fit for much. He deserves recognition as he has worked hard at a very low salary. Love to Dorothy and Cecil. Sincerely yours, Wm Osler. PS. I am sending to the Library a very interesting photograph, which Payne has just given me, of Banister's anatomical lecture, from the painting in the William Hunter Library.

To H. B. Jacobs. Feb. 4.

I am all right again—no further colic or rocks. We were very sorry to hear of Mrs. Gilman's death. She had a splendid life & was a fine figure in the Hopkins history. We are having a busy term. I am deep in Bodley matters—struggling with the underground storage stack. The machinery here needs oiling badly—too many bosses & not enough money. Splendid weather & such bright clear days. Tommy writes in such good spirits from Winchester—no homesickness or worries. As the new boy he has to pay for his gallery (dormitory), & an early duty is to call the boys at 6.30, go back to bed and call them again at 6.35, 6.40 and 6.45. The boys have a special language of their own, nearly 400 words which a new boy—or rather man as the boys are called men—has to learn within the first fortnight ∴ he is assigned a senior boy as Pater or instructor & if at the end of a fortnight the words are not known the Pater has the privilege of spanking the new boy. I shall not be able to order the Æsculapius this year. I have had to subscribe to the new building of the Royal Med. Society, London—pour encourager les autres! & that has taken my spare cash—but it will come later. . . .

'Desolated', as he expressed it, by Revere's absence, they soon motored down to spend a Sunday with him, and came away charmed with all they had seen. 'Splendid school—such nice boys in the house', he wrote in characteristic vein. So he radiated enthusiasm. In one of his wife's letters at that time she says that on coming home from a business meeting at Christ Church he had exclaimed: 'This is a delightful life and place—so many nice men'; and she adds: 'Isn't it wonderful how he adapts himself to these changes.' Adaptability was unquestionably his long suit, and was what made him so acceptable a companion. On the 25th he sent a 'bread-and-butter' note to G. H. F. Nuttall of Cambridge, which says briefly: 'Many thanks for a delightful visit. I enjoyed the dinner so much. It was a great treat. My regards to Mrs. Nuttall & love to those dear children'—in explanation of which Professor Nuttall writes:

He stayed with us at 3 Cranmer Road, Cambridge, coming as my guest to attend our annual dinner in memory of Samuel Pepys. The chief speaker who was to respond to the memory of S. P. failed us at the last moment, and I appealed to Osler to come to the rescue about one hour before the dinner. He consented willingly, and asked for my copy of the famous Diary on the last blank page of which he jotted down some data hastily in pencil—I have the Diary to-day. He made an admirable speech, one of the best, showing a deep knowledge of Samuel and his times, and touching on matters mostly *not* in the Diary.

Osler's own version of this occurs in a letter of the 25th, in which he says:

Allbutt will send you in a few days the Pepys menu, Magdalene College, Cambridge. I was there on the 23rd—P's birthday, when they have an annual gathering. In the absence of Lord Grenfell I had to respond to P's memory—& fortunately had enough to say something. Such a delightful occasion. If A. does not send it, let me know. I will send mine. . . . Ike comes tomorrow for a 'leave out' day. He is very happy at school. I am pegging away at my Lumleian Lectures—Angina pectoris, trying to put together my personal experiences.

The Lumleian Lectures of the Royal College of Physicians were on an ancient foundation—indeed 'in 1581 in the twenty-fourth year of Elizabeth, Dr. Richard Caldwell a former President of the College in conjunction with the Lord Lumley' founded what was 'commonly called in their annals The Chirurgical Lecture, and endowed it with a rent charge of forty pounds a year on their lands and on those of their heirs forever'. Formerly an elaborate yearly course of surgical lectures had been given, but these had long since been done away with and replaced by a series of three with an honorarium of £30, on some subject in the domain of clinical medicine. Osler's lectures on this foundation were given on March 10th, 15th, and 17th. It was not his first appearance before the College in the rôle of one of its appointed lecturers, as his introductory paragraph explains; moreover he had chosen to speak for a second time on a cardiac disorder:

Twenty-five years have passed since I stood here, a much embarrassed junior, as Goulstonian Lecturer. I have always had a keen sense of gratitude to the College for according recognition to a colonial worker at the time of life when such an action counts for so much, and I recall the intense pleasure of my colleagues at Montreal that one of their number had been selected for the honour. The subject of those lectures came within the ken of the younger Fellows, whose work is, or should be, largely in the post-mortem room and laboratory. And now kindly time has moved me among the seniors, and I have to thank you Sir [addressing the President, Sir R. Douglas Powell], for the opportunity to deliver the course distinguished among all others in the College, since in these Lumleian Lectures the incomparable Harvey laid the sure foundations of modern experimental medicine.

I make no apology for the subject I have chosen—Angina Pectoris. In a very special way it is *our* disease, having been first fully described at this College by the English Celsus, William Heberden, and in a manner so graphic and complete as to compel the admiration and envy of all subsequent writers. Like books, diseases have their destiny. Could Heberden return for a month's busy practice his surprise would be not less at the new cohorts of disease than at the disappearance of familiar enemies. How staggered he would be at the *Nomenclature* of the College! And he would be keen to write new commentaries upon old diseases with new names. How the word appendicitis would jar his critical ear, but how rejoiced he would be to see light on that dark malady, 'inflammation of the bowels'. Living through a century of theory, he died at the outset of the great awakening in clinical medicine, bequeathing a precious legacy of experience greatly appreciated by several generations of students, and leaving in this College a precious memory which it is our delight to cherish.

Looking through the famous 'Commentaries', one is impressed with the value, with the rarity too, of the old-fashioned, plain, objective description of disease; and one is impressed also with the great gulf which separates the clinical medicine of to-day from that of our great-grandfathers. Page after page of the 'Commentaries' are as arid as those of Cullen or of Boerhaave, and then we light upon an imperishable gem in the brilliant setting of a master workman, whose kinship we recognize with the great of old—with Hippocrates, with Aretaeus, and Sydenham. Such a clinical gem is the account which Heberden read at the College, July 21st, 1768, 'of a Disorder of the Breast', to which he gave the name 'Angina Pectoris', based on the study of twenty cases. When he incorporated the description in his 'Commentaries' (written in 1782) his experience had extended to 100 cases. . . . For more than a century the chief contributions to the pathology of the disease have been made by members of this society, and to-day our Fellows number many of its best known students, among whom, Sir, you rank *primus inter pares*. And yet so far as I can ascertain, angina pectoris has never been formally considered in one of the College courses. It is, too, a disease for a senior to discuss, since juniors see it but rarely; indeed I had reached the Fellowship before I saw a case in hospital or private practice. And then I take it that in this course the College wishes an expression of opinion on some affection to which the lecturer has paid special attention. . . .

This was typically an Oslerian method of introducing his subject, and the three lectures are coloured throughout with the victims of the history of this remarkable disease of which in its tragic form he had had an experience perhaps as great as that of any living physician. 'It is the quickest death we see,' he said; 'and is that which may have been in John Henry Newman's mind when he penned the lines describing the death of his mother.' And so on, to the end, when with an allusion to the 'De Rerum Natura' of Lucretius—the book he had chosen from T. J. Prout's library the previous December—he closed the last lecture.[1] This burden lifted, he wrote a few days later to H. B. Jacobs:

26th [March]

You will perhaps see Mrs. Osler before you get this as she sailed by the Lusitania on Saturday (20th). Harry Chapin's illness is a sad

[1] One section of the address, which deals with 'Angina in Doctors', deserves at least a footnote. 'A point [he said] that stands out prominently in my experience is the frequency of the disease in our profession. For the same reason, doubtless, that Sydenham gives for the incidence of gout, "more wise men than fools are afflicted", angina may almost be called "morbus medicorum". Thirty-three of my cases were in physicians, a larger number than all the other professions put together. Curtin in his study of sixty fatal cases notes that a fourth were in physicians. This large percentage in my list may in part be attributed to the circumstance of the publication of lectures on the subject in 1897. But the frequency with which doctors die from the disease has become the subject of common remark. From John Hunter onwards, a long list of most distinguished men have been its victims. Not to mention the older physicians, among our contemporaries was Nothnagel, himself one of the ablest students of the disease, whose last act in life was to describe his own fatal attack . . . In

tragedy for the family as he is the pivot member. If she waits I may not be able to get to Wiesbaden, as I should not care to leave Revere alone. The autograph copy of Browne went for £17. Stupidly, I sent a bid for 252 instead of 482, at least they say so, & missed it, but they wired that the man would sell with an advance of £1, so I have it. I have never seen an autograph copy of the R[eligio] They must be very rare. I got the Locke book—of which I had not known & the London edition of the Cenci for 10*s*. We have had the most wonderful weather—nearly three weeks of sunshine. I have been in town a great deal, meetings & my Lumleian lectures. I had the record audiences of the College. Love to Mrs. Jacobs. Yours ever, Wm Osler. I knew you would like the catalogues—some gems among them.

No wonder he had 'the record audiences'. Nothing could have been better than a series of lectures out of his own experience—with only enough allusion to the history of the subject to serve as a background. But they must have given his new secretary a deal of trouble. In subsequent letters he apologized for the fact that his 'Fraülein' had forgotten to forward a certain package of books, saying: 'She must have overlooked it—poor girl—bedevilled as she has been—and still is—with my angina lectures.' This sounds a little more sympathetic than the episode related in the following letter to his little friend Muriel Brock, for whose sake he interrupted for a few minutes the further typing of Lumleian Lectures:

13 Norham Gardens,
March 31, 1910.

Dear Muriel-Marjorie-Maude!—Your mother told me in Rome

---

a group of twenty men, every one of whom I knew personally, the outstanding feature was the incessant treadmill of practice; and yet if hard work—that "badge of all our tribe"—was alone responsible, would there not be a great many more cases? Every one of these men had an added factor—worry; in not a single case under fifty years of age was this feature absent, except in Dr. G., who had aortic insufficiency, and who had had severe attacks of angina years before, probably in connexion with his aortitis. Listen to some of the comments I jotted down, of the circumstances connected with the onset of attacks: "A man of great mental and bodily energy, working early and late in a practice, involved in speculations in land"; "domestic infelicities"; "worries in the Faculty of Medicine"; "troubles with the trustees of his institution"; "lawsuits"; "domestic worries"; and so through the list. At least six or seven men of the sixth decade were carrying loads light enough for the fifth, but too much for a machine with an ever-lessening reserve . . .

last winter that you were first baptized Marjorie, and only on account of some objection on the part of your grandmother your name was changed to Muriel. And then because of your other grandmother not liking either of these names so well as the one with which she was baptized for the first time in 1806, when in Scotland, having been accidentally born there, much to her disgust, she wished you to be called Maude ; so now I am going to call you whichever I wish. What I liked about your letter particularly was the spelling. It shows the advantage of having nice parents and good teachers, and hard work at school. I cannot come to Rome this spring ; on the even-alternate years my wife is very cross in the spring, and only allows me out every other day, and I could not possibly get away as far as Rome. Let me know when you come to England. The picture on the back of your letter was exceedingly rude. Hermanda Jane's left leg should have been straight out from her side, not as you have got it with a rectangular obliqueness.

Give my love to your father and mother, for whom I am always awfully sorry, and you know the reason why ! I am awfully sorry to hear that you have had oldmonia ; how horrid of you. I suppose that Dante-esque old rival of mine, Professor Stewart, has quite stolen your heart ; he is a thoroughly bad man, given over to all sorts of wickednesses in philosophy. I have not had a decent cup of tea since last winter with you and those angelic friends of yours. Give them my love. [The letter is type-written up to this point ; and he continues in script :]

My boy is so horrid—has turned into a Winchester man ! He has just come home. I had to go on in ink with this, as my fluffy-headed stenographer struck her fist on the table, and said she did not come here to take down nonsense—not she, not from any man ! What do you think I said ? Nothing—but I gave her a basilisk look, & she fainted dead away & is groaning with her fluffy head in the waste-paper basket & there she can stay until I finish this. Mrs. Osler has gone to America leaving me in charge of a black-eyed Canadian girl, my grand-daughter once removed, who is leading me a pretty dance. Your affec. friend, Wm Osler.

PS. 1. My love & sympathy (to and with) your poor parents.

PS. 2. The fluffy-headed vestal still groans. An envelope & two sheets of paper protrude from her mouth—the basket just fits her head.

PS. 3. I have just had a photograph taken of her.

PS. 4. She has recovered & I am leaving quick—Good-bye.

Meanwhile preparations were in train for the many meetings which crowded themselves into the late spring and early summer months; one of them he mentions in the following letter:

NATIONAL ASSOCIATION FOR THE PREVENTION OF CONSUMPTION AND OTHER FORMS OF TUBERCULOSIS

Annual Meeting and Conference in Edinburgh, July 2nd–5th, 1910

President of Conference, Prof. Osler, M.D., F.R.S.

13 Norham Gardens,
April 15, 1910.

Dear Jacobs,—. . . I wish you could see how beautiful the country is beginning to look. I shall not go to Wiesbaden; Mrs. Osler does not return until the 19th, and the meeting begins on the 18th, so that I would have to leave tomorrow. I shall probably join you in Paris later for a week. It was delightful to get the account of the Welch dinner. What a splendid occasion! There is nowhere in the world where such things are managed so well.[1] Mrs. Osler wrote me that she was delighted with the bronze [for Osler Hall]. I have not half thanked you and Mrs. Jacobs for your kindness in the matter. Revere has been off in Wales for a week, and had some very good fishing. Your rod has been a great delight to him. He went with one of the crack salmon-fishers in England, so that he is getting some good lessons. You will see by this paper-heading that we have an annual meeting in Edinburgh, of which I am the President. We had an interesting conference yesterday, young Waldorf Astor has undertaken to finance an active anti-tuberculosis campaign. . . .

From among those who at one time or another had more or less intimately crossed Osler's path there were several losses at about that time. Isabel Hampton Robb had ended her splendid career on April 15th; on the 21st Mark Twain had died of the disease the subject of the Lumleian Lec-

[1] The Welch dinner was held at the Belvidere Hotel, Baltimore, on April 22nd, his election to the presidency of the American Medical Association being the excuse made for it. As Osler said, nowhere do they manage these things better, and in no place are they so apt to pay tributes other than posthumous ones. There were five hundred guests; Thayer presided, Councilman, Halsted, Flexner and others of the 'old guard' spoke—most amusingly, be it said, and with many reminiscences of the early Hopkins days; Weir Mitchell read a poem; Leonard Wood spoke; and it was the small hours of the morning when it came the turn of Welch to reply and to acknowledge the gold medallion which had been presented to him, replicas of which all the guests received. Osler lamented greatly his absence, sent a cable of congratulations, and wrote an appreciation of Welch which was published in the *American Magazine*, Aug. 1910, lxx, 456.

tures; his old Montreal friend and colleague Arthur Browne had gone not long before; on the 20th Mrs. Osler's brother-in-law died; King Edward on May the 6th; Robert Koch on the last of the month; and J. F. Payne was nearing his end. The scholarly Payne, of whom Osler probably had seen more than of any other member of the Royal College of Physicians, had shortly before retired from the Harveian librarianship because of ill health and gone to his country home at New Barnet, whence there issued many letters to Osler relating to their common historical and bibliographical researches:

You asked me [Payne wrote on April 19th] whether I knew of any good sketch of the evolution of medicine in Great Britain. I must confess I know no such work either good or bad. Aikin and others tried to do something of the kind, but never got further than biography, which is not the same thing. There are really not the materials. I find in my A. S. [Anglo-Saxon] Lectures that we had neglected the History of English Medicine even more than the History of Medicine in general. But when we get Power's John Arderne, and Cholmeley's Gaddesden, with my F. P. [Fitz-Patrick] Lectures on some more people, there will be some materials for such a history, if any one will take the trouble to write it.

And again on the 27th Payne wrote: 'I was quite taken aback by the flattering proposal in your letter that I should sit for Sargent, and that this very great honour was intended for me by the Library Committee, including yourself, whom I strongly suspect of having originated and advocated the scheme.' This business of getting portraits painted or drawn was no new thing for Osler: he was not one to wait for their demise before venturing to pay a tribute to those he admired. So he now dragged in Mr. John S. Sargent when he could; and the artist no longer appears to have stencilled the Regius Professor's letters as he did on a former occasion. Indeed not many weeks elapsed before Osler wrote again:

Dear Sargent, Could you arrange to do a Black and White of my friend Dr. Musser of the University of Pennsylvania: he is at the Piccadilly Hotel for two days & could call at any time. Send him a wire. Do you think it would be possible for you to give us a sketch for our tuberculosis campaign that could be reproduced on a postcard? Anything would do from a caricature of J. Wm White to the bacillus attacking a modern Mona Lisa. The general verdict at the College is that you have hit off our good friend Payne to the life.

In the waste-paper-basket letter to 'Muriel-Marjorie-Maude' he had mentioned being in charge of a black-eyed Canadian girl, his 'grand-daughter once removed'—in reality the daughter of his old McGill schoolmate, H. P. Wright. She and an actual niece had been staying all the spring at 13 Norham Gardens, to the not inconsiderable distraction of the Rhodes scholars. These young ladies were to have been presented at Court—Canada could not possibly have produced better representatives—but this had been prevented by the King's sudden death, and to atone for their disappointment Osler took them, later on, to the Continent for a week's frolic. All this is made clear in a letter on a 'Monday' to H. B. Jacobs:

Harry Chapin died on Saturday—poor fellow. 'Tis awfully hard on them all. He was a trump & such a helpful man to so many people. In such a disease it is better to have it over quickly. We had thought of going to Holland first, but now our plan is to go direct to Paris about the 1st. We shall take over two girls—Nona G and Ottilie W—both plain, but very sweet; our style! It is awfully sad about the King, but at 69 a short, sharp illness is a mercy. King George will be all right; he seems a very sensible fellow. It will be so nice to see you again & to have you with us in Edinboro.

On May 16th he wrote to J. William White, who was spending his summer energetically at St. Moritz:

I was under the impression that I had written to you from the Athenaeum Club after seeing Henry James. It may have been only one of my many good intentions. He has been in a very bad way, profoundly depressed about himself, with no positive delusion, but awfully blue and unhappy. His nephew Henry James Junior, came over and stayed with him for a time, and now William James has been here and has temporarily left Mrs. James in charge. W. J. does not write very hopefully. . . . It is a very sad business, more so as he has greatly improved physically. He wrote to me about eighteen months ago describing certain unpleasant anginoid symptoms; these have disappeared entirely. I do hope you are coming over; the influence of your personality on him might be very salutary. For two or three days after my visit to him in town he seemed a different man, was able to get about, and promised to come down and stay with us; then he suddenly lapsed, and decided

THE TERRACE AT 13 NORHAM GARDENS

to go home [to Rye].[1] Do let me know when you arrive. My boy is at Winchester working hard at cricket and entomology, but I am afraid like his father he is going to be a frivolous loiterer through life. Love to Mrs. White. . . .

It was a strange friendship—that of White and Henry James. Two men could hardly have been more unlike in their characteristics and tastes—no three men, indeed, more unlike than James, White, and Osler. But another man whom White greatly admired and who possessed an equally volcanic type of physical energy had emerged from the wilds of Africa not long before, and was now enjoying himself big-game hunting in Europe. Roosevelt, between his visits to crowned heads, for whom in their jobs he expressed great sympathy, had already lectured at the Sorbonne on 'The Duties of the Citizen in a Republic'; the day before King Edward's death he had given at Christiania his Nobel Lecture in which he suggested a 'World Court', the checking of armaments, and a League of Peace; had spoken in Berlin on the 11th on 'The World Movement'; and was now due in Oxford for the Romanes Lecture, to which the following refers:

From Rudyard Kipling to W. O. Burwash,
May 18, 1910.

Dear Osler,—It is extremely kind of you to think about us for the Romanes Lecture (I thought you were in Canada or I'd have written you). The Vice-Chancellor has just wired me that the date is changed to June 7th, and says he is writing. He asked us to stay with him, and hear the lecture, which we greatly want to do. No (talking of lectures), I did not get the lectures on Servetus or 'The Nation and the Tropics'. Please send 'em along. I've just finished my new book of children's tales and shall be curious to see whether the profession will spot Dr. Nicholas Culpeper and René Hyacinthe Laennec as I have drawn them. With the best regards to you both,
Ever yours sincerely.

---

[1] Henry James's nephew writes of this visit: 'Osler frisked around him, jollied him, poked fun at him, told him (in Greek) that his only trouble was that he was revolving round his belly-button, &c. He prescribed a reasonable regimen and imported a nurse who was to give massage. But that involved the sort of mistake I don't believe Osler made often. It would have required constant and authoritative supervision to make my uncle stick to any regimen. Still, it was a reassuring and refreshing episode.'

The Romanes Lecture was postponed until June because of the national mourning for the King, whose funeral did not take place until May 20th. Meanwhile, what is more pertinent to this memoir, Osler had a lecture of his own to deliver. This was given at the request of Professor Gilbert Murray, who writes: 'Every year I organize a course of lectures on Greek subjects outside the general course—Greek Medicine, Greek Astronomy, Greek Mathematics and the like, in which I invite specialists to come and lecture. Osler was always interested in this course and helped me more than once.' Accordingly, on the 29th of this month, Osler spoke on 'The Lessons of Greek Medicine', using doubtless the same material which had served him at York the preceding October. 'The tap-root of western civilization sinks deep in Greek soil, the astounding fertility of which is one of the outstanding facts of history.' So begins the lecture, the MS. of which is among Osler's many unpublished papers.[1]

Philosophy, as Plato tells us begins with wonder; and, staring open-eyed at the starry heavens on the plains of Mesopotamia, man took his first step in the careful observation of Nature, which carried him a long way in his career. But he was very slow to learn the second step—how to interrogate Nature—to search out her secrets, as Harvey puts it, by way of experiment. The Chaldeans who invented the gnomon, and predicted eclipses, made a good beginning. The Greeks did not get much beyond trained observation, though Pythagoras made one fundamental experiment when he determined the dependence of the pitch of sound on the length of the vibrating cord. So far did unaided observation and brilliant generalization carry Greek thinkers, that there is scarcely a modern discovery which by anticipation cannot be found in their writings. Indeed one is staggered at their grasp of great principles. Could Democritus give the opening address at the new electrical laboratory he would maintain that his well known exposition of the physical world had received renewed support by all the recent studies. Man can do a great deal by observation and thinking, but with them alone he cannot unravel the mysteries of Nature. Had he been able, the Greeks would have done it; and could Plato and Aristotle have grasped the value of experiment in the progress of human knowledge the course of European history might have been very different.

---

[1] He extracted some of its paragraphs for subsequent addresses, as for his Edinburgh 'lay sermon' of July 2nd.

And from this he proceeded to deal with what he considered to be the great lessons to be learned from Greek Medicine, stressing that 'what Socrates did for philosophy, Hippocrates did for Medicine'; and that the special merit of the Hippocratic school 'may be said to lie in the development in the powers of observation, and on the strong, clear common sense, which refused to be entangled either in theological or philosophical speculations'.

> But the high-water mark [he said] is reached in that remarkable document, the Hippocratic Oath, which has been well called a monument of the highest rank in the history of civilization (Gomperz). For twenty-five centuries our 'credo', it is in many universities still the formula with which men are admitted to the Doctorate. At McGill we used the old Latin modification, and with it, when Registrar of the Medical Faculty, I had to swear into the Guild the members of the graduating class with uplifted hands.

It is probable that the finishing touches of this address were never added because of other things, one of which had to do with a form of therapeutics perhaps never so successfully practised as in the temples of Epidaurus—a subject which he necessarily had thoroughly ventilated before Professor Murray's class. 'When one looks through the list of the recorded cures at Epidaurus,' he had written, 'it must indeed have been a house of Rimmon to such a man as Hippocrates or to Eryximachus': for the first lesson and one of the most important (to be learned from the Greeks) was the emancipation of medicine from religion, mysticism, and superstition.

The *British Medical Journal* for June 18, 1910, was given over to a series of articles on so-called faith-healing. Since the days of Huxley, Tyndall, and Herbert Spencer, a great change had come over the profession in regard to this matter—a change perhaps due in large part to the extraordinary growth of Christian Science—something which is neither Christian nor science, yet has supplied for certain people a prop which provides some measure of mental poise in the presence of ill health and disease. What Osler had to say on the subject has been given in the brief quotation from the recent edition of his Text-book; and this or something else stirred the editor of the Journal to gather some authoritative expression of opinion in regard to those bodily ills that yield to these methods of treatment. Sir Clifford Allbutt furnished some reflections on the subject; Sir Henry Morris, in a philosophic spirit, discussed the 'miracles' of Lourdes and the 'cures' of Christian Science; Mr. (later Sir) H. T. Butlin, then President of the Royal College of Surgeons, was another contributor; and Osler's paper on 'The Faith that Heals' was the last of the series:

> Nothing in life is more wonderful than faith [he began]—the one great moving force which we can neither weigh in the balance nor test in the crucible. . . . To each one of the religions, past or present, faith has been the Jacob's ladder. Creeds pass; an inexhaustible supply of faith remains, with which man proceeds to rebuild temples, churches, chapels and shrines. . . . Christendom lives on it, and countless thousands are happy in the possession of that most touching of all confessions, 'Lord! I believe; help Thou my unbelief.' But, with its Greek infection, the Western mind is a poor transmitter of faith, the apotheosis of which must be sought in the religions of the East. The Nemesis of faith is that neither in its intensity nor in its effects does man find any warrant of the worthiness of the object on which it is lavished—the followers of Joe Smith, the Mormon, are as earnest and believing as are those of Confucius!

But these were generalities, and one must get deeper in the essay to learn something of the author's personal views on the healing qualities of faith; for Osler, as may be added, was through his personality one of the most successful—albeit unconsciously—of psychotherapeutists. The jocular saying of some one that the treatment in his medical wards consisted of a mixture of hope and nux vomica had some basis of truth.

> Apart [he said] from the more specific methods to be dealt with, faith has always been an essential factor in the practice of medicine. . . . Literature is full of examples of remarkable cures through the influence of the imagination, which is only an active phase of faith. The late Daniel Hack Tuke's book, 'The Influence of the Mind on the Body', is a storehouse of facts dealing with the subject. While in general use for centuries, one good result of the recent development of mental healing has been to call attention to its great value as a measure to be carefully and scientifically applied in suitable cases. My experience has been that of the unconscious rather than the deliberate faith-healer. Phenomenal, even what could be called miraculous cures are not very uncommon. Like

others, I have had cases any one of which, under suitable conditions, could have been worthy of a shrine or made the germ of a pilgrimage. For more than ten years a girl lay paralysed in a New Jersey town. A devoted mother and loving sisters had worn out their lives in her service. She had never been out of bed unless when lifted by one of her physicians, Dr. Longstreth and Dr. Shippen. The new surroundings of a hospital, the positive assurance that she could get well with a few simple measures, sufficed, and within a fortnight she walked round the hospital square. This is a type of modern miracle that makes one appreciate how readily well-meaning people may be deceived as to the true nature of the cure effected at the shrine of a saint. Who could deny the miracle? And miracle it was, but not brought about by any supernatural means. I had the good fortune to be associated for five years with Weir Mitchell, and saw much of the workings of that master mind on the sisters of Sir Galahad and the brothers of Sir Percivale, who flocked to his clinics. His extraordinary success, partly due to the rest treatment, was more largely the result of a personal factor—the deep faith the people had in his power to cure. And it is in this group particularly that the strong man armed with good sense, and with faith in himself, may be a power for good. And the associations count for much. Without any special skill in these cases, or special methods, our results at the Johns Hopkins Hospital were most gratifying. Faith in *St. Johns Hopkins*, as we used to call him, an atmosphere of optimism, and cheerful nurses, worked just the same sort of cures as did Æsculapius at Epidaurus; and I really believe that had we had in hand that arch-neurasthenic of ancient history, Ælius Aristides, we could have made a more rapid cure than did Apollo and his son, who took seventeen years at the job!

'Once again', he said, 'old beliefs are in the melting-pot. . . . A great gulf has opened between pastor and flock, and the shepherdless sheep at large upon the mountains have been at the mercy of anyone who could pipe new tunes.' And after a sympathetic and understanding portrayal of the Christian Science cult and of the 'Emmanuel Church Movement', which had also originated in Boston and which he described as 'an honest attempt to bring back that angelical conjunction, as Cotton Mather calls it, of physic and divinity', he concluded by stating that, to him, 'not a psychologist but an ordinary clinical physician concerned in making strong the weak in mind and body', the whole subject was of intense interest; and that 'our attitude as a profession should not be hostile, and we must scan gently our brother man and sister woman who may be carried away on the winds of new doctrine'.

The week of May 29th saw them in Paris—a week entirely given over to the 'plain [!] but very sweet' niece and 'grand-daughter once removed'. They joined Dr. and Mrs. Jacobs there, and Osler saw to it that some other young people were attached, but it is apparent from all accounts that he was the life of the party. There was little that Paris afforded that was left undone and unseen. There was a trip to Fontainebleau with Cecil Harmsworth; they saw Rostand's 'Chanticleer' just produced; heard Scotti in 'Falstaff'; attended the races at Auteuil; dined at the famous restaurants; shopped to their hearts' content; saw the sights, from the Louvre to Notre Dame, where, as one of the party recalls, 'W. O. dropped some coins in the box marked "Prayers for those in Purgatory", saying that he had many friends there.'

They were back in Oxford in time to hear Mr. Roosevelt's Romanes Lecture on June 7th, 'The Biological Analogies in History'—a rather stiff subject—and to see him receive his D.C.L., on which occasion he was twitted not a little in very excellent Latin by the Vice-Chancellor whose guest he was. Subsequently, at the American Club, Mr. Roosevelt atoned for his somewhat indiscreet statements in London the week before, by stating that the relations of American and British peoples were now so cordial as to permit of frankness of speech, and that what he had said in his Guildhall speech could only have been said by a sincere friend and well-wisher. But, all told, he had, as Mrs. Osler wrote, a very wonderful reception, and she added: 'Our chauffeur drove him from 10.15 a.m. to 6.30 p.m. and was very proud.' Oxford was said to have been in festive mood and to have thoroughly enjoyed its day of hero-worship.[1]

Towards the end of the month a letter to H. B. Jacobs says: 'We have been having a very busy time, so many people coming and going, and an invasion of the Examiners this week. If you reach London by the 1st do come and meet the American clinical surgeons—30 of them will be here

[1] A few days later, one more was added to Osler's many honorary degrees, namely a D.Sc. from the University of Leeds.

and they dine with us on the terrace that evening.' But despite the 'people coming and going', he is found doing the sort of thing which so greatly endeared him to people. The June number of the little Saranac publication, the *Journal of the Outdoor Life*, was given over to a series of testimonials to Edward Livingston Trudeau. Likely as not, the idea had arisen during the recent week of play in Paris, for Lawrason Brown, its editor, had been a member of the festive party there. Osler's contribution reads in part as follows:

How true sometimes is the paradox of the Gospel that to save his life a man must lose it! Out of the depths—'from our desolation only may the better life begin'. In that best of all medical autobiographies, 'Jugenderinnerungen eines alten Arztes', Professor Kussmaul tells the story of his student days and of the happy beginning of a busy life as district physician in the Black Forest—plenty of work, good health, and a happy home with wife and children. Then the overwhelming disaster—sudden paraplegia, a long struggle in adverse circumstances, and a final victory wrought out of the very elements of defeat. Would that the story were more common! And yet how often does ill health, the bridle of Theages as Plato calls it, concentrate a man's resources and bring out qualities of work, the fruits of the spirit, which may be missed in the hurly-burly of the work-a-day world. The issue is not as a rule a man of affairs, but rather the fiery soul of the artist or poet 'fretting the pigmy body to decay'. Of all the blows of circumstance that *may* help to temper a man's metal, chronic illness is the most uncertain in its effects. Those fortunate ones win out who early learn to work in limitations which seem intolerable to the robust, who wish to take the kingdom of heaven by violence. The late W. K. Brooks told me that he attributed any success he may have had to the recognition of a permanent (congenital) weakness of the heart; and surely of his Chelonian race any swift-footed son of Thetis might be proud! Now and then men are fortunate enough to overcome the worst foes encountered in the battle of life—chronic ill health, and an enforced residence in a paralysing environment. The attitude of mind so splendidly expressed in Henley's verse, 'Out of the night that covers me', scoffs at the menace of the years, and unafraid, with unbowed head, the happy possessor of the unconquerable soul of this sort feels that

> It matters not how strait the gate
> How charged with punishments the scroll,
> I am the master of my fate;
> I am the captain of my soul.

And this is the lesson of Edward Trudeau's life—the lesson of a long and successfully fought campaign. An implacable foe, entrenched within his own citadel, has been often brought to terms of truce, never wholly conquered. . . .

I like now to admit to the select company on my shelves only the literature that has a personal interest to me, or epoch-making works of the masters of medicine. When the 25th Annual Report of the Sanitarium appeared I had it bound, and it reposes in my library between a work of Laennec, and the story of the early days of the Johns Hopkins Hospital. I wrote on the fly-leaf, 'A triumph of optimism. This shows what a badly crippled man may do single-handed, once let him gain the confidence of his brethren, medical and lay. Trudeau had the good fortune to be made of the stuff that attracts to himself only the best, as a magnet picks out iron. Of an unselfish, sympathetic disposition, he secured the devotion of his patients, to whom he was at once a tower of strength and a splendid example. . . .'

And in a letter of acknowledgement on June 24th, Trudeau wrote, saying: 'I have been in the Grip of the Tiger and in bed now for five weeks, but if my body is harassed and shrivelled by disease my soul is full of joy, and after reading these wonderful tributes in the *Outdoor Life* I feel I *must* get on my feet once more, for life with such friends cannot but be worth living under most any conditions!'

Getting timely portraits painted, writing tributes of the sort just given, distributing books to libraries and friends who would appreciate them—these were oft-recurring episodes. There were so many repetitions of them, indeed, that it is hardly possible—or necessary—to mention them all, even if more were known. But another kindly thing he did so often as to make the reiteration tiresome was to attend medical meetings in provincial districts, when the presence of the Oxford Regius was certain to act as a great stimulus. So, on June 28th, when busy preparing for the Edinburgh meeting of the next week, he was the guest of the Nottingham profession, invited to open with an address their new club and library.[1] There, after presenting to Mr. Smithurst

[1] In this address entitled 'Organization in the Profession' (*British Medical Journal*, Feb. 4, 1911, i. 237), Osler used the figure of speech so apt and so descriptive of one of his own great functions in life that it may be regarded as unconsciously autobiographical. 'Of the value [he said] to the local practitioners of a medical society and of a library we are all agreed. How common the experience to enter a cold cheerless room in which the fire in

a piece of silver in recognition of his long and faithful service of fifty-seven years as librarian of the society, he, from all accounts, said the old things with which we are now familiar, about library, laboratory, and nursery—things directed particularly to the seniors about their relations to one another and to their juniors—that the hospital should be made into a post-graduate school—that 'without post-graduate work a doctor was stale in five years, in the rut by ten, and by twenty in so deep he could never get out'. Two days later, on the afternoon of Friday, July 1st, an avalanche of American surgeons who were making a tour of the British clinics descended upon Oxford and partook of Osler's hospitality, little realizing that he had come back from Nottingham for the purpose, instead of going on to Edinburgh, where he was booked to give an address to the students in McEwan Hall on the Sunday. No hint of this conflict of engagements shows in his brief letters written after the crowded week was over. One of them to Dr. White follows:

[13 Norham Gardens] Saturday [July 9th]

Dear J. William, Shall you be in town on Monday p.m.? I have been in Edinboro for a week trying to stir up Tuberculosis work at

---

the grate has died down, not from lack of coal, not because the coal was not alight, but the bits, large and small, falling away from each other, have gradually become dark and cold. Break them with a poker, get them together, and what a change in a few minutes! There is light and heat and good cheer. What happens in the grate illustrates very often the condition of the profession in a town or county: singly or in cliques the men have fallen apart, and, as in the dead or dying embers, there is neither light nor warmth; or the coals may be there alive and bright, but covered with the ashes of discord, jealousy, and faction. Like the poker bringing the elements together, the medical society may do three things. It is the most important single factor in the promotion of that unity and goodfellowship which adds so much to the dignity of the profession. I have no idea of the state of the atmosphere in Nottingham—whether you are united and harmonious, or whether you fight amongst yourselves like cats and dogs—but the large "turn out" this evening suggests that the former condition prevails. In this matter, so far as my observation goes, everything depends upon the influence of the seniors, whose attitude of mind determines whether the young men grow up in a state of wretched discord or in one of pleasant comradeship. I have known a clever old Shimei, of a quarrelsome disposition, ruin the profession of a city for a generation; on the other hand, a strong old man with a good heart and a smooth tongue may keep the peace, even among Ishmaelites.'

our National Association. Send me a wire & I will call—Love to Mrs White. Yours sincerely, Wm Osler.

This laconic reference does scant justice to the Edinburgh meeting, the preparations for which, as he was President of the association, had occupied much of his time during the spring. It is not surprising to find introduced a departure from the established custom of holding the annual meetings in London, by no means the best way to propagandize the crusade, as he fully appreciated. Edinburgh, moreover, had long been engaged in a local combat against tuberculosis; but there were other reasons for the choice, one of them the desire to call public attention to the Victoria Farm Colony, a project which Dr. (now Sir) Robert Philip of Edinburgh had promoted. He, indeed, as far back as 1887 had established a tuberculosis dispensary—the first in Great Britain—and for years had been prominently identified with the movement in Scotland to provide proper care for consumptives.

Though the actual sessions of the conference did not begin until Monday, July 4th, a tuberculosis exhibition was formally opened on the preceding Friday, in Osler's absence, by the Countess of Aberdeen, whose successful campaign in Ireland during the three years since the Dublin exhibition had been started on its travels entitled her to this honour. A 'tuberculosis morning' was held on Saturday in all the Edinburgh schools, unquestionably the best place to start the work of popular education; and later in the day a visit was paid to the new Farm Colony. On the Sunday there was an afternoon service [1] for the university students, who crowded McEwan Hall to the doors to hear the man who just missed being Lord Rector, deliver what was termed a lay sermon—'Man's Redemption of Man'. Osler chose as his text the two verses from Isaiah, beginning, 'And a man shall be as an hiding-place from the wind'; 'And the voice of weeping shall be no more heard in her':

To man [he said] there has been published a triple gospel—of his

[1] It was in part a memorial service for Robert Koch, concerning whom, after Osler's sermon, Hermann Biggs of New York, Professor Woodhead, and Dr. Robert Philip, Osler's host, all made brief addresses.

soul, of his goods, of his body. Growing with his growth, preached and professed in a hundred different ways in various ages of the world, these gospels represent the unceasing purpose of his widening thoughts.

The gospel of his relation to the powers unseen has brought sometimes hope, too often despair. In a wide outlook on the immediate and remote effects of the attempts to establish this relation, one event discredits the great counsel of Confucius (who realized what a heavy yoke religion might be) to keep aloof from spiritual beings. Surviving the accretions of twenty centuries, the life and immortality brought to light by the gospel of Christ, remain the earnest desire of the best portion of the race.

The gospel of his goods—of man's relation to his fellow men, is written in blood on every page of history. Quietly and slowly the righteousness that exalteth a nation, the principles of eternal justice, have won acquiescence, at any rate in theory, though as nations and individuals we are still far from carrying them into practice.

And the third gospel, the gospel of his body, which brings man into relation with nature—a true *euangelion*, the glad tidings of a conquest beside which all others sink into insignificance—is the final conquest of nature, out of which has come man's redemption of man, the subject to which I am desirous of directing your attention.

He worked into the sermon a good many paragraphs about the triumph of Greek thought, which he borrowed from his lecture in Gilbert Murray's course, and this may in part explain why that lecture was never completed for publication. He then went on to say (one wonders what 'Father' Johnson would have thought):

My generation was brought up in the belief that 'Man was in his original state a very noble and exalted creature, being placed as the head and lord of this world, having all the creatures in subjection to him. The powers and operations of his mind were extensive, capacious and perfect'—to quote the words of one of my old Sunday-school lessons. It is not too much to say that Charles Darwin has so turned man right-about-face that, no longer looking back with regret upon a Paradise Lost, he feels already within the gates of a Paradise Regained. . . . Within the lifetime of some of us a strange and wonderful thing happened on the earth—something of which no prophet foretold, of which no seer dreamt, nor is it among the beatitudes of Christ Himself; only St. John seems to have had an inkling of it in that splendid chapter in which he describes the new heaven and the new earth, when the former things should pass away, when all tears should be wiped away, and there should be no more crying nor sorrow.

There followed the fascinating story of the growth of modern sanitary science; and finally he referred to the memorable phrase of the Greek philosopher Prodicus: 'That which benefits human life is God', suggesting that it may come to be a new gospel of the glorious days of which Shelley sings.[1]

On Monday the conference commenced in earnest with a succession of papers from Sims Woodhead of Cambridge, J. G. Adami of Montreal, James Ritchie, Professor Tendeloo of Leyden, and others. A luncheon at the College of Physicians followed; and the afternoon sessions were devoted to a consideration of the administrative control of the disease. Hermann M. Biggs of New York recounted his experiences with the control of tuberculosis in that great city; and other papers followed by the medical health officers of Glasgow, of Edinburgh, of Liverpool, of Sheffield, and so on. The well-attended sessions continued for another day, when tuberculosis in children was dealt with, the afternoon being devoted to the working-man's relation to the disease. Finally a resolution was drawn up, 'to represent to his Majesty's Ministers the advisability of considering a scheme of national insurance against tuberculosis', after which with a few words of congratulation Osler adjourned the meeting. This becomes an old story, but it is one which may have to be again repeated—for he will soon be similarly engaged with the Oxfordshire association. A review of the busy ten days is given in the following characteristic letter from Oxford on Sunday the 10th:

> We had a great day with the Surgeons. We met them at 3 with motors—saw Ch Ch, Magdalen & New then to the Radcliffe for tea—then to the Museums & laboratories & here for dinner at 7. We had 52 at round tables in the drawing-room. . . . Pig! to get a Ketham before me. I have been looking for a good one for a long

---

[1] Osler's rendering of the phrase from Prodicus led evidently to a good deal of discussion among his philological friends. Gildersleeve must have written to him about it, and Osler evidently sent the letter to Herbert W. Blunt, the Librarian at Christ Church, who wrote that 'Prodicus states as a fact of anthropology that our ancestors held as gods those things which are beneficial to men', and quoted from Cicero's 'De Natura Deorum' in favour of Osler's rendering of the passage.

time. I am bankrupt, having bot.·all the Leonardo Anatomical volumes, the aviation and the generation. These are getting scarce and some of the vols. are limited (100). See 19th Century Magazine for July—good article on his aviation. Just back from Edinboro, great T.B. meeting. I had a 2500 audience in the Hall on Sunday & *preached* to the students on 'Man's redemption of Man'. We sail on the 29th. . . . Open Arms full—6 over Sunday.

One cannot escape the feeling that Osler's greatest professional service was that of a propagandist of public health measures. His beginnings in this direction, seen even in his youthful days in Montreal, were actively continued in Baltimore, where he was constantly crusading against malaria and typhoid, not only in his wards but on public platforms; and he left there just as the anti-tuberculosis crusade was getting under way. With this same movement, as can be seen, he energetically allied himself while in England; nor was his a voice in the wilderness in this rôle he chose for himself—a rôle as important as that of the laboratory scientist whose cloistered studies supplied the knowledge on which our whole public health movement is based. Certainly no man of his time came in closer contact than he with workers in all fields of medicine. No wonder that a group of American surgeons made a pilgrimage to Oxford; and when his addresses before the Army Medical School in Washington are recalled it is not surprising to find him making a presentation speech to accompany a subscription gift for Sir Alfred Keogh on his retirement from the position of Director-General of the Army Medical Service. This event took place at the Royal Army Medical College, London, on July 18th, and in the course of some well-chosen remarks, concerning the reorganization of the College which had taken place during Keogh's administration, he went on to speak of the medical and nursing departments of the Territorial Army in which he himself had been enrolled:

Here [he said] I had personal experience of your [Keogh's] admirable tact, your unfailing optimism and your sane judgement. To you we owe it that the medical side of Mr. Haldane's scheme is now working so smoothly and efficiently. Your term of office as Director-General came too swiftly to a close, and one cannot but regret that the services of a man of your youth and energy should be lost to the country; but you have the satisfaction of feeling that you have inaugurated a work which others can carry to completion. We are glad that the responsibilities of the new post [1] which you have accepted are beset with the difficulties likely to bring out your special capacities, and that there will be work enough to keep you idly active. . . .

Little did he realize that four years later the man whom he was addressing would in a great emergency be recalled to his old post of Director-General of the Medical Service.

Thus he had met with provincial practitioners, surgeons, public health officers, and army medical officers—all in the course of a few weeks; and on July 22nd at Oxford he was called on to address a group of specialists at the opening of the Ophthalmological Congress. The manuscript of the address entitled 'Specialists and Specialism', found among his unpublished papers, shows that he had given time and thought to the situation in which the ophthalmological surgeons, among the first to specialize, find themselves. 'To two great groups of minds', he said, 'the world has been indebted for its progress—the hypermetropic, the wide-visioned men of the type of Aristotle, Darwin, and Spencer; and the myopic—the men of concentrated penetrating vision of the type of Pythagoras, Vesalius, Harvey, and Pasteur. Who shall say which is the more important?' And, perhaps with memories of his own quondam intent to become an ophthalmologist, he continued as follows:

Those who think that at the present day specialism has run riot, are purblind critics who cannot see that we are safe so long as each generation in each department produces a few men with hypermetropia enough to synthetize the work of their colleagues, and so far these have never been wanting. The medical profession has become a mere congeries of specialists and upon you is the blame! In the forest of general practice you first blazed the way, and a good one too, which others have been ready enough to follow. Not that ophthalmic specialists are new—contrariwise, they flourished in Egypt and Greece, and indeed in every age of the profession, but you took the lead in showing how a special branch of medicine should be studied, practised and made successful. It is a far cry from the days of the genial Pepys, in the seventeenth century, who tells how the eye doctor, whom we all execrate as the man who

[1] Rector of the Imperial College of Science and Technology.

LINACRE, HARVEY, SYDENHAM AND OSLER

made him stop writing the immortal Diary, had never seen an eye dissected until he visited Lower at Oxford. For one great work we are thankful to you—breaking down the barriers of prejudice which existed in the profession, against any one man knowing any one thing better than his fellows. It was a hard fight, and you may think it not yet a fight to the finish, as there remain a few who diffuse an atmosphere of the glacial period in the presence of a specialist. Shades of Tobit ! Think of the contrast even within my memory between the general surgeons who practised ophthalmology, and the specialist who to-day practises ophthalmic surgery. I still shudder at the remembrance of those ' good old days ' at the Montreal General Hospital, when cases of pneumonia, fractured legs and cataract were jumbled in the same ward, under the care of the same man ; and it was not without qualms of conscience that the staff consented to the appointment of an ophthalmic surgeon, my friend the late Dr. Buller. When I studied at Moorfields in 1872, Bowman and Critchett were the only men who did not hold surgical positions in other hospitals. We all recognize how much the science is indebted to general surgeons who have made ophthalmology a study, and to all of us at once will occur the name of that veteran—the greatest generalized specialist of his generation—Jonathan Hutchinson, the last of the polymaths, the man at home in all spheres of medical science. Few will be found now to lament the change, and fewer perhaps who do not feel that it would have been better to recognize earlier the pressing demands of specialism in a subject of such complexity.

For the closing paragraph he borrowed passages from his ' Remarks on Specialism ', published eighteen years before :

In the cultivation of a specialty as an art there is a tendency to develop a narrow and pedantic spirit, and the man who year in and year out corrects errors in refraction, removes prostates or takes blood pressures without regard to the wider basis upon which his art rests is apt insensibly, but none the less surely, to reach the attitude of mind of the old Scotch shoemaker who, in response to the Dominie's suggestions about the weightier matters of life, asked : ' D'ye ken leather ? ' But every special branch carries with it the corrective of this most fatal tendency. Problems in physiology and pathology touch at every point the commonest affections, and exercised in these, if only in the earlier years of professional life, a man is chastened, so to speak, and can escape the deadening effect of routine. The other radical defect of specialism is a failure to recognize that it deals as a rule with partial truths which must be correlated with facts obtained by wider study. . . .

The rest—with Plato's words which ' embody the law

and the gospel for specialists'—has already been quoted (Vol. I, p. 361).

All this was very serious and worth thinking about, though, curiously enough, what those in attendance chiefly seem to remember was an afternoon on the terrace at the 'Open Arms'. This perhaps needs a word of explanation. One may picture a sweltering morning in June, with W. O. flying off after breakfast and announcing, off-hand: 'There'll be a few men here to tea this afternoon'; and in response to the rejoinder of how many—'Oh, about twelve.' Later in the morning one of the inevitable young visitors at the house discovers by chance on his desk the programme of the ophthalmological meeting in which it is stated that in the afternoon at 4 there will be a garden-party given by the Regius Professor and Mrs. Osler at 13 Norham Gardens. And so, instead of going to the river and spending the hot afternoon in a boat as intended, some rugs are moved on to the lawn, sandwiches are made, buns purchased; and by 4.30 seventy-five people have arrived, most of whom, enjoying themselves hugely and believing it was a function long prepared for, remain on until 7. And they also recall that the Regius Professor was present and spoke at their annual dinner that evening, making some very amusing remarks, admirably fitted, as intended, to put every one in a cheerful mood to hear any subsequent harangue with equanimity. And it was hardly noticed that his chair was soon empty after the ball had thus been set rolling, for he was due the next morning in London to attend an important conference in connexion with the annual meeting of the British Medical Association which had opened there the same day.

On the evening of the 23rd he wrote to Thayer: 'We sail on the 29th. I may have to return with Mrs. Osler on the 6th of September: Winchester school opens on the 10th, and I have a few lithogenous twinges again in my stone quarry and it might be wise to go to Contrexéville; this will cut off my proposed early week in October with you all, much to my grief. Send a line to Pointe-à-Pic, Murray Bay.' But Osler wasted no time in planning for his annual visit to America and had still much to do in this remaining week, apart from the sessions of the B. M. A. The following letter, probably of this date, was shortly to be read before the Henley Rural Council :[1]

Oxfordshire County Association for the Prevention of Tuberculosis.

May I ask you on behalf of the above association, to lay this letter before your Council at its next meeting? In view of the prevalence of consumption, and the absence of any adequate means for its relief or prevention, the Radcliffe Infirmary has determined to devote certain hours of its out-patient department each week to the treatment of consumptives only, coming from all parts of the district. It will mean a large increase of its work, and this association is undertaking to make good to the Radcliffe Infirmary any loss it may thereby incur. A doctor will be in charge who will devote himself solely to this department and to preventive work in consumption, in close co-operation with the Infirmary, and the sanitary authorities. The Oxford City Council has granted £100 a year towards his salary. The association would ask the district councils throughout Oxfordshire to co-operate in this work by making yearly grants of perhaps £10 to £15 according to the population they represent—suggesting that councils representing over 5,000 persons should contribute £15 a year—and by this means to provide a fund of £150 a year, which will be needed to raise the doctor's salary and allowances to £250. Will your council give the matter its serious consideration? An early answer, if it be favourable, will make the immediate appointment of a doctor possible, and he can enter without delay on the special training which this work will need, either at Edinburgh or in some centre where preventive work in consumption is already in full activity. I am, yours very truly,

Wm Osler.

On the 25th he sent this note to Miss Mabel Price :

Lady Wantage, whom I saw yesterday, is very sympathetic, and I am writing to-day to ask her for a specific subscription. I enclose you a note from Mason and one from Fleming. Could you not come in this evening about nine o'clock : Dr. Mallam and I are to meet Stobie here. Yesterday at the staff meeting I nailed them down specifically to open the dispensary on Friday, October 7th. The Executive Committee were to be asked to arrange preliminaries with Stobie, and to guarantee to pay him his salary until we can get arrangements completed. I enclose you my cheque.

What Osler's moral support meant to the 'Committee of the Oxfordshire Branch of the National Association for

[1] 'Tuberculosis in Oxfordshire'. *British Medical Journal*, Sept. 3, 1910, ii. 646.

the Prevention of Tuberculosis', of which for many years he was President, may be told in Miss Price's own words:

We (my family) left Oxford in 1900 to live for some years at Headington, outside the town to the East, where there is a population of nearly 2,000 people, mainly Oxford working people. We started a small Charity Organization Society Committee there, and very soon came on the underlying cause of most of the sickness and distress there was. About 60–70 cases of consumption came to our notice. We realized what a difficult and almost insoluble problem it presented. No means existed of getting the special forms of treatment and help they needed; no measures of prevention were in force. It was a burning question, and soon after Sir William Osler came to Oxford I went down and laid the whole matter before him, only to find that he already knew all about it. He knew the question in all its aspects—social and medical—its difficulties, the prolonged nature of the illness, the patient living the ordinary life of the people, half disabled himself and a danger to others for many months of the year—to end at last, hidden away, to die slowly, often forgotten by the outside world. There was nothing sensational about it—the people had come to accept it as fate and took no precautions against it. Sir William instantly took the matter up. As a member of the Council of the National Association in London, he arranged that their exhibition should be held in Oxford within the next few months. I saw him in June 1909; the exhibition was opened in the University Examination Schools in November. He organized lectures, medical conferences, and two big general meetings in connection with it. Many thousands of people came to it and the association was formed. As an immediate result, in 1910, the first dispensary was opened in Oxford, a medical officer [Dr. William Stobie] specially trained in the School of Sir Robert Philip, and two nurses trained in tuberculosis were attached to it.

Within the next two years seven other dispensaries were opened in the county. Sir William went himself all over the county to raise interest and get financial help.[1] We went in this way to Lady Wantage, Sir Charles Rose, Mr. T. F. Mason, Mr. Fleming, Mr. Brassey and many others. During its early years patients came from Berkshire and Buckinghamshire to the Oxfordshire dispensaries. The Reports I am sending you show how rapidly the work grew,

---

[1] He probably faced no little opposition in some quarters. On January 18th of 1911, he was at Witney with the proposal that one of the central dispensaries should be established there, and met with the usual criticism that Witney could care for its own consumptives but did not wish to endanger its people by importing others.

and Sir William scarcely ever missed the fortnightly committee meetings. We made many efforts to get a small sanatorium-hospital for ourselves, and Mr. Phipps made a gift of £500 to Sir William for this purpose. Mr. Mason gave another £500. A property was bought on Shotover where the hospital was so badly needed and could have been built, but rival interests have always prevented it, and we are still without any hospital for consumption in the county.

Up to the last months of his life Sir William Osler was steadily at our back in the work of the association, giving advice, help, encouragement, and generously of his time. His unflagging support helped us in what was often uphill work. As long as the dispensaries were in the hands of the association (in 1916 they were taken over by the County Council) he came regularly to the Oxford Dispensary—generally one morning in the week at 10; and saw patients there in consultation with the Tuberculosis Officer, taking the clinic himself if the latter was away for any reason. If a particularly difficult or sad case occurred in the county he would go himself and see it. Early in 1916 before the Government scheme for the care of consumptives was as complete as it became later, a discharged soldier was dying in a lodging in a very poor house in Banbury. I told Sir William of this and he at once went off to see him; the man had been turned out of one lodging after another; finally a woman had given him an attic in her house and was doing what she could for him; but the conditions were impossible. Within a few days the man was removed to a War Office Hospital in London.

This is a bare outline of what he did for us. An expression of the committee's appreciation is in the beginning of the Report for last year [1920].

On July 28th he wrote to his invalided friend, H. P. Bowditch of Boston:

So kind of you to remember my birthday. I have had a very busy summer, a great many things on hand, & scores of people coming and going. I hope to see you before long; we are sailing for Canada tomorrow and shall be in Boston towards the latter part of August. As soon as I reach Boston I will telephone to find out if you are at home. I saw Lauder Brunton the other day; he asked after you. He seemed quite himself again. With love to the family.

Except for the allusion to Lauder Brunton one would hardly gather from this that he had been engaged in London almost every day since the 23rd, and more particularly on the 27th and 28th. A month before, the following notice had appeared in the journals regarding the Medical Library Association (over the names of the joint secretaries, Dr. I. Walker Hall of Bristol, and Dr. C. E. A. Clayton of Manchester):

Sir,—By the kind permission of the British Medical Association the second annual meeting of the Medical Library Association, under the presidency of Professor Osler, will be held at London University during the last week of July. Two short sessions will be held on the mornings of July 27th and 28th, at which papers will be read dealing with matters likely to be of practical interest and assistance to medical librarians, members of library committees, and readers.

It is also intended to hold a bibliographical exhibition in connection with the meeting, as this proved such a successful feature of the meeting held in Belfast last year, and we shall be glad to receive offers of loans to illustrate the following sections of the exhibition: (1) Incunabula. (2) Books by London medical men up to 1600. (3) Photographs of and papers relating to medical libraries. (4) Special collections, &c.

The meetings were held in the old School of Science, South Kensington, and at the first of them Osler spoke in familiar phrases, 'on the different types of medical libraries to be found in the British Isles, on the value of co-operation between them, and the way in which this might be promoted.' To the subsequent programme of the meetings the librarians of the Royal College of Surgeons, of the Royal Society of Medicine, Sir Thomas Barlow of the Royal College of Physicians, and others, contributed. It is to be hoped they had an audience worthy of their subjects, but this is doubtful.[1] The occasion is reminiscent of another meeting held in Saratoga, N.Y., in 1902, when, however, the Professor of Medicine at the Johns Hopkins had at his beck and call more young men with whom to fill empty benches than had the Oxford Regius in 1910.

Osler has noted in his account-book for the year: *July 29.* 'Sailed for Quebec *Empress of Ireland* with Grace, E. R. O.,

[1] The association [writes Dr. Hall] did not gain the support of the London Librarians, as it seemed to them unnecessary. For a time it stimulated library work in the provinces, and an attempt was made in 1910 to make a catalogue of the medical and scientific periodicals in British libraries. Considerable progress was made, and though the project was temporarily dropped it is satisfactory to note that a catalogue has at length been completed (1923) by Professor Leiper and his assistants. The interest in the association flagged gradually, and finally disappeared with the outbreak of war.

Ottilie Wright and Nona Gwyn [the 'grand-daughter once removed' and the niece].' *August 4.* 'Arrived Quebec 5 days 21 hours.' *Sept. 6.* 'Sailed *Kaiser Wilhelm II.*' *Sept. 12.* 'Arrived Plymouth 6 a.m.' *Sept. 13.* 'Oxford 2.30.' His peregrinations in the intervening six weeks may be gathered from a few of his many brief notes; it was little more than a series of calls upon his old friends, but the impression he made on some one who met him for the first time at Murray Bay is this: 'He was like a happy boy out of school, full of life, energy and good fellowship, and fairly radiated with the joy of living.'

To H. B. Jacobs in Newport. The Spinney, Pointe-à-Pic, P. Q.
Tuesday, [August 9th]

Dear Jacobs, We had a splendid trip. Revere is off fishing with Campbell Howard in camp about 40 miles north of Quebec. I start on my rounds next Sunday—Montreal, Belleville, Toronto & Hamilton. Then to Boston about the 21st. I will come to you (Newport) for a day or two on my way to Baltimore. We sail on the 6th. I shall go to Contrexeville to irrigate my rt. kidney as there have been twinges from time to time. Campbell Howard has had a splendid offer from the University of Iowa—Dept. of Med., another benefit of the [Abraham Flexner's] Carnegie Report. I have urged him to accept though the school is small and it is far away, but they give him carte blanche, a good salary and two assistants at $2,000 and $1,500. This is a glorious place almost as bracing as Oxford and full of charming people.

From F. J. Shepherd's house in Montreal he wrote a week later to Dr. Maude Abbott: 'So sorry to miss you to-day—but I was hard pushed and had some 10 calls to make and the new M. G. H. plans to talk over. I am delighted with the prospects of the new Museum. Do let me know if I can be of any use'; and on the 16th from Craigleigh, his brother's house in Toronto,[1] to Mrs. Brewster:

Welcome to your new home—may you have much happiness in it. Could I come on Friday (p.m.) Sept 2nd or on Saturday & spend

[1] Reference has been made in previous chapters to the characteristic reticence of the Oslers regarding one another, and family matters in general. It is unusual, therefore, to find, in a letter written a month later by W. O. to a Toronto physician whom Sir Edmund seems to have befriended, this fraternal tribute: 'Thank you so much for sending the picture of E. B. O. with the children: he never lets his family know what he does; he has got the best heart and the freest hand of any man I ever met.'

Sunday? We sail the following Tuesday. Mrs. Osler will be in Baltimore that Sunday & Revere off fishing with his Uncles. I wish you could see him; perhaps they could motor out on Monday afternoon. I have had a very happy visit seeing old friends in Murray Bay & Montreal. Now I am trying to see the new generation of babies everywhere, & such darlings. Give my love to Sylvia. It will be delightful to see you all again. Mrs Revere, Canton, will always find me. I shall be at the 'Glades' for a few days next week & I must go to Bar Harbour to see Weir Mitchell.

Baltimore was no less torrid than usual in mid-August, and Washington likewise, but he nevertheless made a special trip there to the Surgeon-General's Library to see Dr. Fletcher, the Librarian, active as ever, though eighty-seven years of age. Then to 'The Glades' on Massachusetts Bay, whence he wrote on August 25th: 'I have had a lovely time—seeing the families—three days in Baltimore—how the town is booming. Hot as Hades here—S.W. blowing; flies & mosquitoes galore.' The 29th found him at Little Boar's Head, New Hampshire, spending the day with his quondam playmate of Rome, Susan Baker; though when he found that his beloved 'Rosalie' was no longer to be produced, he threatened to leave. Then Canton for a day with Mrs. Revere; Newport with Dr. and Mrs. Jacobs; Mt. Kisco for a visit with the Brewsters in their new home; and on the 6th, from New York, they sailed, as he writes, 'in a swelter!'

What for them was a comparatively quiet month followed upon their return. A few incidents only need be noted. Among their early visitors were Dr. and Mrs. J. W. White, who had just returned from St. Moritz with the Abbeys; and White particularly wished to consult Osler regarding the resignation, being pressed upon him, of his university position, which he was loth to relinquish. On his departure, Osler wrote: 'What I feel about you is just what I feel about Tyson, that it would be a thousand pities there should be any rumpus after such a long and devoted service. You are popular with the class, yet for the Professor of Surgery not to operate, and not, so to speak, be in the arena with the younger men is an anomaly—and that no doubt is what some of them feel.' Dr. White evidently acted upon this advice and handed in his resignation.

The following exchange of letters on another matter tells its own story:

From Henry Phipps to W. O. Sept. 9, 1910.

Sorry to have missed you in Oxford and America. I have been trying to get a number of copies of the 'Life of Pasteur', by Vallery-Radot, in two volumes, but though the bookseller has advertised extensively he has not been able to get a copy. Now it occurs to me that it might be a good idea to print two hundred and fifty copies for distribution, some through you and some through the Johns Hopkins University and other institutions. The price quoted is 14/ per copy in quires, and I would have the work done through a bookseller with whom I deal in London. If you could spare the time, and were inclined, I would be glad if you would write an introduction to the reprint. At your leisure please give me your views on the subject.

From W. O. to Henry Phipps. Sept. 21, 1910.

We must have passed each other on the Atlantic. When your letter came I was on the point of writing to Mrs. Guest to find out if you were still in England. Your idea of reprinting the 'Life of Pasteur' commends itself to me very warmly, and I should be only too glad to write an introduction. The consent of Longmans & Co., who own the copyright of the translation, and published the book, would have to be obtained; I have written to them and will let you know their answer. I spent a morning at the tuberculosis dispensary at the Johns Hopkins, and was delighted to see the work progressing so rapidly; it has really become a very important centre. I was glad to find several post-graduates there from other towns. We are making a renewed effort to stir up public opinion here, and have started an influential Appeal Committee to enable us to put three more exhibitions on the road. . . .

Osler was mistaken as to the publishers, for it was Constable & Co. and not Longmans who had this particular copyright; but the matter was finally settled; a special edition was printed for Mr. Phipps and distributed the next year in ways to be told. So Osler's name became coupled with the great story of Pasteur's life just as it became, first and last, with other volumes under circumstances less well known. Many books were dedicated to him; others inspired by him; and in his library is a copy of 'Rewards and Fairies' inscribed to him with the quotation: 'Excellent herbs had our fathers of old', and in it is this note of October 3rd from Bateman's, Burwash, Sussex:

Dear Osler,—Herewith my book of Tales. I wouldn't bother you with it except for Nick Culpeper and Laennec for whom I feel you are in a way responsible. Yours very sincerely,

RUDYARD KIPLING.

Plans were already being laid at this time for the International Medical Congress meeting to be held in London three years later, and it would appear that pressure was being used to get Osler to accept a position on the central committee which would naturally have resulted in his being made President; but he turned this aside in favour of his friend Sir Thomas Barlow, and wrote as follows on October 4th to Professor Wenckebach:

Pavy has recently resigned his place on the International Committee. The College of Physicians, having been asked to nominate someone in his place have appointed me, so that I shall go to the meeting in Berlin on the 13th. I have not yet had any word as to the hour and place of meeting. I shall of course be glad to do anything I can to help on the work, but *on no consideration would I accept the Chairmanship*, as you have suggested; someone should be appointed who knows French perfectly, and my languages are hopeless, so please do not think of me as I could not accept under any circumstances.

Much more to his taste was a meeting such as that which came two days later—the Caius quater-centenary celebration at Cambridge. As Norman Moore reminded those present, John Caius was the first of three great founders of homes of learning who were members of the medical profession, John Radcliffe being another, and the third Sir Hans Sloane, whose collections formed the nucleus of the British Museum. But the princely benefactor of the 'new college of Caius' was more than physician, having been a Professor of Greek as well, and those who gathered to honour his memory were distinguished in many walks outside of medicine.[1] Meanwhile at 13 Norham Gardens the usual procession of people were coming and going. A note scribbled on October 10th at the Hotel Metropole, London, and left for his old assistant, Charles D. Parfitt, who had been well enough to pay a visit to England, tells the usual story:

Dear Parfitt, Desolated not to meet you. Could you not come

[1] In connexion with this quater-centenary of Caius's birth, the Cambridge University Press published an edition of his works which appeared the

and spend the night with us at Ewelme? I go back by the 5.05 train from Paddington. I will join you at the 1st class ticket office at 5 minutes to five. If you are not there I will take it for granted that you are detained by other engagements. Come tomorrow. Address Ewelme Oxon. Wallingford is the station. Telegraph and we will have you met. Yours Wm OSLER. Would call again but I am busy at Committee all day.

Parfitt, happily, was making a winning fight against his infection, but, alas, another, to whom Osler had been more outspokenly devoted than to any of his assistants before or after, just now reached his end, and with wet eyes he must have written the following letter to Thayer on October 14th:

We had word this week of dear old Jack Hewetson's death. Of course it was not a surprise as in his last letter to Mrs. Osler he complained of growing weakness. It brings back memories of those happy days when we learned to love him so dearly. What a tragedy that he should have had the blighted life! Would it not be nice if a few of us put up—or arranged—some memorial of him at the Hospital? Put me down for $100. Talk to Barker and Smith about it. Anything that you suggest will I am sure be acceptable to all his friends. We have had a quiet month since our return. Since Sept. 1st I have had no twinges on my right side so I hope the bit of gravel may have slipped away. I did not go to Contrexeville as I had intended. Ike is off at school again, very happy, but loathing Latin and Greek. . . . Yours ever, W. O.[1]

A series of entries in his account-book at this time read as follows: *Oct. 16. Sunday*: 'In bed with cold'; *22nd. Saturday*: 'Not well all week, cold hanging about, in bed to-day and Sunday'. *Nov. 3*: 'Newcastle'; *Nov. 14*: 'Return of cold'; *Nov. 17*: 'Cambridge Lecture'; *Nov. 25*: 'Cold room, Examiners' meeting'; *26th. Saturday*: 'Return of cold'; *Nov. 27–Dec. 3*: 'In bed all week with mild bronchitis, very little fever, moderate cough, have never got quite over cold of six weeks ago.' These brief entries perhaps need a little amplification.

following year, and which Osler reviewed in his 'Men and Books' series (*Canadian Medical Association Journal*, Nov. 1912, ii. 1034–6).

[1] His tribute to Hewetson with an account of the early days at the Johns Hopkins Hospital, published in the *Johns Hopkins Hospital Bulletin* for December of that year, has in part been quoted in Vol. I, p. 335.

There is no trace in his letters of his being under the weather; rather he is thinking of others :

To C. P. Howard in Iowa City. Oct. 20, 1910.

It is very nice to have your letter and to hear such good accounts of the work. I knew you would be busy as a bee from the start; you will have difficulty in finding time for your work. I am getting the slides ready: they will go next week by the American Express. Some of them I am afraid have faded a bit. The set showing the rashes in infectious diseases will be most useful; I have forgotten who sent them from Cleveland to me, but they make a stunning set for demonstration. The abdominal tumours will do for outside lectures. I am sending first the box with the thirty-eight or thirty-nine slides of infectious diseases this week, as you may need them at once. They really give a splendid picture of the rashes; I wish I could remember the kind fellow who sent them to me. The students I know will appreciate them. So glad you have seen the Perkinses. I have had letters from the Chicago men about you, from whom I am sure you will get a good welcome. Ike was back yesterday for his 'leave-out day', looking very well. . . .

And a few days later he wrote to Dr. J. A. Nixon of Bristol, whose plans to start a medico-historical club were being laid: 'I would rather meet ten or twelve modest fellows like you at home than a hundred ordinary citizens. Of course I will come. Early in December would suit me best. Why not call yourselves the Linacre Club?' So he loaned himself unhesitatingly; and the chance 'Newcastle' entry in the notes just taken from his account-book refers to a similar occasion—a meeting of the Northumberland and Durham Medical Society before whom he gave an address on 'The Hospital Unit in University Work'.[1]

He had doubtless chosen this subject for the reason that the Royal Commission on University Education had just begun to hold its sessions under Lord Haldane's leadership. Osler had been notified that in due course he would be called upon for evidence before this commission; and as a précis would be expected, he probably was already assembling his views on the matter. Though the commission was to consider the subject from a national standpoint, Lord Haldane's programme was largely concerned with an effort to put the University of London on a more practical and

[1] *Lancet*, Lond., 1911, i. 211–13.

effective basis and, of this, the improvement and standardization of medical education was no small part. Naturally, therefore, what had been done at the Johns Hopkins Hospital and Medical School during their first two decades was to be thoroughly ventilated. The subject of medical education at that time was at the boiling-point in the United States. Abraham Flexner's report [1] upon the conditions he had found in the course of a comprehensive survey had just been issued and been received with a howl of protest from the many schools of low grade, whose organization, equipment, and standards he had severely castigated—effectively so, be it said, for the report was influential in the rapid elimination of the poorer schools and in levelling up the character of the work done in the others. In this report the Johns Hopkins had been held up as a model; but even models may be found to have defects, and these ere long were pointed out in a privately printed letter to the Johns Hopkins authorities, though it was not until the next year that the air, already electrified by the question of full-time positions for clinical teachers, became surcharged. It was a matter on which Osler, as will be seen, had very definite opinions.[2]

In his Newcastle address Osler endeavoured to answer the questions—'What is university work? What is a hospital unit? What connection have they with each other? And what interest have they for us and for the community at large?'

All are agreed [he said] that a university has a dual function—to learn and to advance learning. I use the word 'learn' in the old

[1] 'Medical Education in the United States and Canada.' Bulletin No. 4 of the Carnegie Foundation for the Advancement of Teaching.

[2] It was on March 3, 1910, that John D. Rockefeller announced his intention to endow a body of trustees with the balance of his fortune, 'for the promotion and dissemination of knowledge; the prevention and relief of suffering'. This in time has become restricted largely to preventive medicine, sanitation, and medical education on a world-wide scale—a far-reaching effect of Osler's 'Practice of Medicine', 2nd edition. Mr. Flexner, meanwhile, as the expert of the Carnegie Foundation, had made and published a survey of the conditions of medical education in Europe. He became in 1912 an Assistant Secretary of the General Education Board of the new Rockefeller Foundation which financed the full-time academic programmes at the Johns Hopkins clinic and elsewhere.

sense—met with in the Bible and still used colloquially—as it expresses the mental attitude of the student towards his Alma Mater, '*totius litteratorii studii altrix prima*'. In mind, manners and morals the young man seeks life's equipment when he says to his Alma Mater in the words of the Psalmist, 'O learn me true understanding and knowledge'. To learn the use of his mind, to learn good manners, and to learn to drive Plato's horses, form the marrow of an education within the reach of every citizen, but to which universities minister in a very special way; and it should be comprehensive, fitting a man, in Milton's words, 'to perform all the offices, private and public, of peace or of war'. The other great function of a university is to advance learning, to increase man's knowledge of man and of nature. Looking over the lecture list of any modern university, one is impressed with the bewildering complexity of subjects taught, from Homer to Victor Hugo, from Tamil to internal secretions; but they may be roughly grouped into those dealing with man and those dealing with the cosmos about him. At any time these 800 years this division has been recognized, and though we have travelled a long way from the seven liberal arts which once comprised the whole range of study, it is not so much the nature of the subjects or their division that characterizes modern education, as a new spirit, a new attitude of mind towards them. No real progress was made until we returned to the Greek method—the pursuit of knowledge for its own sake. Out of the laboratories, as the result of work done by men absorbed in study and usually without the slightest bearing upon practical problems, came the three great revolutions of the nineteenth century—the annihilation of time, the substitution of the machine for the hand, and the conquest of disease. Physics, chemistry, and biology have given us control of the forces of nature. Faraday has harnessed Niagara, the power of which is now transmitted hundreds of miles away; the Curies have found the magic *vril* of Bulwer Lytton's 'Coming Race', and Pasteur has revealed one of the greatest secrets of life.

It is characteristic of modern conditions that, hovering on the borders of the charmed circle of pure science, are those keen to turn every discovery to practical use. What good is knowledge unless it can be utilized in the service of man, asks a utilitarian age? The university of to-day, while ministering to the advancement of learning, is ready to teach how to make the learning profitable, so that everything in practical science, from household economy to aviation, finds its place. Schools specially adapted to special needs stand out as dominant features in the new programme, and Oxford and Cambridge, as well as Newcastle, Leeds and Bristol, have felt the strong impulsion to develop the science which deals with human well-being. Of the old faculties which made up the *studium generale*, medicine has been the one most profoundly affected by the growth of modern science. What a revolution in our generation! Anatomy, physiology and pathology with their sub-divisions of histology, embryology, physiological chemistry and pharmacology, are now housed in laboratories controlled by specialists, whose ideals and work differ in no respect from those of their colleagues in the departments of physics, chemistry and biology; and in many places large separate institutes are devoted to these subjects. The urgent need to-day is to extend this type of university work into our medical schools, so that *all* branches of the curriculum are included—medicine as well as pathology, surgery as well as anatomy, midwifery and gynaecology as well as chemistry. But here comes a difficulty—the practical schools which deal with these important subjects and their sub-divisions are not under the control of the university, or at best have a very feeble affiliation. . . .

From the account in the Newcastle *Chronicle* next day, the address, of which these are the opening paragraphs, must have been largely given without following his manuscript. He put his finger clearly, in the last sentence quoted, on the weak spot in the British system of medical education—indeed, of medical education, as yet, in most countries, when he spoke of the loose affiliation of the clinic with the university. They were either independent corporations, as he believed was the case in Newcastle; or the hospital had evolved the medical school, as in London; or there was a mutual arrangement between university and hospital such as existed in Edinburgh. Good work was done under these systems, but there were bad features about each of them, particularly as they affected the small hospitals where too many physicians and surgeons for the number of beds bred discontent in the outside men who claimed hospital privileges. The 'hospital unit' he was to describe met the needs of the situation, he believed. As for the medical students, he is quoted as saying, he would make them serve two and a half years in the hospital and two and a half years in the medical school. He would make them understand that a hospital was an organization that went on perennially. The beds had no holidays: neither should the medical students [laughter, and cries of 'Shame']. Well, he would give them a few days at Christmas and a few days at Easter, and he was sure they would not want more than a couple of weeks in the summer.

Continuous work was really a necessity to keep a student in good mental condition.

But to return to the written address. It contained much wisdom in regard to the duties of the professor who is to be head of the ideal unit; in regard to his workshop, the clinic, and laboratories; in regard to his staff, to teaching, and to research work.

> Upon one thing [he said] I would insist—that every assistant connected with the clinic taught. A few exceptional men, like the distinguished physicist, the late Professor Rowland, are really too good to teach; but for the majority, daily contact with students, and a little of the routine of teaching, keep us in touch with the common clay and are the best preservatives against that staleness so apt to come as a blight upon the pure researcher.

In the evening there followed, of course, a large banquet in the King's Hall of Armstrong College; and Osler, after indulging in some banter with his friend, Principal [now Sir Henry] Hadow, late of Worcester College, Oxford, who had become Head of the College the year before, went on to say some wise and serious things about the general practitioner, the man who does the most important work of the profession and comes in contact with the people; and told how his status could be benefited by opening free courses for him at the Royal Victoria Infirmary in Newcastle—a benefit to staff and patients as well.

Osler's allusion in the address to Professor Rowland recalls that the Johns Hopkins, at this very time, was in the throes of formulating new policies concerning the relation of the clinician to his 'hospital unit'—a matter which in Osler's day had apparently been so satisfactorily solved; and he was being appealed to for his views by parties on both sides of the controversy. But medical education was not the only thing on which his opinion was sought, as is evident in the following note from the Curator of the Hunterian Museum:

From Prof. Arthur Keith to W. O. Royal College of Surgeons of England, 15th Nov., 1910.

Dear Osler,—Please help me: I am puzzling over the relationship of the 'Evelyn' to the 'Harvey' Anat. Plates. Evelyn never heard of, nor saw, such preparations until he went to Padua in 1646 and seems firmly of opinion that his were the first made in Padua. Did Vesling's assistant (Leonaenas) humbug him? There were no such plates at the College of Physicians in 1650 and Cowper (1687) seems to think Evelyn's were the only plates in England. Did you see such tables in any of the Museums of Italy? Was there a real trade in those things or are the Harvey-Evelyn Plates the only examples known? Forgive me my importunities and Believe me Yours sincerely, A. KEITH.

In those days one could hardly speak of medical history and of book-collecting without the name of Joseph Frank Payne coming to mind. Payne rather than Osler would possibly have been the one immediately able to answer Arthur Keith's question; but that Payne was ill and had retired to New Barnet has already been told.

I found your letter on my return from Cambridge [Osler wrote to Mrs. Payne on the 18th]. The sad news was not unexpected, as Sharkey told me this week how ill he was. I am so thankful now that I went a few weeks ago, & shall always carry the most happy recollections of that visit. Do you know that he was one of my oldest friends? I met him in 1873, & in 1874 we attended together several meetings of the Medical Microscopical Society. He was always so kind in writing about my papers. He had a happy & useful life in the profession, and for years, since Dr. Greenhill's death, he has been recognized as *the* English Scholar in Medicine. We shall miss him sadly at the Club and at the College. But our loss is nothing compared with the sad gap it will make in the lives of his loved ones at home. My deepest sympathies are with you. To my deep regret I shall not be able to pay my last respects tomorrow. I have been fighting a heavy cold for nearly a week & yesterday I had to go to Cambridge to lecture. Today I am much worse, & Mrs. Osler forbids me to think of going out of the house.[1]

---

[1] Osler describes his last visit to Payne in an obituary notice (*British Medical Journal*, Nov. 26th) which opens with this paragraph:

'The dominant feeling in the minds of many of us is not so much regret at the death of our dear friend Dr. Payne—for had he not reached the Psalmist's limit?—but a deep sense of the tragedy of the extinction in the grave of so much sound learning. For Payne belonged to that small group of men in the profession of this country who not only possess an interest in the history of medicine, but the scholarship necessary for fruitful work at the records. In our generation he was the worthy successor of Adams, Greenhill, and Ogle—the last-named happily still with us. Practical men who, like myself, dabble in these subjects as a pastime, owe an immense debt to these experts who maintain in the profession the fine traditions of the scholarship of Linacre, Caius and Freind.'

He was entitled to be a little depressed—as much as he ever was—housed with a persistent cold, grieved by Payne's death, disturbed over the rumours of disquiet in Baltimore. At the end of a dictated letter sent on the 19th to one of his old assistants, he adds in script this after-word—often the most interesting portion of his meagre letters:

> All well here—very busy—academically. Ike happy—except classically. Often wish I were back, but—Did you ever by the way read Voltaire's famous *But* letter. I have just been reading his life. I suppose had I remained it would have been out at the cemetery, and this is better! Still I had a splendid innings—nothing to regret and no blur on the picture as I look back.

Little has been said, during the account of this and the preceding year, of the routine university business and the machinery whereby it is conducted, all of which interested Osler greatly. An opportunity to call this to mind is given in the following note written in Osler's copy[1] of Macray's 'Annals of the Bodleian Library', describing the annual visitation which always fell on November 8th:

> Before the visitation today, and after the Latin speech in honour of Sir Thomas Bodley, the Curators and the V.-C. met the President and Fellows of Magdalen College in the Picture Gallery where a portrait of Dr. Macray was presented to the Bodleian. Dr. Macray was present, a fine, hale-looking old man of 86 years. Warren, the President of Magdalen (Macray's College) made the presentation and referred to the long services of Dr. Macray who entered the Library in 1840 and retired in 1905. Dr. M. responded and spoke of his life-long affection for the place and the happiness he had had in doing so much for its archives.

'There is really a great deal to do here', he wrote apologetically to one of his friends who apparently had pictured him as leading a life of academic ease. Hints of some of the things he was finding to do appear in the following two letters—the first of them written on November 18th to Weir Mitchell:

> I am sorry you did not see my boy this summer. I wish he could have had a few lessons in fishing from you. He got some good trout with Frank Ross, about 80 miles back of Quebec. He is taller than

[1] This volume, bulging with his intimate notes regarding the affairs of the Library, was bequeathed to the Bodleian.

I am & very well and strong. He likes Winchester, but he has no aptitude for study & loathes classics. He is interested in butterflies & may take to science in some form, not medicine. We are very happy still & very busy—so many people coming & going. Last Sunday there were 32 visitors not counting three week-enders. A parson from Baltimore, two young men from Toronto, Mrs. Admiral Belnap with the wife of a Capt. Kranter U. S. N., two Cotton Spinners from the North, the Hon. Gorell Barnes, Sec. of the Divorce Commission, a Doctor from Indianapolis with an English-Literature Professor from one of the Western Colleges—& a group of undergraduates, chiefly Rhodes scholars. Sunday eve. I always dine in Hall, at Christ Church & have a couple of guests. We have a very pleasant company, 33 last Sunday. Monday I went to Midhurst in Surrey to pay an official visit to the Sanatorium. Tuesday I have my clinic at the Infirmary from 2–4—chiefly for the Doctors in the neighbourhood. Wednesday, meeting of the governing body of Christ Church, & in the afternoon the Endowment Fund Trustees at the House of Lords. Thursday, at Cambridge, when I lectured on French Medical Education at the Medical School. To-day, I got back in time for the Standing Committee of the Bodleian at 12, a weekly meeting at which we discuss all matters relating to the Library; & at 2 pm the weekly meeting of the Managers of the Clarendon Press. This eve, the Junior Scientific Society. Tomorrow a very busy morning, & two week-enders, Dr. Leonard Guthrie (whose book by the way J. K. should know, Nervous Disorders of Childhood) and McMonagle (& Mrs M) from San Francisco, old friends. There is really a great deal here to interest one. I see a fair number of patients—chiefly stranded Americans & colonials.

You will be sorry to hear of Payne's death—much sound learning goes to the grave with him. He had a fine library which will probably be sold by auction. I will let you know if there is anything very special which you or the College might like. I had a nice talk with de Schweinitz about the College this summer. I have agreed to come out for the S. W. Mitchell lecture in 1912. What a comfort it must be to you to feel that your work has been so successful there—and so appreciated. I have just had a letter from Keen saying that he fears a growth in the colon & has gone to Rochester for operation. I do hope all may go well.

And the other letter he writes on November 23rd to *The Nation*,[1] giving a description of an Oxford Congregation of the preceding day in which was debated the burning question of 'compulsory Greek'. As it records

[1] New York, Dec. 8, 1910, xci. 544.

his own feelings in the matter it deserves reprinting in large part:

That no conservatism is so strong as in a democracy is well illustrated by Oxford and Cambridge, the two oldest democracies in Europe, which to-day, as in the Middle Ages, are in control of the Masters of Arts, whose voice decides everything from the election of a Chancellor to the disposal of a five-pound note. In Oxford the resident M.A.'s and professors, with the heads of the colleges, form a body called Congregation, and these, with all M.A.'s, resident and non-resident, on the books of the colleges, form Convocation. The former has 526 members, the latter about 7,000. Every Tuesday in term at 2 p.m. these bodies meet to transact university business, prepared by a smaller body called the Hebdomadal Council. As a rule, the attendance is small—a handful of men—but when an important question is before the university several hundreds may be in Congregation, while the outside M.A.'s from all over the country may swarm to Oxford (even in special trains!) to *placet* or *non placet* a contentious measure.

In theory it is a magnificent thing, this democracy of learning, this Athenian demos, 7,000 strong, every one with his vote, but it is a cumbrous machinery with which to manage a university—though a grand sight in session! No finer academic function is to be seen than the Sheldonian Theatre packed to the roof to hear Congregation or Convocation debate some burning question of university reform. Except the upper gallery reserved for undergraduates (only a handful of whom were lured from sport of another and more pleasing kind), Wren's splendid building was well filled yesterday with Grecians and Trojans, repeating sixteenth-century history, fighting again a battle over Greek. Then it was a struggle to restrain the introduction of the new learning, believed to be tinctured with heresy; now the battle is over the retention of this same old learning, i. e., Greek, as a compulsory subject for the entrance examination. The Trojans carried their case in the Hebdomadal Council, and a statute was framed, the preamble of which reads:

> Whereas, it is expedient to amend the statute relating to the examination in stated subjects in Responsions (entrance examination) so as to provide (1) that Greek shall no longer be a compulsory subject, (2) that every candidate must, in order to pass Responsions, satisfy the Masters of the Schools in Latin and Elementary Mathematics, and also either in (a) Greek or in (b) two other subjects, one of which must be a Modern Language, etc.

After the passing of a few decrees, the registrar read out the preamble and the battle began. It was, as I said, a fine sight—virtually the whole teaching body of the university, professors, tutors, nearly all the heads, many ancient Dons, not often seen in the house, and youthful M.A.'s. And it was not a 'black brigade', not a gathering made up of the country clergy, who have been known to pack Convocation. These questions have to come first before Congregation, composed of the local M.A.'s and doctors who reside within a mile of Carfax, the centre of the city. The Vice-Chancellor, newly elected, Dr. Heberden, the principal of Brasenose (great-grandson of the famous William Heberden, the English Celsus, whose 'Commentaries' is still a famous book), presided with grace and dignity. The semi-circle below him was gay with the scarlet of the Convocation habits worn by the doctors of the various Faculties. In the matter of words the Englishman has a wonderful self-restraint, and the gift of taciturnity is nowhere better seen than in these Oxford discussions. *Opera non verba* is the motto, and in an hour or two questions are settled which would take Frenchmen or Americans days to discuss. They come to vote, not to talk, knowing that sensible people make up their minds on a question, and are not much influenced by eleventh-hour speeches. The battle is really fought in the pamphlets and statements circulated a week or ten days before the meeting.

Mr. Percy Matheson of New College, a leading Trojan, who had brought up the question eight years ago, introduced the preamble in a strong speech, in which he urged that in our modern conditions Greek should no longer be required as a necessary subject for a degree in Arts. He pointed out that it would not apply to the famous honour school of *Literae Humaniores*, or the School of Theology, and it was stated that particular Schools could reserve their rights. A general education without Greek was better for some boys than a general education with Greek, for which the modern languages offered a proper substitute. The President of St. John's College, Dr. James, who has just come from Rugby School, opposed the measure as a weak concession to popular demands, and a sop to the scientists. If Greek were discarded to-day Latin would follow tomorrow. The greatest rulers of England—Canning, Peel, Gladstone, Salisbury, Milner, and Asquith—were products of the classical teaching of Oxford. Sir William Anson, the Warden of All Souls, thought the preamble of the statute too uncompromising, as it made Greek optional for everybody. The Regius Professor of Greek, Gilbert Murray, while in favour of differentiating in the Faculties, could not support the statute as it favoured universal exemption from Greek. After four other members of the University had spoken a division was taken with the following results: *non placets*, 188; *placets*, 152; majority, 36.

This is the first 'knock out' for the reformers, who are trying to rearrange the constitution of the University and its studies, in accordance with the suggestions made by the Chancellor, Lord

Curzon. Two weeks ago the preamble of the statute reconstituting the Faculties was passed, and the reformers were pretty confident of success on this old question of compulsory Greek, which was decided adversely eight years ago. Had the statute been differently worded, making a differentiation in the Faculties, I believe it would have carried.

While in favour of relaxing the present regulations, I should like to see Greek retained in the older universities as a qualification for graduation in theology, medicine, and law. Under present conditions in England it is no hardship to ask a young man who is seeking a medical degree in Oxford or Cambridge to have a knowledge of Greek. Taught as it is to-day, it may not be of much use, but if for no other reasons, reverence for the memory of Hippocrates and honour of the labours of Galen demand that we should have some men in the profession with a knowledge of the language of our origins. Could the student be taught the dead languages 'without the perplexities of rules talked into him' (Locke), could we but cease from 'forcing the empty wits of children to compose themes, verses and orations' (Milton), could we but adopt the rational method by which Montaigne learned Latin and Greek as he learned his native tongue, these languages might become working instruments, keys to great literatures and to the minds of great masters; and the student would read his Celsus and Hippocrates as freely as his Watson or Trousseau.

This winter will decide whether Oxford is able to reform herself in accordance with the elaborate plan submitted by the Hebdomadal Council. Many feel that only by a Parliamentary commission can the necessary changes be enforced. The conservative element in the democracy may be—as to-day—too strong. The problem is how to unite in due proportion the monarchical element of an American university with the principle that gives a share in the government to the graduates. It is like the two mother forms of states of which Plato speaks, the one monarchy, the other democracy. 'Now if you are to have liberty and the combination of friendship with wisdom, you must have both these forms of government in a measure'; and this holds good for a university as well as for a city.

Perhaps nowhere was Osler likely to miss Payne more than at the monthly dinner of the College Club to which, as told, he had been elected in December of 1904.

My real intimacy with Osler [writes Sir George Savage] began when he was appointed Regius Professor of Medicine at Oxford. From that time we constantly met at the Athenaeum and at various medical meetings. I also visited him at Oxford. We both belonged to a very restricted inner dining circle of the Royal College of

Physicians, called the College Club, which dined once a month for seven or eight months of the year. Osler was frequently there, but his official duties at Oxford not infrequently kept him away. When present he used to spend the night with me. At those dinners he generally sat near one or other of the Fellows most interested in the history of medicine, such as Norman Moore, or Frank Payne. He was overflowing with antiquarian interest, and nothing on these lines was alien to him.

In Osler's library among the books on clubs and societies is a copy of Payne's privately printed 'History of the College Club'; and in the volume have been inserted several interesting clippings on the general subject of 'blackballing'. As is true of many old clubs—and the College Club goes back to the days of Anthony Askew, William Cadogan, and Richard Warren—it had become increasingly difficult to elect new members. Except in the case of the Oslers of the world, some one is likely to harbour a grudge, and it has been cynically said of most clubs of long standing that if the members should all resign and come up for re-election no one would fail to receive a black-ball. There were twenty-two members of the College Club, and at the October meeting each year three Fellows were nominated for each existing vacancy, to be voted upon the following month. In the end of Payne's volume Osler had made a number of entries, thus:

Oct. 31, 1910. We have not been able to elect anyone for the past two years. At the preliminary selection of names, A——, F——, R—— and—I forget who—headed the list, but at the ballot in November no one could be chosen. Someone has 'pilled' each one and as it requires a full vote, two blackballs excluding, it is hard to get unanimity. I was very mad last year and felt like resigning when three such good men as A. F. & R. were blackballed. I doubt if we can elect next month. I suspect Polonius and Hibernicus do the pilling.

Nov. 30th. I could not go to the Nov. dinner as I was laid up with a cold. Savage writes that R—— and D—— were elected. Payne died this week—a great loss to the club.

His November 25th entry—the 'cold room at the Examiners' meeting' which put him to bed for a week—doubtless is what accounted for his absence. But, even when laid up with bronchitis, pleasant things may happen to pass the time; and Bodley's (then) sub-librarian saw fit to inoculate him with a desire for some ancient manuscripts which ultimately found their way into his library and served, furthermore, to introduce him to a Dr. Sa'eed of Teheran, Persia. Bibliomania has well-recognized stages —from books, to incunabula, to manuscripts.

To Dr. A. E. Cowley from W. O. Dec. 1st (in Bed !)

Dear Cowley, Luke iv. 8 ! Is not this December, the leanest month of the year? Are not the times very hard? Is not the voice of Ll—— G—— heard in the land? Is this, think you, a time for MSS.? What a heartless brute to mention them! But—I do love Dioscorides—even in Arabic! Did he not 'peep and botanize' up & down the Thames valley? Is he not said to have gathered Digitalis where the Radcliffe Camera (or the Infirmary) now stands? Considering these things I would like to see the MS.—but I am in bed, with a mild Bronchitis. Could you send it to me by my fraülein & say if you think it a good example of an Arabic MS, & also if the price (the December price!) asked by the son of the Prophet is reasonable.

From Dr. Cowley to W. O. Bodleian Library,
Dec. 1, 1910.

The MS is a very good specimen of Arabic writing—especially Vol. I, but the pictures make it specially valuable. The Arabs did not run to such things much. The portrait of Dioscorides himself has been partly erased by a pious owner (as being idolatrous) and then restored, with the halo turned into a turban—so typical of modern progress! The volumes belong to a Persian. They have been brought to England by a man (New College) who was Brit. Consul in Shîrâz. He has offered them, on behalf of the Persian, to the British Museum who have named a price. He has not told me what it is. I think £20 would be cheap—and it is what I should offer if I could—but I should hardly expect to get it for that. I am very sorry to hear that you are laid up—but I don't wonder. I hope the sight of your ancient predecessor will really do you good. Will you let me have him back in the morning?

'Offer £20—if refused, I might go a bit higher—& take to porridge for a month.' The volumes returned to Persia —but found their way back to Norham Gardens in 1912.

It is not unlikely that his inability to shake off his cold may have sent him the next month to Egypt to recuperate and to get the chill of examination rooms out of his bones. Of this possibility, which would take him through Italy, he hinted on a Christmas-card sent to 'Muriel-Marjorie-Maude' in Rome:

My wish for you is: that I may see you next spring. The British Ambassador has asked the Chancellor of Oxford University to send some one to Rome to lecture on Table Manners to the English & American children, as the Mayor of Rome, the Pope & the King of Italy have been very much worried about the subject, having heard of the conduct of certain little girls whom I shall not mention. I have consented to give a course of six lectures & demonstrations!

Some things important to medicine which had been happening, as well as a sidelight on English politics—a subject rarely touched upon in Osler's own letters—may be gleaned from the December letters of his frequent correspondent, Weir Mitchell:

. . . Nothing is new here in science that I can tell you, except the very amazing story, that Rockefeller having given Ehrlich for three years Ten Thousand Dollars a year, someone left the German a million of marks, upon which he wrote to Mr. Rockefeller that he had no longer need of his pension and did not know how best he could reward such generosity, but finally concluded to send him one thousand doses of '606'. This comes from Flexner, and I have no doubt it is true: or, I rather think, however, it comes from Welch. I may add that Noguchi, it is said, has found means of cultivating with some preparation of liver the specific organism of syphilis. This would be the final triumph in this chain of wonderful discovery. I think this is calculated to produce enormous influence upon the civilization of the world, on the efficiency of armies and navies, and on the hygiene of the next generation or two. . . .

We are all well at home, very busy, College prosperous, etc. I have finished a novel which has been lying on my summer desk for three years, and which like all my books has one medical portrayal—a paranoiac. It is not a book which will be popular or widely read. I do not think I shall reprint it in England. It is really not worth while. For some reason our books have in England so small a sale that it is not worth while to bother with additions to the literature of a declining nation!!! Upon my word, what the deuce is happening to you in England. I quoted to my friends the Misses Lawrence, in irony, Tennyson's lines:

A land of fair and long renown
Where freedom slowly broadens down
From precedent to precedent.

Surely you are far away from this and are taking a header into bewildering revolution. I don't like it. I want the House of Lords preserved, I want the big old houses preserved, and I want some of the old things guarded for the enjoyment of the American of this later day. As for your Mr. Asquith, it seems to me he has the characteristic political morals of a ward politician. It is a little dangerous, I know, to talk of the politics of another land, even a land so near as England, as one may make mistakes. . . .

And a few days later he wrote again, saying: 'Alas, *Great* Britain! All who love England feel sorry the shillelagh has become so potent in her politics.' Evidently this troubled Dr. Mitchell more than it did his friend on the brink of this 'bewildering revolution'. Certainly life in Oxford sounded peaceful enough, to judge from the following Christmas letter:

To H. B. Jacobs from W. O.

Dear Jacobus, I wish I could look in at No. 11 this eve. Could you return the call, you would find a festive scene, a dance!—R. and his young friends. We have a niece and her children with us & Palmer Wright from Ottawa. R. has grown so much—just my height. He is an awful duffer at his books, but he is a dear good fellow & not the slightest trouble. I suppose Welch has told you that W. A. Marburg will make an offer for Payne's library. I went to New Barnet the other day to look over the collection. I am afraid we cannot get all for the sum M. names, but it will cover, I hope, the medical books without the 15th century herbals, which nowadays bring fancy prices on account of the old wood-cuts. They could be sold separately & after all have only a typographical interest. 'Tis a choice assortment—many books of the greatest variety & many not in the College of Phy. or in the S.-G. [Surgeon-General's] Library. He has also a splendid Milton collection—the best in England after the British Museum. He has been buying with great care for 45 years.

Many thanks for the book—I like C. so much—also for the Shelley, when it comes. I may go to Egypt for six weeks. My brother, E. B., starts for Cairo with a boat party, to be on the river a month. 'Tis too good an opportunity to miss. He wants Mrs. Osler also but she does not care to go so far from the boy. Miss Woolley may come over while I am away. By the way Payne left me the Restitutio Christianismi of Servetus, the 1790 reprint, now almost impossible to get. I have the Calvin—a lovely copy. It too, is scarce—my copy sold in Paris about ten years ago for frs. 1500. I shall be glad of the Harvard Journal. Jim Putnam's article on James in the Atlantic Monthly is most interesting. So glad to hear Mrs. Jacobs keeps well. Happy New Year to you both.

CHAPTER XXXI

1911

THE BARONETCY

'I was very sorry to hear of the death of Frank Frick—ultimus Romanorum of the old guard at Baltimore, a fine set of men, a better is not grown anywhere.' So begins a letter of early January to a member of the Maryland 'Faculty' to whose library Mr. Frick had so generously contributed; and Osler continued: 'Is it not splendid to hear of the success of the Appeal? I feel rather mean not to have given anything, but to tell the truth I got involved more deeply than I had intended in the new building of the Royal Society of Medicine.'[1]

For one whose name was still apt to appear on subscription-lists for all medical projects started in Toronto, Montreal, Philadelphia, and Baltimore, and who for this very reason, perhaps, felt that he must give no less generously in his new home, he must many times have been conscious of the cobwebs in his pockets. And he says again, later in January: 'I suppose you will move to New York for the Hoe sale. I have not yet seen the catalogue, but Quaritch has promised to send me one as soon as they are out. I am afraid I shall be too poor to bid on anything special.' For a bibliophile this was a hardship, but on the whole life did not owe him very much, as he was apt to say; and at this juncture his brother came to the rescue and took him to Egypt, away from the temptation of book catalogues and sales. None too soon: for on January 26th he was actually to be found in the lion's den—of all queer places for a Regius Professor—in attendance at the annual dinner of the Inter-

[1] It was decided by a resolution passed at a special general meeting of the Fellows, February 1910, that an effort should be made to raise the whole amount of the cost of the handsome building to be erected at the corner of Wimpole and Henrietta Streets, by means of voluntary gifts from Fellows of the Society, the members of the Sections, and the friends of Fellows and members—a difficult job.

national Association of Antiquarian Booksellers at the Criterion Restaurant, Piccadilly, at which he is quoted as having said:[1]

I feel very highly honoured that the toast of the evening has been assigned to me. And really it is out of the deepest spirit of Christian charity that I propose it; because you see here before you a mental, moral, almost, I may say, a physical wreck—and all of your own making. Until I became mixed up with you I was really a respectable, God-fearing, industrious, earnest, ardent, enthusiastic, energetic student. *Now* what am I? A mental wreck, devoted to nothing but your literature. Instead of attending to my duties and attending to my work, in comes every day by the post, and by every post, all this seductive literature with which you have, as you know perfectly well, gradually undermined the mental virility of many a better man than I. Had it not been that there is so much more moral ferment in the Celt than there is in the average Saxon, like our Chairman [James Tregaskis], who poses as a Cornishman; and you have only to look at his face and then at mine, to know there is no more Celtic blood in him—it is simply an accident that he calls himself a Cornishman; he has got a 'Tre' in front of his name[2]—had it not been for the saving remnant of the Celtic blood in me I really would not have been able to get up enough Christian charity to propose the toast that is assigned to me here. But I have the greatest satisfaction in feeling that I am going to have my revenge, and I noticed the first indications of it the other day. I saw in one of the catalogues 'Osler's Principles and Practice of Medicine'—the first time I had seen it in an Antiquarian Catalogue. But just think of what will happen in the next generation; and I only hope our Chairman may live—he is certain to—until the great dissolver loosens and frees from the libraries the 125,000 copies of that work which at present are busily engaged in helping the practitioners on the other side of the water, and some on this side of the water, to look after your bodily health. Better than that—that is bad enough—you know what it is to have a book like that come in constantly; it is an awful worry and bother. I know it, but I am not sorry for you. But when you think of that System of Medicine in seven volumes, seven volumes! each one weighing several pounds; just think when that gets on to your shelves—it will not be worth the paper! Then I know perfectly well that I shall have had my revenge. . . .

There was more of this, which appears to have highly enter-

[1] *The Bookseller*, Feb. 3, 1911, p. 144.

[2] 'By Pol, Tre and Pen
You may know the Cornishmen.'

tained his auditors, to one of whom, Mr. B. H. Blackwell, the Oxford bookseller, he paid at the close of the speech a handsome tribute to the effect that around him rotated much of the intellectual life of the undergraduate. On this very day Osler had finished his promised Introduction for a volume more likely to find a ready sale in old book shops than an out-of-date text-book of medicine:

To Mr. Henry Phipps. 13, Norham Gardens, Jan. 26, 1911.

Constable and Co. sent 25 copies of the little sermonette [Man's Redemption of Man] to you some time ago; I daresay they have reached you; I have written asking about them. They are pushing ahead with the printing of the *Pasteur Life*, the introduction to which I have got ready. We are making headway in this country in our tuberculosis fight, and have established a dispensary in connection with the Radcliffe Infirmary, very much on the lines of the Phipps Dispensary at the Johns Hopkins. We hope to get in touch with all the tuberculosis cases of the county. We have a young Scot as physician, who scours the country on his motor 'bike.' I enclose you the cards of our meeting to day. I am off to Egypt next week for six weeks with my brother. I hope you will have a very comfortable winter at Palm Beach.

The 'Life of Pasteur' was subsequently distributed to all Anglo-American medical school libraries, where copies dog-eared from much reading will still be found, in each of which is inserted a presentation note from the Oxford Regius.[1] In his 'Introduction', after a review of what Pasteur had accomplished through his researches, Osler went on to say:

In his growth the man kept pace with the scientist—heart and head held even sway in his life. To many whose estimate of French character is gained from 'yellow' literature this story will reveal the true side of a great people, in whom filial piety, brotherly solicitude, generosity, and self-sacrifice are combined with a rare devotion to country. . . .

This is a biography for young men of science, and for others who

[1] The translation from Vallery-Radot which was used, was the well-known one of Mrs. R. L. Devonshire, first published in a two-volume edition. Since Osler's 'Introduction' was prefixed there have been at least six reprintings. In this 1911 edition Osler explained how at Mr. Phipps's request he had come to write the preface, but the explanation has been omitted by the publishers in subsequent reprintings.

wish to learn what science has done, and may do, for humanity. From it may be gleaned three lessons. The value of method, of technique, in the hands of a great master has never been better illustrated . . . In the life of a young man the most essential thing for happiness is the gift of friendship. And here is the second great lesson . . . And the last great lesson is humility before the unsolved problems of the Universe. Any convictions that might be a comfort in the sufferings of human life had his respectful sympathy. His own creed was beautifully expressed in his eulogy upon *Littré*: 'He who proclaims the existence of the Infinite, and none can avoid it—accumulates in that affirmation more of the supernatural than is to be found in all the miracles of all the religions; for the notion of the Infinite presents that double character that it forces itself upon us and yet is incomprehensible. When this notion seizes upon our understanding, we can but kneel. . . . The idea of God is a form of the idea of the Infinite. As long as the mystery of the Infinite weighs on human thought, temples will be erected for the worship of the Infinite, whether God is called Brahma, Allah, Jehovah or Jesus; and on the pavement of those temples, men will be seen kneeling, prostrated, annihilated in the thought of the Infinite.' And modern Pantheism has never had a greater disciple, whose life and work set forth the devotion to an ideal—that service to humanity is service to God. . . .

The future belongs to science. More and more she will control the destinies of the nations. Already she has them in her crucible and on her balances. In her new mission to humanity she preaches a new gospel. In the nineteenth-century renaissance she has had great apostles, Darwin, for example, whose gifts of heart and head were in equal measure, but after re-reading for the third or fourth time the 'Life of Louis Pasteur', I am of the opinion, expressed recently by the anonymous writer of a beautiful tribute in the *Spectator*, 'that he was the most perfect man who has ever entered the Kingdom of Science'.

Sir Edmund and his party reached Naples on February 4th, as is evident from Osler's letter of expostulation to *The Times*, written on this date, regarding the unsanitary condition of the carriages of the *train de luxe* which he said were 'fit only for the scrap heap'. But this was quickly forgotten—not only by the *Compagnie Internationale des Wagons-Lits* but by the expostulator, if one may judge from the shower of enthusiastic postcards and notes which in a few days issued from Cairo: cards to people as remote from one another as Bodley's Librarian and the 'mother' of Rosalie:

Shepheard's Hotel, Feb. 14, 1911.

Dear Nicholson, Greetings & good health! I spent an hour with Dr. Moritz in the Khedival Library this morning. I am off up the river tomorrow. Yours sincerely, Wm OSLER.

Cairo [no date]

Dear Susan, My love to the darling Rosalie. The bulrushes have gone & so have Moses and the daughter of Pharaoh but they show the place all the same. Love to Mother and Dad. Yours W. O.

But the hospitals interested him no less than the Khedival Library and Gizeh, and in a later letter to W. S. Thayer he says:

We had a week in Cairo where I saw much of interest medically. Looss showed me all his ankylostoma specimens. They have not yet organized a crusade against the disease & it really seems hopeless as no one wears anything on the feet in the country, & the conditions about the villages could not be more favourable for its spread. At every landing-stage one can pick out the victims. Bilharzia is even worse—very common & more hopeless.[1] The Hospital has a score or more of bladder cases & as many of the intestinal form. The clinics are not properly organized, & men of the Griesinger stamp are needed. I was glad to see the old man's portrait [2] in the Library. I am to meet the Board of Education on my return and hope to stir them to the point of spending more money.

They finally went up-river on a boat which had 'every possible comfort including the most jovial dragoman in Egypt', and for once in his life Osler really writes some long letters—long enough to satisfy even Weir Mitchell, who about this time had threatened to cease corresponding unless he could get something better than a p.c. in return. Thus from the s.s. *Seti* on February 22nd, posted two days later from Luxor:

Such a trip! I would give one of the fragments of Osiris to have you two on this boat. Everything arranged for our comfort & the

[1] It was this disease, so widespread in the Nile valley, that caused the military authorities chief apprehension when large bodies of troops had to be sent to Lower Egypt in the Great War. A special commission under the direction of Dr. R. T. Leiper of the London School of Tropical Medicine was sent out to investigate the life cycle of the parasite causing the disease, and it was ultimately found that a variety of snail played the part of intermediary host.

[2] Theodor Bilharz (1825–62), German helminthologist.

dearest old dragoman who parades the deck in gorgeous attire with his string of 99 beads—each one representing an attribute of God! We shall take about 10 days to the Dam (Assouan), 580 miles from Cairo. Yesterday we stopped at Assiut & I saw the Hospital of the American Mission—200 beds, about 20,000 out-patients. Dr. Grant is in charge with 3 assistants and many nurses. I found there an old Clevelander . . . who had fallen off a donkey and broken his ribs, and on the 8th day had thrombosis of left leg. He was better, but at 76 he should have stayed at home. The Nile itself is fascinating, an endless panorama—on one side or the other the Arabian or the Libyan desert comes close to the river, often in great limestone ridges, 200–800 ft. in height; and then the valley widens to eight or 10 miles. Yellow water, brown mud, green fields, and grey sand and rocks always in sight; & the poor devils dipping up the water in pails from one level to the other. We had a great treat yesterday afternoon. The Pasha of this district has two sons at Oxford and their tutor, A. L. Smith, a great friend of his, sent him a letter about our party. He had a secretary meet us at Assiut & came up the river to Abutig. We had tea in his house and then visited a Manual Training School for 100 boys, which he supports. In the evening he gave us a big dinner. I wish you could have seen us start off on donkeys for the half mile to his house. It was hard work talking to him through an interpreter, but he was most interesting—a great tall Arab of very distinguished appearance. A weird procession left his house at 11 p.m.—all of us in evening dress, which seemed to make the donkeys very frisky. Three lantern men, a group of donkey men, two big Arabs with rifles, & following us a group of men carrying sheep—one alive! chickens, fruit, vegetables, eggs, &c., to stock our larder. We tie up every eve about 8 o'clock, pegging the boat in the mud. The Arabs are fine; our Reis, or pilot, is a direct descendant, I am sure, of Rameses II, judging from his face. After washing himself he spreads his prayer mat at the bow of the boat & says his prayers with the really beautiful somatic ritual of the Moslem. The old Pasha, by the way, is a very holy man and has been to Mecca where he keeps two lamps perpetually burning & tended by two eunuchs. He is holy enough to do the early morning prayer from 4 to 6 a.m. with some 2000 sentences from the Koran. It is a great religion—no wonder Moslem rules in the East. Wonderful crops up here—sugar-cane, cotton, beans and wheat. These poor devils work hard but now they have the satisfaction of knowing they are not robbed. We are never out of sight of the desert & the mountains come close on one side or the other. To-day we were for miles close under limestone heights—800–1000 feet, grey and desolate. The river is a ceaseless panorama—the old Nile boats with curved prows & the most remarkable sails, like big jibs, swung on a boom from the top of the masts, usually two and the foresail the larger. I saw some great books in the Khedival Library—monster Korans superbly illuminated. The finer types have been guarded jealously from the infidel, & Moritz the librarian showed me examples of the finer forms that are not in any European libraries. Then he looked up a reference and said—'You have in the Bodleian three volumes of a unique and most important 16th cent. Arabic manuscript dealing with Egyptian antiquities. We have the other two volumes. Three of the five were taken from Egypt in the 17th century. We would give almost anything to get the others.' And then he showed me two of the most sumptuous Korans, about 3 ft. in height, every page ablaze with gold, which he said they would offer in exchange. I have written to E. W. B. Cyclops [1] Nicholson urging him to get the curators to make the exchange, but it takes a University decree to part with a Bodley book! Curiously enough I could not find any early Arabian books (of note) on medicine, neither Avicenna or Rhazes in such beautiful form as we have. I have asked a young fellow at the school who is interested to look up the matter. . . . I am brown as a fellah—such sun—a blaze all day. We reached Cairo in one of those sand storms, the air filled with a greyish dust which covers everything & is most irritating to eyes and tubes. This boat is delightful—five-six miles an hour against the current, which is often very rapid. The river gets very shallow at this season, & is fully eighteen feet below flood level. I have been reading Herodotus, who is the chief authority now on the ancient history of Egypt. He seems to have told all of the truth he could get and it has been verified of late years in the most interesting way. Tomorrow we start at 8 for the Tombs of Denderah—a donkey ride of an hour. We are tied up to one of Cook's floating barge docks; squatted outside is a group of natives, & the Egyptian policeman (who is in evidence at each stopping place) is parading with an old Snider & a fine stock of cartridges in his belt. . . . PS. 24th. Have just seen Denderah & the Temple of Hathor. Heavens what feeble pigmies we are! Even with steam, electricity and the Panama Canal. . . .

A letter to W. S. Thayer on March 1st tells of his further impressions:

The country is wonderful—sun, sand, rocks, and crops, a lovely green belt, between the river & the desert. We had four days at Luxor, the ancient Thebes, the ruins of which are wonderfully impressive. No such monument of human effort exists as Karnak. It is simply staggering. St. Peter's and the Colosseum are toys beside it. Notre Dame could go inside one of the courts. We had a glorious day at the Tombs of the Kings—only 47 of them!—cut

[1] Nicholson had a cast in one eye.

in the solid limestone, long sloping corridors about the size of the covered one at the J. H. H., lateral chambers and then 300–500 feet in the heart of the mountain & 500 from the surface the mortuary chamber; and in one Seti I rests peacefully in his mummy case, with his hands folded and his features as clean cut as when he was embalmed 3500 years ago. Poor devil! Had he thought that troops of tourists would come & stare & that an electric light would flare in his face, he would have preferred a 'burning burial', and he took such pains to hide his tomb, false passages, and an 80 ft. deep well to divert the robbers! Only about 10 years ago the opening was found. We make about 50 miles a day, stopping anywhere for the night, tying up to a mud bank. There is scarcely a mile of the river without some place of interest. Temples everywhere—and from all ages. . . .

Four days later, on March 5th, he says in a letter from Assouan to H. M. Thomas:

. . . Everything here is so new and so old and so strange. By Jove, I should like to have seen Thebes in the palmy days 1500 B.C. The ruins are simply staggering. Had they developed in other sciences as in mechanics and architecture, not much would have been left for the Greeks or for us. We are here at the first Cataract, across which is the great Dam, a bit of work of which even the old Rameses II would have been proud. If the ordinary Egyptian could be made sanitary the country would be a paradise but it is dirty beyond description & the amount of ophthalmia & hookworm disease is appalling. And the bilharzia is very bad. I am to see the pellagra cases at the asylum as I return. . . . I wish we could have been taught to pray in the Oriental style. The somatic attitudes are splendid. Before we tie up for the night our Reis or captain spreads his mat at the bow & goes through his devotions in a most graceful way. Allah pervades the East and the Moslem has a great religion. If Mahomet had not been so foolish on the woman question, Islam would have thriven & the crescent would not have waned as it has. Our dragoman is a fine old Arab full of humour. 'Me,' he says, 'I have my Koran, my cold water, my cigarette and my home.' He knows everything and manages the boat like a first-class hotel. The weather has been glorious—sun every day & sometimes very hot, to-day 86 degrees, but the nights are always cool. I hope the family thrives. . . .

Almost every day long letters of this sort were sent off to his friends—to Tyson, with whom he laments over the recent death of Theodore Janeway—'honest as the day—life did not owe him anything but it is sad that he was not allowed a happy old age with his family'; to Edward

Milburn, who got an enthusiastic postcard from nearly every stop while he was ' off on this big spree ' ; to Mrs. McCrae, his niece, describing the heat and a sand-storm, and he adds : ' It seems a very lazy thing to take a long holiday like this, but it was too good a chance to miss and it really has been splendid ' ; and to many others, all expressing the longing that they might be sharing in his delight over Egypt— ' a land of contrasts '.

On the way back to Cairo they stopped again for a few days at Luxor where ' Professor Sayce, one of the leading Egyptologists, and Weigall, the Director of Antiquities, were most kind & gave us valuable hints as to the best things to see '. ' All sorts of chairs &c make the visits to the Tombs so easy & in many places there are carriages but yesterday I was on a donkey for four hours. I was afraid lest I should shake out a pebble but I stood it comfortably.' And on March 10th he writes to L. F. Barker : ' Such weather ! such monuments ! such a revelation of the intellectual development of man 6,000 years ago ! I am a bit bewildered. I have just come from paying my respects to Dr. Imhotep, the first physician with a distinct personality to stand out in the mists of antiquity. I am brown as an Arab. The country has one God—the sun ; & two devils—dust and flies ; the latter responsible I am sure for 2/3 of the disease. The ophthalmia is awful & one sees a great deal of blindness.' And on March 17th, the last day of the trip he writes again to Mrs. Brewster :

Dear Mabel, Our last morning on the Seti—such a glorious trip ! . . . We have had some splendid days on our way down. Abydos with its old tombs, & the ruins of the city of the Horizon which Ikhnäton, the idealist Pharaoh founded in the 15th century B.C. If you wish to read a touching story get Weigall's book about him—published last year, or read Breasted's chapter on him in his history of the Egyptians—the first individuality in history. He tried to introduce the worship of one god, loved nature, loathed war, & devoted himself to his family and friends—and incidentally wrecked a great empire ! Yesterday we spent at Memphis—all that is left of it. The desert covers the site of one of the world's greatest cities—only the tombs remain. I was specially interested in the step pyramid, built about 3000 B.C. by Imhotep, a physician & architect, for Zoser—the earliest stone monument of antiquity. The tombs of the old princes are extraordinary—among the earliest and the best so far as mural decorations and historical value are concerned. One can see, in stone, representations of weaving, baking, brewing, carpentering, boatmaking &c. Many show methods still in use in the immutable land. Sand, sand, sand everywhere, blown in from the desert, gradually covered the ruined city. Excavations are still being made & every day something is brought up. We sail next week—22nd for Naples, & I should get home by April 1st. Let me know your summer plans—any chance that you may come over? After this long holiday I shall have to stay quietly at work. I have my new edition of the text-book on hand, which will keep me very busy.

In Cairo again he searched the libraries in vain for an early Avicenna MS. and says on a postcard to Ira D. Remsen: 'I spent a couple of hours yesterday with the chancellor of this ancient university (10th cent). The teaching is all in the open—& all on the Koran and its commentators. A little geography, law, &c. There are 12,000 students from all parts of the Moslem world. Students stay 1, 10 & even 20 years. It takes a life-course to know the Koran. An extraordinary religion & with great potency.' Then Alexandria, and *en route* to Naples he writes on March 22nd to McCrae a long account of his medical observations on the trip, some of which find their way into a revision of the section on Parasitic Diseases with which the 6th and 7th editions of his Text-book had begun. 'I hope', he says, 'to be back by April 1st & must settle to hard work on the book. We should go to press January 1st which would enable them to have it out completely by October, 1912—the 20th anniversary of the first edition.'

It was his first visit to Naples, and the thrill of the neighbouring coast as far as Sorrento and Capri, of the sight of Pompeii and all else, added to the impressions which ancient Egypt had made on his enthusiastic and impressionable mind, must have begun to affect his sleep, for he writes on a postcard of March 28th to one of his old neighbours at 3 West Franklin Street:

Thus far on the trip. Glorious place—glorious weather. I wish you were *mit*. I dreamt of you last night as operating on Hughlings Jackson. The great principle you said in cerebral surgery is to create a commotion by which the association paths are restored. You took off the scalp—like a p.m. incision—made a big hole over the cerebellum & put in a Christ-Church whipped-cream wooden instrument [mayonnaise beater] & rotated it rapidly. Then put back the bone & sewed him up. H. J. seemed very comfortable after the operation and bought three oranges from a small Neapolitan who strolled into the Queen-Square Amphitheatre! I have been studying my dreams lately & have come to the conclusion that just one third of my time is spent in an asylum—or should be!

He had indeed been making a study of his dreams, to what purpose or effect is not apparent, but there remains a note-book filled with closely written observations upon them, for he seemed always to awaken with most vivid recollections of astounding, amusing, and bizarre somnial experiences. Meanwhile an impatient wife writes from Oxford: 'He has had a glorious time but the heat would have killed me so I am glad I did not go, and another reason I am glad is that I have read in his absence letters from young doctors, old doctors, men of all ages, which made me feel more than ever how wonderful an influence Dr. Osler has been in the profession. How proud I am of him no one can believe. Excuse this outburst, but you both understand.'

On April 2nd once more at 13 Norham Gardens, he writes to H. B. Jacobs:

The Riviera looked delightful as I passed along the Coast the other side of Genoa. Rome was cold and rainy, & of five, we only had one good day at Naples. After Egypt one gets particular. I found nothing in the way of old books in either place, nothing of special note. Dr. Payne's executors have decided to sell the books at auction—at least to have an auctioneer's catalogue made first. I hope to head off a sale by a specific offer—asking to leave out the 15th century herbals. They have a rather exaggerated idea of the value of the library as a whole, but they would find the big prices limited to a few books. After the catalogue is made, I can talk with Sotheby's, & we may come to terms. It would be a great pity to miss it. You and Mrs. Jacobs really must *do* the Nile. I have never had such an enchanting trip. . . .

He came back to a mass of unanswered correspondence; to a helpless and hopeless secretary; to business of the university; to important matters at the Radcliffe Infirmary which had been awaiting his decision; to a 'London in a turmoil getting ready for the coronation'—the Londoner's one idea of decorating his city, as Whistler said, being to cover it up and sit on it. On April 5th he dictates a letter to F. C. Shattuck of Boston:

I do not see how your letter of Dec. 28th is among a batch of February letters, which I find here on my return. . . . It is awfully sad to hear of Henry Bowditch's death. It was a tragedy was it not, for a man of his type to die in that way. He did a good work for the School and for the community. In a letter which I sent to the *Lancet* about him, I remarked that it was men of his type that formed the 11* of a community. Not many are needed in a country; a teaspoonful of such yeast raises a mighty big lump of dough. With love to the family, Ever yours, Wm Osler. [Script] *Leaven —that is a good stenographic mistake—is it not!

With all that was going on, his habit of never letting slip an opportunity to contribute to another library than his own is illustrated by this letter of April 17th to President Lowell of Harvard:

Dear Lowell,—Some time ago in the Hunterian Library, Glasgow, I came upon some interesting Harvard documents, the early lists of graduates, with their theses, etc. When you so kindly took me to the Library, we found that you had none earlier than 1670 I think. I have had the Hunterian set photographed, and they should reach you with this letter. Please hand them over to the Librarian. If you have to be in England this summer we shall be delighted to see you. . . .[1]

The question which continued to agitate the Johns Hopkins faculty leads him to send the following on the 18th to H. M. Thomas of Baltimore:

Dear Harry T,—So glad of your nice long letter. I have not seen 'the Professor' [W. S. Halsted]; when over here he keeps in seclusion in a very funny way. I should like to know at first hand how things are moving. Personally, I feel that to cut off the heads of departments from a practice is a Utopian scheme, admirable on paper; but the very men who would be most in favour of it would be the first to get the professors to break their rules. . . . You couldn't

---

[1] This letter appears on the first page of the first number of *Harvard Library Notes* for June 1920, with the following comment: 'The earliest "Theses" of which the college possesses an original copy, is that of 1687, Dr. Osler's recollection of 1670 being due no doubt to the fact that there is a copy of the sheet for that year at the Massachusetts Historical Society. The Society has also the "Theses" of 1643. These three were the earliest known until Dr. Osler added 1646, 1647, August 9, 1653, August 10, 1653, and 1678. . .'

tie up a group of four or five men, and not permit the public to utilize their special knowledge. Under such conditions a Professor would not remain more than five or six years. It is an experiment I would like very much to see tried, but not at the Johns Hopkins first. It might have been different if we had started so, but I do not believe that there is any possibility of success at present. . . . Revere and Mrs. Osler are off fishing in Wales. He has grown very much, and is thriving in everything except in Latin and Greek, which is rather a calamity. . . .

'I have had a very busy month since I got back,' he writes on May the 3rd ; 'on the road a great deal & very much in London' ; and perhaps as a result of these consultations he may have 'sanctified a fee', for he continues :

I made a great haul last week, a splendid collection of Sir William Petty's Letters during twenty years in Ireland. A case-book of Sir Theodore Mayerne's ; and a fourteenth-century MS. of Albertus Magnus ; all from the Phillips sale (but I am ruined !) I hope to hear about that Vesalius letter, as one or other of us should get it. I wish I could get out to McGill for the opening but June is an impossible month—full of examinations. Revere goes back to school to-day. He did not get much fishing these holidays. He & Grace went to Tenby for deep-sea fishing but it was too rough. I am rewriting sections of the Text-book and hope to get it ready for the press by the end of the year. Notes, please ! Corrections ! Suggestions !

And in the midst of a long and detailed letter to McCrae who was helping him with this revision, now that the System of Medicine was off their hands, he adds :

I hear you are having difficulty in settling the question of all-time clinical men. It would be a great thing for you young chaps, as you would get all the consulting work & all the kudos, & in a big clinic like the J. H. the chances are that in 10 years the head of the department might be the smallest man of the whole group in the eyes of the community & the profession.

He must have been a little hurt by the intimations that the clinical teachers had been exploiting their university positions, for in a postscript to a letter of May 13th, after he had learned that the Trustees had decided in favour of the plan, he says : 'There seems to be a general impression that we clinical men make large fortunes in a few years. I did not take away from B[altimore] a dollar made in practice ! It all got into circulation again ! I got away with a little less than my Text-book brought me—& with what I paid for the house.' Such postscripts appended long-hand to very brief letters taken down laboriously by his amanuensis illumine most of his correspondence from 13 Norham Gardens at this time: thus to one of his young Baltimore friends, 'Do come and take a rest. You must need it sadly. Break away—and soon. The open arms very open! Lovely weather, many people coming and going. Nona Gwyn & Ottilie Wright are here getting ready for presentation at court next week—very busy days.' Such episodes of the summer term as a course of lectures on life in the tropics for Europeans, given for the benefit of the Indian Service probationers, only appear in university circulars, though they doubtless add to the 'busy days'. But for real news one must have recourse to Mrs. Osler's daily letters to her mother. On May 16th she writes:

. . . Of course their dresses are a bother to get fitted—London is in such a muddle. To add to the effort word has come that I am to go to Court the same night the 25th of May. I can't get out of it now so must go ahead, and never should have done it had it not been *for you*. I know you will be interested but just now it is a tremendous effort as I seem to think only of you. I have had a very interesting time today. . . . I received a card for the unveiling of the Queen Victoria Memorial in front of Buckingham Palace—I was very lucky as tickets were being begged for & very scarce. The German Emperor and Empress came over for it. You will see the pictures in the 'Illustrated'. It was a glorious day & superb sight—all men were in Court dress or uniforms, ladies in morning dress—just street things. The Royalties were numerous & it was a brilliant sight. The King is gracious in manner and full of interest in everything. I was really delighted to have such a chance. I send my card, and the Hymn which everyone sang. The card came from Lord Strathcona and had Annie's name on it—poor soul she has been dead over a year—but it was meant for me. When this reaches you we will be in town. The girls are going to a theatre party on the 24th and we will stay for the Court on the 25th. Unfortunately Willie will not see us dressed as he has to be in Swansea. . . .

The only record of the Swansea visit to which this letter refers appears in this note to the *Lancet* from its 'Correspondent in Wales':

At the Swansea General Hospital on May 25th the Regius Professor of Medicine at Oxford University, unveiled a brass tablet which has been placed there as a memorial to his late uncle. The inscription was as follows: 'To the memory of Edward Osler, M.R.C.S., F.L.S., House Surgeon of this Hospital in 1825. Born at Falmouth, Jan. 30th, 1798; died at Truro, March 7, 1863.' Professor Osler, in the course of an interesting address, gave some reminiscences of the life of his uncle, who was editor of the *Royal Cornwall Gazette* from 1840 until his death. He was also a well-known hymn writer.

While this memorial was being unveiled, the following to Mrs. Revere was being written on the edge of a bed at Brown's Hotel, London:

> Behold three females—one aged, fat, old, grey-haired lady, and two beautiful young girls of different types—sitting on a bed waiting for dresses to arrive to go to Court. The dressmaker promised not to worry us but how can they help it when they have such a lot to do. It is a fearful waste of time too—away from Oxford which is more lovely this year than I have ever seen it, and in a punt on the river one can have so much more pleasure than dressed up like a jumping-Jack. I look like *Katherine of Aragon*, the girls like angels. . . .

And this same letter, finished twenty-four hours later, contains a long and amusing account of trains and feathers and veils, not fitted for this biography, though 'it was too bad Willie missed seeing the girls'—and his wife, it may be added, of whom the girls said 'I looked as if I owned the palace and was about to ask the King and Queen to spend a few days'.

At sixty one must expect to see some of one's friends fall out of the ranks, but Osler had been especially hard hit during the last year, and the following letter of June 7th mentions the loss of still another of them—Dr. Charles M. Ellis of Elkton, Maryland, the man he was always holding up to his young friends as the ideal example of a country doctor—'Hippocraticus Rusticus', Weir Mitchell was wont to call him:

> Just back from town [he writes] & have your letter of Monday with the sad news of Ellis's death. He was indeed one of the very best, & one of my oldest friends. I had not been in Baltimore a week when he called upon me, bringing a letter from Weir Mitchell. I then saw him every week for several months in attendance upon McCoy who was a very special friend of his. He had more good clinical sense than any man I know. His life is full of encouragement,

as it shows to what position of esteem the general practitioner can reach. No man in the profession in Maryland could have had a more charming position than he enjoyed. I had a very nice letter from him a few months ago. It is a sad loss to us all & to the profession and the State. . . .

But there are happier things to record, and on June 11th he writes to H. B. Jacobs :

My purchases [from the Van den Corput sale, Amsterdam] came this week. The Laennec items [1] are A. 1 ! two letters & a draft of his obituary notice of Bayle. One of the letters refers (1810) to an unusual astronomical phenomenon observed in Baltimore which had been referred to him. I must send it to the Faculty Library. A 1588 Leyden diploma & a 17th century Russian one & a good many books including an ed. princeps of Mondino. . . . Payne books still hang fire—they may have to be sold unless Marburg raises his figure. Such a rush these days, everyone on the move. Müller comes soon from Munich [to give evidence before the Royal Commission on University Education]. Lizzie Linzee, Mrs. McCagg, the 3 Weld girls are here (partly at Randolph). Dock comes next week and the examins. begin. Huth letters sold this week. I hope to get a Locke item. I shall be ruined, and if Payne's books are sold at auction, shall go into liquidation. I had a long letter from Welch this week—great searchings of heart about the new proposals. We must have a good talk about them. Ruinous to offer the clinical men only $7500. They had much better all migrate. I have a young friend who has just got a whole time Pittsburg billet at $20,000—in charge of big works, not a whit more important than the J.H.H. shop. After all what is a man's value in the community? That is the question for the Trustees to decide. The Hospital will make double the salary, even in medicine, out of the private patients attracted to the individual men. . . . Let us know when you reach London.

From this and other letters of the week one would not have supposed that anything unusual could be impending. He appears to be chiefly concerned over the ultimate disposition of Dr. Payne's library ; sends some seventeenth-century illuminated diplomas to the McGill library, and on Monday, the 19th, writes : 'I wish you could have been here Saturday night. I had the Colophon Club—a sort of inner circle of the Bibliographical Society—at dinner at Christ Church—a very interesting group of men.' On this

[1] Osler made these items the subject of one of his 'Men and Books' notes in the *Canadian Medical Association Journal*, March 1912, ii. 247.

same Monday, from the four corners of the earth, princes and princesses, envoys and ambassadors, were arriving in London for the coronation of King George, and the following morning there appeared in the papers a long list of coronation honours—one marquess (Lord Crewe), four new earls (The Lord Chancellor, Sir Robert Reid; Rosebery, Brassey, and Curzon), four viscounts, nine barons, nineteen privy-councillors, twenty baronets (Osler included), fifty-five knights, and so on, and so on. On this eventful morning Sir William writes to Miss Marcia Noyes, the Librarian of the Maryland 'Faculty':

June 20th.

I am so delighted to hear of the Ellis bequest. I knew years ago of his intention. He was a good soul. I hope you will get the money soon. I will hear from Dr. Jacobs who comes to England tomorrow. I have a little treasure for you in the shape of a Laennec letter—in which he refers to Baltimore. How is Miss Nichols. I have not heard from her for months. I wish she could get some good berth. They have been putting a baronetcy on me—much to the embarrassment of my democratic simplicity, but it does not seem to make any difference in my internal sensations. I do hope you will get a good holiday—You need it I am sure—& deserve it—I am sure.

But it is hardly fair to dismiss the honour in this casual fashion, for though the announcement was not expected until after the coronation, they had known it was coming for several days—since the 11th, in point of fact. On that afternoon, with 13 Norham Gardens as usual full of people, Dr. Osler had walked in with the mail in his hand and tossed to his wife a letter from 10 Downing Street marked 'Confidential'. When they had an opportunity for a moment alone, she said: 'What excuse are you going to give for declining it; you always have said you would', and he replied: 'I think I'll have to accept—Canada will be so pleased—there 's only one Canadian baronet.' Despising anything that savoured of title-hunting, Osler had always pooh-poohed the idea when any allusion was made to such a possibility. They, of course, kept it secret, though a town-house was engaged from some friends for the week's ceremonies. On the 19th Mrs. Osler was in town to make some preliminary arrangements, which must have been difficult with London covered with scaffolding and 40,000 women marching from the Embankment to Albert Hall to hold a demonstration in favour of women's suffrage. At 7 a.m. she was called to the telephone and a voice said: 'The devil: the fat 's in the fire: this baronetcy thing is out! William [the butler] says so.' She sent for *The Times*, where, sure enough, it was, and hurrying back to Oxford she met a brigade of telegraph-boys emerging from 13 Norham Gardens.

In some ways it is a measure of the affection in which a man is held—the number of messages he receives at such a time. On only one other occasion was the house equally inundated by messages from all over the world—these were to be messages expressing grief and condolence—no less an evidence of the place he held in others' hearts. Ordinary mortals may receive signal honours, may suffer bereavement, and their friends applaud or grieve, but not many of them take the trouble to do what every one seemed impelled to do when anything befell William Osler. They came in successive waves—the telegrams, the cables, the English letters, the transatlantic letters—till the household was swamped. People felt that it was a well-deserved honour and they wanted him to know that they felt so. Then, too, his English friends fully appreciated how people from America still clung to him; and as one of them, Sir Thomas Barlow, President of the Royal College of Physicians, wrote: 'You have been all along a peacemaker and a binder-together of the different interests of medicine both at home and abroad, and if for no other reason this distinction would have been fitting and suitable, but I cannot help feeling that in a sort of way it makes you truly belong to us all here more than before, and I trust most fervently that your life may be long spared and that you may go on doing exactly the good work which you have already done.' It was months before his acknowledgements could even be partly completed, and he was exceptionally punctilious about this sort of thing. But he begins with his family:

21st [June]

Dear Chattie, You must have had such a shock yesterday morning when you saw Bill's name in the Coronation honour list. We had word about ten days ago from Mr. Asquith, but nothing could be said. I did not know when it was to come out—I thought not till after the coronation, but yesterday before I was out of bed the telegrams began to rain in & there has been a perfect stream—more than 100 from England, & 49 cables, U.S. & Canada; two from India. Letters galore. Grace was in town with Mrs. McCagg. Nona and Ottilie had been up at a dance so we did not let them know until later. I have had rather more than my share, but these court honours mean so much here. And when in the swim we must take what comes. These things have never bothered me, & we have so much & have been so happy, that we really did not need it as much as some poor fellow who has done more but who has not caught the public eye. I am glad for the family. I wish Father & Mother had been alive & poor B.B. & Nellie. It is wonderful how a bad boy [who could chop off his sister's finger] may fool his fellows if he once gets to work. Ask Bill Lyon how he accounts for it! The girls are greatly excited. They are having such a good time—seeing the world! Nona looks so well. Her presentation picture is so good & as for Grace—it was her regal appearance that settled George R. Love to Charley & the girls Your affec bro.

'Sir BILLY'!!!!!

Whether he had little interest in the Coronation pageant, whether it was because of the illness of E. A. Abbey,[1] or for some other reason, he remained in Oxford while the rest of the household repaired to London for the festivities; and there he continued with his acknowledgements. Thus on the 21st to Dr. Jacobs, who had come to London partly for the Coronation and partly for the Payne sale:

. . . Such a torrent of cables & telegrams! Really one's friends are awfully good. This thing cannot make us any happier, and as we were very contented before, I hope it will not disturb our *Aequanimitas*. Of course, my people will be enchanted. Everyone here is most kind & the whole town has called. G. and the girls are up in town for the fun, I am having a peaceful time at home! I shall ask Phipps for the extra £1000. I do hope the Payne executors will not raise the figure. The collection is wonderfully rich. I shall be heart-broken if we do not get it—purse-broken too, as there are three or four items I must bid for—tho I believe these baronetcy fees are ruinous & may take all my spare cash.

And on the next day to W. S. Thayer:

What do you think of this baronet business for an ordinary Democrat like myself? I suppose it is best to accept the conditions in

[1] J. William White had been hurriedly summoned from America, and Abbey was to be operated upon in a day or two by Sir Berkeley Moynihan.

which one lives, & take what comes and be thankful. I have had a good deal more than my share. We were very happy and contented, & it was quite unexpected. . . . What a time you have had over this Rockefeller suggestion. I have written Welch. I have had no details from anyone—only someone mentioned $7,500 as the prospective salaries; at $20,000 it would be worth while, scarcely at less. It is a doubtful matter. What would the school have been if the clinical men had not been active in the local & national societies. Would whole-time men have the same influence in the profession at large—I doubt it. And in the U. S. could a good man keep himself from the public? If they paid proper salaries I would like to see the experiment tried. I hear that you have declined Jefferson. I told Keen to try. What are you doing this summer? I wish we could see you here. Love to Sister Susan. G. R. O. and the boy are well—both at the Coronation. . . .

So he did not attend the 'Royal Progress' in London, possibly for reasons hinted at in a letter of the 30th to McCrae which says: 'We have been very contented without the embroideries—I hope we may be equally so in the future. Revere seems a bit overwhelmed but it may be a good thing for him in the long run as he is evidently not going to do much with "book learning". I am swamped with letters & telegrams and now that the transatlantic letters begin to come in it seems hopeless.' One of them, from such a remote spot as the Grand Cascapedia, P. Q., Canada, may be quoted:

Tell your son that I killed a 45 pound salmon last week, and two days before three, 40, 39, 29 lbs. Of less importance is it that you are a Bart. What is that to me, for whom you are long ago high in the *peerage* of friendship. A lessening number of survivors, four, only four. Time has terribly dealt with that splendid peerage, Lowell, Holmes, Alex. Agassiz, Brooks, and last Ch. Norton and Aldrich, and I am the last of nine children and one sister. Therefore please to take care of the new Baronet. . . . Keep an eye on any Harvey things for me and quit writing me those half-page scraps of letters. I have seven queries to put at you about Harvey. I spare you. Could I learn at the Heraldry Office when Wm. H. got arms? I hear you cuss. Well! goodbye. Yrs. WEIR MITCHELL.

But other things than Coronation festivities frequently lured him to London, as is evident from a note of July 2nd to Jacobs, who was sojourning there:

So sorry not to have been able to stay today and see you but I had to motor from town this morning with a bevy of boys with whom I was dining last night. We have just had 15 of them to tea—such nice fellows—a club. Three of them went on a pilgrimage to the U.S. hospitals this winter. I will come to see you Tuesday—will let you know the hour. The Payne library yet unsettled. I shall be heart broken to miss it. I am putting the case before Mr. Phipps tomorrow.

And so he did, but Mr. Phipps for the moment felt that he had done enough for the Johns Hopkins and was more interested in other things. In the following letter of July 9th is given something more about the sale which was so exercising him:

Has Welch told you there is a chance that we may get Payne's library? Marburg will go to $10,000. Much depends on what price the valuators put on his Herbals. There is much of first class importance & not many duplicates in the Warrington collection. Mrs. P. will give us the first offer. P. had given away a few treasures before his death—to the College the original Linacres which were not in its shelves. He had left me the Restitutio Christianismi reprint, Nürnberg 1790, which I have been after for years & wh. must be extremely rare.[1] There are some good MSS. & a choice lot of 16 & 17 century English pamphlets. Both the English & the Latin editions of the sweating sickness—the former impossible to get now. S-G Library copy the only one in U.S. I do hope we can get it. If not there will be a fine scramble at Sothebys! I have had some luck lately—several beauties! but next year I must *go slow.* I have spent too much this year on books.

I hope the angels are well. Hugs & kisses all round. Tell Pius he must come over soon in an aeroplane.[2] Bodley's Librarian merely disappeared—he could not die! but has bobbed up serenely. I wish you could be at our meetings—more fun than a circus. Beastly election on.[3] Plague on both their houses! The country is safe—never so prosperous if they would only shoot the newspaper editors.

---

[1] In this volume Dr. Payne had written: 'This is a reprint made in Nuremberg of the original of 1553 of which most copies were burnt along with the author. . . . Very scarce and difficult to obtain. This copy came from Mark Pattison's library, J. F. P.' A full account of this rare book will be found in 'Bibliotheca Osleriana' (in press).

[2] The 'European Aviation Circuit' had just been completed, Védrines the Frenchman arriving first at Hendon, the terminal point.

[3] A political truce had been declared during the Coronation week, but this over, they were at it again, hammer and tongs, over the Parliament Bill. By-elections were necessary to fill seats made vacant by some of the Coronation Honours.

There lives in Reading, the county town of Berkshire half-way to London from Oxford, a doctor with a hobby, a man after Osler's own heart, Dr. Jamieson B. Hurry. Though now a modernized town famed for such things as its biscuits and its seeds, it has an ancient history. Early in the twelfth century Henry I founded there a Benedictine Abbey, which remained one of the wealthiest in England until, at the dissolution of the monasteries, it was despoiled and looted by Henry VIII four centuries later, when the last Abbot, a faithful Papist, was hanged, drawn, and quartered before his own gateway. Dr. Hurry had made the ruins of this abbey his specialty, and being a little shy about this particular fact he was greatly encouraged by reading what Osler had said in his Belfast address in 1909 to the effect that no man is safe without a hobby. In consequence, he had sent to the Regius 'The History of Reading Abbey', one of his five different volumes on the subject of the abbey and its abbots.

This may suffice to explain how on July 10th Osler came to unveil the memorials to 'the first and last abbots of Reading' presented to the Borough as a coronation gift by Dr. Hurry—the memorials consisting of two sculptured bluestone slabs affixed one on each side of the ruined entrance to the old chapter house. A procession headed by the town beadles and sergeants-at-mace started from the Town Hall, followed by the Mayor, the Town Council, and other town officials, the Archdeacon of Berks and many others, including, one may be sure, the little daughter of Dr. Hurry, as well as the new baronet; and all proceeded to the Forbury Gardens. There, it is said, 'Sir William stepped forward, unveiled the memorials, and delivered this address':

> Let me first offer congratulations to this old town in the possession of a romance that appeals to all lovers of antiquity. In your modern prosperity the outside world may lightly forget the glorious history of foundations, now alas, in ruins, which once made Reading the rival of Glastonbury, St. Albans and Osney. These noble remains you devoutly preserve, and through the pious inspiration of one of your townsmen, we enshrine today the memory of the first and last of the long line of men who for four hundred years ruled the destinies of one of the most famous abbeys of England. You see here in stone symbolized the beginning and the end of a great epoch—of a vast

movement to the strength of which our wonderful cathedrals and many superb ruins bear enduring testimony. Marvellous, indeed, was the faith that found expression in such works! Small wonder that the thirteenth has been called the greatest of the centuries, since in it the larger number of these magnificent foundations took their rise. Little could the first Hugh, even amid the vicissitudes of a long and stormy life, have dreamt of the tragedy that awaited his splendid home and far-off successor—a tragedy that stirs us to the quick in the pages of the Abbé Gasquet, or in the brief memorial printed for this occasion. But like an earthquake, the upheaval to which this ruin testifies was the outcome of natural causes, though not always easy to trace in the tangled skein of history. We pity the fate of Abbot Hugh Faringdon, and you may call down curses on the head of King Henry, but they were both mere pawns in the great game which man has for ever to play with the enslavers of his spirit. The one lost a beautiful abbey and his life, the other in losing a reputation saved a nation, and struck off forever from this land the galling fetters of foreign ecclesiastical domination. Much as we deplore the savagery, the injustice, the brutalities associated with the Reformation, into the other balance must be thrown its two great victories—the appeal to reason, and the birth of the spirit of nationality—precious gifts, worth a costly sacrifice.

Still at work, the forces which four centuries ago were relentless enough to wreck this abbey and to butcher its head, have slowly but surely so moulded man anew that he looks on life with new eyes. Even those who regret most acutely the changing of the old order rejoice in a new spirit abroad in the world that has given the individual, whether child, man or woman, a value never before possessed. The recognition of the right to live and to be happy and healthy in this beautiful world is its fruit. But this and much more is the work of the past, of which we are the inheritors, and it is from this past we may draw our keenest inspiration and our surest ensamples. And the lesson lies not in what a man has believed but in how he has behaved. Who cares a fig whether Abbot Hugh Faringdon assented or not to the King's supremacy? The lesson for us is in his blameless life and brave death—in them we find what the poet calls 'the touch divine of noble natures gone'. Consciously or unconsciously, everyone looking on this last scene in which the last abbot stands at the foot of the gallows with a rope round his neck, will in his heart make an obeisance to the man who stuck to his principles even unto death—and in so doing will gain strength for life's daily battle. That we live in a better and happier world is the outcome of the struggle of those of our ancestors who loved the light rather than darkness. To reverence their memory is the best inspiration for our work. We need their help, and it is through just such memorials as Dr. Hurry has here erected, that their benign influence may touch us. As always, Kipling gets to the marrow of the thing in his splendid poem, 'Our Fathers of Old':

If it be certain, as Galen says
  And sage Hippocrates holds as much—
That those afflicted by doubts and dismays
  Are mightily helped by a dead man's touch,
Then be good to us, stars above!
  Then be good to us, herbs below!
We are afflicted by what we can prove;
  We are distracted by what we know—
      So—ah, so!
Down from your heaven or up from your mould,
Send us the hearts of our fathers of old.

The copy of 'Rewards and Fairies', therefore, came in handy and was quickly put to use; and another characteristic thing is that, in the photograph taken after the address, the little daughter of Dr. Hurry occupies with the guest of honour the centre of the group. Two days later, on his birthday, came the sale at Sotheby's of the first portion of Dr. J. F. Payne's library, the 'Early Medical Works'. In his 'Men and Books' series, 1912, Osler wrote:[1]

I was anxious that the library should be kept together, and my friend, Mr. W. A. Marburg, of Baltimore, very kindly commissioned me to buy it for the Johns Hopkins Medical School, for which a few years ago he bought a valuable collection of old books. The executors had placed a reserve price of £2,700, but on the morning of the sale I received an intimation that it would be reduced to £2,500. The collection was to be offered first *en bloc*. With Dr. Henry Barton Jacobs and Dr. George Dock, I went to Sotheby's at one o'clock on July 12th. A more rapid sale I never saw. The bidding began at £2,000, and within a minute it was knocked down to an unknown bidder at £2,300, a figure beyond that which Mr. Marburg had mentioned, but Dr. Jacobs and I were prepared to go to the 'reserve price', had we had a chance!

Later he expressed his satisfaction that the collection 'has been kept together and is well housed in the Wellcome Historical Museum'; and his disappointment in not securing it for the Hopkins must have been lightened the next day after the sale by the addition of a precious volume for his own collection: 'A Declamation in the prayſe and cōmēdation of the moſt hygh and excellent

[1] *Canadian Medical Association Journal*, Mar. 1912, ii. 249.

science of Phisyke, made by the ryght famous clerke doctour Erasmus of Rotherdam, and newly translated out of Latyn into Englyshe', London, Robert Redman, no date. And on the fly-leaf he has written: 'Given me by Mrs. Henry Barton Jacobs, July 1911, again a curious coincidence, just as occurred in connection with my 1st edition of Burton which she gave me. Quaritch had sent a list of some old English books which had come in; among them was this of Erasmus, which I did not know had appeared in English. It was too high priced, I thought. A few days later it was sent with Mrs. H. B. J.'s regards This book is not in the Bodleian or the British Museum, but is in the Britwell Court Library so Gordon Duff tells me. W. O.'

Meanwhile the acknowledgements continued—sometimes merely on a visiting-card, as to his old Toronto friend Adam Wright: 'Many thanks, dear Adam, for your kind letter. Greetings to your good girls—all—and the boy. I still take the same sized hat.' And letters to the 'darlings', like this to one of his special pets, the daughter of an Oxford colleague:

> Dear Monica, Did I answer your sweet letter? The *Boss* says I did not & I am so bewildered and belettered and becabled and bebirthdayed that I have lost count. I th*o*t (which is Scotch) you a darling, which you are, & Harry knows that I know that he knows that you are—so there! Yours, W. O.

Osler admired the Scotch and was very fond of them; 'they are the backbone of Canada' he often remarked; also 'they are all right in their three vital parts—heads, hearts and haggis'. But he was fond of playing pranks upon them, and this same Monica recalls that when she first met him in Oxford he said: 'You are a well brought-up Scotch girl—where does the Book of Hezekiah occur in the Bible?' And, indeed, she *was* so brought up, but was much distressed at her inability to answer the query. She also recalls his saying one day, when he caught her in the pose of obviously trying to make a good impression: 'First cousin of Sapphira, cease your many inventions.'

Ever since the London Congress of 1901, when the Duke of Cambridge had found the Professor of Medicine from the Johns Hopkins so 'joky', the Royal Commission on Tuberculosis had been holding sessions in an endeavour to determine whether the bacilli of bovine and human tuberculosis were one and the same. Meanwhile, with the episode of Koch's pronouncement long since forgotten, the crusade against the disease, as has been seen, had been going on undeterred. The elaborate report of this commission had just been issued, and by a coincidence there appeared in *The Times* of July 14th an article announcing that 'the Executive Committee of the Welsh Memorial to King Edward, which has collected £200,000 to be devoted to a campaign against consumption in Wales, has obtained from Sir Clifford Allbutt, Sir Lauder Brunton, Dr. A. Latham, and Sir William Osler a statement on the value of the sanatorium treatment of the disease'. This statement sets forth in several concise paragraphs, clearly understandable to any lay reader, the way in which pulmonary consumption affects different classes of patients and what is the best thing to be done for each of them. The fact that Osler's name was the last of the signatories suggests that he may have been the author, though, to be sure, the names are given alphabetically; but this is less important than the fact that a group of the leading Welshmen, instead of erecting a bronze figure on a horse to commemorate the reign of Edward VII, decided upon this unusual form of a memorial. The public at last were taking notice, which may have induced another leading Welshman, Mr. Lloyd George, to provide, as part of the National Insurance Act, for the setting aside of a million pounds for the maintenance of existing sanatoria, and a million and a half for the erection of others in districts where they were needed.

Five days later (July 19th) the National Association for the Prevention of Tuberculosis opened its annual convention at Caxton Hall, Westminster. The sessions began with a congratulatory telegram from the King expressing his sympathies with the association's work; Mr. John Burns opened the first Conference; and many subsequent papers were given—all of which indicate what an impetus the crusade had already acquired. Osler not only presided at the afternoon session, but the following morning made some introductory remarks; and is quoted by *The Times* as having said:

. . . that the public, thanks to this association and to the press, were becoming more and more alive to the necessity of dealing with this insidious disease in its early stages. Doctors also needed education. Like the rest of men, they had many sins, and one was carelessness in examination. How many doctors in cases of cough made a practice of always carefully stripping and examining the chest? This carelessness was especially prevalent in that most vicious type of practice which was about to be foisted on us; contract practice as a rule was bad practice. Pleading for common-sense treatment, he said that two years ago a young woman from 'over the herring pond' was brought to him, and as the tuberculous signs were of the slightest he simply prescribed open air, golf, and a rational life. The mother, however, did not like this 'Go, wash in Jordan', and these two years had been spent on the Continent under tuberculin treatment. The patient had stood it wonderfully: she could not have been better if she had not had the treatment. The great majority of people in that room probably had somewhere a little focus of the disease, but were saved by the natural capacity of healing. Probably not 10 per cent. of the tuberculous, even under the new regulations, could be treated in sanatoria, so our energies should be largely devoted to elaborating and perfecting home treatment. The tuberculosis dispensary should not be independent of the general hospital, where a special tuberculosis department could be easily arranged. For one thing, the essential laboratory facilities were greatest at a hospital. He dreaded the growth of a group of men whose whole knowledge and life were in the tuberculosis dispensary; they necessarily became narrow. Even the general physician tended to get into a narrow rut. If anyone wanted to be encouraged, and to feel that the world was getting better, let him visit a sanatorium; and if he was not satisfied of its value he ought to have tuberculosis himself. One thing still lacking was a specific which would destroy the germ without damaging its host, though tuberculin, when properly used in suitable cases, had undoubted efficacy. . . .

A common-sense talk evidently tuned to the ears of his lay hearers. No less so were the remarks he was called upon to give the following day, July 21st, in his testimony before Lord Haldane's Commission on University Education, when, as the Minutes of Evidence show,[1] he dwelt upon the

[1] 'Appendix to the Third Report. . . . Minutes of Evidence. From Nov. 1910 to July 1911.' London, H. M. Stationery Office, 1911, pp. 342–54.

development of university education in medical schools, and particularly, by way of illustration, upon the organization of the medical clinic as it had come to be developed at the Johns Hopkins. These tasks over, he writes from Oxford on the 24th to Dr. (now Sir) Andrew Macphail of Montreal who had just undertaken to edit a new journal, the official organ of the Canadian Medical Association, and who had written more than once for some ' thunder ' :

Dear Macphail,—I do hope by this time your poor eye is all right again. I was very distressed to hear of the accident. What a terrible ordeal it must have been for you! I hope to have something ready for the Journal before long. I have been horribly negligent, but the fact is I have been head over ears in work of one sort or another, and do not seem able to get through much. Do drop me a postcard saying how you are. If you come over please come to us for a while. . . .

There was little chance that Macphail would receive any copy just now, for in another letter of this same day, to H. M. Thomas, Osler says, ' We are having a very busy time, so many people coming and going. It was nice to see the Thayers, and to see Sister Susan looking so well. Dana was here on Saturday, Jim Putnam, and Litchfield of Pittsburg come to-day. I am off to the British Medical Association at Birmingham this evening.'

At Birmingham one of the sessions of the Section on State Medicine was entirely given over to a discussion on the administrative control of tuberculosis in which the same old questions arose—compulsory notification, sanatoria, dispensaries, tuberculin, and so on; and Osler renewed his plea for the association of the tuberculosis dispensary with the general hospital and with the county infirmary. Dull affairs to many, he got great enjoyment out of these large gatherings of his professional brethren, and among other things probably attended as usual the annual luncheon of the Continental Anglo-American Medical Society, which had come to regard him as a sort of extra or honorary President. ' We have had a splendid meeting,' he writes, ' so many nice fellows. Campbell Howard came & we prowled about all day & have seen many men; many interesting things.' Among the ' nice fellows '—a guest of the association—was Professor Russell H. Chittenden of Yale, with whom Osler must have had some words regarding another matter, which accounts for the following letter dictated after his return to Oxford:

July 28, 1911.

Dear Chittenden,—I wrote Hadley as follows:—'The Silliman Lectureship is a great temptation, but I really do not feel that I have anything of sufficient interest to give you. My work has been so entirely technical, dealing with the more practical problems of medical education, that I do not feel that I could make you any really new contribution, such as is worthy of the name of Silliman. A course on the New Medicine and its relation to the Profession and the Public could be made of interest, and of value, but I really do not feel that it would quite come under the provisions of the Foundation.'

This is really very much along the lines you suggest. I could before long prepare a short outline of the headings. It would be a great pleasure to me to stay ten days at Yale, see the work of the University, and I could probably bring out material for two or three extra lectures that would interest some of the men in the Academic Department. Discuss the matter with Hadley and let me know. I should prefer to come in the month of October. They have just postponed the International Tuberculosis Congress until the 23rd of April. It is in Rome and I must attend. . . .

Some two weeks before, and at about the same time from two American universities, he must have received invitations to give a series of important lectures. One of them, dated July 1st, came from David Starr Jordan of Stanford University, California, asking him 'to give a course of three lectures under the West Foundation on the general subject of Immortality, Human Conduct, and Human Destiny'; and the other from Arthur T. Hadley of Yale in regard to the Silliman Lectures. In his letter President Hadley had said:

. . . The number of lectures is not fixed by the terms of the gift; but it is contemplated that the course should be of sufficient length—say from eight to twelve lectures—to form the basis of a volume which shall be published at the expense of the university. . . . Our lecturers have been Messrs. J. J. Thomson, Sherrington, Rutherford, Nernst, Penck, Campbell and Arrhenius; and for next October it is to be Professor Max Verworn. . . . In establishing the foundation, the devisor provided that 'the general tendency' of each of the courses should 'be such as will illustrate the presence and wisdom of God in the natural and moral world'. But he was wise enough to add that it was not necessary that the religious element should be emphasized, inasmuch as he believed that any orderly statement concerning the works of the Creator revealed his presence and wisdom. We thus have our hands free to employ the income of the fund for any course of lectures which is not positively and avowedly materialistic in its conception.

I feel that if you can come to us we shall be able to give you a pleasant time and that you will meet outside the lecture-room even more than inside it a number of students who will derive inspiration from your work and your talk. I think that J. J. Thomson, when he was here as Silliman Lecturer, did more work in promoting the study of mathematical physics by his casual conversations over his beer or his whisky-and-soda at the Graduates Club than he did in his more formal utterances. I very much want our younger men to have the chance to know you, and I hope that if you accept our invitation you will be able to make a reasonably continuous stay here. . . .

It was undoubtedly a great temptation, and Osler, as an indication that he wavered, had written across the top of this letter 'Ans. 21st July '11 The New Medicine'. It would not have been surprising had 'James Bovell' been written somewhere on the sheet, for Osler's one-time master would in all probability have given a course on 'the presence and wisdom of God in the natural and moral world' more satisfactory to the devisor of the Lectureship than would his favourite pupil. How this all turned out will be seen.

Meanwhile something of what is engaging him at Oxford is indicated by this letter from Lord Hythe (2nd Earl Brassey), one of the Trustees of the Endowment Fund, written August 2nd:

Dear Sir William,—Many thanks for yours of the 1st inst. I do not think that there is enough money voted to provide for the revision of the [Bodleian] Catalogue; about £1,000 a year is required. I do not think it would be possible to appeal with success for additional money in Oxford if the resolution proposed by the Chancellor is confirmed. People will say that the Trustees have plenty of unallocated money in hand to do the work. The question of printing, I admit, is not urgent. I think the Trustees will have done well to insist on a proper estimate being prepared for carrying on the work of Catalogue revision, and a responsible Head being put in charge. Mr. Gibson, I am told, has done his work admirably, but when he is working on the Catalogue revision, another Assistant is required for the Library.

Money is necessary to get things done and Osler usually was a successful beggar; but no more so than his heroic friend in Saranac who writes to him on August 3rd:

When that very nice letter you wrote from Egypt came I was on my 'beam ends' again and since I have righted myself somewhat time has passed more rapidly than I thought . . . There is little news with me. I am still on my porch and in my reclining chair most of the time when I am not in bed but the old machine keeps on working still. Saranac and the work there still continues to grow and I still can help it exist and grow. Good as Laurie [Brown] and Baldwin are at doing the work, *they never get any money and money we must have* and here is where I still come in. This year besides the greater part of the support of the institution, I have personally begged so far a new X-ray plant ($2,000), $2,500 for a fund towards the support of the scientific and medical work at the Sanitarium so that Laurie can have a paid bacteriologist and join his bedside observations to good laboratory experiments and records; and last week I got $10,000 for a nurses' cottage where we will train special nurses to care at a reasonable cost for the poor devils who need them and whose name is legion! Yesterday I got $1,200 to build three iron and stone gates at the three entrances for which so far we have never been able to afford any gates. I am sending you three Kodaks I took of the Trudeau family, to recall us to your mind because the one of me is decidedly cheerful for a man who often reads in the papers his own obituary! Congratulations and love from us all. Most sincerely, E. L. TRUDEAU.

Peaceful occupations these—raising money for charitable objects. But it was a peaceful time. On the day this letter was being written in the Adirondacks, Mr. Taft witnessed the signing of an arbitration treaty with England; another was being signed in Paris; Mr. Carnegie was making a peace-speech in Liverpool, and Lord Haldane, the Secretary of State for War, before the University Extension Course in Oxford, was delivering an address: 'Great Britain and Germany: a Study in Ethnology', in which he sought to trace the growth and meaning of what seemed to him the German habit of mind and to point out the difficulties in the way of a mutual understanding and how they might be diminished. Meanwhile, however, Mr. Lloyd George's inchoate insurance bill was before Parliament; the proposed misuse of the royal prerogatives by the party in power was still vexing the country; and the dock labourers were on strike. But probably neither the political upheaval which led Osler to exclaim 'plague on both their houses', nor the social unrest, lessened the crowd at Lords for the annual Eton-Harrow cricket match, or the festivities at Cowes.

The month, from August 11th to September 6th, the Oslers passed at Llanddulas, a tiny village in North Wales, taking with them a large bundle of congratulatory letters still to be acknowledged. From there he soon sends an undated letter to H. M. Thomas, saying:

We are off here at a lovely spot where we have taken a house for four weeks—close to the sea. Ike got back from camp at Salisbury Plain where he had a very happy time. He is 1½ inches taller than I am & looks well. He is no student & never will be. Study is not to his mind, but I am not worrying. He is a good lad & will do well. I was sorry not to see Mary before I left, but I had to go to Paris for two days & had only a day at home before leaving, but your sister wrote that she was better. . . . So glad you have had a good summer at the old place. I remember it on the occasion of my first visit to the Blue Ridge—before I went to Baltimore. Delightful letter from Trudeau with photographs has just come. He is holding his own.

On the 15th this to his old pupil, W. G. MacCallum:

Dear Mac, It was very nice to hear from you. These titles do not seem to make any difference in one's feelings or in the circumference of my head. I had hoped perhaps we might see you here this summer. Campbell Howard told me of his visit to you. He has 'achieved a maid that paragons perfection' to use Iago's expression—or was it Cassio's? Ottilie Wright, daughter of the late Dr. H. P. W. of Ottawa. She has been with us on and off for the past two years & is one of the darlings of my heart, so you can understand how happy we are about it. I am so glad to hear that you are happy in New York. I knew it would not take long to make good! Mrs. Osler sends love.

There follows an undated letter from Ogwen Lake, North Wales, to Mrs. Robert Brewster—a letter really intended for her little girl with whom evidently a new game had been started during a brief visit he had just had with them in Paris:

I hope this may catch you in time to take my good wishes for the voyage home. Revere & I are here fishing for three days, deep in the heart of the Welsh mountains, a lovely spot. R. is off all day in the boat, while I prowl about the rocks & talk to the mountain sheep. He is the most patient fisherman—like all his mother's family. Tell Sylvia that I had a great surprise a few minutes ago. I am writing on a big rock half way up the mountain & just beneath me is a lovely green patch on which a mother sheep and a half grown lamb were having their dinner. I saw something on the back of the lamb, very busy plucking the nice soft wool & rolling it on a reel. It was Flopsy, Mopsy, Dopsy—she changes her name a little every day—I gave a whistle which she knows very well, and she looked, and jumped nearly an inch when she saw me. She said that all her babies clothes were made of Welsh wool from lambs, and they collect it every year and weave it into the softest cloth in the winter. She was so glad to see me, and in a jiffy was in my pocket looking for chocolate. Was it not lucky that I had some? She has never been in America & I told her it would be very nice to go out with Sylvia. I think she will, so look out for her on the steamer. Send me a p.c. when you get home. . . . We have had such peaceful days under the lovely beech trees. Grace is so happy here. She loves to get away from people. You will see her in October I hope. I know she will be charmed with Mt. Kisco. . . . [PS.] Tell Sylvia that this sprig of heather I took from Mopsy Flopsy Dopsy's button hole. She had on the dearest blue suit—serge—very tightly fitting & looked so sweet.

On the 25th from Llanddulas he writes to his friend Shepherd of Montreal:

I do not believe I ever wrote thanking you for your kind letter you wrote about my Bty. I tried to put up a Knighthood job for you on the occasion of the opening ceremonies [1] but it was blocked on the ground that the French & the Toronto people would feel hurt. I will show you the correspondence some day. We are here in a lovely valley—so fresh & green when the whole country to the south is parched. 53 consecutive days of sunshine in the Thames valley—unheard of before. . . . I wish I could look in upon you all at Como. I had a very funny dream about you the other night. The boy is off fishing in the lakes near by.

And on the same day to Howard A. Kelly of Baltimore:

Dear Howard A. I have only recently had sufficient leisure to

[1] This refers to the ceremonies of June 5th, when the new McGill medical building to replace that destroyed by fire had been officially opened. The buildings which contain the library and museum in which Osler's old specimens are treasured were made possible through another gift from Strathcona. Earl Grey, the Governor-General of Canada, presided. Osler had been strongly urged to be present and to give the chief address, but his long trip to Egypt did not justify his being away again, especially during examination week, as he explained.

go into the question of whole time clinical men. I am sending an open letter to Remsen on the subject—which will go to all the Trustees & members of the Med. School. It is a great pity Flexner's Report was issued—full of errors & misconceptions—& I am stating it frankly. You will have the letter about Sept. 20th. I hope you have had a good summer. We are off here in a peaceful Welsh valley after a very strenuous season. The less one has to do the less one does—but we have now so many outside interests that time flies. . . .

This confidential letter to President Remsen, printed by Horace Hart at the University Press and intended for the eyes of the Hopkins faculty only, is perhaps too intimate to publish in full until the still-troubled waters he speaks of shall have temporarily quieted down to await the next beneficial agitation—for benefits are almost certain to come, though the rocking of the boat from the storm may cause discomforts.

Dear Remsen, [he began]—The subject of whole-time clinical teachers, on which I send you the promised note, is one of great importance, not only to universities, but to the profession and to the public at large. It is a big question, with two sides. I have tried to see both, as I have lived both, and as much, perhaps, as anyone, can appreciate both. Let me thank you, first, for Mr. Flexner's Report. As an Angel of Bethesda he has done much good in troubling our fish-pond, as well as the general pool. The Report as a whole shows the advantage of approaching a problem with an unbiased mind, but there are many mistakes from which a man who knows the profession from the outside only could not possibly escape. . . .

[And after a heart-searching review of what he thought a hospital clinician should be and do, he ended with]—These are some of the reasons why I am opposed to the plan as likely to spell ruin to the type of school I have always felt the Hospital should be and which we tried to make it—a place of refuge for the sick poor of the city—a place where the best that is known is taught to a group of the best students—a place where new thought is materialized in research—a school where men are encouraged to base the art upon the science of medicine—a fountain to which teachers in every subject would come for inspiration—a place with a hearty welcome to every practitioner who seeks help—a consulting centre for the whole country in cases of obscurity. And it may be said, all these are possible with whole-time clinical professors. I doubt it. The ideals would change, and I fear lest the broad open spirit which has characterized the school should narrow, as teacher and student chased each other down the fascinating road of research, forgetful of those wider interests to which a great hospital must minister.

Under the same date, September 1st, he wrote this much-treasured letter to the Librarian and staff of the Surgeon-General's Library in Washington:

Dear Friends, Among the 1000 telegrams and letters which I received not one touched my heart more closely than that which you all so kindly sent. Not a little of any success I may have had is due to the enormous stimulus which the publications of your department have had in my work. You who are part of the machine that pulls the profession along little realize the amount or importance of your labours. I dare say the next generation will be able to appreciate better what you have done. I can honestly say that no one of this generation has had a more grateful sense of his obligations than your sincere friend & well wisher, Wm Osler.

To Lewellys F. Barker. Llanddulas, N. Wales, 2nd [September]

. . . Yours with enclosure has just come. I wish I had had it earlier as I have just sent off to the press the revise of a letter which I am sending to Remsen on Whole-time Clin. Professors. He sent me a letter a month or two ago, & with it Flexner's Report. Kelly had sent his copy some time ago but it came when I was very occupied & I had not a chance to read it until a few weeks ago. It never should have been permitted to go out in its present form. You will see what I say & think of it. I am sending the letter to all the Trustees & the teachers of the school, as I believe most of them have had an opportunity of reading Flexner's Report tho not for circulation. Your address will do good & it puts the clinical problem in its proper light—and it must be solved by clinical men not by the pure laboratory people who know nothing of it—as F's Report clearly shows. . . . We are all well, enjoying the peace of this lovely spot, after a horrid racket. A baronetcy is a worrying honour—but fortunately it does not make any changes in one's sensations or in the general outlook on life. Love to Miss Humpton. I have fortunately lost my plantigrade secretary—I did *not* kill her tell Miss H., though often tempted. Revere 1½ in. taller than his daddy—a sweet lad, but no student. . . . I shall not be out this year. I am trying to revise the text book—very hard—It should be rewritten. Miss Humpton could do it! I am getting McCrae to help. We expect them next week. By the way, since I last wrote we had a delightful visit from the Müllers. M. as you will see by my letter is strongly opposed to the whole-time scheme—His evidence at the Lond. Univ. Commissn. was most interesting. It will be published before long—I will send you a copy. . . .

To Frederick C. Shattuck. Llanddulas 4th [Sept.]

Dear Fred S. Your nice letter should have been answered long ago but among the 1000 received I kept special ones to attend to at my leisure. We had a busy season—so much to do and so many people coming & going & then the coronation honour came in the midst of it, very unexpectedly, as I have not bothered my head about these things. When I came over first Broadbent very kindly said he could arrange anything I wished if Strathcona & Laurier gave a sign, but I told him to let matters rest as it would look as if I came in search of a title. These honours are very unequally distributed. Some of the most deserving men never receive any recognition—Hughlings Jackson for example and imagine chucking at 80 a knighthood to Jonathan Hutchinson! We are very well. My quarry is quiet for the time. The boy is taller than his father—no student, but an ardent fisherman. He is this minute beguiling trout in a lovely stream that flows thro the valley. Curiously enough I dreamed of you last night—but you had grown a beard. George was not in it with you & was greatly disgusted. You let out the secret that he had paid you $5000 a year for over 30 years not to grow a beard as it would rival his. You looked patriarchal and very well—really for the first time in your life handsomer than George. Love to the boy—it is nice to see his good work. Greetings to you all in which the Revere girl joins. Ever yours.

So, 'in a quiet Welsh valley away from all visitors, living the simple life', as he writes, 'getting used to saying "Lady Osler" and trying to finish the enormous correspondence that has poured in', a pleasant four weeks was passed.

To Mr. Henry Phipps. 13, Norham Gardens, Oxford. 7th [September]

We returned today from N. Wales where we have had a delightful rest. Many thanks for the cutting descriptive of the new psychopathic clinic. What a unique building! I hope next year when I come out, to see it nearly finished. How glad you will be! Your J.H.H. Dispensary is doing splendid work. I suppose Dr. Hamman has sent you the No. of the Bulletin with the last report—such good work. I am trying hard to get the County here organized—our dispensary is doing well at the Radcliffe Infirmary. We have had nearly 600 cases in 9 mos. How long shall you be in London? I should like to call & have a chat. Have you any extra copies of the Pasteur Life? . . .

A new secretary had been engaged, and with his correspondence no longer in arrears he managed at last to get off an article, for Dr. Macphail's journal, on a poorly understood malady of which he had seen many examples during the twenty years since Dr. George Peabody had first called attention to it.[1] His Text-book revision, meanwhile, was occupying his spare moments, and there were, besides, two addresses (indeed three) to prepare for the next month.[2] The first of them [3] was given on October 4th at the opening of the new Pathological Institute of the Royal Infirmary in Glasgow, of which Dr. John H. Teacher had just been appointed Director. The one-time Pathologist to the Montreal General Hospital, and the man who had spent so many hours in the old dead-house at Blockley, dwelt in this address on what should be the proper ties to bind the infirmary and the university to the pathological laboratory—'the place where the teaching is done, where ideas are nurtured, where men dream dreams, and thoughts are materialized into researches upon the one great problem that confronts the profession in each generation—*the nature of disease*:'

Only in one way lies redemption for the director of any institute or laboratory, he must have associates who know more about certain subjects than he does himself. An Admirable Crichton in these days is a quack, and in the art of delegation, in the subdivision of labour, in specialization among his subordinates, the director will find safety. The patient demonstrator who spends two hours with a group of students at a section has a place of equal importance with the man who is chasing the secret of anaphylaxis. In the hurly-burly of to-day, when the competition is so keen, and there are so many seeking the bubble reputation at the eye-piece and the test-tube, it is well for young men to remember that no bubble is so iridescent or floats longer than that blown by the successful teacher. A man who is not fond of students and who does not suffer their foibles gladly, misses the greatest zest in life; and the teacher who wraps himself in the cloak of his researches, and lives apart from the

---

[1] 'Transient Aphasia and Paralysis in States of High Blood Pressure and Arteriosclerosis.' *Canadian Medical Association Journal*, Oct. 1911. An appropriate place for its publication, since his attention was first called to the condition by the illness of his old friend and colleague George Ross, Macphail's predecessor in the editorship of the leading Canadian journal. See above, Vol. I, p. 168.

[2] At the Centenary Jubilee of the University at Christiania Osler was given an honorary M.D. *in absentia* at about this time.

[3] 'The Pathological Institute of a General Hospital.' *Glasgow Medical Journal*, 1911, lxxvi, 321–33.

bright spirits of the coming generation, is very apt to find his garment the shirt of Nessus. Encourage the students to help in the teaching, and arrange the time of sections not for your own convenience, but for the students and staff. I had a practice of making the clinical clerk tell the story of the case, not read an abstract, but speak it out and tell its difficulties and the diagnosis, right or wrong. It was good for us all, the teacher and the taught, and we met on the same levels as seekers for truth. . . .

And, lastly [he said], this institute exists for the benefit of the public. There is not a patient in the wards who will not be helped by the work done here. Nowadays laboratory methods of treatment and diagnosis are more and more in vogue. This will be the routine of service, but the larger public that pays the piper has the right to call the tune; and the demand which they make, and with just right, is that the resources of the institute should be requisitioned in the fight which science is making against unnecessary disease and untimely death. . . . Given to pessimism, the Briton loves to look on the dark side of things. There is no such medicine for the malady as a study of the health records of our great towns—a story of marvellous progress, better housing, better feeding, better drinking, better health, and, as a consequence, better citizens.

And he closed with the boyhood recollection, already quoted, of the tapping of the spring maples for sugar in the Canadian backwoods—a happy figure of speech as he turned it to fit the old Glasgow Royal Infirmary.

His host in Glasgow was A. Maitland Ramsay, a 'charter' member of that 'North-Atlantic' society of the summer of 1904, who had arranged a meeting of the Glasgow Southern Medical Society to be held the next evening in Osler's honour. Before this body he read in the Faculty Hall a timely and important paper on High Blood Pressure,[1] or what in more modern parlance is referred to as 'hypertension', a symptom which physicians have harped upon overmuch since the introduction of an instrument of some precision has made the estimation of blood pressure reasonably exact. Many people, in consequence, have become unduly frightened on being told that they have 'hypertension', and it was this that Osler's paper was intended to offset. It recalls his article of some years before in which he said that the finding of a small amount of albumin in

[1] 'High Blood Pressure: its Associations, Advantages, and Disadvantages.' *British Medical Journal*, Nov. 2, 1912.

the urine was conducive to longevity rather than the reverse—a comforting and oft-quoted remark to many an anxious soul. At the outset he drew upon his reading of Herodotus and his trip on the s.s. *Seti* for an allegory, saying : 'A man's life may be said to be a gift of his blood pressure, just as Egypt is a gift of the Nile'—and there followed a long comparison between the human irrigation scheme and the forces which keep Egypt watered and drained in order to prevent 'dropsy of the soil'. From his own experience with patients suffering from hypertension, he gave illustrations to show how a philosophical view of the situation would benefit them provided at the same time they could be made to 'reduce their speed from the 24 knots of a *Lusitania* to the 10 knots of an ocean tramp'. And he closed by saying that the clinical picture he had painted was (and it still is) a fair presentation of the subject—'necessarily a bit sombre, but brightened when possible'.

The third promised address was not delivered, for reasons given in his account-book, where is noted : *Oct.* 11—'Heavy cold 2 days. Followed exposure on Sunday p.m.' *Oct.* 13—'Missed address Reading Path. Soc.' The 'grand-daughter once-removed' and the niece had ended their long sojourn at Oxford the week before; and as his wife was about to leave for what proved to be her last visit to her aged and devoted mother in America, he writes on the 13th : 'We are desolated, left alone & now A. G. goes off to-morrow, but I have a deuce of a lot of work on hand. I'm getting thro the text-book at a good rate. We go to press early in January.' And on the same day to A. C. Klebs :

I wish I could be at Vienne on Sunday, but it is impossible. Please send me a good newspaper account and a photograph of the [Servetus] monument. Yes, I would like so much to subscribe to the Arloing Memorial, put me down for 100 francs.[1] . . . I still feel you played us a low trick in not coming here. We had a delightful summer in Wales. . . . Keep an eye open for any old Medical books of the 15th and 16th century. Do you know my friend Conrad Gesner—one of the greatest of the Switzers? I have many but want all of his works. Wonderful man!'

---

[1] In connexion with this contribution to a bronze plaquette for S. Arloing, 1846–1911, 'Directeur de l'École Nationale Vétérinaire de Lyon', Osler's early interests will be recalled.

In a later note he says: 'Thanks for your cuttings about Servetus, over whom they seem to have poured a good deal of oleo-margarine. The difficulty is that the liberals use him as a stick with which to beat the clericals.' His 'heavy cold' had prevented him from attending meetings not only at Reading but also at the Royal Society of Medicine, where, having been made President of the Clinical Section, he was booked to appear on the second Friday in each month for the coming year. He had also been elected to membership in the Samuel Pepys Club; and though this club meets infrequently it added another to the many gatherings he made an effort to attend. His university obligations meanwhile continued unchanged, as did his regular Tuesday afternoon clinics at the Radcliffe Infirmary—clinics, by the way, which were occasionally written up to be published in some medical journal at home or abroad, as was the case, for example, with one on October 24th.[1] He had, indeed, 'a deuce of a lot of work on hand'—even without his Text-book revision.

One section of Osler's library is given over to what he used jokingly to refer to as the 'Death, Heaven and Hell' corner, which contained books, old and new, on spiritualism (with which he had scant patience), dreams and ghosts, on witchcraft, on immortality, longevity, premature burial, pre-existence, resurrection, 'self-murther', euthanasia, embalming, cremation, and similar subjects. Among them, for example, is that amazing volume, 'Words in Pain', written anonymously by an unhappy woman with an incurable malady, 'but with a soul cheered and sustained by its own inward light', and containing a series of letters to her doctor—almost too sad to read; for at the last she took fate in her own hands. All this may serve as a sufficient introduction to the following letter published in the *Spectator* for November 4th under the title 'Maeterlinck on Death':

To the Editor of the Spectator. Christ Church, Oxford.

Sir,—A student for many years of the art and of the act of dying, I read with eagerness Maeterlinck's recent Essay, only, I must confess,

[1] 'Chronic Infectious Endocarditis, &c.' *Interstate Medical Journal*, St. Louis, February 1912.

to be disappointed. A brilliant example of the type of literature characterized by Hamlet in his famous reply to Polonius, there is an unpleasant flavour, a cadaverous mustiness about the Essay which even the words cannot cover; and in spite of the plea for burning burials, one smells everywhere 'the mould above the rose'. To those of your readers who feel after the reading, as I did, the chill of the charnel-house, let me urge an hour in the warm sunshine of the Phaedo.

But I write for another purpose—to protest against the pictures which are given of the act of dying, 'The Tortures of the Last Illness', 'The Uselessly Prolonged Torments', 'The Unbearable Memories of the Chamber of Pain', 'The Pangs of Death', 'The Awful Struggle', 'The Sharpest Peak of Human Pain', and 'Horror'. The truth is, an immense majority of all die as they are born—oblivious. A few, very few, suffer severely in the body, fewer still in the mind. Almost all Shelley's description fits:

Mild is the slow necessity of death;
    The tranquil spirit fails beneath its grasp,
Without a groan, almost without a fear,
    Resigned in peace to the necessity;
Calm as a voyager to some distant land,
    And full of wonder, full of hope as he.

No death need be physically painful. M. Maeterlinck has been most unfortunate to be able to say, speaking of doctors, 'who has not at a bedside twenty times wished and not once dared to throw himself at their feet and implore mercy'; but this is the same type of hysterical statement as 'all doctors consider it their first duty to protract as long as possible even the most excruciating convulsions of the most hopeless agony'. There are no circumstances contradicting the practice of Thomas Fuller's good physician: 'when he can keep life no longer in, he makes a fair and easy passage for it to go out'. Nowadays, when the voice of Fate calls, the majority of men may repeat the last words of Socrates: 'I owe a cock to Asclepius'—a debt of thankfulness, as was his, for a fair and easy passage. I am, Sir, &c., William Osler.

On the fly-leaf of the copy of Maeterlinck's book Osler has written: 'See Avicenna, *Traité sur la délivrance de la crainte de la mort*, 1894', and inserted in the volume is this letter from a physician in such a remote corner of the world as Kokstad, East Griqualand, Cape of Good Hope:

December 5, 1911.

Dear Sir,—When the *Spectator* of Nov. 4 arrived here, containing your interesting letter with its comments on Maeterlinck's 'Death', I had just been re-reading for the first time for 15 years the 'Odes' of Horace. It has often struck me that so few poets of the higher ranks have attempted to translate the Odes. I suppose that, being Masters of their craft, they know that a translation is at its best a failure—and your quotation of Shelley's lines, beginning 'Mild is the slow necessity of Death' I read in the *Spectator* just after reading Ode III—in fact I had laid down my Horace to open the paper; and fresh in my mind were the lines (29–33)

Post ignem aetheria domo
subductum macies et nova febrium
terris incubuit cohors,
semotique prius tarda necessitas
leti corripuit gradum. . . .

Shelley, as skilful an artificer in English as Horace in Latin, translated the words 'tarda necessitas leti' literally. I suppose it is the coincidence of reading your letter and also these lines that has compelled me to write you. Living as I do among black—and also so far as the classics are concerned, white—savages, contributes to the impulse; and also the consciousness that the 'Osler' of my student days has become part of my mental equipment, and its presence by me is a never-failing friend in times of need. Especially for the last reason, I feel myself without presumption entitled to take what in a stranger might be regarded as the uncalled-for liberty of addressing you. Yours faithfully, J. Duncan.

But the story of the individual books in his library must be left for the published catalogue of the Bibliotheca Osleriana, hard though it is to keep off the subject. It was difficult also for Osler himself, as the following letter of November 29th to Dr. Jacobs shows:

We have had great excitement here over the Huth sale, the prices were shocking & all previous records broken, as the average for a thousand volumes, excluding the Shakespeares which were sold separately, was £50. I got the only book I wanted, for a song, Astruc's study of Genesis, from which dates all modern Biblical criticism. He was the famous Montpellier & Paris physician of the first half of the eighteenth century, & a great figure in his day, but he is as dead as a door nail now except among theologians. Nobody apparently knew of the extraordinary rarity of this book which was published anonymously & has not been in the auctions of either London or Paris for fifteen years. Quaritch secured it for me for 17*s*. Welch will know about it as he is an old friend of Astruc's. I got one or two other less important things; and am waiting now for the second part of the Hoe catalogue, there may be something in that.

I wish the Trustees would do something for Miss Bonner, who deserves a good pension. She has done splendid work at the Hospital, particularly in the early days, when she was a bond of peace. I am writing to Smith about it.

It is quite probable that his letter to the *Spectator* remonstrating against Maeterlinck's views regarding the act of dying may have called to mind the fact that years before (June 1888), after reading Munk's 'Euthanasia'—a related subject—he had sent to Ross's journal in Montreal a review in which the same favourite lines from Shelley had been quoted. If this is so, his promise earlier in the year to Andrew Macphail that he should have some 'copy' for the new Canadian journal, may have come to his remembrance and have led him to send off the first of the series of brief papers entitled 'Men and Books' which appeared in monthly instalments during the coming eighteen months. It may be recalled that in the editorial rooms of the *Medical News* in Philadelphia, when in the '80's they were hard put for some copy, Osler always had something worth while which could quickly be whipped into shape for publication; and so with these notes for Macphail, he appeared to have an inexhaustible supply. That he was willing to see them buried in a Canadian journal was not entirely without sentiment on his part, for they correspond to the series of 'Ephemerides' sent from Baltimore in 1896–7 to help out the pages of the *Montreal Medical Journal* which his old friends Roddick and Blackader, with others, were editing, as well as to the earlier 'Notes and Comments' sent in 1888 to George Ross when he was struggling single-handed with the editorship of the predecessor of these journals, in which so many of Osler's early McGill papers had been published. Consequently, with his single seventeen-shilling purchase from the Huth sale to rejoice over, he soon sends off to Macphail this account of 'Jean Astruc and the Higher Criticism':

It is strange how the memory of a man may float to posterity on what he would have himself regarded as the most trifling of his works. Ask in succession a score of doctors, 'Who was Astruc?' and the expression aroused indicates that at least in our profession he is 'clean forgotten as the dead man out of mind'; and yet librarians and dealers in second-hand books know only too well what a prolific writer he was in the first half of the eighteenth century. But ask any theologian, any man interested in the history of the Bible, the same question, and his face at once brightens—or darkens—as he replies, 'Oh, Jean Astruc, he was the father of modern biblical criticism'. And so it is that the man whom we have forgotten, who cut such a figure in the profession at Montpellier and Paris, the enumeration of whose tomes extends through three pages in Bayle's 'Biographie Médicale', is remembered to-day by a small octavo volume, published anonymously in Brussels, 1753, with the title, '*Conjectures sur les Mémoires Originaux dont il paroit que Moyse s'est servi pour composer le Livre de la Genèse. Avec des Remarques, qui appuient ou qui éclaircissent ces Conjectures.*'

Interested in Astruc for some years, having had occasion to refer to his splendid work on the history of syphilis and to his history of the Montpellier Faculty, and incidentally knowing his position as the founder of the criticism of the Pentateuch, I had long tried to get the above-named volume, which I had never seen advertised in any catalogue. It turned up the other day at Sotheby's in the Huth collection. . . .

Astruc's notable discovery was the recognition that in Genesis there are two separate accounts of the Creation and of the early days of the world, the one extending as far as verse 3 of Chapter II, in which the Creator is spoken of as Elohim, the other extending from verse 4 of Chapter II to the end of Chapter IV, in which the Creator is called Jehovah. These accounts differ in important details, particularly in the fact that in the Jahvistic account no mention is made of the sin of Adam, which plays so important a rôle in Pauline Christianity. . . . The work is a small octavo volume, extending to 525 pages, fully one-half of which is taken up with a critical consideration of his views. Small wonder that in 1753 the distinguished physician to the King, and professor in the Paris Faculty, published such a work anonymously, and in Brussels.

In a letter earlier in the year Osler had hinted that his contribution to the building fund of the Royal Society of Medicine was more than he could well afford—a fund, alas, at the time far below the cost of the building then nearing its completion. For the disagreeable task of further begging, J. Y. W. MacAlister enlisted his aid, and to him Osler writes on December 4th:

Dear MacAlister,—Yes, of course, to anything you write I would subscribe, only I do not know how the members would feel having a letter sent out by so comparatively a new-comer as myself. Are there any men you think I could tackle privately? There is a good deal of wealth tied up here and there in the profession. Has anyone attacked T——? Savage might help in that matter. I would take advice about sending out a letter from me, some people might think it peculiar; still, no matter!

MacAlister received a telegram on the 8th saying: 'All right. Osler'; and there follows a deal of correspondence about this distasteful job which, nevertheless, had to be done:

Please send me a dozen of the books & [copies] of my letter. I have written to T—— & to old B—— of Preston whom I know very well, & to the man who is supposed to keep the purse of the Drapers' Company, & will try to stir up one or two others. I do not despair of getting something out of Strathcona. We shall come through all right in the end. Also send a descriptive booklet to J—— M—— Esq., The Carlton Hotel, & put inside with my compliments. It would be worth while to look up carefully the descendants of some of the old worthies connected with the Medical Chirurgical or other societies. Who is enjoying R—— B——'s unearned increment, of which the old man left a very big slice? The heirs might like to fit up a room at a cost of £1,000. Family vanity is a powerful lever which Mitchell has used to great advantage in Philadelphia.

Meanwhile the Text-book is getting on and he writes to McCrae on December 15th:

Dear Mac,—I had hoped to send the Infectious Diseases section this week but the pasting-in and re-copying has been a longer business than I thought it would be. It should go by the Wednesday steamer, or a good part of it. You will not have much difficulty in slipping in your portions. I have decided not to put in the Introductions for the following reason: I have long had in contemplation *An introduction to Medicine* for medical students, a brief account of disease—its study, classifications, type, growth of our knowledge, &c. If I wrote the Introductions it would virtually cover an important part of the ground and Appleton & Co. would not like me to use this material.[1] We shall have enough with the book in its present form. . . .

There were other occupations, too, for he writes to J. H. Pratt on the 15th: 'We are beginning to get things in line for the International Congress in 1913. I am President of the Medical Section, and shall look for the active support of the Inter-urbans.' And the same day he sends Mrs. Brewster a letter which permits the year to close with laughter:

Dear Mabel, Xmas greetings! I hope this may reach you in time but it is a slow steamer this week. I am so sorry Grace did

[1] Osler had in mind the preparation of short introductory statements before the various sections of the Text-book—i. e. to precede the diseases of the respiratory tract, the circulation, &c.

not see you but she could not stay over in New York. I motored to Southampton to meet her, & picked up Revere at Winchester—she was surprised to find us on the dock. I hope Sylvia's big Bible 'All Hail' has come. I am sure she will be interested in the pictures. I have sent you a nice little edition of the Phaedo for your bedside library. The translation is not so good as Jowett. I am very busy—have just finished the examinations, today, and am working at a new edition of my text-book which should go to press next month. I have had no time for much outside reading but I am finishing Bergson on Laughter. Curious that the only two special works of any moment on this very emotional problem should be by Frenchmen—one in 1567 by an old Montpellier physician Joubert, & the other by B. I would give a great deal to look in upon you at the children's hour & have a good laugh & romp with Sylvia. My Xmas greetings to Uncle Ned and his family. Tell him I do not despair yet of seeing him in my rooms at Christ Church. By the way do you know (R. B. will surely) dear old Prof. Lounsbury at Yale? I have just been reading his early days of Browning—delightful & so true. . . .

Which looks as though he must have begun, in preparation for his Silliman Lectures, to orient himself as to the members of the Yale faculty. But Bergson on 'Laughter' evidently interested him even more, and he must have read pen in hand, for a month later a long note was published in Macphail's journal,[1] dealing with the subject—a note which ends with this paragraph :

I cavilled at Bergson's conclusion—that like sea-froth the substance of laughter is scanty and the after-taste bitter. It is not always so. Joubert is right. There is a form that springs from the heart, heard every day in the merry voice of childhood, the expression of a laughter-loving spirit that defies analysis by the philosopher, which has nothing rigid or mechanical in it, and is totally without social significance. Bubbling spontaneously from the artless heart of child or man, without egoism and full of feeling, laughter is the music of life. After his magical survey of the world in the 'Anatomy of Melancholy', Burton could not well decide, *fleat Heraclitus an rideat Democritus*, whether to weep with the one or laugh with the other, and at the end of the day this is often the mental attitude of the doctor ; but once with ears attuned to the music of which I speak, he is ever on the side of the great Abderite, and there is the happy possibility that, like Lionel in, I think, one of Shelley's poems, he may keep himself young with laughter.

---

[1] 'Men and Books. V. Two Frenchmen on Laughter.' *Canadian Medical Association Journal*, Feb. 1912, ii. 152.

CHAPTER XXXII

1912

HARD PRESSED

THE knowledge soon spread that he was planning for a visit to America the ensuing October, and he was bombarded with invitations to speak. He must have shared in the feeling expressed by Weir Mitchell in a letter of that time—'It is an abominable thing that one is not twins—in fact I should like to be numerous.' He wrote on January 4th to F. C. Shattuck that he was very doubtful as to whether he should give the 'Ether Day' address at the Massachusetts General Hospital on October 16th, and added: 'I have the Silliman course at Yale, for which I am taking as my subject the evolution of modern medicine. I shall have to do something at the Hopkins and at Montreal, so that I shall be pretty hard pressed. My old friends have been only too urgent in asking me to lecture at different places.'

He was by now deep in the Text-book revision over which for some months he had been frittering. 'It is just twenty years since I was working at the 1st edition [he wrote]. It 's been a great pleasure and has brought me hosts of friends known and unknown, but putting new wine into old bottles is a difficult job.' Indeed he had become more deeply involved than he realized, and, as his letters make clear, he was procrastinating over the preparation of the Yale lectures which, indeed, finally had to be postponed till the following spring. But hard at work as he was (and continued to be for three months more) in 're-bottling' the chapters of his Text-book, he found relaxation in familiar ways. His was not 'the spade of unenlightened industry'. Just now his attention was engaged with a medical writer of the Reformation who had better fortune than Servetus, which accounts for a paragraph in the following letter of January 10th to A. C. Klebs in Ouchy:

... I am so glad to hear from you, & it is satisfactory to know that you have got some local affliction, which I am sure will chasten you for your good! Of course it is gout! Tissot is well worth looking up. I have several editions of his famous 'Avis'. . . . Of course you well know that the house in which he lived had been occupied by Voltaire. He was not so big a man as Tronchin. Are you going to Rome [Tuberculosis Congress]? I hope to spend the month of April, or part of it, in Italy. I have just been revising the section on tuberculosis in my Text-book, & have found your book of great help. I heard several of the London men speak of it with great praise. I want very much an old picture, engraving or anything would do, & a modern photograph of a little island called Ufenau, in Lake Zurich, on which Ulrich von Hutten died. There must be pictures of the old monastery—possibly too of Pastor Schnegg to whom Hutten went for treatment. Did you ever read Strauss' life of Ul. v. Hutten—splendid! . . . Keep your eye on Conrad Gesner for me. He is a great friend. I am not sure whether he is not the only really respectable Swiss in history! Greet your father. . . .

And later on, in a subsequent letter, he adds:

Are you sure that there is not anywhere in Germany a national monument to Ulrich von Hutten? There surely must be! I have always had the greatest admiration for him, and as a factor in the Reformation he certainly comes next to Luther and Erasmus. . . . I have been on the lookout for years for an original edition of the De Guaiaci[1] but have never met one. I have half a dozen of his other pamphlets & dialogues. He did a great work in the reformation & was the fons et origo of the national spirit of Germany. There should be a big national monument to him on the Island—which might be teutonized for the occasion.

In another January letter he says: 'Revere is home. He has just completed a 5 ft. Atlantic liner, engines and all, which is to be launched this week'; and in a note of the 22nd to Jacobs: 'You will have the catalogue of the remainder of Payne's Library. The herbals and the Miltons will fetch big prices. I have secured a few good items lately, a 1470 Ars Moriendi and an early Avicenna. I have a treasure of a new secretary—a Scotch girl who is going to be a great help as she knows French, German, & Russian well.' And on February 5th:

. . . The 1519 edition [De Guaiaci Medicina] is not very rare, and the arrangement followed in the third & fourth editions, which I have, is not the same as that you gave. I have [a] MS. of the English translation, 1539. It appeared in English twice.

[1] 'De Guaiaci Medicina et Morbo Gallico,' 1519.

At the sale of Payne's library last week I got Hutten's stirring appeal 'Ad Principes Germanos ut Bellum Turcis inferant', 1519. I shall be glad to hear about the monuments. I do not think there is any special evidence that von Hutten lived a more dissipated life than the average man of his period. I am just reading the 'Epistolae Obscurorum Virorum' of which he wrote a great many, & if that gives a true picture of the times, it is not surprising that he dedicated his 'De Guaiaci' to Archbishop Albert. . . .

The latter part of January saw the disposal at Sotheby's of the second portion of Payne's library, an account of which was soon sent off with his monthly instalment for Macphail's journal. In this note, some of which has been quoted above, he says in part:

The working library of a doctor is not, as a rule, worth much after his death; but when a man is interested in books, knows their value, and buys judiciously, the collection which he leaves may form a considerable part of his estate. I know an old doctor living not far from here whose hobby for forty years has been first editions, some half-dozen of which are worth his entire establishment.

A scholar and book-lover of the best type, Dr. Joseph Frank Payne began to collect early, and had wide interests, both professional and literary. There was no one in England better versed in the history of medicine, to which he had made a number of contributions of the first rank, principally on Anglo-Saxon medicine. Shortly before his death he delivered in Oxford a most instructive course of lectures on Greek pre-Hippocratic medicine which it is to be hoped he has left in a state for publication.[1] Part of his library was sold in July, and the remainder at the end of January. . . . The second part of the library consisted of a special collection of about one hundred and sixteen Herbals, a few miscellaneous classical works, and a collection of first and other editions of Milton, and Miltoniana. The Herbals were offered *en bloc*, but the reserve price was not reached. Several of the fifteenth-century Herbals brought a very good price: a 1488 Herbarium, the earliest with figures of plants, brought £96. For years Dr. Payne had been very much interested in Milton, and his collection contained a very large number of first editions. The highest price paid for a single item was for a quarto edition of the famous tract on 'Education', one of the very few copies known in this form, and for which Mr. Quaritch paid £172. The library realized as a whole £4,353, a figure which is rarely reached by modern medical collections.

[1] The manuscript, 'Six Lectures on the History of Greek Medicine', was later given to Osler, and is now in his library.

Osler's letters of the time give evidence that the thorough revision being given the Text-book was the chief thing on his mind ; and though McCrae was sharing the burden, pen, paste-pot, and scissors were busy. 'It is very slow getting in the slips in the proper places,' he writes on February 2nd, but I should be able to have it all within six weeks. I have cut out a great deal here and there. I am afraid they have not been printing and are waiting for the whole of the manuscript. If so they will never get it out by the 1st of October. We could put the whole thing through here at the Press in four months.' . . . And later on he says to his collaborator : 'I wish you would give instructions to use the English spelling of 'centre', 'millimetre', &c. It makes no difference over in America but it does over here. I expect you will have a devil of a job before you have finished with this and will be sorry you ever undertook it !'

On February 10th Lord Lister died suddenly in his eighty-fifth year, from pneumonia ; and on the 16th a memorial service was held in the Abbey where a grateful nation would have interred him but for his express wish to be buried at Hampstead beside his wife.

I have just come from the Abbey service, [Osler writes] [1] —the most splendid tribute ever paid to our profession, and so richly deserved in the person of Joseph Lister, one of the greatest benefactors of humanity. Voltaire saw Newton buried like a king in the same Abbey, and ever after esteemed it one of the glories of England that she was able to recognize the supreme merits of a king among men. To-day's ceremony was England's tribute of heart and head. The nation's Valhalla was packed to the doors ; nurses, students, doctors, and the general public crowded in the nave, while the reserved seats of choir and transepts were thronged with a gathering of representatives from all parts of Europe. As one of the delegates from the University of Oxford, I had a choir seat, which chanced to be next to our own [McGill] Chancellor, Lord Strathcona. The recognition of the international character of Lord Lister's work was witnessed by the presence of nearly all the foreign ambassadors, and representatives of the Académies des Sciences of Russia, Sweden and Norway, Spain and Rome. Among those who occupied seats were the Prime Minister and many of his colleagues, Lord Lansdowne and the Duke of Northumberland. Opposite to me was a group

[1] 'Men and Books. IX.' *Canadian Medical Association Journal*, Apr. 1912, ii. 343–4.

of Lister's old Glasgow and Edinburgh pupils—Macewen, Caird, Littlejohn, Bramwell, Balfour, Playfair, and others.

Just before 2.30 p.m., after the organist had finished playing Chopin's 'Funeral March', there was heard at intervals a distant voice, high above the silence. At first the impression was of someone singing outside. I was waiting for it, having had a few years ago, at the funeral of Lord Kelvin, the same experience. The choir coming through the cloisters sang the hymn, 'Brief Life is here our Portion', and the high note at the end of the third line alone reached us in the clear liquid voice of one boy. For three or four verses this was heard without another note of the full choir (the sound of which was not audible until the last verse), which finished just as the procession entered the Abbey. Preceded by the canons, the coffin was borne through the nave and choir covered with a purple pall and on it a magnificent wreath of orchids sent by the German Emperor. . . . It was a noble and ever-to-be-remembered occasion. And was ever Handel's grand anthem sung more fittingly? 'When the ear heard him then it blessed him; and when the eye saw him, it gave witness of him. He delivered the poor that cried; the fatherless and him that had none to help him. Kindness, meekness and comfort were in his tongue. If there was any virtue and if there was any praise, he thought on those things. His body is buried in peace, but his name liveth evermore.'

Only those who have lived in the pre-Listerian days can appreciate the revolution which has taken place in surgery. In the seventies at the old Montreal General Hospital we passed through it, and it is pleasant to recall that when Dr. Roddick returned from Lister with the technique there was no opposition, but the surgeons patiently practised a laborious and unnecessary ritual for the sake of the better results. As with everything that is worth preserving in this life there has been evolution, but from the great underlying principle on which Lister acted there has been no departure. . . .

But the malady which so suddenly had carried off Lister in his old age may affect the young as well, and early in March some very anxious days were passed by the Oslers in Winchester. In a letter to McCrae of March 11th dealing with the everlasting 'revision', Osler adds:

Revere has pneumonia, but is in very good condition. It started on Thursday morning with a chill & the temperature went up nearly to 106°. He has got involvement of the upper half of the right lower lobe, very little cough, no pain, & the respirations have not been above 32. I have just left him & this is the completion of his fourth day, so that he should be comfortable. I go back again this afternoon. He is in excellent quarters at the College Sanatorium & has two very good nurses.

A few days later he wrote to H. B. Jacobs, saying that Revere had behaved like a gentleman, had had his crisis on the sixth day and was now very comfortable; and to this he added: 'While in Winchester I saw a case with a Dr. Arthur E. Bodington, who turned out to be a grandson of George B., and I wheedled out of him the old man's original account of his tuberculosis treatment. I have been after it for years.' It 's an ill wind that blows no good; and that Osler would not unnecessarily worry over his boy's illness and would find some interests beyond the school sanatorium was quite in train with his character. Equally consistent was it that he should sit down and write for Macphail's journal an account of this historical pamphlet just added to his library:[1]

A generation—two indeed—in advance of his day, George Bodington has at last come to his own, and is everywhere recognized as the pioneer of the open-air treatment of pulmonary tuberculosis. Not that he was the first to send consumptives into the open: Celsus speaks of sea voyages and the advantages of the climate of Egypt, and the horseback cure of Sydenham meant fresh air and exercise. But Bodington recognized that 'to live in and breathe freely open air, without being deterred by the wind or weather, is one important and essential remedy in arresting tuberculosis'. . . . The prevalent method of treatment was to shut the patient up in a close room, excluding as far as possible the access of air, and to drug him with tartarized antimony and digitalis, alternating with occasional doses of calomel, and now and then to take a little blood! For all this Bodington substituted 'fresh morning air, a good dinner to make him fat, an opium pill to make him sleep, and good wine to bring down his pulse'. He had really the idea of sanatorium treatment. 'I have taken for the purpose a house in every respect adapted and near to my own residence for the reception of patients of this class, who may be desirous, or who are recommended to remove from their homes for the benefit of a change of air.' He held that cold was never too severe for the consumptive patient: 'The cooler the air which passes into the lungs the greater will be the benefit the patient will receive. Sharp, frosty days in the winter season are the most favourable. The application of cold, pure air to the interior surface of the lungs is the most powerful sedative that can be applied.' He advocated riding or walking, according to the strength of the patient. Several cases are reported in the essay

[1] 'Men and Books. XI. George Bodington.' *Canadian Medical Association Journal*, June 1912, ii. 526–7.

showing the very favourable results obtained by this treatment. As is often the case, his practice was better than his theory, for he had a belief that the disease was associated with impairment of the contractility of the lungs from loss of nervous power, consequent upon the presence of the tuberculous matter.

The house at Sutton Coldfield still stands, the prototype of the innumerable open-air sanatoria of today. A few years ago Dr. Lawrason Brown of Saranac made a pious pilgrimage to the place, and I am indebted to him for photographs of the house. Bodington was severely criticized by his contemporaries, and he did not live to see the open-air method adopted, but has the great merit of being the first, or at any rate among the very first, to advocate rational and scientific treatment of pulmonary consumption.

The Phipps Psychiatric Clinic at the Johns Hopkins under Dr. Adolf Meyer's supervision was by this time nearing completion and plans were on foot to dedicate properly the building in which, possibly for the first time, the mentally sick were to be accommodated in quarters equal, if not superior, to any that had previously been provided for patients with maladies of other kinds. On March 18th Osler wrote to Mr. Phipps :

Your idea of inviting some of the leading alienists to the opening is a good one, and I hope it can be carried out. It could be made the occasion of an interesting discussion on ways and methods of dealing with the insane, which would stimulate work enormously in America. When is the Clinic likely to be opened? I have the Silliman Lectures to give at Yale in October, so that I hope it may be during that month.

He also wrote to him saying that he would be greatly pleased to learn how enthusiastically the copies of his edition of Pasteur had been received by all the medical schools to which it had been sent, and that he was keeping the letters for him to read. One of Osler's characteristic notes in reply to one of these letters was sent to a former Hopkins pupil, Paul G. Woolley, at the time Dean of the Medical Department of the University of Cincinnati ; it chiefly concerns an old grievance he harboured against the city :

March 21, 1912.

Dear Woolley,—So glad to have your letter, and to hear that the Pasteur book was appreciated. I am sure that you will be able to do splendid work where you are. They have always had a fine set of men there, and they only need a little stimulation and encouragement. I want to see a fine monument to Daniel Drake in Cincinnati, one really worthy of the man. He was a great character, and did a remarkable work for the profession in the West. I hope to see some rich Cincinnatian put up a $25,000 monument to him—he is worth it. He started nearly everything in Cincinnati that is good and has lasted. If anybody will give the amount I will come out and give a regular 'Mississippi Valley' oration.

The end of March saw his burdensome winter's task nearly completed, and on the 27th he writes to W. S. Thayer: 'Just sending off the last of the text-book revision—deuce of a job, but interesting. I have smashed up a good many of the old sections.' Though a deal of proof reading was to follow, the responsibility of seeing the revision through the press was delegated to McCrae, and Osler had time for other things. A note of the 30th to a quondam Baltimore neighbour says:

All well here again. . . . We are off to Italy next week where I hope to join McJacob [H. B. Jacobs] in Rome for the T.b. congress. . . . What a stirring at the J.H.H. . . . Great thing to have an active circulation in an institution. You must come here on your way thro from Germany. I hope to join you but July is a bad month—so much on hand. Old Nicholson died last week. A new Bodley Librarian is to be appointed & [there is] much searching of hearts. Wonderful place. I am beginning to understand it. Ed. princeps of Dioscorides last week at Sotheby's. Love to the darlings—all. . . .

He had long planned to be in Rome for the VIIth International Tuberculosis Congress to be held there the second week in April, and this gave an opportunity to get Revere into a milder climate where his complete convalescence might be assured. So it came about that for the three weeks from April 4th to the 25th the 'Open Arms' was closed. Ten days were passed in Northern Italy—at Venice, Florence, and Padua, to the architectural awakening of Revere, who had already begun to show skill with his pencil and who as a pastime had taken up photography and etching, to his father's great delight; for nothing could have been more remote from his own particular gifts. After a sojourn at the Italian lakes, saddened by the news of the sinking of the *Titanic* on the 14th, Revere was taken back to school, and Osler went on alone to Rome for the Congress. It was not a particularly well organized affair, he thought, though there were gathered from all countries most of the old-time leaders still active in the great crusade—and many new ones besides. Since he had no formal paper to present himself, it may be imagined that he resumed the corruption of his little friend's tea-table manners, and that the old book shops were thoroughly revisited. The trip, during which he had made a list of all the medical incunabula he could find in the Italian libraries, ended with a few days at Cannes with Dr. and Mrs. Jacobs.

Some notes have already been given of Osler's relation to clubs of various kinds, and the ways in which he used them. However, since his marriage his home had taken the place of a club and he greatly preferred to have people gather about him there than to search elsewhere for entertainment. A man's table, like his house, is infinitely communicative, and tells many things besides the figures of its master's income ; and at his home and in his library Osler was at his best. Still, as has been seen, he dined with considerable regularity at Christ Church on Sunday evening, attended the monthly dinners of the College Club, those of the Royal Society and the Colophon Club, as well as the less frequent gatherings of such groups as the Pepys Club. And from this time on there was to be another of these dinner clubs which he possibly enjoyed most of all. It comprised a group of men who for their combination of learning with good fellowship could hardly have been surpassed. The following letter from the Secretary of 'The Club' will tell all that is necessary.

94 Banbury Road, Oxford,
May 3, 1912.

Dear Sir William,—I have the duty, honour and pleasure to inform you that at the meeting of 'The Club' last evening you were with all due ceremony and with entire unanimity on our part elected into the fraternity of the oldest senior Club at Oxford. The antiquity is only surpassed by the famous Phoenix Common Room at Brasenose. Three toasts preceded the election :—'Father Banks', 'The Lady Patroness' and 'To a happy Election'. Then seven spills of paper of precisely equal length were given round, and after an interval collected. Had any of them been dimidiated, tertiated or even decimated, the proposed election was void. As it was, they each exhibited their pristine Procrustean length. I understand from the Principal of Hertford that you already possess a printed list, brought up to date by manuscript entries, of all members of The Club. It only remains that I should remind you that we meet on the 1st, 3rd, 5th and 7th Thursdays of term, that no reply is needed to the notes of invitation unless (*absit omen!*) you cannot come, that a new member is entertained by all the other members before he himself is host, and that the hosts of the three remaining dinners this term are, in order and *secundum Rotam*, the Provost of Worcester, the Warden of All Souls, and Dr. Cowley. I am sure you will be interested some day in seeing the original green book of Records, containing all such rules, rotas and details as are lawful to be set forth in writing, from April 8, 1790 to the present time. With all due felicitations, I am, Sincerely yours, F. MADAN.

In addition to his usual fixed duties in connexion with the Infirmary, the Press, and the Bodleian, he was obliged to be in London the second Friday in each month to preside at the Clinical Section of the Royal Society of Medicine,[1] and at other times to attend the meetings of the Council. In the intervals he presumably was making some sort of a preliminary draft of the Silliman Lectures to which, and to his search for the earliest printed medical works, he frequently refers in his characteristically brief letters on a multitude of subjects. Thus, on May 18th to Dr. J. A. Nixon: 'What is the date of that Mesué of the Bristol Library? Have you any other medical incunabula before 1480? Sincerely yours, etc.' And shortly after, to the same: 'Dear Nixon, that was a very interesting talk of yours. What about the Dover tablet? What took the old reprobate to Stanway to die? Did you get the estimate or was I to get one? I wish you would as I am awfully hard pressed with arrears. Sincerely yours, etc.' Seemingly a conspiracy was on foot to get a tablet erected in Stanway Church, Gloucestershire, to the memory of Thomas Dover ('Physician and Buccaneer'). At this same time, too, he was in correspondence with Andrew G. Little the historian, long interested in the Grey Friars of Oxford, and wrote regarding some MSS. of Roger Bacon which were full of

[1] The new building had been formally opened by the King and Queen on May 21st, the Oslers being among those invited to be present.

good things—'That is a capital remark he quotes from Aristotle that medicine begins where natural philosophy ends—do come & see me about the proposed Bacon celebration.' And on June the 4th to Dr. Albert N. Blodgett of Boston:

Dear Blodgett, Thank you so much for your Gui Patin. What an interesting old character he was! I do wish the new edition could be completed & that you could get out your translation. I have written a little note about him in the Journal of the Canadian Medical Association of last month. Give my love to Brigham when you see him. . . .

Around this, as around almost any one of Osler's brief letters, a long story might be woven—stories indicative of his peculiar ferment, which would link together many people, of many times, and of many places in the world. Thus in October 1908 Osler has been seen in the Bibliothèque Nationale puzzling over and transcribing notes from the Gui Patin MSS. and letters there, with which as a basis he undoubtedly intended to make Patin the subject of an essay. But he must have learned at the time that a Dr. Paul Triaire, a scholarly physician of Tours, was engaged in preparing a new and complete edition of Patin's 'Letters' which was to supersede all others. To shift the scene, there was born in the backwoods of Vermont, some ten years before Osler saw the light in the backwoods of Upper Canada, the man to whom this last letter had been sent. After Dr. Blodgett had worked his way into medicine, his abilities were brought to the attention of Dr. G. C. Shattuck (father of the Shattuck brothers, Osler's friends and contemporaries), who thereupon sent him abroad to complete his training. He became one of Virchow's early pupils and in due course brought home with him a knowledge of the new pathology, long before Harvard was ready to receive these doctrines. Finding no opportunity in Boston to use his new learning, he had gone to Montreal to see Palmer Howard, and here the story may be taken up in Dr. Blodgett's own words. It begins at the time when Osler and H. V. Ogden were living with Buller and were busy with their quest for the brains of criminals:

I had previously formed the acquaintance of the late Palmer

Howard who told me that he had been attracted by the zeal of an exceptionally talented member of the senior class whose name was Osler, but my first interview with Osler was in the month of September 1879. He was busy with the preparation of his lectures and was engaged in some studies on the nervous system, during which he was experimenting with the injection of various alloys of metals to preserve the form of the cavities of the brain without disturbing the relations of the delicate tissues. I was interested in the attempted injection of the choroid plexus which was surprising to me in its completeness though it did not satisfy Dr. Osler himself. . . . I have no available data to fix the time when Osler delivered an address in Boston in which he alluded to the learned Gui Patin, but in his account of this versatile physician he spoke of the voluminous correspondence Patin had maintained with the most celebrated men of Europe in all branches of learning, and of his multifarious interests in all the departments of science of his day. During an interview which followed the address, I mentioned the copies of his 'Letters to M. Charles Spon' and asked Osler if they had been translated. He told me that they had not been translated into English at least, and challenged me to undertake that work; and this challenge I accepted. He continued to ask from time to time of my progress, took a personal interest in the work, and when at last I could inform him of its completion he was desirous that I should await the edition of M. Triaire. . . .

So it came about that during the winter of 1908–9, when Osler was in Paris, he had written to Dr. Blodgett to let him know of M. Triaire's forthcoming publication. As the years passed by and the second volume of the 'Letters' failed to appear, Osler sent off many inquiries, to Gustave Monod and others, asking what had become of it—inquiries which were finally answered by a note in the *British Medical Journal* for February 24, 1912, announcing the death of M. Triaire after a long illness, and expressing a fear that the second volume of his work had been left unfinished. And this leads up to the May instalment for the 'Men and Books' series[1] which Osler sent off to Macphail at that time, and which he began as follows:

One physician we know thoroughly, and one only—Gui Patin, Dean of the Faculty of Medicine, Paris. His ways and works, his inmost thoughts, his children, his wife, his mother-in-law (!), his friends, his enemies—the latter *very well*—his books and pictures, his likes and dislikes, joys and sorrows, all the details of a long and busy

[1] *Canadian Medical Association Journal*, 1912, ii. 429–30.

life, are disclosed in a series of unique letters written to his intimates between 1630 and 1672. But this is not a biographical note—I wish only to lodge a protest and to express a hope.

He went on to speak of the various editions and of the calamities which had befallen them, not the least being the illness which had overtaken Dr. Triaire and prevented the completion of his work. The 'protest' was against one Pierre Pic, 'whom I would like to shake for the disappointment caused by a wretched volume which has recently seen the light'; and he closed with this:

But the chief object of this note is to make an appeal, to express a hope, that the Paris Faculty will at once arrange for the completion of M. Triaire's edition. Much of the work has been done, and it should not be difficult to find someone with the necessary qualifications. They owe it to the memory of one of the greatest of their deans. When completed, an English edition should be forthcoming. From one of the old editions a translation has already been made by Dr. Blodgett of Boston, who, at my request, has withheld it from the press awaiting the completion of Triaire's work.[1]

But here the Gui Patin ferment may be left to do its work.

To H. B. Jacobs from W. O. 13 Norham Gardens, 5th [June]

Yes, my edition of the 'De Trinitate' [Servetus] has the single hyphen & the misspelt word. It is very interesting—I did not know that there had been another imprint. I will slip your letter into my copy. The [2nd] Huth Sale begins to-day. There are very few things of special interest to me, though there is a beautiful 1478 Celsus, which I wish I could have secured for the Library of the Royal Society of Medicine, but Quaritch tells me he has a very high bid for it. Love to you both. Sincerely yours, Wm Osler. I have been going over our Bodleian incunabula: extraordinary collection!

The length of a man's letters are usually in inverse proportion to the number of his correspondents, and if he would retain his friends, old and new, as Osler did, there should be no wasted words. On that same June 5th he wrote to Miss Flumerfelt of Manchester, who was evidently

[1] Dr. Blodgett meanwhile had published a paper in the *Boston Medical and Surgical Journal* for May 16th, giving an estimate of Gui Patin's life and character as displayed in his letters, an article which Osler reviewed for the *Lancet*, July 13, 1912, ii. 131.

planning to change her name, and who has already been introduced during her preliminary medical examination as 'Trotula':

Dear Trotula, 'Twas as I thought & hoped, & knew! Hearty congratulations—only having known *me*, to decide on a Surgeon is a bit hard. You must bring him over here & talk about your plans. Would you not like to be married here? Why bother about that exam? Silly thing! Chuck your head—you will never need it again. I enclose you letters to the Lady Supts. of the two hospitals at Montreal. Best wishes to you both. . . .

And during this same month there were similarly picturesque and brief notes: to his boyhood friend, 'Ned' Milburn; to Adam Wright of Toronto, his fellow student, about a suitable candidate for the Chair of Medicine; to Shepherd in Montreal, acknowledging a barrel of apples; to Casey Wood, an early McGill pupil to whom he gives the first hint of what he planned to do with his library:

Our edition of Helmholtz's life had to be curtailed from the German to bring it into a single volume. I think all students and young doctors should read the lives of Pasteur and Helmholtz. I was glad to see a notice of your ophthalmic library in the last Report of the Librarian at McGill. I am adding treasures to my collection every few months, and it will finally be housed in Montreal. I am collecting on two lines—books that are of historical importance in the evolution of medicine, and books that have interest through the character or work of their authors. In that way I limit the field, which is large enough! Do let us see you here some time. I am sending you with this a photograph—not so artistic as yours. My boy is at Winchester, doing very well.

Also to James Tyson of Philadelphia, lamenting John Musser's death—'how sad to have him leave us so early'; to J. William White about Henry James getting the D.Litt. at the Encaenia; to Dr. D. S. Lamb of the Army Medical Museum in Washington:

Dear Lamb, I am awfully glad to have your two papers, particularly as somebody had the audacity to tell me that you were dead! & I have been worrying at the thought that I should not see you until we foregathered with some of our old friends on the other side of the river! I had a talk with Hrdlička about his South American specimens, & it was he who told me that your hat was still in the ring. With greetings and regards, & my love to old friends at the Museum and Library. . . .

To Leonard Mackall, saying: 'The first Dutch edition of the Religio was 1665. It reappeared in 1683; I have both; then in 1688 a fine quarto edition of the works appeared, and it is this one I am looking for'—the only edition of the 'Religio', be it said, needed to complete his collection; to Dr. Jesse Myer of St. Louis, many notes about his forthcoming 'Life of Beaumont' for which Osler had promised to write an introduction; and to Dr. Adolf Meyer about the opening of his new clinic in Baltimore:

I feel that I am in your hands in the matter. The date you mention—the second half of April—could be arranged. Mr. Phipps will be in London at the end of this month & I could talk to him about it. I am rather shocked at the thought of giving the general opening address; only I suppose it would please Mr. Phipps, for whom I have a warm affection, & then the word 'general' would let me out of any special psychiatric association. I will let you know his feelings.

There was also a succession of letters to A. C. Klebs about the purchase for the Johns Hopkins of the library of Prof. J. Pagel, the Berlin historian—a library which they finally lost; thus on June 15th:

Your telegram came while I was away. I did not wire as I was doubtful how long you would be at Leipzig. Your letter has just come. I should like so much to see the catalogue of the books as I might induce Marburg to buy them for J.H.U. I could not afford it for myself and I daresay there would be many duplicates in my collection. I have written Sudhoff asking him to send me on the catalogue and if there was any hurry I would cable Marburg or cable Welch to see him. That Spanish item is most interesting but it is not the first by any means on Syphilis in Spain. There are several most important 15th century pamphlets. The figure given is ridiculous. I only paid £6 for my 1497 Leonicenus, one of the first Italian descriptions of the disease. . . . I am so glad you saw Sudhoff. I wish we had a few more like him—scholar as well as student. . . . Just got a fine 1478 Celsus—ed. pr.—I have a copy but I could not resist this one—which I must hand over to one of the libraries.

This was all very peaceful and one wonders what Osler and Sudhoff would have felt had they been present at All Souls College, Oxford, on the evening of this fifteenth of

June to hear Spenser Wilkinson, Professor of Military History, give a public lecture on 'The Next War', in which the conflict between the British and German naval policies was clearly pointed out, and the statement made that the British Expeditionary Force would be a smaller army than Wellington's at Waterloo.[1]

As though the Silliman Lectures were not enough, he was beset by invitations to give other courses in the coming year on similar foundations—a course at Johannesburg under the auspices of the South African Lecture Committee, and also to give the Lane Lectures at Leland Stanford University. This latter invitation must have had a particular appeal, for Osler had never been to California; and Sir Michael Foster, Allbutt, Welch, Fitz, Sir Patrick Manson, and others of his friends had already given the series—an ordeal, be it said, for both lecturers and audience, of ten lectures crowded into five days. In regretting, he wrote to Dr. Ray Lyman Wilbur, the Dean and Professor of Medicine:

Dear Dr. Wilbur,—It is very kind indeed of the Trustees to ask me to give the Lane Lectures next year, but I am afraid it is an impossibility. I have to go out to the opening of the new Phipps Institute at the Hopkins in the spring, and there is a big international Medical Congress here in August (at which I hope to see you) so that I could not possibly go out again in the autumn. I am particularly sorry, for I should have liked so much to have given the Lane Lectures—the old doctor was a warm personal friend with whom I had many conversations on the subject of medical education.

---

[1] A new Secretary for War, Colonel Seely, had just been appointed to succeed Lord Haldane, who had become Lord Chancellor, and it was hoped he might be able 'to complete the work designed by his predecessor but dropped for notions of political expediency'. It was earlier in this year that Lord Haldane had gone to Berlin to engage in friendly and confidential communications with those responsible for the control and guidance of German policy. The countries, without question, were drifting into war, but despite a state of nervousness shared by both of them in official quarters over rival naval and military preparations, the British people closed their eyes to these warnings. They were busy with their own domestic troubles: the Home Rule Bill had come up in April; there had been a great demonstration in Belfast and the bitterness of feeling in regard to 'loyal Ulster' was brought home by Kipling's verses; there had been strikes, and the suffragettes had resorted to the breaking of windows and the pillar-box outrages. How Germany felt is shown by Bernhardi's book which appeared during the year; and later on the Balkan ferment broke out into actual war.

This letter makes it evident that the dedication of the Phipps Psychiatric Clinic had been postponed till the spring of 1913, and Osler must have begun to realize that the Yale lectures had better be postponed also, though this apparently was not decided upon till later. Meanwhile Mr. Phipps, his interest in Pasteur having been deeply aroused, had evidently prepared a trip to France in Pasteur's footsteps, as the following note of June 27th indicates:

So glad to hear from you. Unfortunately we cannot possibly leave during the first two weeks of July. We have to be at the Dublin celebration—3rd to 7th—and the next week we have the Congress of the Colonial Universities coming to Oxford. It would have been such a pleasure to join you on an excursion to Dôle and Lille.

The celebration to which this refers was the bicentenary (July 4–6) of the medical school of Dublin University, more familiarly known as Trinity College, which proved to be a most successful occasion, equally fortunate in its skilful organizer, Professor A. F. Dixon, and in its week of sunshine—both worth calling attention to. Among the delegates were a number of former Baltimore colleagues and pupils with whom Osler, and Lady Osler who accompanied him, chiefly foregathered. Evidently they had gone a day early, for he was scheduled for a lecture before the Women's National Health Association—the same body he had so effectively addressed on the initiation of their tuberculosis campaign four years before—his subject on the present occasion being the dispensary treatment of the disease as illustrated from experiences at the Radcliffe Infirmary. The next evening, as part of the bicentenary festivities, there was a large dinner for the delegates at the Mansion House, where Osler was called on to propose the toast of the evening, and made a post-prandial speech such as well deserved publication [1] and will bear quoting. It was largely devoted to the story of the Dublin School of Physic; to its associations with Oxford; to John Locke and the Molyneuxs; to William Petty, 'Oxford's greatest gift to Ireland'; to the chance which had thrown in Osler's way Petty's manuscript letter-book containing a sheet dealing

[1] 'Men and Books.' XIII. *Canadian Medical Association Journal*, 1912, ii. 833–5.

with the famous survey (which Osler appropriately presented to the Library of Trinity College); to the dark days of the eighteenth century and the glorious ones which began the next, when the Dublin School reached the summit of its fame in medicine, midwifery, and surgery; and finally to the imperishable glory associated with the names of Robert James Graves and William Stokes, whose works to-day are 'full of lessons for those of us who realize that the best life of the teacher is in supervising the personal daily contact of patient with student in the wards'. He closed with a personal touch, saying:

This is a graduates' dinner, and at last I come to a part of the toast which I know at first hand. Graduates of this school have been much in my life. To usher me into this breathing world one of them came many weary miles through the backwoods of Canada. Across his *tie*, as he called it, John King, M.A., T.C.D., birched into me small Latin and less Greek. I owe my start in the profession to James Bovell, a kinsman and devoted pupil of Graves, while my teacher in Montreal, Palmer Howard, lived, moved and had his being in his old masters, Graves and Stokes. From the days of Columba, the Irish of all classes have had a passion to peregrinate, and at every step in my career I have met your fellow graduates in Toronto, in Montreal, in many country districts of Canada, in the great cities of the United States, in lonely villages in Virginia and the Carolinas, and now in the very different surroundings of Harley Street and the pleasant villages of the Thames Valley—and everywhere the same intelligent and highly trained men, ever working with the Hippocratic spirit, *caute*, *caste et probe*, and ever leaving their patients if not in better health, at least in better spirits.

His attendance at these bicentenary festivities[1] must have been the final straw, for shortly after his return he cabled to President Hadley of Yale: 'COULD LECTURES BE DEFERRED TILL SPRING. AM FEELING RATHER USED UP HAVING JUST FINISHED REVISION OF TEXT-BOOK. WOULD BE DIFFICULT TO GET READY BY OCTOBER.' Two days later, on July 10th, he writes to Mrs. Brewster, saying:

We have been in a perfect whirl for the past three months. I have

[1] They were spread over the three last days of the week, and on the Saturday afternoon, in the Examination Hall of Trinity, honorary degrees were bestowed upon many of the delegates and guests—the D.Sc. upon twenty-five of them, Osler included.

been reading proofs & at last have seen the title page & index & have finished. There has been a steady stream of visitors—& many relatives. Both my brothers from Toronto have been with us, and this evening we expect my sister [' Chattie '] who has not been in England for 31 years. We go to Scotland August the 5th for a month, to Tongue, the most northerly point in Sutherlandshire. The fishing there is excellent & Revere is a devoted angler. He is very well, and such a dear good fellow—but ' book-learning ' is not in his line. He sketches so well and with very good hands & a good heart life should not worry him. We are very excited about Woodrow Wilson of whom I am very fond. He is sure to catch many mugwumps. I am sorry for Taft, and still more sorry that Roosevelt should have treated him so badly. It was so nice to see Uncle Ned's boy. Unfortunately I was away & returned just as he was leaving. Our garden is splendid, such roses !

One of the steady stream of visitors recalls that he and the Regius—

. . . had gone off somewhere in the country for tea with Dr. Emmet's daughter who was living in a working-man's thatched cottage made over into a charming abode ; that on their return to 13 Norham Gardens they dined in the open air on the terrace, where it was light until 9.30 and still as a forest—the quiet only accentuated by Great Tom's 101 strokes at 9.05 p.m., when the gates of all Oxford colleges are closed—accentuated too, by the occasional note of a thrush and by some owls whose ' to-whit ' in a tree of the neighbouring park was followed by a fluttering flight through the branches to the boundary fence and back to their nest again. And then before bed, an hour in the library looking at the books which were just beginning to be catalogued and which had burst out of the library into the hall, and would soon be in the dining-room. . . .

This excerpt shows that there might be peaceful moments at the ' Open Arms ' even with a houseful of guests ; but even so, the inevitable reference to the library, now being catalogued, suggests the History of Medicine which at this juncture is occupying much of his time. The following letter of July 13th to Fielding H. Garrison of the Surgeon-General's Library indicates that he was concerned with plans for the success of more than his own particular section of the coming Congress :

As you perhaps have seen [he wrote] there is to be a section on the History of Medicine at the International Congress next year. Dr. Raymond Crawfurd (of Tray's Hill, Hornsey Lane, London N.) is Secretary, and Norman Moore, Chairman. Would it be too much trouble for you to prepare for the former a list of the clubs and societies in America that are interested in the subject, and to whom special invitations could be sent? I do hope you will be able to come over. Give my love to the dear old man [Fletcher], and greetings to all your colleagues in the Library. . . .

Nor was this all, for he had launched a project to establish something more permanent, namely a section of the Royal Society of Medicine which would draw together medical men who were historically minded.[1] It is to this he alludes in the following brief note to Dr. Crawfurd, in which also he first makes mention of the classification of his library:

We can 'pull it through' all right, and the scheme will stir men in all the sections. You must spend a week-end here after I return —any one in Sept. I have my bibliographical books concentrated & you will be interested to see how far I have got with my B.P. [Bibliotheca Prima]. I picked up the Ed. Prin. of Plato (who comes in as the *f* and *o* of modern psychology) and of Copernicus (1543). I enclose a review which may interest you.

He had undertaken no light task in either of these projects, and of the first he writes to J. Y. W. MacAlister later in the month: 'I have sent out 168 private letters chiefly to Fellows of the Society & have enclosed with them a postcard addressed to you so that we should get back enough acceptances to give some idea of the number likely to join the new section.' Of this new organization, which was to hold its first session the coming November, Dr. Crawfurd says:

I saw a great deal of Osler in connection with the Section of History of Medicine at the Royal Society of Medicine. He was its father, and I doubt if it would ever have come into existence but for his quickening influence: he acted like a magnet in gathering together a company of original members. He was its first President; his own contributions were few and mainly biographical, and I do not think anyone could have discovered from them how fully he possessed the true historical sense, but his faculty of extracting contributions on every conceivable aspect of medicine from the most unproductive sources was invaluable to the Section; and that Osler was in the chair was a sure draw.

[1] Sir D'Arcy Power states that from time to time a similar project had been proposed but had invariably fallen through. Osler's backing was needed to bring such a plan to fruition.

To Arthur T. Hadley. The Athenaeum, July 15th.

Dear President Hadley, I cabled you last week, not knowing that we were to have the pleasure of seeing you. I asked to have my Silliman Lectures postponed until the spring. I have been hard pressed for the last six months by a revision of my Text-book, unexpectedly forced upon me by the publishers. This has left me rather used up mentally, & I would very much like to have the winter for the better preparation of the lectures. I had arranged the programme with Stokes: 1. Six lectures on the 'Evolution of Modern Medicine'. 2. A general address on 'A Way of Life' to the student body. 3. A couple of bibliographical lectures on subjects in which I am interested. I hope to see you this evening at the Royal Society.

The Royal Society was celebrating the 250th anniversary of the days when, after the Restoration, the 'invisible' philosophers of Oxford had assembled once more in London with the determination of forming a society. On this Monday evening the delegates were given an informal reception at which he must have seen Mr. Hadley and have invited him to the 'Open Arms'. The formal ceremonies of the celebration began the next day with a commemorative service in the Abbey—sufficient to show that the days of conflict between science and theology were about over. Indeed, a special Collect written for the occasion praised the Almighty 'for all those who in every age and clime have added to the sum of earthly knowledge by their discoveries in Natural Science'. It was an occasion not merely of national but of world-wide importance, and it is probable that no building ever contained at any one time a greater number of notable men, representative of all the leading institutions of learning in the world, than gathered at the Guildhall the next evening for dinner, and subsequently to hear the Prime Minister—Mr. Asquith—discourse at great length on 'The Royal Society', Viscount Morley on 'Universities at Home and Abroad', the Archbishop of Canterbury on 'The Learned Societies in the Old World and the New', and several more, with what time was left them, on other toasts.

Mr. Hadley was among the 'foreign visitors' who went to Oxford after the celebration, and while there must have told his host he could give the Silliman Lectures at any season he chose, even though October was the usual time. He could hardly have given any other answer in view of this picture which remains in his mind :

The place where he was at his best was in the little upstairs room of his own house, when he or Lady Osler, or both, talked freely and charmingly with those who were privileged to form part of their household. It was in that upper story that he kept his more precious medical books of bygone days ; and if he happened to be alone with anyone who appreciated them the sight of the books opened a wondrous flow of talk. Well do I remember a couple of hours spent one morning in that study, when each of us ought to have been at work at something else, so that our conversation enjoyed the added flavour which goes with forbidden fruit. It began with Ulrich von Hutten ; I have forgotten where it ended. In those two hours of conversation I learned more about medical history and more about the persistence of certain queer traits in human nature than could be got from months of study by the most approved method of research. What he said was like Smollett and Gibbon : Smollett's frankness without his coarseness, and Gibbon's erudition and lucidity without his conventionality. In talk of this kind I have never met the man who was Osler's equal.

To S. Weir Mitchell from W. O. August 3rd.

So delighted to have your nice long letter today. The American memoir will come in our absence, as we are just off to Sutherlandshire—to Tongue—for five weeks. My boy came back from Winchester yesterday & he hopes to get some good trout fishing, & possibly a salmon. He is a devoted Waltonian, and is already an expert dry-fly fisher. He has grown a fine lusty lad, not much given to books, but a good carpenter, & clever with his pencil. We have had a very busy summer. The Dublin Bicentenary was a great success—a large representation from abroad, and many men of mark. I had to propose the toast of the School and had the good fortune to be able to present their Library (T.C.D.) with the original draft of the agreement of Petty (who was Professor of Anatomy here in 1650) to make the famous Down survey, with a list of the officers who paid him the monies, & the names of the men composing the surveying parties. I found it by accident, bound at the back of a big volume of his letters that I got for a song at the Phillips sale last year. I am sorry you were unfortunate with the Burns letter, for which I suppose Rosebery or one of the other Scotch collectors sent an unlimited bid. Many thanks for trying to get the Browne Travels. I have a copy. I lack only one or two Browne items. I have been working at the earliest printed medical books up to 1480, which form a most interesting group. I will give you a lantern-slide lecture on them at the College when I come out. I have just heard that my Yale lectures are to be postponed until the Spring. I am glad in a way, as I have been hard driven for the past nine months revising that old Text-book—re-writing a great part of it & finding it not easy to get the new wine into the old bottle. I have just sent a nice group of folios to Fisher—Aldrovandus, the old Bologna physician-naturalist. We missed you at the Royal Society celebration. I hope Harrison sent you all the cards &c. The foreign visitors came here after the London festivities & we had a great day at Wadham College—the birthplace in Oxford of the Society. I have sent you a little booklet giving a brief account of the local men of that date. The dinner at the Guildhall was a most brilliant affair—Asquith & the Archbishop made splendid speeches. . . .

I have become more & more involved in the Bodleian, and begin to understand its workings. I am there every day, when possible. We have just completed an immense underground stack, between the Old Bodleian & the Radcliffe Camera, which will hold 1,300,000 books. This relieves the congestion, which has made the working of the library so difficult. You will be interested in the catalogue of the Library of the Royal College of Physicians just printed, with its incunabula & Harvey items. Did you ever get those Harvey letters? De Schweinitz told me you had the money collected for them. We got a few months ago twenty-five Erasmus letters for the Bodleian for £25 apiece! A few of us took around the hat. We had not a letter of his in the library. I am afraid you will be bored with the length of this letter. . . .

The Oslers seem to have chosen the very jumping-off corners of Great Britain for their holidays. Land's End one summer; Llanddulas another; and now, Tongue in the very northernmost part of Sutherlandshire. But in Lochs Craggie and Laoghal as well as in the Kyle there was said to be good fishing, and this was Revere's chief object in life and hardly less so his friend Raleigh Parkin's, who with his sister Alice was added to the party. Professor Somerville also joined them.

To Mrs. Robert Brewster. Tongue, N.B. August 6.

Dear Mabel, . . . We have had as I told you an unusually busy summer—so many people coming & going. One great delight has been a visit from my sister and her husband. After 'raising' nine children—all splendid—& a husband! against heavy odds she has at last got into smooth waters—but as she says sadly, with the nest empty. Two other brothers have been with us, so we have had a family gathering. Revere got home on the 1st—so well & much grown. He is a darling, good heart & good hands but not much at his books. We have come here for the fishing—to the most northerly coast of Scotland—to the Kyle of Tongue where there are good lochs for trout and perhaps salmon. We have been out all day after sea trout—very few fish but plenty of rain. It is a lovely spot—beautiful hills—really mountains. We have very comfortable rooms in an hotel not far from the sea. Grace will not have to speak to a soul—which is her idea of a blissful holiday, & if the fishing is good the boy will be happy. I enjoy the loaf, & read & write. I have been deep in all sorts of out of the way professional reading for these [Silliman] lectures trying to get in touch with men & times & places in our history. 'Tis not easy but the personal interest in the individuals helps over the dull periods. I had a nice letter from Uncle Ned last week, with a definite promise of a visit next year. That story in last month's Scribner was so good. What a true touch he has. Perhaps you will plan a winter trip to Europe? My love to R.B. & a kiss to the lassie. . . .

They probably visited the ruins of Castle Varrich, by tradition the residence of an eleventh-century Norseman; and heard the local tale of the great battle between the clans Murray and Mackay, when the last of the Murrays, caught in ambush, were killed on the slopes of Ben Laoghal which rises in rugged cliffs at the head of the Kyle. But one thing more certain than this is that Osler promptly looked up the local doctor. He soon sends off a letter (undated) to Dr. Thomas in Baltimore:

Dear Harry T. Alas! I am not coming out this fall. . . . I am sorry in many ways. We have had a very busy summer—celebrations galore & visitors innumerable. We have come here to the very end of the Island for fishing. Revere is so enthusiastic about it. The trout are good but wily. The place is enchanting & so quiet, on the moors, on an inlet or kyle. The best doctor has a district 40 by 25 miles—a scattered parish of 1600 people. I spent the day with him yesterday on the road. How sad to hear of Miss Garrett's illness—and so serious. . . . You will have a copy of the text-book before long. It is not all it should be, in parts, but in spots it is up to date. So glad Hal is now at the medical school. He should make a good student. I am enclosing him a letter & a *billy-doo* for luck! Love to the family. Yours ever, W. O.

And the '*billy-doo*' to a young medical student, the only possible way his father could be remunerated for helping with the text-book, reads:

Dear Hal, Tear off the over-leaf & shake it in the face of some banker and he will give you $100.00 in cash—which is the face value of my signature. If he demurs tell him *to go to* — that I was 500 miles from home & had no cheque book. Buy with it your books & anything you need for your studies. I am sure you will do splendidly in the medical school; 5th, or is it 6th generation? Good luck to you.

And on the 14th he writes to 'Trotula', who had just obtained her first 'locum-tenency':

Dear Trotula, Heavens! How sorry I am for you & your patients! and such a slump! after those happy weeks in Cornwall with the L of your L. But it will be a happy—no I mean good—experience for you. Do let me help you about a Hospital appointment—let me know of anything likely & I will write one of my most mendacious letters. When are you to be married? Do not wait too long—please. No man is worth waiting for more than six months. I am writing to the dearest old fellow at Preston—Dr Brown whom you will be delighted to meet. We are here fishing—or R. is—& catching many trout. Come & see us soon. . . .

No Englishman is without *The Times* even in places so remote as Tongue, N.B., and so it is not surprising to find in the issue of August 16th a long letter from Osler to the editor, inspired by an editorial of the week before propounding a scheme for tuberculosis sanatoria which Osler felt 'overreached the provisions of the special clauses of the insurance act'. It was a carefully written argument favouring the use of the dispensaries in connexion with existing hospitals, where doctors and students could be trained for this special work before there should be any great outlay on the part of the Government for sanatoria.

And this plan works well [he writes]. One of the most successful of existing tuberculosis dispensaries I was able to start, by the generosity of Mr. Henry Phipps, in connection with the Johns Hopkins Hospital. It now forms an important part of a great medical school, through which every student as a matter of routine passes as a clinical clerk. If for no other purpose than this, every general hospital with a medical school should have its tuberculosis department. The tuberculosis work of the Oxfordshire branch of the National Association has centred about the Radcliffe Infirmary, the treasurer, committee, and staff of which, with a commendable liberality, have not only given the dispensary accommodation, but have for the past two years set aside from twelve to twenty beds on the balconies for tuberculosis. Doctors, nurses and patients are all the better for this association.

The fishing was good, as he said in all of his letters—'but the rain it raineth every day'. On the 20th he writes to Dr. Thayer:

Dear W. S. So sorry you have not taken in this far away place. You have been far enough! What a trip! We thought of Stornoway when at Kyleakin, but the stormy winds were blowing & the steamer did not look inviting. When do you sail? . . . My lectures are postponed. To tell the truth I have been so busy this summer (with doing nothing!) that I have only three of them ready & to finish them before Sept. 15, when I had arranged to sail, would have cut into my holiday. I have taken a big subject—the Evolution of Modern Medicine—& the reading for it grows. Have you seen Osborn Taylor's Mediaeval Mind? Excellent! He is a New York man, I believe, not an academic, but a genuine student with a great grasp of the subject. If you ever come across him, say I am acting as an advertising agent in this country. Revere has had some very good fishing—hooked a huge ferox this afternoon, but the monster made short work of his tackle. He has been out every day, from 9 to 6.30—burns, lochs and the Kyle. It is a wonderful country, but moist. Such rain as we have had! . . .

On August 24th he writes to A. C. Klebs, who is in England:

I am still dickering with Fock for the Pagel Library, the price of which has gone up steadily. A friend [undoubtedly his brother, E. B. O.] offered me the sum which they first named & I hesitate to tax him for more. As an historical *collection* it is valuable but there are no special items of any great value & at auction it would not bring 1000 marks. The Van den Corput library went for ridiculous sums. If I can squeeze another friend I would give what they ask for the sake of the Pagel family. . . . We are having a splendid holiday here—at the end of the Island. The weather has been awful, 14 days rain, but the fishers do not care. It has been a great experience for Revere, as there are a number of crack sportsmen here. I loaf & read all day—and play a little golf. I will let you know of any change of plan in case I get to London before the 11th.

And in the following to H. B. Jacobs he gives a glimpse of the place and the life:

In spite of the rain we are having a very happy time here. Revere has caught some fine trout—a 3-lb. sea trout today. I wish Mrs. Jacobs could have it for breakfast—they are delicious. He has been out every day 9 to 6.30 often soaked. Three fine days at last. This is a great country—moors, grouse, sheep—& fish, nothing else. It is a splendid life for these men—out all day & good exercise, often indeed, hard work. I wish more would come over and settle down to this sort of summer. Such a nice group of men in the lodge attached to this hotel—fish & shoot all day; one an old admiral of 78. This morning I saw about 200 sheep dipped—precaution against mange; played a round of golf & spent the afternoon with Grace on the rocks & moors. Had tea in a crofter's cottage—fresh scones, raspberry jam & better tea than Rumpelmayers. We joined R. & his gillie at 6. . . . I am going to the B.A.A.S. at Dundee which meets from the 4th to the 10th after which I hope to spend a few days with Schäfer—he is President. Carnegie has asked us to stay at Skibo on our way down & the Howards want us to go to Colonsay, but Revere says he must have a couple of weeks at home.

At the Dundee meeting of the British Association mentioned in this letter, he 'heard Schäfer assault the Vitalists'; and the week of August 27th was passed at Skibo Castle 'seeing the Laird at home'; but there is little trace of this visit beyond a note from Dornoch, Sutherland, to F. H. Garrison of the Surgeon-General's Library, lamenting the indisposition of his senior, Robert Fletcher,[1] 'that dear old gentleman' to whom Osler had long been so devoted, still indexing and proof reading at ninety years of age. Shortly after his return he wrote to Jacobs again about some Laennec books, and added:

We had a week at Skibo with the Laird who is a great old boy, full of interest. The place is delightful—such moors! Revere had good fishing in his lochs. I went to Dundee to the B. A. Ad. Science & saw many old friends. A nice day at St. Andrews—the only British univ. I had not seen. I wish you would try a summer in Scotland. I never saw such blazes of colour as the heather about Skibo—some of the hills literally covered with purple. I spent a couple of hours in the Univ. Lib. Edinburgh yesterday going over their medical incunabula, not very many but some very good. I saw the 3rd copy of the Restitutio Christianismi of Servetus—only the first 16 pages are missing. It was given to the Library in

---

[1] Fletcher was an Englishman by birth, born in Bristol, and Osler had promised J. A. Nixon, one of the editors of the *Bristol Medico-Chirurgical Journal*, to write an appreciation of him for the December number of the journal. In this note Osler speaks of his first meeting with Fletcher in 1881, at the Library of the Surgeon-General's Office in Washington when he was looking up the subject of echinococcus disease. Unhappily the note had to be transformed into an obituary one, for Fletcher, after returning to his desk, died suddenly on November 8th after an illness of a day or two. Another appreciation of Fletcher was written for the 'Men and Books' Series, No. XIX, in the *Canadian Medical Association Journal*, March 1913, p. 227.

1695—where and how it got to Scotland no one knows & it contains the MS draft of a long letter wh. Servetus sent to Calvin. Better weather now. The garden is lovely. Our old friends, the Mallochs came this afternoon & young Archie with them. Poor M. has angina & when he heard I was not coming over, bucked & said he must see me. Fortunately he stood the voyage well, but is badly knocked out in heart & arteries. . . .

And the 'young Archie', then entering his last year at McGill, who kept a journal, notes that Sir William, during their week's stay, and until he saw them off at Waterloo Station on Wednesday the 13th, had 'had an extraordinarily cheering effect upon Papa, so humorous and full of fun; and they had been twice to Frilford Heath for golf and had been all over the Clarendon Press and the Bodleian, the Radcliffe Camera, the Museum, the Laboratories, and the book-stacks below the grass-plots—wonderful!' And he adds: 'He introduced me to Fuller's "Worthies"; showed me where to look up about the skull and cross-bones symbol on poison bottles, and when I went up to bed I found a huge old Materia Medica under my pillow—put there as I had told him of my distaste for therapeutics!'

In all probability Osler had set himself by now to the preparation of his Yale lectures, but with many interruptions, as his brief though innumerable letters indicate. Thus, to his old friend, Dr. Duncan McEachran of the veterinary school in Montreal:

Sept. 9, 1912.

Dear Mac, Do let me know when you reach England. I send this on the chance to the Bank of Montreal. We should be so glad to see you here. Come and spend a night and I will motor you to Banbury the next day. Sincerely yours.

To Dr. E. Libman, a heart specialist in New York, with whom he was in frequent correspondence:

Dear Libman, It would be nice if you could give us a paper on endocarditis at the Medical Section of the Congress next year. I am sure it would be of great interest. The grouping of your cases is admirable. I will look out for your young friend when he comes. . . .

To Fielding H. Garrison, saying that he would like a photograph of Fletcher to accompany the sketch he had promised to write for Nixon, and he asks: 'Is there a separate copy of the medical incunabula in the Surgeon-General's Library? I have become interested in the earliest printed medical books. I will send out a list so you can tick off those you have.' To Dr. Jesse Myer, apologizing for the brevity of the Introduction he had written for Myer's 'Life of Beaumont', adding 'perhaps it is none the worse for that'; and he hoped that the family were still planning to put the Beaumont papers in the Surgeon-General's Library where they could be permanently secure. In a few days he wrote to Myer again to say: 'Now I wish you would turn your attention to Daniel Drake. His family papers and records must be somewhere and should be of extraordinary interest in connection with the history of the profession in the Mississippi Valley.' Then a series of notes to accompany presentation copies of the eighth edition of the Text-book, like this to Dr. Hamburger of Baltimore, a former pupil in the first Johns Hopkins class:

> Dear Louis P. H. Greetings to you & Mrs H—— & the three kiddies. I suppose by this time there are three! It is high time you quit practice for a year & came over for a brain-dusting. I have asked A & Co to send you Ed. 8th of my text-book. Same old friend, I trust, tho the face is much changed. Yours, W. O.

So also to Dr. T. R. Boggs: 'You will have Ed. 8th shortly—much changed, not always for the better. Revere is 2 inches taller than his dad & still devoted to fish. He will never be a student, but he has good hands and a good heart—two out of three essentials so we are satisfied.' As a matter of fact, the other essential, now two inches above his father's, was developing in an unexpected fashion destined to draw them more closely together than ever through a common interest in books.

In a letter of this time to H. B. Jacobs, Osler says: 'I am doubtful about the French meeting as I really ought to stay at home & work. We are in a terrible mess here trying to get the Tuberculosis problem settled. The difficulty is to get any central control.' A few days earlier, on September 10th, he had written to Mr. Phipps: 'I will come up tomorrow about 5 o'clock and have a cup of tea & a chat with you. I may possibly bring Revere as I would like you to see him. I hear from Adolf Meyer that the clinic is getting along rapidly.' Over this cup of tea he must have told Mr. Phipps something about the excellent work that was being done in Oxfordshire in the fight against tuberculosis; how dispensaries, in addition to that at the Radcliffe Infirmary, had been opened at Witney, Thame, and Banbury, to which specially trained staff-nurses and a tuberculosis officer, debarred from practice, had been attached; and how tuberculosis classes were being held, outdoor shelters being provided, and so on. This doubtless explains not only a note of September 19th which says: 'Your generous gift will delight the committee, which meets to-day—we are gradually getting the work in the town and county very well organized and I hope it may serve as a model for other places'—but it also explains the following 'minute' in the Annual Report of the Oxfordshire Association for the Prevention of Tuberculosis:

> Early in December Sir William Osler asked that a sum of £500, the gift of Mr. Phipps of New York, should be divided among the nurses of the association and the many district nurses in the county who had co-operated with them in the care of consumptives; any balance there might be to be given to the almoners of the dispensaries to purchase blankets or clothing for patients in special need.

And it is not at all improbable that Sir William, whose name does not appear that year on the list of donors, may have merged his annual contribution with that of his friend. However this may be, it serves to introduce the following quotation from an article by the Secretary of this small Oxfordshire association, written after the passing of the man who for ten years, as its President and moving spirit, had acted as though the association were his main interest in life:

> . . . The nature and extent of the consumption problem was then only guessed at. No reliable facts and figures were available. Notification was not compulsory, and was strongly opposed: the Insurance Act did not come into force for some years later; no public funds were assigned to the treatment or relief of consumption. Voluntary Hospitals and Sanatoria were springing up all over the country, but the number of beds was totally inadequate and the finances precarious. Sir William was among the foremost to urge the Government to take the matter up. On the Astor Commission he was a guiding force in establishing the principles on which a public

campaign against consumption should be based—principles which have since been embodied in the Insurance Act and in all Public Health Acts relating to consumption. It is difficult to estimate the country's debt to him.

With all his public work he nevertheless found time to devote to the Oxfordshire association; to its fortnightly committee meetings; to the Oxford Dispensary, then held at Bath Court, where he often saw patients himself one morning or evening in the week, and where he was always ready to act in consultation with the tuberculosis officer in any difficult case. Many times he went far into the country to see these people in their own homes, and got to know the hard conditions of poverty and bad housing many of them had to contend with.

Invariably he took the wide view: for him obstacles and difficulties were only made to be overcome. He realized the far-reaching network of consumption, the very life and habits of the country caught in its toils, and while urging on medical research he never forgot that the problem was a social one as well, and in all he wrote and said he appealed to the general public to do their share towards the regeneration that must come before the plague could be stamped out. It is for us especially who have worked in close co-operation with him to carry on in his honour and to his memory the campaign for the cause he had at heart to the victory he predicted.

That a man of Osler's training should have felt impelled to engage in this sort of a public crusade perhaps explains the feeling expressed in a note of this time to Dr. George Dock, who had accepted a 'full-time' clinical position in St. Louis under the Rockefeller programme:

It would be [he said] a very good thing to have a few men at Research institutes, Cole at the Rockefeller for example, devoting all their time to the work, but what I dread is to have a class of clinicians growing up out of touch, and necessarily out of sympathy with the profession and with the public. This would be nothing short of a calamity. There are always men of the quiet type like Halsted, who practically live the secluded life; to have a whole faculty made up of Halsteds would be a very good thing for science, but a very bad thing for the profession.

Bradfield College, Berkshire, a public school founded in 1850, had always kept abreast of modern educational progress. Mr. Edward Armstrong, Fellow of Queen's College, Oxford, had recently been appointed Warden, and it was probably at his solicitation that Osler on October 9th opened the new science laboratory and subsequently 'addressed the boys and a large gathering of parents in the Big School'.

Though he appears to have talked on preliminary specialization in science, particularly as a preparation for Medicine, he nevertheless recommended to the boys that they stick to their Greek, 'because, after all, the Greek outlook on life was the outlook of youth; the Greeks were optimists and saw life with good clear vision'. Though the editors of the daily papers might be pessimists there was no cause for pessimism, for there never was a period in history when young men and boys should be so optimistic; when the poor were better off, and there were fewer poor, and the rich were doing more for them; and when the outlook, if they would look with Grecian eyes, was better for the country and for the Empire.

Those, however, who were present at this ceremony [writes the Warden], will remember rather than the *ipsissima verba*, the mingled fire and kindliness of the speaker, and his thrilling influence upon boyhood. Nor will they ever forget the scene which followed, when boys, masters and parents, clustered in the quiet, leafy Berkshire lane, watched the great physician turn the key which was to open to Bradfieldians, present and future, a more highly perfected home for science than the school had as yet possessed.[1]

The impression should not be gained from this recital that Osler, mind and body, was always on the wing, always flitting, never at rest. Active as was his mind, he appreciated repose, and particularly the restful quiet of a library. It was at about this time that he selected and sent to the Bodleian a beautiful English mantel clock to replace Dr. Rawlinson's, which had worn itself out after 160 years of usefulness. It strikes a soft, unhurried chime appropriate in character for a silentium; and may it measure as many hours as did its predecessor. Under it is the following inscription:

V. c. Gulielmo Osler Baronetto
Medicinae apud Oxonienses Professori regio
Hoc Horologium
Grato animo acceptum refert
Bibliotheca Bodleiana
a.d. VIII. Id. Oct. A.S. MCMXII

[1] It had been Osler's wish to have a really well-equipped science laboratory established in Father Johnson's memory, in connexion with Trinity College School at Port Hope; and the present head master states that had he lived longer he would have seen this project through. In 1918 Osler established

OSLER'S CLOCK AT THE BODLEIAN

At about this same time there was on exhibition in Boston, Mass., a supposed portrait of William Harvey which had aroused great interest—doubtless the same portrait that had intrigued Osler in the summer of 1903. Dr. John Collins Warren had written to him concerning it, and on October 14th Osler replied :

If that is a picture signed somewhat indistinctly, I think by Janssen, with the date 1656 higher up, I know all about it—and the story is interesting. Eight or nine years ago, lunching in Paris with Rupert Norton, he said, 'You must come and see an interesting Harvey picture at Stegelmeyer's.' Sure enough, there was a very fine Janssen, marked as I have described and looking like Harvey. The only suspicion was that it was a very young man for that date. I asked for the refusal of the picture for ten days, for a photograph and for the pedigree. These were sent to me in London. The picture was stated to have come from Colonel Harvey Bramston, a collateral descendant of Harvey, through one of the Colnaghis, who had purchased it in 1895. I showed the photograph to D'Arcy Power and to Payne, the two men who knew most about Harvey, and to Lionel Cust, the expert at the National Gallery, all of whom decided it was impossible that it could represent Harvey who at that date was stricken in years and nearing his end. Moreover it was totally unlike the National Gallery picture taken of him as an old man. Meanwhile I had written to Colonel Harvey Bramston, who replied that he had never owned such a picture, and that if he had it was the last thing with which he would have parted. He was, of course, furious, and wrote to the old Colnaghi in Pall Mall, on whom I also called, but neither of us could get any satisfaction, and a year or so later the old man died. It is a good picture, a Janssen, and Cust said that it was worth the money—£300. For 'ways that are dark and tricks that are vain', picture-dealers can give points to the Heathen Chinee ! My love to John & to Sturgis Bigelow.

He writes to Jacobs early in November : 'I am busy—still deep in this [National] Tuberculosis question so hard to settle here' ; and on the 4th to A. C. Klebs :

Should you by any chance reach Almond's Hotel before Wednesday evening, do come to the Athenaeum Club, where I am giving a dinner to the officers & some of the staff of the Pathological Society of Gt. Britain to meet Flexner. That is No. 1. No. 2 is—if you get to Almond's before 4.30 on Thursday & you would like to hear me discourse mellifluously on 'acute pneumonic phthisis' & see some

---

a Founder's Exhibition in memory of the Rev. W. A. Johnson, 'to be awarded to the boy taking the highest place in honour science at the University examinations.'

superb specimens, come to the Brompton Hospital. And No. 3 is that if you get to London before one o'clock on Thursday bring the 'light of your life' to lunch with me at the Royal Automobile Club, Pall Mall. I hope you will have had a good voyage.

A letter also went to Weir Mitchell about the spurious Harvey portrait, and it adds: 'All goes well here. This is a busy term—so many things on hand, and I have to be in London a great deal.' Of the 'many things on hand', in addition to the fixed obligations which, week, month, and year on end, were cheerfully met, some traces are to be found. A new Department of Pharmacology for the Oxford school was opened on November 9th with appropriate formalities. Dr. J. A. Gunn, the new incumbent, gave an address; and the Regius, who presided, sketched the history of pharmacology in the university, closing his remarks by reminding the Vice-Chancellor (the Principal of Brasenose) that Withering's monograph on the use of digitalis was inspired by the results of its use on a previous holder of his office. Then tea was served in an adjoining department, 'where editions of Dioscorides on Materia Medica were displayed'—a characteristic Oslerian touch.

At about that time, too, a 'school of voice production' was established at Oxford! That Osler was greatly interested in human speech and its dialects has been already pointed out in connexion with his unfinished essay, 'The American Voice', which he always carried with him on his crossings; and one may imagine that it became a topic of conversation on some Sunday evening at Christ Church. At all events, to bring the importance of the subject before the public, a conference was finally held at 'the House', the Regius Professor of Divinity presiding, with the Master of Pembroke, the Rector of Exeter, Sir William Osler, and the Rev. P. N. Waggett as participants—the latter remarking that the 'affected intonation and bad speech of the clergy was really a matter for tears'. Osler must have expressed himself very mildly, to judge from an editorial on the subject, which says:[1]

. . . We note with satisfaction, mingled with some surprise, Sir

[1] 'Voice Training for the Clergy.' *British Medical Journal*, Nov. 16, 1912, ii. 1412.

William Osler's description of the English voice. It is pleasant to know that it sounds sweet and soft to his ears, and this makes it all the more deplorable that it should so often be marred in the utterance. We mumble and swallow our words and distort our vowels in a manner which makes our splendid language sound to the foreigner like a jargon. The reason was long ago given by John Milton in his 'Tract on Education' (1644), where he says: 'For we Englishmen being farre northerly doe not open our mouthes in the cold air, wide enough to grace a southern tongue, but are observed by all other nations to speak exceeding close and inward; so that to smatter Latin with an English mouth is as ill a hearing as law French.'

'We have the first meeting of our new Section of the History of Medicine this afternoon', he wrote to H. B. Jacobs on November 20th. 'About 160 have joined so that I hope it may be a success.' Much time had been expended in preparation for this gathering, and, though Osler had ways of his own, one wonders what has become of the composition of his Yale lectures during all these weeks. At this inaugural meeting he accepted the presidency of the section; Raymond Crawfurd and D'Arcy Power were chosen as secretaries; and among the list of Vice-Presidents and members of the Council occur the names of Allbutt, Ronald Ross, Rolleston, E. M. Little, J. A. Nixon, F. M. Sandwith, and others, who were certain to give the movement support. The introductory remarks of the newly installed President are given in the Transactions, in part as follows:

In thanking the members of the Section for the honour of election as their first Chairman, Sir William Osler remarked that he had at least two qualifications—a keen interest in the subject, and a certain academic leisure, which would enable him to attend to the duties of the position. Physicians held very different views on the subject of the history of medicine. A majority were indifferent—too busy to pay any attention to it; a considerable number were interested enough to read articles or to listen to papers; then there were the amateur students, like himself, who dabbled in history as a pastime; and lastly, there was a select group of real scholars, men like Adams, Greenhill and Payne. It was to be hoped that this Section would form a meeting-ground for the scholars, the students, and for all those who felt that the study of the history of medicine had a value in education.

The Chairman had had sufficient 'academic leisure' to prepare a paper dealing with the William Petty MS. which he had discovered, and to which allusion has already been made. He said that 'in reading Petty's life and works one gets the impression of a man born out of due time; and that his ideas and the practical capacity and energy with which he carried them into execution suggest the twentieth rather than the seventeenth century'. One paragraph from the address may be quoted, to recall the beginning of Ireland's grievances, which in a very short time indeed were to culminate in a threat of civil war—a threat so serious that it was misjudged by a nation wanting 'a place in the sun'.

But Petty [he said] has a third claim to remembrance as the author of the famous Down Survey of Ireland—which 'stands to-day, with the accompanying books of distribution, the legal record of the title on which half the land of Ireland is held' (Larcom). . . . In 1649 Petty had been named Deputy to Dr. Clayton, the then Regius Professor of Medicine at Oxford, and in 1651 succeeded him in the Chair of Anatomy. At Oxford he became an active member of the Club or Society, out of which originated the Royal Society. In 1652 he was appointed Physician-General to the Forces in Ireland, with which country the remainder of a stormy life was to be associated. A masterful, energetic, resourceful man, the first thing he did was to reorganize the medical service. Energy in action was, he said, the great requisite of life, and soon an opportunity offered which called forth all his powers. In 1652 the Irish were conquered—the English won, and as Petty says, 'had amongst other pretences a Gamester's right at least to their estates'. The claimants were: (1) The adventurers in England to whom 2,500,000 acres of Irish land had been pledged for money advanced to raise an army; (2) the soldiers of the New Model Army of Cromwell and Fairfax, who had really done the fighting; and (3) the Commonwealth, which had reserved the Crown and Church, and certain other lands. There were, it is said, 35,000 claimants of land in all. Lots were drawn, and attempts were made at the distribution, but it was found impossible to identify the lot drawn with any particular parcel of land. There was no survey, and matters were soon in a hopeless muddle. The Surveyor-General, also a doctor, a visionary, unpractical man, insisted that a survey could not be made in less than thirteen years. Petty, a strong critic of this scheme, undertook to finish the job in thirteen months, if given a free hand. Registers and valuation lists existed in places, but no maps; Petty agreed to 'survey, admeasure and to map', and so his work came to be known as the 'Down' survey, because it was surveyed *down* on a map. The date fixed was February 1, 1655, and the rate of payment agreed upon was £7. 3s. 4d. per 1,000 acres of forfeited profitable land, and the Church and Crown Lands at £3 per acre. It was a vast undertaking, but Petty had a genius for organization, and was himself a practical surveyor as well as a mathematician and physicist of the first rank. . . .

There followed papers by the newly appointed Secretaries, Raymond Crawfurd and D'Arcy Power; and the 'Section', which was henceforth to hold monthly meetings, had been without doubt successfully launched. Innovations of this sort were more easily introduced in the new Royal Society of Medicine than in the conservative old College of Physicians, which held its second winter meeting a few days later. As usual, the select College Club dined beforehand—and, as usual, 'Polonius' was present, which fact moved Osler to unaccustomed profanity when he made the following note in Payne's volume on his return to Oxford:

Nov. 26, 1912. Election. 20 men present. We *all* thought B—— was sure of election and his name came in first. All the same when I saw that damned old Polonius I knew there would be one blackball —there were two! There was some hitch about the box and the voting had to be repeated—there were 3! Then F—— and K—— were voted for—both had 2 blackballs—so no one was elected. The club felt sore!

The following day, November 27th, the Bodleian underground book-stack in which he had been so greatly interested was formally opened, and before a large gathering of members of Congregation, Falconer Madan spoke of the problems confronting Nicholson, his predecessor, which had led to this subterranean chamber. Here such gigantic series as *The Times* from 1808 and 'some 100 yards of bound ordnance maps', with other things, might be stored to relieve the pressure on the Bodleian Quadrangle, where 'there were now about 1,700,000 separate works, with a daily increase of 200 from one year's end to the other'. Prophesying that within fifty years every college and institution would come to have a similar underground receptacle for its stores, he paid due tribute to the curators of the Bodleian, and the Radcliffe Trustees, who had 'spent a vast amount of time and trouble in solving the knotty problems, both of rights in the site, and details of the construction'.

I am interested to hear of your Linacre finds [he writes to Klebs on Dec. 9th]. There were a great many editions of his translations from Galen. I have the originals, all except the 'De Temperamentis' one of the earliest books printed at Cambridge, where there is a copy waiting for anybody who wishes to pay 45 pounds! I will look up the Goulston, whose books I am always interested in, as he was the founder of the Goulstonian Lecture at the Royal College of Physicians, and he left some beautiful old books to Merton, which I must show you some day. We made an excellent start with our historical section at the Royal Society of Medicine. We have nearly 160 members, and there were between two and three hundred at the first meeting. I am so glad you got in touch with Sudhoff. Stir up the men for the historical section of the Congress next year. There is a very good list of papers, but not enough men from the continent. . . . Quaritch the angel! secured for me at the Hoe sale a superb copy of von Hutten's 'De Guaiaci', the original edition. Like a fool I missed the other day, by not telegraphing, the De Curatione Pestiferorum one of the earliest incunabula printed and for 3 or 4 pounds![1]

'I have had a worrying week,' he writes on the 15th, in explaining his delay in getting some Christmas messages off to America; 'first with a succession of Examiners from outside who have to be looked after, but more particularly with Whitelaw Reid's illness. I had to go to town every evening as I seemed to be of greater comfort to him than his London doctors. He passed away peacefully this morning. He had a long & useful innings & will be much missed here.' Were it not for this chance letter there would be nothing to indicate that he had been having an anxious week, for there is scant reference to his professional activities in Osler's correspondence. Meanwhile, from 13 Norham Gardens there had issued a bushel of letters saying 'Dear Doctor—Have you anything for the Medical Section (of

[1] Not satisfied with his own collection of the early printed medical works, he stirs up other libraries and librarians in the same direction. It was in this December that he incited Mitchell to 'bleed the Fellows' of the College of Physicians of Philadelphia for its fine editio princeps of Celsus (see above, Vol. I, p. 277). J. C. Wilson, the President of the College, made that volume and the story of its purchase the text of his address on May 5th, 1913, at the Washington meeting of the Medical Library Association. Osler at this same meeting spoke on the 'Proposed General Catalogue of Incunabula' (cf. Bulletin of the Association for April 1914), and gave an account of the copies of that (1478) edition of Celsus which he had encountered. (Cf. also 'Incunabula Medica', Oxford Press, 1923, foot-note, p. 17.)

which I am President) of the International Medical Congress to be held in London next August, etc.' This looks a long way ahead, but plans which concerned the whole household must be made, and Lady Osler wrote to some Boston friends: 'We are taking either a house, or rooms in Brown's Hotel—a suite; and you must be with us. We shall have the Müllers, the Pierre Maries, and I don't know how many more. It seems a hopeless job, altogether, and will be hot and muggy I'm sure.'

On the 17th he was given a degree at the University of Durham, but what apparently interested him more than this addition to his academic honours was a search while there for some records of Richard de Bury, consecrated Bishop of Durham shortly before Christmas nearly six centuries before. In the Grolier Club edition of 'The Philobiblon' he made this note on his return: 'Dec. 17th, 1912. At Durham to get a D.C.L. Nothing of de Bury but a MS. of the Philobiblon in the Bishop Cosin Lib. In the Cathedral is the slab on the grave erected by the Grolier Club'; and he goes on to give the inscription and the Latin quotation, which, however, does not appear to agree with what is given in the Grolier edition. That they had a festive Christmas is evident from a note to his never-forgotten boyhood friend, Edward Milburn:

Dear Ned, Thanks for the Rabbi Ben Ezra—a favourite poem of mine, the best of Browning's, I think. I hope you have had a good Xmas. We had a house full—a daughter of E. B. & her three, H. S. Osler & his son from Toronto & a sister-in-law & two nieces from Boston. My boy was 17 last week—growing a big fellow, not much at his books but a very good sort. Thank the lassie for her photograph, very good. She must keep the house lively. I hope to be out in April & should be able to stop over at Belleville on my way from Toronto some time in May. Love to you all Ever yours.

CHAPTER XXXIII

1913

THE SILLIMAN LECTURES AND INTERNATIONAL MEDICAL CONGRESS

'We have had a very busy Christmas—the house full to overflowing', he writes to H. M. Thomas early in January. 'Revere is very happy. He is going to spend the next year with a tutor as he has to make up enough Latin & Greek to pass his [Oxford] entrance examination.' And to another of his old Baltimore friends:

Our new section in the History of Medicine is going to be a great success. . . . I was very anxious to have Allbutt or Norman Moore as President but the younger men would have neither of them, & insisted that I should be elected. I am sorry in a way, as I am afraid Moore was rather hurt: but I have had a nice talk with him about it. . . . They have elected me President of the Bibliographical Society which is a very embarrassing honour, as I feel so horribly amateurish with all these professional fellows like Pollard—but it is a very nice group of men & I have been on the Council for three years as Vice-President.

The feeling of 'these professional fellows' themselves is well enough expressed by the announcement of January 6th from A. W. Pollard of the British Museum stating that after he [Osler] had left the meeting that day he had been unanimously nominated for the post to succeed H. B. Wheatley; that it would be his duty and pleasure as Secretary of the Society to save him all possible trouble; that Wheatley had asked H. R. Tedder [Librarian of the Athenaeum] to dine with the Colophon Club on the 20th with the usual intimation of a resigning President that someone else would be his host.[1] Osler, however, was not the kind of presiding officer to shoulder his secretary with the entire burden of programmes and other arrangements;

[1] In regard to Osler's 'work' as President of the Bibliographical Society—a post he held for the remainder of his life, twice as long as that of any other President—Mr. Pollard writes that '"work" is not quite the right word, for he brought us life and high spirits and would give us no less even to the end'.

and a presidential job of still greater responsibility, namely of the Medical Section of the coming International Congress, was on his hands. The Section was fortunate in having, as one of the Secretaries, Dr. William Pasteur, but even he, perhaps, was hardly aware of the mass of correspondence in soliciting contributions for the lean Historical Section and in pacifying would-be contributors to the overfilled programme of his own, which passed over the office desk at 13 Norham Gardens. But if this was arduous for the officers of a single section, what Wilmot Herringham, the Secretary-General of the Congress as a whole, had to face can be imagined; and it must have been a relief, at least on the score of providing entertainment for the 7,000 prospective participants, when at Osler's instigation the Astors gladly promised to give an afternoon reception at Cliveden for a thousand or so, and Strathcona an evening entertainment for the entire Congress.

'It is this, it is this, that oppresses my soul; it is this, it is this that I dread', was one of Osler's familiar interjections, borrowed from 'The Hunting of the Snark'—an interjection, be it said, as often called forth by missing a book as by anything else. 'I am very unhappy to-day,' he writes, 'having just lost a MS. of Chrysippus and one of Constantinus Africanus—but these are the hazards of the mart.' Though the preparation of the Yale lectures chiefly engrossed him from January to April, he managed to hold the threads of countless other things which called for time and correspondence—the Roger Bacon celebration, for example, planned for the following year; the new edition of Liddell and Scott's Greek Dictionary for which the Press was making arrangements; even such trifles as the Thomas Dover tablet, concerning which on January 27th he writes to J. A. Nixon of Bristol the following characteristic and possibly over-interpolated note:

Dear Nixon,—I was very much obliged for the extra copy of the Fletcher memorial [his own in the *Bristol Medico-Chirurgical Journal* for December]. I wrote to the Editor thanking him for the first one. Will you dine with me at the Automobile Club on Wednesday evening after the meeting [of the Historical Section]? You could get away in time for a late train. Do you know anything about Mr. Robert Dover's [Thomas Dover's grandfather] 'Olimpick

Games upon the Cotswold Hills' ? I see on sale at Sotheby's on February 4th 'Annalia Dubrensia' written by Drayton, Johnson, etc., 1st ed. Colyer-Fergusson [Max Müller's son-in-law and a descendant of Dover] was dining with me last night and was much interested in it and hopes to buy it. What about the *tabloid* to T. D.? Sincerely yours.

'We are having a peaceful time with the house cleared out —we have had an extraordinary winter—the almond trees have been in bloom for a week. I am struggling with my Silliman Lectures which I find very interesting—trying to trace the evolution of scientific medicine.' So he writes early in February, and three weeks later: 'Deuce of a job getting these lectures ready. Have heard from Harvard about the Clarendon Press lecture. Horace Hart is doing fine slides for me.' Evidently he had taken on other things besides the Silliman series, yet on February 26th he writes to the Yale University Press: 'I shall have everything ready for you after the lectures and we should be able to have the book out by October'—a vain anticipation, as will be seen. It was inevitable that a man with so many contacts and interests should be interrupted, even with 'the house cleared out'. It was at about this time that Berry's translation of Gomperz's 'Greek Thinkers', Vol. IV, came into Osler's hands, a work which had delighted him ever since the time twelve years before when he had greedily devoured the first volume of the series during one of his periodic attacks of bronchitis. For a time at least the Silliman Lectures must have been side-tracked, and ere long he sent a review for his 'Men and Books' series [1] which begins in this wise:

Readers of my occasional addresses will have noted frequent references to the work of Professor Gomperz on 'Greek Thinkers',

[1] No. XXI, 'Aristotle'. *Canadian Medical and Surgical Journal*, May 1913, iii. 416–17. Though Osler could thus switch off easily from what would appear to be his major task of the moment, in all probability these side excursions were recreational. He must have written at about this time, also, No. XXII, on 'Dr. Slop', for the same series which he continued to send to Macphail. He was spurred to write this latter note in view of an article he had just seen (in the current number of the *British Journal of Obstetrics and Gynaecology*) by Alban Doran, who had come to the defence of Dr. John Burton in a way which appealed to Osler in view of the 'libellous portrait' left by Laurence Sterne in 'Tristram Shandy'.

Volume IV of which has just appeared. To young men with leisure, young practitioners in the waiting stage, who wish to keep the dough of their minds leavened, let me commend these volumes. An hour a day, or less, for a year, with a note-book, and I can promise the best of company and a stimulating diet, full of intellectual hormones. If it be true that a man is born a Platonist or an Aristotelian, my congenital bias was toward the great idealist, but without, I fear, the proper mental equipment; the cares of this world and the deceitfulness of my studies have driven me into the camp of the Stagirite. And it is a glorious tribe, to be sealed of which, even as a humblest member, one should be proud. In the first circle of the Inferno Virgil leads Dante into a wonderful company, the philosophic family who look with reverence on 'The Master of those who know' —and so with justice has Aristotle been regarded for these twenty-three centuries. No man has ever swayed such an intellectual empire—in logic, metaphysics, rhetoric, psychology, ethics, poetry, politics and natural history, in all a creator and in all still a master. The history of the human mind offers no parallel to the career of the great Stagirite.

On March 1st, in acknowledging a hospital report from G. Alder Blumer of Providence, he writes: 'Very good reading—you seem to be prosperous. That "cash over-invested" sounds fascinating. We never have anything like it here. I've just had two hours over the Bodleian accounts —such a contrast!' And he tells President Hadley, declining an invitation, that he would feel more free at the Graduates' Club, because 'from what I hear there will be a good many of my old students turning up for one or other of the lectures', and they must be looked out for. During these months the meetings of the Clinical Section of the Royal Society of Medicine had of course continued, for one of which, indeed—the meeting of February 14th—devoted to the subject of cervical rib, Osler had advertised in the journals, asking members of the profession to bring their cases for exhibition; again on March 3rd, in support of the German commission which was getting out a general catalogue of incunabula, he sent to the journals a public letter requesting that lists of the medical incunabula which might be in private collections be sent to him. Then came the news of the death on March 11th of another old friend, causing a pang, the greater in that it had come so shortly after that of Robert Fletcher.

To S. Weir Mitchell from W. O. 21st [March]

It is very sad to hear of John Billings' death. You will miss him very much. What a fine life! so full of accomplishment. I have just written an obituary notice for the British Medical Journal. You will be glad to hear that Power has got the Harvey portraits collected, & a study of them will form the first fasciculus of studies from our new section of the History of Medicine of the Royal Society of Medicine. I hope to see you very soon. May I dine with you on Monday eve, April 14th, on my way to Baltimore? . . . It is so nice to hear that you are keeping well. We heard of you in Chicago & of your successful lecture. I wish you could come over to the Medical Congress this summer. I am chairman of the Medical Section & we are getting together a nice group of men for the discussions. You will be sorry to hear that Gowers is very ill—his own disease, ataxic paraplegia, it looks like, & ascending, so that now there are bulbar symptoms. Barlow the other day presented the Harvey letters to the College of Physicians—it is the proper place for them. It was most kind of the Library Committee to send me a copy of Stockton-Hough's Incunabula. It seems very rare. I know of only one copy in this country. You are getting rich in 15th century books. I was delighted that you got that Celsus 1478 as it is the most beautiful copy I have seen. With love to Mrs. Mitchell & Jack, Affectionately yours.

'I am sailing next week', he writes to President Hadley on the 28th, 'and shall go to Baltimore for a couple of days to the opening of the new Phipps Institute, as Mr. Phipps is one of my oldest friends; but I shall be in New Haven Saturday eve the 19th.' At noon on the following day, March 29th, there was a noteworthy ceremony in Merton College chapel, which, three hundred years before, to the day, had witnessed the public funeral of Sir Thomas Bodley. This commemorative service illustrated how 'Osler's ferment continued to work in the Oxford dough'; though to a large extent the programme had been drawn up by the Rev. H. A. Wilson of Magdalen, and the Rev. R. H. Charles of Merton. Its chief feature was an English translation of the Latin oration by the 'ever-memorable John Hales, Fellow of Merton', delivered at the time of Bodley's interment in Merton chapel. On the same day the Clarendon Press published a small volume, 'Trecentale Bodleianum', containing Bodley's autobiography, the early statutes of the Library, extracts from his will, and other pieces.

In Osler's copy of this volume he has made the following note:

March 29th, 1913. The service at Merton was attended by about 150 people. The pro-V.-C. Shadwell, Provost of Oriel was present. Nearly everyone was away. I was the only Curator present & only Hogarth & Bywater representing the Press. Dr Charles a Fellow of M. read the service. Madan, Bodley's Librarian, read the lesson from a MS. of Bodley's, a special translation of the chapter. Skrine read an English translation of Hales' Oration. Did it well—good voice—took just half an hour. Full of quaint, golden phrases worthy of the ever-memorable John. Dr. Macray the historian of Bodley was present, the sub-librarian, the assistants & many of the boys. Altogether it was a memorable & delightful service, & I am very glad to have suggested it to the standing committee & helped Madan get over some of the difficulties.

In company with his colleague William McDougall, and with F. W. Mott, who were to give addresses at the opening of the Phipps Clinic, he sailed, on April 5th, on the *Campania*, and during the voyage must have written, to judge from its context, not only a large part of his Baltimore address to be delivered on the 16th, but also the first portion of the lay sermon to the Yale students which he had promised to give on Sunday the 20th. On the Friday before landing he wrote to Anson Phelps Stokes:

I get to New Haven Saturday eve, 19th. I am sending on a dress suit[-case] to the club with my photographs &c. My address on Sunday will be 'A Way of Life'—about 1/2–3/4 of an hour. I have six lectures on the Evolution of Modern Medicine. I will send a synopsis. The material will much more than cover six but it is a heavy tax on an audience to ask a longer series. I think they will make an interesting book. I have many illustrations. I am writing to Blumer to say I am at the disposal of the Medical School for cliniques & demonstrations every day. I have a lecture on Burton's Anatomy of Melancholy for the English Literature Students. I hope to see as much as possible of the students & professors. . . .

His visit, indeed, had developed into what was to be almost a lecture tour, interspersed with many visits—on Sunday the 13th, the day of his arrival, with the Brewsters; on the next day in Philadelphia to see Weir Mitchell and join a large gathering of his old friends at dinner; on Tuesday in Baltimore at the Futchers'. The next day the three-days' programme of exercises in connexion with the opening of the Phipps Clinic began with his address entitled 'Specialism in the General Hospital'. In the course of his introductory remarks, before entering upon his main theme, he said:

> Only a few impressions of life endure. We use the same cylinders over and over again, the dots and markings become confused, and when we call for a record, a jumbled medley is poured out, a confused message from the past. But certain records are time-fast, and bite in such a way that no subsequent impressions can blur the clearness, and the story comes out fresh and sharp. So it is when I call up those early years so full of happiness, so full of hope. And to have seen in so many ways the fulfilment of our heart's desire is more than we could have expected, more indeed than we deserved. I am sorry for you young men of this generation. You will do great things, you will have great victories, and, standing on our shoulders you will see far, but you can never have our sensations. To have lived through a revolution, to have seen a new birth of science, a new dispensation of health, reorganized medical schools, remodeled hospitals, a new outlook for humanity, is not given to every generation.
>
> By temperament a dreamer, wherever I have worked, visions of the future have beset me, sometimes to my comfort, more often to my despair. In desolate days I have wandered with Don Quixote, tilting at windmills; in happier ones I have had the rare good fortune to dream dreams through the gate of horn, and to see their realization, to have both the vision from Pisgah and the crossing the Jordan. . . .

And from this he went on to speak of the transformation since his day that had occurred at Toronto, McGill, and the University of Pennsylvania. 'Looking back', he said, 'over a somewhat vagrant career, my fission from an academic body has always been a stimulus and has invariably quickened the page of progress.' So now at the Johns Hopkins the scanty seeds of prophecy he had scattered in his peaceful valedictory appeared to have fallen on good ground. For he had spoken of the needs of special departments, hoping that within twenty-five years there would be a psychopathic institute, a children's hospital, and so on. He expressed his confidence that this psychiatric institute would play its part in the national campaign of prevention of mental ill-health—a campaign as important to the public as the great struggles against tuberculosis and infant mortality; adding that 'it would be helpful also to study in a sane, sober and sympathetic way epidemics of mental, moral, and even economic folly as they swept over the country'. And he concluded with the following innocent-enough paragraphs:

The present out-break has not been equalled since the capture of the Roman world by Oriental cults. The same old-fashioned credulity exists that enabled Mithras and Isis, Apollonius and Alexander to flourish then as the new cults do to-day, and for the same good reason. There is still potency in the protoplasm out of which arose in primitive man, magic, religion and medicine. Circe and Æsculapius were probably twins! Historically our fringe of civilization is of yesterday, if we compare the six or seven thousand years of its record with the millions which must have passed since man assumed his present form on the earth. In this vast perspective Aristotle and Darwin are fellow-students; Hippocrates and Virchow are contemporaries.

Primitive views still prevail everywhere of man's relation to the world and to the uncharted region about him. So recent is the control of the forces of nature that even in the most civilized countries man has not yet adjusted himself to the new conditions, and stands, only half awake, rubbing his eyes, outside of Eden. Still in the thaumaturgic stage of mental development, ninety-nine per cent. of our fellow creatures, when in trouble, sorrow or sickness, trust to charms, incantations and to the saints. Many a shrine has more followers than Pasteur; many a saint more believers than Lister. Less than 20 years have passed since the last witch was burned in the British Isles! [See below, p. 555.]

Mentally the race is still in leading strings, and it has only been in the last brief epoch of its history that Æsop and Lewis Carroll have spun yarns for its delight, and Lucian and Voltaire have chastised its follies. In the childhood of the world we cannot expect people yet to put away childish things. These, Mr. President, are some of the hopes which fill our hearts as we think of the future of this new department. . . .

It was an admirable address in his best vein, just what was needed as an introduction to the subsequent series of papers by eminent psychiatrists who did not necessarily see eye to eye with him in the matter. In the words of the local news-sheets, Baltimore was glad and proud to claim some share in this man; and a long editorial in one of the local papers expressed the general feeling as follows:

One sees now, if he never realized it before, that Dr. Osler would have been great in any field—in the pulpit, in politics, in literature, in journalism, in law—because God gave him a great and unexceptional and many-sided mind and a spirit which such minds often lack—the inspiration, the courage and the honesty of the prophet who has walked on the mountain-top and swept the whole world with his eyes, and who can deliver a message that is as unbounded as his vision.

During the three days given over to these inaugural exercises, with the usual receptions and gastronomic festivities that accompany such functions, he not only was the central figure but, as is recorded, supplied the life and spirit which made the occasion memorable. He was naturally drawn into other things—an evening meeting at 'Osler Hall' in the new Faculty building, for example—and the following note to F. H. Garrison shows how he willingly loaned himself to meetings unanticipated in his itinerary:

They have asked me [he wrote] to speak on Dr. Billings' Bibliographical work at the N. Y. Memorial meeting on the 25th. Could you send me (care of Graduates Club, New Haven) a few details: (1) date of origin of the library & mode of it. (2) Any early printed record reference—I could probably get it at Yale; (3) No. of volumes of the Index [Catalogue] which Dr. Billings edited; (4) Is there not a pamphlet about the plan of the Index? (5) How many volumes of the Index Medicus did Dr. B. edit? (6) Any other points of interest about the early days of the Library. Yours gratefully, &c. I shall be at the Library Association meeting May 5th.

Osler must have been an enigma to many people who could have little understanding of the adoration felt by those who were fortunate enough to know him and to come under his spell—to none more than to the tribe of cheap journalists. And one of these, remembering how space-filling had been the Osler 'copy' of eight years before, distorted from his 'Fixed Period' address, had a column in the *Baltimore Sun* of Saturday morning detailing a fictitious interview, which went broadcast from Baltimore to San Francisco, from Winnipeg to New Orleans, headlined 'Osler Shocks the Cardinal'; 'Newest Oslerism arouses Prelate's Indignation'; 'Cardinal Gibbons Scores Osler', &c. It was all based on that innocent paragraph containing the statement that 'ninety-nine per cent. of our fellow creatures, when in trouble, sorrow or sickness, trust to charms, incantations and to the saints'. It was altogether

OSLER, AET. 63

From a snapshot taken in the Hopkins garden

too bad; and though his old friend and neighbour repudiated the interview, tried in vain to get in touch with the victim of newspaperdom, and, failing to do so, wrote him a note of deep regret, it was not a pleasant kind of introduction for the Silliman lecturer.

Meanwhile on the Saturday he had left for New Haven and buried himself in the library of the Graduates' Club, where he managed to complete his address—'A Way of Life'—which was to be given before the undergraduates in Woolsey Hall the following evening. It was not his first 'lay sermon' to students in a university other than his own. Nor does the published address show evidence of the pressure under which it was written. This, however, the manuscript, still preserved, fully betrays, for on the back of it Osler has noted: 'I wrote this on the steamer going to America, from notes that I had been jotting down for a month, but I only finished it on the Sunday of its delivery.'[1] Naturally enough, from these circumstances one can appreciate the source of his comparison when he says:

I stood on the bridge of one of the great liners, ploughing the ocean at 25 knots. 'She is alive', said my companion, 'in every plate; a huge monster with brain and nerves, an immense stomach, a wonderful heart and lungs, and a splendid system of locomotion.' Just at that moment a signal sounded, and all over the ship the water-tight compartments were closed. 'Our chief factor of safety', said the Captain. 'In spite of the *Titanic*', I said. 'Yes', he replied, 'in spite of the *Titanic*.' Now each one of you is a much more marvellous organization than the great liner, and bound on a longer voyage. What I urge is that you so learn to control the machinery as to live with 'day-tight compartments' as the most certain way to ensure safety on the voyage. Get on the bridge, and see that at least the great bulkheads are in working order. Touch a button and hear, at every level of your life, the iron doors shutting out the Past—the dead yesterdays. Touch another and shut off, with a metal curtain, the Future—the unborn tomorrows. Then you are safe—safe for to-day! Read the old story in 'The Chambered Nautilus', so beautifully sung by Oliver Wendell Holmes, only change one line to 'Day after day beheld the silent toil'. Shut off the past! Let the dead past bury its dead. So easy to say, so hard

[1] The last seven of the nineteen pages of the manuscript from which he read, and from which the address was printed, are hand-written on paper of the Graduates' Club of New Haven.

to realize! The truth is, the past haunts us like a shadow. To disregard it is not easy. Those blue eyes of your grandmother, that weak chin of your grandfather, have mental and moral counterparts in your make-up. Generations of ancestors, brooding over 'Providence, Foreknowledge, Will and Fate—Fixed fate, free will, foreknowledge absolute', may have bred a New England conscience, morbidly sensitive, to heal which some of you had rather sing the 51st Psalm than follow Christ into the slums.

'The load of to-morrow, added to that of yesterday, carried to-day makes the strongest falter.' 'Change that hard saying, "Sufficient unto the day is the evil thereof" into "the goodness thereof", since the chief worries of life arise from the foolish habit of looking before and after.' 'The day of a man's salvation is *now*—the life of the present, of to-day, lived earnestly, intently, without a forward-looking thought, is the only insurance for the future.' 'Begin the day with Christ and His prayer—you need no other. Creedless, with it you have religion; creed-stuffed, it will leaven any theological dough in which you stick'—these were a few of his expressions to explain a philosophy of life that he had found helpful in his work, useful in his play.

> The quiet life in day-tight compartments will help you to bear your own and others' burdens with a light heart. Pay no heed to the Batrachians who sit croaking idly by the stream. Life is a straight, plain business, and the way is clear, blazed for you by generations of strong men, into whose labours you enter and whose ideals must be your inspiration.

This was his own philosophy of life which he ascribed to its two most influential episodes—the trifling circumstance that took him to Weston, where he had come under the influence of Father Johnson; and the chance encounter, in 1871 during a period of unnecessary worry, with Carlyle's admonition 'not to see what lies dimly at a distance, but to do what lies clearly at hand'.

There was nothing new in this, but is there anything new in any sermon? From childhood we are told 'never to put off till to-morrow'. Over the portal of the house where Sir Spencer Wells used to live at Golder's Green is the motto, 'Do to-day's work to-day.' Still, few sermons have created an equal interest, and it was said that 'the medical profession might well be proud of a leader who could, without affectation, preach a lay sermon, which an archbishop might not be ashamed to have written'. In a copy of the address in Osler's library is inscribed the following poem, 'The Salutation of the Dawn', with his note upon it:

Listen to the Exhortation of the Dawn!
    Look to this Day!
For it is Life, the very Life of Life.
In its brief course lie all the
Varieties and Realities of your Existence:
    The Bliss of Growth,
    The Glory of Action,
    The Splendour of Beauty;
For yesterday is but a Dream
And Tomorrow is only a Vision;
But To-day well lived makes
Every Yesterday a Dream of Happiness,
And every Tomorrow a Vision of Hope.
Look well therefore to this Day!
Such is the Salutation of the Dawn!

(by whom?[1] sent me 26. vi. 18 by de Havilland Hall to whom they were given by a remarkable woman, Mrs. Jacoby. If another reprint is called for put this on this page. Wm Osler.)

On Monday afternoon, April 21st, his lectures on the Silliman Foundation began, and continued through the week with the exception of Friday, when he attended the memorial meeting for John S. Billings at the New York Public Library, and when Bishop Greer, Weir Mitchell, Welch, Andrew Carnegie, Richard R. Bowker, John L. Cadwalader the President of the Board of Trustees, and others spoke. It was in his address on this occasion that Osler, after referring to the 'Index Catalogue' and the *Index Medicus*, made this interesting statement:

There is no better float through posterity than to be the author of a good bibliography. Scores know Conrad Gesner by the 'Bibliotheca' who never saw the 'Historia Animalium'. A hundred consult Haller's bibliographies for one that looks at his other works;

[1] Said to be from the Sanskrit, the poem was published, as an inserted frontispiece, in 'Words in Pain', Lond., G. M. Bishop, 1919 (see above, p. 298).

and years after the iniquity of oblivion has covered Dr. Billings's work in the army, as an organizer in connection with hospitals, and even his relation to this great Library, the great Index will remain an enduring monument to his fame.

Though over-dined and over-entertained, he entered into the life at Yale with enthusiasm and soon captivated the students. Professor Nettleton, who had known the Oslers in Oxford, recalls that in reply to an invitation to meet some of the faculty members at his house on the Sunday of his arrival, Osler had replied: 'If you don't mind I would prefer meeting undergraduates. I see Dons every day at Oxford but not enough undergraduates from America.' Thereupon they asked some members of the Dramatic Association and of the Elizabethan Club for tea, and he stood at the door to receive them, took each man in turn by the shoulders as he entered and proceeded to give a mock diagnosis of his character. 'The whole thing was carried off with a spirit and humour which cannot be described. At first some of them hardly knew how to take everything that he said, but soon the contagion of his boyish and whimsical spirit captivated them completely, and when he left he invited them to attend his lecture the next day, saying that it was only to be preliminary and would not be *much* over two hours, nor be wholly obscure even to those of limited medical or other intelligence.'

The Silliman Lectures which, as already stated, began on Monday afternoon, were abundantly illustrated with lantern-slides, and being semi-popular were delivered with great informality. They represented, as he once said, 'a sort of aeroplane flight over the history of medicine' from the time of Imhotep, 'the first figure of a physician to stand out clearly from the mists of antiquity', to the days of modern sanitation with its organized crusade against tuberculosis. There have been many histories of medicine written and there will be many more, but perhaps none by an author who loved his subject more deeply and could understand better the human side of its chief actors. A single quotation from the lectures, rescued for publication nearly ten years later,[1] must suffice to give an idea

[1] In accepting his honorarium from the University Treasurer, Mr. George

of the sympathetic manner in which he handled his subject:

The publication of the 'Fabrica' [of Vesalius] shook the medical world to its foundations. Galen ruled supreme in the schools: to doubt him in the least particular roused the same kind of feeling as did doubts on the verbal inspiration of the Scriptures fifty years ago! His old teachers in Paris were up in arms: Sylvius, *nostrae aetatis medicorum decus*, as Vesalius calls him, wrote furious letters, and later spoke of him as a madman (*vaesanus*). The younger men were with him and he had many friends, but he had aroused a roaring tide of detraction against which he protested a few years later in his work on the 'China-root', which is full of details about the 'Fabrica'. In a fit of temper he threw his notes on Galen and other MSS. in the fire. No sadder page exists in medical writings than the one in which Vesalius tells of the burning of his books and MSS. . . . There is no such pathetic tragedy in the history of our profession. Before the age of thirty Vesalius had effected a revolution in anatomy; he became the valued physician of the greatest court of Europe; but call no man happy till he is dead! A mystery surrounds his last days. The story is that he had obtained permission to perform a post-mortem examination on the body of a young Spanish nobleman, whom he had attended. When the body was opened, the spectators to their horror saw the heart beating, and there were signs of life! Accused, so it is said, by the Inquisition of murder and also of general impiety, he only escaped through the intervention of the King, with the condition that he make a pilgrimage to the Holy Land. In carrying this out in 1564 he was wrecked on the island of Zante, where he died of a fever or of exhaustion, in the fiftieth year of his age.

To the *North American Review*, November 1902, Edith Wharton contributed a poem on 'Vesalius in Zante', in which she pictures his life, so full of accomplishment, so full of regrets—regrets accen-

---

P. Day, Osler had written: 'Call me a prophet of Baal if you do not get most of it back in the next three years.' But he had taken on more than he realized—was living, possibly, too much in 'day-tight compartments'. The American trip with its successive engagements and addresses taken at the pace of a man of forty was exhausting. The London Congress followed and, though he set himself later in the year to the task of correcting the galley proofs, checking up his quotations, completing his illustrations, &c., the urge was gone. The war came: he returned his honorarium and the galley lay untouched for five years on the window-sill of his library till it became foxed and sun-baked. The rescue of the lectures and their final publication by the Yale Press in 1921 in their present imperfect form is explained by Fielding H. Garrison in his prefatory note to the volume.

tuated by the receipt of an anatomical treatise by Fallopius, his successor to the chair in Padua! She makes him say:

> There are two ways of spreading light: to be
> The candle or the mirror that reflects it.
> I let my wick burn out—there yet remains
> To spread an answering surface to the flame
> That others kindle.

But between Mundinus and Vesalius, anatomy had been studied by a group of men to whom I must, in passing, pay a tribute. The great artists Raphael, Michael Angelo and Albrecht Dürer were keen students of the human form. . . . But greater than any of these, and antedating them, is Leonardo da Vinci, the one universal genius in whom the new spirit was incarnate—the Moses who alone among his contemporaries saw the promised land. How far Leonardo was indebted to his friend and fellow student, della Torre, at Pavia, we do not know, nor does it matter in face of the indubitable fact that in the many anatomical sketches from his hand we have the first accurate representation of the structure of the body. Glance at the three figures of the spine which I have had photographed side by side, one from Leonardo, one from Vesalius, and the other from Vandyke Carter, who did the drawings in Gray's 'Anatomy'. They are all of the same type, scientific, anatomical drawings, and that of Leonardo was done fifty years before Vesalius! Compare, too, this figure of the bones of the foot with a similar one from Vesalius. Insatiate in experiment, intellectually as greedy as Aristotle, painter, poet, sculptor, engineer, architect, mathematician, chemist, botanist, aeronaut, musician, and withal a dreamer and mystic, full accomplishment in any one department was not for him! A passionate desire for a mastery of nature's secrets made him a fierce thing, replete with too much rage! But for us a record remains—Leonardo was the first of modern anatomists, and fifty years later, into the breach he made, Vesalius entered.

Perhaps the Elizabethan Club, which incidentally houses a rare collection of early English volumes, interested him as much as any of the undergraduate activities of Yale. On the Tuesday evening of April 22nd he was the special guest of the club, and as a memento of the visit left behind him the original edition of Napier's 'Logarithmorum Descriptio'. 'We gave him a dinner', writes William Lyon Phelps, 'and afterwards at the Elizabethan Club he spoke most brilliantly on Burton's "Anatomy of Melancholy". After he had talked nearly an hour he asked how long he should go on, and I replied that we could sit as long as he could stand. It was really a wonderful occasion.' From this address also, as subsequently published,[1] an illustrative paragraph may be taken:

No book of any language [he said] presents such a stage of moving pictures—kings and queens in their greatness and in their glory, in their madness and in their despair; generals and conquerors with their ambitions and their activities; the princes of the church in their pride and in their shame; philosophers of all ages, now rejoicing in the power of intellect, and again grovelling before the idols of the tribe; the heroes of the race who have fought the battle of the oppressed in all lands; criminals, small and great, from the petty thief to Nero with his unspeakable atrocities; the great navigators and explorers with whom Burton travelled so much in map and card, and whose stories were his delight; the martyrs and the virgins of all religions, the deluded and fanatics of all theologies; the possessed of devils and the possessed of God; the beauties, frail and faithful, the Lucretias and the Helens, all are there. The lovers, old and young; the fools who were accounted wise, and the wise who were really fools; the madmen of all history, to anatomize whom is the special object of the book; the world itself, against which he brings a railing accusation—the motley procession of humanity sweeps before us on his stage, a fantastic but fascinating medley at which he does not know whether to weep or to laugh.

With his lectures, these addresses, morning clinics at the hospital, and other engagements, the busy week passed, and on the morning of his last day he wrote as follows to his host at the next stop:

All right. Am leaving by the 10.15 due Back Bay 1.59. Will lunch in train. Have accepted Lane invitation for Tuesday eve [Syndics of Harvard Press]. Great time here. Never had a better week in my life—great place! Splendid fellows. Love to the darlings. Yours, W. O.

Possibly enough has been said in detail of this, which proved to be his last, visit to America; for, after all, the opening of the Phipps Clinic and the Silliman Lectures were its chief objects. It was in other respects not unlike

[1] *Yale Review*, January 1914. Soon after coming to Oxford Osler had evidently conceived the plan of having the Clarendon Press publish a new and carefully collated edition of the 'Anatomy'. The idea must have come to him when in 1905 he began going through the old libraries and first came upon Burton's own scattered volumes. Some correspondence brought the fact to light that both W. Aldis Wright of Cambridge and Edward Bensly of Aberystwyth were working on the project, which he consequently appears to have abandoned. This Yale address he intended to be one of a series of papers on Burton (cf. p. 199, above).

his previous brief sojourns, consisting of a round of visits, and the laconic entries in his account-book for the remainder of the time must suffice. Read between the lines, it is a perfectly good autobiography of four weeks, and hardly needs the bracketed interpolations:

Mon. April 28. Last lec. Dinner Hadley. [Followed by reception in Art Museum.]
Tues. April 29. Boston Lect. at Harvard. [On the Clarendon Press.]
Wed. April 30. Lect. Opening Brigham Hospital. K's dinner.
Thu. May 1. N.Y. Bibliog. Soc. & Grolier Club. [Luncheon and dinner for him.]
Fri. May 2.
Sat. May 3. } Brewsters. [at Mt. Kisco.]
Sun. May 4. Phila. [Weir Mitchell.]
Mon. May 5. Washington dinner & m't'g Med. Lib. Ass. [cf. foot-note, p. 342.]
Tue. May 6. ditto.
Wed. May 7. Balt. Address to nurses.
Thu. May 8. Buffalo.
Fri. May 9. Hamilton and Dundas. [To visit friends and relatives.]
Sat. May 10.
Sun. May 11. } Toronto. [ditto.]
Mon. May 12. Belleville to see Ned Milburn.
Tue. May 13. Montreal. Dinner of Med Chi Soc.
Wed. May 14. Montreal.
Thu. May 15. Sailed 'Empress Britain'.
Fri. May 23. Oxford 3.45. Good trip—clear & cold.

Two out of all these entries may perhaps be singled out for special mention—one has to do with a nursery, the other with a nurse. Of course he did not forget Rosalie and her 'mother', to whom he sends this note:

Wednesday [April 30th]

Dear Susan, I am so sorry not to be able to see you—and your mother—and your father—and the boys—and the dolls, particularly my beloved one! I have only today here & leave tomorrow morning early. The Revere girls come back to us next month. We have great fun together. With love to you all, Your affec. friend

Wm Osler.

And the other was the commencement address[1] to the Johns Hopkins nurses on May 7th, for which he had been

[1] *Johns Hopkins Hospital Nurses' Alumnae Mag.*, July 1913, xii. 72–81.

persuaded to return to Baltimore. It was an extemporaneous talk in which he told of his experiences with nurses in the old days in the smallpox wards of the Montreal General; at Blockley, for which Miss Alice Fisher of cherished memory did so much; at the Johns Hopkins into which Isabel Hampton had entered 'like an animated Greek statue'. And he went on to say:

Some years ago I had the following letter from a member of the graduating class of a Western Hospital: 'Dear Dr. Osler: We have had a discussion whether special virtues, other than those of an ordinary woman, are needed for a nurse. What is your opinion? Please send a list of those you think to be the most important.' To this I replied: 'Dear Westerna: No special virtues are needed, but the circumstances demand the exercise of them in a special way. There are seven, the mystic seven, your lamps to lighten at . . . tact, tidiness, taciturnity, sympathy, gentleness, cheerfulness, all linked together by charity.'

And now for a brief résumé of these seven virtues and their exercise. Tact is the saving virtue without which no woman can be a success in any way, as a nurse or not. She may have all the others, but without tact she is a failure. With most women it is an instinct, her protective mechanism in life. It is one of the greatest of human blessings that so many women are so full of tact. The calamity happens when a woman who has all the other riches of life just lacks that one thing. I remember one such woman in a hospital with which I was connected, who had had the greatest difficulty with the Board of Trustees to obtain a revolution in the matter of training. They were antique, they were obstinate and self-opinionated, and they regarded their hospital as ideal, which it was not. We had appointed a woman who, to all intents and purposes, had all the necessary qualifications for the place. She was well trained, she had a splendid presence and she had a good record in her school, but in six months she had all the trustees by the ears, she had all the doctors against her and all her head nurses up in arms. All due to a congenital deficiency in tact. She simply could not do any one thing right at the right time.

Now as to tidiness it is not necessary to speak to the modern nurse. Neatness is the very essence of her work. It is the prime duty of a woman of this terrestrial world to look well. Neatness is the asepsis of clothes—not the carelessly tied shoe-string or the dorsal infirmity of a waist and skirt too illy joined. . . .

And in like vein he spoke of taciturnity, a gift so much needed by nurses—'if you have heard anything let it die with you'; of sympathy, to be given in full measure but with discretion, for some seek it as a drunkard his dram; of gentleness, a nurse's birthright; of cheerfulness, than which there is no greater blessing in the world; of charity—'gently to scan your brother man, still more gently your sister woman; to judge no man harshly, to live as closely as possible to the counsels of the Sermon on the Mount, may enable you to live in the true spirit of nursing. These riches shall not fade away in life nor in death decrease.'

Then, too, his 'Phila' entry on May 4th must have been occasioned in response to this appealing note:

> My dear Osler,—I hope to learn that you will be here again before you go home. My friends are fast falling by the way, and this last loss was a far more serious calamity to me than would seem likely to hardened old age. The sentence is bad but will be clear to you. I grow not less but more sensitive as time runs on. The stated engagements of the Carnegie Trust once a month brought Billings and me together so often that we were not separated as busy men are apt to be. I have always dreaded the Arctic loneliness of age, and now alas! Yours sincerely, S. WEIR MITCHELL.

And Osler writes to him from the steamer: 'It was good to see you again & in such fine form. I never heard you speak more clearly & to the point than at the Billings meeting. How I wish I could see you on the river tackling a salmon! So long as you can do this do not talk of old age. You have done more in the past twenty years than many an active-minded man in a lifetime.'

During his sojourn he must have had ample opportunity to get first-hand information regarding the status of the programmes for 'full-time' clinical teachers, one of them about to be inaugurated in Baltimore, another in the Brigham Hospital at whose opening he had officiated in Boston. Before leaving England he must have promised to write for the *Quarterly Review* something on the medical aspects of the recently issued report of Haldane's commission, together with a conspectus of Abraham Flexner's volume dealing with 'Medical Education in Europe', which he had not as yet had time thoroughly to peruse. To this task he apparently set himself during the voyage.[1]

[1] *Quarterly Review*, Lond., July 1913, ccxix. 204–30. 'London University Reform. (1) Final Report of the Royal Commission on University

It is a remarkable fact [he says] in the history of medicine in England that a complete medical faculty of a University did not exist until well into the last century. Neither Oxford nor Cambridge has ever had one, nor has London, for the University of the greatest city of the world's greatest empire is a compound educational polyzoon, the units of which, like the polypoides, though highly organized and with admirable vegetative and reproductive organs, are without heart or central nervous system. This higher organization the Commission proposes to supply in the remodelled university; but, in the case of medicine, problems of extraordinary difficulty have to be met.

These extraordinary difficulties he proceeded to discuss, and to show how they could be met in ways the Commissioners, largely influenced by Mr. Flexner's convincing testimony, had proposed. And he concluded by saying:

There is a new outlook in Medicine, and a new science is moulding both thought and practice. Vested interests are powerful, old associations and ways are strong, but stronger still, we hope, will be the public and professional opinion in favour of the changes suggested by the Commissioners. London should be the most important medical centre in the world. That it is not this, is due to lack of organization and cohesion. To unite into a great Faculty its scattered forces is one aim of this able and far-reaching report, which will have the active support of all but those whom fear of change not only perplexes but appals.

'I have had a wonderful trip in America', he writes from Oxford, 'and enjoyed it immensely—everybody was so kind —too kind in fact! But I kept in pretty good condition and got through my lectures safely. Yale is a wonderful place. The men are charming.' He had returned to find the Secretaries of the XVIIth International Congress of Medicine in a state of distraction, and he must pass judgement on countless matters like the following:

It will evidently not be easy to alter the foreign titles of our discussions. The heart one is the only one that is not satisfactory. The revised German is 'Die Pathologie der Herzschwäche'—the revised French, 'La pathologie de l'asystolie'. Do you think these

---

Education in London. Lond., Wyman, 1913. (2) Medical Education in Europe. A Report to the Carnegie Foundation for the Advancement of Teaching. New York, 1912.' These were two separate reviews, neither of them signed, but the second, which deals solely with university problems of medical education, was written by Osler.

may stand or shall we try to get them altered to: 'Der Wesen der Herzschwäche' and 'Les formes différentes de l'asystolie?' [etc., etc.].

[And again:] The enclosed from Herringham is the reply of headquarters to my query whether our Council would be in order in inviting selected members of the Section to dinner. This was confirmed by Barlow at the R.C.P. this afternoon. They appear to be very anxious that all public entertainment should be on a simple scale so as not to set a pace which it might be difficult for some foreign countries to keep level with. It appears that many men only accepted office on the assurance that it would not involve them in much expenditure.

[Likewise]: Halliburton writes to say that Friday Aug. 8th would suit the Physiologists for the discussion on Internal Secretions. On receipt of your approval I will write him our acceptance. Have you had anything further from von Müller and Widal? Do you propose holding another meeting of our executive before the holidays? The only matters outstanding are to complete the list of openers and to appoint the two sub-committees and agree on the letter to be sent by the council to the various medical departments of universities and hospitals.

[And another:] As you propose sending a personal letter to each member of the Clin. Museum Com., I will not send out a notice as well. But I will convene my co-secretaries for 4.30 at the R.S.M. on Monday 30th June. I will call at 1 Wimpole St. tomorrow to book a room. Should there be any difficulty about it I will send you a wire. I conclude that you propose to get through all the business at one meeting. It may have to be rather a long one.

[Still another:] There is a growing feeling amongst us that we are not doing enough as a Section in the way of entertainment. Other Sections are making rather elaborate preparations. It is suggested that we should have a Council Meeting early in July to consider the question, and incidentally it will give the executive an opportunity of telling the Council what is being done. I shall be glad to know one or two dates convenient to you for this meeting.

[And more urgent:] I communicated your reply about F——'s [a German contributor's] paper to Herringham. He writes to say that he thinks we do not quite appreciate the position, which is this: 1. the matter is urgent. 2. conciliatory letters have already passed. 3. F—— says that he will not give an independent communication to any one section, and will only give it to a combination of the three sections—Neurology, Psychiatry & Medicine. Herringham is anxious to know as soon as possible if we agree to a joint meeting of the three sections, one of the afternoons, as F—— would like an answer by the end of the month. I do not know the man or his work sufficiently to express an opinion whether it would pay us to sacrifice one fifth of our independent communications to hear him...

Naturally there were innumerable questions which needed prompt and definite decisions, and that Osler did not waste much ink in his replies is evident from the answer to this last inquiry:

Dear Pasteur, I think such a thing is out of the question—to have a joint session of three sections for one man! He must be a megalocephalic crank! Sincerely yours.

Meanwhile he was having other responsibilities. The Prince of Wales, who appeared to be a delicately built boy, had taken up residence at Magdalen the preceding October, with directions that he should be put under the care of the Regius Professor of Medicine. Soon after his return to Oxford Osler was called in, for during his absence the Prince had had an attack of influenza; and he has left in his account-book notes of this and all subsequent visits. The silver inkstand from a grateful patient some time later makes it seem probable, taken with other indications, that his advice was acceptable; and the two appear to have understood each other from the first.

On June 16th, evidently in reply to some queries regarding the Yale Medical School, he writes to Mr. Stokes expressing the conviction that should the proper steps be taken Yale might do what Jena, Heidelberg, and other German universities had done—have a medical school as good as the best; and he proceeds to outline clearly what the situation needed, giving advice which has borne good fruit. And in a letter of the same date to the Yale Press he says: 'I am delighted with the paper & page which will make a splendid book. Send me the proofs please in galley form as there will be a good many things to add here & there.' Too many things, be it said, for him ever to complete. 'I have been much tied up with the exams—only just free, & half dead', he writes on June 24th to A. G. Little; but he nevertheless engages himself (for the proofs of the Silliman lectures have not yet come to warn him of his rashness) to write one of the essays for the memorial volume to be published as a feature of the Roger Bacon Commemoration projected for the next year.[1] Appeals of this sort were impossible for him to refuse, and he soon accepts, saying:

Dear Little,—Yes, I could have the article ready by next February. I have your MSS. and could send them whenever you wish. When I have a little leisure I would like to go over them carefully. Allbutt would write a good article, but I do not know that it would be necessary to have more than one person dealing with the medical side. He could do it well—probably better than I can. I understood that mine was to be in the form of a lecture, for which Bacon's position in the history of medicine would be very suitable. Later I would like to see the prologue of the d.R.S. [De retardanda senectute.] It might be well to have a meeting of the Committee.

This proved an idle promise. He little realized how his engagements were piling up. One of them had to be met at this juncture, for at the instigation of Sir Henry Burdett he had been elected President of the British Hospitals Association, an organization of hospital administrators who held their annual conference this year in Oxford on June 27th. In his address before this conference, after stating that the country at large might congratulate itself on having an admirable hospital system, he went on to say, with the National Health Insurance Act in mind: 'Do not be over-anxious that you have fallen upon troublesome days; that, as managers, you are full of worries—it is good for you, and I hope that your worries may be increased by what I am going to tell you this morning. It is well to be thoroughly chastened when the rod is upon you!' He proceeded to enumerate the four points he wished particularly to dwell upon—that they must give up the voluntary system; that they must provide laboratories; that there should be a physician in charge who is not engaged in general practice; that the county hospitals should be used for post-graduate instruction. It was the sort of sermon Osler could drive home fearlessly and effectively; and his telling and picturesque phrases, evidently spoken impromptu,[2] are reminiscent of his manner

[1] A large international committee had been organized, with an executive committee of twelve, of which Osler and Mr. Little were both members.

[2] Subsequently published from stenographers' notes; *The Hospital*, London, July 5, 1913, liv. 411.

of addressing Lady Aberdeen's people in Dublin. His theme savours of the present-day agitation for hospital standardization: for example, in emphasizing his second point, he said:

> Excellent as are the general hospitals of this country in regard to the care of the patient, the nursing and the general arrangements—always clean, always tidy, always looking well—when I go to a general hospital I am usually asked to see the wards and the kitchens. I say 'No, I do not want to see them, they could not look better here than they did in the last place I visited; show me your clinical laboratory; show me your pathological laboratory.' And then the manager has an engagement. He says, 'Will you kindly show him that room in the basement?'—and he goes away with a blush that leaves a radiance. And that is what I would emphasize before this Association. You may just as well know the truth, and it is this—that so far as your clinical and pathological laboratories in the county hospitals are concerned, I will not say that they are out of date, because they never were in date, but I say they are shockingly behind the times. You may as well know the truth, and you have got to reform it; you have got to change it. You have got to rearrange your ideas because many of you are ignorant on this question. . . .

There was much more of this, and in an enthusiastic editorial, Sir Henry Burdett agreed with all he had said and spoke as hopefully as he could in regard to the deep-rooted conservatism which enfolds the English hospital system. But it is noteworthy that in the reports of the meeting the association was said to have been especially interested 'in the new wing of the Radcliffe Infirmary which will give the institution the most complete clinical and pathological laboratories yet attached to a county hospital in this country—a development to be traced no doubt to the influence of the Regius Professor of Medicine': all due, as has been learned, to a certain specified contribution to the Oxford Endowment Fund.

On July 7th he writes to Dr. Klebs: 'I have been swamped with work for the past two weeks—so many meetings, & the Congress details. Are you coming on for it? If so do save the evening of August 6th for my dinner to the foreign members of my Section at the Royal Automobile Club. I will get you to help me with the seating as you know a good many of the men [&c.]'; and to

Jacobs two weeks later: 'We have taken rooms at Brown's and hope to have the Müllers, Sudhoff, and others with us. I wish I could join you at a game of golf. I have had no time for months.'

Though the rumble of that vast undertaking, the Congress, had by this time come to obliterate most other sounds, one may, while awaiting its arrival, stop to mention two comparatively small happenings—a sad and a pleasant one. There is a bound essay in Osler's library by Francis Gotch entitled 'Two Oxford Physiologists', in which on July 19th Osler has written: 'We buried poor Gotch today—a good colleague & a good friend'; and there follows an account of his long illness, during which Osler had cared for him. And in relief the pleasant happening may be recorded—the arrival from Persia of a rare manuscript on which was written, 'Copied in the year A. H. 761 (1360) by one who carries back his ancestors to a man who studied directly under Avicenna himself in Hamadan the last home of the great Philosopher. Presented to Sir W. Osler to whose sound teachings the profession all the world over owes so much, by M. Sa'eed, July 1913.'

To Dr. M. Sa'eed from W. O. 13 Norham Gardens,
August 1st.

Dear Dr. Sa'eed,—It is exceedingly kind in you to send me that beautiful Avicenna manuscript [the 'Ishârât']. I have just shown it to Mr. Cowley at the Bodleian who is delighted with it, and says it is in an unusually good state of preservation. Let me know please, at any time, of others that may be offered for sale, and I would particularly like a manuscript of Avicenna's poems. Mr. Cowley tells me that he thinks modern volumes of his poems have been issued. I would like very much if you could have someone take a good photograph of the tomb of Avicenna, and send me a memorandum of the cost. I am interested also in Rhazes. How long shall you be staying in Hamadan? I should like to send you a copy of the new edition of my Text-book (1912).

The XVIIth International Congress, likely to be the last of those unwieldy periodical gatherings of medical men from all over the world, was held in London from Wednesday, August 6th, to Tuesday the 12th, under the presidency of Sir Thomas Barlow. Thirty-two years before, in 1881, another of these great congresses had been held in

London, which Palmer Howard of McGill and his protégé William Osler had attended, and which was graced by 'the presence of the Prince of Wales and the Crown Prince of Prussia'. Both were now in their graves, and so also were all the great figures that made notable a congress at which Pasteur and Bastian had tilted over spontaneous generation, and at which Huxley, Lister, Virchow, and Koch had all spoken. Comparable to these, there were no outstanding figures at this second London congress, whose transactions, comprising a staggering list of subjects, may be said to have been based almost entirely on the further development of the researches of those giants. There was one exception perhaps, the most picturesque figure of the congress, a German from Frankfort, Paul Ehrlich, the discoverer of salvarsan, whose brilliant career was to end just two years later, and after only twelve months of war, believing to the end that his Kaiser was an upholder of peace.

Into the whirlpool of huge assemblages of this sort are always drawn other gatherings which have no official connexion with the main body. Thus there met at the Royal College of Surgeons, on the day before the great congress opened, the International Association of Medical Museums, an organization which had received Osler's warm support and whose existence was largely due to the enthusiasm of Dr. Maude Abbott of McGill. Professor A. S. Warthin, of Ann Arbor, Michigan, presided; and Osler, prefacing his remarks by a warm tribute to the late Sir Jonathan Hutchinson, 'at whose wonderfully popular museum at Haslemere the results produced by the classification of well-chosen material along any line might be seen', went on to speak in favour of an international association of workers along similar lines. He took the trouble, moreover, to write to Strathcona, telling him about the work at the McGill Museum and of the proposed association, and, as a result, ere long, was able to forward to Dr. Abbott a cheque for £1,000 in support of her most worthy project.

It was a brilliant and memorable scene when, on the morning of August 6th, in the Albert Hall, packed to the doors and ceiling, Prince Arthur of Connaught, speaking for the King, formally opened the congress. He was followed by Sir Edward Grey, who spoke for the Government; and then came addresses from twenty-five or more official delegates from several countries, picturesque in uniform or academic gown. If nothing more, it showed what a vast labour of organization in providing for 7,000 participants had been put on the shoulders of practically one man, Dr. Wilmot P. Herringham. The whole congress, indeed, was on such a scale as to make any subsequent attempt to rival it appear hopeless. Indeed, Professor von Müller, who, with his wife and daughter, was among Osler's special guests at Brown's, and who was chosen President of the succeeding congress (which, but for a cataclysm unforeseen, would have been held in Munich in 1917) expressed himself despairingly in regard to the possibility of competing with it. That things were going well is evident from a card scribbled in the course of the week to H. B. Jacobs:

> I send you the Congress medal—not Gallic! but the Lister is good. Such a time as we are having. Great success. I had 196 men of my section at dinner at the R. A. C. [Royal Automobile Club] on Wednesday [i.e. August 6th] & we are seeing a host of your old friends here. Section work A.1. Yours in haste, W. O.

The British can hardly be outdone in bountiful hospitality, and what was probably being duplicated in countless other places went on at Brown's Hotel, where, during the ten days, in a large sitting-room two round tables seating eighteen people were filled to overflowing twice a day—for both luncheon and dinner. Nor was this all, for at tea people came uncounted. Among them one afternoon was the 'Uncle Ned' of the Brewster letters, who in one of the most charming of journals [1] describes his few contacts with the person he therein calls 'Sir Richard Holter':

> I found Sir Richard, and his wife too, and his niece from North America as well, all at the end of a week full of a prodigious discourse on matters medical and a vast entertainment of the visiting doctors, but with life and hospitality still left in them. They gave me tea, and as much assurance of interest at my coming as though they had not had innumerable doctors to dinner the night before; and they invited Jane and me to dine with them on Sunday night when they would be back from the country.

---

[1] E. S. Martin's 'Abroad with Jane.' N. Y., Charles Scribner's Sons, 1914.

And on the Sunday night, at Brown's:

We dined with the Holters, in luxury and pride as it turned out, at the commodious, domesticated London tavern there they had established themselves in apartments suitable for the entertainment of all the doctors. They gave us meat and drink and friendship and hospitable discourse. Sir Richard questioned us about our intentions and revolved them in his helpful mind. They included a progress through Holland and Belgium. 'Do you like legs?' he asked me. I told him 'Yes, of course.' 'Then you should take a look at Ostend. Don't forget it.' So I fixed Ostend in my mind as an improving place, recommended by a physician, not to be overlooked, but all this, of course, is confidential.

And, in order to introduce the successor of Mr. Whitelaw Reid, this journal for a moment may be continued to Monday:

At the American Embassy at half-past one I found the Ambassador, and discussed with him the state and prospects of our country at the time I parted from it; the state, prospects, inhabitants, habits and climate of Great Britain; and the expediency of having the Rockefeller hook-worm movement brought to the attention of the doctors at their closing session that evening. Then the Ambassador, who is not yet a proud man (except perhaps in the season), walked along with me, expounding his satisfaction in getting back since the first of August to informal clothes and hats, remarking, as we passed Buckingham Palace, on the politeness of the sentries in saluting his automobile (which bears the arms of the United States) when he rode by in it, and their consideration in letting him pass unobserved when he went afoot. But, after all, I suppose their consideration is due to his neglect to wear our national cockade on his hat.

But this is getting away from an occasion in which Mr. Page does not properly figure—the Congress. In the course of its proceedings Ehrlich gave a memorable address on chemotherapy, and another was given on the last day by the Rt. Hon. John Burns of the Local Government Board, who spoke on the national health, and incidentally, as a labouring-man, on the wastefulness of armaments; though this is not the reason why he was being heckled by a scattering of suffragettes who one by one were bodily extracted from the assembly by some stalwart 'bobbies'. But, like all other gatherings of the sort, the congress was chiefly interesting on its social side. There were magnificent dinners—one of 500 guests at the Hotel Cecil given by the

Government, and at which John Morley, Lord President of the Council, presided—and another at the Savoy, given by the President of the Congress. There were conversaziones at the South Kensington Museum, and by the Corporation of London at the Guildhall. There were receptions at Windsor Castle, at Lambeth Palace, at Strawberry Hill, and at all the London hospitals. On Sunday there were excursions to Oxford, to Cambridge, and on the river, and, for the more pious who remained, a special service at St. Paul's and another at the Abbey. But perhaps the most picturesque of all the entertainments was the evening fête on August 11th given by Lord and Lady Strathcona in the Botanical Gardens at Regent's Park, which were decorated like a fairyland by Japanese lanterns pendent from long bamboo poles, and where there was music from the Royal Artillery band, and where the pipers of the Scots Guard played, and a folk-song quartette provided entertainment. There a wonderful old man just approaching his ninety-third year stood under a marquee at the head of the receiving line, prepared to shake hands with approximately 5,000 people who approached in a sinuous queue without apparent end, until Osler in desperation, after this had gone on for more than an hour, entered into a conspiracy with his wife, who sent word to their host that she wished to speak with him. So chairs were brought, and during the process of his extracting from her a promise that they would visit him at Glencoe later in the summer, the endless queue was broken and diverted to the supper tent.

The transactions of no other medical congress had been so thoroughly reported in the lay press ; and as an aftermath not only the newspapers but the Government, in consequence of Ehrlich's address, calling a spade a spade, faced for the first time the open discussion of venereal diseases, with the result that a Royal Commission was appointed to consider this great national menace. Another aftermath was a letter in *The Times* of August 13th in which Sir Henry Morris expostulated against some statements expressed by speakers at the congress concerning the development leading towards whole-time professional services in hospitals and medical schools. Osler promptly took up the gauntlet, and from the

Athenaeum that night sent the following letter to the Editor in reply:

Sir,—Sir Henry Morris's opinion carries the weight of his distinguished position and long experience as a teacher, but I am afraid he does not realize the changed and changing conditions—certainly in medicine—or he would not speak of the head of a modern clinic as a 'Jack-of-all-trades'. Let him visit Krehl at Heidelberg, Kraus or His at Berlin, von Müller at Munich or, should he prefer a surgical clinic, that of the Mayo brothers at Rochester, Minnesota, and he will understand what organization under a 'Jack-of-all-trades' means. In the rearrangements of London University it is very important to have the active co-operation of such men as Sir Henry Morris; and of this I am sure—that a visit of a week or two to any one of the clinics I have mentioned would make of him a strong convert to the scheme suggested by the Royal Commission, so far as the hospital work is concerned.

That night the Oslers left for Scotland with some friends, to escape for a few weeks from 'the world and his wife'. They went first to the Culag Hotel, Lochinver, an old shooting-lodge of the Sutherlands, where with a delightful company was found peace for themselves and abundant fishing for Revere. From there a week later he wrote to L. L. Mackall:

We have had a deuce of a business with this congress & only just escaped alive. This is a delightful spot—sea & moor & loch. We loaf & read while Revere fishes all day. He will be charmed with the Walton facsimile. I cannot say yet about my German trip. I am doubtful on account of the death of our Professor of Physiology & I am chairman of the Board of Electors. It may be impossible to leave.[1]

But there was no escaping from *The Times*[2] even in

[1] Charles S. Sherrington was appointed to the Waynflete chair to succeed Professor Gotch on November 7, 1913.

[2] The issues of August 14th, 15th, and 16th contained a series of two-column articles by Sir Henry Morris, entitled 'The Training of Doctors', and the articles probably voiced what others felt. The last one of them ends with this question: 'Why should an attempt be made to thrust on the University of London such a series of recommendations as those concerning its Faculty of Medicine—a set of ornamental cast-iron professors in a miniature faculty, figuratively feeding a few students in a sort of doll's-house "Constituent College" with fertilizing ideas, forming a section of an ideally perfect university with German foundations and a Maryland crest, and flying the Banner of the Great Ideal? Why should it?' A succession of letters by others in similar vein appeared in subsequent issues, one of which in the issue of August 23rd upheld the training of the so-called 'practical' doctor.

this 'delightful spot', and that Osler was still in a combative mood regarding the 'training of doctors' is evident from the following letter on Culag Hotel paper which he preserved but evidently thought better of forwarding. It said:

I have waited for a teacher more familiar with London students to protest against the Philistinism of Mr. C-G. whose letter appeared in your issue of August 23rd. As the London hospitals train our students, Oxford & Cambridge teachers have a direct interest in the problems of medical education in the metropolis. From my point of view there is only one intellectual infection of any permanent value to the medical student—the scientific spirit, & outlook, & attitude of mind, which he gets, often unconsciously, from his teachers and fellows. If good, it leavens his life's work. That he may be steeped in it and be at the same time thoroughly practical is the experience of scores of teachers & of scores of pupils, of men of the type of Bowman & Paget. The practical man [whom Mr. C-G. had lauded] was well defined by a general practitioner in my company a few moments ago as one who never learns anything after leaving his hospital. I should be precious sorry to have any student in whom I was interested come under the influence of a man who in these days could say that 'scientific education may be excellent as an ideal but I doubt if it materially assists the average practitioner in the treatment of disease'. Mr. G. represents a type—the men who jeered at Harvey, scoffed at Pasteur & scorned Lister—the carpenters in surgery and the pill-mongers in medicine, without vision beyond the bench or the counter. The tragedy is that the type persists.

His outing was evidently doing him good, and on August 25th he wrote to Weir Mitchell:

We are having a delightful rest in this lovely spot. I loaf & walk & we usually join Revere for lunch or tea at one of the lochs. The season has been so dry that both the salmon rivers are too low for fishing but the trout are fairly numerous. We go to Glencoe next week with the Strathconas & then home, I hope in time to see Welch. I wrote last week about the Congress. My section was excellent, a great many good papers, and the foreigners were well represented. Chauffard, & Vaquez of Paris, Kraus & His of Berlin & Müller of Munich were the stars. . . . Brunton kept up well, but he looks aged. You know he has a serious heart trouble, which limits his activities. Bridges lives near Oxford but a letter to Yattendon should reach him as his mother-in-law lives there. His appointment has given great satisfaction. We have just published at the Press a collected edition of his poems. I will have a copy sent to you. . . . I have been studying the earliest printed medical books to 1480 to get a picture of the professional mind of the period. I have traced about 140 & have photographs of the more important. All are 13th century, Arabic, Salernian, or contemporary. The Greeks had not come to their own—only the aphorisms of Hippocrates & one small tractate of Galen! I shall make it my presidential address at the Bibliographical Society. Our historical section of the Royal Society of Medicine is doing well. Jastrow is coming over to lecture on Babylonian Medicine. . . .

So from Lochinver to Inverness, down the Caledonian Canal to Ballachulish, and from there by motor into the awe-inspiring solemnity of Glencoe—' the glen of weeping ' where once Ian Macdonald lorded it over the country and where, as Macaulay tells us, was perpetrated the atrocious massacre by royal troops of the unsuspecting and hospitable Macdonalds; and where to-day, as in 1692, the view from Mount Royal, Strathcona's residence, is said to be the most gorgeous from any human habitation. But though they found a house-party, and though Revere had fishing to his heart's content, the Laird, their host, was away; for Strathcona, on learning that Lord Haldane was going to Montreal to address the American Bar Association, promptly decided that the High Commissioner of Canada, in spite of his ninety-three years of age, should be there to greet a Lord Chancellor of England. Accordingly he cabled to have his Montreal residence opened, took passage on the *Lusitania* early in August, kept open house for five sweltering days in Montreal, and having done his duty returned on the same ship, reaching Glencoe, however, too late to see this particular group of guests.

There followed a peaceful few weeks at home for the Oslers before term began—the only really peaceful time they could look forward to, when Oxford was comparatively empty and when every afternoon he and Revere could jump the fence and go down for a swim and frolic in the pool at ' Parson's Pleasure '. But even during September there were visitors. Among them was Mrs. Brewster's ' Uncle Ned ', who gives this account of his pilgrimage: [1]

. . . But, as I said, people are apt to have erroneous ideas about

[1] ' Abroad with Jane ', p. 111.

what they are really doing and to lose sight of the end in the ardour of their attention to the process. There was Sir Richard Holter, whom Jane and I visited over Sunday at Oxford. I would not dare assume that Sir Richard has delusions about anything, but whatever he thinks, he gives out that he is a professor in Oxford University. Well, he is; but his great line is the direction of human life. I went about with him for a day and a half, and wherever he went he was always directing human life, and wherever he touched it it seemed to go lighter and more blithely.

It was not term-time when we were in Oxford and the studious youths were not there, but a dirigible war balloon dropped in about the time we did, and camped on a college common [the University Parks] over Sunday, and that filled up the place a little. I was glad to see a dirigible, though it seemed a mighty modern bird to be resting in the grounds of Oxford University. Sir Richard showed me the Bodleian, and its new and admirable device for storing books. It had too many—all the great libraries have too many—and instead of crowding in an enormous library to contain them, it dug out a large hole under a venerable building nearby, put stacks in it, connected it by a suitable passage, and there they can have a million books or so, available, harmless, and inoffensive to the landscape.

Next day he took us to church in Christ Church Cathedral, a duodecimo cathedral but very worshipful, and afterwards showed us many things—rooms, halls, chapels, windows, more libraries and the like, venerable and edifying. And after lunch, with one of the kind ladies of his family he motored us twelve or fourteen miles over to Ewelme, where about five hundred years ago, when our forebears were still inhabitants and part owners of England, the Earl and Countess of Suffolk founded a 'hospital' for the care of a dozen or two old people, and built a church beside it. There it all is as they left it, and the Countess's effigy, very handsome and perfect, on her tomb in the church. Sir Richard directs the life of the hospital *ex officio* as one of the details of his Oxford occupation. The Earl of Suffolk is not buried there. He got into politics and his body was not recovered.

And among other pilgrims to 13 Norham Gardens who appeared at this time was a foreign-looking physician, Dr. M. Sa'eed, who bore under his arm an illuminated MS. of the Canon of Avicenna, wrapped in a Persian shawl almost as old, together with two other books without which, as he said, he never moved—his Bible, and Osler's 'Practice of Medicine'; and it is certain that all the Arabic MSS. in the Bodleian were got out for inspection and there was much talk about Avicenna and the plan to get his dilapidated tomb repaired.[1]

On his return from Scotland Osler had found the galley proof of his first Silliman Lecture awaiting him and wrote to the Yale Press to send the others, saying: 'Please yourself about the bindings. Send me a dummy. We shall be able to have the book out by Christmas.' And on September 30th to Anson Phelps Stokes: 'I will get on with the lectures at once. There have been shocking delays but I do not think it will do the book any harm.' But even in this state of mind he did not hesitate to promise himself for still another task, and accordingly wrote to Dr. J. C. Comrie, the lecturer on the History of Medicine in the University of Edinburgh, who was proposing to edit a series of medical biographies:

I think I could take the Sydenham & the Boerhaave. Streeter might be willing to do the sixteenth-century Anatomists as he knows Vesal so well. W. G. MacCallum of Columbia could do Malpighi; Power, Harvey; Paget for Paré—unless you wish new men for these two—Mediaeval Medicine, Norman Moore. I don't know whom to suggest for Greeks & Arabians. Save Browne of Cambridge, I don't believe we have an Arabian scholar in the profession—it is time we tried to breed one. I am delighted to hear that the post-graduate course has been so successful.

'It is time we tried to breed one'—the feeling there expressed may in a measure explain this note written by Professor Morris Jastrow of the University of Pennsylvania, who says:

I owe much to his encouragement. When he heard that I was

[1] Osler's efforts to get governmental authorization to repair Avicenna's tomb in Hamadan would make a long story. He had prepared a sheaf of letters on the subject, with Dr. Sa'eed, Dr. J. Arthur Funk, Mr. A. R. Neligan of the British Legation, Professor E. G. Browne the Persian scholar, Sir George Birdwood, and others. Osler attempted to arouse the interest of the profession by letters to the journals; by getting Dr. Sa'eed, on another visit to England, to speak at the Historical Section on the subject; by arousing the interest of the Persian Society; and even the war and its aftermath did not cause him to leave off. Meanwhile Avicenna's tomb continues to disintegrate. Of it Dr. Sa'eed wrote at this time: 'The date of 1294 A.H. at the top is the date of renewing the place by the daughter of the Shah. The dome also was built by the Princess but is decaying and needs attention. Inside it is black with the smoke of wood opium and Hashish used by the Dervishes who take shelter there.'

interested in Babylonian-Assyrian medicine, he invited me to open a course of lectures on the History of Medicine at the Royal Society of Medicine in London. That was in October, 1913. I stayed with Sir D'Arcy Power and spent the week-end at Sir William's. Before my departure for home, he gathered a most distinguished and interesting company of scholars: Orientalists, physicians and others, to meet me at a dinner at the Athenaeum Club; while at the meeting of the society at which I read my paper, he had a most remarkable group of physicians and other scholars from London, Oxford, Cambridge, etc. This, of course, is merely one of a thousand such things that he was doing constantly. It was as though he wanted to ensure the continuity of research by encouraging the next generation to go on—in every field. '*Nihil humani ab illo alienum erat*' can be said of him in a sense that applies to few others.

At the opening of the winter session at St. George's Hospital on October 1st, Osler gave an introductory address on 'Examinations, Examiners and Examinees'. It was a vigorous appeal for reform—be it said, by a man who as an examiner notoriously favoured the victims of the tests. Soon after coming to England he had been asked to examine in Cambridge, which he enjoyed, as it gave him the pleasure of a semi-annual sojourn with the Allbutts, until conflicting duties obliged him to resign. According to his brother Regius, 'he leaned generally to the indulgent side, but never in any disproportion to the whole issue'. It is said that the Oxford examiners, who always stayed at 13 Norham Gardens during the June and December examination-week, were likely to hear him remark, after they had lunched the last day and were to pass on the books, 'There 's just one thing to remember—be lenient!' His attitude, needless to say, met with strong opposition from those entrenched in the old system of examinations which, like the French *concours*, kept men during their best years continually meeting tests on subjects they had long left behind. Certainly something was wrong with a system of accumulated examinations which in the case at least of one of the examining bodies could reject sixty-nine per cent. of the candidates.

Difficult as the examiner's job might be, it was the examinee who had Osler's chief sympathy. This he made clear in his address. To put a quart measure in a pint pot

THE REGIUS AND THE UNDERGRADUATE

From a snapshot taken in 1913

was impossible—infinitely more kind to stop a student in his career than to allow him painfully to struggle on and submit to the humiliations of successive rejections.

The conclusion of the matter is [he said], the student needs more time for quiet study, fewer classes, fewer lectures, and, above all, the incubus of examinations should be lifted from his soul. To replace the Chinese by the Greek spirit would enable him to seek knowledge for itself, without a thought of the end, tested and taught day by day, the pupil and teacher working together on the same lines, only one a little ahead of the other. This is the ideal towards which we should move. The pity of it all is that we should have made an intolerable burden of the study of one of the most attractive of the professions, but the reform is in our own hands and should not be far off. A paragraph in an address of the late Dr. Stokes contains the pith of my remarks: 'Let us emancipate the student, and give him time and opportunity for the cultivation of his mind, so that in his pupilage he shall not be a puppet in the hands of others, but rather a self-relying and reflecting being.'

That Osler nevertheless was an admirable examiner there is abundant testimony not only from the victims of the system, whose general intelligence interested him more than their cubby-holed store of knowledge, but also from examiners themselves, though to many of them his informal methods were caviare. Professor J. A. Stewart writes:

The John Locke Scholarship was founded by the late Henry Wilde, F.R.S., for 'the promotion of the study of Mental Philosophy among the junior members of the University of Oxford'. . . . The examiners and electors are (1) the Regius Professor of Medicine, (2) the Waynflete Professor of Moral and Metaphysical Philosophy, (3) the Wykeham Professor of Logic, (4) White's Professor of Moral Philosophy (throughout the whole of Dr. Osler's tenure, the writer of this memorandum), (5) the Wilde Reader of Mental Philosophy. 'Each of these officers, if he think fit, may appoint some other person of the Degree of Master of Arts at least, and approved by the Vice-Chancellor, to act in his place.' Dr. Osler occasionally appointed some one so to act, but, as a rule, he examined himself. He evidently enjoyed the opportunity thus given him of coming into direct touch with the humanistic side of Oxford work—indeed, it was as a humanist, even more than as a man of science, that he seemed to me to contribute to the efficiency of the Board of Examiners. Among the papers set in the examination—(1) Essay, (2) Philosophical Questions, (3) Logic, (4) Mental Science (general), and (5) Mental Science (special), with History of Philosophy as an alternative paper—the two Mental Science papers (general and special), of course always contained questions involving knowledge of physiological principles on which, as a man of science, Dr. Osler spoke with authority; but what I remember best is the value which I learned to attach to his judgement on candidates' answers to questions belonging to moral and political philosophy (questions about which he amused us by protesting, year after year, that he knew nothing at all!)—and especially to his judgement on the Essay, perhaps the most important part of the whole examination. Here his keen eye for native ability, and for the style in which it expresses itself, was one of the most valuable assets which the Board of Examiners possessed during the period of his membership.

So examinations might not always be simply a chore to be got over with. Enjoyment might be got out of them—even fun; and he was not infrequently guilty of composing fictitious ones. The following, for example, was sent to two young ladies known to the 'Open Arms', who were studying in Oxford:

ST. THELEMA: English Literature: Honour Paper

I. In the poem beginning 'I sing the progress of a deathless soul' justify the author on Evolutionary views for starting its progress in an apple.

II. How far did Democritus Junior draw upon Democritus Senior for the foundations of his immortal book?

III. Trace the influence of the life of Thomas Hobson on John Milton.

IV. Write, and justify, an imaginary love letter from Damaris Cudworth [1] to John Locke.

V. Write a bibliographical essay on the vicissitudes of 'Queen Mab'.

VI. Sketch the life of Rose Aylmer and explain physiologically how Charles Lamb was able to live for weeks on Landor's verses to her.

EGERTON YORRICK DAVIS,
Senior Examiner.

It will be recalled that during one of Osler's summers spent at 'The Glades' he had made friends with a number of Bostonians whom he found companionable. One of

[1] Damaris (Lady Masham) was the daughter of Ralph Cudworth, one-time Master of Christ's College, Cambridge. Osler had become interested in the legend of her attachment to John Locke, and had a water-colour painted showing the two sitting together under Milton's mulberry tree in the Master's garden at Christ's.

them was staying at 13 Norham Gardens at this time while giving a course of university lectures; and this accounts for a characteristic epistle which appeared shortly in the New York *Nation*, entitled 'Charles Francis Adams at Oxford'. It reads in part as follows:

Oxford, November 4th.

The University did herself great honour to-day when she enrolled this distinguished American among her graduates. There are several occasions when honorary degrees are conferred—at the Encaenia, or Commencement, in June; at one of the many degree days during the term; at special gatherings or congresses, such as the British Association, or at any one of the weekly meetings of Convocation during term. The preliminary procedure is slow, taking four or five weeks. The name is first proposed to the Hebdomadal Council, the next week the case is stated, the following week the voting takes place, and in the next *Gazette* an announcement is made under University Agenda. . . .

Oxford University is governed by a democracy of doctors and masters who week by week meet in Convocation and Congregation and pass upon the business prepared by a group of eighteen men, who with the Vice-Chancellor and proctors, make up the Hebdomadal Council. A degree may be conferred in one of three places, the Divinity School, the most beautiful room in Oxford, dating from the fifteenth century; the Convocation House; or in the famous Sheldonian Theatre. By a piece of good luck there was a contentious meeting to-day, so that Convocation had to meet in the theatre. Robed in a scarlet gown with grey trimming, Mr. Adams was first escorted by the Regius Professor of History to the Divinity School to await the decision of Convocation. At two o'clock sharp the Vice-Chancellor, Dr. Strong, escorted by the four bedells, entered a fairly well filled theatre, the senior bedell saying: '*Intretis in Congregationem Magistri, intretis*.' Taking his seat, the Vice-Chancellor declares '*causa hujus convocationis est, etc*.', and immediately proceeds to the first business in hand, on this occasion the reading of the proposal to confer the degree; and asking in the old phrase, '*Placetne vobis Domini Doctores, placetne vobis Magistri?*' Unless the question is doubtful one rarely hears a '*placet*' or a '*non placet*'; and as no objection was raised the bedells went for the candidate and escorted him to the steps leading to the Vice-Chancellor's seat. It was a glorious day, and the sun, streaming through the window of Wren's majestic building, lit up a memorable scene, the centre of which was the alert, vigorous-looking old veteran, an historical representative of all that is best in American life, to whom the mother of English universities paid homage.

As the public orator, Mr. Godley, had not returned from Princeton, his deputy, Mr. Powell, Fellow of St. John's College, made the presentation in the following Latin speech, many passages of which called forth hearty applause . . .

And after giving a translation of Mr. Powell's complimentary and stirring words in presenting Mr. Adams, 'an American citizen, for admission to the Degree of Doctor in Letters, for Merit', Osler concluded his account as follows:

By an interesting coincidence, Mr. Adams's lectures appeared from the Oxford Press this week. A most unfortunate date was chosen for their delivery—Eights Week, devoted to the boat races, when a Gibbon or a Mommsen would not have drawn good audiences. It is to be hoped in future that the October term may be selected for these lectures on American History. The value of the volume, so it seems to me, is the presentation of the subject, 'Transatlantic Historical Solidarity', by an active participant in a great struggle. It is an inspiring volume for young men to read, and I trust the old veterans will rejoice in the splendid tribute which the distinguished lecturer paid to his old foe, Robert E. Lee, for whom he rightly claims admission 'among the world's great—one more American Immortal'.

In sending a 'bread-and-butter' letter after his return to Washington, Mr. Adams referred to this 'elaborate and kindly communication' as having given him 'what is commercially known as a "first-class send-off"'; and he added:

I was glad you accompanied your presentation of the speech in the original Latin with a translation, for I can only say that on the occasion referred to I found myself somewhat deluged by Latinity, and was almost painfully reminded of how rusty my Latin had become. Of this, by the way, I was still more forcibly reminded by a lapsus in my Oxford lectures, or in the language of Virgil: '*Infandum, Regina, jubes renovare dolorem*', which, translated, signifieth in this connection: 'Doctor, let me confide to you my unspeakable mortification.'

In the eyes of classical Oxford, I am no better than that eminent explorer, Dr. Cook, and stand convicted of the unpardonable. I have made not only a bit of bad Latinity, but a false quantity, two sins altogether unpardonable in the eyes of Oxford. If you will turn to page 154 of my lectures you will see to what I refer, in the line there quoted from Lucan.

Under the chairmanship of Mr. F. T. Gates, whose

interest had been aroused, as has been told, by the reading of Osler's Text-book, the General Education Board of the Rockefeller Foundation announced, this autumn of 1913, that the sum of a million-and-a-half dollars had been given to the Johns Hopkins Medical School 'for the purpose of so organizing the departments of medicine, surgery and paediatrics that the professors and their staffs might completely withdraw from private practice in order to devote their entire time to their respective departments'. Osler's position in this particular matter has been rather emphatically expressed in some earlier letters, and though he hedged a good deal about it subsequently, his own extramural activities had been of such a nature that he tended to sympathise with those who were opposed to the rigid Rockefeller programme, and would have offered a compromise. He wrote at this time a letter to the *British Medical Journal*, dated November 5th, in which he again expressed what he thought would be the dangers from what he termed 'a life of clinical and laboratory seclusion, though it is a great attraction and appeals to many men'. In this letter he speaks of the most gratifying feature of the endowment, namely, that it was to be associated with the name of William H. Welch, saying: 'No man of his generation in the United States has so deeply influenced the profession, not only by his administrative ability and his stimulating work in pathology, but much more by a personal, unselfish devotion to its highest interests.' He must have sent this communication to Welch before it was printed, for in the following issue of the same journal there is published a reply dated November 10th and signed 'W. H. W.', which fully answers Osler's apprehensions, and outlines the scheme which in later years has come to be adopted by a few of the London hospitals, whereby, adding unquestionably to their prestige, they have affiliated themselves with the University of London. What may have passed privately between these two men is not known, but Osler had had sufficient experience during fifteen years in Baltimore to appreciate that even if he and Welch might not entirely agree on some programme, Welch's plan at least was well worth trying.

However much he favoured the ‘ hospital unit ’ scheme, with a paid incumbent, he apparently did not wish entirely to debar the professor from a certain amount of private consultation work, feeling that what had been true in his own case would undoubtedly apply to others ; that it would not interfere with a teacher’s university work and would encourage him to keep more in touch with the profession as a whole. There was of course much to be said on both sides. In his own case, the friendly doctor-and-patient relation was a pleasure and stimulus—more cherished as a source of friendships than of income ; people came to him from most remote places. Thus in his day-book on November 29th, under the name of the two patients he saw in consultation on that day, he has written : ‘ Curious coincidence. These people knew each other well in Winnipeg ; both came over on purpose to see me and met on my doorstep 4000 miles away.’

That Osler missed no opportunity for campaigning in aid of the reform needed in medical education can be judged from his remarks at the annual dinner of Sheffield University earlier in November, on which occasion he was the guest of the university. From all accounts he made a stirring plea for the linking up of the universities and hospitals in order that medical science might be advanced. For the medical schools no less than the universities needed that ‘ subtle, imponderable element, a sort of educational radium, an emanation not easy to analyse, known as the university spirit ’. He paid a warm tribute to his friend Herbert Fisher, the new Vice-Chancellor, late of New College, Oxford, saying that he had three justifications for his office—mental eyes such as very few Vice-Chancellors had; a heart, which was so important for an institution dealing with the young ; and, lastly and most important, an ideal Mrs. Vice-Chancellor. Unfortunately he lacked one important qualification, and that was the element of dulness, which Fuller had declared was essential in the head of a college—but of course he was talking of Oxford and Cambridge. Mr. Fisher, who, three years later, was to become President of the Board of Education under the Coalition Cabinet of Mr. Lloyd George, writes as follows of Osler's relations to the education-reform movement in England:

Others will tell you, with more authority than I can command, of his services to medical education in England. Of course we, at the Board of Education, made the fullest drafts on his experience and enthusiasm, and many were the conversations we held together after I took up official work in London. One of Osler's great ideas was to create a scheme under which country practitioners might be given regular opportunities of keeping in touch with clinical work in the hospitals; another was the further development of the clinical unit system of teaching in our hospitals and university schools; a third was the great development of post-graduate education. It was not his business to think out practical details, and I should doubt whether his strength lay in administration, but as his mind was always alive and moving, and as he was never frightened by the size or novelty of a plan, his counsels at a time of active concern for educational progress, were always of value, even if it might prove impracticable to give effect to them in every particular. His remarkable evidence given before the Royal Commission on London University was specially important as helping a professional opinion in favour of the clinical unit system of teaching which he had himself perfected at Johns Hopkins, and is sufficient to give him an enduring importance in the history of English medical teaching. Until his death he was a distinguished member of the two committees which successfully advised the Board of Education and the Treasury in the distribution of State grants to the universities, and was thus brought into contact with all the medical work of an academic character which was proceeding in the country. In the end I doubt whether there were many men in Europe or America who had so good a synoptic view of the contemporary state of medical education in the world at large.

All this may in a measure account for his procrastination in revising the proofs of the Silliman Lectures. On the day after his return from Sheffield he wrote to Mr. Stokes, saying: 'A little more patience, please! Am at it now —hard, & you will soon have the proofs. Forgive the unpardonable delay & tell Mr. Day I am in sackcloth & ashes for my delinquencies.' But there were many things to interrupt him, as he admits in the following, written on November 21st to Weir Mitchell:

I have owed you a letter for some time. I have to thank you for the delightful story ['Westways'], which I read on a long journey into Shropshire. I liked it so much. The picture of the divided family is so good. Gettysburg too was fine. Lady Osler read it with special interest as both Dr. & Col. Revere lost their lives in that great battle. We have had Charles Francis Adams here. I am sending you his lectures on the war. He is a fine old veteran & in great form. At the Royal Automobile Club he astonished the members by taking every morning the high dive, about 14 feet, into the swimming pool; very few attempt it. We are very busy—so many people coming & going, & I have got mixed up with London affairs so that I am there two or three times a week. Lauder Brunton is better, but looks badly. Poor Gowers is a sad wreck. I go in & have a chat with him as often as possible. I hope you liked the Harvey portraits. Our Historical Society is a great success. Revere is home to-day, for what is called a 'leave out'. He is thriving but finds Latin & Greek not very easy. He has nice tastes & good hands. He is getting ready for the University. Your letter from the Hot Springs was full of marrow. I like such details about your work.

On December 4th he gave before the Abernethian Society at St. Bartholomew's Hospital his address on 'The Medical Clinic: a Retrospect and a Forecast'—an address from which many quotations of an autobiographical nature have previously been given. He began as follows:

Unrest and change are the order of the day, and it may be taken as a good sign that the medical profession is bestirring itself about many problems, one of the most important of which relates to the future of our medical schools. Those who have followed the discussions of the past few years will have noticed that two diametrically opposite opinions have been expressed. On the one hand, there is a group thoroughly satisfied with existing conditions—and with themselves—the teaching was never better, the students never more contented, and any change could not but be for the worse. On the other hand, there are those who say that the existing conditions in our large hospitals are inadequate to meet the modern needs of student and of staff, that the teaching is defective, that the rejections at the examinations are shockingly high, that there is inadequate provision for research, and that an entire change is needed in the organization of the clinical departments of our medical schools.

He went on to tell in retrospect the story of the organization of the medical clinic at the Johns Hopkins, of his own methods of conducting his classes there, of what, as he saw it, were the real functions of a medical clinic, and in his concluding paragraph ventured on this forecast:

I designedly took this subject for my address because the future is with you young men, who are certain to see within the next few years radical changes in the medical schools of this country. There are two important problems. Is it possible to organize in the English hospitals university clinics such as exist on the continent, and such as those which we had at the Johns Hopkins Hospital? There are difficulties, of course, but they are not insuperable, and once started, clinics of this type will be instituted in every school in the kingdom. Only let them be complete ; the chief in full control, responsible for the teaching, responsible for the work of his assistants, and let them be well equipped with all modern accessories for research. The other problem is more difficult. Shall the director of such a clinic devote his whole time to the work, or shall he be allowed to take consulting work? For the former many advantages may be claimed, though the plan has nowhere yet had a practical trial. The amount of work in a modern clinic is enormous, quite enough to take up the time and energies of any one man in conducting the teaching, treating the patients, and superintending the researches. Then it is attractive to think of a group of superclinicians, not bothered with the cares of consulting practice, and whose whole interests are in scientific work. It is claimed that as much good will follow the adoption of the plan of whole-time clinicians as has followed the whole-time physiologists and anatomists. Against it may be urged the danger of handing over students who are to be general practitioners to a group of teachers completely out of touch with the conditions under which these young men will have to live. The clinician should always be in the fighting line, and in close touch with the rank and file, with the men behind the guns, who are doing the real work of the profession. The question, too, is whether the best men could be secured ; whether academic and scientific distinctions would satisfy these men. Then for the hospital itself, would it be best to keep our best in clinical seclusion. Would there not be the danger of the evolution throughout the country of a set of clinical prigs, the boundary of whose horizon would be the laboratory, and whose only human interest would be research? I say frankly that I am not in favour of the whole-time clinical teacher. This is not surprising, as my life has been largely spent in association with my professional brethren, participating in the many interests we have had in common. At the same time let me freely confess that I mistrust my own judgement, as this is a problem for young men and for the future. I know how hard it is 'to serve God and mammon', to try to do one's duty as a teacher and to live up to the responsibility of a large department, and at the same time to meet the outside demands of your brethren and of the public. And if added to this you have an active interest in medical societies, and in the multifarious local and general problems, the breaking-point may be reached. I had had thirty-one years of uninterrupted hard work. William Pepper, my predecessor in

Philadelphia, died of angina at fifty-five; John Musser, my successor, of the same disease at fifty-three! After listening to my story you may wonder how it was possible to leave a place so gratifying to the ambitions of any clinical teacher: I had had a good innings and was glad to get away without a serious breakdown.

Seven years later, at the hospital where this address was given, the 'unit system' for one of the medical and one of the surgical services was put in operation—even to the feature of having 'whole-time' appointees, regarding which, as Osler says, he mistrusted his judgement. And had a four-year war not intervened, the experiment would probably have been made earlier. But with all this concerning medical education in the London Hospital schools, it must not be forgotten that there were Oxford obligations to be met, at the Infirmary, at the Press, and particularly at the Bodleian which he was to get to know thoroughly. The agenda papers of the curators' meetings were far less likely to have James Bovell's name scratched over them than had been those of the Hebdomadal Council whose sessions he had so faithfully attended some years before. But stated meetings were not the only things that took him to Bodley, where from chief to 'Bodley boys' all were enlivened by his visits. The appointment in 1882 of the former Librarian, E. W. B. Nicholson, marked the beginning of a period of reorganization, which transformed the somewhat old-fashioned institution into a working library on modern lines. There is evidence of his administrative ability in the small but amazingly detailed Staff-Kalendar, first published in 1902. After a prolonged period of failing health he had died on March 17, 1912.[1] His successor, Falconer Madan, with whom Osler came almost daily in contact, wrote the following letter on December 4th, which records another contribution to Bodley's history:

Dear Sir William,—I am very much obliged for your suggestion about a *Bodleian Quarterly Record*, to contain Notes and News. Up

---

[1] In Osler's copy of Macray's 'Annals of the Bodleian Library' (1868) he had inserted from time to time many letters and personal notes relating to Mr. Nicholson and his final illness during which he cared for him. The volume consequently has an historical value and Osler made special disposition of it (cf. foot-note, p. 250).

to the present I have been working to get the chief Accessions printed, and part of that plan is to allow us four extra quarto pages or so of Bodleian news. But I am bound to say that this plan drags heavily, even in view of the time approaching when we shall *have* to settle the gigantic question of printing our Catalogue. Now your timely suggestion may lead to a more modest but hardly less useful *beginning*. It is only too patent that we are much behind the times in not *printing* more about ourselves. There is very little in evidence to show outsiders that we are alive. The Annual Report is somewhat stately, and nothing approaching to liveliness can possibly be allowed in it. . . . Can you bring this before the Standing Committee tomorrow, and make some suggestion about ways and means? I do not forget that *you* first suggested the Bodley Memorial Service, the public opening of the Underground Bookstore, and the Exhibition of some of the Chinese books (now in a case in the Picture Gallery). I am, Sincerely yours, F. MADAN.

Thus were laid the plans of the 'B. Q. R.', of Osler's part in which there might otherwise be no record. Others who had spent their lives there might have known the library better, but certainly it never had a better publicity agent, for even an institution like the Bodleian needs to give evidence of progress and activity. But Osler's object was more than Madan's letter indicates, for better than any one else he probably knew and sympathized with the junior workers on the library staff, and unquestionably his chief reason for advocating the 'Quarterly' was to provide convenient pages for the publication of their occasional brief papers which would make them feel that they had some small voice at least in Bodley affairs.[1] As Mr. Madan wrote a few years later in the same periodical:[2] 'The

[1] This publication had an effect beyond the Bodleian itself, as is evident from the first item in the *Harvard Library Notes*, No. I, 1920, which reads: 'Sir William Osler should have whatever credit may come from the printing of these *Notes*. No one would have welcomed them more encouragingly than he, or have awaited future issues with keener interest. It was his guarantee of support that enabled Falconer Madan, who retired a year ago [1919] from the post of Bodley's Librarian at Oxford, to start the *Bodleian Quarterly Record*. Its first number was dated April 23, 1914, and Dr. Osler had much to do with keeping it going regularly during the distracting years that followed. These *Harvard Library Notes* are frankly modelled upon "B. Q. R.".'

[2] 'The Late Sir William Osler, Baronet, M.D.' *Bodleian Quarterly Record*, Jan. 1920, ii. 298.

Library was his [Osler's] admiration and delight, and as a curator and a member of the Standing Committee he had considerable influence on its administration. He promoted the establishment of the Room for Medical Students, as well as the Science Research Room at the Camera; and when a good opportunity for a special purchase presented itself he was among the first to offer liberal support, and to engage the interest of friends.' But what, after all, is more important comes later on when the writer speaks of his 'unmeasured friendliness and sympathy' as the larger feature of Osler's life: 'If he came to you as a friend, he had a way of drawing up his chair to yours, as though all his time were at your disposal, with looks and words of infinite compassion if you were in ill case, of helpful encouragement if you were striving against hindrances, and sympathetic comprehension if you were in doubt and difficulty. These qualities are akin to the divine.' And there were places beyond university circles where these same qualities akin to the divine were met with. One of them, to which Miss Price testifies, was the monthly meeting-ground of the Oxfordshire Branch of the Tuberculosis Association. At the annual meeting on December 17th, the President of the society spoke as follows:

The difference between what men hope for and what they get is often a source of worry and discontent, but yet in politics and in other aspects of life they generally get what they deserve, neither more nor less. A couple of years ago we hoped for great things in the way of tuberculosis organization in this city and county—a well equipped sanatorium on Shotover (for which we have the land), a hospital for advanced cases, a complete organization of dispensaries, a thorough co-operation of all the public health and voluntary associations; and it seemed an easy matter. This is not a large county, the city is not large, and their association with each other is extraordinarily close; the population is homogeneous, and the Radcliffe Infirmary is an exceptionally excellent medical centre. But here we are, still muddling, after having considered some half a dozen schemes, not one of which has driving power behind it to blend the scattered and sometimes antagonistic interests.

No army can enter upon a successful contest without a first-class general staff, and in this tuberculosis warfare the one thing lacking is a central organization with power, a body that will be able successfully to dictate terms to the local authorities, a general staff that will mature a plan of campaign and hand it over to the subsidiary commanders to carry out. As it is now, there is no organized scheme for the country at large, but a happy-go-lucky method, every county, every town, with its own. Is it too late here to hope that the City and the County may yet join forces? If there is not enough glue in the local pot to get them together, perhaps the Local Government Board may provide what is lacking.

One thing is certain, that an efficient scheme must include the insured and their dependants, uninsured, and Poor Law patients. The present status is as follows: there is neither sanatorium, nor hospital, but the Radcliffe continues to treat cases on the balconies. The association is continuing the work of the county, and, as the Report will show you, we have had a very successful year. I wish anyone interested would visit the Bath Court Dispensary at eleven o'clock on Wednesday or Saturday morning, or one of the local dispensaries scattered about the county. The educational value of the association has been enormous, very largely through the visits of the tuberculosis officer and of the nurses who have been untiring in their efforts and deserve our warmest thanks. We are only holding on until a scheme is matured. The association is at the command of the health authorities and of the public, but we are ready to hand over the work at a month's notice. Meanwhile it is gratifying to note the remarkable decrease in the deaths from the disease throughout the county. It is perhaps early to attribute this to any special efforts of the association, but it comes in, I think, as part of the general improvement that is taking place everywhere in the health of the community.

In contrast to all this concerning medical education and the tuberculosis campaign, a letter written the next day may be given. It was to James J. Walsh of New York, who was composing a book on 'The Century of Columbus':

Dear J. J. W. . . . I will ask at the Bodleian what would be the best piece of Oxford architecture of the last half of the fifteenth century. I should think the superb Divinity School. I will let you know. I am glad you had such a nice visit. It was awfully nice to see you, but I wish you would not appropriate all the reprobate Protestants like Shakespeare[1] in your wretched out-of-date community. Why don't you take Bacon and that old rascal Calvin who burned my friend Servetus! Sincerely yours, Wm Osler. I have just seen Madan who says the Divinity School is the thing. If you wish I could send a picture.

---

[1] Cf. 'Was Shakespeare a Catholic?' By J. J. Walsh.

On the 20th he wrote to Fielding H. Garrison:

> Our history section has been doing very well. Jastrow's lecture was a great success & we have had a good talk on Egyptian Medicine from Elliot Smith. Caton lectured this week on the Greek temples. My [Silliman] Lectures have been delayed. I have been so busy this term I have not had time to finish the proofs. They are semi-popular & represent a sort of aeroplane flight through the centuries. . . . I hope before long to print my paper on the early printed books up to 1480, dealing with them as illustrating the mind of the profession during the early years of printing. I have been getting some treasures lately.

In a Christmas letter to H. B. Jacobs he says: 'The house is full and a very merry party. My books are streaming in & such treasures—a Newton Principia the other day to add to my ed. principes of the 17th century'; and in this letter he speaks for the first time of the new interest which had come over his Waltonian boy: 'Revere has taken to the auction room & sent his first bid to Sotheby's, £1 for Landor's Pericles & Aspasia & got it! He is taking such an interest in good literature. He got his etching out for Christmas and has just started to copy one of his Florence sketches.'

And in his own Christmas mail was the last letter he was to receive from his constant correspondent in Philadelphia, in acknowledgement of 'A Way of Life' which had come as a Christmas gift, saying: 'Many thanks for the booklet, and more for the M.D. who can fearlessly speak out for the wholesomeness of a Christian life. May the New Year be kind to you and yours, and so I remain with all good Xmas wishes loyally your friend, S. Weir Mitchell.'

CHAPTER XXXIV

1914

WAR WITHOUT WARNING

THE year opened with sad tidings; and in a copy of Weir Mitchell's 'Ode on a Lycian Tomb', a poem written as a memorial to his daughter, Osler inserted on January 4th a note stating that he had just had a cable from 'Jack' Mitchell announcing the death of his father, 'one of my dearest friends—had I been a son he could not have been kinder to me during the five years of my life in Philadelphia'. And in a long obituary appreciation sent off to the *British Medical Journal*, he says in part:

The 15th of next February would have been his eighty-fifth birthday. When I saw him last May he had begun to show his age, but mentally he was as keen and alert as ever. Of no man I have known are Walter Savage Landor's words more true: 'I warmed both hands before the fire of life.' We have to go to other centuries to find a parallel to his career, not, it is true, in professional work—for others have done more—but in the combination of a life devoted to the best interests of science with literary and social distinction. He reminds one of Mead, who filled so large a place in public and professional life in the early part of the eighteenth century. And of Mitchell, Dr. Johnson's remark of Mead is equally true: 'No man ever lived more in the sunshine of life.' But a much closer parallel is with the great seventeenth-century Tuscan, Francesco Redi, in the triple combination already referred to, of devotion to scientific study and to *belles lettres*, and in the position which he enjoyed in public esteem. . . .

On January 19th he wrote to F. H. Garrison, who was gathering material for a Life of John S. Billings:

I am taking no steps about the Avicenna tomb until I get an estimate; then I will arrange a committee and send a circular. I am getting a great deal of information out of your History & it will be a great bibliographical help. Mitchell had a fine life. I wrote a very hurried sketch of him in the British Medical Journal. No, the initials 'J. S. B.'[1] are of Sturgis Bigelow of Boston, who was

[1] In Note 3 of 'Science and Immortality'—properly 'W. S. B.'

a great orientalist. I will ask Miss Acland about the letters from B. [J. S. Billings] to her father. He wrote a great deal to Miss Acland—not much I think either to Brunton or to Burdett. I am just trying to finish my early printed books (to 1480) paper for the Bibliographical Society. I wish you could see the fine exhibit I have got together for this evening, but I dare say the S. G. L. has the majority of them.

What was said of another Student of Christ Church, Ingram Bywater, Gilbert Murray's predecessor as Regius Professor of Greek, that he 'acquired knowledge with an easy deliberation and kept it by mere tenacity and a sure instinct for selection', was no less true of Osler. His interest in the early medical incunabula had been a by-path followed in the preparation of his Silliman Lectures to give him 'a mental picture of professors and practice of the time, from the characters of the books they thought it worth while to have printed'. And a trail of this sort once taken up he pursued with a keen scent in spite of red herrings innumerable. It was natural, therefore, that he should have made 'The Earliest Printed Medical Books' the subject of his presidential address before the Bibliographical Society, with a discussion of the influence of printing from its dawn till 1480 upon the art of medicine—a period, admittedly, of greater typographical than scientific interest.[1] In an early paragraph of the address Osler explains his personal relation to his subject as follows:

. . . Not an expert bibliographer, but a representative of an ever-increasing group of ordinary book-lovers, I have tried in the casual studies of a life devoted to hospital and consulting practice to glean two things, the book biographies of the great men of science, and the influence of their books in promoting the progress of knowledge. The anatomy of the mind of a man as shown in his book, and the physiology of the book itself, so far as it has had a definite

[1] For an abstract of this address, see *British Medical Journal*, Jan. 24, 1914, p. 205. Osler's intention to print a complete list of the early medical incunabula led him into difficulties which only the bibliographers of incunabula can appreciate. The task was finally handed over to Mr. Scholderer of the British Museum to complete, and the volume, 'Incunabula Medica', from which the above quotation is taken, was eventually published by the Bibliographical Society in 1923, nearly four years after Osler's death. It contains a preface by A. W. Pollard, Osler's address, and a bibliographical list of 217 books (1467-80).

function, though not perhaps bibliography proper, serve to illustrate its story. And this plan of study has its place. Revolutions are more rapidly effected in the arts than in the mind. A new process, a new discovery in practical science progresses more in a decade than does a new thought in ten. Harvey's demonstration of the circulation of the blood was scarcely accepted by his own generation, but within a few years after Jenner's discovery the civilized world was vaccinated. It is not surprising to find the invention of printing spread so rapidly that, before the close of 1480, it had been introduced, as Pollard tells us, into twenty-two towns in Germany, forty-nine in Italy, four in Switzerland, eight in France, thirteen in the Low Countries, five in Austria-Hungary, six in Spain, and four in England, a total of 111 places, and some 350 printers had been at work. It is estimated that the total output of the early presses in the fifteenth century amounted to twenty million copies. The art of the scribe was by no means easy to displace. Long after printing became common distinguished scholars continued to send to their patrons their shorter works in manuscript. Erasmus, who had long practice as a scribe, followed this custom, and Nichols states that not until 1499 did he write in the Letters familiarly of printing and printers. . . .

Of the essay Fielding H. Garrison writes: 'Almost any other hand would have made a stupid, dry-as-dust job of it, and again Sudhoff's remark comes back to me, that an essay of Osler's is worth many ponderous tomes of dry erudition.' Certainly there could be no more delightful presentation of the story of early book-making than that contained in the address, from its opening sentence to the following paragraph which brought it to a close:

Taking a survey of the period as illustrated by the output of the press, one cannot say that for the first twenty-five years of its existence printing did much, if anything, to free the profession from the shackles of mediaevalism. Not until the revival of Greek studies did men get inspiration from the true masters of science, and for at least two generations they were too busy looking for the fountains to explore for themselves the virtues of their waters. The accurate observation of Nature which Aristotle taught, the searching out her secrets by way of experiment which the Alexandrians and Galen practised, were the great achievements of the sixteenth and seventeenth centuries, as exemplified in Vesalius and Harvey. I have taken you through a somewhat arid period in our history, but the sympathetic student will look beyond the printed page to find in the lives of these men the spirit of helpfulness which gives to the profession of medicine its value to humanity. This has never been better expressed than by Kipling in the verses at the end of his sketch of Nicholas Culpeper:

> Yet when the sickness was sore in the land,
> And neither planet nor herb assuaged,
> They took their lives in their lancet hand,
> And oh, what a wonderful war they waged!
> Yes, when the crosses were thick on the door—
> Yes, when the terrible dead-cart rolled,
> Excellent courage our fathers bore—
> Excellent heart had our fathers of old.
> None too learned, but nobly bold,
> Into the fight went our fathers of old.

On January 21st his old friend whom he had known in Montreal as Donald A. Smith died in his London home, at 28 Grosvenor Square, and six days later the body of this simple and homely man was borne without pomp to his last resting-place in Highgate Cemetery, where his wife had preceded him only a few months before. There had been a national service at the Abbey, to be sure, where indeed he might have been interred had he not willed otherwise. Osler was one of the ten pall-bearers, chosen owing to their personal ties—the Duke of Argyll, the Principal of Aberdeen, the Governor of the Hudson Bay Company, the Colonial Secretary, the Lord Mayor, and Lords Aberdeen, Lichfield and Lansdowne. Thus ended a career so picturesque that had it been found in fiction it would have seemed a story overdrawn. A man whose exact birthplace and age were uncertain, and who had begun life counting musk-rat skins at Lachine, yet by the time of the South African War, in the words of his Queen, had become one of the Empire's greatest benefactors. John Hay once said that the modern British imperialism as a popular force was largely the joint product of four men—Joseph Chamberlain, Lord Strathcona, Rudyard Kipling, and Lord Northcliffe. To neither Chamberlain nor Strathcona was it given to see what latent endurance and loyalty underlay this federation of peoples when put to a supreme test.

The time was drawing near when the Empire was sorely to need men like Strathcona, of resolute and optimistic type—men accustomed to triumph over difficulties. There could not be too many of them, for even now the affairs of

Britain were in a troubled plight. Strikes were prevalent and the Prime Minister was beset on the one hand by Labour delegates who advocated railway nationalization and protested against compulsory military service or any increase of armaments ; on the other hand he was dodging militant suffragists who were terrorizing the country, smashing windows, damaging pictures—among them Sargent's portrait of Henry James—burning railway stations and country houses, even setting off a bomb in the Abbey. Nor was arrest and imprisonment a deterrent, for the hunger strike followed, and a dismissal under the 'Cat and Mouse' Act. But these were trifles compared to the spectre of civil war. The Ulster crisis was coming to a head, and to all appearances Home Rule would be enforced at the point of the bayonet, though Lord Roberts, himself an Irishman, had said that the use of the army to coerce Ulster was unthinkable. There were worse things than a court-martial, and officers in the Curragh had handed in their resignations—a course even followed by Colonel Seely, the Secretary for War, though this was not until the end of March. How greatly Osler was himself disturbed by these things does not appear, though in a letter to a colleague in London, by whom he had been asked to see a militant American in consultation, he writes:

W—— says she is not certifiable, so what are we to do ! I have written to her brother urging him to come over & take her out of the country. These ancient cynophilic vestals should be segregated by Act of Parliament. The Government should buy Iceland from Denmark and deport them there automatically at the menopause.

Meanwhile he writes to J. William White in reply to a letter from somewhere in the Far East :

We have had a very busy winter so far—a great deal doing, so many people coming & going. Awfully sad to have dear old Mitchell leave us, but he had a wonderful innings & died the death of the righteous, with a minimum of that 'cold gradation of decay' through which so many of us have to pass ; & it is perhaps just as well that Mrs. Mitchell followed him so soon. Revere is getting ready for his exams, & hopes to come here in October. He has taken to sketching & books but is still devoted to fishing. I had a nice morning with John Sargent the other day. He made a splendid crayon sketch of me which will go in a couple of months to the College of Physicians, Philadelphia.

And .to Camac on February 25th, that the Historical Section of the Royal Society of Medicine was getting into very good shape; that their plans for the summer were uncertain—'I had hoped to get out early, but the National Library Association meets here at the invitation of the Curators of the Bodleian at the end of August & I cannot possibly leave until afterwards. I do not know what Grace and Revere will do.'

The world in general at this time seemed to be filled with people who, like the woman he had seen in consultation, were 'uncertifiable', and Osler with a number of others was victimized just now by one of them through the publication of 'The Family Encyclopaedia of Medicine', a work which appeared on February 26th and was widely advertised in the daily press. On March 4th there was sent to him by the Registrar of the Royal College of Physicians the following note:

The President and Censors deeply regret to observe that your name appears in this advertisement, a copy of which I enclose, and in a similar advertisement in the *Daily Telegraph* of Thursday, the 29th ult. (enclosed). They desire also to draw your attention to an article in the *Daily Mail* of the same date (enclosed). They hope to receive from you an assurance that your name has been inserted without your knowledge or consent. They further desire to draw your attention to a Resolution of the College, dated February 2, 1888. I enclose a copy of this Resolution [pertaining to personal advertising]. They hope that you will communicate at once with the Editor and publishers of the 'Family Encyclopaedia of Medicine', requiring that your name be withdrawn from the advertisements, and from succeeding numbers of the publication, if you have not already done so.

To this he replied on the following day:

Dear Mr. Registrar, Your letter, with its lurid enclosures, is the first intimation I have had of the existence of 'The Family Encyclopaedia of Medicine', in connection with which the use of my name was entirely unauthorized. Six months ago a Dr. R—— asked me to look over a paper on typhoid fever, to which I replied I was too busy. When three months later a type-written article appeared I looked him up, & finding that he was a Cambridge man of apparently good standing, I glanced it over and made a suggestion about typhoid carriers. I made no written corrections. There was nothing on his letter-paper to indicate that he was connected in any way with a popular publication, of the existence of which your enclosure of to-day is the first & only intimation I have had. I have written to Dr. R—— that I consider the use of my name was unwarranted & obtained by means of subterfuge, & that he has grossly abused what was meant to be a kindly act to a younger colleague. Sincerely yours.

His mother's admonition—Remember, Willie, the shutters in England will rattle as they do in America—must have come to his mind during the trying weeks that followed, when the matter lay before the Board of Censors of the College. The affair apparently culminated at a meeting of the Comitia on April 6th, of which Osler has left the following note:

At the College meeting to-day (6th) I raised the question of the responsibility of the College to defend its members. D—— made a Pecksniffian address in which he said the honour of the College had been dragged in the mud. P—— said it was not customary for the C. to defend individual members. The President asked if the C. wished to take any action—no reply. I have sent in my resignation as a protest against this attitude. In this matter I am not the galled jade and if the College is prepared to discipline me in a perfectly innocent action they should be prepared to defend me when it is clear I have been the victim of fraud and subterfuge. W. O.

Four days later, April 10th, he appended, to an accumulated bundle of correspondence, this note:

The day after I sent in my resignation the President called me up by telephone & asked if he could come & see me the next day, & begged me to say nothing about it as the matter was very complicated. The College could not well take action, as it was not altogether certain how far the Editor of the F. E. M. had compromised some of the younger Fellows. I saw Barlow in town yesterday and talked over the whole business. He much regretted D——'s remarks and explained why it was impossible for the College to take up the matter. Very reluctantly I agreed to withdraw my resignation.

All this need hardly be mentioned except to show that Osler was capable of acting on an impulse of indignation, and the episode may indicate that people in general were perhaps over-sensitized in those early months of 1914. It may have been something more than a coincidence, too, that Osler should have caused to be published at this time an article [1] containing a long letter written in 1684, in which John Locke the philosopher expatiates on 'the arbitrary and unjust expulsion' from Christ Church he had recently sustained under the Deanship of Bishop Fell:

> This opinion of me [Locke wrote] I thought time and ye contradictions it caryed with it would have cured, & that the most suspitious would at last have been weary of imputeing to me writeings whose matter and stile have I believe (for pamphlets have been laid to me w:^ch I have never seen) been soe very different, y^t it was hard to thinke they should have the same author, though a much abler man than me.

Osler no less than Locke could meet episodes of this sort with equanimity. They were, indeed, of rare occurrence, and as he was not built to harbour a grievance nor willing to let misunderstandings grow into alienations, his life, 'sloping towards the sunny side', went on unaffected.

With all his multifarious interests it must not be forgotten that the Regius at the same time was a consulting physician and had professional duties both to prince and pauper, though it is difficult to see how he fitted in time for his consultations. He notes in his account-book on March 10th that he had seen the Prince again; while, in contrast, Bateman the parlour-maid takes over the telephone a cable message, handed in at Calcutta, to 'OSLER OXFORD': 'SAVE MY SON GEORGE HALLORAN GOD WILL PAY ALL EXPENSES', which indicates that an Indian student, who was being well attended to, had met with an accident. God pays many a doctor's fee.

He presided as usual on March 13th at a meeting of the Oxford and Reading Branch of the B. M. A. held at the Radcliffe Infirmary, giving a paper on 'The Diagnosis of Early Pulmonary Tuberculosis'; and a few days later he wrote to his old friend James Tyson of Philadelphia:

[1] 'Locke's Expulsion from Christ Church.' *Oxford Magazine*, Mar. 12, 1914, p. 254. The Locke letter had been procured at Sotheby's the preceding July. It was one of some two hundred unpublished letters written by Locke to Edward Clarke and his family, subsequently acquired *en bloc* by Dr. Benjamin Rand of Harvard. Dr. Rand intends to publish these letters, together with the replies, which he succeeded in finding in the possession of Lord Lovelace.

'I am a great deal in London for one thing or another. We shall have a big dinner next week for Gorgas, and the University has decided to give him an honorary degree.' No opportunity to do unexpected and kindly things of this kind for people coming through England did Osler miss. Early in the year he had learned from Gorgas, who had been on a mission in Johannesburg, at the invitation of the Transvaal Chamber of Mines, to investigate the cause of the high death-rate among the native labourers, that he would return through England some time in March. Osler had immediately written to Sir Ronald Ross, saying: 'Would it not be nice if the 'Tropicals' gave Gorgas a dinner when he returns from South Africa? I think we could easily get sixty or seventy men'; and to J. Y. W. MacAlister suggesting that the Royal Society of Medicine ask him to give an illustrated lecture, to be followed by a reception. He wrote also to Sir Rickman Godlee to inquire whether the Royal College of Surgeons ever gave honorary fellowships on special occasions, because Gorgas, who had just been appointed Surgeon-General of the U.S. Army, would soon be in London—'a man whose work in Cuba and Panama has probably been the most important ever done in tropical sanitation'; also to Major G. O. Squier, the military attaché at the American Embassy, to stir him up in the matter. Then to Gorgas himself on March 16th:

Dear Gorgas,—I hope you will fall in with the somewhat active programme which has been arranged, of which MacAlister, the Secretary of the Royal Society of Medicine, will send you full particulars. I will see you on Wednesday evening at the Army Mess dinner. Friday and Saturday I have to be at the Association of Physicians at Cambridge. I think we shall have a very good gathering at the public dinner to you on Monday—the Colonial Secretary, the leading members of the profession, the Archbishop of Canterbury, Lord Bryce, Lord Moulton and others will be there. Wire me on arrival where you are staying. Greetings to Darling and Noble. Sincerely yours, &c.

So it came about that the evening of March 23rd saw a distinguished gathering for dinner at the Savoy Hotel, and Sir Thomas Barlow, who presided, in calling on the first speaker, said that the dinner had been first suggested by a man who was 'always striving to promote the friendship between the two great branches of the Anglo-Saxon race'. One of the speakers of course was Mr. Page; another Lord Bryce, who referred to medicine as 'the only profession that laboured incessantly to destroy the reason for its own existence'; and there was much more which must have warmed the modest heart of the guest of honour, who doubtless accepted it as a professional rather than a personal tribute.

It was a highly characteristic touch that Osler should have had engrossed and illuminated on parchment, copies of the addresses made by the public orator, Mr. A. D. Godley, and by the Acting Vice-Chancellor, Sir Herbert Warren, when Gorgas was given his D.Sc., *honoris causa*, at a special Convocation in Oxford the following day; and that he should have had copies made and sent to the *Journal of the American Medical Association*, in which they were reproduced as companion pieces to Gorgas's report of his 'Recommendations to the Transvaal Chamber of Mines'. Few people would have taken all this trouble even to pay a deserving tribute to an old friend. But Osler never paused to consider trouble; he took troubles of this kind as a practised runner takes a hurdle with no apparent effort. And the story has a sequel, for Sir John MacAlister states that had it not been for the example of Osler's generous and happy thought leading to this complimentary dinner in 1914, the suggestion that the nation hold a military funeral and a service at St. Paul's after Gorgas's sudden death six years later in London would never have been thought of.

This was merely a typical episode, one of many, which has perhaps taken too long in the telling. There were plenty of other things to occupy him: a meeting of the Association of Physicians in Cambridge; book sales in London; and March 27th was given over to the entertainment of a group of surgeons. For, following the example of the American inter-urban clinical societies, an English club of a similar sort had been formed—the Association of Provincial Surgeons—and they were entertained much as the American Society of Clinical Surgeons had been four years before, a great display of volumes relating to the history of British surgery having been got out from the

Bodleian stores for their edification.[1] That a group of surgeons should make a pilgrimage to spend a day with a physician, chiefly known to be an ardent bibliophile, is in itself worthy of comment, especially as this physician just now was smarting under unmerited censure from his own guild. But Osler not only had a catholicity of mind but of friendships as well. One need not be surprised, therefore, at finding him a month later (April 27th) the guest of honour at the dinner held in London in celebration of the twenty-first anniversary of the Jewish Historical Society of England. Lord Reading, the Chief Justice, presided, and in responding to the toast of Science, Osler gave a noteworthy speech, of which a few paragraphs at least should be retrieved from 'Men and Books', and the Jewish periodicals into which it subsequently found its way.[2]

In estimating [he said] the position of Israel in the human values, we must remember that the quest for righteousness is Oriental, the quest for knowledge Occidental. With the great prophets of the East—Moses, Isaiah, Mahomet—the word was, 'Thus saith the Lord'; with the great seers of the West, from Thales and Aristotle to Archimedes and Lucretius, it was 'What says Nature?' They illustrate two opposite views of man and his destiny—in the one he is an *angelus sepultus* in a muddy vesture of decay; in the other he is the 'young light-hearted master' of the world, in it to know it, and by knowing to conquer. Modern civilization is the outcome of these two great movements of the mind of man, who to-day is ruled in heart and head by Israel and by Greece. From the one he has learned responsibility to a Supreme Being, and the love of his neighbour, in which are embraced both the Law and the Prophets; from the other he has gathered the promise of Eden to have dominion over the earth on which he lives. Not that Israel is all heart, nor Greece all head, for in estimating the human value of the two races, intellect and science are found in Jerusalem and beauty and truth at Athens, but in different proportions. . . .

In the early Middle Ages the Jewish physicians played a rôle of the first importance as preservers and transmitters of ancient knowledge. With the fall of Rome the broad stream of Greek science in Western Europe entered the sud of Mediaevalism. It filtered

[1] 'Some MSS. and Books in the Bodleian Library, illustrating the Evolution of British Surgery.' *British Medical Journal*, April 11, 1914, i. 825–6.

[2] *Canadian Medical Association Journal*, Aug. 1914, iv. 729; also *Jewish Comment*, Baltimore, Dec. 18, 1914; &c.

through in three streams—one in South Italy, the other in Byzantium, and a third through Islam. At the great school of Salernum in the tenth, eleventh and twelfth centuries, we find important Jewish teachers: Copho II wrote the Anatomia Porci, and Rebecca wrote on fevers and the foetus. Jews were valued councillors at the court of the great Emperor Frederick. With the Byzantine stream the Jews seem to have had little to do, but the broad clear stream which ran through Islam is dotted thickly with Hebrew names. In the Eastern and Western Caliphates and in North Africa were men who today are the glory of Israel, and bright stars in the medical firmament. Three of these stand out pre-eminent. The writings of Isaac Judaeus, known in the Middle Ages as Monarcha Medicorum, were prized for more than four centuries. He had a Hippocratic belief in the powers of nature and in the superiority of prevention to cure. He was an optimist and held strongly to the Talmudic precept that the physician who takes nothing is worth nothing. Rabbi ben Ezra was a universal genius and wanderer, whose travels brought him as far as England. His philosophy of life Browning has depicted in the well-known poem, whose beauty of diction and clarity of thought atone for countless muddy folios. But the prince among Jewish physicians, whose fame as such has been overshadowed by his reputation as a Talmudist and philosopher, is the Doctor Perplexorum—*dux, director, demonstrator, neutrorum dubitantium et errantium*!—Moses Maimonides. . . .

In like fashion he went on to trace the influence of the Hebrews through the centuries—and some of their tribulations as well, in the schools of Montpellier and Paris; their intimate relation to some of the popes; of Abraham Conath's printing-press at Mantua whence the first Hebrew works were issued; of Jean Baptiste Silva, one of the physicians Voltaire did not ridicule, and to whom he gave the copy of the 'Henriade' which Osler's messmates in the 'Ship of Fools' presented to him in 1905; of the outburst of scientific activity among the German Jews of the nineteenth century, crowned by Paul Ehrlich's revolutionizing researches; and he closed the address by saying:

I have always had a warm affection for my Jewish students, and it has been one of the special pleasures of my life the friendships I have made with them. Their success has always been a great gratification, as it has been the just reward of earnestness and tenacity of purpose and devotion to high ideals in science; and, I may add, a dedication of themselves as practitioners to everything that could promote the welfare of their patients. In the medical profession the Jews have a long and honourable record, and among no people is all that is best in our science and art more warmly appreciated; none in the community take more to heart the admonition of the son of Sirach—'Give place to the physician, let him not go from thee, for thou hast need of him'.

'We are very busy and enjoying a wonderful spring', he wrote to Mrs. Brewster late in April. 'I never saw the country more beautiful and the sun has had his own way for three weeks.' And in a letter soliciting from his old friend Ogden another 'Alkapton' paper for the Quarterly Journal, he urged him to come over, for he could breakfast in bed and browse in the Bodleian to his heart's content, adding: 'Revere is just back from Scotland where he has been after his beloved fish. He passed Matriculation fortunately and comes up to Christ Church this autumn.' They had been in town for a week, he said in a letter of the 27th, amusing themselves while the house was cleaning; and on their return he wrote to J. Y. W. MacAlister—'the poker of the fire'—about organizing a Vesalian celebration for December, the coming 400th anniversary of his birth, and added: 'Another matter! I see in the Hodgkin sale early in May another 1478 Celsus. Could we not bleed some fellows to the tune of about £30 and send a bid? It is one of the great books of the profession, which the library should possess. I will go a fiver. Who are the men likely to help in it? I will attack them.'

During all these past few months there had also been correspondence without end regarding the repair of Avicenna's tomb, and on the departure of Dr. Sa'eed, who had been making a long sojourn in England, Osler wrote on May 1st:

I had a note this morning from Mr. Funk with the estimates—repairs at £100 & £300 to provide an income of £15 a year for a caretaker. This amount I am sure we could raise. Would it be possible to have it done under the auspices of the Regent or of the Shah, so that we could put at the head of the circular 'under the auspices of His &c., &c.'? I am writing to Funk & to Neligan at once, asking them as to the names of men in Persia who should go on the committee. In this country we would ask the President of the College of Physicians, the College of Surgeons, the Royal Society of Medicine, Dr. Cowley, Professor Margoliouth, the two

Regius Professors of Medicine at Oxford & Cambridge, & Professor Browne—and we may think of some others. In Paris the President of the Academy of Medicine & the Dean of the Medical Faculty, & the President of the French Society of the History of Medicine. Good-bye! I hope you will have a very comfortable journey. It has been so nice to see you. Do let me hear how everything progresses. I suppose your address is Hamadan.

On Saturday, May 2nd,[1] he writes to H. B. Jacobs: 'We have the Hadleys with us. He is giving the course of lectures on American History. The first one yesterday was delightful.' The successor of Charles Francis Adams in this lectureship, Arthur T. Hadley, has written this recollection of his visit:

My real acquaintance with Osler began after he had left America and made his home in England. He acted as a sort of *proxenos* for Americans in Oxford, and Mrs. Hadley and I more than once enjoyed the benefits of his hospitality. The household was a most delightful one. The Oslers had a positive talent for making people feel at home. The house stood at the north edge of Oxford, with some open ground about it and a beautiful view of the university cricket fields through the trees at the back of the garden. Life at that house combined all that was most charming in city and country, in England and in America.

It was our good fortune to spend two weeks in this house in May 1914, when the English springtime was at its best; and among

---

[1] According to *The Times*, on this same Saturday was held 'a discussion of great importance not only to agriculturists but to the medical and veterinary professions and the public in general', which took place at a meeting of the Berks and Oxon Chamber of Agriculture. It was called to act on a resolution—'that further research in swine fever should be undertaken at one or more university centres as well as at the Government Laboratory at Alperton.' Osler's interest in comparative pathology, which went back to his early Toronto and McGill days, may be recalled; and the agitation seems to have arisen from the question whether universities—and particularly Cambridge, where Dr. George H. F. Nuttall was especially fitted to undertake research in this direction—should participate in it, or whether it should be a purely governmental affair, for under these circumstances research was apt to be biased and its results often pigeon-holed. Osler is quoted as saying at the meeting that 'there was nothing like a row for doing good. Until the pool was troubled by the angel the waters had no healing. Therefore they owed the Chairman [the President of the Chamber] a debt of gratitude; the problem of swine fever would benefit and no harm be done. The officials of public bodies did not take offence. They were thick-skinned.' To this Sir John McFadyean replied: 'One needs to be.' And Osler answered: 'I know, and you are.'

all the visits I ever made this stands out pre-eminent in my recollections for the many kinds of pleasure which it afforded. As Osler himself well said at the time, there is no place like Oxford for a man who has passed his most strenuous years and wants to combine occupation with enjoyment. He had them both in plenty. Quite apart from the professional calls on his time, which were rather more numerous than he wished, he was extraordinarily active in dealing with the administrative problems of Oxford University. Even in the quiet halls of Oxford, reform had begun to make its disturbing presence felt; and for advice Oxford instinctively turned to Osler as one who knew the habits of the intruder and was familiar with the measures which were necessary to keep him quiet. His work was purely advisory, but his advice was almost always taken. . . .

And Oxford appreciated Osler. He seemed to me to have a kind of hold upon the respect and affection of the place in its entirety which few men have attained. You felt this wherever you dined in his company; not simply in his own college of Christ Church or among men of his own age, but in every college and with men of every generation. For Osler was a man to whom differences of years meant little. He had a catholicity of social instinct which enabled him to say the right thing to the youngest freshman and to the oldest Don alike. For the moment, he was always of the same age as the man with whom he spoke—not talking down to one or talking up to another, but instinctively taking the other's point of view and being actually interested in the things that absorbed the other's attention. Nor was it in university and college circles alone that he made himself popular. He was in contact with the civic life of the community. His spirit of personal friendliness and understanding did more to remove sources of tension or friction than could have been accomplished by any measures of organized co-operation, however wise.

One of the most delightful days of my life was spent with the Oslers in a visit to an alms-house at the ancient village of Ewelme. . . . Previous incumbents of the office had been content to take the stipend without going near the alms-house more than once or twice a year; Osler addressed himself seriously to the duties of the place, perhaps one day each week; and by so doing won not only great credit in Oxford but, what was at once more picturesque and more desirable, great affection from the old men after whose welfare he looked. Many of these duties were of a kind particularly congenial to Osler's mind and tastes. The fifteenth-century cloister round which the dwellings grouped themselves; the charming little church with the rooms and yards adjoining it; and, above all, the old books, long neglected, with their ancient manuscripts and bindings and royal seals;—all these afforded Osler never-ending delight, and gave his friends who visited the place with him a wonderful background against which his face and figure stand out as clear as that of Saint Jerome.

To Rudyard Kipling from W. O. May 9, 1914.

Dear Kipling, The Roger Bacon celebration is on June 10th. There is to be a presentation of a statue at the Museum which will be received by Curzon. Bridges has promised to write a brief ode which would be recited at the Museum, in which he says he will deal only with philosophy & that he might not mention Roger Bacon at all. Merton College gives a lunch & the Committee empowers me to ask you to write & recite something for us at the luncheon, dealing particularly with the personality & tragedy of Roger Bacon. Do please accept & come to us & bring Mrs. Kipling for a little visit. . . .

To W. O. from Rudyard Kipling. May 10, 1914.

Dear Osler, I can't tell you how shocked I am to find the practice of medicine at Oxford (Roger's own university) so grossly behind the age. It was Galen who laid down that 'anger at meat' (by which he meant all mental emotion save of the mildest) is the mother of evil; and here are *you*—Regius Professor—counselling me to recite my own verses 'at' not before or after, but *at*—a bountiful meal. May I refer you to 'Libellus R. B. A. &c, &c, de retardandis senectutis accidentibus et de sensibus conservandis' (Oxford 1590) But seriously, much as I should love to be of use to you I fear I am no good in this matter. I don't know Bacon except from the popular legend; I have no Brewer and I can't get up to Oxford on the 10th and I am up to my eyes in work and arrears of work of all sorts. Forgive me, and send me, as soon as you can, your paper on R. B. to file with my old doctors. Nicholas [Culpeper], who could write even if he couldn't cure for nuts—says at the beginning of his Herbal, 'I knew well enough the whole world and everything in it was formed of a composition of contrary elements, and in such a harmony as must needs show the wisdom and power of a great God.' That seems to me to cover Roger Bacon's outlook and I present it to you for a quotation. The wife joins me in kindest regards to you both and I am, Yours ever sincerely, RUDYARD KIPLING.

And another exchange of letters of about this time followed upon a telegram of May 14th from Oxford saying: 'THANK YOU SO MUCH BUT IMPOSSIBLE TO ACCEPT NOMINATION. I HAVE WRITTEN. OSLER'—

From J. Y. W. MacAlister to W. O. Royal Society of Medicine, London, May 20, 1914.

My dear Mr. President-nominate,—Your telegram has given me a cruel shock, and I must earnestly beg—I should say implore—

that you will reconsider your decision. You were nominated yesterday by the absolute unanimous vote of the whole Council of the society, and, unless you prevent it, your election follows as a matter of course. It is not for me perhaps to say anything about the honour this is, for you have achieved such honours in your brilliant career that there is practically nothing left that will enhance them; but if you knew the traditions here you would understand what a special honour the election to the presidency of this society in your case means. It is for the first time in its history an entire departure from tradition, which demands that the presidents of the society shall be the best of those *who have served it longest*. How strong this tradition is you will perhaps understand better if I tell you that some years ago a proposal to make Lord Lister President of the society had to be withdrawn. It is in some ways even a greater honour than the presidency of the College of Physicians, for the Society is more broadly representative of the profession.

But I know that all that will count for nothing with you; but what I hope will count is the fact that many of the leading men of the society have been looking to you for some time as the future President, whose indomitable energy, progressiveness, and large mindedness would help to place the society in the position that properly belongs to it, and it would be a bitter disappointment if now that the opportunity has come you hold back. The society wants a man who is above tradition and who will make precedents for himself, and there is none other who can fulfil that need as you can. In saying this I am not disparaging others, for your really unique position in the profession, and in the public estimation gives you opportunities of *doing things* which other men, however willing they might be, have not got.

I do not know if you have ever realized how much the Amalgamation owed to you. I remember, as vividly as if it were this morning, how at a time when I had practically given up hope, you came into my room at Hanover Square, and I told you of my dreams, and you urged me to 'go right ahead, that the time was ripe, and I was not to worry about the old fogies'. Your encouragement gave me just the stimulant that I needed at the time—for I was physically as well as mentally ill—and I went 'right ahead', and even then hoped to see you President of the reformed society, and I cannot well express the bitter disappointment and discouragement it will be to me personally if you refuse this opportunity, which may never come again.

Do not be afraid of the work, I will guarantee to save you all that; and you are so often in London that to preside at a monthly Council Meeting (the times for which can be fixed to suit you) should be no tax upon you. To parody the posters—'it is your inspiration we want'. Up to now the presidencies have worked out in a perfectly rhythmical order, and this is the exact psychological moment for your presidency. Church was the necessary Amalgamating President, as he had presided at all the Amalgamation Meetings, and the Sections had to learn what amalgamation meant; then began the move and the new building, for which Morris was the best man, and did yeoman service; settled in the new building the next thing that had to be done was to break the stupid old tradition, which prevented a specialist from occupying the chair, and Champneys as head of his specialty has done his duty well; and now, having amalgamated, built, and got rid of its fetters, what the society needs, and must have, is a new and inspiring energy to give it a good start on the great work that lies before it. It is your clear duty to accept, and for duty's sake you must not refuse. Yours sincerely, and very anxiously, J. Y. W. MacAlister.

To J. Y. W. MacAlister from W. O. The Athenaeum, Pall Mall, [undated]

Dear MacAlister, Awfully sorry I cannot accept the nomination. It is not my job. I need not go into reasons. It is good of you to think of me. I see your hand in it. Sincerely yours, Wm Osler.

A good many other people who knew and had worked with Osler felt that they would like to see his influence exerted in other fields than the one he had chosen. A hint at this will be found in the following note of May 29th to his colleague of the University Endowment Fund:

Dear Lord Hythe, I shall be glad to be at the meeting. I am not quite sure that any words of mine would be of value, so that I would rather not speak. We Colonials occupy rather an anomalous position here in the political world. I am in favour of a preferential tariff for the colonies and strongly against any coercion of Ulster. I have sent the slip on to Heberden. . . .

Then too, not long after, on the death of Sir William Anson, the senior member of Parliament for the university, he was waited upon, as he says, 'by a deputation of the caucus of both parties asking me to stand as an independent member & that there would be no contest; but remembering Michael Foster, & still having some sense left, I told them it was not my job. There would have been nothing in it for me but worry'. What Leslie Stephen in his 'Hours in a Library' says of Sir Thomas Browne, is equally true of Browne's modern representative, Osler:

He would have been hopelessly out of place on the floor of the

Senate, stirring men's patriotism or sense of right; for half his sympathy would always be with the opposition. He could not have moved the tears or the devotional ecstacies of a congregation for he has too vivid a sense that any and every dogma is but one side of an inevitable antinomy. Strong convictions are needed for the ordinary controversial successes, and his favourite point of view is the centre from which all convictions radiate and all look equally probable. But then instead of mocking at all he sympathizes with all, and expresses the one sentiment which may be extracted from their collision—the sentiment of reverence blended with scepticism. 'It is a contradictory sentiment, one may say, in a sense, but the essence of humour is to be contradictory.' . . .

Osler was never a strong protagonist: his sense of fair play, his charity for the other fellow's foibles and failings, and his sense of humour, would have made him unsuccessful as the great leader of a cause. As pointed out by some one, great leaders of men and of causes, with perhaps the notable exception of Lincoln, have been conspicuously without any sense of humour.

There were other things enough, and more to his fancy. It will be remembered that on his earlier visits to Cardiff he had prodded the natives on their financial neglect of the university and its medical school. The seed apparently had not fallen on barren ground. Meanwhile the Report of the Royal Commission on University Education had been carefully studied by some prominent Welshmen, and a deputation representing the university had waited on the Chancellor of the Exchequer with the proposal that the Government should come to their aid in establishing the 'unit system' at Cardiff, where an anonymous donor had given a magnificent sum sufficient to complete the necessary buildings. As an outcome of this, a small committee was appointed by the Board of Education to act as advisers of the Treasury, and it may be noted that the 'anonymous donor' had included among the terms of his gift 'the last and most important condition—and upon this mainly depends this offer—that the grant made by the Treasury shall in the opinion of Sir William Osler the Regius Professor of Medicine at Oxford be an adequate one for a first-rate, up-to-date medical school'. Thus it came about that Osler makes the entry, '*May 22–23.* Cardiff Med. School' in his account-book—an entry, be it said, which under different dates is to appear many times during the succeeding years.[1]

There were other things of like kind which took him afield. On June 4th he is found at Bath giving an address at the opening of the Pathological Laboratory, when he emphasized the great opportunity the famous old place offered for the scientific study of arthritis in its many forms. A hospital was no new thing at Bath, for Beau Nash and Dr. Oliver (he of the 'Bath Olivers') had first started one, but never before had there been a laboratory. On this occasion, again, Osler prodded the local pride, saying: 'There are three further things needed—a good museum where physicians can come to inspect every known type of arthritis, a modern X-ray department, and, the third, a well-equipped and up-to-date library. I am a great believer in books as tools and shall be glad to give £10 toward the founding of such a library.' His old friend 'Jimmy' Johnson (now the Rev. James Bovell Johnson of Fiddington Rectory, Bridgewater) came over to Bath for this occasion, and recalls that there was a large and distinguished gathering of locally prominent people, including

[1] I was Chairman of the Royal Commission [writes Lord Haldane] which reported on the University of Wales about 1916 and Sir Wm. Osler was my colleague. Our field of inquiry was a wide one, and one of the difficult questions was how to found an adequate College of Medicine in the reformed university. For ideas on the subject we turned to Sir William, and he took a very active part in framing and negotiating a scheme. There were two views: (1) that the college should be an independent one in the university, the sphere of which was the whole of Wales; (2) that it should be a college affiliated to and largely controlled by the University College of Cardiff. The commission was unanimous in holding the first view, which Sir William supported very strongly. The desire was to give the largest importance to the college. But unfortunately it had to be connected with the existing chief centre of medical instruction in Wales, and this was the existing Medical College and Hospital at Cardiff, standing on land belonging to the University College there. It was difficult to get over the claim of Cardiff. Not all stuck to one recommendation, and even now the matter is not wholly settled, so far as I know. Sir William persuaded a well-known lady, I think Miss Talbot of Margam, to give £50,000 as an endowment for the new college, and, with the conditions attached, obtained a leverage. It may be that the compromise will result in a large measure of independence in the government of the reorganized medical college being conceded. Cardiff is a great centre, but a difficult place to deal with.

the Marquis of Bath and others; and a public dinner at a famous restaurant. But they slipped away, meanwhile, and went through the libraries and the old book shops, where Osler tracked down some volumes dealing with the medical worthies of the locality.

On June 9th and 10th came a curious conflict of engagements between the two old universities, one of which had on its rolls the name of Francis Bacon and the other his prototype in the interrogation of nature, Roger. After all the trouble and interest he had taken, as a member of the executive committee, in helping to prepare for the Oxford celebration when, among other ceremonies, a monument to the 'Doctor Mirabilis' of his contemporaries was unveiled in the Museum, Osler himself was absent in Cambridge.[1] And so was Sir John Sandys, another member of the Roger Bacon Committee, for, being Public Orator at Cambridge, he must be there for the conferring of degrees. Then, too, the Romanes Lecture was made a feature of the Oxford ceremonies, and this took Professor J. J. Thomson away from the Cambridge celebration.

The opening of the new physiological laboratories in Cambridge on the 9th was the culmination, for the Cambridge School of Physiology, of the small beginnings made when in 1870 Michael Foster was transferred from University College shortly before Osler was there at work under Foster's successor. It was a ceremony not to be missed, despite the conflicting Oxford meeting; and, what is unusual for such occasions, when Prince Arthur of Connaught, who officially opened the building, admitted the guests, the new laboratory rooms were found equipped and in full operation; and demonstrations were made by the workers—by Professor Langley, by Miss Dale, G. R. Mines, R. A. Peters, A. V. Hill, W. H. R. Rivers, Joseph Barcroft and his collaborator C. G. Douglas of Oxford; by Walter Fletcher, W. B. Hardy, Keith Lucas, and

[1] This monument and the volume of essays edited by A. G. Little alone remain as evidences of the elaborate programme to commemorate the 700th anniversary of Friar Bacon's birth. Although a start was made to republish his works (e. g. the 'Communium Naturalium' by Robert Steele), the war checked the fulfilment of the project. A volume of Bacon's medical treatises by Professor Little and Dr. Withington is in course of preparation.

others—many of whom were soon to be swept into far more serious fields than those of academic research.[1]

Then in the Senate House, cheerful with its scarlet gowns, the following degrees were conferred—a LL.D. for Prince Arthur of Connaught, Lord Esher, Lord Moulton, and Colonel S. M. Benson, Master of the Drapers' Company, which had provided funds for the new building; the Sc.D. upon Osler, David Ferrier, E. A. Schäfer, and E. H. Starling, four men who 'had contributed to the advancement of physiological science'. It would be difficult to say whether the Cambridge dedication or the Bacon centenary celebration at Oxford had drawn together the more eminent or interesting group of people. Among the Oxford celebrants was the Rt. Rev. Abbot Gasquet, President of the English Benedictines, who is singled out for a special reason. For on the evening of June 30th from the Athenaeum Club Osler writes: 'Just in from a dinner by the Bibliographical Society to the new Cardinal — Gasquet — all the literary book men in London—such a charming company.'

Abbot Gasquet was the member of the Bibliographical Society who instead of Osler would probably have been elected President the year before to succeed Richard Garnett, had it not been that his work in Rome as head of the Commission on the Vulgate led him to decline. He had just received his cardinal's hat, and Osler, with A. W. Pollard and other friends, gave him the complimentary 'Book Lovers'' dinner to which the note refers. As Mr. Pollard has said of this,[2] the second year of Osler's

[1] One of them writes: 'How little we thought that day of what was coming! We thought the big new building would become a busy hive at once. All of us had plans for work in that Long Vacation, and several good Germans and Austrians were coming; but from August and for five years more it stood almost empty, with poor Langley working away in a couple of rooms. Keith Lucas killed flying, and poor Mines, were never to return. Peters was winning his Military Cross and Bar in France; Douglas was in charge of Gas Services in France; Barcroft had the Chemical Warfare Camp at Porton; Hardy running the Royal Society War Committees in London; Fletcher in charge of the Medical Research Council; A. V. Hill running a team of mathematicians improving ballistics for the navy and anti-aircraft guns.'

[2] Preface to Osler's 'Incunabula Medica, 1467–1480', Bibliographical Society, 1923.

presidency of the society, it was unwontedly gay not only because of this dinner but in 'bursting into a summer meeting at Cambridge'. 'Under Sir William's presidentship', he adds, 'both festivities were delightfully successful.'

'We are having the usual busy spring season—just at present in the midst of examinations', Osler writes to H. B. Jacobs on the 23rd. 'This evening we have all the Pages coming, as tomorrow he gets his honorary degree at the annual celebration.'[1] And he adds: 'We are in a nice mess here with the Irishmen. I wish they would tow the island into the mid-Atlantic & let the Orange & Green fight it out between them.' The spectre of civil war which so long had hung over the country was growing daily more real, for there was 'no compromise and no surrender' in Ulster. But not even to this, nor to the railway strike, was so much space given in the press as to the victorious polo team; the crews at Henley; the American Cup trials; the open golf championship; cricket at Lords; tennis at Wimbledon; a negro prize-fighter who had won another championship; and the incident of Lord Brassey's 'arrest' at the Kiel Regatta. Even the fact that on June 28th a fanatic Serbian student threw a bomb, which had a more far-reaching effect than the mere killing of the Archduke Ferdinand and his wife, was soon overshadowed by the death of Joseph Chamberlain, by the *affaire Caillaux*, and other happenings at home and abroad.

Early in July Osler attended as usual the annual meeting of the Tuberculosis Association at Leeds, where on the 8th he gave an address intended to shock his hearers into action. He emphasized anew that much must be done in the homes, since there was only room for a third of the present cases in sanatoria; and in conclusion said:

In no way can you mark the lintels of your doors that the Angel of the White Scourge will pass with certainty. Despair would fill the heart if it were not for the splendid efforts of officers of public health, who in fifty years have cut in half the mortality from tuberculosis. But, after all, this is a wonderful campaign in which we are

---

[1] At this Encaenia the young Duke of Saxe-Coburg, W. H. Page the American Ambassador, Lord Bryce, a German jurist Dr. Ludwig Mitteiss, and Richard Strauss the musician were all given degrees.

engaged. We have tracked the enemy, and know his every stronghold, and we know his three allies—poverty, bad housing, and drink. But though the ravages have been reduced it remains the most powerful amongst man's innumerable enemies. Before us is a long, slow, hundred years war, or even longer, in which, however, co-ordination, co-operation, and enterprise will win out just as surely as it has done against typhus and typhoid.

The Oslers took advantage of this meeting for a week's outing, of which he writes in the following letter to Mrs. Brewster on July 10 from the Lamb Hotel, Ely:

The summer is getting on, & I shall soon be facing west. I have my passage by the Aquitania, Sept. 7th. Grace & Revere sail to Quebec on the 30th of this month. I am kept by the Library Association which meets in Oxford the first five days of September. . . . I go on to Boston as soon as possible as Grace & R. sail about Sept. 20th. He has to be back by October 1st to get ready for his first term. What would you have thought had I gone into the puddled pool of politics? Sir Wm Anson, the senior member for the University died about a month ago, & delegates from both liberal & conservative caucuses asked me to stand unopposed as an independent University man. It was awfully good & kind of them, but I was not even tempted. No new job at my time of life, thank you! As it is I have more now than I bargained for, & a good deal of work that I should like to do has to be neglected. We are off for a week's motoring in Norfolk, & tomorrow pick up Revere at Quidenham, where he is still with his tutor, & on to Norwich, Cromer & round the coast to Peterboro & back to Cambridge, where I stay for a few days at Magdalene College to work over the Pepys Library & to preside at the first peripatetic meeting of the Bibliographical Society. I wish you could have been with us today. The country is superb. This Cathedral is wonderful.

One of the members of the Bibliographical Society says that the mental photograph he most constantly recalls is that of Osler welcoming the London contingent at the gate of Magdalene College, where they were given lunch on this unwonted excursion. No doubt it was this group of book-loving friends—if any of his groups of friends can be singled out—in which he took chief delight; and though during this July at the instigation of Ingram Bywater he was made a member of the Roxburghe Club and attended their meetings occasionally during the war,[1] it by no means

[1] He was also elected later in the year to membership in the Baskerville Club—a book-publishing club of Cambridge men 'for encouragement of

supplanted the Bibliographical Society, of which he was re-elected President each year until the end. It would appear that the idea of the *Bibliotheca Osleriana* must have taken form while he was browsing in the Pepys Library during this Cambridge visit. Mr. Charles Sayle of the Cambridge University Library, of whom he saw much at this time, became interested in the project, and they had many a subsequent exchange of visits in Oxford and Cambridge, during the course of which the plan of a 'Bibliotheca Prima', 'Bibliotheca Secunda', and so on, came to be crystallized. And innumerable letters on the subject during the coming months passed between the two.

During the next five years the cataloguing of his library on these new lines became Osler's engrossing interest, and in the trials and tribulations of those years it was his refuge and salvation. It was a novel project—this attempt to make a sort of bio-bibliographical catalogue raisonné of his books—at which professional bibliographers shrugged their shoulders; and as the work progressed the difficulties and complexities which they had foreseen merely added to the fascination of the task which was leading Osler on by the nose. He intended that the catalogue should be something more than a mere impersonal list of books, and should have some of the features his great forerunner, Conrad Gesner, the father of bibliography, had put into his 'Bibliotheca Universalis'. He was possibly influenced, too, by Haller's 'Bibliotheca Medicinae Practicae', but far more by the 'Bibliotheca Chemica' of John Ferguson, the Professor of Chemistry at Glasgow, which had been published a few years before.[1] On the death of Professor Ferguson, two years later, Osler paid a tribute to his memory at a meeting of the Bibliographical Society (November 1916), saying in the course of his remarks some things which perhaps unconsciously reflected the views he was formulating in regard to his own collection of books:

> Though an absorbing and profitable study, the results of bibliography are too often recorded in big tomes of intolerable dulness.

bibliographical studies', and to which his recent Cambridge degree now made him eligible.

[1] 'A Catalogue of the Alchemical, Chemical and Pharmaceutical Books

There are at any rate two works on the subject full of the marrow and fatness of books—one is James Atkinson's 'Two-letter Bibliography'; the other is John Ferguson's 'Bibliotheca Chemica', a catalogue of the library of the late Dr. James Young, now in the Glasgow Technical College. While not large, the collection is extraordinarily rich in works on alchemy and sixteenth- and seventeenth-century books on chemistry, and just the sort of library for a man of Professor Ferguson's training to catalogue. It is the most useful special bibliography in my library, and scarcely a day passes that I do not refer to its pages. The merit that appeals to one is a combination of biography with bibliography—beside the book is a picture of the man sketched by a sympathetic hand. Would that in other subjects, students as accurate and as learned could be induced to follow this example! There is an interesting paragraph in the preface which illustrates the spirit in which Professor Ferguson undertook this work: 'The history of chemistry, as indeed of all science, is but a succession of epitaphs upon forgotten men and forgotten discovery. What then, do these men not owe to him who gathers up their works, and in so doing recalls their achievements, and thus labours to lift that icy pall of oblivion which descends on everything human, just because it is human, imperfect, temporary, and has to be forgotten to make way for something else? It was to mitigate that fate as far as human effort can, when it has to strive with the eternal law and necessity of change, that this gathering of the writings of bygone thinkers and workers was made. That they were struggling with error-obscured vision towards the light of reality should cause not neglect of them and contempt for their shortcomings and failure, but should arouse the fellow-feeling and interest of those who at the present moment are engaged in the same struggle, and whose turn for neglect and contempt is coming. Dr. Young realized this, and the library is his effort to awaken and foster such sympathy and remembrance.'

Upon the author of a really good bibliography the iniquity of oblivion vainly scattereth her poppy—to use an expression of Sir Thomas Browne—and the 'Bibliotheca Chemica' will prevail as potently for John Ferguson as has the 'Bibliotheca Britannica' for his great townsman, Robert Watt.

At about that time he wrote to H. S. Birkett at McGill:

I am delighted to hear that you have been appointed Dean, as you have got plenty of glue in your composition, a much needed element in a large faculty group. . . . As I dare say you know, I hope my collection of books will go to the college. It will be particularly rich in historical works & the original editions of the old masters of

---

in the Collection of the late James Young of Kelly and Durris, Esq., LL.D. F.R.S.' Glasgow, Jas. Maclehose & Sons, 1906.

the first rank. Of course, many of these rarer things I could not myself have afforded to buy, but my brother E. B. has given me in the past two years about £1,000 for the purpose of purchasing incunabula & the more expensive editions. Let me know who has been appointed acting librarian as I should like to keep in touch with him, or her. . . . I wonder if we could not have Shepherd's portrait painted by Guthrie in Edinburgh? Is there any example of his work in Montreal? I think he is the best portrait painter on this side at present.

A happening of July 16th betrays one of Osler's characteristic acts, for on the evening of that day a dinner attended by the old house physicians and surgeons of the Radcliffe Infirmary was given at Christ Church to Mr. Horatio P. Symonds, who had served there since 1878. A portrait sketch of the guest of honour, which now hangs in the Infirmary, was presented by Osler, who called attention to the fact that Mr. Symonds was the seventh surgeon in direct succession from Richard Symonds of Atherstone, Warwick, whose family for three generations had served the public in that part of England; and he also read a gracious letter from Mr. John Sargent who had drawn the portrait. The following day, in furtherance of the plan to arouse interest in the repair of Avicenna's tomb, Osler and his colleague, Professor Margoliouth, attended a meeting in London of the Persian Society, when both of them spoke—a futile interest it would seem just at this time, when one considers that on the same day there was a test mobilization of the three British Fleets at Spithead. Winston Churchill at least was not going to be caught napping, but the possibility of a European war, however disturbing were the rumours of Austro-Serbian relations, seemed far less probable than war in Ulster.

'I am shockingly full of engagements', he wrote to his friend Shepherd at that time. 'I cannot get away on account of some local meetings. Grace and the boy leave by the *Calgarian* on July 30th. I sail September 7th to New York and shall be a week in Baltimore at the time of the celebration. I wish you could see our roses which Grace gathers by the bushel.' He had made a promise, also, to McCrae to give an introductory lecture to his students at Jefferson on the opening of the school year, when he evidently intended to 'sound a note of warning to the average school' in regard to the full-time programme,[1] for he wrote to Dock that 'the danger will be of getting "half-baked" clinicians who do not know chickenpox from measles. Ewald tells me that there is a good deal of growling in Germany about the ignorance of the ordinary clinical details on the part of the younger men.'

The week of July 26th saw two large medical gatherings in England. A horde of American surgeons had invited themselves to London; and at the same time the annual meeting of the British Medical Association was held at Aberdeen. Both these meetings were as well attended as if nothing unusual was in the air; and at both of them were a number of foreign guests, including some eminent Austrians. Osler was at Aberdeen during the week, the guest of Professor A. W. Mackintosh, who recalls that—

> He arrived on the Monday or Tuesday, and left I think on the Friday (July 31st) for Colonsay. He was in splendid form; full of life and interest in all that was going on. He summed up in his usual clear way a discussion on Artificial Pneumothorax which was introduced by Dr. Rist of Paris. At the annual dinner of the association on the Thursday night he proposed the health of the President (Sir Alexander Ogston) in a few admirable sentences. His behaviour and his speech were simply those of the old Osler. It is an astonishing fact that I at least never for a moment realized during that week that there was any possibility of war for us, and I believe that Sir William was quite in the same position: we scarcely looked at a paper—there was no time for it. We did hear, I believe, that there were no Austrians at the dinner, as they had been 'recalled', but this seemed natural as the original dispute concerned Austria. I believe that this fully explains Sir William's naïve act in starting for Colonsay. No man could have been more natural and delightful, throughout.

---

[1] He managed to get off a letter to McCrae which was read to the students, and from which some quotations reminiscent of Bovell have already been taken. In all probability the address he had prepared was in large part the same that he sent to Henry W. Cattell, the editor of *International Clinics* (Phila., 1915, iv, pp. 1–5), in the 25th anniversary number of which it appears as the leading article. In this paper—The coming of Age of Internal Medicine in America—occurs a paragraph which begins: 'The burning question to be considered by this generation relates to the whole-time clinical teacher'; and he proceeds to express himself emphatically and finally on the subject.

In Osler's account-book, opposite the dates 'Sunday August 2nd–Saturday 8th' he has jotted down, 'Colonsay with the Strathconas. On Monday heard of the declaration of war with Germany [the ultimatum ?]. Grace & Revere sailed on the 31st. I was to follow on the Aquitania Sept. 5th.' Things had moved rapidly during those memorable days when it became evident that the peace of Europe depended upon whether Germany saw that her opportunity had come. On the 29th Austria had declared war against Serbia; Grey's proposal for a peace conference had been refused by Germany, and the possibility of a spread of the conflict hung by a thread. On July 31st came the Russian mobilization; on August 1st Germany's declaration of war; on August 3rd her troops entered Belgium. Then the avalanche. But Osler by this time had reached the Strathconas' remote island, and something of his feelings are expressed in a letter of August 6th from Colonsay House to Mrs. Brewster:

Here is a nice mess! Goodness knows when you will get this, but you will have had a cable. I cannot leave as I have to help in organizing the medical dept. of the Territorial force. Grace and Revere sailed on the 31st. She will be furious to have the ocean between us, & she has been on the committee of the nursing dept. If a steamer is available they will return at once. I am so sorry for the poor souls stranded on the continent. I have a niece & her daughter at Aix. I hope they have got to Switzerland. It all seems very unnecessary, but the nations are still in the nursery stage, squabbling & fighting like children. I do hope you will see Revere if they sail from New York, Grace is sure to telephone you, but it is very uncertain & they may decide to stay until it is perfectly safe to cross. I am stranded in this far away island about forty miles from the coast, with the Strathconas. We have been trying to get away, but the trains from Oban south have been too crowded. We leave tonight. I am so disappointed not to see you all. But it is a small matter in comparison with the tragedies that are inevitable in the families of friends. . . .

It all seems very unsuspecting of Osler. Indeed, on Friday, July 30th, while the B. M. A. was in session in Aberdeen, a War Emergency Committee had been formed at the London offices of the association, 'to organize the profession in England, Wales and Ireland in such a way as to enable the Government to use every available practitioner to serve the country in such a manner as to turn his qualifications to the best possible use'. On the memorandum which must have been sent to Oxford the same day, Osler's name headed the list of the committee-men appointed by the representatives. On August 4th, the day after Germany violated her neutrality pact, came England's declaration of war; and in a few days the vanguard of the 'Contemptibles' was on French soil.

On getting back to Oxford Osler found much to do. On the 10th he wrote to H. M. Hurd in Baltimore: 'It will be impossible for me to leave in these troublous times and to my great sorrow I shall have to give up my proposed visit. Lady Osler & Revere sailed 10 days ago just before war was declared. We shall be here in the centre of the hospital work, as the plan is to utilize the university and college buildings. Already within the week the big Examination Schools have been converted into a hospital—nearly 300 beds are ready and we could take patients in a few days. I am trying to get in touch with Welch who I fear is stranded somewhere on the Continent. Miss Nutting too is there.' The number of beds apparently grew rapidly, for on the same day he wrote to D'Arcy Power: 'I wish you could see the Schools!—never put to such good use. About 350 beds in already.' Also on the 10th, to Winford H. Smith: 'Fortunately the country has been expecting this & the organization has been remarkably prompt. We have converted the Examination Schools into a hospital for 400 beds.' And four days later to W. S. Thayer: 'The country is extraordinarily calm and it looks as if we should be able to hold the seas. In the short space of ten days we've turned the Schools into a big hospital ready for 480 patients.' It had become a 1,000-bed hospital before many weeks elapsed. Meanwhile, in order to pick up the rest of his family, a letter written by Lady Osler on August 16th on the R. M. S. *Calgarian* may be quoted:

When I found out that W. O. was not intending to come with us but was waiting in Oxford for the meeting of a Librarians' Asso'n I was annoyed and said I would not go without him, but he insisted that he wanted Revere to see his uncles & Campbell so we started on the 31st. Sir William was in Aberdeen at the British Medical

Association, and if my brother-in-law E. B. O. of Toronto, who was in London standing by the Dominion Bank, had only told me of the conditions we might have been saved this muddle and worry. We landed at Rimouski and went to Cacouna where we found the excitement intense, as nearly all the Montreal business men have houses there and were telegraphing their wives. . . I could get no word from Oxford until Sunday when a cable came saying 'COME WHEN SAFE'. We left at once for Murray Bay to see Campbell, and I telegraphed my people. Mr. Allan of this line was at Cacouna, and said he would sail this ship on which we came over, on Thursday. We went on to Quebec, and the Reveres and Susan Chapin met us there. Campbell came from Cap à l'Aigle, and Nona Gwyn too; so we saw some people, hysterical though it was. We are now half-way over, and thus far quite safe. The ship is painted black, and every port and window covered with blankets at night. The whole situation is too horrible; of course one cannot take it in as yet. I expect soon to be very busy, as I am on the Hospital Board at Oxford. . . .

And on her return she found a man 'quite different from what I have ever seen him'. Osler had a premonition from the first, that the war somehow was to bring home to him a great sorrow, as well as to bring 'the inevitable tragedies in the families of friends'. But this never appeared on the surface, and recourse must be had to the letters of others, to disclose something of his movements and reactions at the outset of what to him was an abhorrent and unnecessary strife. Few men could have loved peace more than he, and during this troubled time he went calmly about his business, making a practice of leading conversation at his house and table away from the gossip of war. There follows a contrast of two letters, both written from 13 Norham Gardens on August 22nd, the day the Germans had occupied Ghent. The first, to Dr. J. W. Wigmore of Bath in pursuit of the two Dr. Olivers, one of whom has come down to posterity on a biscuit:

Dear Wigmore, Why were the biscuits called Bath Olivers? Did Oliver ever give a description of them &, if so, where? Sincerely yours, Wm OSLER. Has his original formula ever been published?

The second, on the same date, was from Lady Osler to her sister in Boston:

We reached Liverpool just too late to catch the 9.30 Oxford

train. There was no special, so we had to wait until 11.30. After getting off the luggage, helped by our ever-useful Great Western man, we went to see the cathedral, this calm proceeding being more to Revere's liking than seeing soldiers. There were plenty everywhere—on the dock and in front of all public buildings. The trip to Oxford was uneventful; we took on two carriages of recruits at Birmingham and left weeping wives and mothers in the station. At Oxford we found W. O. looking very fit and well and evidently thankful to see us, never once saying 'Why did you come back?'; and listening patiently to the tales of our experiences, and apparently satisfied that Revere had seen one aunt, two uncles, two godfathers, four babies, two godsons and many friends. Oxford looked the same, and it was hard to understand why we had rushed back. Tea was on the terrace; the garden a mass of gorgeous bloom—a fresh crop of roses, and wonderful snapdragons.

First *I* talked, and told our experiences; and then W. O. told his. He left Aberdeen the day we sailed, and went to Colonsay that evening in the yacht. Monday, Harry Howard arrived, and brought the news. They tried all of them to get away that night but couldn't. All wires were cut off, and trains used only to move Scotch soldiers, and no reservations could be made. They never got to London until Friday morning I think. Donald Howard has gone to Belgium with his regiment; Harry waiting for his commission. I think Willie went directly to London where he found Edmund, [his brother] worried to death about Isobel Meredith and the bank. W. O. evidently spent the following week mostly in London where there is a Canadian Committee to arrange for the applications coming from Canada, and he undertook to do what he could about the medical and nursing applications. Then, here, a most wonderful work has been done. The Examinations Schools have been turned into a thoroughly equipped hospital—operating room, p.m. room, chapel, and every detail complete—the courtyard with pavilions built to contain beds—the large picture of the Kaiser put in the cellar. Opposite, the Masonic Hall has fifty beds, part of the same organization; Magdalen School is turned into a hospital; eighty beds in the Infirmary grounds; 1,000 Territorials in Christ Church. Balliol and Keble have been moving on into camps; everyone has come home; all heads of colleges but Brasenose, who is lost in Germany. All helping, all working like slaves. The plan is for our hospital to receive patients who are in Netley the big army hospital near Southampton—I mean patients there now from the regular army. They want that free at once, to put in the wounded coming across the Channel; then gradually others will come to us. These military hospitals have been established all over the country—3,000 beds in Cambridge, etc. Willie says that the quiet, calm way in which it has been done could never be believed without seeing it.

Red Cross workers are everywhere. Professor Thomson turned his big laboratory into a work-room and Mrs. Melville Lee and Mrs. Arthur Thomson started a work-room at once. I could not begin to tell you what they have done. I spent nearly all day there yesterday, and as Mrs. Lee has given out I have been made the Chairman. It is in the Museum. They have furnished the hospital with night-shirts and day shirts enough to start with; and I could not tell you the other things for the soldiers who have started. Friday morning I reported at the hospital, and shall hope to have regular work there, but fancy this work-room will take much time for the present. Everybody looks very serious and earnest, W. O. quite different to what I have ever seen him. The newspapers are so unlike the American and Canadian papers—no pictures, except in the small cheap ones. An enormous number of troops has been moved across the Channel, no one really knows how many. Of course we know so many men; I hardly dare think of the *young ones.* Revere meditates and is very quiet. He will join the Training Corps in college at once. I was obliged to go to London this morning, and it is strange to see the Red Cross on Devonshire House.

You would never believe the stories and experiences of people getting home. . . . This town is full of Americans waiting; and London too; 2,000 left yesterday on the *Olympic.* Our nice secretary has enlisted but not gone yet; Benning and William [the butler and the chauffeur] are here. We are only using the motor for necessity and to help tired people. I am cutting down all expenses so as to have money to use for other things; *napkin-rings* and *bare table*, no sweets, and two courses for dinner. The first week, prices went up in the skies but are better now.

Monday night. I have been all day at the work-room; sent off 200 shirts and started much work. We are beginning things for women and children at odd moments. Nearly all the large houses in London are used for different good works and hundreds of country houses are turned into hospitals already. All this Red Cross training has been splendid. It is almost impossible to explain the feeling: the world is so occupied with the cruelty to Belgium that one's own troubles and fears seem forgotten—even Mrs. Max Müller calling the Kaiser a 'mad vicious brute'. I was glad to find the dear lady alive, I feared this would kill her. Her son arrived Saturday from Budapest, coming through with the returning Ambassador. The Bucklers were at a chalet in the Savoy Mountains and were really without a penny. Mr. B. managed to get through, and has gone back on a bicycle with gold. I could write on and on, telling what I have heard, but you would be exhausted. To-day the news is bad, but one cannot really trust anything. I am sending a copy of the 'White Paper'—the report of the diplomatic transactions, and you can see how Sir Edward Grey fought against it. We went to Ewelme for church yesterday. Thirty men have gone from the village and hardly any left in the choir. . . .

Even from Ewelme! Just as they had gone with the husband of Alice of Suffolk from Ewelme to Agincourt. No wonder the descendants of those men saw visions of the 'Bowmen' on their retreat from Mons. So these daily letters continued, full of details of work; of rescuing friends on the Continent; of the sewing-room in the Town Hall—'not an idle person about'; of the bad news from the Somme; and on the 27th:

. . . We have no patients yet. Willie is ordering a Colonel's uniform as he can't go into the wards without it, and is Honorary Colonel of the Oxfordshire Regiment. He is Consulting Physician to a hospital in Devon paid for by Mr. Singer and being arranged by Lady Randolph Churchill and other Americans; also a Canadian hospital supported by Canadian Masons near Netley; and 100 Canadian nurses coming. Revere has gone up the river with Jack Slessor for a few days; there was nothing for him to do here and he looked pale and worried. . . .

Meanwhile the first 100,000 of 'Kitchener's mob' was being recruited and trained, for England was plastered with Kitchener's posters—'Father, what did you do in the Great War?' &c. But there was no Mr. Britling about Osler. He knew from the first, without waylaying authorities, what his job would be, and quietly went about it without fret or fuss.[1] He, with others, appreciated the menace from congregating large bodies of men, but such a thing as compulsory vaccination for the troops the Government was unwilling to advocate, and an appeal to the men themselves was the only recourse. To this task he promptly set himself. So on that same evening of the 27th, while his wife was writing that 'the army order of

[1] When the 'Territorials' were first organized by Lord Haldane and it was decided where the chief hospital bases were to be, Osler was made [1908] an honorary Colonel, but he was never 'called up' even during the war. He only wore his uniform when on official hospital visits—indeed he ordered a Lt.-Colonel's uniform by mistake and never took the trouble to have the insignia changed. He held a unique position, and could go to War Office or Head-quarters much more comfortably in mufti—an action which would have brought rebuke on almost any one else. 'Swank' and 'swagger-stick' might be for others.

THE VILLAGE OF EWELME

400 night-shirts is finished', he prepared this letter for *The Times*:

Sir,—In war the microbe kills more than the bullet. Malaria, cholera, typhus, typhoid, and dysentery have been the scourges of armies. From the first three our soldiers are not likely to suffer; but it will be very difficult to prevent outbreaks of dysentery or of typhoid fever, of which in the South African War more men died than were killed in action. Against this we now possess an effective vaccine, and I write to urge that antityphoid vaccination should be made compulsory in the army. The very simple procedure is followed by a slight and not often incapacitating indisposition and there are no harmful effects.

The work of the French army doctors and of British army surgeons, particularly in India, has shown conclusively the remarkable reduction in the incidence of typhoid when vaccination is thoroughly carried out. The experience of the American Army is of special value, as the disease is so much more prevalent in the United States. . . . Fortunately, in this country typhoid fever is not common, but in camps it is difficult to avoid contagion from 'carriers'—men who harbour the germ while well themselves. Abroad the men are sure to be exposed, and I would urge most earnestly that vaccination be made compulsory. Sir William Leishman in the *Lancet* last week has pleaded for the adoption of the practice. The Vaccine Department of the Army Medical College, Lister Institute, and many of the pathological laboratories throughout the country have a plentiful supply. Pending the issue of a compulsory order, it is the duty of the medical officers of the Territorial Force to urge as many men as possible to be vaccinated [etc. etc.].

But there was great opposition on the part of that still-powerful group, the antivivisectionists and the anti-vaccinationists, to any compulsory legislation of this nature. Hence it was necessary to appeal directly to the newly enlisted men, and one of Osler's many heart-to-heart talks given to the officers and men [1] in the camps at Churn, on the Berkshire Downs, has been preserved:

What I wish to urge [he said] is a true knowledge of your foes, not simply of the bullets, but of the much more important enemy, the bacilli. In the wars of the world they have been as Saul and David—the one slaying thousands, the other tens of thousands. I can never see a group of recruits marching to the dépôt without

[1] This brief address, an appeal to the men's patriotism, he entitled 'Bacilli and Bullets', and as one of the penny war pamphlets issued by the Oxford Press in 1914 it was widely circulated.

mentally asking what percentage of these fine fellows will die legitimate and honourable deaths from wounds, what percentage will perish miserably from neglect of ordinary sanitary precautions? It is bitter enough to lose thousands of the best of our young men in a hideous war, but it adds terribly to the tragedy to think that more than one-half of the losses may be due to preventable disease.

And he went on to tell in simple terms of the sad experience of the South African War; of the Spanish-American War; of what vaccination meant; of Almroth Wright's discovery and how it had been successfully introduced into all other countries but their own, and in some was compulsory; and he ended by saying:

It is not a serious procedure; you may feel badly for twenty-four hours, and the site of the inoculation will be tender, but I hope I have said enough to convince you that, in the interests of the cause, you should gladly put up with this temporary inconvenience. If the lessons of past experience count, any expeditionary force on the Continent has much more to fear from the bacillus of typhoid fever than from bullets and bayonets. Think again of South Africa with its 57,000 cases of typhoid fever! With a million of men in the field, their efficiency will be increased one-third if we can prevent enteric. It can be prevented, it *must be prevented*; but meanwhile the decision is in your hands, and I know it will be in favour of your King and Country.

He was a little naïve, possibly, in regard to some of the consequences of the war, and could not believe that it would affect either the friendship or the humanitarian attitude of individuals on whichever side they might be. For at about the same time that ninety-three German 'intellectuals', Ehrlich among them, were preparing to sign their famous 'appeal to the civilized world' to believe as untrue that Germany had caused the war, had trespassed in Belgium, had treated Louvain brutally, &c., and on the same day as his letter had gone to *The Times*, Osler wrote:

Dear Ehrlich,—Do you think it would be possible to arrange for the manufacture of salvarsan in the United States under your direction. I have had letters and have been asked to communicate with you through the American Ambassador in Berlin. Perhaps Flexner has already communicated with you. No doubt the Rockefeller Institute would undertake the control and arrange that your financial interests were protected. Very sincerely yours,

Wm Osler.

This letter was enclosed to Mr. Page, asking if he could forward it to Frankfort, and explaining that Professor Ehrlich was an old friend, and that the matter was really one of national importance. On September 1st, with the Germans in Amiens, Lady Osler wrote to her sister :

Never have I seen in England such wonderful weather as we are having now—clear, fresh and sunny, day after day. It seems almost mockery when everyone is so depressed and worried. You would not notice anything different here, though of course the streets seem rather empty because women are busy inside. There is a general feeling that Kitchener's call for a 'New Army' has not been responded to promptly. I think men in villages do not understand—they seem to feel we have gone to help France and there is not the obligation. I don't believe they lag behind. It seems as though *I* should expire with that awful *loyal feeling* running down my back; and I loathe being a woman and sixty years old. . . . We have had such a *talking* week-end, Isobel Meredith and the two girls telling their experiences coming in a motor from Aix to Boulogne; Orville Bullitt who came for Sunday telling of his, from Munich to London, and being arrested as a German spy at Southampton. Edmund was here too; his predictions for the future are very gloomy—financially I mean. Willie too listless to talk—except German atrocities. . . . All my letters have been returned from Murray Bay, and I see how dreadfully anxious W. O. was. Poor dear, in one he said 'You had better stay a month', and on the same page, 'I hope to hear you are coming at once.' . . . Our hospital has no wounded yet, except men injured in camps near here. The Canadians in London are managing a hospital. W. O. of course, and Donald Armour, are on the Committee; and probably W. O. has to go this week to Southampton about the situation, near Netley I think. The Queen of Belgium has brought her children to England, —came yesterday, and will leave them with Lord Curzon. I wonder if you have seen in your papers that Lady Lansdowne and some others have suggested only wearing a white or mauve band on the sleeve for mourning. It seems so wise. Mr. Merry's sister told me to-day she had one son in the Fleet and two in France and was so glad. I feel a coward when each day brings us nearer December 28th, Revere's 19th birthday. I have read and re-read the Revere memorial [Gettysburg] and hope to have courage.

Though as a territorial officer Osler had his own official area in Oxfordshire, his services were eagerly sought by American and Canadian enterprises beyond his district. Thus in August, when the Canadian Hospital was started in London by Canadians and Anglo-Canadians, and also when the Queen's Canadian Military Hospital was established at Beechborough Park, Shorncliffe, near Folkestone, he was made Physician-in-Chief, with Donald Armour Surgeon-in-Chief, posts which they held till the end. On the outbreak of the war, too, the American Women's War Relief Fund organized and maintained an auxiliary hospital of 250 beds at Paignton, and subsequently (1917) opened an officers' hospital at Lancaster Gate. To both of these places Osler acted as consultant; and Lady Harcourt, who had much to do with their organization and, as she says, came in constant touch with Sir William, writes that 'to every one—medical officers, matron, nursing staff and patients, his visits were like a ray of sunshine. His oversight was what made us efficient; his sympathy and enthusiasm smoothed our path'. And long after, when, on January 1st, 1918, these hospitals of the 'A.W.W.R.F.' came to be taken over by the American Red Cross, Osler was given, 'in token of their gratitude for his invaluable services', an inscribed gift.

Then there was the Daughters of the Empire Hospital for Canadian officers, and the Duchess of Connaught's Canadian Red Cross Hospital at Taplow, which he regularly visited each week throughout the war; and when the Canadians first arrived and were stationed on Salisbury Plain and went through an epidemic of cerebrospinal meningitis he was often among them. It is a universal comment that whenever a difficult case turned up, or whenever any one wanted help or advice, Sir William was sure to be on hand. But this is getting ahead of the story. Even in those dark days—the darkest in the history of modern times—when the French Government had withdrawn to Bordeaux and people were fleeing from Paris, he writes to Thayer: 'Things are looking blue for poor old France, but the position to-day is very different from that of 1870, and we are all confident that in the long run the Allies will come out on top.' Others might be filled with gloom, but he would be sure to add a postscript to his letters, whatever their subject-matter—'spirit here splendid' or words of this purport. So he was one of those who played a leading rôle of optimist during the next five years. To his old friend 'Ned' Milburn he writes: 'I was to have sailed to-morrow, but of course I cannot leave with this wretched war raging. We shall win out in the end. How splendidly Canada is doing!' There were too many people in those first months of the war who did little but sit back and criticize: any one would serve as a target—Haldane, Kitchener, Winston Churchill, Woodrow Wilson, Joffre, the Government, the Army, the Navy, the campaign. But there was one happening of the early days of the war which touched him to the quick. 'What a cursed act of vandalism to destroy Louvain!' And he was apparently the first to set in motion the idea, expressed in the following note of September 2nd to A. W. Pollard, that the Library be restored:

> Do you think we [the Bibliographical Society] should do anything about the Louvain outrage in the way of sending an official letter of sympathy; & when matters quiet down I am going to suggest that we help them in a small way in the restoration of the library. I would like to undertake with some friends to replace the books of Vesalius who perhaps after Erasmus is the greatest name on their list. . . .

A succession of letters, chiefly to American friends, on the same subject followed. 'Of course,' he says, 'nothing could be done at present, but an Anglo-American committee should be formed so that when these modern Huns are out of the country we could put matters into shape. I am particularly interested in helping with the library.' All of this came in due time to fruition, though Osler's part in it has been lost.

> These are stirring times in old England [he wrote to Mrs. Brewster on September 4th]. At last the country is ablaze and recruiting going on everywhere. We are very busy—Grace particularly as President here of the Soldiers' Guild. She leaves the house at 9 & is away nearly all day. We are starting two hospitals for the Canadian Contingent, and as I am on the executive committee I am in town nearly every day. It is very nice to see how warm the American sympathy is with England & France. Such trials as people have had in getting out of Germany. Some of our Oxford Dons have been captured & put to work in the fields! The first sad list of casualties came out to-day—two young Oxford friends have fallen. Good will come of all this horror if it wrecks for ever the cursed militarism of Germany. How I wish I could be with you for a weeks peace at Mt. Kisco.

The relief from a month of suspense which came after 'the first Marne' is unnoticed in his letters. Military operations interested him little, and he did not waste time studying movements of troops and putting pins in maps. 'I have been trying to get into touch with Van Gehuchten & Denys, so as to offer to take charge, here in Oxford, of the members of the families of the professors,' he wrote to L. F. Barker on September 9th. And the same day from Oxford went broadcast this printed letter signed by the Vice-Chancellor, the Principal of Brasenose, Osler, Miss Mabel Price, and Mrs. William Max Müller:

Oxford, 9th September, 1914.

Dear Sir or Madam,—With the approval of the Belgian Minister a small committee has been formed at Oxford to aid our colleagues of Louvain University. A number of people have expressed their willingness to help by taking temporary charge of members of the families of the Professors and Tutors. If you wish to join this movement please send your name to the Secretary, Mrs. Max Müller, 7 Norham Gardens, and say whether you could take a man, woman, or child, and for how long.

From Lady Osler to Arthur T. Hadley. Sept. 13, 1914.

I have just written to Mr. Stokes asking him to try to raise some money for the professors from Louvain who have taken refuge in England. Many are coming to Oxford, and are being taken into private families, but where there are families of five children it is difficult. Incomes here are reduced and undergraduates are not returning. At Magdalen only 47 coming; Christ Church about 100; Keble 70; Oriel 80; so you see what it means. About 350 lodging-houses are vacant. We hope to board some of these people, and help them until they can get on their feet and find their friends. I am sure the university's sympathy will be great and some may like to feel certain the money will be properly used. If you will help at Yale it will be a great assistance. I have asked Mr. Stokes to send anything to my banker in Boston. . . .

There was, of course, a most generous response from all sides when the Oslers asked for anything, but it is doubtful if their American friends had any idea of how they were being pressed, and of their anxieties. He was importuned to compose a message of greeting to atone for his absence from the reunion the Johns Hopkins graduates were about to hold in celebration of the twenty-fifth year of the hospital. And this he did; though he could have had little heart for it, even unaware that there was considerable pro-German sympathy in Baltimore at the time. His long letter [1] read at the reunion by W. S. Thayer contains only this brief allusion to the war: 'It is a small matter that I am not with you. "When the greater malady is fixed, the lesser is scarce felt" expresses my feeling in the present crisis.' This was all. And in his note of September 11th which accompanied the message he says: 'The country here is in fine spirits, and ready for tremendous sacrifices. Grace is working early and late. She has got the true New England spirit. A university regiment of students will be organized at once and they will be under military discipline. Revere of course will join.'

The university indeed, and its colleges, had turned their undivided attention to the war. War is chiefly a matter of young men, and of course the colleges were emptied, but this applied no less to other institutions like the Bodleian and the Press. In some way they must carry on, as they did, for example, at the Press, where Mr. Cannan, the Secretary to the Delegates, with the volunteer help of his three daughters, kept an office running, while those too old to serve worked at the presses. On September 14 the famous volume 'Why we are at War' was issued, quickly went through ten impressions, and was translated into six foreign languages! The host of Oxford Pamphlets followed. There are few records of what led up to this; there was little time for records, and Mr. Cannan must have made his arrangements verbally with H. W. C. Davis in the first week of August. The present Secretary, at least, finds no records, and merely recalls that when he got back to Oxford early in September he met Osler on the station platform, and that Osler played with his six-months-old baby as if no war was on. So these two letters:

Sept. 11th.

My dear Osler,—Advance copy sent herewith shows *Why we are at War*. The general public won't know why until Monday. We

---

[1] Subsequently published under the title of 'Looking Back', in Macphail's journal, among what he called his 'Books and Men snippets'. This, and a review of the 'Life and Letters of Nathan Smith', both forwarded on Sept. 25th, were the last two papers (Nos. XXV and XXVI) of the series.

are sending a copy to Spring-Rice. If you want us to send a copy to anyone in U.S.A. telephone tonight. To-morrow is too late for the mail.

Sept. 15th.

Dear Chapman, Thank you so much for the advance copy of the Red Book which I did not see with your letter until this eve. My secretary telephoned a list for me this p.m. Greetings to that baby—anything sweeter I never saw. You must have been reading Quillett's Callipaedia ! Yours, [etc].

And it is probable, to judge from the following, written on the same date (the 15th) by Lady Osler to her sister, that the list of names included that of Woodrow Wilson :

Of course we are feeling hopeful to-day over the retreat from Paris, but one hardly dares put too much faith in it. The news was posted on the Town Hall Sunday morning when we came out from the Cathedral. The Yeomanry stationed in Christ Church were at the service and Scott Holland preached a wonderful sermon. Poor dear Reggie [W. O.] can't go to church—he says he can't endure the prayers and hymns. To me it is a relief to get ready to burst and not be able to. The attitude W. O. is in seems more unreal than anything else—he allows everyone to abuse the Germans and even says vicious things himself of the Kaiser. He is sending letters and books to President Wilson and all the prominent men—about Germany's lying attitude. It is really extraordinary to hear him. We have seven Louvain people in the house. The enclosed will show you what we are doing—I have written several people to help. . . . The Pooles have a Professor with his wife and two babies who just escaped, and *one manuscript* from the Library—the only thing saved from the University. He gave us the address of the Professor of Bacteriology in Folkestone and we asked him to come with his wife and family. To my horror I found at 9 p.m. Friday that there were five children and they were due at 11.15 Saturday—Parsons, Lizzie and William away ! We hustled about and had all ready—went to meet them and only Professor D. came. When he found he was not to pay board he would not bring his family. It seems they were at the seaside near Ostend and got away easily bringing money and clothes, and two maids. So they have a decent place at Folkestone. I am getting him a house and they will come for the winter. The two Professors lunched here and the stories were awful. Anything more wonderful than the kindness of people here I could never imagine. Letters are pouring in with offers of hospitality—but money for clothes, etc., is very important. The lodging-houses here will all be empty this winter and we shall have to help these people. . . . The big lecture-room is full of wounded Germans. In our work-room we are making clothes for Belgians, night-shirts for a hospital, and in a rush 500 sacks to hold straw for recruits to sleep on in College halls. When you read these things you will feel as though Oxford would look changed, but it doesn't—only people look so worried and anxious. . . . Now I am going to bother you. Will you arrange to have the enclosed [Belgian appeal] put in the papers—whichever you think best, and receive subscriptions which can be put to my account? . . .

Probably few who thought they knew intimately the blithe Osler and his ready sympathy fully realized his real depth of feeling and tenderness. Under ordinary circumstances he could conceal his emotions, but he 'could not endure the prayers and hymns'. His collection of books came to be his solace when the day's work was done, and he used them habitually to camouflage his feelings and to divert conversation from the otherwise inevitable topic of war.

To J. William White from W. O. Oxford, September 21.

Dear J. William, Sorry to be detained here instead of sailing as I had intended but it was impossible, of course, to leave in this scrimmage. The spirit of the country is A.1, & at present things look very favourable. Grace is working about eight hours a day on shirts, &c. Revere joins the Officers' Training Corps, &, as soon as he is ready . . . 67 wounded Germans came in last week—fine looking fellows all of them—the bullet-wounds trivial, but the shrapnel horrid. I am lecturing at various camps on the typhoid question. I enclose you a proof of the lecture. We are getting a group of Louvain professors here—Denys, the well-known bacteriologist, & his wife come to-day. They tell a gruesome tale. Send me two or three of your reprints: one on *White's operation* & *Operation per se*, and any other special ones. I do not want the catalogue of the Bibliotheca Osleriana without your name in it—to appear 10 years hence! If you have any of the early papers of Hayes Agnew to spare, send them also. I am gradually getting a great collection, which if all goes well, will go to McGill. Many thanks for your card. . . .

In every letter he speaks in this same off-hand way about his son—'as soon as he is ready'. But the agony which underlay this casual remark never appears. 'All here are working', he writes on the 25th to the son of his old friend, Archibald Malloch. 'The spirit of the country is splendid. We have had several young Oxford friends killed. Revere enters the training corps on the 1st and will apply for a commission as soon as he is fit. I am very busy—in town three days a week getting a Canadian Contingent Hospital organized.'

Meanwhile he had been inspecting hospitals, and though 'bombarded with anti-vaccination literature' he continued with his lectures on health and personal hygiene to the new batches of recruits at the camps within reach of Oxford. And yet he writes to Anson Phelps Stokes that he will 'go on with the Silliman Lectures at once'.[1] And again on October 2nd to J. William White, who by this time had forgotten his cardiac neurosis and wanted to help:

> I should think there would be no difficulty in your getting work in connection with the Red Cross. The wounded are beginning to come in. We have about 400 in the Schools—only a few serious. The country is in fine form, recruits pouring in, everybody working, and extraordinarily little fuss. We have got seven or eight Belgian professors here & their families, & some of them, poor devils, absolutely penniless. We are trying to get them settled in lodgings & small houses. Many of them are charming people—& some absolutely destitute. If you can squeeze a few hundred dollars out of any of your friends for them we shall be very much obliged.

Indeed White could; and these appeals to their American friends in Boston, Philadelphia, and Baltimore were promptly and generously responded to, so that money and boxes of clothes began to pour in. Meanwhile he writes on the evening of October 3rd to L. L. Mackall: 'While you are in Holland just pick up that quarto edition 1688 of Sir Thomas Browne—it must be loafing about on the shelves somewhere'; and to F. H. Garrison: 'If you ever come across copies of the Congressional Reports dealing with the anaesthesia question please remember me'; and to Dr. Neligan of the Legation at Teheran: 'There is nothing to do but postpone matters relating to Avicenna's tomb, and keep your eye open please for any good MSS. I am very anxious to have one of Rhazes.'

On October 9th Lady Osler writes: 'This is the day Revere goes into college and it is all so different to what we had expected. My heart aches for him for he is not

[1] In a letter a year later he says: 'I have bought off the Yale book by returning my honorarium. I was doubtful about them [the lectures]. I suppose I have got critical—possibly hyper-critical! the deeper I get into medical history.'

doing what he thought would have been better—but has not complained once—only said, "I will do what Dad thinks best and train here this term." Willie runs if I speak of it.' Every one knows what 'it' implied, and 'it' was being faced by parents throughout England even for immature boys below military age. On this same day Osler says in a note to Macphail: 'We are looking out for the Canadian Contingent—I shall go down and see them as soon as they arrive. I hear they are to be seasoned here a bit before going to the front.' And it may be said that the third generation from Canon Osler was so well represented among them as to occasion an editorial in a Toronto paper entitled 'The Osler Volunteers'.

The idea must have occurred to more than one thoughtful person, even in these anxious times, that provision must be made for a proper collection of army medical statistics by ensuring more convenient records of the sick and wounded than is usually provided for by a Staff whose chief duty, after all, is to prosecute the war. In reply to a letter from J. G. Adami, who was greatly interested in the matter from the Canadian standpoint, Osler wrote on October 9th: [1]

That is a very interesting suggestion. As far as I can see from the work at the Base Hospital here, the histories & reports of cases

---

[1] Early in October 1914 (writes Sir Walter Fletcher) Lord Moulton and I called upon Keogh and suggested that the Medical Research Committee might be of help. Keogh said that the routine records of the hospitals and other units would be well done in France by the well-trained Expeditionary Force, but might be badly done in the Territorial hospitals and elsewhere.... A week or two later the Army Council officially accepted our offer and notified all the units accordingly. We worked out a new card system. I remember my surprise at finding that a million cards (our first order) weighed 6½ tons. We took a house in Bloomsbury for the purpose, and that was occupied and in use before Christmas 1914.

On October 27th Osler wrote to Moulton (as Chairman of the M. R. C.) to suggest that the M. R. C. should help in the collection of statistics. I answered him by return, and he wrote on the 29th to say he was glad to hear that we had already arranged this. He had seen the need for this at once on his visits to Territorial and other hospitals at home.

There was never any difficulty with the War Office about this. The Army Council backed us up through thick and thin. The work outgrew the Bloomsbury house, was transferred to the British Museum, and thus we compiled an alphabetical card index to all of the admission and discharge books of all hospitals in all areas at home and overseas, and of all other units of wounded, of which we have had about 600 already, & the reports on the operations, are very good. The difficulty is that they are all filed away, & nobody has the time subsequently to work up the material as a whole. I am afraid we will at once get up against the Red Tape in the army, but I will send on your letter to Keogh, the new Surgeon-General. A letter to the Lancet on the lines you have written would be very helpful.

General Sir Alfred Keogh, who has recently been seen the recipient of a complimentary dinner on his retirement from the army, had been called back into service as Director-General of the Medical Service. He responded favourably to the proposal of ‘ Colonel ’ Osler, who wrote to him again on another topic a few days later, using anything but military formulas :

Dear Keogh, If I can be of any service in a health campaign in the camps let me know. I have been doing a little of it, and as you say, it is a most important business. I am preparing a demonstration of books & articles illustrating the evolution of our knowledge of military & naval preventive medicine. It is a good story for the country. I visited on Saturday the Convalescent Home that Mr. Mortimer Singer has opened at Milton Hill about twelve miles from here. If you would like to see an ideal spot come down. I could motor you over. It is a splendid piece of work. . . .

There was a good deal of talk in England about ‘ business as usual ’, and this to many people meant play as well as business. But Osler had no heart for other than the day's work. When asked by the College of Physicians to give the FitzPatrick Lectures for 1915 he promptly sent his regrets. And when some one suggested the continuance of one of the Oxford dinner clubs he replied : ‘ I think we should not meet during the war : at any rate I am not going to dinners, public or private.’ Lady Osler wrote on the 15th :

The refugees are pouring into England—Willie was at Folkestone today and said the streets were packed solid. Lights are reduced here now at night and only one lamp allowed on a motor. In London they say it is awful at night—rows of lights are put in

---

from field ambulances and hospital ships, available both for reference and for tabulation by modern mechanical methods. When the card index left our custody it weighed over 240 tons. It and the clerical staff passed to the Pensions Ministry, where it is now an indispensable index of reference for checking pensions claims. . . .

Hyde Park on the grass to divert the attention of airships from Westminster Abbey and other treasures. I want Willie to send his books to America but he laughs and won't believe it. Our work-room has been delving for a week over 300 bed-jackets for the hospital, and children's clothes, and *shirts*! We are tremendously busy over the Louvain professors—they are coming with a rush now. Some people have taken them in and we have taken rooms and houses for others, but none here except for the night—it is too trying for Willie and he must be protected in every way—all the horrors and war-talk nearly kill him and he often looks ill and worried.

To W. S. Thayer from W. O. October 16, 1914.

Dear Thayer, Thanks so much for the cable. It was a great worry not to be at the Celebration. We are very hard at work here—particularly Grace who is at it early and late. We have twelve Belgian professors, sixty-one in all with their families. It has been a job to settle them comfortably. Many of them are destitute. This Belgian business is an awful tragedy. I was at Folkestone yesterday, & saw the horror of it on the station platform—old men, women, children, all with their little possessions tied up in bundles, the whole town full. Fortunately they are being well cared for. We have opened our Canadian Contingent Hospital [Beechborough] near Folkestone—a lovely old place. They sent us a batch of Belgian wounded the night before last, so I had to go down to see that everything was going smoothly. Did you ever read Baron Larrey's 'Life and Memoirs'?—a great book! I am trying to stir up among the Territorial medical officers the importance of the health in the camps. We have had such wonderful weather for the last two months that there has been little or no sickness so far. Revere is up at Christ Church & has joined the Officers' Training Corps. Love to Sister Susan. Sincerely yours, W. O. By the way, we have Miss Macmahon in charge of our Canadian Hospital.

By this time the Germans had come to realize that their long-planned blow to take Paris in a short campaign had miscarried, and in their underground fashion were putting out feelers for peace proposals in Washington. It was feared in England that Mr. Bryan, an ultra-pacifist, would welcome anything to end hostilities, whatever the terms. This, with the President's insistence on neutrality while German-Americans apparently were left free to carry on their plots, caused much uneasiness which Mr. Page vainly endeavoured to dispel. Any word from the States, at all consoling, was eagerly received, so Osler on October 21st sent a note on 'Emerson on England' for publication in *The Times*:

Sir,—A valued American correspondent writes: 'The President's order of neutrality is wise, given our mixed population, but you know where our hearts and hopes are, and what toasts we drink in private life. If you have any half-hearted spirits among you, please read them the enclosed sentiments of our greatest man of letters, written in 1856, and still felt—oh, how strongly now—by all who are worthy of the great cause our race represents.' Yours, &c., WILLIAM OSLER.

England. 'I see her not dispirited, not weak, but well remembering that she has seen dark days before; indeed, with a kind of instinct that she sees a little better in a cloudy day, and that in storm of battle and calamity she has a secret vigour and a pulse like cannon. I see her in her old age, not decrepit, but young, and still daring to believe in her power of endurance and expansion. Seeing this, I say, All hail! Mother of nations, Mother of heroes, with strength still equal to the time; still wise to entertain and swift to execute the policy which the mind and heart of mankind require at the present hour, and thus only hospitable to the foreigner, and truly a home to the thoughtful and generous, who are born in the soil. So be it! So let it be!' RALPH WALDO EMERSON ['English Traits', 1856].

It is not improper now to say that the 'valued correspondent' was Fielding H. Garrison of the Surgeon-General's Office in Washington, to whom Osler wrote his thanks on the same day, adding:

I am suggesting at the Council Meeting of our Historical Section to have a series of bibliographical demonstrations & talks illustrating the evolution of naval & military hygiene. I have been reading Baron Larrey—a fascinating life! We are very full of work. Between 600 and 700 wounded have passed through our Base Hospital here—only one death—that from tetanus. We have fourteen Belgian professors in Oxford, all but one stranded financially & even sartorially. They are a eugenic lot with large families. Lady Osler has roused her American friends & got a very good bank account for them & the Rockefeller Foundation has made a splendid offer for the Louvain science men. But, it is an awful tragedy! The country is in fine form. Nearly 700,000 recruits have come in. I do not think there can be any doubt as to the outcome but there is a long road ahead. Do not forget my anaesthesia wants.

'The country is in fine form', yes: but during those late October days little did the country, outside the War Office, know of the thin khaki line valiantly holding out in Flanders against far superior numbers; until on the 31st the impossible happened and, with the recapture of Gheluvelt by the 2nd Worcesters, Calais was saved.

To J. William White from W. O. Oxford, October 28, 1914.

What an angel you are! It is perfectly splendid! [$3,000 from Philadelphia]. We have got, I think, now enough, as this Rockefeller Foundation offer to help the science professors will help with five or six out of the fifteen who are here; but we are hearing of new ones every day & there are twenty at Cambridge. The new recruits are getting into shape rapidly. I saw a magnificent camp last week near Brighton. The wounded are pouring in & the hospitals are filling rapidly. They do remarkably well.... I am trying to stir up the antityphoid inoculation & have had a great time in addressing open-air meetings of the men in the camps. I wish you could have seen us at the King Edward Horse camp near Slough. I addressed the men from beside a big oak tree, they sitting on the ground about, & afterwards all the officers were inoculated as an example. These sons of Belial, the 'anti's', have been preaching against it....

The 'Sons of Belial' indeed had even been permitted to put up recruiting posters in the shop windows: MEN OF THE EMPIRE ENLIST BUT REFUSE TO BE INOCULATED. So there were 'anti's' at home as well as abroad to be opposed. It was enough to make any one have bad dreams. Of one he writes in this letter to L. F. Barker:

I am sending you a reply from this country to the German letter [1] & a bundle of Oxford pamphlets. One of the tragedies is really the mental attitude of our German friends. Still, I suppose one has to stand by one's country, right or wrong; but there is the plain fact that Germany has been progressively preparing for this conflict for twenty years. In spite of the shocking mortality & the general feeling of distress, the country is in good spirits and very hopeful. The soldiers are turning out far better than one would have expected. Some of the old stuff is in the country, apparently. Curiously enough, I had a dream of you last night. You were just as you looked that day when you first came to see me at 83 Wellesley Street. You were sitting on the edge of a bed in Ward F. all alone, with

[1] This was apparently written by Gilbert Murray, and was signed by Osler and many others. In America, meanwhile, the personal reply by Samuel Harden Church in the form of a letter to Professor Schaper of Berlin, one of the German signers, had been published and circulated broadcast.

a most ingenious apparatus by which you were drawing the blood out of the veins of a man into flexible capillary glass tubes. The whole bed & the floor beside it was just a network of these capillary tubes filled with blood. You said quite gravely that this was the only possible way to get enough blood for cultures. The man was nearly dead! I wonder how the modern Joseph (Freud) would interpret this!

'Of course we feel terribly about Antwerp', Lady Osler wrote on October 22nd, 'and Winston Churchill has been blamed for sending our marines—however, one can't tell. We have got ourselves schooled now and don't listen when people tell tales—or try to—and believe nothing but official statements. We expect the worst and try not to think about it. I allow no one to abuse Kitchener or the Admiralty to me and find these rules make life much less fatiguing; I no longer mind when women put in shirt-sleeves hind-side before.'

With its cheerfulness, its warm hospitality, its precept of healthy optimism, its example of self-sacrificing hard work, the 'Open Arms' from the beginning to the end of the war radiated the fine spirit at its best which saw England through her trials. Always—'the country is in fine form'. Rarely did Osler write anything more pessimistic than this line to Professor Josiah Royce of Harvard: 'It's the deuce of a mess, this old humanity has got into. We will never be any different. I don't suppose we are a bit better than the Greeks—in some ways not so good. My chief comfort is to think that after all we are living in the childhood of civilization. What are the few thousand years since Hammurabi in comparison with the millions since the Stone Age.'

Whatever may be said of 'old humanity' Osler could never be any different, war or no war. 'The Regius is keeping up', writes his wife. 'He inspects and writes and preaches—and *hopes!*' That he had not lost any of his customary reactions is evident from the following on October 29th to the President of the Vancouver Medical Association; and his offer, it may be added, was promptly taken up:

Dear Keith,—That is a very interesting programme of your medical association. I have only one criticism—that you should have had it in the King Edward High School! The city is now large enough for the profession to begin to think of its own home, and do what has been done in Toronto and so many of the American cities, and done so successfully. Begin quietly with your own rooms where you can have the journals and the medical library, and start a building fund, for which bleed freely your friends inside and outside. I am willing to be bled to the extent of 100 dollars to help you make a beginning. I have seen in so many cases the enormous advantage of a home for the general profession that I commend the scheme to you most heartily. . . .

They received consoling letters, of course, from many sources,[1] and to their old friend, H. V. Ogden, Lady Osler wrote on November 4th:

It was very nice hearing from you and I am sure that you are all so English your sympathy goes out most sincerely to us in the midst of this awful war. Every morning we read of friends being mown down, all the youth and glory of the country, the young men we have known up here; and our only boy training in the park under our eyes—except that I can't look. Work is the only salvation, and I keep at it from 9.00 a.m. to 11.00 p.m. W. O. is busy and trying to be cheerful; hard work sometimes.

And on the next Sunday evening from Christ Church, when presumably those at the high table have set an example of cheerfulness to the uniformed boys below, Osler wrote in his turn to Mrs. Chapin:

Dearest Sue, All goes well—Grace working like a Trojan & making others work as well. You have been splendid in getting money for the poor professors. Grace's fund now amounts to nearly $10,000 & the Rockefeller Foundation has offered $20,000 for the science men directly as a result of her letter to Dr. Welch. She really has been splendid. You must come over soon. Revere is very happy here. I have just been at his room. Such nice companions. He & Bobby Emmons are great chums. They are off at Iffley this afternoon sketching. He drills every day. He & I must have a snap-shot in our uniforms. I only wear mine when I go inspecting the camps & hospitals. I spent two days near Torquay at the Singer American Hospital, 200 beds in a huge mansion. The other brother has a convalescent home near here for 150—such an ideal spot. I dare say Grace has told you of it. Do let our Boston friends know

[1] And sent letters of condolence, too—even for a time into Germany (via the United States), as ere long to Frau Professor Ewald in Berlin on learning of her husband's death. Ernst Lissauer's 'Hymn of Hate' was incomprehensible to English people.

that they never gave money in their lives that will be of greater help to more deserving people. It was simply ghastly, the plight in which some of these nice people arrived, & now in their own homes they are so happy. It has been a fine bit of work. . . .

The Canadians had come, and were on Salisbury Plain for the winter. Apparently each and every one had letters to the Oslers, and appeared at the 'Open Arms' to get themselves washed and fed and petted while on leave. McGill, meanwhile, was organizing a base hospital unit of which Birkett the Dean was C.O., and Osler was expected to intervene for them at the War Office, for of course they wished to go to France. Countless people, too, were pressing him for jobs as though *he* were the D.G.M.S. rather than Sir Alfred Keogh. He wrote on November 12th to J. William White, who was growing violently restive :

Keogh tells me they have had to sit severely on all outside independent hospitals & units for the front, as they found it was not possible to control their work. The English provisions for the front & at the base hospitals seem excellent, but the French need help. The best work is being done apparently through the American Hospital in Paris. Should I hear of anything specific, I will let you know, or even cable you.

'Things are going well here and the country is in really very good form', he repeats to F. H. Garrison in a letter of November 16th. 'I got the other day the "ether number" of Littell's Living Age, 1848, which is full of interesting material.' And he goes on to describe the war exhibit of books they had gathered at the Royal Society of Medicine, adding that, 'we are starting here an interesting thing at the Bodleian and have devoted one of the alcoves at the Radcliffe Camera to the history of science.' Then, too, there must have been some criticism of the Historical Section of the Royal Society of Medicine, for in defence he writes on November 17th to J. Y. W. MacAlister :

It is not a good way, to pull up the turnips to watch their growth. We cannot make medical historians in a couple of years. If your friend will look over the material presented to the Section, while perhaps it does not indicate much research, I do not think there is much that could be called folk-lore or gossip. What is wanted in this country is not dilettante students like myself & some others but real scholars, & your friend will be interested to know that some of these are at work on serious medical research. Thistleton-Dyer, for instance, is doing for us at the Press a splendid piece of work in Greek botanical terms &c.; Withington is making a special study for us in Galen and Hippocrates for revision of the medical terms in Liddell & Scott. We have formed at the Bodleian a separate little department for the study of the history of science & medicine at which at present five are working: one making a comprehensive study of the English medical manuscripts; Singer is doing a very interesting unknown MS of Manfredi; another is collating and will edit an unknown MS of Maimonides; another is working at the Spanish medical MSS in the Library; while we have one of the Belgian professors at work on some interesting iatromathematical literature. Of course, this is the sort of stuff we need. I think it is quite possible that we may gradually get associated with the history section a group of scholars capable of doing spade work. If your friend wants a job in the historical branches send him along. The harvest is plenteous but the labourers are few. Thank you all the same for his criticism, but if he looks over the papers he will come to my view that it is a bit bilious.

As is so apt to be the case, the funds for the new science room at the Bodleian had been provided by the workers rather than by the University, and ere long the chief one of them, Dr. Charles Singer, whom he dubs 'that Socratic gadfly, your husband', very properly enlists, and Osler writes to Mrs. Singer: 'You must come here when he goes off, & run the Science Room & do the proofs & lay wires & act generally as medico-historical hormone.'

He gave an important and timely address in London on November 20th, before the Society of Tropical Medicine, on 'The War and Typhoid Fever'. It was nearly the last [1] of his separate papers on typhoid, over thirty in all; and meanwhile he had seen typhoid reduced to the vanishing-point even in Baltimore, where by now there were not enough cases to teach over. But here was a new danger, and for this address he had assembled and reported every case in which any untoward effect had been produced as the result of inoculation. 'It will be a great triumph', he said, 'to go through the war without a devastating experience of typhoid fever. While with our present know-

[1] There was one later paper, on Typhoid Spine. *Canadian Medical Association Journal*, 1919.

ledge we cannot but regret that inoculation has not been made compulsory, let us hope that a sufficient number have taken advantage of the procedure to make impossible a repetition of the enteric catastrophe in South Africa.' And he closed with a moving comparison between 'the needless slaughter of the brave young fellows—allies and foes alike'—which was now going on, and the fight being waged by the great army of sanitation 'which claims allegiance only to Humanity'. On the same day there was written from Buckingham Palace this very pleasant note:

My dear Sir William,—I am desired by the Prince of Wales to write and tell you that a small souvenir is being sent to you in recognition of your valuable services during his Royal Highness's residence at Oxford. He had intended to write himself, but the souvenir was not ready; then came the orders for him to join the staff [A.D.C. to Sir John French] and almost at the same moment the bad news of Cadogan's death [the Prince's Equerry]. The result was that he was more than busy and I persuaded him to leave the writing to me. A framed photograph will follow the souvenir in a short time. It is too sad that we should have lost our last term at Oxford: it would have been such a happy and successful one. But we must all feel the pinch caused by this world earthquake. One of the pleasantest memories of our two years at Oxford will be the friendship that was made with you. I feel that in this sad time your cheery help will be invaluable to many. With my kind regards, Yours v. sincerely,

H. P. Hansell.

In one of his brief notes of this same November 20th, Osler said to W. S. Thayer: 'Very busy and very hopeful. Ike in the training corps, Grace working like a galley-slave & I knocking about & seeing much of interest.' And to Mrs. Brewster: 'Just a line to say that all goes well—only the heartache for friends whose fine boys have been killed. It is sad reading every morning. So many of our young friends here have been taken. Oxford is one big camp & hospital. Our Belgians are doing well.' It was characteristic that he should have spoken in his London address of 'the brave young fellows, allies and foes alike'. He found it difficult even to believe the first-hand stories of some of the refugees. So in a letter of November 23rd to Dr. George Armstrong of McGill, he says:

I have urged Keogh, the Director-General, to take your unit as soon as possible. There are difficulties, as the question of holding the coast is still doubtful. I have been looking over the photographs of atrocities and of mutilations and have asked in the various hospitals, and one can never get anything closer than this damned third person [1] whom I should like to mutilate personally. I suppose there have been atrocities, particularly in the sack of Louvain, but in other parts they have been grossly exaggerated. Love to all. . . .

To Simon Flexner from W. O. November 23, 1914.

It is very difficult to get these Belgian professors to move. They are all so upset and distracted that I have not been able to induce any one to accept either the Harvard or the Chicago offer. It is a deuce of a problem what to do with the people here. The Government is bringing over another 50,000 from Holland, and it is very difficult to fit them in. We have fifteen professors here with their families, all settled in their own houses and most of them at work. I do not know what we should have done without the Rockefeller help, though our friends in America have been very liberal. I am afraid it is going to be a long job and the great majority of the people are entirely without resources. We have had to provide everything. Two of our rooms upstairs are a sort of old-clothes shop. People here have been very kind. Denys and his family are charming. He is busy with a big research on tuberculosis. I shall hope to see Rose and James. Love to the family. . . .

'So many people coming and going.' Among them was the son of Osler's old Hamilton friend, A. E. Malloch, to whom he wrote on November 24th:

Dear Malloch, Archie arrived in very good form & we have enjoyed his visit here very much. He is just getting over his second antityphoid inoculation, which knocked him over a bit, but he is all right to-day. Mrs. Guest has arranged for her hospital somewhere east of Calais, where I think he will see plenty of good work. As you know, she is the daughter of Henry Phipps & wife of the Hon. Freddy Guest, Controller of the King's Household. She and young Howard Phipps are going over & Archie will be very comfortable with them. Of course, Mrs. Guest is delighted with him. He looks A.1. in his uniform. We are seeing all sorts of interesting cases here. The nervous injuries & the chest cases are what I am looking after specially. Love to Mrs. Malloch and to Olmsted. . . .

---

[1] There had been an editorial in the *Spectator* on 'The Third Person'. In another letter, to Adami, Osler said: 'There have been all sorts of rumours and statements but I do not believe there has been a single case of mutilation brought to this country. I am sick to death of the newspapers. I wish the Government would suppress them during the war and issue a weekly bulletin.'

Our [Belgian] professors are very plucky and trying to get to work [wrote Lady Osler on November 25th]. The wives and children are nervous and much upset—it requires much tact to find out their wants as they are proud and sensitive. Mrs. Max Muller and I do the work and W. O. smiles and signs the cheques. I believe we will have them for months, they haven't a penny. Those who had a few francs have gone through it, so we shall need every penny we have got. Clothes alone for 100 people are an item. Life is very tragic at present. And one can hardly take it in. I saw twenty-nine huge lorries just now in front of St. John's College ready for an East Coast invasion, to motor troops across the country. That seems a fear at present. We have a base hospital here with 1,000 beds, and it all keeps one busy. Nearly all the large private houses in London are full of wounded. . . .

Meanwhile there were Canadian relatives and sons of friends on Salisbury Plain to take care of, and on December 1st she wrote to her sister : 'I have such a nice time sending things to Campbell Gwyn and the eight men in his tent. Two roasts of meat, cakes, potted ham, etc. ; books galore and papers ; so they may keep cheered up.' Osler meanwhile : 'I have at present a perfect avalanche of correspondence and do precious little else but write letters.'[1] Many of them evidently were acknowledgements of gifts to the Belgian fund, and on December 2nd he wrote to his friend White :

Thank you so much for your last contribution ! You really have been wonderful. I have written to nearly all the Philadelphia subscribers. I wish you could look in here and see how comfortably Grace & young Mrs. Max Muller have settled these people. Our house is nothing but a junk-shop. We have packing cases arriving every week & our drawing-room is a sewing-room for the wives of the professors, most of whom are making baby clothes, as they are an extraordinarily eugenic lot. I hope something will come of your offer to Jusserand. On the French side they seem to be in want of help. I will have your Primer of the War put in proper hands for review. Yesterday the committee asked me to express to you again our warmest thanks for all you have done.

Such things as White's 'Primer' were much needed in

[1] Nor by any means were all the letters in his 'avalanche of correspondence' purely personal. A good deal of it was propaganda like the long letter to the *Journal of the American Medical Association*, dated December 4th, which the journal (p. 2303) entitled 'Medical Notes on England at War'. A series of these letters followed.

England to offset the distrust for America which was taking hold, despite all Mr. Page's efforts; and Osler writes enthusiastically about its reception:

I have distributed them with private letters to the *Morning Post*, the *Spectator*, the *Saturday Review*, *The Times*, the *Daily Telegraph* & the London *Nation*. I hope they will give it the notice it deserves. Young Max Muller, who has just been in, says the copy he took has been circulated. I wish you would send me another half-dozen, as I should like to send to Grey, Asquith, Haldane, Lloyd George, Earl Crewe, Harcourt, & Lord Iveagh; or, what would be better still would be for you to send copies with a private letter, saying, if you like, it was sent at my request. . . . Things are going very well. Treves, whom I saw on Friday just back from the front, says that the organization is something that he never dreamt of when he looks back upon the South African experiences. . . .

Meanwhile his regular tasks continued, even the Tuesday and Sunday clinics at the Radcliffe Infirmary, and he actually wrote an account of one of them at the behest of the editor of an American journal.[1] 'W. O. has been two days in bed with a cold', Lady Osler tells her sister. 'He got it at Paignton when he went to inspect the American Ladies' Hospital. Of course he's preaching at all these places about a medical history of the war and has started records, etc., and has got the War Department at it.' Even on a Sunday evening at Christ Church he writes letters. Thus to Colonel Birkett, the C.O. of the McGill Hospital Unit:

6th [Dec.]

Dear Birkett, I had an interview with Keogh, the Dir. Gen. yesterday & cabled his views. He had not heard of the offer!—these things come through very slowly. The position is this. There are five or six large English Base Hospitals, as many as can be dealt with from the front. They are chiefly at Boulogne & neighbourhood—but the tenure of the coast is just now so uncertain that the War Office cannot undertake any new hospitals in this region. He says if you all came over at this time there would be only delay & disappointment. As it is the Canadian nurses have been kicking their heels—& no doubt cussing!—in London for some weeks & are only now getting drafted into work The French are sadly in need of help & I have written to Chauffard asking if the French Govt. could

[1] 'Remarks on the Diagnosis of Polycystic Kidney, Radcliffe Infirmary, Nov. 23, 1914.' *International Clinics*, Phila., 1915.

utilize a Hospital unit raised in Canada of men speaking French—but of course not mentioning names. It will be some time, I fear, before the Canadian contingent will be fit to leave. K. insists that half-trained men only embarrass the Generals. Things are going pretty well. The country is in fine spirits & 'tis surely a good omen that in the end of the 4th month the Germans have not yet finished with Belgium. We are very busy. I am seeing a great deal of interest. Keogh was greatly touched with your offer & not a little surprised.

On December 10th Lady Osler wrote that the Medical Examiners had been there over Sunday and all the week; that the ladies were busy putting warm sleeves into 1,000 waistcoats and making pyjamas for the hospital; that the chauffeur was ill with bronchitis, which was inconvenient, as they had so many trips to take; that one of the Belgian ladies with five children under seven was expecting another and would go to the Acland Home—'they haven't a penny except what we give them and the children only speak Flemish'; that each day there was some one to help in a different way—'as for Willie I hardly know how he lives, people ask so many favours of him'; that they were not sending any Christmas presents, for 'the money simply flies here in the many things one wants to do'. And again she wrote: 'I have just come from town—third class—and must go again Tuesday for a Canadian concert, and after that I hope not for months; London gives me the blues.' One member of the family was too much in London already, as he indicates in the following note of December 7th:

Dear Lord Iveagh, I am very sorry, but it would be quite impossible for me to take the Chairmanship of the Governing Body of the Lister Institute. As it is, I have undertaken in London far more than I can attend to properly. With many regrets [etc.].

Slowly and ponderously Great Britain, having started unprepared and without an army, was summoning her resources. The East Coast affair had amounted merely to a raid which came off on December 16th, when innocent people were killed at Scarborough and elsewhere by long-range naval guns. But this and the few early air-raids had thoroughly aroused the country. It must be finished this time, once and for all, was the feeling that had slowly made its way into every English household—no more German militarism for us—no more Deutschland über Alles; no talk of peace without victory here, whatever Mr. Wilson may say; for should the German War Party remain in power this might easily happen again. Osler knew this as well as those at the American Embassy. 'The horror of it no man knows', wrote Mr. Page to Colonel House on December 12th. 'The news is suppressed, but four of the crack regiments of this kingdom—regiments that contained the flower of this land and to which it was a distinction to belong—have been practically annihilated twice. Yet their ranks are filled up and you never hear a murmur. Presently it'll be true that hardly a title or estate in England will go to its natural heir—the heir has been killed. Yet not a murmur: for England is threatened with invasion. They'll all die first.'

Among his Christmas letters Osler wrote on the 14th to Mrs. Brewster:

This should reach you Xmas Eve by the Lusitania—if she has luck; & takes our greetings. . . . We are struggling through the winter in fairly good spirits & everything looks more hopeful. We see too much of the tragedies to make life very happy. I wish you could look in on our drawing-room—turned into a Galleries Lafayette for the wives of the Belgian professors, who work at their clothing every morning from 9–1. Grace has a dressmaker for them & half a dozen sewing-machines We have nearly 100 in 16 families Poor things! it is an appalling tragedy for them, & there are such nice women among them. Then G. bosses one of the big laboratories with fifty of the University women working for the soldiers. These N[ew] E[ngland] women are full of vitality.

Revere has been in the Oxford Training Corps but has not had enough for a commission. His heart is not much set on the military life. Literature, books & art. He and I are so congenial mentally. It is delightful to have him take to these things spontaneously. I could not filch one of his little etchings for you—he says they are not fit to send to anyone. . . . Uncle Ned's book on the war is A.1. He sent six copies & I have passed them on to Asquith, Edward Grey, Harcourt & Haldane & one to the secretary of the publicity dept. I am very sad about all my good German friends. I wonder where Truth is?—bottom of an artesian well these times! I wish I was sailing on the Lusitania. Love to R. B. & the darlings. Yours affectionately, Wm OSLER. I do not know what we should have done without the packing-cases of clothing from America—and the money. G. has raised $15,000.

And on the same day to H. B. Jacobs: 'It will be rather a sad Christmas over here for so many people, but on the whole there is much to be thankful for. Things are a great deal better than any one could have hoped—well on in the fifth month of the war & Belgium not yet finished with. There are fully 1,000,000 men in training here & the spirit of the country is A.1.'

The spirit of the 'Open Arms' was equally A.1. 'I had an unusually busy time last week', Lady Osler wrote to her sister at Christmas time. 'We had so many orders at our work-room: three dozen shirts, 500 surgical dressings, two dozen felt mits for the navy, 200 hold-alls and 200 "house-wives". Mrs. Balfour got appendicitis, and Mrs. Thomson's brother died, so I was much rushed.' And then she continued:

It was a business getting the presents distributed—325. I got the names, sex and ages of all the professors' children; then tied and marked them all, and tied each family's and addressed it to the mother. Then I sent what was left to the General Committee and to various people who had Belgians to look after. The other cases have not yet arrived. I had a case from Marjorie of shirts, socks and woollies, which were sent off mostly to the front and to the Canadians at Salisbury Plain. Jack McCrae was here on Sunday and said his men needed socks badly. While I was packing them off there came a message from Mrs. Griffiths next door to know if I could help her with a box for her nephew in the trenches;—that 's the way all the time; and shirts, heavy scarfs and jerseys are always in demand.

Accompanied by young Dr. Malloch, who was on Christmas leave from Depage's hospital at La Panne, Osler went to an auction in town the day before Christmas, and Malloch wrote in his journal: 'Sir William so pleased that he got Aristotle's 'Opera', and bought Jonathan Hutchinson's collection to give to the J. H. H., some American paying for it at £80—about 10,000 drawings. We decorated a small Christmas tree in the evening, and Sir William told of his school escapades in Dundas and of being expelled.' And a day or two later, in a letter to Adam Wright of Toronto, Osler says: 'Some of the Canadian contingent spent Xmas with us. They have had a deuce of a time with rain and mud—the worst winter we have had for years. The country is in fine form and very hopeful.' And his wife's long letter to her sister on Christmas night tells of the morning spent at Ewelme; of a cheery luncheon at home to which the Max Muller children came in for dessert; and of the afternoon in the hospital and Infirmary, where the wounded had a wonderful day, though 'one hardly dares to think of the men in the trenches—it 's cold here and must be ghastly there.' Of these and other things—one particularly close to his heart—Osler writes in the following New Year's letter to Mrs. Brewster:

Dear Mabel, What a darling! Such a merry happy face! You must be crazy about her. I can imagine the family worship of you & R. B. & Sylvia. I am sorry not to see her in this stage as there is nothing so adorable as a jolly healthy baby. We have had a full house for Xmas. A nephew & his friend, privates in the Canadian contingent, a great-nephew who is at school near Oxford, & a young Canadian friend whose husband is in the trenches. We all went to Ewelme for church & distributed the Xmas dinners to the 13 old men. Grace has not had time to think of anything but the Belgians & acting as a distributing agent for American presents. Really it is wonderful! Every week big packing-cases come. Yesterday 24 barrels of apples were unloaded from a van at the door, for the wounded soldiers at the Base Hospital. We are having a very happy holiday with Revere—such a chip of the old block in his devotion to books. He has developed so rapidly, & you never met anyone with a more delightful taste in literature. It is a shame to have his studies interrupted, but he goes on with the military training & will take a commission when ready. My library grows apace—all sorts of treasures come in—a beauty this week, the Editio princeps of Aristotle 1495 bound by Derome. My bountiful brother E. B. sends an occasional fat cheque to meet my extravagances, as he knows my medical and scientific books are being collected for Canada. Awful weather! the worst winter we have had. The raids & bombs are doing much good—except to the poor sufferers—in rousing the country. The American Commission in Belgium is doing a marvellous work. We had one of the committee here yesterday—49 vessels have already reached Rotterdam! Love to the darlings & blessings on you all for 1915.

And Revere. A chip of the old block in his growing devotion to books; but far more like his great-great-grandfather—of the midnight ride—in his tastes and occupations, skilful with tools and with his pencil, a self-taught etcher; even more skilful with his rod. 'Revere's heart is not in drill or in the war', writes his mother; 'a great question must be decided about him soon, and of course he will do his duty when the time comes.'

Revere Osler to H. B. Jacobs. Dec. 27th.

Dear Dr. Jacobs,—Thank you very much for your card and your kindness in remembering me amid all this excitement. In spite of everything we have had a happy Christmas. Mother is well as usual & so likewise Dad and myself, 'for which', as Pepys would say, 'God be praised'.

Dad has given me (I am telling everyone I meet this, out of joy) a first edition of Iz. Walton's life of Herbert—a perfect gem of a book, uncut, unsoiled and just as it left the hands of the printer and perhaps of Walton himself. You will pardon my enthusiasm for you no doubt know it yourself.

The fishing goes well & I find that in proportion as one's skill increases so does the Thames appear the more unworthy of the abuse which it is customary to bestow upon it. Some day I hope you will come and we will make an expedition with rods and good Waltonian bait to New Bridge or Eynsham, or some other famous place on its banks. My regards to Mrs. Jacobs. Yours affectionately,

REVERE (discip. Iz. Wa.)

CHAPTER XXXV

1915

NERVES AND THE 'CONSOLER-GENERAL'

In his address on the 'Religio' given at Guy's Hospital ten years before this time Osler had written :

> In civil wars physicians of all men suffer least, as the services of able men are needed by both parties, and time and again it has happened that an even-balanced soul, such as our author, has passed quietly through terrible trials, doing the day's work with closed lips. Corresponding with the most active decades of his life, in which his three important works were issued, one might have expected to find in them reference to the Civil War, or, at least, echoes of the great change wrought by the Commonwealth, but, like Fox, in whose writings the same silence has been noticed, whatever may have been his feelings, he preserved a discreet silence. His own rule of life, no doubt, is expressed in the advice to his son : 'Times look troublesome, but you have an honest and peaceable profession which may employ you, and discretion to guide your words and actions.'

There can be no doubt that he wished to shield Revere so far as he legitimately could—not so much for the boy's sake as for his own. It was an instinctive and uncontrollable reaction of defence. Why should his peace-loving boy have to fight and kill ? 'Revere has become devoted to art and literature', he writes, 'and is following in my footsteps in a love of books.' He was not yet ready for the sacrifice. It is all too apparent in his letters to his friends, in which he never fails to make the most of what Revere is doing, and what he will have to do 'when he is ready'; and though outwardly cheerful when things were darkest and they were hardest worked, he would say to his wife, 'Never mind, the worst is yet to come.'

Revere's heart was not in the drill. He had failed to get his commission. 'Too immature', the O.T.C. officer had reported. He was now of military age, and the alternative was to enlist in the ranks. This was the boy's own conclusion, but he must have been fully conscious of his father's unspoken agony. Many a home in England with an only child, and that a son, must have suffered in this way till the final plunge was made.

Revere has had his 19th birthday and has made up his mind about the first step to take [Lady Osler writes early in the year to her sister]. He simply can't talk with his father, but talked wisely, oh so wisely, with me. . . . To-day he brought home his books from Christ Church and his lovely room must be dismantled. What a strange fate after our fear that he might never get in! So that is done for, and the only hope is that the war may some day be over and he can return. Of course dear sister it is useless to say 'don't worry for us' because I know you will feel it all terribly, but with you to look up to and the women I was brought up among I shall do my utmost to hold out and have a cheerful face for the poor dear unselfish angel who is breaking his heart over giving up his boy to this awful risk—that 's all.

On January 4th Osler writes to Mrs. Brewster:

That is a lovely clocklet—thank you so much It adorns my bed-side table, tucked in among volumes of Lucian, Gomperz, Jowett & others from whom I am trying to catch a little Greek fire. Did you ever read Lucians Dialogues? Perhaps I sent you the four little volumes we issued a few years ago from the Press? If not let me know. You would enjoy the last of the Greeks & the first of the Moderns. I wish you could be here to see the wonderful activity in this old land—every one working & so hopeful. Revere is leaving college & going into the Universities Public School Regiment, at first as a private so as to know the drill & then he will apply for a commission. I hate to have him go & it is a shame to have his training here interrupted, just as he was developing so splendidly. I enclose a proof of his book-plate which he has just chosen—a bit rough, but his own design. Mine is still waiting until I can find some one who can put in a moderate space something distinctive of the four Universities with which I have been connected. I have been talking this afternoon to 600 soldiers on health in camp & field. I enclose you proof of a very much medicated letter to the Jrnl. of the Amer. Med. Association. . . .

On this same January 4th he writes to the C.O. of the McGill Unit, which had been fretting all these months in Montreal:

Dear Birkett, I am delighted to hear that the Unit has been accepted. By Jove it reads well in your report and should be A.1. Should you get into a Typhoid district I shall come as a Super-Col. & Campbell's Assistant. It is awfully good of you to offer to take Revere as your orderly. By the time you get over he will have had a good deal of training & could take messages. He is busy now working at French. Have you had any word direct from the war office here? Let me know if it would be worth while speaking to Keogh again. They are still doubtful about the coast, tho. it looks better every week There has been great slackness during the past month. We have not been pressed here or at the American Hospital. The boys have had a deuce of a time at the Salisbury Camp—Soaked in rain & knee deep in mud. Finley was here for a few days & Ellis from Toronto this week end. They have brought cerebro-spinal meningitis of wh. there have been about 30 cases. Greetings to Mrs Birkett & yourself for the New Year.

To be Colonel Birkett's orderly: here was a possible way out, one which might satisfy the boy's conscience and give his father a little more time. Two weeks passed. The Public Schools camp had proved unsatisfactory and Revere was just about to enlist in the Inns of Court Corps when a cable came from Montreal with a definite offer which the boy promptly accepted, and he returned to the O. T. C. at Oxford for further training until the arrival of the McGill Unit.

'We are all hard at work for the soldiers', Osler writes to a Francis niece on January 11th. 'Poor chaps, it is awful weather for them. The conditions in the trenches are unspeakable & the Canadians are finding out what England can do in the way of rain. We have not had such a winter for years.' With it came the unlooked-for outbreak of cerebrospinal fever—a new anxiety added to the fear of typhoid; for though the camps in England had been kept remarkably free from enteric there was much of it in France; Dr. Malloch indeed had brought word of some 3,000 cases in the Dunkirk district. The antivaccinationists were still active, and Osler sent to the editor of *The Times* another letter on the subject:

Sir,—May I through your columns issue this appeal to our soldiers? In this grave crisis all are anxious to render the greatest possible service to our country. You are leaving your homes and occupations in defence of principles for which your fathers fought and died. It is your bounden duty to keep yourselves in as perfect a state of health as is consistent with the hardships and exposure incidental to every campaign. In war it is not alone the enemy in the field who has to be considered; your worst foes have always been those of your own camp—the diseases that have proved more fatal than powder and shot. . . .

Then with a fresh assembly of arguments in favour of inoculation and its reasonable guarantee of protection, he drew upon new statistics such as those from the Valcartier camp, where out of 22,434 Canadians vaccinated only 22 had symptoms other than the usual malaise and headache. In conclusion he had these two questions to ask of the soldiers in training:

(1) Will you believe the statements of misguided cranks who are playing into the enemy's hands by purveying their misleading literature, or will you hearken to men who have devoted their lives to the service of humanity, and who have no wish in the matter other than your good?

(2) Against a transient indisposition will you put in the balance the chance of a protracted and costly illness, possibly an untimely death?

Osler would have made almost as good a Director of Propaganda as did the man to whom he sent a few days later the following note:

Dear Lord Northcliffe,—These full-page anti-inoculation advertisements are doing a great deal of harm, and the Societies for the Abolition of Vivisection and of Vaccination are carrying out a most energetic campaign. If the *Daily Mail* could give me a full-page advertisement at a reasonable rate I should be willing to issue a counterblast. Please pass on my letter to the manager and ask him to let me know. Meanwhile I have arranged an interview with 'Answer' as suggested by you to Mr. Blackwood. . . .

And on the 14th he wrote to Dr. White, who was also propagandizing:

Dear J. Wm, I enclose a very nice Review from the Spectator. Strachey was delighted with your book. I hope you have got a publisher here—tho. from what Strachey (whom I asked) said they are rather 'fed up' with war items. Thanks for the Repplier-White paper & pamphlet—A.1. You have just wiped the floor with him. Send me half a doz. copies please for the papers & friends. I have been away for a week—at the Can. Hospital Folkestone & at the Canadian Camp Salisbury Plain investigating an outbreak of cerebro-spinal meningitis—not extensive but very alarming & it may retard their crossing. They have had a devil of a time in the mud—Such weather! floods too all over the country—Oxford is a lake. Love to Mrs. J. W. Excuse this hurried letter but I want to catch the Lusitania & I am tired out. Yours ever . . .

'Poor Willie, he never has a chance to breathe he is so

busy helping', Lady Osler writes to her sister at the time. 'His interest even in wounds and the results of wounds is intense, and I think the new edition of the "Practice of Medicine" will be a war volume. He is all the time urging men on about the case histories and is conducting a campaign on typhoid inoculation.' As she says, everything aroused his interest and attention, and no less his pen— the cases of trench feet, the early examples of war neurosis, the brain injuries, the irritable hearts, the early 'shell-shock' cases, and so on.[1] They had a visit during the month from Robert Bacon, an old friend who at this time was endeavouring to get the American Commission for Belgium to put him in the way of helping the French behind the lines, and 'who says he shall burst if he doesn't get into khaki'. Many a month passed before this wish was fully gratified, but meanwhile Mr. Bacon was doing yeoman service, as he had done from the very outset; and just now he had a new project. He had much to do with the establishment early in August of the American Ambulance at Neuilly, Paris, where an arrangement had been made the first of the year to have one of the hospital services taken over by successive groups of surgeons and nurses from some of the American medical schools. A unit from the Western Reserve under Dr. Crile was already there; to be followed in three months by one from Harvard; and in turn another from the University of Pennsylvania which was to give J. William White the outlet he sought. Could not something of the sort be done for the British, whose hospitals in France were certain to be overcrowded and undermanned as soon as the spring campaign opened? This programme Osler and Bacon finally worked out together, as will be seen; and it was a very timely act, for Anglo-American relations at the moment were unduly strained by the recent American 'Notes'. Were copper and petroleum and food from American ports destined for Germany 'conditional contraband'? If so, they were liable to seizure, and Sir Edward Grey pointed out that

[1] These things and many more Osler described and discussed in his 'Medical Notes on England at War', published from time to time in the *Journal of the American Medical Association* as well as in two of the Canadian Journals.

the copper exports from America to Dutch, Scandinavian, and Italian ports had grown prodigiously.

'I opened *The Times* yesterday', writes Lady Osler on the 21st, 'and saw in large letters: "Sir William Osler offers his services to Canada", and was soon inundated with messages and notes. It of course means nothing more than his offering to help with the organization &c.[1] All Revere's papers are filled out and sent in and the cable sent to Ottawa about his commission. Willie feels very satisfied about it and Col. Jones who has all the Canadian medical affairs in his hands says he prefers a chap who has a brain and no experience.' On this same January 21st Osler wrote to the Princess Louise, evidently in reply to a query regarding the situation at Salisbury Plain:

Dear Princess,—There were four cases [of cerebrospinal fever among the Canadians] at Valcartier, three on the voyage, and there have been about twenty-five in the camp of which I saw eleven at present ill. They have opened a special hospital which is very comfortable, a laboratory for the examination of the contact cases, and they have an excellent staff of doctors and nurses—one doctor in particular, a young Canadian from the Rockefeller Institute, New York, who fortunately is an expert in matters relating to the serum treatment of the disease. I do not think the epidemic will be severe. I may mention, too, that there have been cases at the Shorncliffe camp near Folkestone, which I am going down next week to visit. The conditions on the Plain have been most unfortunate but the disease is one which may break out in the best of barracks and camps. I have been taking a great deal of interest in the McGill Unit and hope to go over and help them get established somewhere in France. I hear they do not arrive until the end of April. I have a very happy remembrance of your good husband and of all he did for Canada, particularly in the days when he founded the Royal Society of which I was one of the original members, and on the Committee with him. He had a life full of usefulness and we Canadians must always feel very grateful for what you and he were able to do in shaping the early destinies of the Dominion. . . . Please do not mention the slight outbreak at Shorncliffe, as it is not yet known. . . .

[1] Osler promptly wrote to the Editor of the *Lancet*: 'Please take no notice of that newspaper canard about me. It arose from a harmless statement I made to Birkett that when they had their hospital organized in France I would go over and help them should they have any serious typhoid outbreak.'

He had had abundant experience with cerebrospinal fever in the epidemics which occurred in Maryland in 1893 and again in 1898—indeed the following year he had made it the subject of his Cavendish Lecture in London. The War Office as well as the profession were greatly disturbed over this outbreak and Osler wrote for publication [1] a short but reassuring paper in which he gave the history of the disease as it occurs in encampments; also some sensible hints regarding the best means of preventing contagion, which was largely a matter of 'contacts' when men live nine in a tent as they were living on Salisbury Plain. It was an alarming epidemic with high mortality, and though Simon Flexner some years before (1906–7) had elaborated at the Rockefeller Institute a protective serum which had been successfully used by Dr. A. G. Robb of Belfast, it was little known in England, which had been remarkably free from the disease in pre-war days. Treatment with the available serum (afterwards found to be worthless) had dismally failed, and the error was not really redressed until the Medical Research Council finally put Mervyn Gordon to work on the subject, much time having been lost meanwhile.

Tired out and thoroughly chilled at one of his visits to the camps, Osler wound up the month with one of his bad colds, which housed him for a week but gave him time for other things. 'You are always a good bibliographical tonic', he writes to L. L. Mackall. 'I am struggling to finish my paper on the Early Printed Medical Books. It 's rather a heavy job.' And to Jacobs a few days later: 'I have not written for a long time. The days and weeks fly by. We are so busy with so many things but fortunately the back of the winter is broken.' And he adds: 'I forget whether I told you of my election to the Roxburghe Club which is a sort of blue ribbon society of its kind.' Also to F. H. Garrison that 'our Bibliographical Society were so pleased with their medical President that they elected me for another period! Everything goes on smoothly here. Frost-bites, cold-bites, and cerebrospinal fever are the

[1] 'Cerebrospinal Fever in Camps and Barracks.' *British Medical Journal*, Jan. 30, 1915.

things which have been interesting me chiefly.' And to a Fellow of the Royal College of Physicians: 'I think the President of the College should be a man resident in London. I have had enough of these things & am not especially ambitious in this direction. To tell you the truth, I think the business would bore me to death. All the same, it is awfully good of some of the Fellows to think of me.'

In other letters he expresses himself quite emphatically regarding Anglo-Teutonic relations. 'So glad to hear of Sudhoff & Müller', he writes to A. C. Klebs, 'but it's a hopeless job to think of getting any truth between the two sides. I wish they would hang a few of the newspaper editors. You seem to have been pretty fortunate in Belgium for we have had very different stories told us by Americans over there, particularly by one of the members of the Commission who called here last Saturday. Everything will depend upon our control of the sea, & if that goes then it will be a question of how long before the Teutonic & American eagles are at one another's throats.' And on January 27th he writes to W. G. MacCallum:

Dear Mac, Sorry not to have answered your nice letter before but this house is nothing but a branch post-office & I am tied up with all sorts of things besides being on the road a great deal. One can't help feeling very sad about our old German friends, but there will be an awful gulf between this country & Germany for the next two generations. Their hate is nothing to the loathing expressed here on all sides. Of course the atrocities have been grossly exaggerated & Klebs tells me just the same stories about English troops. Unfortunately there seems to be no question about the Belgian horrors. We have about 21 professors here with their families 130 people in all & they are living on good American money, partly what we have collected ourselves & partly from the splendid Rockefeller gift. . . . The poor Canadians have had a devil of a time at the Salisbury camp—mud to the knees & the weather has been appalling. . . .

Then, in reply to some peace resolutions passed by the Federation of American Biologists, which had met at the end of the year, expressing 'the hope of an early and enduring peace without permanent cause of rancour, ensuring to each nation the glories of scientific and humanitarian achievement ', and so on—to this he sends Professor Graham Lusk an acknowledgement :

Dear Lusk, Many thanks for the copy of the resolution. It is a pious wish, but there is an intellectual gulf wider & deeper than the Atlantic being built between Germany & this country. It is very sad, & it is hard to know just what to do about old friends. I never saw that copy of Müller's letter. I should like very much to read what he said. I suppose in a way it is most fortunate that they can get into such a mental attitude. After all, it would be a terrible tragedy if they did not believe their own country was right. . . .

In October of 1914, as we have seen, steps had been taken by Osler, Fletcher, and others, whereby the army records relating to casualties might be standardized for statistical and other purposes. It was, of course, evident that these records would be invaluable were a satisfactory history of the war ever to be written. Moreover, Adami, who at this time was still Registrar of the McGill Unit, was most eager not only that the Canadians should set a high standard for medical records but also that an arrangement should be made for a proper collection of pathological war specimens. This was desirable not only for the Canadian Corps but for the British as well, and he naturally was anxious to work in co-operation with the Research Committee. Hitherto, provision for things of this sort had received scant consideration. Indeed there had been no proper medical history of any British campaign, not even of the Crimea nor of the war in South Africa—nothing, in short, to be compared with the official medical records of the American Civil War. Sir Alfred Keogh, the Director-General of the Army Medical Service (for convenience the ' D.G.M.S.') and his staff at the War Office had been working at intense pressure throughout these early months. The demands for hospitals, ambulances, and new medical units were insistent, and there seemed at first little hope that the War Office could possibly yield even to Osler's strong representations.

Osler was keen [writes Sir Walter Fletcher] that particular men should be chosen at the outset to write up special subjects. He felt that if they were warned beforehand they would do better than if asked unexpectedly at the end of the war (we all thought then of a war of a few months or of a year or two). He was anxious that selected men should begin writing at once for the information and guidance of others, and there he was quite right. The War Office at first thought it might be left till later. On the 7th of December I wrote to Keogh formally to suggest his appointing a committee on the Medical History of the War, and suggested names for it after consulting Osler, Leishman and others. In spite of War Office congestion, the proposal was acted upon favourably and on January 8, 1915, formal invitations to serve were sent out by Keogh to the proposed members.

Osler was doubtless drawn in, not only from the British but from a Canadian standpoint as well, and at his suggestion Adami addressed a letter to the *Lancet* at about the time the 'D.G.M.S.' issued these invitations to a conference (cf. p. 437 *n.*). It was obvious that the Medical Research Committee, already granted the privilege of gathering statistics, was in a position favourable not only to the collection of data for a future history, but also in a position to make itself responsible for the conducting of researches into war diseases. With the assurance that his overworked staff would not be burdened with any added responsibilities, Sir Alfred Keogh was persuaded.

So it came about that at a meeting called for the 9th of March, over which Keogh presided, a committee of twelve [1] to provide the necessary co-ordinating authority for the compilation of an adequate medical history of the war was appointed. At the time of this meeting Osler pointed out the importance of allowing for the prompt publication and dissemination of memoirs dealing with the practical side of military medicine, and offered to supply the names of particular men in France who might be asked to give attention to such subjects. The question of collecting pathological specimens was also raised, but these were secondary matters. The War Office agreed, subject to the exercise of appropriate censorship over publications. Capt. F. S. Brereton was put in charge of an office in which the medical war diaries of the different units in the field, war maps, and other documents bearing upon medical activities

[1] The members were—*Medicine*: Robinson and Osler; *Surgery*: Pilcher and Burghard; *Statistics*: Barrow and Brownlee; *Hygiene*: Horrocks and Beveridge; *Pathology*: Leishman and Andrewes; *Secretaries*: Brereton and Fletcher.

were assembled. Fletcher was appointed as his co-secretary, a matter of major importance in view of his influential position in the service of an existent organization.[1] This committee never officially met again until after the war, when it was revived by Keogh's successor, General Goodwin (cf. p. 654). Meanwhile, countless inquiries and scientific researches were set on foot, nominally on behalf of the Medical History Committee. None too soon had the War Office recognized an agency in touch with research, for not many weeks elapsed before 'chemical warfare' was first introduced by the enemy. To find some prompt means of defence against chlorine gas, British scientists were called upon in a panic, and from that time on there was no question as to the place of research in the future conduct of the war.[2] So the powers given to the Medical Research Committee came into being—a committee which played no small part in the highly creditable record made by the Royal Army Medical Corps. And though Osler disappears from the scene, only to be called upon from time to time when needed, it was in this, just as in everything else—when things were going well he let them alone and passed on to help somewhere else.

Meanwhile things of quite a different sort were going on at Oxford, and from there Lady Osler wrote to her sister on February 13th:

To-day I have just been wild with despair about it all; the heart-strings are nearly pulled out with sympathy. . . . A Professor Thonan,

---

[1] This organization (the Medical Research Committee) was a novelty, perhaps tainted by health insurance unpopularity, and had still to earn the knowledge and respect of the army. As a part of Lloyd George's National Health Insurance Act, provision had been made at the instigation of Dr. Christopher Addison (who later, in 1919, became the first Minister of Health), whereby a generous sum was to be devoted each year to researches in connexion with the public health. Dr. Fletcher shortly before the outbreak of war had been called from the Physiological Laboratory in Cambridge to supervise the disposition of this fund.

[2] The full utilization of medical scientists by a military Corps in which the officers' duties were supposed to be limited to the reception, treatment, and evacuation of the sick and wounded, nevertheless took time. Professor C. S. Sherrington, for example, Osler's colleague in the Chair of Physiology at Oxford, might have been seen as late as the autumn of 1915 working ten hours a day, seven days a week, calibrating shells in a Birmingham munition

geologist from Louvain who has been living at Merton College some time, has now been given a house and brought his wife and baby. Yesterday she came to say that the landlady had left no linen for change, etc., so I went to see her and have made her quite happy. I took her out to buy pots and pans. Fancy her experience: her first baby born one day; Louvain bombarded the next; she and the baby moved into the cellar, and from one part of the cellar to another as the house fell in. Finally they were in a vegetable bin for three days, then the water-pipes leaked in and they crept out and took refuge in a church; and finally got away. Not a vestige of their house left, nor a rag of clothing. Her people lived at Ypres; they reached there but were driven out, and all came to England. Now the parents' house is ruined, and they are just heart-broken and worn out. . . .

And in a postscript she added:

Monday. I have just come from town where I have been on a queer errand. An old friend of Willie's died suddenly;[1] he was going to the coroner's inquest, and to arrange for the cremation, etc., but was called to Sheffield and asked me to go. I have always such queer errands in London: ovarian tumours; cremations; Belgian babies; almost anything. I am worried nearly ill over America and Germany.

There was reason for worry. London and Washington had been arguing the 'conditional contraband' and 'continuous voyage' questions, with increasing heat on the American side and firmness on the British, even though the questions involved a considerable rewriting of international law. Germany had nationalized all food supplies, and Britain answered by making food-stuffs contraband. To this Germany countered on February 18th by announcing a blockade, and by the end of the month came the declaration by Great Britain of a counter-blockade against Germany, imperfect though it must be. Meanwhile the military operations of the winter following the 'first Ypres' had amounted to a stalemate. Apparently neither side could win that way and the war was resolving itself into one of 'attrition'. Colonel House was in Europe to put out

factory—not the most useful place, even during the war (unless for the sake of example), for the future President of the Royal Society.

[1] This was T. Wesley Mills, Osler's one-time assistant in the physiological course at McGill, who had died with scant warning in an attack of angina, as W. O. explains in a letter the next day to F. J. Shepherd of Montreal.

feelers for peace, and the British were preparing for the disastrous attack on the Dardanelles. On February 23rd Lady Osler wrote to her sister:

> Lieutenant R. Osler leaves for Canadian Military Hospital at Cliveden tomorrow. It is hard to realize what it means. Sometimes I have felt he should have been encouraged to fight but he is better fitted for another kind of usefulness. Independent of that I do not feel that Willie who has given his life for others should be subjected to the risk of giving up this boy in the other way. Their companionship is wonderful and the vacancy in the daily life of rushing in and out will be hard, but I must not dwell on it. . . .

Theirs was indeed an unusual companionship for father and son. Like father, like son—even in the matter of harmless practical jokes. One of them, recounted by Sir Walter Fletcher, who was also victimized, took place on the Sunday before Revere's departure; and the chief victim was so delighted that he inserted records of the occurrence in his copy of Rabelais's 'Catalogue de Saint-Victor', Paris, 1862,[1] which contains Gustave Brunet's 'Essai sur les Bibliothèques imaginaires'. Among the documents is the following letter in crabbed script addressed to Mr. Revere Osler, ostensibly from a certain 'Bookseller and Dealer in Antiquities' at Norwich:

> Dear Sir,—I take the liberty of sending you a small but select list of books which have lately come into my possession. You may remember perhaps an old gentleman who lodged in a room above my shop: I think that he once gave you a book from his collection—or was it your friend, Samuel Leake? About a week ago he called me into his room and told me he was dying, which was indeed evident from his appearance, and that he would like to sell me a few of his books 'dirt cheap', as he said, that I might sell them with a good profit in remembrance of any kindness he had received from me. The remainder of the library was privately sold on Thursday last to Maggs of London, bringing about £2,000. The old man himself died yesterday quietly in his chair, holding a Bible in one

[1] Also inserted is a long list of imaginary titles as they appear on the backs of artificial books in the library of Lord Astor. An accompanying note in Osler's script says they were 'prepared by E. H. Dring of B. Quaritch and given me by him'. The following are examples: 'Shells and Mollusca' by Lloyd George; 'Adventures of Captain Kettle' by T. Pott; 'Did he Mean It?' by B. Shaw; 'Why Noah liked Pears' by Sope; 'Tu Oldat Forte' by Osleregius; &c.

hand and his much loved Aldine Horace in the other, both of which books he has left to me. The list of books by his instructions, is to be sent only to certain people who he thinks will appreciate any of them they may buy. Both you, Sam Leake and James Thorrow are among the number. Hoping you will find something to your taste among these, I remain yours respectfully,

J. R. T——, Norwich.

Accompanying the letter was an amazing 'list of books belonging to the late Elias Brumley of Norwich'. Needless to say it was a hoax. Revere had first tried it out with success on his friend 'Bob' Emmons; then the two with even greater success on Lady Osler; and finally when his father and Fletcher came in he told them the whole story of the old man he used occasionally to see while tutoring in Norwich the year before, who lived above the shop where he used to purchase fishing tackle. '*A bas* the Medical Research Committee! We'll go up there to-morrow with the boys', was the prompt reaction of his hearers. Finally Revere read aloud the list of books, and came to:

AVICENNA. A manuscript, small folio. I know nothing of this, as Dr. Watley the only Persian scholar in Norwich is away and I have no means of getting information. However, since I only paid 10/- for it I am willing to let you have it for £1.0.0.

At this W. O. looked at Revere very hard, took the paper from him, put on his glasses—and, in a moment—'You young scoundrel, you've fooled your Dad!'

To H. B. Jacobs from W. O. Oxford, [undated]

Dear Jacobs, You will be amused at this joke by Revere on the old man. The Sunday before he left he got his friend Bobby Emmons & Grace very much excited with a letter of which I here send you a copy. I had dining with me that night a well known bibliophile Dr. Fletcher of Trinity College, Cambridge, & when we came back from dinner Revere read the letter & the list of books, & we were getting our telegrams ready & Bobby Emmons & Revere were arranging to go off to Norwich in the morning, when I began to smell a rat about the Avicenna. The joke really went off very well, & you will be greatly interested in the list, as it shows how much Revere has picked up in the way of bibliography—how & where Heaven only knows. The names of the men referred to are a couple of old booksellers at Norwich, whom he knew. . . .

Osler made the most of these incidents—anything to get

his mind off the war during his hours at home. And though the house almost always contained one or more young war-worn Canadians eager to tell of hair-raising experiences and horrors, to none of this would he listen. So it was not purely accidental that, as though nothing unusual was going on, he should send out early in March to many a surgical clinic in America a gift accompanied by a note of explanation such as the following:

March 4, 1915.

Dear W. J. Mayo,—Your clinic will never be truly prosperous until under the patronage of St. Cosmas and St. Damian, the saints of surgery, of whom I am sending you a coloured lithograph! Several years ago at Rome, in the Mother Church of the West, I was delighted to find wrapped in a parcel among the precious relics the very instruments with which in the third century A.D. these famous surgeons had performed the transplantation of the thigh operation—and successfully, too—antedating Carrel about 1,700 years! It is a cheap print, as you see, but the merit of it is that it comes direct from the shrine of the saints. I was glad to see Crumley over here at the American Hospital. He seems a very nice fellow. With best wishes to you, and special greetings to your brother. . . .

At home, meanwhile, Osler continued 'preaching, writing, inspecting, hoping'. He saw life steadily and saw it whole. Though there were many engagements relating to medico-military affairs, the meetings of the Bibliographical Society were kept going, for people in their leisure moments must not let themselves dwell upon the war. The Historical Section of the Royal Society of Medicine of which Norman Moore was now President, also kept on with its sessions, with Osler as usual behind the scenes. The exhibition of books on the history of military hygiene had been held early in the year, and at the February meeting Sir Alexander Simpson of Edinburgh, though an octogenarian, was prevailed upon to come and read a paper on Jean Astruc, the subject of Osler's first 'Men and Books' sketch (quoted above, p. 301). In the discussion Osler also took up the cudgels in defence of Astruc, whose character some old-fashioned theologians had recently assailed.

He had arranged, too, for a special meeting at one of the sections of the Royal Society of Medicine, to discuss the epidemiology of cerebrospinal meningitis—a meeting held on February 26th which he opened by saying he hoped it would 'allay the growing apprehension in the minds of the public, and help to stimulate among the profession an interest in one of the most remarkable of epidemic diseases'; and he went on to speak of the sources of infection and of the serum therapy in regard to which many letters had been passing between Simon Flexner and himself. It was an important ball to set rolling, and an active discussion on the subject lasted over two following meetings of the section. Meanwhile Osler himself was much on the road, as is indicated in a letter to Sir Dawson Williams: 'I will see your man at Salisbury on Thursday and do anything I can to help him. I hear the cases have been very numerous in the civil population. In London, too, it is spreading. Do come down and spend a quiet week-end before long.'

His clinics at the Radcliffe Infirmary also continued. One of them on the subject which had long interested him—Arteriovenous Aneurysm—found its way into print [1] after being given on March 26th for the benefit of the local medical officers. His letters of the period were much like his life—a few hopeful words about the progress of the war—mention of his boy—and then he abruptly switches off to his library and the book-mart. On March 7th he wrote to Mrs. Brewster:

All goes well here, & things begin to look brighter. The German blockade seems a farce, & we hope for a peaceful solution of the neutral shipping question. There has been a lull in the stream of wounded, & preparations are in progress for a great advance in the spring—100,000 beds in France! It is appalling to think of it, but such is war! Revere went off about 10 days ago. He has a commission in the Canadian contingent & has been assigned for

---

[1] *Lancet*, London, May 8, 1915, pp. 949–55. In this article Osler made a plea that the war (pathological) specimens be sent to Millbank and to the Museum of the College of Surgeons, as well as careful reports of the cases to the statistical bureau of the M. R. C. Subsequently, to avoid confusion about the disposition of museum specimens, Fletcher with Adami and T. R. Elliott got Keogh to issue a special order (of 14th June, 1915) directing that in future all specimens be dispatched to the College of Surgeons, in care of the Medical History Committee. There, as Army property, the war collection remains, superbly prepared and displayed by Sir Arthur Keith and his staff.

duty at one of the Canadian Hospitals as orderly officer. He is to join the McGill Unit when it comes over in April or May & will be Col. Birkett's orderly officer. They will have charge of one of the new Hospitals in France. He will do ambulance & supply work. I have four nephews at the front & five other relatives come over in the 3rd Canadian Contingent, so that we shall have our anxieties—I enclose you a printed slip of a memorial service which we held at our College this afternoon in memory of the Oxford men who have fallen. Eighteen of our undergraduates already—several of them we knew quite well. It is a shocking business, & it does seem a mockery to hold services but I suppose it is a comfort to the poor relations. A congregation of 1500 sang Abelard's hymn 'Oh what the joy'. I could not help thinking of the nice German women singing this afternoon Ein fester Burg ist unser Gott as I used to hear them in the Cathedral in Berlin. Thank Uncle Ned for his nice article in Life. . . .

The Canadian hospital near Taplow to which Revere had gone—one of the best equipped and most successful of the privately endowed war hospitals—was erected on the grounds of the Astors' beautiful place at Cliveden on the Thames. Osler's official visit as consultant was made there every Monday morning during the remainder of the war, and from the senior medical officer, Colonel F. H. Mewburn of Calgary, Alberta, an old friend, down through the shifting list of junior officers, sisters, and men—all seem to look back upon these inspections, and the cheer they invariably brought, as one of the bright incidents of their long-drawn-out period of service at this hospital. The War Office, to judge from the number of beds it was assembling in England and France, was making provision for an immense number of possible casualties in connexion with the expected spring offensive, and many units which had been organized to run hospitals of 520 beds found to their dismay that a unit of 1,040 beds had been accepted as a standard. Apparently Osler and Robert Bacon had already made overtures regarding some help from the American universities, to judge from the following note of March 11th from Sir Alfred Keogh:

My dear Osler,—I wrote you last night about the Americans. I wish, however, that MacAlister had been more explicit about them. At present we had better not do anything. I hope the McGill Unit will not delay. Everything points to our wanting them as soon as possible. They *might* have to wait here, but their presence in England would make us feel safer.

It was two months longer before the McGill Unit finally reached England, and Revere meanwhile was put to work in the Quartermaster's department at Taplow. There he had such minor chores assigned to him as marching the men to church, all of which he accepted cheerfully, even though in his heart he knew that something more serious than this comfortable billet must come if he were really to 'do his bit'. On March 15th Osler wrote to George Dock in St. Louis:

. . . We are having a busy time here medically. I have been greatly interested in this cerebrospinal outbreak in various parts of the country. I was at Salisbury last week for a couple of days. The disease has spread there from the camp to the civil population. I saw some 15 cases, & lectured to nearly 250 doctors from the country. Naturally the public is very much stirred up about it. I am struggling, too, with this typhoid inoculation question, against which the antivaccination cranks are making a strong fight. About 95% of the men are protected. It is curious that paratyphoid is prevailing so extensively. We only had about twelve cases here at the Base Hospital, seven of which were paratyphoid. I hear that among the Indian troops in France it is almost entirely paratyphoid. I lectured at Chester, too, last week to the North Wales Medical Society on the soldier's heart. There are a great many instances of the old-fashioned irritable heart of Da Costa—of worry, tobacco, & too much exercise. The library continues to grow. I have made several great hauls lately—the Withering papers (letters and journals, &c), a MS Peregrination of Andrew Boorde, a unique copy, from which Hearne printed in 1733—Aristotle ed. prin. Aldine. Revere has joined the Canadian Contingent. He has taken hard to books & to literature. How are the boys? Lady Osler is well. We have got twenty-two Belgian professors here & their families, all living on good American money. Things are beginning to look hopeful, but it is a long and worrying business. . . .

And in a letter of March 28th to H. B. Jacobs, from the Grand Hotel, Torquay, he says:

I am here for a few days inspecting the American Hospital at Paignton which has been a great success. There are three nice Hopkins men on the staff. We are all feeling very hopeful. The blockade is a farce—2 vessels caught last week out of 1500 that reached port. The new army has turned out much better than anyone would have supposed possible. The tussle will be during the next four months. Germany is immensely strong & war is her business so I fear we are in for a long siege. Did I tell you that I have got the minutes of the Medical Society that Jenner & Parry founded—chiefly in Jenner's hand? I must send it to you to show at the Historical Club. . . . I got the Mesué 1471 last week, the 3rd or 4th medical book printed . . . This about expends my E. B. O. fund which has enabled me to get some treasures. . .

For four interminable months little change had occurred in the allied front in Flanders and Northern France, and how the troops of Kitchener's First Army had endured life in the constantly shelled, waterlogged, and accursed trenches during that awful first winter passes understanding. 'The winter evenings in Flanders are long, how long, O Lord!' Those were the days when 'Gott strafe England' was the slogan of Germany, and 'Tipperary' was being sung in England. 'If you have the chance', wrote Osler to L. L. Mackall, who was preparing to return to Germany to resume some studies there, 'give my hearty greetings to the Ewalds in Berlin & to the Müllers in Munich. If they do not treat you well in Jena we will give you a separate alcove in the Bodleian.' Those were days too, when, as the following letter indicates, the provisions of the Geneva Convention were being observed by at least one party:

To President Lowell from W. O. Oxford, April 3, 1915.

Dear Lowell,—You doubtless know that several universities have sent members of their surgical staff to the French hospitals. Do you think Harvard University would offer to staff a British war hospital for 1040 beds:

'for work either in France or in England. This means a personnel which I enclose on the paper "A". We do not ask them to bring equipment, though doubtless surgeons would prefer to bring their own surgical instruments. We will pay them their salaries if they wish this. The rates which we pay are enclosed on "B". We cannot give the personnel commissions, though I am not quite certain of that, but I do not suppose they care. The status is the same whether they have commissions or not. I cannot for the moment say whether they would work in England or in France. So much depends upon future military events. . . . If the offer be made, we shall have to get the consent of the enemy. (See Article XI of the Geneva Convention)'.

This quotation is from a private letter of the Director-General, and should, of course, not be printed, but I thought it best to give

& have to be away a great deal, but the work is most interesting. The Canadians have covered themselves with glory. Everybody is talking about their bravery. We are getting back a lot of wounded, among them my sister's son, Campbell Gwyn who has a bullet in his arm. . . . We are expecting the McGill people over at any time. I think they will take charge of a large hospital somewhere in France.

Then came on May 7th the news of the sinking of the *Lusitania*, and this with the enemy's employment of chemical warfare not only worked an extraordinary transformation on the good-humoured and tolerant British soldier in Flanders, but it stirred the country to its depths as nothing else could have done. A reconstruction of the Government soon followed—a Coalition Cabinet with a Ministry of Munitions under Mr. Lloyd George; Sir Edward Grey and Lord Kitchener alone remaining at their original posts. England had rolled up her sleeves at last. During these past months Osler had begun to make notes on the blank pages of his account-book where in other times appointments for professional consultations would have been entered. Thus, opposite April 29th to May 8th he records:

One of the busiest ten days I ever had. Harrogate on the 29th, interesting case of chronic jaundice. Leeds, Friday, saw Teale and the hospital; back in the evening. On Sat. General Jones of the Canadian Contingent spent the day here & went over the local hospitals. Adami was with us. Sunday, Cheltenham to see a case of hematuria. In eve went to London so as to be able to leave early Monday for Woking to see young Wilkes with septic pneumonia following a fracture. While there a telegram to see Mrs. Burns in London. Saw her in p.m. where up again Tues. a.m. In p.m. went to Cliveden to see medical cases at Canadian hospital. Wed. London again. Thurs. London. Friday London, and in p.m. Chatham where lectured to 1500 soldiers. Dinner in eve by medical officers of the garrison. Sat. a.m. saw the Fort Pitt Hospital; made rounds with the young doctors. P.m. went to Bromley to inspect new Canadian convalescent hospitals. I travelled in all 1260 miles which reminded me of old American days. W. O.

Likewise, the next week: *Mon. May 10*, Cliveden. *Tues. May 11*, Gosport. *Wed. May 12*, Folkestone. *Thurs. May 13*, London. And from the Athenaeum Club on this last morning he sent the following note to a newly elected Fellow of the Royal College of Physicians:

THE COLONEL AND THE LIEUTENANT

the Ladies' College, Cheltenham, where Miss Fegan was then running her little school of librarianship; and then spent a wonderful afternoon among the treasures of the Phillipps manuscripts. Gloucester was reached that evening, and after service on Sunday there was a visit to the Cathedral library. The afternoon brought the little party to Malvern for another wonderful time, with Mr. Dyson Perrins's illuminated manuscripts. In the midst of it the inevitable happened and a telephone message from Oxford called Osler to a patient farther north. He insisted on his friends completing the programme, and they had a happy morning at Worcester Cathedral Library and a delightful drive back to Oxford. The memory of those three days in the midst of the stress and anxiety of the war remains ineffaceable, all the more so because before the war ended the three friends who shared that brief holiday were united in the deeper community of pain. The holiday is mentioned here because, amidst his strenuous war work, to have planned this bibliographical week-end for himself and his friends shows how great was the refreshment which Osler found in his love for books, and how generous he was in sharing it with others.

On Thursday, June 26th, Lady Osler wrote to her sister:

I think Bob [Robert Bacon] and W. O. had a long talk about the hospital [Harvard Unit], and then Willie went to the War Office and arranged matters. Dr. White goes to Neuilly with the Penn. University Hospital lot. . . . We had our first letter from Revere yesterday. Colonel Birkett has written so nicely about him. No address was on the letter—near the sea somewhere. I have had the blues about the war for several days. I feel perfectly hopeless, everything seems at such a standstill but it may be all right. . . .

But this was only for a sister's ears, and rarely for them. Far more characteristic of the spirit at 13 Norham Gardens, even when things were at the worst, is the following letter —The Mobilization of Faith—published in the London *Times* for June 22nd:

Oxford, June 19th.

Sir,—May I protest against the pessimism of the letter which appeared in to-day's issue of *The Times* under the above heading? My friend Mr. Burroughs writes from the cave of Elijah. It is not true that 'since August our faith has wavered and our light has failed'. Can he not hear above the tumult of the wind, the earthquake, and the fire the still, small voice which has stirred the Empire to its depths? If, as he says, 'such spiritual forces as were then at our command have been broken and scattered', it means they were not the weapons of Gideon, but Egyptian reeds fit only to be cast away. The faith worth having in the present crisis has been mobilized, a faith everywhere manifest, whose work is made perfect in sacrifice. In these troublous days, when to many even God's providence seems estranged, it behoves us all, clergy and laity alike, to strengthen the weak hands and confirm the feeble knees, and to look back on the past ten months with thankfulness for what has been accomplished, and to face the future with a courage begotten of confidence in ourselves and in our cause. I am, yours, &c.[1] Wm Osler.

A spirit of this sort was what England greatly needed. It was a period of great depression, and the Rev. E. A. Burroughs had merely voiced the general feeling. The blockade was proving a serious menace. What would America do? Anything but write notes? 'The news of the Leyland Liner being torpedoed has just come', wrote Lady Osler on the 30th, 'and I believe it will settle America now. Heavens, isn't it horrible!' Huge advertisements were appearing in the papers—AN URGENT CALL FOR HELP IN THE MUNITION CENTRES—accompanied by a picture of the new hard-working Minister of Munitions; YOUR COUNTRY NEEDS MORE AIRCRAFT, &c. The Government went so far as to pass a Registration Bill, and this was better than nothing, but unless the whole nation should be mobilized for compulsory service as in France and Germany, about all that Kitchener and the Government could do was to appeal—to appeal for thrift in the household; to the farmer to raise more food; to the working-man not to strike; and to every one to invest in the great war loan at four and a half per cent.! This was the best a nation could do which still adhered to the principles of voluntaryism, even though it was evident to all that the cream of the country was being skimmed off and that the cost of a soldier under this system had become nearly prohibitive. The labour situation, too, was most serious, with disputes on the Clyde and Tyne; at Cardiff where 200,000 miners walked out; even the railway workers were demanding higher wages. 'There is a sensation over everything', she wrote, 'that

[1] Osler must have written at about the same time his article for popular consumption on 'War, Wounds and Disease' in the *Quarterly Review*, London (July number, p. 150), containing an especially vivid paragraph on the venereal peril; but the whole tenor of the article is optimistic.

seems like a thunder-cloud ; no one quite knows what it is but I call it depression, and with good reason.' On July 10th Osler wrote to Dr. White :

Dear J. William, I have written to Makins & to Bowlby [Consultants to the Army in France], both of whom will be delighted, of course, to see you on your way back. They are having a very slack time at present. I hear the hospitals are empty & the men here are twirling their thumbs in idleness. No doubt it will all change very soon. I shall be here on & off all the summer. I am going over to the McGill Unit when they get settled & when they get any patients. I have had suggestions from several quarters that satisfactory help could be given by supplying house officers for the hospitals here. Garrod of St. Bartholomew's has interested himself in this & has already had correspondence from a number of men in America. You could discuss the matter with him when you come. . . .

As he said, it was 'a slack time' so far as the hospitals were concerned, and nothing was worse for the R.A.M.C. than to sit back and twirl their thumbs in comparatively empty hospitals during lulls. The method practised by Osler under these circumstances was to encourage his young friends to engage, as he did himself, in some literary research to take their minds off the war. So in a note written in the middle of July, he says :

Revere writes most interesting letters. He and his chief seem the only two with much work, as they have not yet opened the hospital. We are in a quiet period. There were 25,000 empty British beds in France last week & 500 vacant here (Oxford) ; but there will be work enough later on. We have had Norman & Campbell Gwyn here & Archie Malloch who has just gone to open a new hospital at Burley-on-the-Hill, the home of the Finches. I have got him interested in Sir John Finch & Sir Thos. Baines, the David & Jonathan of the profession in the 17th century. This is a most interesting story—look them up in the D.N.B. when you have a moment. Archie has been working at the Bodleian & has got out all sorts of interesting facts. I hope he will get a number of Finch's letters at Burley.[1]

---

[1] All this led to the publication by Captain Archibald Malloch of a monograph on Finch and Baines (Cambridge University Press, 1917). In the introduction to this 'pleasant but novel task' the author says : 'I have gone to him [Sir William Osler] in every difficulty that has confronted me in this work and in spite of the immense demands on his time he has ever proved to be, as he has been called before, "the young man's friend".'

There were meanwhile many things to be done. The Belgians, of course, were still in Oxford, and by natural processes increasing in numbers. The 'work shops' continued with their output of pyjamas and so on—also increasing in numbers. And Osler in his not infrequent teasing moods would refer to his wife as a woman of 'push and go'—that at least was the sort of person the Minister of Munitions said the country needed. His own obligations even during slack times were many, in addition to that of being 'Consoler-General' to the army. One finds traces of his footsteps in familiar places. Thus:

A conference was held at Oxford, under the auspices of the Oxfordshire Association for the Prevention of Tuberculosis, on July 17th. Representatives of sanitary authorities, Insurance Committees and other bodies attended. Sir William Osler, who presided, moved resolutions urging that the retention of the dispensary system should be regarded as essential in any scheme for dealing with tuberculosis in the county; that no tuberculosis scheme in the county could be considered complete or adequate which did not make provision for co-operation with a voluntary-care and after-care association on the lines suggested by the medical officers of the Local Government Board, etc., etc.

On July 29th he wrote to his Quaker friend, H. M. Thomas, in Baltimore:

Dear Harry T. How's thee? & how's the family & the medical student & Trudeau & Margaret? I wish you were over here in this orgie of neuroses & psychoses & gaits and paralyses, &c. I cannot imagine what has got into the C. N. S. [central nervous system] of the men, & I see it is as bad in Germany. It is a sort of psychical decerebration. You never dreamt of such gaits—the craziest, un-text-book things. One fellow was just like Blondin on a tight-rope. Hysterical (?) dumbness, deafness, blindness, anaesthesias, galore! I suppose it is the shock & strain, but I wonder if it was ever thus in previous wars. It is a horrid business but we have much to be thankful for at the end of a year. The Germans have not carried out their programme; we have 2 1/2 millions of men under arms and the navy is in command, but the country begins to realize that it is a long affair, 2 or 3 years more, unless there is a sudden smash somewhere. If we go under, Johnnie get your gun! Your turn next. Revere is off with the McGill Unit, Asst. Quartermaster & working so hard. There are 13 members of my family over. Norman Gwyn has been with us with a broken ankle & his brother with a bullet through his chest. One is dead & one a prisoner. I am very busy & getting a good deal of education, but I am longing for a time when I can spend some hours of each day at the Bodleian. Tell Zoe I wish she could see our garden. Such roses! Grace has been such a worker. Her shop in one of the museum laboratories is a sight. We have 153 Belgians (professors & families) 22 professors, & heaven knows what will become of the poor devils. 'Tis an awful tragedy. Love to you all.

After his service at the American Ambulance J. William White paid them a visit in August, and Lady Osler wrote to his wife: 'I think he has done everything he wanted to do except go down in a submarine, and that he cannot accomplish. It has been as good as a play to hear our husbands going for each other and calling each other the most awful names.' White had rewritten his war pamphlet, and Osler wrote to him two weeks later: 'Just back from Burley-on-the-Hill. Your New Edition is A.1. & should have a great run here. It is full of good stuff. Will write you a steamer letter. D. the K!' He and Lady Osler had gone for a short visit to Burley in Rutland, where Mr. Phipps's daughter, Mrs. Guest, had recently established a convalescent hospital, of which 'Archie' Malloch was in charge; and it was there that Malloch's Finch and Baines quest had started. A little later, too, they spent a few days with Lady Wantage at Lockinge House near Oxford, 'to meet the Archbishop of York; and came away exhausted. There were twelve people, and all talked about the war, its horrors and mistakes. Willie looked a ghost and could not divert anyone.[1] No more visits for us.' It was while there that the Regius began the following to Mrs. Brewster—evidently a little depressed by the war talk to which he had been forced to listen:

24th [August]

We are off for a day in one of those Anglican paradises in which I hope some day to see you & R. B. & the children. Such gardens & flowers & trees. Still, I wish it were Avalon! It seems ages since I was in America & goodness knows when I shall be able to get away. This awful business gets worse & worse & if the U. S. comes

---

[1] Much more to his taste was the visit paid this same month in company with Mr. John Lane to Lord Sherborne to see a supposed portrait of his hero, Sir Thomas Browne.

in the complications will be worser! Things look very serious, and we are anxiously waiting. I have a feeling that Germany will back down at the last moment. We are all very depressed about Russia but the truth is she is no match for the highly trained Germans & Krupp is winning. The outlook is much better here, & to have 3 millions of men in training is very hopeful. Munitions are piling up & the feeling in France is optimistic. But it is going to be a slow business. The house keeps full, another wounded nephew back & a cousin with shell-shock & a nephew with an infected hand. Grace is hard at work, but there has been much less to do lately as the Hospitals are empty. Revere writes very cheery letters from Etaples. I hope to go over shortly to see the Hospitals & stay a week with the McGill men. We are thankful he is not in the Dardanelles. I have been a great deal away—Cardiff, Paignton & Folkestone. The household is depleted, chauffeur, butler & secretary all gone. I am in despair about the latter as I had just got him properly trained in the Library work. I hope to steal another young chap from the Bodleian

28th No steamer this week so I brought the unfinished letter home. Such a busy day—Dr. Camac from N. Y. & Dr. Morris from Phila, then Dr. Van Dyke from the Hague & Mr. Yates Thompson & a stranded Johns Hopkins M.D. who has married a German wife, who has refused to go to America; then a new Belgian professor asking help. So you see we have plenty to distract us. Tomorrow the Pages come to lunch on their way thro to Broadway. He has done so well in London & Mrs. Page is a dear. The Embassy staff too is a great credit, particularly Col. Squier who has made such a strong impression in scientific circles. Kiss the darlings for me. The photos are on the mantelpiece in my bedroom & Grace often talks to that bright-eyed baby. What a delight she must be!

Early in September he paid his long-promised visit to the McGill Unit, the first record of which is on a postcard to Mrs. Brewster from Montreuil-sur-Mer, saying: 'Here with Revere. Such a lovely walled town—the first stopping-place of Sterne on his Sentimental Journey. Am sending you a full account of my trip.' The account follows:

No. 3 Canadian Gen. Hospital Camiers,
Sept 7th [Tuesday]

You would be amused to peek through the fly of a tent and see me sitting up in a camp bed with this pad on my knee! Such a comfortable billet! I have not slept in a tent for forty years. Its a bit breezy, & cold & cramped but snug enough—considering. I crossed yesterday from Folkestone to Boulogne as they sent word the Hospital was full & in good working order. Three miles out from

Folkestone we passed close to the Cable boat, the Monarch, potted at 2 a.m. by a submarine, the masts out of water & surrounded by trawlers. They have never got one of these fast trans-channel boats that cross twice daily. Col. Birkett, Maj. Howard, Billy Francis (a nephew) & Revere met me on the dock. R. looking so well & brown. The McGill unit is stationed at Camiers about twelve miles south of Boulogne, with six other general Hospitals, all in tents. It is close to the sea from wh. it is separated by sand dunes while behind the Downs rise to about 300–400 feet. In the camp are about 8000 people, so that from the top of the Downs the spread of white tents makes a most attractive sight, and far away towards Etaples one can see a second group of tents & huts. The McGill men are so nice, many of them old students & all old friends. They have been here for about three months getting settled & having a very quiet time, as there has been no fighting. Revere is assistant quartermaster and has got into the job very well. He has about 40 men to control & has to do with the supplies &c. He sometimes feels that he should be off in the fighting line & of course if he wishes we shall not oppose it; but he is not much cut out for a soldier's life & loathes the whole business of war. The hospital tents are from India, holding 40–50 beds & the inner lining is of that attractive Cawnpore material of various colours & patterns. Such a nice set of nurses—all from the Royal Victoria or the Montreal General Hospitals. Capt. Law the quartermaster is an old family friend. Next to us is the Harvard Unit with 800 beds & at Etaples is a Chicago Unit with the same number. The wounded & sick come from the Ypres district every few days & are the result of the casual fighting (& the ordinary illnesses—now & again a typhoid). I shall make an inspection of all the hospitals in the District. The weather is glorious and we all sat outside the mess tent until 10 p m

Sunday eve. We have had a splendid day. Church parade at 10.30, excellent sermon from the Chaplain who explained that war wiped out all sects in camps! Then we motored to a lovely spot Hardelot for lunch—Campbell Howard, Billy Francis, Revere & I. Nice old inn with tables on a lovely lawn. Then across country to Montreuil *sur mer* (once, it is now 10 miles inland!) a walled town of extraordinary beauty One wonders not to hear more of it. I never saw such walls & moats in such good preservation. Revere is devoted to the place as it was at the inn, from which I posted a card to you, that Sterne rested the first night of his Sentimental Journey. At M. are about 1000 of the Indian troops many in hospital. Poor devils, they look very much out of place. This is no country for them —too cold & wet.

Wednesday eve. Such an experience! I had not asked to go to the Front as I knew permission was not granted; but the dear old Commandant at Etaples said he would send me: so at 8 a m yesterday

Col McCrae, who has been thro the whole district & Capt Rhea & I started off. If you look on the map we went northeast to Merville to see a big dressing station and mobile laboratory, in charge of two old friends. Here we saw the wounded brought in from the trenches among them the Speaker's son—Maj. Lowther. Shot thro the chest. It was a sad business but the nurses & doctors seemed to know their work, & the officers' wards were very comfortable. Many of the men are sent on in the big ambulance trains the same eve. Then to Armentières which is a great centre & to Nieppe, the Canadian headquarters, where I saw many old friends. Stationary balloons, aeroplanes, soldiers, camps, billets in farms, brigades of artillery on march—such a scene! In the field next to the chief med. officer's house a big new German aeroplane was brought down the day before our visit. We had hoped to be able to go the upper road to Bailleul & Hazebrouck, but it had been shelled the day before and was impassable, so we kept along the second line of trenches & in the eve. saw many returning & going to them. Here for the first time we heard the boom of guns, every few minutes. About 3 miles from Nieppe we saw the bombardment of aeroplanes by the German aircraft guns. The first one was 3000–4000 feet up at the edge of a light cloud, & within 5 minutes 42 shells had exploded near it. We could see the bright flash & then a puff-ball of black smoke, quite circular which gradually increased to about the size of the moon & took 15–20 minutes to disappear. Within half an hour we saw another, much closer—122 puff-balls could be counted against the clouds, many seemed so close, but the aeroplane sailed about taking the usual daily observations. It was a great sight the most wonderful I have seen. Miles & miles of motor lorries line the roads waiting to go up in the eve. The whole country is alive with troops. The peasants are hard at work getting in their crops, even between the lines of trenches. We visited Hazebrouck & on to St. Omer the headquarters. Col McCrae has been fighting all thro the district and took us to several spots on which his battery was stationed. Everywhere great squares of graves—marked with the names of the men of the Regiments. The villages do not look much battered except at one place, just where we crossed the Belgian frontier, but there was scarcely a church left standing. Except for the soldiers St Omer seems untouched by the war. We passed the big aeroplane camp, just outside the town. We have done about 190 miles & not a mile of bad road, in spite of the heavy traffic

Thursday. We had an experience last night 11.30—a big convoy came, 15 steel cars—all beautifully fitted 34 beds in each, nurse & doctors. We went to see the men unloaded. Splendid organization—about 30 ambulances. The men were lifted out 4 in 4 minutes & I got into an ambulance with them, an Irishman wounded in the head, an appendicitis, a typhoid & a bad shrapnel wound of leg. All were smoking! It took 7 minutes to the Hospital & the 4 were in bed within 27 minutes from the arrival of the train. I have been to Wimereux, north of Boulogne to see the big infectious hospital & I shall stay a day there on my way back, as they have all the typhoid & paratyphoid cases of the whole district centred there. Extraordinarily few for the enormous number of men.

And a week after his return home he added this postscript:

I had hoped to finish & send this off but I got back to a press of work & have been away almost every day. It was a wonderful experience & I wish I could have stayed longer, but I have engagements in Leeds Oct. 1st, two addresses, which I have to write within a week. Grace has been away with friends in the south of England, her first holiday for a year. I am very well & very brown. I must send you a copy of my father's journal & papers which my brother E. B. has had printed here. You will be interested to look it over. It is a private, family affair, not for distribution. R. B. will see in it a good bit of our Clarendon Press work. How I wish I could be with you at Mt. Kisco. I do not believe this horrid business will ever be over, but we are keeping up our courage. Love to the darlings & to R. B. & Uncle Ned.

A cheerful enough letter—just the sort many people wrote after their first visit to France. Meanwhile seemingly one of the Belgian families had left Oxford for Holland:

. . . They insisted on going [Lady Osler wrote to her sister] and said they could not stay on charity any longer. At 9.30 Thursday morning I was to be seen in the car going to the station with 9 P——s and their bags—followed by a cart full of luggage and another Belgian with a male and female bicycle. I should think it had been a prosperous year for the P——s: they came with five children and two Gladstone bags; they left with six children (one in a hat box), four trunks, a cradle and two bicycles. The N——s have left too. My wee house is empty now but we shall put some others in soon I think.

And it may be added that ere long another Professor's family left, with seven bicycles, 200 white mice and guinea-pigs!—and lost one bicycle and four guinea-pigs between the Banbury Road and Liverpool Street. Even tragedies of war may be amusing. But enough of this. The Harvard Unit had come, had gone to France, and was not faring well. New campaigners are apt to be restive in war, and in hospitals idle times and empty beds breed dissatisfaction.

As usual, the Consoler-General enters the scene, and from the Athenaeum the day of his return he wrote to President Lowell:

Dear Lowell, I have just come back from France, where I paid a visit to the Harvard Unit, & I am sure you will like to know my impressions. The quarters are good, tents of the fine Durbar variety, the wards are most attractive. At first patients were scanty, later they have been numerous & many important cases have been treated. The Commandant, Sir Allan Perry, is a charming man who has done all in his power to make things run smoothly. The staff is A.1. I saw the work in several of the departments, & could not but be impressed with the very valuable experience it has been for the men, so varied and so unusual. The X-ray work is just what one would have expected from the well known expert of the M. G. H. The Dental men have been a revelation & I saw several cases of terrible mutilation of the face on the high road to repair. The nurses have done splendidly. I was delighted to meet them at a tea kindly given me by the matron. It was a peculiar pleasure to dine with the mess & to meet so many men of the younger generation, all of whom seem treading the footsteps of that great group—the Warrens, Jacksons, Bigelows & Bowditches—who made Harvard famous in the past. I do hope arrangements have been made to continue the work. It would be a thousand pities if the younger men lost this unique opportunity. . . .

On Wednesday the 29th he wrote a line to Adami, saying: 'I am off to Leeds, Newcastle & Manchester to-morrow—back Tuesday. Come for next week-end, 9th—do. All sorts of things to talk to you about.' The Canadian Medical Corps, it may be added, was having its troubles. But meanwhile at Leeds, at the opening of the medical school, he gave on October 1st the two addresses he had spoken of in an earlier letter. Sir Berkeley Moynihan—'Carnifex Maximus'—with whom he stayed, recalls that Osler remained in bed during the morning and wrote the Nerve and Nerves talk given before the Leeds Luncheon Club—'a little medical advice on how to get the best work out of the human machines of the nation in these times of stress and strain':

The other day I asked a battle-bronzed veteran fresh from an inferno of shell fire if he thought any single factor would decide the war. 'Yes,' he said, '*nerve*; the men who can best stand the racket will win.' I must confess to a little surprise, as I expected him to say men, or money, or munitions. . . . The phrase is a good one, dating from the days when English bowmen fought where now not arrows but shell and shrapnel darken the air. It means command of the machine and all its resources. . . . Some years ago, at Columbia University, New York, I heard that American Socrates, William James, deliver a remarkable address on 'The Energies of Men', in which he contended that our organism has stored up reserves of energy ordinarily not in use, but that may be called upon; deeper and deeper strata of material ready for use, on tap if we care to call upon it. . . . Our energy budget has really never been exploited. Kipling has the secret in a verse in the famous poem 'If':

> If you can force your heart and nerve and sinew
> To serve your turn long after they are gone,
> And so hold on when there is nothing in you
> Except the Will which says to them: 'hold on'.

As with the individual so with the nation. Nerve is a special trait of the Briton, who has always displayed a dogged determination and a capacity to hold on, so well expressed in the lines I have just quoted. The nation, too, has its reserves of energy, upon which in the present trial we must call. We are standing well the change of gear. New and unthought-of levels of energy are available, on tap at *will*. . . .

There is a state the very opposite of that of which we have been speaking, seen in man and nations, and best described by the word *nerves*, a word not in the dictionary. It is slang, but we all know the meaning, the unstrung state, the inability to get work, or the best work, out of the machine, a jumpiness and instability. A man may inherit a weak, irritable nervous system, another may spoil a good one with bad habits or bad training, or a good one may be shocked out of action by the blows of circumstance. . . . Unfortunately, it is not a matter for the individual alone. 'Nerves' may attack whole communities. We are all apt to be swayed by states of mind which are rarely associated with any clear consciousness of their causes. They may be nothing more than moods, but they spread like measles, or any other infection. What a contagion is fear, a state in which the nerves are unstrung. How its voice rings through history. The spirit of fear may come on a people like pestilence and in the Middle Ages was responsible for that black record of witches and witchcraft. Waves of emotion play on man's nerves as the wind on an Æolian harp. . . . We get 'nervy', and lose control of the machine. Judgement becomes difficult, and we are swayed by emotions that sweep over the crowd regardless of any basis in truth. We become weak-minded, and believe anything any Ananias says. Who would have dreamt that so early in the war there could have been so many liars in the country as the men and women who saw

Russian troops ![1] An instability of this sort leaves us easy prey to the Yellow Press. . . . The 'Liar' of Lucian should be reprinted and spread broadcast as the true model for these modern Cretans.

Collectively, we need steadying, more self-control, more cultivation of the *will*, which alone has the key to our reserves of unused energies. We should avoid everything that artificially stimulates, and so irritates the nervous system. It indicated a certain lack of nerve, an oyster-like flabbiness in the nation, not to have followed the King's example in the matter of alcohol. Nothing so weakens the will of the worker, of mind or of muscles, as leaning upon that Egyptian reed. Too much tobacco also increases the irritability of the nervous system, and many of our young soldiers smoke far more than is good for their hearts or brains. Another serious promoter of 'nerves' is the combination of gossip, gabber and gas which we have dealt out by the penny dreadfuls, and too often poured by people into our too willing ears. I wish we could catch and intern one person, a lying knave, an Autolycus, who flits from house to house, in most, alas! very welcome, called 'a friend of mine'. That appalling third person is responsible for apprehension and mistrust where confidence should reign, and very often for a limp, flabby public opinion instead of 'nerve'—that well-strung state so needful for our final victory.

But 'Science and War', the other address, delivered before the Medical School that afternoon, was not written in a morning in bed. Some of its paragraphs show his state of mind:

Our young minds are trained to regard warfare as one of the prerogatives of Jehovah, the Lord of Hosts, who 'teachest my hands to war and my fingers to fight'. With man's conception of a great war in Heaven has passed into current belief one of the strongest of popular dogmas—that of a personal devil. Nurtured on the Old Testament, I recall as a child my terror at the recital of the slaughter of the thousands by the Israelites, when they spared neither man nor beast, woman nor child. After the ears of my understanding were opened it was but small comfort to know that these countless thousands existed only in the imagination of the historian of petty tribes of Palestine. The pride, pomp, and circumstance of war have so captivated the human mind that its horrors are deliberately minimized. The soldier embodies the heroic virtues, and the camp is the nursery of fortitude and chivalry. The inspiration of the nation is its battles. Crécy and Agincourt, Trafalgar and Waterloo,

[1] There is a story, perhaps apocryphal, told by Sir Walter Raleigh, of how Osler at the time maliciously scattered the ends of some partly consumed Russian cigarettes on the tracks at the Oxford station.

are more notable events in history than Magna Charta, the execution of King Charles, or the Declaration of American Independence. . . . For more than a century the world had been doing well—everywhere prosperity and progress. The French Revolution and the founding of the American Republic seemed to lift humanity to a level on which might be realized practically the brotherhood of man. There had been bloody and grievous wars in the nineteenth century, but there were such hopeful features that the new century opened with peace congresses and peace palaces. Remarkable and unheard-of incidents seemed to indicate a change of heart among the nations. . . . An intellectual comity had sprung up between the nations, fostered by a growing interchange of literature and maintained by gatherings whose Pentecostal character lent hope to the dream of Isaiah of a day when in the spirit of wisdom and understanding Ephraim should not vex Judah and Judah should not vex Ephraim.

And some of us had indulged the fond hope that in the power man had gained over nature had arisen possibilities for intellectual and social development such as to control collectively his morals and emotions, so that the nations would not learn war any more. We were foolish enough to think that where Christianity had failed Science might succeed, forgetting that the hopelessness of the failure of the Gospel lay not in the message, but in its interpretation. The promised peace was for the individual—the world was to have tribulations; and Christ expressly said: 'Think not that I am come to send peace on earth; I came not to send peace but a sword'. The Abou ben Adhems woke daily from their deep dreams of peace, and lectured and published pamphlets and held congresses, while Krupp built 17-inch howitzers and the gun range of the super-Dreadnoughts increased to eighteen miles! . . . Professor Haverfield shocked me the other day by remarking that the Greeks, with all their refinement, were a match for the worst of us to-day. This drove me to Thucydides, where I found a parallel with Belgium in the treatment of Melos by the Athenians. He gives the wonderful dialogue in a cold, clear style befitting the hard barbarity of the transaction. The delegates from Athens urged: 'What is right is estimated by the quality of power to compel.' 'The powerful exact what they can, the weak grant what they must.' The Melians wished to remain quiet and to be friends, and to force them to take sides they said would only make enemies of all the neutrals—and then there were the gods! To which the Athenians replied: 'As regards the favour of heaven, we trust that we, too, shall not fall short of it: they always maintain dominion wherever they are the stronger.' It was the case of the Walrus and the Carpenter, and the Athenian delegates retired with the remark: 'We bless your simplicity; we do not admire your folly.' And Book V concludes in a twentieth-century 'might is right' fashion: 'They surrendered at discretion to the Athenians who put to death all the male adults, and made slaves of the women and children, . . . as for the country, they inhabited it themselves.'

In spite of unspeakable horrors, war has been one of the master forces in the evolution of a race of beings that has taken several millions of years to reach its present position. During a brief fragment of this time—ten thousand or more years—certain communities have become civilized, as we say, without, however, losing the savage instincts ground into the very fibre of their being by long ages of conflict. Suddenly, within a few generations, man finds himself master of the forces of nature. In the fulness of time a new dispensation has come into the world. Let us see in what way it has influenced his oldest, and most attractive occupation. . . .

From this he went on to speak of 'the influence of the new dispensation of science on the old practice of war'—first of science as a destructive agent, and he told of his recent impressions in France; and then of science as an agent in the prevention of disease in war, a subject far more after his own heart. 'Apollo, the far darter, is a greater foe to man than Mars.'

And what shall be our final judgement [he said in closing]—for or against science? War is more terrible, more devastating, more brutal in its butchery, and the organization of the forces of nature has enabled man to wage it on a titanic scale. More men will be engaged and more will be killed and wounded in a couple of years than in the wars of the previous century. To humanity in the gross, science seems a monster, but on the other side is a great credit balance—the enormous number spared the misery of sickness, the unspeakable tortures saved by anaesthesia, the more prompt care of the wounded, the better surgical technique, the lessened time in convalescence, the whole organization of nursing; the wounded soldier would throw his sword into the scale for science—and he is right.

To one who is by temperament and education a Brunonian and free from the 'common Antipathies' and 'National repugnances' one sad sequel of the war will be, for this generation at least, the death of international science. An impassable intellectual gulf yawns between the Allies and Germany, whose ways are not our ways and whose thoughts are not our thoughts. That she has made herself a reproach among the nations of the earth is a calamity deplored by all who have fought against Chauvinism in science, and a bitter regret to those of us who have had close affiliations with her, and lifelong friends among her professors, whose devotion to science has made every worker in every subject the world over their debtor. . . . With death war dies, and there is no hatred in the grave. . . .

It was a noble motive that prompted the Warden and Fellows of New College to put upon the roll of honour in their hall the name of a German Rhodes scholar, one of her sons, though an enemy, who had fallen in battle for his country, an action resented by certain narrow-minded Philistines in the press. I should like to pay a last tribute of words to Paul Ehrlich, one of the masters of science, who has recently passed away. . . . The brilliant labours of such a man transcend national limitations, and his name will go down to posterity with those of his countrymen, Virchow and Koch, as one of the creators of modern pathology. . . . This old earth has rarely had a worse year than that through which we have just passed. Men's hearts are failing for fear, and for looking after those things which are coming upon it. Though final deliverance from strife will not be in our day, let us not despair. Only just awake, the race is sore let and hindered by passions and practices, strong as animal instincts, which millions of years of struggle have ground into its fibre. I have just finished reading Henry Osborn Taylor's last book, 'Deliverance', in which he sketches the ways in which our ancestors of all times and countries have adapted themselves to the fears and hopes of their nature. From such a story of incessant and successful adjustments one may take a Pisgah-sight of a day when 'nation shall not lift up a sword against nation, neither shall they learn war any more'.

Without a secretary, Osler's brief letters of the period were usually on postcards. They meant much to the receivers thereof, as did one, for example, addressed to R. Tait McKenzie, Farnborough, Hants; and Professor McKenzie writes a page of explanation of how, during his early work with the War Office in the establishment of command depots for the re-training of wounded and damaged men preparatory to re-enlistment (work which was taken over long after by the organization under Sir Robert Jones), Osler came to see him and subsequently sent Sir James Mackenzie, who stayed a week to study the effect of graded exercise on the heart cases. Meanwhile recourse must be had to Lady Osler's letters to learn that slack times were over for the hospitals in France. She had written to her sister on October 5th:

They are terribly busy [at Camiers]: patients in and out, night and day. Revere has been happier since being so occupied, but when he has leave I am sure he will apply to be transferred. The battle is raging, but nobody expresses excitement. The losses are too terrible. I think there were four hundred Oxford boys in *The Times* list to-day—I mean men who live here, like the Williams's son at Summerfields School, and two Lynam masters. There are 1040 wounded here now and the streets are full. Mrs. Boyce Allen came back to the work-room yesterday after weeks of absence, and asked tenderly for you. Her son is safe still; I believe the Canadians have not been in this advance yet. . . . Mrs. MacM. was from Baltimore, and he from Montreal. They came to live in England just as we did. Friday word came the *only son*! was killed in France. The girls went home for the night, and back Saturday p.m. to work. They came to see me this morning—pathetically brave. . . .

The summer months in Flanders, where trench warfare was by this time a highly specialized science, had till now been Paradise compared to what had been going on in Gallipoli, where, too, was what amounted to a military deadlock. Most disconcerting news, meanwhile, was coming from the east where Hindenburg was settling his score with the Russian armies, which were in full retreat. The long-expected offensive by their allies on the western front to give them some measure of relief, had been delayed from want of munitions until September 25th, when came the French attack in Champagne followed by the British thrusts at Hooge and among the slag-heaps at Loos and La Bassée. All it amounted to was a few more wrecked villages and a few more salients to consolidate, after regiments such as the 9th Black Watch had been piped back with only 100 men and one officer surviving. 'A success but not a decision', said Head-quarters. 'Poor staff work', said the rank and file. But with 200,000 casualties the hitherto idle hospitals had no time for 'grousing'. The young assistant quarter-master at Camiers learned, from what he then saw, that, so soon as opportunity offered, he must join the combatant forces. Osler meanwhile kept his head clear and his hands full at home. Typhoid was under control, but new diseases, against which they were not protected, were appearing among the soldiers in England and overseas. The following cryptic note of October 8th to H. D. Rolleston indicates that he was alert for these things:

Dear Rolleston, I will send word to Davis-Taylor—so pleased to have the case—Have been in Leeds—gassing! & Manchester—Many diarrhoea cases from the Dardanelles at Cliveden—

1) simple, which all seem to get, no reaction to Flexner or Shiga

2) def. Bac. dy. symptoms & reactions

3) Amoebic—one doubtful case. A N.-Z-der with bad dys. profound emaci. &c, gave also ParaTy-B reactions, very marked. P.M. shoe-leather colon—many typic. typhoid ulcers in Ileum.

We have 24 Enterics in one ward from the East 22 P-Ty. [paratyphoid] B. 1 P-T. A & one plain T.—all clinically Typhoid Bismuth & charcoal large doses—seems to do best I must try to come down before long Could not you both get off for a week-end?—do. Love to Mrs. R. . . .

And he promptly wrote to J. Y. W. MacAlister: 'We should have more *specific* war meetings: (1) Paratyphoid Fever, (2) The War Nephritis, (3) Trench Fever, (4) The Dardanelles Diarrhoea, (5) The Soldiers' Heart—are army medical subjects which need discussion.' And on the 13th he wrote again:

Dear MacAlister, Dreyer will open a discussion next week or week after on P-Ty [paratyphoid] Infections. He has been at the Infectious Hospital, Wimereux for the last 3 mos, & knows the whole business. He thinks Dawson will come. Will you wire him? in yours or my name or both. Torrens has just been back & would not be able he thinks to get away. Failing D. we might find an Army man, failing these I could give our experience of about 30 cases dealing with the Clinical aspects. It is a very important matter—questions are to be asked in the House as to the incidence of T. and Para-T. in the Dardanelles. The present group of 24 which I have under observation are from the East. Dreyer will be here thro' the 1st week in November. . . .

And again on the 21st he wrote: 'I saw Garrod to-day. Failing Dawson I will open but D. is the man & he should be asked. It is a most urgent problem. I will ask to-morrow at the Army Med. College for any man who knows Para-Typ.'[1] All this led up to an important meeting at the Royal Society of Medicine—one of the series of meetings, indeed, which he promoted and engineered. The first of them was held on October 19th,[2] dealing with cerebrospinal

[1] Typhoid, though rampant in the East among uninoculated troops, had been effectually controlled in France; but many new and obscure fevers had begun to appear there among the troops—fevers conveniently recorded in the hospitals as 'P.U.O.' [pyrexia of uncertain origin]. Among them were the paratyphoid and trench fevers, polyneuritis, infectious jaundice, &c., which gradually became differentiated.

[2] Osler opened the discussion. Dr. Gardner Robb followed with an

meningitis; this was followed by the meetings of November 9th and 23rd devoted to paratyphoid fever, a malady which, akin to typhoid, had become so prevalent that it was causing anxiety at Head-quarters.

One of the many sojourners at the 'Open Arms' during those days entered in his journal: 'Sir William has a big job with his letters and no secretary. Mr. Hill from the Bodleian comes in the p.m. to work on the Catalogue. But in the evening he and Lady Osler write letters up in the sitting-room and have to buy stamps by the £5-worth.' From the sitting-room earlier in the month there had issued a batch of long-hand invitations 'requesting the pleasure of your company to meet Dr. Beal of the American Hospital, Paignton, at luncheon, 1.15 Wed. 13th, at the Imperial Restaurant, Regent Street'. And in a letter of October 15th to her sister, Lady Osler says:

> ... Wednesday, W. O. did one of his angelic strokes. He had a luncheon of twenty-two for Dr. Beale who is leaving Paignton and returning to Worcester. He has really done very well, and the ladies of the committee have made him a presentation of silver. Dr. Penhallow is taking the job; he had just arrived when we were there. Did I tell you that Mrs. Whitelaw Reid is paying for Dr. Penhallow and about twelve nurses? Why has the Red Cross 'gebusted'? Well, the luncheon was in London, of course. Mr. Page was there; Sir Alfred Keogh of the War Office; the head Naval Med. Man, I forget his name; and all the most important and representative men. Just a simple luncheon. They toasted the King, and Sir Alfred Keogh thanked Dr. Beale, for England, for the work done at Paignton. ...

Nor were Canadians and temporary American volunteers the only ones to occupy their thoughts. There were English Tommies as well, one of whom, Osler's 'boy' in the Oxford Museum, wrote from somewhere in France on October 25th:

> To Lady Osler.—My Lady, Thank you very much for the parcel which arrived to-day. It is very kind of you to keep me so well

---

account of the Belfast epidemic in which Flexner's serum had been used with most favourable results. H. D. Rolleston, Michael Foster, and others also participated. The discussions, revised and amplified by the participants, were published as a series of articles in the *Practitioner*, January 1916. There Osler attributes the failure to get results with the serum treatment in the British camps to the fact that inert sera had been used.

supplied in tobacco. The jersey will be very handy as it takes up very little room in my pack. Judging from the temperature to-day, we shall want all the clothes we can possibly wear! It is a dreary wet day and we have just come back from an inspection by the King and the French President. Had it been a fine day, it would have been a very gay scene, with the many different coloured uniforms. We are back at the village resting now, and go back into the trenches in a few days' time. We have a very good time back here. There is a barn rigged up as a library, with all the most recent periodicals and newspapers. We generally have a concert and one or two footer matches each time we come back for a rest. We are out trench-digging most days, but find time for a game at bridge or a quiet read most nights. We had a rather rough time up in the trenches the last time. The Germans shelled our front line with some very heavy shells and 'Minewerfers' [Whiz-Bangs]. We had one or two narrow escapes, but managed to come up smiling as usual. The 'Minewerfers' are huge things, something like an oil drum, filled with high explosive. You can actually see them coming through the air. They make a peculiar droning noise, and one gets flat down in the bottom of the trench and hopes for the best. One burst in the next traverse to us, when we were going along the communication trench, and I quite expected the trench to fall in on top of us. We were hard at work all night repairing the parapet and barbed wire, which were knocked about pretty badly. I am sorry to hear Benning [the chauffeur, who had been invalided home from Cairo] has cracked up. I am afraid a good many will be down with pneumonia this winter! I hear from William [the butler] occasionally and he seems very keen on coming out here. So were we, but I don't think any of us would grouse at the monotony of Writtle or any other village in England! I am glad to say that Mother keeps very well, although she worries rather because I have not been home on leave yet. The leave goes on slowly but surely, so I hope to be home for a few days, if it is not till 1916! I did not find a scarf in the parcel, but a pair of mitts instead. Yours very respectfully, A. TAYLOR.

That Osler had begun to feel uncomfortable about his son's protected position is not apparent from anything he says himself, but confession of this constantly appears in his wife's letters. 'General Jones asked to see Willie the other day and said he had heard Revere was uneasy, and proposed since they were all so fond of him in the C.A.M.C. that he be transferred to a field ambulance, which means the danger zone at the front. I would sacrifice anything to know the boy's conscience was at rest. Poor Willie simply won't or can't talk about it.' On November 4th Osler wrote to J. William White:

Thanks for the Leidy drawing in anticipation. What an artist he was! I had his Rhizopod book in the Lab. only yesterday showing the amoebae pictures to a girl who is working at pyorrhoea. I am glad you are going to Canada. Tell them not to listen to the newspapers & the politicians—but to send along the men & the money. I had a great visit in France—was in your tracks very often. You ' took the cake '. Dear old Makins was delighted. We are very busy. I am on the road three or four days of the week—twice already this week to Cliveden where we have a most interesting set of para-typhoid cases—to-day the rounds of 3 camps seeing inoculated men who have had the triple vaccine at one dose, typhoid para A & para B. A majority of the cases from France & the Dardanelles are paratyphoid & have already been vaccinated against ordinary T. I was at the Asquiths' on Sunday. A. has been wretched & Mrs A. He has a hard team to drive. Mrs. A. asked about you at once. A. was chuckling over the Baltic business as they scarcely expected the submarines would do so well. This Cavell business has been a great aid in the recruiting. [Edith Cavell had been condemned October 11th and executed the following day.] I know her sister very well at Henley. Grace is at it hard. More than 100 workers now in two laboratories. Revere is well, but they have not enough to do. Sometimes worked day & night when big convoys come & then two weeks of idleness. We hope he will get a few days at home before long.

Revere's long-expected few days' leave finally came, one exciting incident of which is recorded in his father's account-book, as follows:

Th. Nov. 11th. Narrow escape of the library. Grace awakened 3.30 a.m. with smell of smoke in the house, went downstairs & found the dining-room on fire; deuce of a time, 25 minutes before the fire brigade arrived. Meanwhile we got many of the more important books into the drawing-room annex. Unfortunately the Incunabula & MSS were in the room above the dining-room which was full of smoke & very hot. Revere & I went in with wet towels over our mouths & got out three or four shelves & then had to stop. Fortunately the firemen got it under control easily, but it was a narrow escape. The MS of Paul Sarpi & the one belonging to Grimani [1] were in the dining-room & got badly scorched.

---

[1] In this volume, a fifteenth-century astrological work, Osler has written: 'This MS. had come back from Maltby with the old binding repaired. I left it with another in the dining-room and both were badly scorched. . . . The old parchment covers were curled and baked.'

It was a close call—this fire, which threatened his collection of books. A little more and the ceiling would have fallen. It must have given them all a great shock, but their reaction to it was characteristic. Lady Osler's next letter to her sister gives an amusingly tragic account of what went on during the half-hour's turmoil before the arrival of the Oxford firemen, who said: 'Good morning, have you a fire?' After a pick-up breakfast that same morning the Regius and his son went off to town as though nothing had happened; and in the library of Mr. Thomas J. Wise, Hampstead, N.W., pursued their favourite recreation, leaving the 'woman with push and go' to begin clearing up the mess—a matter which took many weeks. They lived meanwhile in other parts of the house, and when finally they could return to the dining-room, this, the only room not previously lined with volumes, now had shelves the length of one wall, soon to be filled up with books of reference convenient for 'the flighty purpose'. The episode recalls Osler's reaction to other fires, for example his telegram urging Trudeau to take courage and remember the phoenix. Similarly, when the house at 1 West Franklin Street was threatened he took it philosophically; and when McGill suffered from the fire which nearly ruined the valuable collections in the pathological museum he cabled his congratulations to the governors. He seems to have been pursued by fires. There was to be another at Dundas in which all his home letters were burned.

> How goes it J. W.? [he writes to Dr. White on the 18th]. I hope better. Drop a p.c. occasionally & report progress. Revere home for 5 days. Looking very fit. He is off to a field ambulance near Poperinghe. Burnt out the dining room Friday 3^{30} a m. Deuce of a scare but no books lost. Love to Mrs. W. Yours, W. O.

Revere had gone back on the 13th to rejoin the McGill unit, which was having its troubles, and Osler as usual was playing the rôle of adjuster and intermediary. He writes to Adami on the 24th that he is told the Jesuit College back of Boulogne to which they are assigned is a hopeless hole, but not to worry Jones about it. 'They have been living in a beastly spot as it is, but I have written Birkett to do what he can to make the old place of service. It is not a good thing to get a first class group of men disgruntled and unhappy.' Revere's transfer, meanwhile, was postponed until the hospital should be moved—an event which did not take place till Camiers had become a sea of mud ; and one black and stormy night all the big marquees, with their 'attractive Cawnpore material', more fit for service in India, pulled out their tent-pegs and were levelled to the ground. 'It is rough on Willie', writes Lady Osler, 'to have all these university units who get muddled appeal to the War Office through him and he is dreadfully cut up about the McGill ill luck.' In years to come many another unit, American and Canadian likewise, while meeting the varied and trying fortunes of war, used him—the Consoler-General—as an intermediary to the War Office in forwarding similar protests against their apparent ill luck. On November 25th he writes to H. M. Thomas :

> 'Tis sad to hear of Trudeau's death, but he made a fine & successful fight. It was in *The Times*, but I only glance at the papers these days, so missed it. I heard of it in London on Tuesday & just had time to write a brief obituary note for the Lancet of this week. You will miss him sadly. What a strong man he became & how helpful to others. Few men have done better work & what an example to invalids. We are all well—still very busy. I wish you could see these nerve cases, terrible wrecks from the shell shock & such unusual symptoms. Grace is at work all day. We had the dining-room burnt out last week. Only precious thing lost was that nice Vernon plaque of me which melted to a ball. Revere was at home . . . he is so well. There is not enough to do with the McGill Unit & he feels that he should be at the front. No daylight yet in this horrid mess. Recruiting is wonderful. There will be 3–4 millions of men under arms soon. All will be needed. It is going to be a long business. The loss among our friends is shocking—Schafer, Moore, Rolleston, Garrod, Handford, Herringham & others have all lost boys. There are practically no students here—only 20 at Ch. Ch. Love to all at home. I hope Hal is in good form.

In his obituary tribute to Trudeau he quoted from the letter in which Trudeau had written : 'Are there no other ideals than efficiency and success ? I know you hate sentiment ; but with some of us sentiment stands for a good deal and is a real factor in the problems of life.' And Osler, perhaps on the very day these words were quoted, made a mark for the loss of another son against the names of one of his friends. For thus, opposite the list of 'present members' in his copy of Payne's 'History of the College Club', he checked off the losses as they were sustained—in one case, before the end, three marks for as many sons. His own turn was to come. But the fathers of newly dead boys and boys still alive in those days in England, however much they ached for one another, made no outward sign, exchanged few letters of condolence, but struggled on with their day's work uninterrupted. To learn the most about Osler one must have recourse again to the letters of others :

You ask how he looks [Lady Osler writes to her sister on December 1st]—very well I think, except just lately perhaps, because I know his heart aches about the new danger to Revere, but as I said yesterday, we have not heard yet where he is. Everyone says W. O. looks well, but why he is not worn out I do not know. His correspondence alone is too dreadful. If he would let me I could give up everything and help him a lot—but he won't. The thing that wearies me, and him too but he won't say so, is the continual strain of talking. Every day for weeks there has been an extra person at luncheon—someone wanting something. Today a female doctor from Boston, who came for a letter to a Swiss doctor as she is going to work in Zürich. Yesterday it was a Canadian nurse wanting a job. Tomorrow it will be a parson wanting to go to France, and Friday it will be all the Harvard Unit at luncheon in Christ Church Hall and tea here at 4.30. The demands on him never stop. At Cliveden if he doesn't go every Monday they are dreadfully annoyed and Nancy telephones to know why—and says her children are weeping for him. . . .

And on that particular Friday, December 3rd at 4.30 p.m., she writes to another who would be interested :

I am waiting to receive the Harvard Unit for tea, and enclose programme [1] of the day's proceedings. I fear some may come in ambulances—for they must be dead. I wish you could have seen

---

[1] A printed card : HARVARD UNIVERSITY UNIT. *2nd Contingent. Visit to Oxford. December 3rd, 1915.* This gave an itinerary of the hospitals, laboratories, &c., to be visited between 11.30 a.m. and 5.0 p.m., ending with an 'exhibition of 20 of the works that have chiefly influenced Science and Medicine'. As can be seen, he took a vast deal of trouble to give these volunteer organizations a good start and a pleasant impression. It was a great disappointment to him that the Johns Hopkins people did not send a unit. He writes to the Dean : 'When one has lived a completely comfortable life, to be wet and cold and muddy for weeks at a time, tests a fellow's mettle', and he adds : 'all the same get your boats ready—if we go under you come next.'

the luncheon tables in Ch. Ch.—the Hall and pictures never looked more wonderful. I went to see them at 12.30—64 places—and all the Imperial old silver and gold vases, tankards, etc., on the tables, with chrysanthemums, oak colour, to harmonize with the wood, and two huge fires sputtering and snapping. I am sure they must have loved it. Dr. Cheever and Dr. Bremer came with their O.C., Sir Allan Perry, to lunch Sunday. They only arrived Saturday night and *were* so nice. I hope and pray all goes well in France. It is simply horrible, the weather over there, and I am terrified about the men being cold. I am providing them with sleeping socks to their knees. . . . Socks are the most needed of all things, and *khaki* mufflers. The McGill men are having the *devil's* own time with wind and cold; they are being moved outside Boulogne and I hope will be comfortable. Revere as you know is going nearer the front—to No. 3 F.A. as quartermaster. I hope he may be happier. The war is too muddy and worrying to write about.

Later. The men all came and have had really a wonderful day. I think they thoroughly appreciated it—arrived at 11, left at 6.

It was now Revere's turn to tell how muddy the war really was, for instead of going to No. 3 Canadian Field Ambulance as expected, and perhaps at the very moment when 'two huge fires were sputtering and snapping' in Wolsey's dining-hall at Oxford, he was writing the following letter to his aunt, Mrs. Chapin:

No. 3 Canadian General Hospital, B. E. F.
Dec. 3rd.

Dear Aunt Susie,—Just a line to wish you a happy Christmas and to let you know my prospects of the same. I am still with No. 3 which nearly a month ago ceased to be a hospital and which has since become a turbid mud hole, rank with unrest and discontent. The canvas hospital proved, as everyone expected, a decided failure, and not only was our three months' hard work undone by the winds of a night but the ground from being an arid waste of grassless dust was changed in the course of a week to a sea of mud, which was and still is, black, putrid and unwholesome, to sit, sleep or stand in. So after a good deal of hesitation and a still greater deal of correspondence it was brought to the notice of some red-hatted, brass-buttoned, elegant gentleman that No. 3 Canadian Gen. Hospital was undergoing a process of gradual *enlizement* and would very likely disappear altogether. Orders came to evacuate all patients, which was done immediately, and to prepare to move at a moment's notice. A suitable building was found in Boulogne and it seemed evident that we were to make it our winter quarters. All this is now in the days long ago and the red-hatted authorities must have forgotten us. It would be an act of heroic kindness to remind them again of our existence and to point out that 30 officers, 250 men and 70 nurses have for five weeks sat in cold and draughty tents with the mud oozing through the floors and the rain dripping from the roof, without a thing to do but fight the wind and the rain and stoke the smoking stinking braziers. . . . I wish you could see us here. Some of the officers I think you must know. Bill and Campbell Howard of course, and Dr. Russel and Dr. Little whom you probably remember from Baltimore days. We are all assembled round an old oil-can full of hot coke which pours volumes of dismal smoke through a ventilator in the roof of the tent. There are several comfortable chairs and three card-tables which Muz sent from England. There are also two plain tables covered with blankets, a letter-box, a notice-board and two pails. Over all, in my eyes at any rate, a mist of impenetrable gloom seems to hang. In an adjacent tent are two long board tables with chairs on either side. In this we eat 3 times a day. Behind is a shed, built by the Engineers, with a stove and a sink. It makes a good kitchen and turns out daily at least one first-rate meal. We all sit round the oil-can every day. Sometimes someone goes away for the day, sometimes someone writes a letter and usually two or three couples are playing cards with a pile of sous in front of them. The strange thing is that no one complains. I have explored the country pretty thoroughly and found a good deal of interest. There is little chance of talking French except on walks when one meets peasants on the road ; even then they speak a strange dialect of their own. I think there is a good chance of No. 3 leading this same life for several weeks more. The Boulogne expedition seems very distant and I am very glad to be getting away and trying the excitement of proximity to our old friends the Germans. It is said that they have unheard-of means of dispelling gloom. I hope you all have the same happy Christmas that we used to have at Canton and that you can forget the war for that one day at least. My best love to all whom I know in Canton. Your loving Revere.

PS. Do you not think that you could stow yourself, Susan, Margaret and the uncles on board the Peace Ship which your eminent compatriot is about to launch upon the sea of blood? At any rate give him my love and a split pea for the dove. (May it choke him !)

Loathe the war as they did, evidently neither Revere nor his father were ' peace without victory ' men. On December 10th the Regius writes to H. B. Jacobs :

. . . It is sure to be a long war. Finance may stop it and leave the issue undecided, which would be unfortunate. Either we or the U.S. have to smash Germany. If we go under she will be at your throats within a year. Ships, ships, ships ! what would we do without the navy & it may be the navy that will decide the war. The difficulty is to turn a democracy into a fighting people. It is very slow work. Ld. Derby has apparently done the job without conscription. The recruiting has been wonderful. There will be an army of 4 million within 6 mos. Lack of proper organization is sadly felt. You cannot grow a big general staff in a few months any more than you can build a Krupp's in a year. On the whole the country has done wonderfully and if we could only shut up the politicians & editors & put the war into the hands of a few good men, she would do better still. . . . Revere is well, but there is not enough to do at the McGill unit, so he is going to join a field ambulance & will be near Poperinghe. Poor laddie, he longs to be back at Ch. Ch. with his books. Oxford is empty—we have 20 men at Ch. Ch. instead of 280. The losses have been fearful and so many friends have lost boys. . . . Extraordinary people, such self restraint —no murmur or discontent. Grace is working at high pressure—120 women in a big laboratory. . . . I am picking up a few treasures —nice XIII Cent. MS of Platearius—one of the Practica of Bernard de Gordonio. The Catalogue grows. . . .

In his batch of Christmas letters to America, for good reason sent off early in the month, he gives some details of what happened at the fire; as in the following note to Mrs. Brewster:

. . . It was so good of you & R. B. to send that fat cheque [for the Belgians], which Grace acknowledged. People are wonderfully kind & send all sorts of things—95 barrels of apples! came last week for the Canadian wounded soldiers. Revere had leave for 5 days—looks so fit. He is joining the Field Ambulance as the Hospital work is too monotonous & he feels it rather a soft job. He will be at the front We shall have to take our worries with the others. Poor laddie! he loathes the whole business. We had a horrid scare the other night—fire in the dining-room Grace woke with the smell of smoke 3.30 a.m. We kept it in one room until the engines came. It was a narrow escape. . . . No serious loss, but another hour & the whole house would have gone. I suppose you are glad now to have had the fire at Avalon. When I opened the door & the black smoke puffed into my face the thought came 'nothing that cannot be replaced', but then I rushed upstairs to get the MSS & incunabula. I enclose a photo. of the wreck taken next day. The country is at last awake. Recruits pouring in—munitions abundant—outlook good on the western front, very bad in the east—very good at sea, better in America! So let us be thankful. The English are awful pessimists I suppose it is the climate. . . . Letters are very uncertain just now but this should reach Avalon in time to wish you all a very happy Xmas.

The year ended with one of his familiar broncho-pneumonic attacks, a little more prolonged and serious than usual. He entered in his account-book opposite Dec. 26th—'Cold hanging about for two weeks, began in larynx, then went to head; out on & off. Last few days bronchial & coughed a good deal at night just before going to sleep—no fever.' This barred him from active participation in the Christmas gaieties, for the house as usual was full of young people 'on leave'. Indeed on the 30th he writes that he is 'still housed with influenza'. Nevertheless he can write cheerfully enough, as this to Mrs. Chapin on the 26th indicates:

Dearest Sue, We have had a happy Xmas but have missed Isaac so much. I hope Grace sends on some of his letters which are often very amusing. Grace is wonderful—such energy & industry. She is the life of that big Red + work-room; & she seems to have money galore for everything. You have been an angel to collect so much. Things are going well in the country, which at last recognizes the gravity & greatness of the task. So long as the Navy holds the seas Germany is in a tight place, no matter what she does on land—but an inconclusive peace would be a disaster, & mean a repetition of all these horrors in another ten years. . . . Fire has done much good—as usual, but what an escape for my books! Your loving W.

It was at about this time that the widespread system of espionage, one purpose of which was to blow up with bombs vessels carrying munitions of war to Europe, had been uncovered in the United States. Though the Austrian Ambassador had been recalled, the more clever German Ambassador remained and was engaged on the one hand in the plot to dislocate American industry, and on the other was letting loose *ballons d'essai* of peace, one expression of which was the amazing expedition of the 'Oscar II' with its 'out of the trenches by Christmas' slogan. Peace would be welcome in England, but not 'at any price'. The disconcerting news of the failure at Gallipoli alone, coupled with an attack of broncho-pneumonia following influenza, should have been enough to depress ordinary mortals. Nevertheless Osler can write on the last day of the year, 'The country is going strong. Hit any man on the head for me who says "peace"!'

CHAPTER XXXVI

1916

THE CANADIAN ARMY MEDICAL CORPS AND OTHER THINGS

'W. O. is on the rampage again—Liverpool, Torquay, Paignton', writes his wife early in January. But before making this round of visits he had to attend the Conference of Educational Associations, a significant gathering, for the war had intensified the sense of responsibility in their work among teachers of all grades. That Sir Oliver Lodge should preside over the Conference as a whole served to give a flavour of science to the deliberations, even affecting the component societies, of which there were thirty. Over one of them—the Association of Public School Science Masters—Osler presided. As likely as not, it was his vigorous address at the Bradfield School three years before that led to his having been chosen for this post, but that he was a known champion of preliminary science courses properly given, even at the expense of Greek, was of itself enough. Osler's presidential address,[1] given on January 4th, began with a

[1] This, as published in the *School World* (Feb. 1916), has for its title 'Intensive Work in Science at the Public Schools in Relation to the Medical Curriculum'. Apparently it was delivered under another title, to judge from the following illuminating comment upon it in *Nature* (Jan. 1916, p. 548): 'The pervading sense of national responsibility was perhaps most intense at the meeting of the Public Schools Science Masters, who met, as did also the Mathematical Association, at the London Day Training College. The president, Sir William Osler, gave 'The Fateful Years, Fifteen to Seventeen', as the title of his address, . . . which had much literary charm as well as commonsense merit, and was well received, the general feeling of the members being clearly in accord with their President. It was pointed out, however, that the real obstacle to the plan suggested was the faulty regulations of the university in which Sir William Osler is Regius Professor. The schools tend to send their best boys to Cambridge and London, because Oxford will not allow the medical course to begin at once. . . . The irony of the situation is heightened by the fact that the university has just sent an appeal to the head masters on the lines of Sir W. Osler's request to the science masters. The situation would be humorous at another time; but at the present moment it is of the most obvious importance that every

description [1] of Father Johnson's influence on the development of his boys in the days at Weston; and at the end, in facing the inevitable objections that would be raised against specializing too early in the schools, he said:

Nature is never special, and a knowledge of her laws may form a sound Grecian foundation upon which to build the superstructure of a life as useful to the State, and as satisfying to the inner needs of a man, as if the ground-work were classics and literature. The two, indeed, cannot be separated. What naturalist is uninfluenced by Aristotle, what physician worthy of the name, whether he knows it or not, is without the spirit of Hippocrates? It has been well said that instruction is the least part of education. Upon the life, not the lips, of the master is the character of the boy moulded; and doubtless the great master of masters had this in mind when he said: 'It may be, in short, that the possession of all the sciences, if unaccompanied by knowledge of the best, will more often than not injure the possessor.' (Plato, *Alcibiades*, ii.)

It has been already stated that men of Osler's type rarely become great leaders of a 'cause'. Such men can see both sides too clearly, and theirs is a different rôle. So now, even though a better and more general preliminary education in science will undoubtedly be of benefit to the nation, for reasons other than the more effective conduct of future wars, Osler must leave, with his address under discussion, to go on his 'rampage'.[2]

To J. William White. 4th. On train.

Dear J William Worried not to have had a line saying how you are. Ask Mrs White to write. I do hope the sciatica is better & that

---

encouragement should be given to aspirants to a medical degree, and that every hindrance to rapid and thorough qualification should be removed. The discussion will, it may be expected, cause the rescission of the offending regulation.'

[1] See above, Vol. I, p. 33.

[2] As an aftermath of this meeting, a small committee of the Public School Science Masters' Association was promptly chosen; and 'the unsatisfactory points of science in the schools and the ancient universities' was memorialized in *The Times* over the signature of 'thirty-six distinguished men of Science'—*Osler one of them.* Subsequently a reorganization committee was formed and met on May 3rd at Burlington House, Lord Rayleigh presiding—a meeting at which other than scientists were present. This was followed by another letter to *The Times* of May 4th, signed by representatives chiefly of the humanities—*Osler one of them.* Bryce, Cromer, Curzon, H. A. L. Fisher, Trevelyan, F. G. Kenyon, Gilbert Murray, and

you are convalescing. What an aggravation to be knocked out just at this time when you had so much to do. Was it not splendid that they gave Henry James the O. M.—really the greatest literary distinction in England. Everybody is delighted. Mr Asquith was asking for you the other day. Your Martian mind made a great impression on these politicians. I wish you & Roosevelt were in the Cabinet. I have been laid up with a heavy cold. Revere was home for a few days looking so fit. The house is still a junk shop—190 barrels of apples & $2000 came to Grace from Canada & the U.S. at Xmas! We had the house full of men from the front, chiefly relatives. 18 members of my family are over. I have been gassing today to the Public School masters on rearranging the science work, & am now on way to Liverpool. . . .

And from Paignton a day or two later he sends a card to reassure Mrs. Whitelaw Reid: 'All goes well here. Staff working smoothly & the hospital in very good order.' Almost too smoothly, for he slipped on the tile floor of the operating room, fell, and hurt his hip, so that he came limping home at the end of this particular 'rampage'. One of the various Canadian officers at the 'Open Arms' for the following week-end notes in his journal under Sunday the 9th: 'Dr. Penhallow here from Paignton. Sir William wrote 40 letters and cards this morning. He limped and hopped about when Charlie and Johnnie Max Muller came in for lunch, pretending this was the result of his fall. "Isn't William funny?" says Johnnie. Later at the Wrights' for tea: "Don't bully me, Doccie-O," says baby Muriel,' &c.

To be sure, some of the forty cards and letters were merely cryptic messages such as this: 'A.1. This looks hopeful. The old Scoundrel! But he evidently repented. Strange not to have heard from Norman Moore. W. O.' Perhaps, too, during this narration of more serious things, not enough has been said in regard to Osler's spare moments devoted to children. Their appeal grew stronger as years went on, and he was apt to make a house-to-house visit among them after his tea and at about their bed-time, when

others were among the twenty-three signers. (Cf. 'Science and the Humanities in School and University', *School World*, June 1916, pp. 215–19). It is quite probable that the seed of Osler's presidential address before the Classical Association in 1919 was planted in his mind at this time.

he was invariably the youngest and most hilarious person in a succession of neighbouring nurseries.

'You're a child, Doccie-O', the babies said,
  'For we hold you and lead you in thrall;
And we laugh at the knowledge that 's stored in your head,
  Because you must come when we call.'

'In my childhood', said Doccie-O, 'I was like you,
  Just as naughty, if not even worse:
For children must frolic, and old folks must stew,
  But the man who won't laugh is a curse.'

In the companionship of children one could most easily forget the war. And next to children—in that of books. Books, indeed, were apt to colour affairs even of a serious nature. This the following two letters illustrate. The D.G.M.S., as will be remembered, had been pestered a good deal already, but just now he was being pressed by Osler and some others to establish a special hospital for the study of the many peculiar disorders of the heart exhibited by the soldiers. The request had been made to have these cases segregated in what was an ordinary military hospital at Mount Vernon, Hampstead (now the National Institution of Medical Research). The War Office, however, strongly discouraged any idea of setting apart hospitals for special complaints. It seemed hopeless, but finally Osler, Allbutt, Mackenzie, and Fletcher together bearded Keogh in his den; and this, as Fletcher says, 'did the trick.' He adds that Osler the same night sent him a book inscribed 'with cardiographic greetings', accompanied by this letter:

Oxford 11th Jan.

That was a bit of good work, & I hope all will go well. Do let us insist on A.1. men in charge who will live in the Hospital & have full control of their own cases and assistants. We should be able to get good juniors—and then arrange Team work. I would transfer temporarily my cardio-vascular collection, books & pamphlets, & we can arrange clinical conferences, &c to which the men of the other Hospitals will be invited. I hope you have induced Lewis to join. Opened a quarto parcel this eve.—so disappointed, tho it was a rare item, the translation for a second *Religio Medici* by Sir William Browne (B. of the Medals) of Isaac Hawkins Browne's *Fragmentum.*

'As I walked away from that meeting with Keogh,' writes Sir Walter, 'I found the first edition quarto of Ferriar's

'Bibliomania' in Charing Cross Road, and sent it to him. Osler wrote in reply:

Oxford. Friday a.m.

'Tis a beauty! How could you have had the heart to part with it, & a large paper copy!

> 'And first the Margin's breadth his soul employs,
> Pure, snowy, broad, . . .'

A thousand thanks! It must be very rare. I have never seen it in a catalogue. F. must have sent it to Dibdin in MS. as D's Bibliomania is dated June 1809 & F's April. I have just wired Jones about Meakins, who I hear is in the country. One of the assistants should be picked for X-ray knowledge. Allbutt's name should precede mine—as older, wiser, & better to look at! Do not ask him, as he has a foolish notion that the Oxford Regius has precedence of the Cambridge.

All this must have happened on Osler's return from Shorncliffe, where, according to a letter, he is finding 'much of interest in the paratyphoids dysenteries and hearts'. On the 12th he writes to Dr. E. C. Streeter of Boston:

Where is your Aristotle paper? A friend of mine has just edited for Loeb's classics Galen's De Nat. Facultatibus & he wishes in a brief bibliography to put together recent articles dealing with Greek Science & Medicine. Your A. paper might come in here—as A. really had the *key*. Please get a year off & come to our Science-History room at Bodley. The war has upset us badly as 3 of the 5 workers have gone. I am struggling with my incunabula paper but get very little time for work at it. I conduct a correspondence bureau for Doctors & Nurses wishing jobs as they seem to have a notion that I am in charge of all the Hospitals here & in France! I am working at my library at spare moments—but my man has gone & progress is slow.

Almost any one of Osler's scraps of letters contain hints which intrigue the curiosity of an unintended reader. On January 26th he wrote Mrs. Whitelaw Reid:

Dear Mrs. Reid, I enclose letter from Keogh. You see the Authorities at Washington must ask. Shall I write to Gorgas or Wood? I enclose also a list of Med School Libr. to which it would be nice to send copies of the autobiography [Trudeau's]. If you like I will write a little slip which Lea Bros could have printed & enclosed in each vol. Shall you be at home tomorrow for lunch—if so I could come & have a talk. Send me a line to the Athenaeum Club. Sincerely yours, Wm OSLER.

To do justice even to this scrap one must turn to the attitude of mind of the 'authorities at Washington'. Nowhere has this been better explained than by Mr. John Buchan [1] in his chapter on 'The Straining of American Patience', brought about by Mr. Bryan's 'vapourings' and the incredible 'blundering of German diplomacy'. Mr. Wilson considered it his business merely to interpret the opinion of America at large; he had not the personality to mould that opinion and had decided that the temper and interests of the country were on the side of neutrality. But phrases like 'too proud to fight', and the German reaction to this attitude by a continuance of her submarine activity, were unquestionably changing the temper of the country. Still, it does not appear that this as yet had affected either the President or Mr. Bryan's successor as Secretary of State, who appeared to be equally exasperated with the Allies and the Central Powers. Osler's conference with Mrs. Reid was doubtless what led to his writing on the 30th two letters to be forwarded by Mr. Page, one to General Gorgas, in the course of which he says:

. . . Keogh is favourable but says it must be asked for by the U. S. Govt. She & he (K) are most anxious that *you* should come. K. says that every facility will be given to see everything. Do you think, (1) that it would be useful, & (2) that the plan is feasible? If official the Gvt. would have to pay expenses but Mrs W. R. is anxious to do this. Privately I should say that the opportunity *should not be missed.* I am writing to the President & have asked him to confer with you & Wood.

To Woodrow Wilson from W. O. Jan. 30/16

Dear Mr. President, The Medical Services of the U. S. Army and Navy should not miss the opportunity the war offers of studying certain problems of organization. An American lady has offered to pay the expenses of two or three men from each service & Sir Alfred Keogh, the Director-General, assures me that every facility would be given. Permission would have to be asked, of course by the government. Personally I feel the matter to be of sufficient importance to bring to your notice. If you agree, please talk the matter over with Wood & Gorgas. With greetings & regards, Sincerely yours.

Efforts had been made before this to get the President's authorization for the sending abroad of military observers,

[1] 'A History of the Great War.' Lond., Thomas Nelson & Sons.

but on the grounds that it would be an unneutral act he had refused to give his sanction even for volunteers from the Medical Corps to go in an unofficial capacity. Writing as an old acquaintance, it was perhaps purposeful rather than naïve of Osler to suggest that the matter be talked over with Leonard Wood, whose 'preparedness' campaign with its officers' training camps was meeting with no official favour. However this may be, it was a timely suggestion even though action was not taken for some weeks, for in the interval, on February 10th, Germany had announced that from the 1st of March all armed merchantmen would be treated as belligerents and attacked at sight. The Government at Washington had reached what appeared to be the cross-roads of its neutrality path and must take one or the other turning. While awaiting a reply to these letters Osler was busy with other things. On February 2nd he wrote again to White:

I was very glad to have your long account this week. What a remarkable condition! Just like a Doctor to have something out of the way & puzzling. . . . If you could get over here in the spring it would be an easy matter to get a house in the neighbourhood with a nice garden & we could look after you. It would be such a pleasure. I shall be here, except for a couple of weeks which I hope to spend in the Hospitals on the other side. I asked the other day about Henry James but he was not well enough to see anybody. I am so glad that Henry Jr. is coming over. I will see him & send you his report. It is too bad. They say he has worried terribly about the war. We are doing about the same things—Grace with a big workshop which does all the dressings &c for the group of Hospitals in this district. I am on the road a great deal. . . . Things are going well in the country—nearly 4 millions of men! The Zeppelin raids are a great stimulus & so far the damage is far below the Lusitania level—133 men, 133 women & children and not a single important building touched. Do let us hear how you are—as we are always looking for news. Just a postcard at times.

It was on the night of January 31st that a fleet of Zeppelins had crossed over the English midlands and penetrated as far as Birmingham—by no means the first of these raids, but from the enemy's standpoint perhaps the most successful of all. Terrifying as air-raids may be, their effect was to rouse English people to anger rather than to frighten them.

Naturally there was a demand from many quarters for reprisals, and a column in *The Times* was given over each day to letters on the subject, one of which Osler contributed—a heated note written from the Athenaeum on February 11th, possibly after he had overheard some wild talk of vengeance:

Sir,—The cry for reprisals illustrates the exquisitely hellish state of mind into which war plunges sensible men. Not a pacifist but a 'last ditcher', yet I refuse to believe that as a nation, how bitter soever the provocation, we shall stain our hands in the blood of the innocents. In this matter let us be free from blood-guiltiness, and let not the undying reproach of humanity rest on us as on the Germans. Yours, &c., Wm Osler.

More like him is the following letter to L. L. Mackall on the 7th:

. . . The Library grows in spite of the hard and harassing times. Paré's *Anatomie Universelle* 1561 came in this week—not in England or S. G. L. Why so rare I cannot imagine. Malgaigne could only find two copies in France (1840). I suppose as one of the first anatomies to be printed in French the students used up the copies.[1] Keep an eye open for my Bibliotheca litteraria—books outside of Med. written by Doctors. I am getting a good many & the list is most interesting. I suppose when the war is over about 1920 it might be possible to get the journals in which the few medical articles occur written by Schiller. My secretary has gone & the precious William the butler, & the chauffeur. Revere is with the McGill Unit but he will exchange to the artillery & take his chances with his chums. He has become devoted to books & put up a great bibliographical joke on some of us. I am very busy seeing all sorts of interesting cases—My early printed books paper hangs fire—I get very little time for work. If you wish to see a fine bit of American scholarship take a glance at Curtis' 'Harvey's Views on the Use of the Circulation of the Blood'. A.1.[2] Willie F. was here at Xmas—'fat

[1] This was a book to delight Osler's heart, and he wrote an account of it for the *Annals of Medical History* (1917, vol. i, p. 424), a quarterly publication which was started in the spring of 1917 by Dr. Francis R. Packard of Philadelphia. Osler's note ends with the following statement: 'The fitness of things demands that this copy should return ultimately to France, to the great collection of the Ecole de Médecine.' One may recall his favourite saying that 'every book has its natural habitat'.

[2] He had sent to the *Lancet* (Feb. 19, 1916, pp. 416–17, 'A new Commentary on Harvey') a long unsigned review of this masterpiece of Professor John G. Curtis of Columbia, published posthumously by his successor, Frederick S. Lee. It was a glowing appreciation of one scholar for the work of another, and Osler knew full well from the experience with

& well liking' as the Scripture says. Oxford is deserted—only Rhodes scholars & invalids.

'Only Rhodes scholars and invalids'—in the University; but with the colleges and streets full of soldiers—many of them invalid Tommies in their blue coats and red ties—and with 5,000 Derby recruits gathering in the Parks, the city of Oxford was anything but deserted. Of the American Rhodes scholars, three or four were taking the medical course. One of these, Dr. W. C. Davison, was Secretary of the American Club, an organization which formerly brought together every Saturday night the Americans studying in Oxford. This club in no sense rivalled the 'Open Arms', used pretty much as one by all Americans and Canadians, students and otherwise; for at the 'Open Arms' was a tennis-court and tea every afternoon on the terrace, at which attractive young people were certain to be encountered. Besides, it had the additional advantage of having no dues—in which connexion it may be well to quote from a letter Lady Osler sent to her sister at this time. It says: 'Margarine at 10*d.* tastes as good as butter at 1*s.* 8*d.* and gran. sugar is as good as cut. One does not need dessert or cakes and it's really a pleasure to surprise the servants. One must try to save in view of the future.'

It was not dessert or cakes that drew Rhodes scholars, among others, to 13 Norham Gardens. A sufficient attraction was the Regius Professor of Medicine, who, to return to the American Club after this digression, accepted at this time an invitation to attend the meeting of February 12th. According to the Secretary's report, 'the guest spoke informally and humorously', drawing lessons from his experiences in life which might be useful in their careers. 'Born seventh in a missionary's family in the backwoods of Ontario with twins ahead I did not have an auspicious financial outlook', &c. To such an occasion as this Osler could effectively rise, fully concealing from the young people before him that his sympathetic heart was heavy. A day or two before, he had written to F. J. Shepherd:

So glad to hear from you & to know that you are not worse optically.

---

his Harveian Oration how nearly impossible it was 'to present anything new about William Harvey or even to colour anything old with new tints'.

Very sad about Yates who never should have come over. Camiers was no place for him—cold as Greenland, mud to the knees & wind & rain every other day. I knew it would prove a hole of the worst description. They have all been very plucky about it. I have been so sorry for Birkett. The new place is turning out much better than they expected. Revere is leaving them to take a commission in the British Army. He does not feel it right not to be in the fighting line. They have been so kind to him. He has turned out a most satisfactory boy, devoted to literature and books. He and I have great fights in fun as to which books of my library are to go to McGill. I am getting my catalogue in good order and many good things come in. Archie Malloch is doing well at the General Office, London. He comes here every week end. I see a number of our old graduates at Cliveden (Taplow) every Monday. That movie which you saw was taken here. I hope Elliott Galt keeps well. I am trying to get into touch with him this week as I see Maggs Bros have 40 letters & an MS of his grandfather for sale. Love to Dorothy & Cecil. I hope you will come over in the Summer. I have not heard of or from Sherry for a long time—I suppose his boys are out. My doctor friends here have been hard hit. Rolleston, Norman Moore, Garrod (2), Herringham, Power, Handford (2) have lost boys. 'Tis a horrid business & the end is not in sight.

With eighteen relatives in service the Osler family in Canada and England must have been kept pretty much on edge. One incident Lady Osler mentions in her home letter of February 13th:

A most extraordinary thing happened last week. Wednesday eve a cable came from Toronto from Willie's cousin Ernest Osler saying that his nephew Stewart Thorne was very ill in Hospital at Shorncliffe, and to please see him and report. He decided to go, wired the hospital, and word came back that Thorne was dead, 'but please come and make arrangements'. So off he went. I telegraphed Campbell Gwyn to meet him, which he did and they made all the arrangements. W.O. was spending the night at the Beechborough Hospital. Late in the evening the undertaker called up about the name and it was discovered that the man was another Thorne altogether—a man from Nova Scotia. Willie had arranged the funeral, guns fired, etc. It was an escape. The other man, our Thorne, was on leave in London and perfectly well. We really couldn't help laughing.

Osler's suggestion to J. Y. W. MacAlister for a series of symposia at the Royal Society of Medicine had been carried out. So at one of the January meetings the Soldier's Heart had been under discussion, and on February 15th Trench

Nephritis had its turn, with W. Langdon Brown as the principal speaker on the subject of this previously unrecognized disorder. But these set meetings were only incidental to the many unexpected calls which kept him ' on the road ' and made him liable to exposure. At about that time Lady Osler wrote : ' We are having some coldish weather, which is sad for daffodils and lilac buds, but they should have known better.' ' Coldish weather ' was equally bad for the Regius and perhaps he, too, should have known better. His account-book opposite *Feb. 24th* states :

Got stuck in snowstorm returning from Cheltenham. Could not get up the hill & had to stay the night. Could not motor back the next day—too much snow. Very cold & got chilled. Had bad cold Friday. Began in larynx then went to head, felt badly, much stuffed up, little or no fever.

This by now has a familiar sound, but he had difficulty in shaking off this particular attack, and it kept him a week in bed, which let him put his mind on other things. On the 26th he wrote a characteristic letter to F. H. Garrison, whose ' History of Medicine ' he had evidently been reading from cover to cover :

I am in such a muddle over my letters that I forget whether I wrote about your bibliography address—copy please—two, in fact ! 'Tis A.1. I have written McCulloch, rather in favour of bibliographies & special monographs. Klebs writes about his incunabula work—I hope he will include a list, at any rate, of those in Phila, N.Y. & Boston. I wish I could get my list to 1480 finished. I get no time for work—incessant calls of one sort or another. . . . I enclose you a list of Corrigenda—not very long. The book seems to have taken over here. I see it very often and recommend it everywhere.

Eighteen months over—now for another period, of the same length or longer ! The Zeppelin raids have done great good—only the pity of women & children butchered ! No single important structure damaged ! I wonder does Klebs really know what damned barbarians they are. I am answering his letter—and then no more ! Greetings to all old friends. Yours, Wm Osler.

P.S.1. It is wonderful that the errors should be so few when one sees the extraordinary number of dates & names.

P.S.2. You will see by the list that I have read the book. It has been most helpful, too, in my ambitious schemes of cataloguing my library on a plan of my own, at which you will be very much amused.

P.S.3. We are having a great Shakespeare exhibit at Bodleian. Wonderful treasures, I did not know we had so many.

P.S.4. Excuse these scraps but I am writing in bed with a cold. I was stalled the other night in a snowstorm in the Cotswolds.

P.S.5. What a great contribution is that of Curtis. I wrote an editorial in the Lancet.

And there follows a long list of Corrigenda such as: 'p. 204. Petty—for "who took the first census of Ireland" read "who made the first great survey of Ireland". See his relations with Graunt. There is a recent paper, I forget when, dealing with the point. He was the father of pol[itical] economy in England.'

To Dr. J. Collins Warren from W. O. [March] 3rd.

Dear C. W.—Macartney's things went to Cambridge. Here is MacAlister's letter—write him—which gives the information you wish. 'Tis an interesting story. No doubt the life M. speaks of is in the Library. By the way, MacAlister has written a fine life of Macartney, who must have been a rare old bird. Have you read John Curtis' book on Harvey? best bit of historical work on Medicine done in America for years & good reading. 'Tis a direct outcome of John C. Dutton's influence on Curtis. D. was a trump—just as good as his M.G.H. brother. I suppose this Curtis came of the old N. E. [New England] stock. Tell George & Fred Shattuck to read it. I believe John & Edward C. were Harvard men—& if so about your time. All goes well here & in the long run we shall come out on top. Revere is leaving the McGill Unit. . . . He will join the Imperial service, probably the Royal Field Artillery. . . . Excuse this writing but I am abed with the grippe. Love to little Johnnie, in which Grace joins. Yours ever, Wm Osler. Send the Memoir—am shocked not to have it. I 'lay out' every Boston man with that Vol. in which are bound the papers of 5 generations of the Warrens. 'Tis really a unique item in my library.

On this same day Lady Osler wrote: 'We have had a terrific (for here) snowstorm. Willie got caught on a hill outside Cheltenham in a hired car; had to go back and sleep in a damp hotel where he got a miserable cold, and has been seedy ever since. As usual he is in bed and working all the time. . . . The fighting in France now is horrible and the hospitals are filling up. I suppose our turn will come.' Yes, while these comparatively trifling things were going on in Oxford, the fighting in France *was* horrible. The appalling and titanic struggle for Verdun was under way—the longest continued battle in history—and the accompanying diversions along the British front, which in other times might have seemed major operations, were obscured thereby. The centre of the scene had shifted from Ypres to Verdun—always the two nodal points of the western front. 'On ne passe pas.'

The papers for Revere's transfer from the Canadian to the British army finally went through after the interminable delays which departmental red-tape rendered inevitable. He had behaved exceedingly well in his quartermaster's job and the Canadians were loth to have him go, but there was no longer any doubt in the minds of his parents. 'A wonderful letter he wrote to Bob [his book-loving friend] about patriotism just settled me when I read it', wrote his mother. 'He has just come from town [March 7th] where he went to the War Office and put in his artillery application, then he and Bob had a day in old book shops. All this interest in literature must now be set aside and perhaps *never* taken up, but I'm proud of what he 's doing.'

So just now for a few days, while his application with other untold thousands was filtering through the meshes of the War Office, Revere had a few days at home, and his parents' letters naturally make much of it. 'He has got his line in life—perfectly devoted to literature & to books—a great comfort to me,[1] as considering his parents, it might have been to dice or horse-racing! We have a great time together', wrote W. O. to his old friend Wm. Gardner of Montreal. But it was over all too soon, and on March 13th from his mother: 'Revere left on Saturday to report at Folkestone and await his orders. He and his Dad were glued to old books all the time he was here, and reading to each other every evening; Bob joining in, sitting on the arm of Revere's chair with his arm around him. But Revere now seems years the older.' Father and son did 'have a great time together'—Osler always spirited and full of fun when young

[1] Revere must have been browsing over the Aubrey manuscripts in the Ashmole collection, for under the date iii/29/16 on the back fly-leaf of Osler's copy of the 'De Motu Cordis' (1628), in Revere's fine script is a note which must have greatly pleased his father, viz. an extract from Izaak Walton's account of Walter Warner who claimed to have 'discover'd to Dr. Harvie' the circulation of the blood.

people were about ; fond of relating amusing reminiscences of his boyhood, as when Canon Osler and a clerical visitor were each mischievously told how deaf the other was and how they roared at each other all the evening.

Six weeks had elapsed since his letters went to President Wilson and General Gorgas. Finally on March 15th he was able to write to Mrs. Whitelaw Reid :

> I had a letter from President Wilson to the effect that the matter was under consideration & this morning Page writes that the appointments are to be made. Have you had any word from Gorgas? He has not replied to my letter in which I made mention of your generous offer. I suppose if they come over officially the Govt. will pay all expenses. I dare say by this time you have heard from Gorgas.

And soon General Gorgas wrote, saying that ever since Osler's letter of January 30th had come, he had been working hard over the proposal. Glad as he would have been to go himself, this was frowned upon, but the names of three candidates from the Medical Corps had been sent to the State Department for action. 'It will be a great gain to us', he added, 'to get these three men detailed and to give our officers an opportunity to see something of actual conditions in Europe. The matter could not have been arranged except for your personal appeal to the President.'[1] And Osler promptly wrote to Mrs. Reid: 'It looks as if your kind suggestion would bear good fruit. I will take the men myself to the War Office & see that they are put in the right hands in France.' Gorgas himself could not be spared, for America was still 'waging peace' as Mr. Roosevelt expressed it, in Mexico; and two months more elapsed before the officers of the detail finally reached England.

To the Osler household there had been added a grand-niece, Miss Joan Mackenzie, who not only made herself a great favourite but became a voluntary secretary, bossing W. O. about his untidy desk and helping him with 'the correspondence bureau'. This, however, continued to be largely in longhand. 'We keep busy', he writes. 'I am on the road a great deal—in London 2–3 days a week. Grace

[1] The medical officers of this detail were Colonel A. E. Bradley, Major C. S. Ford, and Major W. J. Lyster of the army; Captain F. L. Pleadwell was also sent over as a representative of the navy.

has a big shop & is a sort of universal provider. The Zeppelins do much good in stirring up the people & bringing home the realities of war. 'Tis sad to have the poor women & children butchered. A bad business & old humanity should be ashamed of itself. I 'spect Crile[1] is right.' They had been much distressed by the torpedoing of the *Sussex*, on which were several of their friends, one of the Rhodes scholars, as well as Professor Baldwin and his family, who had been visiting them only the day before.

Our next excitement [Lady Osler wrote to her sister] has been the Zep. Friday night I had just gone to bed; Revere was at home, and talking with his father on his bed when the signal went—a hooter at the station. Of course I meant to go out, and much to Revere's disgust Joan said so too. We walked as far as Balliol when we were challenged and told to go home and to the cellar. The streets were absolutely silent except for soldiers at the corners and about the big buildings; fire engine at the Bodleian, etc. Not a vestige of light anywhere, except sometimes a wee glimmer at the edge of a cellar window. We finally returned to bed, and at three o'clock the electric light was turned on. I believe the warning is given when the Zeppelin is within fifty miles. Last night the same thing happened, but I stayed calmly in bed and mean to do so in the future. It is wearisome to be up every night. W. O. of course remains peacefully in bed and reads.

Off and on during all these months he had been working on his Text-book—the 9th edition had indeed been due in 1915—and, with the help of Thomas McCrae in Philadelphia, a revision (still called the 8th edition) sufficient to satisfy the publisher was issued in 1916.

Incidentally [he wrote to J. J. Walsh] I am trying to pick up a little education. I am working at the earliest printed medical books, & am reading some of your old friends. I have just finished Vincent of Beauvais' sections on Med. The [volumes of the] R. Printer's edition in the 70ties are the biggest incunabula known. Things are going well here—'tis a hard business to stir a democracy. The Irish problem is difficult. The settlement is really in N. Y. Until Hibernia Magna recognizes the folly of Irish independence there must be trouble.

Ireland, indeed, was playing traitor and the Sinn Fein movement gaining momentum. And it was scarcely a

[1] G. W. Crile: 'A Mechanistic View of War and Peace.' N.Y., The MacMillan Co., 1916.

month later that Sir Roger Casement was captured, when his transport, a disguised German auxiliary cruiser, was sunk in the act of landing arms—the signal for the outbreak of the Irish rebellion of Easter week and the summary execution of its leaders. It is a far cry from Roger Casement to St. John the 'golden-mouthed', but Osler's brief letters touch on many and diverse things. On March 31st he wrote to President Lowell of Harvard:

Pass this on to your Librarian—a Greek MS circa 1200 of St. Chrysostom has been sent from Naples to the Bodleian. We have several tho not identical. It has been looked over by Brightman, the leading expert in liturgical MSS, whose report I enclose. The rascal asked at first £500; but I have got him down to £100. It would have to be bound, which could be done better here than in America. Greek MSS of this date are rare. Some friend of the Library or of the Theological School might like to purchase it. A suitable binding would cost about $25. Do not bother about it yourself but pass this letter on to the library. I hear from Sir John Rose Bradford that the Harvard Unit is doing A.1. work.

Two new interests came at this time to engage his attention. In a letter to W. S. Thayer of April 1st he says:

The French are doing splendidly & this country is in fine form—if we could only choke some of the politicians & editors. We have started a big Army Heart-Hospital [Hampstead]. Allbutt, Mackenzie & I have had the selection of the staff & have been put in control as active consultants. We visit once a week each, & determine the policy &c. There are to be 4 services. Lewis has one, Parkinson & Meakins (of Montreal) the others, & we hope to be able to get Fraser for the 4th. Such interesting cases—chiefly neurotic, but many mitral & a few aortic. Typhoid has slumped—very few dysenteries. Nephritis persists & is most interesting. . . .

On the same day that this was written came a letter from 10 Downing Street, stating:

I have pleasure in proposing, with the King's approval, that you should be a member of the Royal Commission which he has been pleased to appoint to inquire into University Education in Wales. The terms of reference are as follows: 'To inquire into the organization and work of the University of Wales and its three constituent Colleges, and into the relations of the University to these Colleges and to other institutions in Wales providing education of a post-secondary nature, and to consider in what respects the present organization of University Education in Wales can be improved and what changes, if any, are desirable in the constitution, functions, and powers of the University and its three Colleges.'

Among those who were invited to serve were Lord Haldane, Sir Henry Jones, the Hon. W. N. Bruce, Miss Emily Penrose, and a few others representing various fields of education. Into this new job Osler threw himself with eagerness, and a shower of letters, mostly undated, soon poured in upon Mr. [now Sir] John Lynn-Thomas, the surgeon, of Cardiff:

Monday

Dear Thomas, Get your mind on the question of a national post-graduate scheme in connection with the school. The Commission will visit Wales in June (end of) & I should like to hold meetings of the profession at Bangor, Aberystwyth & Cardiff. Please help in this when the time comes. We could bring the Tuberculosis men &c.

Sunday

You are moving along! The report of the Hospital meeting shows a good spirit—I was glad to see the suggestion of an Election Committee. How can we get into touch with the Profession whose confidence should be sought? Is there not a Principality Branch of the B. M. A.? It will be a great matter to have everything cut & dried for the Commission. The Hospital must be made to feel that *it* is the Medical School for the last three years. Yours sincerely.

So from now on, every two months or so, a few days must be passed with this commission which, as Sir Henry Jones testifies, 'gladly leaned on his experience and strong common sense not only in all matters that concerned medical education, but was largely influenced by his liberal views on education in general. Moreover, the gentle playfulness at the back of his mind made him as ideal a committee-man as a companion, and because of his sympathetic understanding of the Welsh people their debt to him is deep.' That it was far from an uncongenial task would appear from the following letter of April 12th to his nephew, W. W. Francis, who was still with the McGill Unit, which Archibald Malloch had also joined:

Dearest Billie, How goes the work? I hear you are the *staff* of the unit. Meakins was talking of you yesterday. He is very happy at Mt. Vernon [the Heart Hospital] & getting into very good work. He & Cotton will get a great deal out of their experience as there is much to be done & we have such a nice set of fellows. . . . All well here. Revere is expecting notice any day to go to Newcastle for training. I wish he was going to Exeter. It has been a slow job. Joan & her Douglas [who had been convalescing at 13 Norham Gardens] are beaming. He is all right again. I am on the Welsh University Royal Commission—for my sins—& will have a job in settling the new medical school at Cardiff. It is interesting work, & with such nice men. When are you coming? 'Tis time surely for leave. Yours affec. W. O. Look after Archie Malloch—good lad & keen on literature.

Though wages had risen and taxes were heavy, the early months of 1916 was a period of renewed confidence throughout England. The resolution to pursue the war to the end had been stiffened by the Zeppelin raids and by the stories which had filtered through of the treatment of prisoners at Wittenberg and other internment camps in Germany. Moreover, Washington, after the sinking of the *Sussex*, had at last shown impatience and actively threatened a severance of relations. Meanwhile, to help the French in their desperate defence of Verdun the British had taken over the western front from Ypres to the Somme with their largely improvised army, now of five million men, most of them as yet untrained in actual warfare. But of these military operations on varied fronts Osler apparently read little and said less, though a number of his relatives were actively engaged. 'We are kept anxious now most of the time', his wife wrote on April 12th, 'with all the Oslers and Gwyns at the front; seven in the midst of it, and the Canadians are holding a bad salient.' They were indeed, for from February to June, in the desperate and largely unrecorded fighting for a better foothold in the line drawn about Ypres, the Canadians had been heavily engaged. And on Sunday the 16th she wrote again saying: 'Willie is holding out so well though the house goes on in the same mad way. When I open the front door there is always someone waiting for a job or for a letter of introduction to the War Office.' The following gives a glimpse of the household on this particular Sunday:

We now have Mr. Penfield the Rhodes scholar who was on the *Sussex*, with a fractured leg in plaster, established in the blue room, and he will stay as long as he wants. Bob is here too, in a tremendous state of excitement as he has a job to drive an ambulance at the front. Also Archie Malloch. Just as we finished luncheon a motor arrived with Ralph Osler (Frank's son) and another officer; then Dinah Meredith and her friend Wanda Gzowski, drenched through. An early hot tea was scrambled for them, when in the midst arrived some people from Florence (Italy) whom W. O. had asked and forgotten; and a gentleman from Cardiff, and several hospital nurses. They all seemed quite happy, but life is queer. . . . All officers on leave now have suddenly been called back and one trembles to think there may be a horrible repetition of last year's fighting.

Among those 'suddenly called back' was Ralph Osler, who was never to see England again. And with all this going on, Dr. Malloch's journal relates that 'W. O. gave his usual morning clinic at the Infirmary and in the evening read aloud parts of Fuller's sermons.' It was the same sort of steadying spirit which led to the holding at this time (on April 24th, the Monday after Easter, and the day the Germans attempted to unload arms in Ireland) of the Shakespeare Tercentenary Exhibition at Bodley in which Osler's hand can be seen. The Turbutt folio, of course; the 'Venus and Adonis' of 1593; the poet's reputed copy of 'Ovid'; and many other similar treasures, of which the Press had issued an elaborate illustrated catalogue, were naturally all placed on view. And it is interesting to contrast a cabinet 'crisis' in London holding sessions behind closed doors, with a meeting at Oxford the same afternoon in the Divinity School, where the speeches were on a subject far removed from politics. Osler had prepared an address for the occasion—'Creators, Transmuters and Transmitters, as illustrated by Shakespeare, Bacon and Burton'. It was in his happiest vein and, were other more important things not happening, might well deserve reprinting here in full. A paragraph for the Baconians must suffice: [1]

History repeats itself. Greek philosophy, lost in the wandering mazes of restless speculation, was saved by a steady methodical research into nature by Hippocrates and by Aristotle. While Bacon was philosophizing like a Lord Chancellor, two English physicians

[1] Lond., Oxford Univ. Press, 1916. Privately printed. It is proper to add that Osler said man owed his world-dominion to the transmuters; and the following shows what they meant to his library—'Only by the labours of transmuters has progress been made possible and their works will fill the shelves of the concentrated *Bibliotheca Prima* of the future.'

had gone back to the Greeks. 'Searching out nature by way of experiment' ('tis Harvey's phrase), William Gilbert laid the foundation of modern physical science, and William Harvey made the greatest advance in physiology since Aristotle. Recking not his own rede, Bacon failed to see that these works of his contemporaries were destined to fulfil the very object of his philosophy—the one to give man dominion over the macrocosm, the world at large; the other to give him control of the microcosm, his own body. A more striking instance of mind blindness is not to be found in the history of science. Darkly wise and rudely great, Bacon is a difficult being to understand. Except the 'Essays', his books make hard reading. In the 'Historia Naturalis', a work of the compiler class, one would think that a consideration of Life and Death would so far fire the imagination as to save an author from the sin of dulness. Try to read it. A more nicely tasteless, more correctly dull treatise was never written on so fruitful a theme. There is good sense about medicine and nature, but with the exception of the contrast between youth and old age, which has a fine epigrammatic quality, the work is as dry as shoe-leather, and the dryness is all his own, as other authors are rarely quoted. Only a mollusc without a trace of red marrow or red blood could have penned a book without a page to stir the feelings and not a sentence with a burr to stick in the memory. Bacon students should study the lengthy consideration given in it to the spirits, and then turn to Schmidt's 'Lexicon' to see how very different in this respect are the motions of Shakespeare's spirit. The truth is, Bacon had in a singular degree what an old Carthusian (Peter Garnefelt) called 'the gift of infrigidation'.

More might well be given, but the following note from the journal of a week-end sojourner perhaps tells enough—even to 'Up Jenkins' with the young people—a game of concealment Bacon is supposed to have played:

> We saw the Shakespeare exhibition at Bodley. Sir Sidney Lee, Sir Walter and Lady Raleigh, Professor and Mrs. Firth, Mrs. Max Muller, Mr. FitzRoy Fenwick (present owner of the famous Phillipps Library near Cheltenham) came to lunch. Addresses at the Divinity School by Mr. Madan, Sir Walter Raleigh, Sir Sidney Lee and Sir William. Splendid. We sat on the platform. Dinner at the Wrights', and Sir William played 'Up Jenkins' with us.

Besides the creators, transmuters, and transmitters, there is another class he did not mention—the inspirers or animators—a group to fill almost as few benches as the creators and to which Osler himself belonged. It is more difficult to trace those who stimulate others to create, transmute, and transmit, though they are always much more loved by their contemporaries than those of the other groups. 'The Bodleian is a huge mausoleum', Osler said. He was speaking of books, 'not one in ten thousand of which survives its author.' It is also a mausoleum of personalities, but many a day will pass before the inspiration of his daily visits will be forgotten by Bodley's staff of workers.

There followed much correspondence on familiar topics—the disposal of a copy of Raynalde's 'Birth of Mankynd', 1545, which he had managed to resist, but which must find its proper place; letters to persons regarding the future programme of the Welsh University Commission, the gist of them being: 'We must get the profession of the principality at the back of the movement', and this he set out to do. As for the war, he said as usual: 'All goes well—if we could only have the country run by the soldiers & not by the politicians. We are really waiting for either a Lincoln or a Cromwell.'

To Surgeon-General Gorgas from W. O. 4th [May 1916]

Dear Gorgas, Page sent on Lansing's cable. I am so glad you have arranged it. I remember Bradley well. I have asked to be notified at once of their arrival & I will take them to Keogh, who will make all arrangements. They should arrive just in time, as things should begin to get lively by the early summer. Very little disease among the men in France. Typhoid has practically disappeared. Much shell-shock & odd nervous conditions. Yours sincerely, Wm OSLER.

It was the first trickle, the coming of these four medical officers, though the significance of the detail could not have been realized at the time. Osler left no stone unturned to give them a welcome and show them attention. They were met on their arrival with a card saying: 'So glad to know you are over. Could you come next Thursday for the week-end—4.45 train from Paddington?' And other numberless and undated notes follow, such as these to Surgeon Pleadwell, the first to reach England:

Tuesday.

I enclose cards for the R S M Lib, 1 Wimpole St & the R C Surgeons Lincolns Inn Fields—both good. Get interested in the

Museum at the R C Surg. wonderful You can give yourself a clinic of the first class with the specimens & the cards. Ask to see Prof Keith who is a genial Scot.

26th

Any spare mornings, Lewis & his colleagues at the Mount Vernon Military Hospital, Hampstead, would be delighted to show you any of the heart work which is in progress. I am writing to Major Meakins of Montreal who is in charge of one of the departments. Ask for him.

5th

Keith will give a demonstration to the Harvard Unit at R. C. S. at 11 tomorrow—I hope you will be able to go.

19th

So glad—see Birkett at the McGill Hospital & Sir John Rose Bradford, Etaples to whom I have written. Let me know if I can be of help.

[undated]

How I should like to !—but I am tied & bound with the Welsh Royal Commission & have several other claims about me—head & heart & legs ! W. O.

In the midst of all this, shortly after their arrival, he and Sir Alfred Keogh gave 'the Mission' a dinner at the Athenaeum attended by the American Ambassador and many officers high in the councils of the R.A.M.C.—an event which fell on Empire Day and escaped notice in the press. Though why should the advent of four American medical officers in mufti make any difference to the war? America was good at an exchange of 'Notes', as though the war was a debating society. She could supply munitions and food ; but not much else.[1]

On May 12th he wrote to H. M. Hurd : 'It 's a horrid business but no one here wants peace unless at our terms. We must go through with it now if it takes another five years. We cannot do it over again. Things look more hopeful but a democracy is a blundering cyclops at war.' And he added : 'The strain is terrible on the young fellows.

[1] The R.A.M.C. as well as the Navy at this time was greatly in need of medical officers. There is a long letter on the subject in the *Lancet* for May 6th signed by Allbutt and Osler. Osler meanwhile had been in correspondence with some of his American medical friends regarding the sending over of a large number of unattached young men, recent hospital graduates, who could get unusual opportunities for work in the understaffed London hospitals. They began to appear in December.

One of my nephews was here to-day—he and another were the only officers of his regiment unwounded at St. Eloi a few weeks ago. Revere has joined the Royal Field Artillery and is getting his training.' He was 'desolated'—it is his usual expression—on losing at this time two of his little playmates—the 'Doccie-O' children, one of whom, little Muriel, he particularly adored and whose miniature he always carried. They had been spending the winter with their grandmother and must now return to their parents in the States. It is a relief, therefore, to have this account of a restful day given in Lady Osler's home letter of May 26th :

Stow-on-the-Wold on the Broadway Road.

Dear Sister,—W. O. had a consultation about eight miles beyond here and insisted on my coming as he had hired a motor. He dropped me off here and I took a walk and have been sound asleep in a field under a white May-bush, with daisies, buttercups, clover, forget-me-nots and many others under my feet. Such a fine view across the Cotswolds with Kingham and Chipping Norton in the distance. I have loved it, and we are now to have tea in a nice old inn. I only wish you were here. The day is too superb. I believe my condition of mind is peculiar; I almost resent the glory of the country and the blue sky when I think of the horrors across the Channel and the misery in the hearts everywhere. I believe it is easier to bear when the clouds are gray and the rain coming down, although that is selfish for it is dull for the wounded to be shut up in the hospitals. Campbell Gwyn came on Sunday. He looked years older and seems so weary. The Canadians are in that perilous Ypres salient, and all the officers say it would have been better to have given it up last autumn and have straightened the line. Since last April (1915) when the Canadians saved Calais they have been kept there and the last few months the Guards have been there too. With his good-bye he said: 'Aunt Grace, for Heaven's sake keep Revere back if you can, as long as possible.' . . . All the men who come back are perfectly optimistic and say of course it is all right—go on sending 'men and guns; men and guns'. Campbell says huge guns are coming all the time, and not yet used; preparing for the future. Isn't it ghastly to speak of the 'future'? W. O. is simply wonderful; he reads more in the papers I think than he used, at least he pretends to, but rarely talks of the war. He has so many interests: spends all day Monday at Cliveden, and the officers tell me they live for this Monday visit. . . . Don't let people say England is not doing anything. The other afternoon I went out for an hour. The first house was the Burrows'—the son a prisoner since October 1914, the nephew who lives with them wounded; then over to the Acland Home to see a country friend—one son killed, one with leg stiff and two inches short from wound; afterwards to the Wrights' where there are three sons serving, and Mrs. Blake there with two. Then to the Sherringtons' to condole with her as her only child of eighteen has just gone to France; then to see Mrs. MacDonell—only son killed, and found Mrs. Symonds with her whose only child had left Salisbury without being able to come home. After that I tottered home and wondered what fate was in store for the Oslers.

It is fortunate that Osler had his library to turn to as a refuge. On May 27th he wrote to Charles Sayle:

Splendid—I am so glad. Sorry to have forgotten about the paper—I send two more—the other a 'chatter' at our Shakespeare meeting. Revere is in the R. F. A. at Fenham Barracks, Newcastle, getting licked into shape. We had him with us while he was getting a transfer. You will be delighted with his keenness in English literature. The year in France with books in place of 'bridge' has done him so much good. The Library thrives—the revision of catalogue is nearly complete. My secretary was called up more than a year ago & there has been much delay. The B. prima grows—in mind & in shelves. By the way, is there a full bibliographical description of your Averroes? Lady Osler has been very busy—the hotel full but always a vacant bed for you.

And again on the 29th to Robert Gunther about the 'Richardson Correspondence', which Oxford would have lost but for his intervention:

On Friday there is a remarkable collection of letters, &c, relating to the old Oxford botanists (Sherard amongst others) to be sold at Sotheby's. I hope to induce the Radcliffe trustees to allow us to spend £100. The Bodleian will give us £50 & I am trying to get an extra £50, that we may send a limit bid of £200. Do you think you could persuade Magdalen to help?

These things were much more to Osler's taste than the talk of war which was scarcely to be avoided with one or more youngsters just out of the trenches almost constantly in the house. 'With all the Bath, Osler, and Francis connection', wrote Lady Osler, 'there are fifty men serving.' This in one Canadian family alone! No wonder in England women by now were doing men's jobs—acting as conductors on the buses and workers in the fields. Naturally the feelings in the Norham Gardens household were more or less coloured at that time by what was happening to the

Canadians. 'House full as usual; I never thought war could increase the demands on the "Open Arms" as it has', Lady Osler wrote on June 11th. 'Such a nice Sunday with Dr. Hugh Cabot and George Shattuck en route for France.' And she adds: 'Our hospital is full of wounded Canadians, and just now so many Canadian friends in the casualty lists we felt the whole business was up; but on the other hand Joffre is in London and Kitchener has started for Russia so one tries to take fresh cheer.' But on the 19th she wrote: 'These have been strenuous days and the beginning of Osler sorrows. Ralph Osler, Frank's only child, was wounded Tuesday night at Ypres, taken to the clearing station, operated upon—an abdominal wound—and died Thursday. Of course this is the beginning, and we shall all have our turn.' Some time before this, in regard to the first visit of the Welsh Commission, Osler had written to Lynn-Thomas:

> I shall be in Cardiff June 21 & 22 and I think it would be important to hold a gathering of the medical profession, at which we could have a full & free discussion on the Medical School problems. Who is the chairman of the Cardiff Medical Society? I am going to Aberystwyth & Bangor the following week. To whom should I write in those places to organize meetings? Would it not do you good to come up there and play the missionary? The first thing is to get the entire profession of the principality interested in the medical school. . . .

And so for the larger part of a week he was campaigning in Wales, arousing the profession with the slogan of 'Pick your men—men are the important thing. The day is long past when big buildings mean a big university or a big college—pick them for two things, for their enthusiasm and for their work as researchers.' To develop a university spirit, in short, some inspirers and creators were needed rather than transmitters. But there is little trace of all this except that he influenced a wealthy native to endow a Chair of Hygiene and Preventive Medicine; nor does a reminiscent letter such as the following from Treborth, Bangor, help greatly:

> After his visit to Penhesgyn he used to send sweets to the children —or money to buy sweets. I used to write to thank him and tell him about them. He always stipulated that the naughty ones should get as many as the good. I told him once of a tiny little two-year-old we had who could curse and swear like a trooper and said she was quickly

being cured by a double dose of his sweets. He replied: 'Glad to hear such good accounts of the children—a little coprolalia stimulates the nurses & the parson. That one must be a gem.'

Early in July he spent a few days at Revere's training camp, and on Sunday the 9th, from Durham, he wrote to Mrs. Chapin:

I am having a very happy week-end with Revere who loves this place. We had a splendid afternoon in the libraries & to-day will see the Dean & a great collection of a friend of mine who lives near. R. is so well & getting into the work. It is not very much to his liking but he has made up his mind to go through with the horrid business & take his chances. The war has been a terrible mental shock to many sensitive young fellows. It is bad enough for hardened old sinners like myself. When are you coming over? it is high time.

And a few days later from Newcastle-on-Tyne to Mrs. Brewster:

I am here to see Revere who is in the Royal Artillery Barracks getting his training. . . . We had a glorious day at Durham which he knows well and we had great fun browsing in the Cathedral Library. He goes to Shoeburyness in a few weeks for gunnery, and then may be drafted at any time for France. I hope it may not be for several months. You can imagine how anxious we shall be. My brother Frank lost his only son two weeks ago—such a fine fellow. Six other nephews are in the thick of it at present. The losses are heart-breaking, but we must go on to the bitter end. The outlook is more hopeful, but it will be a long business. Grace keeps well & is working as hard as ever. We have wounded in our Garden every afternoon, many of them Canadians, & her workshop is booming, 80–100 people every day. These New England women are drivers, when once started. I am away a great deal, always three days a week & lately I have had extra work with the Royal Commission on the Welsh universities. We have just returned from a two weeks inspection of the colleges. . . . A most interesting people—a nation apart in thought & in tongue. I was surprised to find Welsh such a living language. I am sending you Hilaire Belloc's new book on Lafayette. Love to Uncle Ned. What splendid work he does for the country & for the Allies by his strong articles.

In a narrative of a man's life, if he is like Osler, who above all things loved his home, it is necessary to give some picture of it; and this the following 'bread-and-butter' letter from a sojourner supplies. It was forwarded with a note from Osler to his sister, which says: 'I enclose a gushing letter written to Grace—so true that I have filched it & send it on to you. Saw Revere on Sunday—very good form & getting into the work. He 's a darling. I am very well & very busy & keeping a grip on myself amid all these worries. Things look bright.' The 'filched' letter reads as follows :

I cannot tell you how much I enjoyed my week-end with you. I have inherited from some miserable Anglo-Saxon ancestor the unfortunate quality of being too shy to express my appreciation, face to face. But from this distance I can tell you frankly what I feel, and that is, that you are simply wonderful. You keep open house ; you are always 'en evidence' as it were. You are always the same, welcoming them in and speeding the parting guest, whether they are maids, matrons or children. You do the right thing always. You must be tired, bored, at times sick to death of it, but you never appear to be. You spend your life looking after other people, looking after the sick and the afflicted, helping the lame dogs over the stile. Your whole life is lived for others and the fact that you get a certain amount of unselfish pleasure out of being able to do it doesn't alter in the least the fact that you are 'wonderful'. I tell you candidly, there is no woman that I have as great an admiration for as I have for you. My mother, Aunt Jennette and you are the three that make my ideal. And none of you ask for praise or applause, or expect it. You probably think I am ridiculous to write like this, but I mean it, and I think we all make a mistake sometimes in not expressing appreciation. I love the artistic side of your house—the garden, the roses, the ease, the comfort, the blue carpet on the stairs, though it may be worn ; the birds in the morning, the comfortable bed, the towels worked in blue ! the writing-table with everything on it, the books. All is perfect, but behind it all I appreciate you, and the organizing power. Other people, many of them, appreciate this but they don't know why. I do—it is YOU. I take off my hat—with love—

And, in due time : 'Fancy that letter going to you ! It was shocking of Willie, for it is a pack of exaggerations. I am quite the biggest coward and most useless person in England and so utterly disgusted with myself that I can hardly endure seeing myself in the glass. She is very anxious about her boy who is flying in France ; and his chum was shot, and killed by the fall, last week.'

In addition to his being an honorary colonel in the Territorial Forces and an official consultant for the military hospitals in Oxford, Osler from the early weeks of the war came to occupy a unique position in relation to the Canadian Medical Corps. It was purely accidental and quite unofficial, but as each successive Canadian hospital was established in England he by common consent became its advisory medical head. ' To see him sitting on a stool in the laboratory at Bulford talking to his old students and friends—advising, cheering, encouraging, without apparent effort, but with deep effect; to picture him thus is the epitome of all his relations with the C.A.M.C.' Thus writes more than one Canadian officer: ' From the difficult days on Salisbury Plain to the end, his presence inspired confidence, gave courage and stimulated work.' For special cases, moreover, his services were always to be had, and when the matter was more intimate and personal the stereotyped cable which came to be sent by the Canadian medical authorities— ' HAS BEEN SEEN BY OSLER CONSIDERS DOING WELL ' brought comfort to many an anxious Canadian home. It was a task self-imposed and one which drew heavily upon the strength of a man generous of his sympathies. And not only were official cables sent but letters followed:

> I saw your boy to-day [he wrote to one of his old McGill colleagues on July 17th]. I had not heard that he had come over until I had a telephone from Armour asking me to come up to-day. The mouth wound has healed almost, he is still anaemic from the loss of blood, but the complication of importance is a pleuro-pneumonia at the left base, with an aggravating cough. They are to put in a needle as the whole thing may be a septic pleurisy. The general condition is good & he will do well. He is most comfortable at the new hospital. I sent you a cable to reassure you. I will keep you posted.

He found time to send a series of letters about this one boy as if there were no others and he had little else to do; though as a matter of fact Lady Osler writes at this particular time that ' he has been rampaging around like mad and looks very weary but insists he is not '. And finally, after a month of anxiety a note of August 10th to the boy's bereaved father gives all the sad details; and another to his mother, telling how good and patient he had been; that there had not been much suffering; how the night before his death the boy had asked the others to leave, and spoke about the chances, which he feared were against him—

'poor fellow! I did what I could to comfort him. There was such a look of you in his eyes. Just as I remember you as a girl. I can realize how you feel. Our boy will be at the front very soon & we shall have to steel our hearts for the worst.'

This in every military hospital was a common enough episode—'died of his wounds' was the only official entry required. But fortunate the hospital which had the services of one who could alleviate suffering distant from, as well as at the bedside. It was this difficult and distressing rôle for which he was much called upon in the Canadian hospitals. The 'Consoler-General'. During the two years to follow, literally hundreds of telegrams or cables came from Canadians, known and unknown: 'MY SON REPORTED SERIOUSLY WOUNDED CAN YOU MAKE INQUIRIES'—'MY HUSBAND REPORTED ILL EMPYEMA DOULON CAN WAR OFFICE TRANSFER TO ENGLAND'—'CAN YOU INFORM OF BROTHERS CONDITION REPORTED IN CASUALTY LIST', &c. Even a death in so remote a place as Mesopotamia touched him; and though he and Sir Victor Horsley, one of the many victims of that disastrous march by the Tigris, were as unlike as two mortals could be, he took time to write the fine obituary tribute, which appeared in the *British Medical Journal* for July 29th.[1]

But the world is not made up of purely unselfish people, and at this point must be faced the recital of a depressing story which stirred to the depths the entire Canadian Army Medical Corps, in which he was merely an honorary consultant. It is an episode of political rivalry and of the

[1] It must not be overlooked that during all this time, so far as other engagements permitted, Osler had been regular in his attendance at many society meetings. Apparently only one of them (the Association of Medical Librarians) lapsed on account of the war. The meetings of the Historical Section of the R. S. M. continued, as well as of the Bibliographical Society; and on July 25th at the annual meeting in London of the National Association for the Prevention of Tuberculosis he gave a most timely address on 'The Tuberculous Soldier', who was becoming an important military problem, particularly in view of pension claims. Osler made some important suggestions regarding a more searching examination in the case of recruits, with provision for the study of doubtful cases before discharge, urging that a national organization with subsidiary branches in each county undertake this work in co-operation with existing societies.

misunderstandings which war breeds between the powers at home and those struggling with problems almost beyond human capacity three thousand miles away. It had better be forgotten, were it not that it affected Osler so deeply. For he saw an injustice being done to a member of the profession, which aroused his indignation; indeed he does not appear to have been so stirred since his resentment over the injustice done to John S. Billings in 1885 when Billings's work for the International Congress was undermined.

To keep things going smoothly and to foster a good spirit in the corps, Osler had planned in his characteristic way to celebrate the second anniversary of the arrival in England of members of the C.A.M.C. by giving a dinner to their Director-General, invitations to which he issued quite unaware that the affairs of the corps were about to be subjected to an investigation. The Canadian Minister of Militia, who at the time was acting to all intents and purposes as Commander-in-Chief of the Dominion troops, appears to have gained the idea that the British Army was effete and that the time had come to separate the Canadian from the Imperial forces. As an entering wedge, steps were taken, not only in contravention of British regulations, but over the head of the Canadian Surgeon-General, to concentrate the sick and wounded of the Dominion corps into special Canadian convalescent hospitals. For the purpose of showing that Canadian soldiers had been neglected, he appointed a commission of inquiry, the composition of which is said to have been most unfortunate, not to say partisan.

It was not, however, until August 20th that the matter was brought to Osler's attention, and on the basis purely of fair play he wrote a friendly letter to the head of the commission, whom he knew personally, asking whether the body had been appointed without previous consultation with the Surgeon-General as to its advisability or to its personnel. This request was looked upon as an impertinence, and meanwhile the commission, whose chief had had no military experience, inspected the Canadian hospitals, saw only the inevitable mistakes which had been made, listened to the stories of disgruntled people, and after some three months submitted a lurid and damaging report, the main purport of which was given out to the press.

The implication that Canadian wounded were badly cared for in British hospitals, and with it the recommendation that they be segregated in their own special hospitals—a recommendation, even if wise, almost impossible to carry out because of administrative difficulties—was enough to strain the good relations between Canada and the Mother Country. The Surgeon-General of the C.A.M.C. was recalled, the members of the commission stepped in, took over his office, and put themselves virtually in charge of the C.A.M.C. An ancient rivalry between the Canadian 'grits' (Liberals) and Conservatives, represented in the persons of the Surgeon-General of the Medical Corps and the Minister of Militia, was supposed to be at the back of all this, and as Osler wrote regarding the action of the inspecting committee, 'really nothing more Gilbertesque has ever happened in the profession—a group of a man's subordinates sit upon his work, turn him out & take on his job.'

It is a long and complicated story, which concerned the affairs of all the Canadian hospitals with which Osler had been connected, and even led to the dismissal of the Matron at the Duchess of Connaught's hospital at Taplow (Cliveden), an injustice which Osler particularly resented as he could not see how she could in any way have been implicated in a case of malfeasance which had been uncovered there. Osler, deeply interested in the welfare of the corps, though his official connexion with it was purely voluntary, felt so strongly in the matter, even before the report of the commission was finally issued, that when the Surgeon-General's removal became rumoured he cabled to Sir Robert Borden that were this action taken he would regard it as a disgraceful proceeding and would at once resign all consultation appointments at the Canadian hospitals and appeal to the profession for fair play. Apparently he handed in his resignation on or about October 20th, and sent to his old friend Sir Hugh Graham of the *Montreal Star*, for publication, the following letter of explanation:

My resignation as Consultant to the Canadian hospitals was

a protest against the injustice done to the Director in the mode of procedure in appointing the Hospital Commission. The profession and the public should suspend judgement until General Jones's report has been printed and given to the press. I have not, as stated, resigned from the Canadian hospital, Beechborough Park, which is under Imperial authority. During the past two years I have had many opportunities to see Canadian wounded in British hospitals in which I have everywhere found them well treated.

Wm Osler.

The Minister of Militia, who appears to have precipitated all this, finally decapitated himself by an ill-advised speech, so 'contrary to the public interest' that Sir Robert Borden was compelled to request his resignation. Subsequently, Sir George Perley was appointed Canadian Minister of War overseas; he called a second board of inquiry, over which Sir William Babtie presided, and on which Osler was requested to serve but refused. This Board reviewed the criticisms made in the report of the first commission, in all essential respects reversing its findings; and the Surgeon-General was exonerated. It was a long-drawn-out and wretched episode, over which Osler lost much weight, and for almost the first time in his life outwardly showed some signs of depression, though this may in part have been due to the fact that Revere's battery meanwhile had been ordered to France. Nor was the affair concluded until early in 1917, when after the report of the Perley board and the reinstatement of General Jones, Osler's resignation was withdrawn.

How all this harrowed Osler probably no one but his wife really knew. In a letter to his nephew, W. W. Francis, at No. 3 Canadian General, where a great hospital out of reach of boards of inquiry was being erected around the ruins of the old Jesuit college, she wrote: 'I have only two duties in life: to keep on cheering the wounded, and to keep W. O. fit for his tremendous amount of work and strong enough to bear the parting with Revere.' And ere long Captain Francis, on returning to his unit after a period of leave, carried with him to his C.O. a gift which shows how Osler loved to plant a seed where he knew it would grow:

Dear Birkett, I am sending by Billy Francis a bit of silver for the mess which please ask the men to accept with my love & best wishes as a souvenir of my visit last year. I wish after the war that you will hand it over to the Medical Faculty of which I hope it may become the nucleus of a collection of table silver, to be used at the Faculty dinners!

Revere by this time was nearly through with his period of training. 'He is well and likes the work—in a way', wrote his mother, and she added: 'Do you suppose he will be spared to us? The streets are full of legless and armless men. We have an officers' hospital now; about 260 beds, and it is pathetic to see men we have known in college so full of life, now on crutches or being pushed about in chairs.' And on September 10th she wrote to Mrs. Chapin:

I wish you were here now for the garden is lovely and we are having glorious days after that awful rain. I do not know when Revere goes. He should have four days before reporting at Southampton, but sometimes they don't get that. It will be hard if we don't see him again. Willie is with him now. He went to Newcastle last Wednesday for the British Association and was to stay with the Bishop. I was asked, but knew I should hate it and only have glimpses of Revere. He is very busy; has had command of the battery several days since he went back there. They were to go further north yesterday with a literary friend to see some famous old library, so they have been happy together.

In his own letters Osler treats the matter lightly. On September 19th he wrote to his former assistant, C. D. Parfitt, who had helped to organize in Baltimore the first tuberculosis clinic:

I was so pleased to have your last letter with an account of your progress. I know what an up-hill battle it has been for you. What a delight to get your own place. I am sending a cheque to the Angel of the House to spend for any little extras in the way of bedroom accessories, trays & cups & saucers—she will know. We are all well. Revere goes over in a few weeks to take his chance with the rest. He likes the artillery. Love to the lassie & to you both from us both.

And on a postcard of October 5th to F. H. Garrison:

I am sending impressions of a perfect gem of a touch-piece (Elizabeth) which is in the possession of the descendants of Sir John Harington (of W. C. fame). Pass it on to the collection. I must get impressions for Storer as well. I hear from Jacobs that the old man is in good form. All goes well here. My incunabula list practically complete (to 1480). I will put in S. G. L. Have you any additions since you sent the list? When does the new edition appear?

And on the 10th to Mrs. Brewster, while in the very thick of the C.A.M.C. disturbance:

I am so pleased to be asked to be Godfather to the little man, & am counting the years with wonder if I shall hear him the Creed, the Lord's Prayer & the Ten Commandments 'in the Vulgar tongue'. I hope so, tho 'tis a bit doubtful. Give him my blessing. Sue Chapin is sending him a Paul Revere porringer, which please have marked with his name. How I wish I could see you all at Avalon. I have been sharing your anxiety about the infantile paralysis, but I feel sure you are taking all precautions. You will be late in the country but all the better for the children. Revere has come for three days leave before going to the front. How I wish you could see him! He has developed so much, & we are boon companions, & he takes such an interest in my books. We shall be terribly anxious of course, but the cause is worth any sacrifice. Grace is slaving and the Hotel is full as usual—so many coming & going. A delightful Texan, convalescing from fever and a nephew with an ankle cracked in a German dug-out are with us at present. I am away a great deal—Hospitals & this Welsh Univ. Commission; but I keep well.

Well might he have wished to be at Avalon, in one of the few parts of the world the war had not reached. Teheran it had reached, and Dr. Sa'eed, in acknowledging a letter, wrote at this time: 'As you see by the address I was compelled to escape from Hamadan about four months ago for the Turks led by the Germans were coming and the fanatic Kurds too were ready to put an end to this apostate Kurd.' Small chance for the tomb of Avicenna.

'The old people are bearing up bravely', Lady Osler wrote on October 29th to Archibald Malloch. 'My sole object now is to keep Sir William well enough to meet any great worry that may come, but he careers about so and spends so much time in London over that Education Board that I can hardly keep my finger on him.' And on the same day, Osler, to J. Y. W. MacAlister: 'You are a good friend but a bad diagnostician. I have had a series of very unpleasant worries chiefly about the Canadian Hospitals, but I have sealed up the door and am free. The next time you see me I hope you will say the broad arrow has left my forehead.'

All through the spring and early summer, while the French were holding at Verdun and the Canadians were fighting for a few hundred yards of quagmire here and there at Ypres, great armies had been gathering and guns were being massed in Picardy for an offensive movement on a colossal scale. The great battle of the Somme had begun on July 31st, and into this maelstrom Revere's battery, a mere atom, had been swept two months later. 'He is busy,' says his father, 'and writes cheerily of mules and ammunition wagons.'

The 'Picardy summer' by that time had broken. October was a succession of gales and drenching rains, and in reaching their new front the troops had to traverse some four miles of nearly impassable ground which had lost all cohesion. Revere had reached France on October 17th, had promptly been sent to the front with an ammunition column, and was soon ordered to join a battery of field artillery with which during the rest of October and November he participated in the last stage of that great battle, which in numbers and duration had exceeded even the battle of Verdun. The supposedly impregnable German lines had been pushed back between the Ancre and the Somme by desperate fighting to a depth of six to eight miles in places—but with what loss to the flower of the British nation!

The casualty lists were long during all these days, but Osler plodded on 'cheerily', as he said Revere was doing. He wrote to Garrison on November 21st, saying that the night before he had attended at Fenny Stratford the 183rd Patronal Festival in honour of the Willis family, and that he had talked about 'old Thomas', adding: 'It was a most interesting occasion, and the 'Poppers' popped at intervals throughout the day in honour of Thomas and his grandson, the famous antiquary.'[1] Nevertheless, two days later, in a letter from London to W. S. Thayer, he admitted that:

> We have had an anxious time of course—so many of the family are here, & in the fighting line. My bro. Frank lost his only son,

[1] In his address on this occasion, 'before the villagers who gathered from miles around', there was no mention of war. It has been published in full, together with an account of the festival, in an article by Dr. Henry Viets, who was then studying in Oxford and who accompanied Osler (*Annals of Medical History*, N.Y., 1917, i. 118–24).

such a fine fellow who had been Shaughnessy's (C P R) private sec. Norman Gwyn has been doing good work at No. 1 General near Boulogne. Revere is on the Somme in a dug-out, just 100 yds from the German lines, & the chief occupation seems to be the exchange of gas bombs. He has taken to the practical work very kindly, writes very cheerfully & seems keenly interested but as a disciple of Izaak Walton the whole business is very distasteful. You remember Miss Parsons—she died the other day near Reading—a most faithful soul. I will write to Sister Rachel about her. I continue to see a great deal of interest—something new every day; but I get very tired of the wounded & of sepsis. I am here at the Welsh Univ. Commission of wh. Haldane is Chairman. We meet twice a week & are taking evidence. The proposal is to start a national school of medicine at Cardiff. [And he returns to a more important subject :] Revere is in the thick of it—in this last push on the Ancre. He is in the 59th Brigade Battery A. Dirty business for a decent lad, but they have to go thro. with it. Of course we are terribly anxious but—the seen arrow slackens its flight as Dante says & we are steeling our hearts for anything that may happen. Love to you all.

The Miss Louisa Parsons to whom he alludes had been the first temporary Superintendent of Nurses at the Johns Hopkins, a woman of military ardour and a true disciple of Florence Nightingale. She was afflicted with an incurable malady, and Osler for the past several weeks had kept in touch with her, visited her frequently, kept her old friends in America posted as to her condition, attended her funeral, having sent a floral tribute in the name of 'The Staff and Nurses of the Johns Hopkins Hospital, America', and wrote for the *Johns Hopkins Nurses' Alumnae Magazine* a note appreciative of her career. He said in part :

November 6th, the parish church of Shinfield, Berkshire, witnessed an unusual scene, unique in its history of more than 1,000 years. It was a beautiful autumn day and the rumour of something special had brought a large gathering from the neighbouring villages. Shortly after the appointed hour there was seen along the Reading road a military escort with a gun carriage, on which covered by the Union Jack was a coffin with the remains of Louisa Parsons, a woman endeared to many of us who were associated with the early days of the Johns Hopkins Hospital. I had never before seen a military funeral for a nurse, but for a veteran of the Egyptian and South African Wars it had been very properly ordered by the War Office....

It was merely one of the countless small things of a similar sort with which neither the Welsh Commission nor worries over the C.A.M.C. could interfere.

It was very good of you to send a nice fat cheque for our poor Belgians [he wrote to Mrs. Brewster on November 24th]. We were beginning to get a little uneasy about the financial outlook. Fortunately last eve word came from the Rockefeller Foundation that they would help again for 1917. They take the scientific people while Grace's fund helps the other professors. Sue Chapin has come for a few months which is a comfort. Revere . . . likes the artillery, but it is a gruesome business for a laddie with his temperament. A letter from him has just come by the evening post, & as I am sure you would like to have first hand news I copy it. . . . I am keeping well—away from home a great deal, chiefly in London.

And painstakingly he copied out Revere's letter written after the final attack in the prolonged battle of the Somme, of which John Buchan says: 'on the 17th we again advanced, and on Saturday the 18th in a downpour of icy rain, the Canadians, attacking from Regina Trench, moved well down the slope towards the river while the centre pushed close to the western skirts of Grandcourt. This concluded the fourth stage of the battle and the weather now closed down like a curtain upon the drama.'

Saturday eve [18th]

Dear Dad,—I would have written yesterday had I not had so much to do. I relieved the brigade forward observing-officer at 5 p.m., and spent the night observing. We take out two bombadiers, as look-out men, and two telephonists. It was a bitter cold night, freezing & snowing until 12 o'clock. I took my turn at watching and then retired to the dug-out leaving the bombadiers on watch. I had two blankets, a thermos full of tea, and some wood, and had several hours' sleep thirty feet under ground. It is a rum little dug-out about the size of your small room but lower & not quite so broad. With a fire & three others, we were quite warm and comfortable. I rather fancy there were some German critters about of the Berlin variety so I shall have a good shake at my clothes tonight. At dawn I watched our barrage of shrapnel put up on the German trenches; then a pause, a re-elevation and rush; and then the prisoners began to come, and were herded in a big trench to my right. They looked at first supremely happy but were soon frightened by the shells from their own lines, which were dropping all about. Our own wounded then began to straggle past, looking very sorry for themselves, poor fellows. I was relieved at 9.30 a.m. by another officer, and the Major who had come up to observe. Unfortunately just after I left the trench a shell burst near him, a splinter of which caught him on the head. The signaller got him back to the battery and the surgeon has just tied him up; and he is now sitting at the brazier, as cheerful as can be. Anyone else would have gone to the hospital. I do hope he may be all right but I fear the shock may upset him. There is a good deal of talk about going to rest billets, and I think we shall move within a week. It will be delightful to see trees and grass again, and to get away from this pandemonium.

No letters yesterday, but I expect them tonight when the pack-horses come up. Everything comes to the battery by pack and the letters come with the rations in the late evening. It is raining now and much warmer, which is a comfort, for the cold is almost worse than the mud. We have a brazier in the mess now and are burning about ten ammunition-boxes a day. It is really very comfortable. I am thankful to be here among such delightful men. There is a good atmosphere about this battery. Good-night, much love. Do not let Muz worry. Revere.

Not only was Christmas drawing near, but Battery A, 59th Brigade, which all this time had been at Mouquet Farm, one of the most fought-over spots on the Somme, had been moved well forward in the newly captured region, as the following letter from Osler to Charles Sayle would indicate:

I send books at Xmas to about 100 of my old students, and this year I have selected your 'Ages' & the just-issued edition (trans.) of Galen's 'Natural Faculties'. Do not bother please—I can get them through ordinary channels. Revere has been in this recent push. He writes: 'We are literally living in bombs as our dug-out is built in an old trench, which must have been used for a bomb store. It is impossible to turn up a shovel of earth without finding some old German or English grenades. Just below us in a great hole is a heap of old mortar bombs, ammunition of all kinds, grenades, broken rifles, & every describable variety of death-dealing weapon, all broken & twisted with the shell-fire and absolutely valueless. I never quite realized how tremendous was the wastage of war until I saw the quantities of once valuable material lying here & gradually being engulfed in the mud. In front of the battery is a tank which fell through a dug-out & had to be abandoned. I had a look at it to-day. The insides have been removed so that it was disappointing, & very unpleasant because what was once a German is sticking his boots out just at the door. This has been a bad place for Germans. The poor fellows lie all around us, with very little on their bones but a few tattered rags of flesh & these are being gradually cleared away by the rats which are plentiful & hungry. We hope to have their bodies cleared up very soon.'

For a man of sixty-seven, however young his appearance, alert his mind, elastic his arteries and his step, Osler had been careering about almost too much, and with his loss of weight was easy prey to one of his bronchitic infections. This caught him on December 2nd, but was shaken off less easily than usual, turned into a bronchopneumonia, and for the remainder of the month he was confined to the house and much of the time in bed, some rather ominous entries meanwhile being made in his account-book. It gave him opportunity to write more and longer letters than usual, many of them having on the margin : ' In bed—pen & pad '. He was really ill this time, but made game of it and proved a most obstreperous patient. He little minded a few days in bed ; made all manner of fun of his malady ; called for his milk 'poultice' (toast and hot water with milk and sugar—the way his mother used to make it—' *a castle* ') ; surrounded himself with books and papers—on the coverlet, the floor, the bedside table ; and one may picture him propped on pillows cheerily answering his mail. So on December 4th to J. Collins Warren of Boston :

Dear C. W. What a delightful extract ! [1] It goes in my famous B. Franklin edition of the *De Senectute* which was given me at that N. Y. dinner. All goes well—only *no peace for us*. No one wishes it, except on our own terms—Reparation, Restitution & Security. Revere [the usual story]. . . . My Anaesthesia collection grows. I made a fine haul of original Simpson pamphlets, & this week I got Vol. VI of 8th edition of the Brit. Encyclopaedia to cut out his chloroform article. . . . I lack—and want badly—the Bost. Med. & Surg. Journal for 1846. Tell Mrs. Myers at the M. G. H. (if she is still with you) that there are several copies I am sure, among her duplicates ! And I want Bigelow's paper on Simpson. I have written to Sturgis B. about it. So nice to hear about the grand-children & particularly about another Joseph Warren. . . .

I hope this will reach you in time for Xmas greetings [he wrote on the 5th to Mrs. Brewster]. The boats are so uncertain now & letters are often 3 weeks in transit. We continue to have such cheery letters from Revere who has never been so happy since the

[1] Extract from an interview with C. H. Parker in his ninety-third year, from the *Harvard Alumni Bulletin*.

war began! He likes the men of his Battery & he seems to stand the hard work & exposure very well. The incessant row of the guns & shells tells on the young & old & they try to send them back for a few days to the base every three weeks. R. has just gone back, to his great joy for a bath & clean clothes. 'Tis a piggie life as they may not have a chance to change for weeks. I have sent you an anthology of the Ages of Man, written by a friend, in which you may be interested. For 60, he has taken my rude remarks. Heavens! that was a long time ago! Every month of the past two years seems a year in itself—and the end is not in sight. There will be an appalling mass of battered humanity to be taken care of. Without any big battle the wounded continue to pour in. We have 1500 beds here—always full. I expect a group of 68 American doctors next week. We have asked for 250 young men who will be placed in the various Military Hospitals & relieve men who can go to the front. It is marvellous how much comes into this country every week from the U. S. Tell Uncle Ned to cheer up. Uncle Sam is doing more than he knows. . . .

And the next day to H. B. Jacobs:

Xmas greetings to you both. This should reach you in time, but boats are few these days & submarines plentiful. We plod on much the same, only with the added anxiety of Revere on the Ancre, but he writes so cheerily & seems wonderfully happy. 'Tis a dirty business though for a laddie of his type, but I suppose he will get used to it & return to the stone age with the rest of them. . . . Have the library all rearranged and shelf-marked and the catalogue up to date. My secretary is still away, but Hill from Bodley comes every evening & a vestal who has been helping me with my incunabula study has come to work permanently on the catalogue, with a view to printing (ultimately). Sue Chapin is with us. Norman Gwyn has had trench fever. Rolleston is much better & with the grand fleet. We had the three Maggs brothers here for a day—to see the Shakespeare exhibition—such nice men.

And on the 11th to L. F. Barker:

We were I feel rightly hurt by Wilson's statement that the objects for which the nations were fighting were the same—this rankled. Very ill-timed too. There can be no peace & there will be no peace until we are either smashed or victorious. Why leave the nightmare on the world of another great war, just as soon as Germany is ready. Good word from Revere—but very hard work—night & day business with the guns & mud to the knees.

He entered in his account-book opposite Dec. 17–23: 'In bed all week. Cough better. Rather weak and knocked out.' Yet he could write cheerfully enough, and as a tonic there came just in time a copy of the 'excessively rare' 1683 'Miscellany Tracts' of Sir Thomas Browne, which he had bid for and lost some years before and which now gave him, as he expressed it, 'an acute paroxysm of bibliomania'. This volume had been sent by a number of his old Hopkins friends, to one of whom, Dr. Thomas R. Boggs, he wrote on the 19th:

I wish you could see me T. B.—abed with that priceless copy of the Miscellanies, and all my Brunonian literature about it. I was just paralyzed—vasomotorically—when I opened the parcel, & at a glance saw what it was. For I had the volume in my hand the day before the sale & left a bid, but the man from N. Y. was too much. And now to think that it should have come back! & in this delightful way. 'Twill be the chiefest of my Browne treasures. And so well coffined. I am in luck! Only a few weeks ago there came in from Holland No 3 of the 1644 Latin editions, about the existence of which I began to feel doubtful. I now lack only the 1688 Dutch complete ed. Am in bed with a heavy cold—much better. Revere well—on the Ancre pounding away night & day with a battery. He is with such nice men & has enough to do to keep him from worry. You would not know the boy—so developed mentally, & with such a keen eye for books & good literature. I hope you will have a booklet I sent for Xmas.

To each and every one of the sixteen contributors to the gift there went a long letter of like kind, with its characteristic expressions. To one: 'I would give my top hair to drop in on you all this evening.' To another: 'I have coughed my Pacchionian bodies loose and split my central tendon in two places. Am all right now.' And again: 'Bad time over here for the Dove of Peace. I wish Wilson's note (arrived this a.m.) had been shot on the way. Peace at this time would mean another big war within ten years. We must go through with this one now to the bitter end and either come out on top or go under & leave the future of democracy to the U. S. I think we can hold out another 1½ years or longer. The country is at last alive to the business.' And a few days later: 'Poor Wilson's peace kite has come a cropper. I am so sorry he sent it just now. I hope he will be answered with Abe Lincoln's words—wonderful how Father Abe is quoted here and his example held up as a model!'

In every letter is something about his collection—'Library thrives—catalogue finished and all shelves marked—a 1673 apocryphal ed. of Le Malade Imaginaire came in yesterday—I can find no reference to one of that date.' And again: 'You will have about the end of Jan. a coloured sketch of a bookworm that will open your eyes—caught him at work.' And every letter of course had something about Revere, who 'has become an abandoned bibliophile & is collecting Walton & his friends and the Elizabethans', and meanwhile is 'pounding away on the Ancre—a devil of a mess. I wonder if we shall ever see the end'. That he had lost none of his spirit, even though he had coughed his 'Pacchionian bodies loose', is evident from the following Christmas message, entitled 'The Silent Unit', which appeared among others in *Lloyd's Weekly News* the day before Christmas:

There was a famous paradox in antiquity—a grain of wheat falls noiselessly to the ground, the same thing happens with the second, the third, the fourth, and so on, for the thousands of grains that make up a bushel. But collect the grains again, and drop the whole bushel, and behold! a great noise. It seems difficult to explain how the sum of many thousands of silences could result in one great sound.

The silent unit, the single grain, will win the war. In this world's crisis it is the spirit of the individual worker—in trench or camp, factory or farm—that keeps the mouth shut, the heart fixed, the hand steady.

The call is for silent sacrifice, of time, of habits, of comforts, of friends, and of those dearer than life itself—the sacrifice of sanctification in the old Hebrew sense. It has come. Do we not feel in our heart of hearts that only a rich anointing of the spirit of the Fathers could have so stirred the Empire from the centre to the circle? My blood was thrilled the other day by the Honour Roll of the Consumers' Gas Company of Toronto—386 men at the colours from one corporation, of whom twenty-five have been killed, thirty-seven wounded, and eight taken prisoners! Why? The answer is in the words of the Prophet-Poet of Greater Britain:

'Because ye are Sons of the Blood, and call me Mother still.'

Let this message be heard above the din of battle and the clash of machinery, the silent unit will win—'In quietness and in confidence will be your strength.'

He was up and dressed for a short time on Christmas Day, and wrote: 'We have the house full but of course our hearts are empty with Revere away. I have been laid up for 10 days—a very unusual experience, but it has given me a good rest & I am going to take it quietly for a month. Grace & her sister are at the Hospital helping with the Xmas dinners. They are *drivers*—I wish you could see the big workshop', &c. So he 'takes it quietly' on the 25th by writing many letters to old friends—as to Miss Noyes, the Librarian of the Medical and Chirurgical Faculty of Maryland:

Dear Sister Marcia, I wish I could spend an afternoon with you in the Library—seeing all the changes & improvements. What a great work you have done for us! I wonder whether you appreciate it. I really believe the doctors do! Think of those old days—of such small things—but we had hope. And old Dr. Cordell! How nice to think that his devoted old age was cheered by the prosperity of his much beloved Faculty. My library grows. I have a very ambitious scheme for a printed catalogue, but it will mean years of work—& I have so little time. Greetings to all your staff & best wishes for 1917. . .

And on the 28th he wrote a letter which, much soiled, came back to 13 Norham Gardens in a soldier's kit a year later, and which reads in part:

To my son on his 21st Birthday.

First—regrets that you are not with us—but these are the only ones; and the most satisfactory of all the feelings I have is that no regrets cloud the clear past of 21 years—and this is a good deal to say. You have been everything that a father could wish, a dear good laddie. And it is not often I am sure that father and son have been so happy together. . . . For the Future—everything is too uncertain to make any plans. We can only hope for the best. But a few years ago your Mother, with her usual good sense, began to save something so that you could have your own money when you came of age. . . . It will be transferred to your name. This will be enough to pay your average expenses at College and there will be extras if necessary—and an occasional 'rake-off' I hope. It is always so much better for a fellow to have his own money, when possible. Many, many happy returns of the day and I hope when this tyranny is overpast we may have more happy days together—you and I and Muz. Your loving Dad.

And on that same day there was being written to his 'dear Dad' a letter from an ex-German dug-out thirty feet under ground, below the ruins of a church which represented the

Battalion Head-quarters of the South Staffords. It tells of a forty-eight-hour liaison duty with that battalion—a very cheerful letter which ends by saying : 'I can't help feeling that at this time next year we will all be together again. I hope Lloyd George doesn't stop us buying books ! I am very happy considering it is my birthday ! I have no regrets except for my own shortcomings, only endless love and gratitude for you both.'

CHAPTER XXXVII

1917

THE SILENT SACRIFICE

'The call is for silent sacrifice, of time, of habits, of comforts, of friends, and of those dearer than life itself.' So Osler had written in his Christmas letter for publication. It expressed the spirit of the country during this trying winter. December had seen a change of Government. Asquith was out. And in the saddle at the head of a special War Committee of Five sat Lloyd George, a man desperately in earnest who with the simplicity of genius talked in terms the people could understand. Great Britain (bar Ireland) at last was really mobilized for war and the Dominions were called to the council table. 'Because ye are Sons of the Blood and call me Mother still!'

Harassed by the Somme battles and by Nivelle's easy recapture of the ground France had lost at Verdun, Germany made new overtures for peace—maladroit as usual. 'We have been wringing the neck of Wilson's peace dove,' Osler wrote later in the month; 'he will be answered in Lincoln's words. We do not want peace except on terms that will guarantee its permanency and we all realize what they are.'

Germany had failed in her original purpose and now sought some compromise. She made an empty offer, a 'combination of bluster and whine', which admitted of no possible agreement, and meanwhile was deporting the Belgians to work in her factories and fields. Mr. Wilson had been re-elected, seemingly on the grounds of having kept the United States out of the war and on a platform embodying the tenets of a League to Enforce Peace. The two were incompatible. What he had really meant by his 'Note' of December 18th, asking the belligerents to declare their rival aims—a note which so annoyed Osler on his sick-bed—only time can tell. The Allies made a dignified and prompt response. Germany replied by the resumption of a ruthless campaign under water; and this was her undoing, for it was what terminated America's patience.

The 'silent unit' meanwhile at 13 Norham Gardens goes on in its usual way. Oxford was full of wounded; the great war loan enforced unusual economy, and food was reckoned in terms of calories. One merely tightened one's belt. Carmelita, aged fifteen, had a wounded brother in one of the Oxford hospitals, and Osler wrote:

11th [January]

Dear Carmelita, That is a lovely photograph—just like you, strange to say! & we love it. Thank you so much. Please come again soon as there are several other poems you really must learn. Unless you get all the good ones into your head (& heart) before you are twenty they do not stick. Winfred came to lunch to-day & spent the afternoon upstairs with Milton—Paradise Lost & Gilbert à Beckett's Comic Histories & the Dictionary of National Biography. He is coming again tomorrow. He is looking much better & can stand on his legs—which seems a natural thing to do! Love to the parent Yours aff^{ly} Wm OSLER.

And probably Winfred Nuttall was entertained, too, by being shown the living specimen of *Anobium hirtum* with which Osler had long been amusing himself; for the parasites of books, though less common, may be no less destructive—and for that matter no less interesting—than the parasites of man and animals, as to which his curiosity, aroused by Father Johnson, had never been lost. It gives an opportunity to recall that, war or no war, institutions like the Bodleian—unless the fate of Louvain befall them—go on largely unaffected. Even the Quarterly Record continued to be published, for as the Editor stated: 'Although we are not yet self-supporting we hope to be so after the war, and meanwhile the generous help of Sir William Osler and other friends prevents it [the *B. Q. R.*] from being a burden on the Library finances.' Apparently it was during his December illness that he wrote for the February issue his account of the living bookworm he had found tunnelling in a copy of the 'Histoire abrégée de la Dernière Persécution de Port-Royal', whose provenance indicated that the worm came from the south of France. Quite a contrast to the sapping, mining, and burrowing going on in the north of France just then, though Osler draws no such comparison, and his interesting account is written as in time of peace:

. . . Only once before, in the University Library, Utrecht, had I seen a living bookworm. The picture of the opened book was so striking that Professor Poulton, to whom I showed it, urged me to have a sketch made by the well-known artist Mr. Horace Knight, of the British Museum. Mr. Knight writes, September 4, 1916: 'Herewith the drawing of the bookworm which more than a year ago you asked me to make. It has been waiting in hopes the larva would pupate, but it has not even commenced to make a case, and Dr. Graham thinks it may go another year. . . . There are no eggs of this species in the British Museum and no drawing of any value.' Mr. Knight's beautiful sketches are so superior to anything in the literature that Mr. Madan has kindly consented to have the plate reproduced in the *Bodleian Quarterly Record*. . . . Insect bookworms are rare in Oxford, even in the most secluded libraries. Mr. Maltby, the well-known bookbinder, has the largest collection I have seen, made during the past twenty-five years, all of *Anobium domesticum*, except one unknown Lepidopteran larva. There are a few in Mr. Madan's possession. Though many of the old books in Oxford libraries are badly wormed, recent ravages are rare. One of the least used collections is that of Bishop Allestree, housed so quaintly above the cloisters at Christ Church. There books have been badly damaged, but at a recent visit I could find no worms in the books, but one shelf had plenty of borers whose sawdust covered the tops of the books below. It may be mentioned that the *Anobium* is the genus of the 'death watch' beetles which make a clicking sound in wood, so that there is some basis for the statement of Christian Mentzel, an old seventeenth-century worthy, that he heard a book-worm crow like a cock. Bodley is singularly free from the ravages of bookworms—confirming the remark of Charles Nodier, 'La bibliothèque des savants laborieux n'est jamais attaquée des vers.'

But the B.Q.R., and the Science Room, and the Shakespeare exhibit, and the repurchase of the First Folio, and the 'Richardson Correspondence'—'all these are trifles!' as some one has written. 'His best work for the Bodleian was of a personal kind: helping the wheels go round. He was loved by the staff and the curators alike, and his kindly words in season often prevented friction that from time to time appeared inevitable.' Osler kept his word, and 'careered around' very little during January. 'He has been angelic', wrote Lady Osler; 'only two or three times to town.' The letters of the time show how great a solace and refuge was his library. He sent out countless flying missives on cards, such as these to Dr. George Foy of Dublin:

Most interesting. Do try to run down the references. I see a good notice of Higgins in the Dic. Nat. Biography. Is there a good 2nd hand book shop in Dublin? I want any of the works of Dr. Paul Hiffernan (1719–1777) particularly his 'Dramatic Genius. In Five Books'. W. O.

Many thanks. Why not write up Higgins. It has not been done properly. Let me know if I can look out anything in Bodley. Y'rs W. O.

I wish you could find an account of that last Witch Trial in Ireland 1895. . . . I have picked up two plays of Hiffernan. W. O.

And many more follow about this case which occurred near Clonmel in 1895, and in which a peasant, wishing to get rid of his wife, had induced his neighbours to burn her as a witch. Nor did his interest in other people's affairs flag. He writes to Dr. John C. Hemmeter of Baltimore:

Thanks for the Haller references. I have read Hirzel's Tagebücher &c. I will look up the others. He was a fine character. Glad to hear you are getting out your collected Historical papers. Thomas Young (not Sir Thomas—he was beyond titles!) was an extraordinary genius. I gave a lecture on him at St. George's Hospital ten years ago. England has produced no one to equal Harvey in our profession. W. O.

And on January 24th to Dr. Pratt of Boston, who was keeping up his tuberculosis work there:

Dear J. H. P. That is a fine record! The papers came this morning & I have read them with the keenest interest. I am afraid one element you have not laid proper stress upon—your own personality. Confidence & faith counts for so much with these cases. The personal supervision & care is all important, & not taking too many cases. I will speak of your results at the annual meeting of our County association next week. Gout papers of course interest me—the incidence of the disease depends on the eyes of the doctor in charge of the hospital. I was told by a well known Scotch physician—'Oh, gout has disappeared from Scotland!' I found tophi in two of his chronic rheumatic cases. The multiple gouty febrile arthritis is not uncommon here. I have seen two cases, both with tophi, in soldiers. All well. Revere we hope is back in rest billets. His battery has been in action continuously since Oct. 21st. . . .

And on the 30th in an encouraging note to A. D. Blackader, who planned as a memorial for his son to found a library of works on the latter's profession of architecture:

Dear Blackader, I am so glad you have decided to hold the C. M. A. meeting. It is a great mistake to let them lapse. I will speak to Russel & one or two of the likely men who could send papers. Archibald could give a splendid account of his heart work & he & Mayo have wonderful specimens. In the B. M. J. you will find reference to every article published on the Insurance Act & the Med. Profession. The best part about the act was the establishment of the Research Committee which is doing first class work. I will bear the matter in mind & let you know. It was a great regret to me not to see Mrs. Blackader, but I was very hard pressed & much bedevilled over that C.A.M.Corps row. My love to you both. I realize how your hearts must ache. Our laddie has been for three months on the Ancre, with his Battery in continuous action. He keeps well, but the worst is yet to come. I will remember the memorial library What a nice thing to do! What a fine fellow he was! My love to his little wife—such a brave soul.

And there soon followed a rare volume of Vitruvius from a book sale to add to the Gordon Home Blackader collection at McGill. On a postcard of February 1st he wrote to H. V. Ogden:

Do send the paper of Farmer to us for the Quart. Jr. of Med.—Garrod is away in Malta. Poor fellow! few have had such knocks. I knew the boys well, such likely chaps. Good word from Revere—back in rest-billets after 3 months continuous fighting on the Ancre. I am all right again. My attack was pure pneumococci. W. O.

On January 22nd Mr. Wilson had made his famous 'Peace without Victory' speech before the Senate, and a few days later the United States was called upon to face the long-feared crisis, when Germany on the grounds of the rejection of her peace overtures withdrew her pledge relating to submarine warfare. It was a desperate throw, and though Mr. Wilson still hoped for a peaceful settlement there was no alternative but to hand the German Ambassador his passports. On February 6th Osler wrote to his old colleague Henry M. Hurd of Baltimore:

. . . The action of the U. S. absorbs all attention here. It was inevitable. We shall have a hard time possibly, but a little tightening of the English waist-band will do no one any harm. I should like to see the plans of the Hurd Library. The situation you mention is admirable. I should like to have been able to leave my collection to the [Johns Hopkins] School, but it seems more appropriate to give it to McGill, where it is much more needed. After all for the older and rarer books the Hopkins has the Surg. Gen. Library at its door. . . . Revere is back in rest billets, about 20 miles from the Front. They have had three very hot months on the Ancre—salvoes & barrages day and night. It is wonderful that the guns stand it. He keeps well & writes cheerfully. We may hope for a decision one way or another before the end of the 3rd year, but Germany is not yet beaten and is very strong. What a cruel shame that her rulers have made outlaws of such good people as we know—at least in the profession. Lady Osler and her sister are hard at work and the hotel keeps open as we have many Canadians stationed here in the Flying Corps.

On the next day he wrote to his bibliophilic Bristol friend, J. A. Nixon, who had just finished his period of leave and returned to his military duties :

Dear Nixon, Glad you have got back safely. So sorry to hear that there are enough self-inflicted injuries to have a separate camp. We are deep in winter—three days of regular Canadian weather—bright & clear getting towards zero. Creech was a rare old bird well known here—a Wadham man, a great translator, a disciple of Burton, profoundly melancholic and in 1700 sent his soul to ? thro' a noose. The Lucretius was very popular—orig. ed. 1682—many reprints, best 1714. D. N. B. says that 'for six mos before his death he studied the easiest mode of self-destruction'! This would be interesting—perhaps Wood gives details. Let me know at any time should you need special books. Yours sincerely W[m] OSLER.

P.S.1. The two New England women are rejoicing in the news from the U. S. & send martial greetings

P.S.2. Lucretius comes in my Bibliotheca prima for his vision & for the atomic presentation & for the 'natural man' view *de rerum natura*.

He engaged his young friends in literary pursuits whenever he could. It kept them from talking war ; and just now the Cambridge Press had sent him an advance copy of Malloch's monograph on Finch and Baines. So on February 17th he wrote to the author, at No. 3 Canadian General Hospital : ''Tis an A.1. bit of work—hearty congratulations. A story well told & brim full of interest. I will see to a good review in the *Lancet*. How delighted your father will be.' And he saw to both of these things when a month later the volume was issued:

Dear Malloch, By this time you have had Finch & Baines, & I am sure you will be delighted with the first serious product of Archie's pen. It does him great credit—a bit of solid work well done. We have had great fun with him over it. The story of the friendship has always interested me, so I am greatly pleased to have it so well portrayed. The Christ's College people are so delighted—Shipley, the Master, said to me the other day—is it not strange that we should have waited all these years to have the story told & then to have it done by a young Canadian. The work has been a good training for Archie & has brought him into contact with many nice people. It represents a lot of hard digging. The illustrations are splendid & the general 'get up' of the book is A.1. I am sure it will have a good sale though this is not a good time for books. All well here—I had a bronchitis at Xmas which housed me for three weeks, but the rest did me good. Revere has had a hard winter on the Ancre and instead of getting leave they have had to follow up the retreating Germans. . . . Fortunately he has kept well, but it is an anxious business.

He forgot neither friends nor friends' children, and on March 1st wrote to Mrs. C. P. Howard in Iowa City:

Dear Ottilie, We have just been talking of you & the darlings and I have just had out the lassie's picture which your mother gave me. Is it not good! We miss you all so much. How I wish you were all at No. 64 Banbury Rd. Tell Muriel not to forget Docky-Wocky & give the boy a tickle for me. Your mother & Marion were here a few weeks ago—both so well. We expect Jean shortly. I am enclosing a letter to Campbell. Leslie Pearce Gould has just been here, asking of course for you. Is it not tragic about poor Collis! Such a dear fellow. Grace is heart broken. Isaac writes cheerfully but it has been a weary winter I fear for him. He hopes to get leave before the Battery goes back into action. We are doing well on our rations—and the belts not yet tightened! Your loving Doccie-O.

All this time, in spite of the absence in Malta of its chief worker, Captain Charles Singer, the Science Alcove in the Radcliffe Camera had been tided along,[1] and on March 3rd Osler wrote to him:

Dear Singer, So nice to have your letter. I envy you the experience. I am afraid Mrs Singer will not be able to join you. She is

[1] In spite of all handicaps the first volume of Singer's 'Studies in the History and Method of Science' was published by the Clarendon Press

working hard & looking well. What a trump she is! I think the Sc. room scheme will go through the Faculties at the next meeting. I am taking all the Sc. Professors to see the place. Balfour was very enthusiastic. I have nearly finished the Rel. Med. [Religio Medici] MSS. and it will be ready before Schiller's paper is printed. I will pass your letter on to Marett with the photos, as they will interest him very much. We must get him actively with us in the Seminar scheme. A year from next summer we should be able to have it. Two weeks intensive lectures & demonstrations—& the whole summer for any special research students. We should get at least 6 men from the U. S. every summer. It will be a great missionary effort & you and that v. m. better partner can do the job. Love to Garrod—fine type—good sense and no d——d *non*-sense. . . .

During these weeks since February 1st America was being irresistibly swept in. There had been sinkings; finally the *Laconia* was torpedoed; and at about this time a German plot to embroil Mexico and the United States was uncovered. A bill empowering the President to adopt a position of 'armed neutrality' had passed the House and was being held up on the last days of the Session by a 'filibuster' of twelve irreconcilables in the Senate. On March 7th Osler wrote to Thayer:

Dear W. S. Yours of 20th here to-day. The boats are coming in—this is the 4th American mail this week. We are so excited about the news in America. What a pity that a doz. men should be able to block all legislation. It looks hopeful, & if America comes in the moral effect will be immense. Germany is not beaten yet

---

during the year. The volume, as Osler says in his Introduction, was 'the outcome of a quiet movement on the part of a few Oxford students to stimulate a study of the history of science'; and he goes on to enumerate the pieces of work which were under way, saying that 'with rare enthusiasm and energy Dr. Singer has himself done a great deal of valuable work, and has proved an intellectual ferment working far beyond the confines of Oxford. I have myself found the science history room of the greatest convenience, and it is most helpful to have easy access on the shelves to a large collection of works on the subject. Had the war not interfered, we had hoped to start a *Journal of the History and Method of Science* and to organize a summer school for special students—hopes we may perhaps see realized in happier days. Meanwhile, this volume of essays (most of which were in course of preparation when war was declared) is issued as a *ballon d'essai*.'

Osler had intended as his own contribution to the volume to collate the various manuscripts of the 'Religio', and though the work had been started he did not wish to have the volume held up for this paper.

& we are not in sight of the end. I expect to see Teddy over here with a big Division. All goes well here. We are worried all the time about Revere, who has been in the Ancre fighting ever since Oct. We hoped that he might have leave but I am afraid his Battery has been moved up towards Bapaume over the very bad country which the Germans have had sense enough to leave. He has kept well & writes very cheerfully. . . . I shall look for your article. Mrs Chapin is still with us Rolleston was asking for you the other day. He has done splendid work & as leading medical consultant to the Fleet his opportunities have been exceptional. . . .

On March 16th he wrote to Fielding H. Garrison:

I shall expect the 2nd ed. before long which you so kindly promised to send. I hope it did not go down in the Laconia. What a stew you must be in at the Capitol! We are following events with deep interest. It is hard to see how you can escape war. We had on Sunday a group of 16 nice Harvard men who braved the submarines to join their unit in France. It was a very sporting thing to do in the face of strong opposition from friends & relatives—17 nurses too. Singer is off in Malta—stirring the pool there. He is full of ferment. We are getting the science room in good order in the Bodleian & hope to make it a useful place for study. I am struggling with a proper catalogue of my library & have an ancient Vestal at work. My secretary has gone—& I am lost—our butler has just died of pneumonia in a war hospital—a perfect jewel, whom we can never replace.

I still lack Morton, Letheon, 1846, and his other pamphlets on Mode of Admin. Ether & on the Phy. effects. Keep your eye open please for them. Greetings to dear old Klebs who must be in despair. Have you heard anything of Sudhoff? What a chasm the war has opened—we shall not live to see it bridged. The boy has been on the Ancre since Oct. 1st & is now 'following up' with his battery. It keeps us anxious & worried. But that is the normal state. Greetings to the librarian & to all old friends. . . .

'I am struggling with a proper catalogue of my library.' 'Keep an eye open, please.' With these oft-repeated phrases in mind the reader may be permitted briefly to forget, as did Osler, submarines and the Ancre, and to turn to the cards of the catalogue which are being arranged and copiously annotated.[1] Also to the volumes on their shelves. In the *Litteraria* section is a book of poems

[1] Reproduced herewith is one of the cards from the *Secunda* section, which shows not only Osler's original note, but also traces of other hands which have latterly been engaged in getting these cards ready for the publication of the catalogue, 'Bibliotheca Osleriana' (now in press).

MEAD (RICHARD) ~~cr. ref. CATALOGUE~~

3369 Bibliotheca Meadiana, sive catalogus librorum Richardi Mead, ~~M.D.~~
Qui Prostabunt Venales sub Hasta ... 1754. Iterumque ... 1755 ...

(1) & totals added with prices in MS. London (1754). 8°.

"H... Dr Richard Mead was ever really described by his witty colleague John Arbuthnot, as the Mae(d) Maecenas Me(d)dicorum, it was a happy instance of the combination of sound & sense of jingle and justice. For of all the numerous scholars, men of letters, collectors, antiquarians and intellectual benefactors, whom we owe to a profession which has fostered the learned Linacre (described by his friend Erasmus as "vir non exactitantum sed severi judicii"); the gentle Caius, that zealot of universities; the genial, the ingenious Arbuthnot; the bibliophile Askew; and the Medical Annalist, the Ovidian Garth; Radcliffe, the founder of mighty libraries, and Watson, the last of the race of Grands Seigneurs de la Médecine – Mead stands pre-eminent as patron, collector, the friend of arts & letters, of artists & littérateurs, the stimulator of mens bodies & minds alike" (AA.3.4)

Over

Bernard Quaritch. A Dictionary of English Book Collectors Part XIII, 1899

(2)

One of the commonest, & one of the most interesting of 'priced' catalogues.

There is scarcely a page which does not illustrate the bibliographic philistinism of the period. Think of the 1468 de Civitate Dei for £3.13.6 and 15 guineas for a set of 18th-century religious works; a Lactantius 1468, for £2.12 & and, on the same page, Calmet's Commentaire, 1724, for £10.16.0! The 1478 ed. princeps Celsus fetched £4.5.0 and the Continens of Rhazes, 1509, £10. One shilling for Gilbert's famous de Magnete 1s, while Lister's Historia Conchyliorum went for £6.16.6. The Aldine Aristotle, ed. princeps £5.5.0; & the Vesal Epitome, 1543, on vellum — £8.12.6. (run on)

The sale lasted from Nov. 18 to Dec. 19, 1754, and from April 7 to May 8, 1755, & the total realized was £5540-7-6

(3) The coins medals busts & museum specimens were sold separately (see no. 3370.) ~~(17). 8 — 99.~~ 11

[W.O.]

Calmet's 'Comm' 1724. p. 8

Vesal Epitome 1543 p. 239

Lister Gilbert p. 37

~~Continens~~ Rhasis 1509 £10 p. 62.

(5)

Catalogues, sale (priced). Physicians, libraries of.

entitled *First and Last*, by George B. Wood, one-time Professor of Medicine in the University of Pennsylvania, and the uncle of H. C. Wood, whose relation to Osler's transfer in 1884 to Philadelphia has been told. In this Osler writes: 'Received March 31st from my dear old friend. . . . This is the second copy I have had. H. C. W. gave me one about 1890. I happened to mention it to Weir Mitchell who . . . immediately claimed the volume for the Library of the College of Physicians. I very gladly gave it to him. It is not in the S-G. Library.' Inserted is this letter from H. C. Wood:

Dear Osler,—I am still alive, for which I do not thank God, but the Devil. I am much pleased that your boy has escaped injury. Right opposite to me lives an old man, now 87, who fought in the ranks and later as a non-commissioned officer, in 122 engagements during the four years of the Civil War; had his clothes many times cut with bullets, but never had the skin broken. Fate seems to be fate. I wish to God I had died young instead of living to be old and suffering. My secretary, Miss Paul, says I have two copies of George B. Wood's poems, so I will send you one, with a statement regarding it on the fly-leaf. If you want rare books, this book is a rara avis. Though rarity is liked by many in beef, I would rather be the author of a book like the last edition of the U. S. Dispensatory, of which twenty thousand copies were sold before it was out.

If we had but a President who was a MAN! Roosevelt would have settled this thing months ago, but it does look this morning as if the country was going to settle it. For 103 years the rules of the U. S. Senate have been that one man could prevent the taking of a vote on a subject simply by talking. It is on record that Senator La Follette some years since talked eighteen hours on a stretch; then a friend took up the talk; and so it went on until no vote could be taken; but this rule was yesterday altered so that the bills to arm American merchantmen will certainly pass into laws.

In another book of verse by a physician, 'Men-Miracles, with Other Poemes by M[artin] Ll[uelyn] St. of Ch. Ch. in Oxon.', 1656, one finds a note of purchase dated 23/iv/17, and, written six months later:

Revere was much interested in this little volume and knew the Song (p. 53) 'Breake thy rod'. The marks in the book are his. He had been reading Cartwright and read the volume for the references to him. W. O.

[And still later:] At my suggestion we bought the first edition 1646 for the Ch. Ch. library for £5.5 June 1919. W. O.

It is unseemly to intrude even in a biography any more than necessary upon a man when he is under emotion. But Osler laid bare the secrets of the heart in the covers of his books, and these he had left for all to read.

Mention has already been made of his relations to clubs, his manner of using them, and his somewhat detached interest in their various regulations. The histories of the more notable ones are come upon in a small section of the library—even the annual membership lists, in many of which he made personal notes. As may be recalled, he had been elected to the Athenaeum under a rule which permitted the election each year of nine members whose names did not have to come through the long waiting-list of candidates for ordinary membership. So in his copy of the 'Rules and List of Members for 1916' there is written a long account of an election held on March 12, 1917, at which time the name of some one he had proposed came up to be voted upon :

> . . . The club [the note reads] is a very sensitive body reacting promptly against any suspicion of bad breeding or poor morals on the part of a candidate. Many men have been stupidly put up by their friends who should have known that they had not the ghost of a chance. . . Some have regarded rejection as an honour : e.g. the late Henry Stevens of Vermont, the founder of the well known house of booksellers. In his 'Recollections of Mr. James Lenox,' 1886, on the title-page, among his distinctions occurs, 'Black Balled Athenaeum Club, London' [etc. etc.].

Membership in the Athenaeum is, of course, a mark of distinction, and admission by the usual portals represents so long a wait that members are apt to have their sons' names entered when they go up to college ; and so, on his matriculation as a commoner at Christ Church, the name of Edward Revere Osler came to be placed upon the list of candidates, alongside of many others who lie in France.

Even among books the war cannot completely be forgotten. And now another volume, 'Human Temperaments', by Charles Mercier, is found to have on its fly-leaf under the date 30.iii.17, the following note :

> Mercier was (is) a remarkable man, with marked individuality and a keen brain. A good talker, an incisive writer, he was the terror of

careless correspondents and of half-baked theorists. For the past three or four years he has been raking the psychoanalysts fore and aft. Some of his letters in the Lancet have been rich reading. Poor fellow! he has had Paget's disease for some years and is now much crippled, with a large and knobbed head and greatly bowed spine. He was with us recently on a visit to Oxford, and was in fine form, telling good stories, and so keen about everything. In spite of the increasing disability, a stone in the bladder, frequent haematuria, he insists that he is still in the ring and fit to do anything. He has had two operations for stone and says a third won't kill him. He says he is going down with all flags flying. My respect for him, which has always been great, is enormously increased. The letter here appended is an acknowledgement of a box of cigars I sent him.

And the amusing 'letter appended' reciprocates the gift by sending 'a certain quantity of piffle to amuse idle moments, if so busy a man ever has an idle moment'. Mercier did go down 'with all flags flying' two years later—and still writing; but if one were to pursue this distinguished alienist further in Osler's library it would lead to the 'Death, Heaven and Hell' corner already mentioned in these pages. For his 'Spiritualism and Sir Oliver Lodge', published at about that time, stands on the shelves beside 'Raymond', a book which just then was making an extraordinary appeal to many heart-broken people. With the wave of spiritualistic revival which spread over the afflicted world as an almost inevitable reaction to the losses of war Osler had little sympathy, and felt that it had done many people enormously more harm than it had brought them comfort. There was nothing new in it. Saul had consulted the Witch of Endor. Osler's curt rejoinder was that Lodge should 'put up or shut up'. Pasted in the back of his copy of 'Raymond', catalogued among the volumes on spiritualism, witchcraft, and so on, are the verses 'Non tali auxilio', which begin:

> 'Have we not earned our rest?' Oh, hear them plead
> Whom death has drawn across the dividing line.
> You should have kept their memory as a shrine,
> A holy place, where he who runs may read
> The lovely record of a noble deed . . .

So Osler's library constitutes an intimate record. His communings were reserved for his books alone. Spiritualism was distasteful and appeared to him to be unreligious: just as psychoanalysis appeared to him undesirable and often unprofessional. But, as Mr. Hadley said, one is likely to be late for his engagements if he permits himself to browse among Osler's books; and meanwhile much had been happening during this month of March.

No leave had been granted to young artillery officers on the western front; not since October; and there were often many anxious two-week intervals between letters—then a bundle of them all at once. At 13 Norham Gardens was a household into which telegrams and telephone messages poured even in peace times; and now any one of them might bring bad news. But even the little telegraph boy of the district knew what was apprehended, and from afar would shake his head to reassure one who saw him from the gate or chanced to meet him in the street. And when word did come, Osler writes: 'Very good letters from Revere, whose battery has been with the division following up the Germans. It has been a case of single blanket, rubber sheet, & bully-beef for three weeks. He keeps well & writes in good spirits.' The Somme offensive, indeed, had been pressed, weather permitting, during the entire winter; and now Revere's battery was among those on the heels of the enemy, who from Arras to Soissons were being hustled in the great retreat back to the newly prepared Hindenburg Line. If there are two things mentioned they are always the library, and Revere. Thus on March 28th to Professor G. H. Nettleton:

> Many thanks for your suggestion—most useful. I hope I have not bothered you, but I always get something & several on your list I had not got. . . . I am hoping to make the Bibliotheca litteraria a strong section of my library—the literary works of medical men & the medicated works of literary men. All goes well here—waistbands tightening a bit, but that will do us good. The boy has been on the Ancre since Oct 1st & is now in the thick of the 'follow up', which keeps us anxious. Greetings to the family & to Phelps.

On April 2nd the United States Congress had been convened in extra session, and in his message Mr. Wilson stated that 'the present German warfare against commerce is warfare against all nations', and asked for an immediate declaration of war. The next evening Osler wrote to Mrs. Brewster:

This is a wildly excited household tonight. I have just returned from town, and found the front porch bedecked with the Union Jack & the Stars and Stripes, & the Revere girls dancing with joy. Wilson's speech is A.1. How glad Uncle Ned must be that he has come out so well. America has already done splendidly over here. I wish you could have visited with me to-day the American women's war hospital for officers—room for 50 & so well arranged. Lady Harcourt, who was a Miss Burns, has been the moving spirit. It is a branch of the big Hospital at Paignton. No word from Revere for five days, but we hope his battery has come to rest. He is with the advanced division & they may be moving on as the German retreat seems now to be forced. We have had some hard whacks lately—one of our very best boys has gone, such a dear. He was in & out constantly when up here, & we became so devoted to him. Another of my best friends has lost his 2nd boy. Hard days on the heart! I am glad your laddie has not twenty more years to his credit. Love to you all.

'Hard days on the heart' indeed. Little could he know what was going on in the region of Arras, the northern point of the Hindenburg Line, where on the 9th the Canadians swarmed on to the crest of Vimy Ridge. No word of this had come on Easter Sunday, when again he wrote to Mrs. Brewster:

One bright spot to-day—your photograph came as we were at breakfast! Such a delight to see you looking so well & with such a splendid boy. Is he not a darling? How proud and happy you must be! I have spent the first unhappy Easter of my life. We have had no letter for ten days & only know Revere's battery is 'on the move', so that we cannot but be worried. Still we keep up our courage & hope for the best. We are so rejoiced at the turn of events in America. You can scarcely realize what it means for the Allies. The moral support will be immense & I fear we shall need all the financial & physical help possible before the ghastly business is over. I am looking forward to 'Life' for Uncle Ned's editorials. How splendid they have been! He has sense enough for a syndicate of editors. I wish 'Life' was read more over here—though I should like to poison some of the writers who malign my beloved profession! . . . I will send a p. c. when we hear from the boy.

And the next 'p. c.' states: 'Two letters from Revere to-day, dated a week ago—hurrying north for the new offensive, so I suppose his battery has been in the thick of it. No news since is good news & we hope for the best.' But the taking of Vimy Ridge took its toll. The casualty lists were heavy, and it was not for some days that the Roll of Honour carried the name of 'Major Campbell Gwyn, Canadian Infantry, son of Col. Gwyn of Dundas, Ontario. Killed in action on the 9th April'.

Dearest Sister, This will be a hard blow for you to bear—the first of your children to be taken. Few Mothers have had an unbroken family of such size for so long; but to give up a dear fellow like Campbell is heart-breaking. We became very much attached to him and he got to feel very much at home with us. We had been dreading the past few days & opened every telegram with anxiety. Only a few days ago we had been hearing of him from one of his men who is in the Hospital here; & who spoke of the affection they had for him & what a splendid officer he was. He was a born soldier & knew his job thoroughly. It will be very sad for the girls who had really seen more of him than the others.... We are steeling our hearts against the possible blow to us, as Revere's Battery is in the thick of this fight. The anxiety is very wearing. Grace keeps up splendidly, but she feels the loss of Collis & now of dear old Campbell. Poor Charlie will be hard hit as he must have felt a special pride in him Keep up your heart dear—he has died in a good cause....

But outwardly one would never have known that Osler was so deeply affected by these blows. 'I am back in my old paths', he wrote later in April; 'away four days last week, very busy time about the hospitals and rearrangements. America will save the situation!' His business was to show only a sunny side, and this he lived up to, as did many others, in spite of the aches and anxieties within. A cable came on April 25th that a fund had been established in his name for the purchase of books for the library of the Maryland Medical and Chirurgical Faculty, and he promptly wrote to H. B. Jacobs:

Your cable just received bowled us over completely. Did ever anyone have such friends! I am deeply touched. You know how much I love the old Faculty. I do not think that anything in Baltimore gave me greater pleasure than to see it established in a proper home & to watch the progress of the Library. Think of the old days in those dismal rooms under the Hist. Soc! Dear Cordell! what a fine loyal soul he was! And Ashby, always so full of hope, & Randolph Winslow, a bit doubtful about the money! How much we owe, too, to those older men, Christ[r] Johnston, Donaldson, Chew

& Miles who made us, strangers, so welcome. Welch & Martin & Remsen paved the way, & it might have been so different! The Faculty was really the stock in the soup. I will write to the President as soon as I have the particulars. . . .

The hospitals kept him busy: '300 malaria cases here from the East last month—all convalescent but they started a blackwater case with intensive quinine—fatal with anuria.' Thus he wrote to George Dock on May 2nd; but his letters are mostly about Revere, and the growing Bibliotheca. 'The Persian Embassy sent me a fine Rhazes MS in Arabic the other day. I expect it came from my friend Sa'eed.' After an exposure in the camps at Folkestone he contracted another bad cold which laid him up for a week; and from Sidmouth, Lady Osler wrote to one of their past Rhodes-scholar friends:

Sir William and I are down at the sea for a rest and a little change. I think we both needed it badly. This is a lovely spot in South Devon, and it is hard to realize the war here. Dear old Oxford is busier than ever, such an enormous number of men training and flying. The hospital is packed. The Randolph Assembly Room is being used now. Briscoe has been turned into a ward for pensioners, mostly Oxfordshire men, I believe, who will be sent to their homes when fit. . . .

The much needed change at Sidmouth probably found him writing his Fothergillian Oration [1] which was delivered on May 14th, and which he introduced as follows:

With the flotsam and jetsam of the sale-room there came to my library the other day a book for the times, with the title 'A Discourse of Constancy . . . written in Latin by Justus Lipsius. Containing Comfortable Consolations, for all that are afflicted in Body, or Mind'. London, 1654. To have known of the 'Discourse' through two admirable articles by Basil Anderton, of Newcastle, gave an added welcome to Humphrey Moseley's 12mo in the original state. In the dialogue, the two friends discuss the miseries of the age, which had made the Low Countries almost as desolate as they are to-day, and the great Louvain Professor a homeless wanderer. To the despairing Lipsius his friend urged that 'equal calamities and far greater had already fallen on the race', and that after all it was the lot of man, his destiny, and that cities and people owe their ruin to 'Commission of Providence'. As a tonic to their constancy

[1] The annual oration before the Medical Society of London. 'The Campaign against Syphilis', *Lancet*, Lond., May 26, 1917.

they rehearse through many chapters the wonderful slaughters, the strange cruelties, the plagues and famines and rapines; and the conclusion reached was that Good comes out of Evil, and that the righteous are never forsaken. Having accepted this comfortable consolation, hard for us to read anywhere except on the title-page of the book, our neo-Stoical friends went to dinner!

A disciple, himself, of the neo-school of Zeno so far as Stoicism implies self-control and fortitude, Osler was not content to remain inactive in the process of letting good find its way out of evil. His subject was the antivenereal campaign; and he spoke openly and effectively about 'the most formidable enemy of the race—an enemy entrenched behind the strongest of human passions, and the deepest of social prejudices'. Nothing better, more appealing, more sympathetic, more hopeful could have been written on the subject, and it is a pity that the address should have been intended for professional ears alone. His closing paragraph is as follows:

> Most hopeful of all is the changed heart of the people. At last the sinner is to receive Christian treatment. Above the mantelpiece of his library hung what the founder of my old school, the Rev. W. A. Johnson, used to call the Magna Charta of humanity. In the centre of the most dramatic scene in the Gospels stood the woman taken in adultery. About her thronged the Scribes and Pharisees, with eyes turned from her to the Christ, stooping as he wrote with his finger on the ground the watchwords of the New Dispensation—'He that is without sin among you, let him first cast a stone at her'. I should like to see a copy of this picture in every one of the new clinics in testimony that we have at last reached the full meaning of the priceless message, 'Neither do I condemn thee; go, sin no more'.

However the address may have been written, it must have been given with a light heart, for Revere had come home—on his first leave in seven months. 'He went away a boy and has returned a hardened man'; and the next day his father writes:

> To our great joy Revere got home yesterday, on ten days' leave. His battery was dug in opposite Bullecourt & the Colonel thought they would be there for a fortnight & that he could be spared. You never saw such a burly looking fellow—so grown & filled out, with hands like a navvie & a face weather-beaten like leather. He has literally been in the open since October & physically it has done him

no end of good. He is in very good spirits & has had a wonderful experience, as his brigade was the first to cross the advanced trenches beyond Arras. They had five weeks of incessant fighting & never more than two days in the one place. His nerves are A.1. but it has been a hard experience & it is not easy to get him to talk much. I do wish you could see him.

Though he would not talk of the war, other than to tell of the congenial friends in his battery, Revere 'Discip. Iz. Wa.' had a happy ten days angling with success both for fish and for books—one day landing a record trout at Cornbury Park Lake. 'He is beside me now', Osler wrote on the 17th, 'with his latest treasure bought at auction yesterday—Philemon Holland's 1603 Plutarch's Morals—a great book.' But this was over all too soon. Artillery officers were needed in Flanders. And once more telegrams must be dreaded and the casualty lists scanned with concealed apprehension. On June 4th the boy's father wrote to F. J. Shepherd:

Yours to hand this eve. I have sent word at once to Ernest at No 4 General, & will see him if he is still there but your letter was dated May 2nd! We are getting letters thro' now in about 2 weeks—as a rule. I will let you know about E. We had Revere home for ten days—his first leave since Oct. Such a big hardened fellow. He had not slept in a bed for seven months. Fortunately he is with such nice fellows in the R. F. A. It keeps us anxious. I have just lost another nephew. I hope the Robertson (of Montreal) whose death I see is not your nephew. Love to the girls. . . .

The French attack on the Chemin des Dames during April had been a worse failure than people were permitted to know, and now the British were preparing for a series of offensives on a huge scale for the ridges of Messines and Passchendaele—and then perhaps the Belgian coast! The latter part of May saw the vanguard of the American Expeditionary Force, consisting of medical officers and engineers, for these were what the Balfour Mission in Washington said were most urgently needed. Certain base hospital units were the first to arrive, all of them officered by university teachers, old-time friends of the Oslers, for whom 13 Norham Gardens was a natural magnet. No bother was too great to take for them. 'CAPTAIN NORRIS AND SEVEN MEMBERS OF PHILADELPHIA UNIT CAMBRIDGE ON TUESDAY

COULD YOU AND SHIPLEY LOOK AFTER THEM' he wired to Nuttall. The 'Open Arms' was a far better place than the Army Stores to get warm pyjamas 'the kind Revere finds best', and long bed-socks, and mufflers—for the nights in France are cold for people unaccustomed to bell tents. And busy as he was, he acted as intermediary between these raw medical officers and the much harassed War Office. 'If there are any special worries let me know, as Keogh likes to hear of them quickly.'

The month of June saw the storming of the Messines Ridge, and Osler wrote: 'Interesting letter from Revere about the Messines battle; evidently a great success; they had 48 hours of constant work & were half dead of exhaustion noise & heat.' Meanwhile, examinations were on in Oxford, though one would not imagine from his notes that 13 Norham Gardens was filled with examiners and convalescing Canadian soldiers—nor from replies to his notes. Thus from Adami, who had been giving the Croonian Lectures at the College of Physicians, probably to empty war-time benches: 'It is like your dear good self to send me this note about your not being able to turn up; not one man in a thousand would have thought of this act of kindness and it goes to one's heart's core.' Then, among the shower of his postcards are the following to J. Y. W. MacAlister:

For 25 or 30 years there was a Medical Botanical Society in London (of which I just learned). I saw advertised in a catalogue their minute books, and it seemed a shame to have this record of human effort adrift, so I sent for the volumes. Not of much value but someone will wish to know about the Society. Will you give shelf room to the Vols. Hope to see you Wednesday.

[Again:] Sorry could not see you this week too busy. Have we the De motu cordis 1628? If not fine copy at Pearson's sale. Will fetch £30. I will go £5.

[Again:] Why discourage me? Not to have the 1628 Harvey in the R. S. M. is a reproach which I should like to see removed. I believe it is an exceptional copy. I will try. Will join you 4 p.m. Wed.

[Again:] The Harvey has come & is really a beauty. The title page had to be repaired, and the leaf of Errata has been put in in duplicate. Like all copies it has been badly cut. When is the next meeting of the Library Committee at which I will present it?

Have you issued the circular to those U. S. hospital units? It would be most acceptable I know. Col. Bradley, U. S. Leg. can give you their addresses.

And meanwhile the following laconic messages are among many that passed to Charles Sayle of the University of Cambridge Library:

Medical diplomas—Cambridge. Have you a good list in the Library? Were they always of one form? When did they begin? *And* when are you coming to pay us a visit and inspect the B.O.

[Again:] I mean the 'parchments' issued by *the Univ.* M.B., M.D. or Diploma entitling men to practise. One came in the other day, 1681, I think. If you are good & come over soon, and if the Univ. Lib. has not got one, I will leave it in my Will! I collect diplomas —when possible—of different Universities.[1] If you cannot come this month, the *mt.* must go to *Md,* as there are important queries —but I wish *you* would come. Revere's battery back in billets— two guns smashed to bits.

[Again:] I am sending the Diploma for your inspection. We do not appear to have any Oxford ones in Bodley. There should be somewhere a good article on Univ. Diplomas—of course the North Italian form is attractive and appears to be the most common. Do come over—I wish you would make it a *professional* visit and let me use your bibliothecal brains for consultative purposes as I would an engineer. There are some points on which your wide experience would be most helpful.

[Again:] In Bib. Litteraria would you put the biography of a man? e.g. under Locke would you put the Fox-Bourne Life with Locke's books? Just a card please.

[Again:] All right. I think too the Life should go with the man's books, and a reference under Biography. The Camb. Diploma came from E. Williams, 37 Newtown Road, Hove. R. pounding away— 4 barrages daily & nightly.

During his leave Revere had extracted a promise from his parents that they would get away for a breathing spell —from 'the people coming and going'. So from Swanage at the end of a brief sojourn, Osler wrote on July 3rd to Mrs. Brewster:

Here for a bit of rest & change. Delightful spot—the Isle of Purbeck—where we spent two summers when Revere was young. Such a sea & beach—I wish you were here with the darlings. How

[1] He had been sending many of these old illuminated diplomas to McGill as he had picked them up from time to time.

they would love the sands. Revere keeps well—got thro. the Messines fight safely & their brigade got called up for special praise. He is full of admiration for the men who stood 48 hours of incessant pounding before getting thro. He is now back in the wagon lines as in the beautiful German dug-out with great steel & concrete emplacement for the guns the position was too exposed. They had 100 rounds a day on their position and lost three guns. We have been delighted with the American Hospital Units—men from Columbia, Harvard, Cleveland & Phila have been with us. It is splendid to see their enthusiasm. The two Boston women are beaming with delight. The final decision rests with the U. S. Germany is not beaten yet. Love to the children & to R. B.; and to the wise man!

It was a brief outing, for he had to be in London on the 4th and 5th for a meeting of the Welsh Commission, and while there sent from the Athenaeum a letter to George H. Simmons, enclosing 'A Note of Warning to Examiners of Recruits', for publication in the *Journal of the American Medical Association.* It concerned 'the unfit who furnish a large contingent in our hospitals and a needless burden of transport, care and pension—the mouth-breathers, the neurasthenics, thin-chested'. 'Cut out unsparingly the owners of these. If lungs and heart are not in a good case the head is of no use in war . . . is the experience of one whose work has been largely with the wastage of the recruiting office.' There was a succession of meetings of the Welsh Commission, doubtless with a good deal of scribbling of 'James Bovell M.D.' on the agenda by one of the members during the prolonged sessions. One gets a better glimpse of him in the diary of a Canadian M. O. who on leave preferred 13 Norham Gardens to London and the theatres:

Arrived Oxford. Sir William in London finishing up Royal Commission on Welsh Education. He returned after dinner, looking, I think, a bit thin but much better they say than before his holiday in Swanage. His two volumes of Vincent of Beauvais' 'Speculum Naturale' printed by 'R' printer in 1473 [?] have arrived—huge. Bought from Davis and Orioli in Italy about seven months ago. He talked to us about the Catalogue which is to be very much '*raisonné*' and books all bearing on the same subject, or suggesting it, will be found together, a method open to criticism, but it will be as Sir William wishes to have it. The History of the Council of Trent will be found under Harvey. Why? Because Paolo Sarpi is its author and he is one who has been put up as the discoverer of the circulation. Then there will be found W. O.'s views on the book, or note as to author, donor, former owner, bargain, price, etc.

And the diary goes on to tell of dining at the Max Mullers', and of Sir William playing cricket with the children afterwards. The week of July 29th–August 4th found him again in Wales, at Cardiff and Aberystwyth on the business of the Commission. On the last day of the month, the day of the first fateful battle for the Passchendaele ridges, he gave in Aberystwyth an address on 'The Library School in the College' at the opening of the Summer School of Library Service.[1] It was a new thing for the British Isles, such a school as he proposed, though they had been successfully established elsewhere; and being a matter close to Osler's heart it must have been a gratification that he could have played a part—perhaps the major part—in launching this one small feature of the work of the Welsh Commission in addition to his help in organizing the medical department.

His theme was the profession of librarianship, and he laid stress on the haphazard way that librarians for the most part had, in the past, come into being—not five per cent. of them college bred. 'The condition confronting us', he said, 'is that between two and three thousand persons, actively engaged in an all-important work, are in backwaters, and not in the broad stream of educational life. This is bad for them, bad for the libraries, and worse for the public.' He spoke of bibliography, of classification, of cataloguing; and in the last section of the address went on to elaborate his pet scheme of a 'School of the Book', concerning which ten long years before he had been writing to D. C. Gilman. Such a school, he went on to say, 'would prove an active ferment in the departments of literature and history.' And in a vein reminiscent of his own methods,

[1] *Library Association Record*, Aberdeen, Aug.–Sept. 1917, xix, 287–308. A 'School of Librarianship' on the basis of suggestions received from the Council of the Library Association, was subsequently opened by Sir Frederic Kenyon in October 1920 in connexion with the University of London, at University College. It was organized very much on the lines which Osler had laid down, though the prospectus makes no allusion to his earlier movement.

with which Revere had been so successfully inoculated, he continued :

Take Milton, for example. The booklet with 'Lycidas'—what a story in its few pages, and how it completes the fascination of the poem to know the circumstances under which it was written ! Only a few libraries possess the 1638 edition, but in an enterprising seminar, one member would get a photograph of the title-page, another would write an essay on these college collections, so common in the seventeenth century, a third would discourse on Milton's life at Christ's College, while a fourth would reconstruct the story of Edward King. The 1645 edition of the Poems, with Milton's famous joke beneath the ugly reproduction of his good-looking youthful face, would take a term, while the Paradise poems and the prose writings considered bio-bibliographically would occupy a session. How delightful to deal with Erasmus in the same way ! how helpful to the senior students ! how stimulating to the teacher ! Think of the virtue that would permeate a classroom if the teacher held up a first edition of 'The Praise of Folly' and then threw on the screen Holbein's illustrative pictures. The man cannot be separated from his books —both must be taken together to estimate properly his position and his influence. A term could be spent with Sir Thomas More and his books, and the student would take, on the way, much of the helpful history of the Reformation. The great advantage of combined biographical and bibliographical concentration is seen in the awakening of a vital and enduring interest in which alone is the taste for good literature encouraged. The dry formal lecture rarely touches the heart, but in the conversational method of the seminar, or on the quiet evening at home with a select group and a few good editions of a favourite author the enthusiasm of the teacher becomes contagious. How different would be the attitude of mind of the average student towards the 'Essay on the Human Understanding' if the splendid story of Locke's life served as an introduction. The man and the book must go together ; sometimes, indeed, as is the case with Montaigne, the man is the book, and the book the man !

His theme, too, evidently recalled to his mind the days in London thirty-five years before, when, uncertain as to his future movements, disappointed in his desire to take up ophthalmology, he had been advised by Bowman to enter Sanderson's laboratory—days when he perhaps, like the majority of mankind, spent too many odd moments on ephemeral literature :

It is not often [he said] that one has a vivid enduring impression of a newspaper article ; but one day in October 1872, in a Tottenham Court Road tea-shop, I read in *The Times* a statement of Ruskin to the effect that no mind could resist for a year the dulling influence of the daily paper. Doubtless as an exclusive dietary the press and the magazine do lead to mental conditions the counterpart of what we know in the body as the deficiency diseases, scurvy, rickets, etc. The library through you supplies the vitamines which counteract the mental lethargy and anaemia which come from a too exclusive use of Northcliffe and other patent foods.

Back in Oxford, he wrote on August 7th to Sir John Moore of Dublin that the address was 'purely educational, not medical', and therefore not suited for a medical journal, and he added: 'I am grieved to hear you have lost your boy. How terribly the profession has suffered in the war. Our boy is in the thick of it with the R. F. A.'

The Passchendaele battles were taking their heavy toll. Hospitals were again over-filled, and in the casualty clearing stations, placed some few miles back of the line, surgical teams detached from the American base hospital units then serving with the B. E. F. were getting their first experience of the real horrors of war. These American medical officers were all friends, not a few of them intimates, of the Oslers, and to one of them on August 19th Lady Osler wrote:

Revere was safe on the 14th. How badly you would feel if you should see him brought in wounded; but what a mercy it would be for him. He is near St. Julien I believe. One of his men passed through the McGill Hospital, wounded, and Billy Francis saw him. His captain is in a hospital in London. They are terribly busy and the weather has been too awful—mud as bad as the Somme, and no dry rags for days on end. Poor W. O. is almost a skeleton and keeps busy every moment but sometimes can't sleep and it makes one very anxious. I dread the winter for him, to say nothing of Revere, if it is to be as bad as last year.

On the 25th Osler wrote to Mrs. Brewster:

All goes well—so far. Revere writes very cheerfully & has stood the hard times of these recent battles. This last affair beyond Ypres was complicated with torrents of rain which kept them soaked for four days. Their Major & Capt. were both wounded so the subs had to take charge. We hope if a lull comes that he may get leave, as he has only been home once in the 11 months. It keeps us very anxious but we hold on & hope for the best. The Boston women came home last week from the parade of the American troops in London in a state of wild excitement. They had both cried hard on the curb-stone opposite the Embassy. The men took London by storm. Do let us know if any of your friends come over. We are having a stream of American visitors—so many over on special duties. How I wish I could have a peaceful visit with you all at Avalon! I just hate not to see the children as they grow up. I tried to send a recent photograph of Revere but they do not allow pictures by post. I will get a chance by some friend.

Among two million men massed within and back of the dreaded Ypres salient, that any two of different arms of the service should chance to meet would be small; so Lady Osler was written to for the number of Revere's battery, and replied on August 29th:

I have wired Revere's address as far as I know it. His O. C. has changed and I do not know his name; could not wire it if I did. I have an idea he is beyond [deleted by Censor]; he might get to you for a day on his horse. . . . He was all right on the 23rd, taking two quiet (?) days off with a gas whiff inside. What a life you must be leading! We are nearly drowned here and blown out of bed. I must send you a warm jersey to sleep in, later.

That same afternoon, Battery A of the 59th Brigade got 'a direct hit'—too trifling an episode for the *communiqués*, but what happened has been told in a diary:

From their position just beyond Pilckem, between Langemark and St. Julien, two or three hundred yards this side of Hindenburg Farm, they were preparing to move up the four batteries to-day on to the ridge. Major Batchelor, Lt. Osler, and eighteen men were bridging over a shell-hole in preparation for the move of the guns in their battery. It was about 4.30 in the afternoon and there had been no shelling. They were so busy they did not even hear the scream of the first shell, which dropped in their very midst and wounded or killed eight out of the twenty. It was difficult to get the wounded back, but they finally were brought to the dressing station at Essex Farm on the canal, a 3,000-yard carry; and then a short distance on an ammunition narrow-gauge; then the advanced post of the 131st Field Ambulance in front of Canada Farm, and finally by ambulance to No. 47 C.C.S. which was 'taking in'—a matter of four hours.

To the officer who leaned over him, Revere's first word was: 'This will take me home.' How often were those words—'a Blighty one'—hopefully spoken by the wounded of whatever rank! His field ambulance card, attached at the forward dressing station, read: 'G. S. W. multiple—

chest, abdomen, thigh.' Late that night an operation was undertaken; and a blood-transfusion from one of his own less-seriously wounded men brought in at the same time. All in vain; he died before sunrise on the 30th.

The diary continues:

We saw him buried in the early morning. A soggy Flanders field beside a little oak grove to the rear of the Dosinghem group—an overcast, windy, autumnal day—the long rows of simple wooden crosses—the new ditches half full of water being dug by Chinese coolies wearing tin helmets—the boy wrapped in an army blanket and covered by a weather-worn Union Jack, carried on their shoulders by four slipping stretcher-bearers. A strange scene—the great-great-grandson of Paul Revere under a British flag, and awaiting him a group of some six or eight American Army medical officers—saddened with thoughts of his father. Happily it was fairly dry at this end of the trench, and some green branches were thrown in for him to lie on. The Padre recited the usual service—a bugler gave the 'Last Post'—and we went about our duties. Plot 4, row F.

Personal messages over busy official wires are slow to get through, and Osler working in his library that afternoon had just been writing to H. M. Hurd:

Congratulations and thanks for the [William H.] Welch Bibliography. It was a capital idea to have this done as his writings are so scattered. The book is a great credit to the Press. I am writing a note to Burket [the Editor] about it. I hope your eyes have improved. Trust you are able to use them a little. We have been delighted with visits from members of several American units. The Hopkins men went through [to the A.E.F.] without stopping. We are kept anxious of course about Revere as he has been in all these heavy battles since April. Arras, Messines, Bullecourt, & now in the fighting near Ypres. He keeps well. His Major & Capt. were both knocked out & the battery has had a pretty hard time. He hopes to get leave when the fight slackens a bit. He has only had 10 days since last Oct. . . .

At 4.15 p.m., as he noted in his account-book among the consultations and engagements, London, Folkestone, Cliveden, Torquay, Paignton, Cardiff, &c.—the dreaded message came. One may hope 'the seen arrow slackened its flight'. And, possibly late that night, he made this entry:

I was sitting in my library working on the new edition of my text-book when a telegram was brought in, 'Revere dangerously wounded, comfortable and conscious, condition not hopeless.' I knew this was the end. We had expected it. The Fates do not allow the good fortune that has followed me to go with me to the grave—call no man happy till he dies. The War Office telephoned at 9 in the evening that he was dead. A sweeter laddie never lived, with a gentle loving nature. He had developed a rare taste in literature and was devoted to all my old friends in the spirit—Plutarch, Montaigne, Browne, Fuller, and above all Izaak Walton, whose *Compleat Angler* he knew by heart and whose 'Lives' he loved. We are heart broken, but thankful to have the precious memory of his loving life.

He began that very night to shield others—his wife, his friends, the medical officers whose efforts to save his boy had been futile. 'Poor Grace! it hits her hard; but we are both going to be brave & take up what is left of life as though he were with us.' Notes, telegrams, cables expressing grief and sympathy, of course poured in—chiefly from his countless American friends. The English in these days sorrowed in silence for one another. It was too common a story—one merely mentioned these things in an off-hand way:

31.viii.17.

Dear MacAlister, So glad to hear that you are better Harrogate is a great place for the Primae viae ductus vitae. I will write to the G. A. Hard blow to-day News of the death of my boy in France Fortunately his great friend was at the C.C.S. when he was brought in. He was a great lover of books and a son after my own heart Yours sincerely W. O.

'Thank you and dear Mrs. Page for your kind message of sympathy', he wrote to the Ambassador; 'we are hard hit but the blow must be taken bravely—others have had to suffer more.' With his intimates he did not await their first words of condolence. 'I wish you could have seen him of late years—so full of interest and mentally so matured', he wrote to Mrs. Brewster. 'I will get my nephew Col Hugh Osler to take out a photograph to you. He "chose for you" do you remember that day in the nursery in Baltimore when he was a little boy.' Also on the 31st to Dr. and Mrs. Jacobs, wishing that he 'could have spared them the grief the sad news would bring', and adding that after all these long years of prosperity in heart and head, for no man living had ever been so blest in his friends, the Fates had hit him hard at last. 'Poor laddie! the war was an awful trial. He had not the heart to shoot a partridge. The men and horses were his only solace—trying to make their condition less hard. Only his love for us & a sense of duty took him among the combatants. Fortunately he has been much happier of late and has been devoted to his men for whom he had the greatest admiration.' And on the same day to his special protégés, the children of Palmer Howard and Harry Wright:

Dearest Campbell & Ottilie, You will be desolated, as we are, at the loss of the dear boy. We have been steeling our hearts for the blow, but now it has come the bitterness is much more than we thought. Dear laddie! he loathed the whole business of war, and I dare say is glad to be at peace out of the hell of the past six months. Was it not a blessing that H—— was with him? This really softens the blow. We have had no details so far. We shall take up our shattered life & do the best we can. All our other dear children, among whom are your dears, will be a consolation. A little letter came from my darling Muriel—to whom give love & twenty kisses and some to the dear boy. Your loving Doccie-O.

For a day at least they had hoped to be left alone with their grief, and had wired, cancelling their engagements; but a Swiss physician, an old Philadelphia pupil who was attending the Empress Eugénie, failed to get the message—came to lunch, paid a long visit afterwards, and from Benning the chauffeur, now a cripple after his own period of service, he first learned on his way to the station of the shadow over 13 Norham Gardens. And Osler's neighbour, Dr. Whitelocke, tells of meeting him that afternoon in the corridor of the Acland Home and Osler calling out: 'Hello, Whitelocke, how's my dear boy getting on?' Dr. Whitelocke—so taken aback that he did not realize for a moment that it was his own son, Hugh, whom Osler was asking about—then told him that Hugh had been sent from Syria back to Egypt with dysentery; and Osler said: 'Be sure and let me know if I can do anything for him. You'll be glad to know that poor Revere fell into the hands of some of our American friends. Such a comfort. Do keep me posted about Hugh. Good-bye, old chap.' And Dr. Whitelocke says that in wonderment but with an aching heart he turned 'to watch him pass down the corridor—not a trace of emotion—a lesson in manliness, restraint and breeding'.

This could be carried out by day, even though at night he would be overwhelmed in the deep waters of sorrow. And occasionally even by day. On the next Monday, September 3rd, he went to Taplow as usual, and the following letter of more recent times shows how difficult it is for his friends to speak moderately of Osler:

I wish that I could have seen you and told you of our beloved Sir William at the hospital. Like all things that are wonderful and true and different, it is almost impossible to write of him; or to say in language worthy of him what one would want to. He made the whole difference to the hospital. Of course to the staff that was natural, but the patients waited for him and accepted his word as final, and it was never one of discouragement. I only saw him cross once—a young M.O. said before a patient that his case was practically hopeless, and that of course annoyed the Chief. I always felt that no case was hopeless and I waited for him to come and say so, too. That was the wonderful part about him, he really brought Healing and Health, Life not Death.

Then after Revere died—I shall never forget that day. We wondered if he could come back at once. We knew he would come soon, but at once ——. Yes, there he was in less than a week after he got the news which I feel really killed him. The men saw what had happened and we all knew his heart was broken. He went through the wards in his same gay old way, but when he got to the house—for luncheon alone with me—he sobbed like a child ——. It was so hard for us who loved him.

I know you only want from me something about his work at the hospital. It was like his whole life, wholly unselfish; and each Tommy got the attention which the Prince of Wales would have had from him. Colonel Mewburn could tell you about it, and Major Vipond in Montreal. He was so devoted to his Canadians, and he used to write me such wonderful letters about my kindness to them. They are too full of praise to be published, but he was never too busy to thank me for some trifling thing, while he himself was doing small kindnesses all day, along with the big things he had to do.

I wish I could really write about him, but you see I can't. My children adored him. They waited impatiently for his Monday visits. He called them 'the Darlings' and spoilt them most outrageously. . . . I can't really think of him without the feeling that all one can do in this brief passage is never really enough. He made us all want to give more. Waldorf shared my admiration for him, but my love began when I was fifteen, a patient at the Johns Hopkins.

Sincerely,

Nancy Astor.

On the 7th they went again to Swanage for two weeks, taking with them as companions Mrs. Chapin and the little Max Muller boys, who always called him 'William', as though he was their own age. 'We came here to-day', Lady Osler wrote shortly after, 'because we had promised Revere to do so, and we needed the change badly. Sir William seemed to be shrinking away into nothing, but I think he seems better. He writes letters; goes out to walk; writes letters; plays with the Max Muller boys; and writes letters.' True, most of them were brief: 'Thanks, dear Perley, for your kind message of sympathy. We are hard hit but shall face the blow bravely.' But not all of them. On the 13th to Mrs. Brewster:

You will be anxious to hear how we have stood the hard blow—well, better than we could have anticipated. Ever since the outbreak of the war 'Fear at my heart, as at a cup, my life-blood seemed to sip'. I never saw a wounded man without thinking of Revere, & since Oct. when he went out every telegram has been opened with dread. The difficulty is to realize that he has gone, and that we shall never see his dear face again. It was most fortunate that Dr. Darrach & Dr. Brewer of New York were at the Casualty Clearing Station, . . . which is a great consolation. He was terribly wounded in chest & abdomen & I do not think there was much suffering. We have had such touching letters from all the men. I am copying an extract from Major Davidson's letter. Dear laddie! he was always so cheerful and he kept all horrid details from us as much as possible. We have come here for a couple of weeks rest & change Love to you all Affectionately yours, Wm Osler.

Ext. from letter of his Battery Commander. 31.viii.17.

. . . He was simply splendid the whole time. I feel rather shy of putting this down on paper when so many officers write letters to relatives of men who have fallen in action, which they could not have written had this not been so. Your son was as delightful and cheery a member of the mess as he was reliable, hard-working and efficient at his work. Nothing was too much trouble to do for the Battery. It was never too dark or late or wet to go out to the guns and do the various small duty jobs which abound out here, and the doing of which well, makes all the difference to a battery. He was always the same whether checking the sights of the guns or the 300 S.O.S. fuses which are kept always at hand and set ready for any enemy attack, or unloading ammunition, or riding all over the country to get tarpaulin, timber, roof-wire, etc., for the gun pits and the dug-outs. He worked with all his heart and looked for no praise. He had not an atom of conceit and never lost his head or his temper with the men when things went wrong, which so many do. I hope I have not said too much but I feel my mother would like to hear any good about me when I get killed, and we all feel about your son what I've tried to express.'

Is not that a nice letter to have been written from the dug-out the very day word reached them that he had died? W. O.

By the 19th Mrs. Chapin could write: 'W. O. is sleeping better and I think he will be all right but his heart is broken and he cannot cease weeping; poor darling, it is so cruel for his later life. His great diversion has been having the little Max Muller boys with him. He has dug in the sands, driven donkeys with them, and then turned to answering notes—over 500 Grace tells me he has written. We can't help him, and as yet the American letters have not begun to come.'

They stopped in London for a day or two on their return; visited Revere's wounded sergeant, who by then had been evacuated to a London hospital; and it was probably at this time that Osler at the Athenaeum opened the book which contains the list of candidates for membership, and under the entry 'No. 10466. Nov. 6th, 1914. Edward Revere Osler, Christ Church Oxford. Undergrad.', wrote in a tremulous pencilled hand—'dead'. If a tear did not fall on the page it surely fell in the deep recesses of his heart. But it was no unusual thing—such an addition to this list of youthful candidates; and as Osler so often repeated in his brief letters, 'others have had to suffer more'. On the 25th, from Oxford, he wrote to Captain Malloch:

Dear Archie, We are back, and at work, as usual, only the sore heart for the poor laddie. I knew it would come but that does not make it less hard. I shall get a specimen page of each section of the library and of the index. Miss W[illcock] has been away finishing her vacation. Unfortunately Miss Walpole has gone to the Athenaeum but I shall try & get someone else to help. Push on with the Pneumonia work. Love to Bill and the boys. . . .

The first American mail came—greatly delayed—it had taken a month. To acknowledge all the messages that the postman carted into the house would have been impossible, and he was reduced to having some one typewrite a form: 'Thanks, dear Friend, for your letter of sympathy. It is a bitter blow but we must face the world bravely however much our hearts may ache.' And as though this expression of feeling did not appear on the sheet, he would often add something utterly irrelevant below, in his own hand—'I do not believe I ever thanked you for that nice book—full of good sense', for example. Or to H. M. Hanna: 'You must feel a proud man at the position the Cleveland school has taken. *We owe this to one Mel Hanna!*' Careless always about addressing envelopes, some of the notes found their way back to him, and he sent them again as though they were something quite impersonal. Thus to W. C. Davison, a former Rhodes scholar, to whom they were devoted:

> This has been returned to-day. I suppose wrong address. All well, very busy. Americans are pouring thro. & we catch a glimpse of a few old friends. 250 here in flying corps. We have 30 each Sunday for tea. Love to the L. of your L. Yours, W. O.

There is no indication in this note of how they had gone out of their way to give a home to these young American aviators billeted in the villages around the Port Meadow. It is betrayed, however, in an earlier letter from Lady Osler which, in mentioning their arrival, says: 'I spoke to some of them in the street yesterday afternoon and they took me for a German spy, but finally six ventured to come back with me to tea.' So they picked up the threads of their life. 'We are taking the only medicine for sorrow—time & hard work', he wrote to one of his former assistants. He took an active interest in the unveiling on October 10th of the Roger Bacon tablet on the south face of the city wall—'as near as might be to the actual resting-place of the great philosopher.' On October 13th he sent off a reassuring letter to the *Lancet* on the subject of 'Home-bred Malaria', which was agitating the community not a little:

> . . . There are no grounds for alarm. A colony of patients from Salonika has fluttered the academic dove-cotes in Oxford where mosquitoes are prevalent—even anopheles have invaded the bed-room of the Regius Professor of Medicine! Every precaution has

been taken by Major Ormerod and Captain Dale, under the direction of Sir Ronald Ross, and, so far as I know, no infection has occurred. In temperate climates districts from which malaria has disappeared have not, to my knowledge, been re-infected. Italian labourers brought the disease to the New England States and there were a few cases but no serious outbreak; nor was the progressive fall in the incidence of malaria in Baltimore interrupted by the importation of many infected Italians. The slight risk, then, from our malarial soldiers in this country may be faced cheerfully. The same may be said of Canada, to which country many infected soldiers have returned. Parts of the Province of Ontario were hot-beds of the disease, which within my memory has disappeared from the districts about the western end of Lake Ontario and the northern shores of Lake Erie. The marshes are there and the anopheles are there, but the disease has gone. As in parts of Italy, the important factor appears to have been the cinchonizing of the inhabitants. I retain lively recollections of the buzzing ears of my boyhood from the large doses of quinine administered to us in the spring and autumn.

Then there were the usual obligations to the Bibliographical Society, to the Radcliffe Infirmary, to the Press, and to the Bodleian. On November 8th, after returning from the Annual Visitation, he made this note in the back of his Macray's 'Annals':

Bodley Speech & Perlustration. Always at 12 the Speech in Latin is delivered in Convocation House by one of the Students of Ch. Ch., one of the younger men. This year X, a classical tutor, who had once before delivered the address was the orator (Orātor Madan called him). The Dean was there & one outsider, & of the Curators, Wilson, Allen & myself. The V.-C., bedells, Registrar & Proctors came in at 12 sharp. The speech which is to be (see p. 105) 'in praise of Sir Thomas Bodley & as a panegyric & encouragement of Hebrew studies', was good in substance but I never heard such a delivery. . . . He dealt chiefly with the events of the year—the benefactions &c. & had the kindness to mention me in connection with the Bodleian Record. After the speech we all went to the Selden End for a meeting. The usual impression is that Bodley's Librarian is locked up for this meeting. We do meet without him at first & then one of the Curators fetches him. He gives an account of the losses of the year in books. This year he reported 32—Most of which are misplaced—none important. Then we perlustrate, visiting special portions of the Library selected by the Standing Committee. W. O.

Osler makes no mention of an incident, related by another

Christ Church Student, who describes it as 'typical of the inimitable combination of unfailing good humour and kindliness which made Sir William's frequent visits to the common room such a joy to his colleagues of the Governing Body of the House'. The Dean, hard put to it to lay his hand upon any younger man, for the Don population owing to the war was at a low ebb, bethought him of one who knew little of Bodley and nothing of the Hebrew tongue. The candidate, with misgivings, consented to fill the breach; consumed much midnight oil racking his brains for forgotten tags of Latin prose; and duly presented himself at the Divinity School, oration in hand. The story continues:

Almost the first individual there to meet his somewhat troubled gaze was the Regius Professor of Medicine, whose familiar figure was sure to be seen at any function where the interests of the Bodleian, of which he was a Curator, were concerned. Osler stepped across to him, as he walked up to the Orator's desk, and with a face as grave as a judge, thrust a paper into his hand saying: 'Look here, X, if you're hard up for something to say about Hebrew, this might be useful to you.' On reaching the desk there was just time to glance at the paper before the Vice-Chancellor and Proctors took their seats. It was covered with the calligraphy of the heathen Chinee, and was in fact a Chinese washing-bill.

He plunged into a proper revision of his Text-book, largely neglected during the war (cf. p. 522). He even accepted an invitation sent on October 21st from Gilbert Murray in behalf of the Council of the Classical Association that he should act as the alternate President in succession to Lord Bryce. Work enough for the days, though his nights were still ghastly. One may control one's emotion before others, but not when alone. His wife, whose own loss was wellnigh forgotten in sympathy for him, could hear him sobbing night after night, till overcome by a restless sleep. Though 'a shadow of his former self' he found solace in three things—in his avocational studies; in keeping young people about him; in his devotion to other peoples' little children:

We are busy as usual [he wrote to Dr. George Dock on November 17th], & greatly interested in so many Americans who are here. I am tied up with all sorts of Bibliographical affairs. My Catalogue of Incunabula to 1480 is under revision at the British Museum. I shall hope to have it out next year. I send you an Address on The Library School in connection with the College. Our historical section keeps up. I made a good haul at the Dunn sale a few weeks ago—ten Incunabula, among them the Ed. prin. of Averroes, which is excessively rare. I am sending you one of Revere's books with his book-plate drawn & etched by himself. It is a bit rough but he meant to do it more carefully later. Dear laddie! he loved his books dearly.

'With a hobby a man is reasonably secure against the whips and arrows of the most outrageous fortune'—an expression he used some months later, in a review of a volume which Parkes Weber had dedicated to him; but there were other things besides his hobby to engage him, things of which he made no mention to Dr. Dock, and for which one must turn to Lady Osler's letters. 'Sir William has pitched in hard at his Text-book revision, and is working at other things as well', she wrote. 'I could better bear this grief were it not to see him suffer; such a tragedy for the end of his wonderful life.' And on November 18th she wrote: 'Yesterday Sir William had all the American doctors working here,[1] fourteen in all, at luncheon at Christ Church; and then took them to the Bodleian where the Librarian showed all the treasures and W. O. gave them a talk on Radcliffe; a wonderful chance for them, and I am sure they appreciated it.' And again: 'We are going on

[1] These were 'casual' medical officers who had been sent over to work on the reconstruction of the wounded under General Sir Robert Jones, who had organized this important branch of work in the War Office. Captain Girdlestone was in general charge of the orthopaedic work in Oxford, and with him Major Erving and the other Americans collaborated. Osler was most enthusiastic about this reconstruction work, and wrote on 'The Problem of the Crippled' for Lord Charnwood's journal, *Recalled to Life*, which had just been started—a journal devoted 'to the dissemination of information as to the care, re-education and return to civil life of disabled soldiers and sailors'. Osler pointed out in his article that the mind as well as the body of the soldier long hospitalized needed re-training, and in his last paragraph says that there is still another side to the problem. 'Plato talks of a friend whose ill health had kept him out of the hurly-burly of public life to the great benefit of his mind. This "bridle of Theages", as he calls it, may have a real value. A physical burden bravely borne makes a strong man, whose moral force in a community is worth a score of mere men-machines.' So likewise a mental burden bravely borne.

as usual, with the flying men here on Sunday afternoons in groups of thirty. They are most amusing and so happy to be in a home. It is a struggle, but I feel we must keep at it. . . . We are so fortunate as to know two Oxford nurses at a casualty clearing station near Revere's grave. They have done everything, and write me constantly. It comforts a woman's heart.' On December 4th Osler wrote to the little grandson of Palmer Howard:

Dear Palmer, Revere was your godfather & loved you very much, so Aunt Grace & I are making you & Bruce share the small savings he left. We are so sad that he has been taken away from us in this cruel war. You will know more about him when you grow up. I am sure you will be like him, so good & kind. Your loving Doccie-O.

There had been a fire at Dundas which had burned down the old homestead of the Gwyns and with it many family records, including all of Osler's home letters carefully preserved by his mother. Of this he writes to his sister:

7.xii.17.

Dearest Chattie, What a blessing to burn down the old house! So you will say when you move into the new one & get it into good order. It must have been a bit of a heart-wrench all the same to see it go up in smoke. Grace will have kept you informed of the life here. We are very desolate at heart, but keeping up the old ways—as there are so many to help & make as happy as possible. She is splendid and has stood the trial so well. It is a great thing to be busy. 'Twill be a sad Xmas for us all with our laddies lost and gone. Your affectionate brother, Willie.

He did one of his kind acts on December 14th. The Library Association was giving a complimentary dinner to the President, J. Y. W. MacAlister, and nothing would satisfy the members but that Osler should preside. He did so, and probably few were aware of his heavy heart. In speaking of Sir John MacAlister he used again the 'man with the poker' illustration,[1] and MacAlister in response told of how Osler with his cheery optimism had put fresh heart in him at a time when he had despaired of success in his project regarding the Royal Society of Medicine—' so that without him that piece of work would

[1] *Library Association Record*, Feb. 15, 1918, xx. 49–51.

have ended in failure '. And Osler promptly followed up the dinner with a note saying : ' It was a great pleasure to have an opportunity of saying a few plain truths about you only I wish it had been before a medical audience. You have done a great work for us. I hope we shall see you tomorrow. Shall you be at the meeting ? '

Then the first vacant Christmas, and soon Revere's birthday—days demanding particular fortitude. On December 26th he wrote to Mrs. Brewster :

> Such an Xmas ! with desolation in our hearts, & as usual, the house full—a nephew, two wounded friends, Col. Futcher (of Johns Hopkins) & Mrs. Chapin. In the evening 14 American doctors who are stationed here in training at the Base Hospitals. We have had to ' carry on ' as usual, but it has been so hard, with our thoughts every moment on the dear laddie who has gone. Poor Grace ! I wonder how she stands the double life. I wish you could have seen those nice boys last night—it was such a pleasure to have them. We were allowed extra rations as they were American soldiers. . . . Sue Chapin is in charge of the American Red X distribution work in London & only comes for Saturday & Sunday. U. S. troops are pouring thro—the censor would not I fear allow me to say how many last week. We are always told by the station-master as the trains go thro. Oxford from Liverpool to Southampton. They will finish the war but dear me ! 'twill be a long business—but patience, courage & hope & all will be well. Is Uncle Ned's boy over yet ? Let us know as we like to get in touch with our friends in France & this house is a regular distribution depot for comforts.

It *was* a double life they were leading. ' Those nice boys last night—such a pleasure to have them.' One of them recalls that ' we were at the Oslers' our first Christmas night overseas, a great crowd of us ; and Sir William was very lively and entertaining '. But some one else wrote the next day : ' I don't see how Willie stood it. He looked like a ghost and I thought every minute he would break down and have to leave the table.'

CHAPTER XXXVIII

1918

KEEPING THE FLAG FLYING

He began the year bravely, and says in a letter to J. Y. W. MacAlister: 'I am hiding for two months trying to finish the revision of my text-book. 'Tis urgent & I am refusing everything but duty-calls so you must excuse me.' So in his letters to his friends, young and old, he sometimes managed not to mention Revere's name: thus on the 1st he wrote to his old colleague, James Tyson, whose malady was advancing and who was feeling his years:

Dear J. T. How is it with you? Best wishes for the New Year. We are keeping well & very busy; so many people coming & going, & always cases of interest at the Hospital. We have 14 nice American surgeons stationed here. They all dined with us on Xmas day. Gwyn is in charge of the Medical Dept of No 1 Can. Gen in France. Love to you all—ask Nell or Mellor to drop me a line, should you not feel up to writing. Ever yours. . . .

And a few days later to Captain Malloch at 'No. 3 Canadian', where Revere had been Assistant Quartermaster:

Dear Archie, That is a V. G. paper, well reported. More please of the same sort! Do get the Pneumonia work together. Why not get [Lawrence] Rhea to give us a joint paper for the Q. J. of Med. Say the April No. which is sure to be late. Can I send you any literature? Did you see that Typhoid spine case at Taplow—there for 10 months & at a V.A.D. Hospital for 8 months before—typical case? Yealland, a Toronto wizard at Queen Square, made him walk in ten minutes! A regular Lourdes miracle! [1] Catalogue goes well. Got Joule's papers this week. Must have a conser. of energy section, & Dalton's fine orig. papers! The Dunn sale brought the Ed. Prin. of Averroes—a gem. The Incunabula list is complete, & is being revised item by item at the B. M.[2] Pollard would not risk any

[1] This was the 'case of Sapper C——' which interested Osler greatly, as it supported his early views regarding the hysterical nature of many cases of so-called 'typhoid spine'. He gave a clinic on the case at No. 15 Canadian General Hospital on January 17th and subsequently reported it in the *Canadian Medical Association Journal* for June 1918, pp. 490–6.

[2] Cf. foot-note, p. 394, above.

mistake. The Harvey Group in B. prima is well, yum, yum! Love to Bill & the boys. Yours, W. O.

Osler had lost nearly two stone in weight since September, and had an ominous interest in the post-influenzal pneumonias on which his young friend was working. Even so, he could be spirited, and to Dr. Andrew Henderson of Powell River, B. C., an old school-friend, he wrote on receiving a photograph:

It was myself, Andy, that was glad to see that dear old mug of yours with the same old Rabelaisian smile, just ready for a joke as usual! Those were great old days at the M.G.H. Hell has broken loose now, but we shall hope for a new heaven & a new earth after the Germans have been smashed—which is going to take time & all Uncle Sam can do to help. We are hard hit—I forget whether you ever saw our boy. Poor laddie! I wish we could have gone in his stead. I have had a good innings. Love to you all. Ever your old friend [&c.].

Giving much of themselves as the Oslers did to the young people 'coming and going', it was inevitable that added sorrows should come to them during the nine months to follow. They had gone to town on the first Sunday of the year—the day appointed by the King as a day of National Prayer—to attend that memorable service at St. Paul's, but Osler could not trust himself there. He wrote to Mrs. Brewster:

Dear Mabel, Friday eve on my return from town I found the delightful Robin Hood volumes—such beauties! & the whole story so fascinating My mother used to repeat to us many of the very ones in this edition, which she had learnt as a child. And then the tears came, as I thought how the dear laddie would have loved them. He had become so interested in the old ballad literature & one of the last books he bought was an old edition of 'Percy's Reliques'. While I was turning the pages with delight Grace (who had been to town with me) uttered a cry of grief, as news had been sent from the aerodrome that young Ely of Rochester, N.Y. had been killed in the morning with a young Canadian. Ely was a Harvard man ('17) who had just come here for special training, & we have been seeing a great deal of him, as his father, the late Dr. Ely of Rochester, was an old friend of mine. The poor chap came last Sunday for lunch, & as he had a day off we kept him & he did not leave until ten o'clock. Such a charming fellow. An hour ago young Kissel from N.Y. whom perhaps you know, called up from the aerodrome. He had flown over from Salisbury Plain to spend the night with Ely—his college chum—of whose death he had not heard! Such a tragedy. We shall keep the poor fellow for a couple of days, as he is completely knocked out. Our hearts just ache for these dear lads, so far from home. Do let us know of any in whom you may be interested. Love to the darlings all. . . .

P.S. At the big service at the Cathedral this p.m. Grace says the Bishop read as part of the sermon Lincoln's Gettysburg speech. It is wonderful what an inspiration Father Abraham is! He brings courage & endurance.

A chapter could be devoted to the story of these two young boys alone—William Ely and his chum, Gustav Kissel—and their relation to the 'Open Arms'. Kissel stayed for the 'couple of days', got his balance, was sent to France and was shortly afterwards killed in his turn. On January 11th Osler wrote to Henry M. Hurd, who had been prodding him to make a contribution to the history of the Johns Hopkins Medical School:

Thanks for your letter of Dec. 4th. I will get on with the story of the Medical Clinic. Mall's death is a terrible loss. Now comes the sad news that Janeway has gone.[1] This will hit the School very hard. I suppose Mrs. Mall will have a good Carnegie pension. Are the plans for your library yet out? I should like very much to see them. I send you a Library School address. I have become very much interested as you will see in this question of Library training. It sadly needs developing here. If there is any preliminary programme of the School of Preventive Medicine please send it. They are starting a National School of Medicine in Wales at Cardiff, & a lady has just given £30,000 to endow a Chair of Preventive Medicine, one of the conditions being that I name the Committee to appoint the Professor. All goes well here; we are very busy, a great many people coming & going all the time. . . .

On the 14th he wrote to Dr. F. C. Shattuck:

. . . All goes well except for the aching heart. Americans are pouring thro. Every week brings in someone who has just landed. The Am. Orthopaedic Surgeons here are first class, 14 of them. I have not heard a word lately from George. I hope if he gets leave he will come to us. Love to Geo. B. [P.S.] Drop in at Goodspeeds & jog his memory about the Bost. Med & Surg Jr. *Vol. 35* which has

[1] See the *Lancet*, Lond., Jan. 12, 1918, i, 80, for Osler's obituary of Theodore C. Janeway, and the issue of Dec. 1st, 1917, for his tribute to Franklin P. Mall.

the ether papers & I want BADLY Morton's original papers. Love to you all.

Written statements to show the multifarious duties which kept him occupied are few. A postcard of the 21st to Sir D'Arcy Power indicates that he had missed a meeting the week before: 'I was very sorry not to hear your paper on Wed.—but I had to be in town M. & T. & a third day was too much. I shall read it with interest. Thanks for Ward—more please.' He does not say that 'M. & T.' had been of themselves too much, but this appears in a note the same day to Adami, with whom he was shortly to go to the Canadian Club luncheon: 'I have asked Armour and Colmer to look after you next week as I am abed with the flu, not bad, but I shall not be out for a few days. So sorry. Tell Sister Radcliffiana [Adami's daughter] to let us know when she returns.'

He appears to have taken to bed with him an unusual book, the 'Essai de Bibliographie Hippique' by General Mennessier de la Lance, the last volume of which had recently been published. How he learned of these volumes does not appear—possibly the Bibliography part of the title drew them into his net—it could hardly have been the Horse—he does not appear to have ridden one since the day in Dundas when he 'got the sack'. But the books went to his heart. The retired French General had succeeded in doing for the literature of his subject precisely what Osler hoped to do with his own library. And his review of the volume, which begins as follows, was written with his old zest:

Not naturally dry, bibliography is too often made so by faulty treatment. What more arid than long lists of titles, as dreary as the genealogies of the Old Testament, or as the catalogue of the ships in Homer! What more fascinating, on the other hand, than the story of the book as part of the life of the man who wrote it—the bio-bibliography! Such, for example, is the recent bibliography of Samuel Johnson, issued by the Oxford Press, from the pen of that master of the subject, the late William Prideaux Courtney, which shows us, even better than does Boswell, the working ways of the great lexicographer. To be of value to the full-fed student of to-day a bibliography should be a *Catalogue raisonné*, with judicious remarks and explanations. In our great libraries this is impossible from lack of space, but the plan is followed with great advantage in the special bibliographies, of which the work before us is a model of its kind. . . .

He goes on to tell how he had put the volumes to the test, all of which indicates with what delight he had gone through them, doubtless with his own bibliographical project in mind; and after commenting on the high plane of veterinary science across the Channel, he ends thus:

Students of the horse in all its relations owe a deep debt of gratitude to General Mennessier de la Lance for this comprehensive and valuable work, so full of accurate and careful scholarship. As a former teacher in a Veterinary College I may be permitted to offer him on behalf of the profession in Great Britain our congratulations on its completion, and our heartfelt wishes that he may be spared to see final victory crown the Army of which he has been so distinguished a member.

It is curious how at these times when housed with an illness he delighted to tell, with variants, to the young people who were about, the stories of his boyhood—how he was expelled from school—how they smoked out the 'old girl' at Weston—how he killed the pig. No sorrow should be allowed to show itself before them, and there was always something of interest for their entertainment, like the pomander-cane which had just come, purchased from two needy old ladies in Maida Vale, in whose family it had been for 150 years. One could still get a whiff of the aromatic 'four thieves' vinegar which once filled the receptacle at the top.[1] And when 'Ned' Milburn's daughter, a Canadian nursing sister, came, the old stories of 'Barrie's Bad Boys' were revived. Thus 13 Norham Gardens tried to forget the war—a difficult task with the messages which came in—just now one from No. 3 Canadian General telling that poor 'Jack' McCrae was no more. 'To you from failing hands we throw the torch; be yours to hold it high.'

So the house was kept filled with young people, if for no other reason than that they did not yet dare to let themselves be alone. To the Canadians, friends from the United States were now being added in increasing numbers, many of whom came through England on their way to the A.E.F.

[1] The cane was handed on to the collection at the College of Physicians of Philadelphia.

'Where are the dear boys?' was his frequent message to American parents. 'Do tell them to come here as to their home if they get a chance.' On February 22nd he wrote to W. S. Thayer:

> . . . We are keeping well and very busy. It is very hard to get time for any continuous work—there are so many calls one way & another. I have been in London four days this week—meetings & committees & sick Canadians. I am so tired of sepsis & of chest wounds, & glossy nerve hands & feet. They will be glad to see you at G.H.Q. Give my love to Bradley. Let us know of anything you want—for yourself or the men with you. . . . Do let us have a line as to your movements. . . .

The library was growing meanwhile. Most of the early anaesthesia papers had finally been secured for the Bibliotheca Prima which he felt was nearly complete, and he was working on the less important but no less interesting sections—the Bibliotheca Litteraria, &c. Thus on February 28th to Sarah Orne Jewett's sister:

> Only this week I have read the 'Country Doctor' which you so kindly sent & am perfectly charmed with the very true & sympathetic account of a man of the highest type in the profession. As I told you I am collecting for my library the books which give an account of the social & literary side of professional life. I hope to publish a catalogue of my collection. Under the 'Country Doctor' could I state that this was a picture drawn from your Father's life & work? If so will you please send me the date of his birth, his graduation, where he practised & date of death. . . .

Osler left some fragmentary notes on 'The Doctor in the English Novel', evidently intended for the cards of the Bibliotheca. One of them relates to Miss Jewett's novel:

> It is a sketch of her father—a good and helpful story, for Dr. Leslie is a man who had had the Jacksons, Bigelows, the Shattucks & Bowditches as teachers and friends. It is Jacob Bigelow who really speaks: 'We must look to the living to learn the laws of life, not to the dead. A wreck shows you where the reef is perhaps, but not how to manage a ship in the offing' (p. 109). No pleasanter picture of the woman medical student exists than Nan, who at last married George I am sure. The ending as it is is most untrue to life.

In a letter to C. D. Parfitt of March 3rd he said: 'A three months "cure" in Muskoka would renew my youth. We have a deuce of a life here—so much on hand always and so many coming & going. I never seem to get time for any work.' The reason is apparent: for one of the several week-end sojourners on this very day supplies a fragment from a diary which says:

'Open Arms' full as usual. Among others Col. Sir James Fowler who has just come and quickly gets into mufti. Also an uncouth Canadian signaller who has been convalescing from a wound here for two weeks and who happens merely to be the nephew of a Canadian nurse once at the J.H.H. Many drop in for tea, and afterwards Charles Singer of the Science Room whose book is just out; then a shriveled Prof. of Spanish with some rare incunabula under his arm concerning which he wants information. Sir William though a shadow of his former self sails through these interruptions as though they were the very things he cordially longed for. But anyone can see that his desk is piled high with unopened and unanswered letters—still no secretary, and there are books and papers everywhere. We slipped away at six and he made a round of visits on people with children—his many darlings who find things in his pockets and cuddle about him while he tells another chapter of some imaginary tale before they go to bed—all over in ten minutes and he flits to the next, where there is the sound of a desperate pillow-fight and great hilarity at the head of the stairs.

Supper, and a quiet evening over books. Thomas Bodley and his 16-page autobiography one of the best ever written; and W. O. tells how Bodley got his friends to bring books, and they in turn told their friends who might be visiting Oxford to carry an armful: since many of these visitors were prelates they pilfered the church stores of MSS. and so to-day the Bodleian holds rare treasures from Exeter and Cairo and other places—really stolen treasures which these other libraries have moved heaven and earth to get back. In spite of the war the Bodleian seems to occupy much of his time and thought. Indeed just now he with the Librarian and Mr. Pollard of the British Museum is engaged in preparing a list of English books printed between 1501 and 1640. . . .

There was much else; but finally at ten, as of old, he goes to bed, which gives an opportunity to copy from its card, as a sample, the note he had just written regarding a recent acquisition—the 1482 folio of AVERROES. . . . Also, as another sample, this gem among his notes on incunabula:

'Thanks to these illuminating researches [of Diepgen and of Fincke] the heretofore somewhat shadowy personality of Arnold of Villanova now stands out in relief as one of the strongest characters in a decadent age and one of the most notable figures in our history. While alive few physicians have been so honoured, few when dead have been so traduced. The friend, counsellor and ambassador of kings, the physician and intimate of popes, a great teacher at the greatest medical school of the period (Montpellier), a prolific writer, he appeals to us rather, now that the full story of his life is known, as a *vir ardentis ingenii*, whose passion was to reform the Church and society. Fearless to indiscretion, he was a preacher of righteousness to a perverse generation, and a denouncer of judgement to come. A scene on the 26th October, 1309, fires the imagination, when the now ageing physician before a conclave of Clement V and his cardinals at Avignon denounced the abuses of the Church, and appealed for a restoration of evangelical Christianity. It recalls a yet more famous occasion fifty years earlier before another Avignon Pope when the great clerk of Lincoln, Robert Grosseteste, made a passionate appeal for personal holiness in the clergy, and for political honesty in the Curia. Truly, in all ages, of such as Grosseteste and Villanova has been the Kingdom of Heaven. Zeal for reform and devotion to mystic theology brought no peace to Arnold, and the sleuth-hounds of the Inquisition were only held in leash by his powerful friends. Once dead they wreaked vengeance on his writings, and sent his memory down the ages tainted with accusations of heresy and magic.'

While I was copying these notes he came in, in dressing-gown and slippers, and placing beside me a small vellum-bound book went out without a word. I could hear him sobbing as he went back up the stairs. It contained the list of Revere's book purchases, with the dates and occasions. It had such entries at this: 'I sent the bid for this from Mouquet Farm on the Somme, *Dec. 6th, '16*. Poems on Several Occasions; Chas Cotton, Lond. 1689, 1st ed. Sotheby £3–12–6.' The last note was one of those made during his leave: '*May 14, 1917*. Dobell's Meditations on the four last things, Death, Judgment, Heaven, Hell, 4th ed^{n}. £2–2–0.'

In a letter of March 16th to Archibald Malloch he says: 'So sorry you are having a slow time lately. I have been on the jump—two days at Cardiff straightening out the Talbot Chair [Department of Hygiene] affairs.' Things doubtless appeared 'slow' in the Boulogne hospitals during early March, but they were not so for long. The Germans were massing troops for their supreme effort—an effort which made it look for a time after March 21st as though even Boulogne might have to be evacuated lest its camps and hospitals, No. 3 Canadian General included, be pushed into the sea.

Mr. Wilson's manifesto of January 8th with its 'fourteen points' had served to drive a wedge between Prussianism and the German people, among whom there were strikes and discontent. To counteract all this, Ludendorff, as the eastern front was no more, made his last throw with the intent to separate the French and British in the west —and so nearly successful was it that Sir Douglas Haig, not given to emotional speech, told his army a short four weeks later that they had their backs to the wall and must fight to the end. These were dark days for England. Fortunately, Osler had other things to think of. 'I have been bedevilled to death lately [he writes on the 25th]. Charlie Bath had a smash at Winchester, forehead knocked in and very bad. Then John Archibald has had pneumonia and I have been up every day since Thursday. Both lungs involved but he is recovering.'

On the 31st he wrote to Dr. Shepherd:

I did not answer your cable as I was unable to contribute at the time. The Income tax had just been paid & had left my bank account very low. You have done splendidly & it will put the old M.G.H. in good form. The Carnegie gift to the College will be a great help. We are keeping well & doing what we can. I have to be away a great deal—meetings & war cases & odd jobs. The Library grows & I am getting the Catalogue in good order; but my secretary is away & I have only a woman & an extra from the Bodleian. I wish you could see my divisions & arrangements. I dare say Birkett will tell you about it, as he was much interested. Now that Revere is gone I shall be able to leave the College some money for its up-keep. Love to the girls. I am glad E. is still at Bramshot—out of this present battle.

He gives no sign that he has been ailing and depressed, though this is apparent from one of Lady Osler's letters:

. . . Sir William is thinner than ever but very brown as he spent two days last week on the roof outside my door. . . . I have taken rooms at Sidmouth in Devon from April 24th for three weeks and hope to keep him there and out of doors. The conditions in France have depressed him dreadfully and I think he has been very pessimistic. We talk quite freely of visits from the Müllers and Ewalds, should the Huns reach England. I daresay he would welcome them kindly—Saint that he is.[1] We had an awful week or ten days with

[1] It may be mentioned that when Revere's kit, forwarded by the Padre at the C.C.S., finally reached home there were found in his wallet together with his father's twenty-first birthday letter, notes addressed to Professor Müller and others to be mailed to them in Germany, in case the boy should be taken prisoner!

so many near friends ill and injured, and ending by his getting a cold. He went at once to bed with aspirin and a lemonade with hot whiskey, —the first I ever knew him to take, and we headed it off.

Nothing of this appears in Osler's own notes written on the same day. 'We keep much the same here, with a house full all the time, so many coming and going we have not (fortunately) much time to think.' And to another: 'Do come should you return via England—any day will suit us as we have an indiarubber house, but bring your meat ticket.' And to Malloch on April 4th: 'All well—very busy—much bedevilled by many things as usual. Love to Bill—and the Kaiser should he reach Boulogne.'

On April 11th he wrote to C. P. Howard that 'all goes well here—except for the gnawing sorrow in our hearts for the dear laddie. We are distributing Revere's small savings & I will send a cheque for $500 Bk. of Montreal for Palmer. Invest it for him please.' And on the 17th again to Malloch:

Thanks for Cabanès but you should have opened the parcel & cut the leaves. The illustrations are A.1. Sir D. MacAlister, Principal of Glasgow University was here last week end, & picked up your book, with which he was delighted—one of the most interesting stories he had read for years. He was much gratified to hear of your Glasgow affiliations. Have you heard anything of the Occupation paper? All here much disturbed by the news, but all will come out on the right side I am sure. It is disheartening, of course. Catalogue is booming—the anaesthesia section doing well, & will be A.A.1. I am picking out a lot of Revere's books for you & Bill. Call on Phoebe [Wright] & ask her if she will please be married from the 'Open Arms'?

As promised, they left on April 24th for a period of quiet at Sidmouth, though repose just now, physical or mental, was difficult. Things were at their worst in France, but England, in spite of her war-weariness, rose to the emergency. 'Never so dangerous as when heart-sick of a business', as John Buchan says, she raised the limit of military age to fifty, gave the Government power to set aside the ordinary exemptions, and extended conscription to Ireland. As a result nearly half a million men, many of them with more than one wound-stripe on their sleeves, were poured into France. But the Irish held back, forfeiting thereby the esteem of the world. The Roman hierarchy in Ireland made a false step by openly assuming the right to interfere as a Church in politics; and Osler must have been so moved by the articles on the subject in the morning papers, that on reaching town he sent from the Athenaeum to *The Times* a letter entitled 'The Curse of Meroz':

Sir,—In Ireland the kinetic drive, to use an expression of the physiologists, is dual—Rome and America. Rome has spoken; now let America speak. Possibly the solution of the problem is with her. Let Cardinal Gibbons and the strong Irish Catholics in the United States and Canada convince their brethren at home that two things are vital—to abjure publicly the dream of an Irish Republic, and to join heartily in the prosecution of the war. Then she may win for herself an enduring peace—the peace she can never have with a perennial Home Rule trouble in Ulster; a peace she will not get, much less deserve, with the curse of Meroz on the land, the curse with which the English-speaking world will curse her bitterly because in the hour of trial she 'came not to the help of the Lord, to the help of the Lord against the mighty'.

He must have been very much keyed up, for this brief note was apparently boiled down from a long 'Appeal to Hibernia Magna' found among his papers, and which, as likely as not, he had written on the way to town. With it is the rough draft of a letter to Cardinal Gibbons, which reads:

Dear Cardinal, Claiming the privilege of an old friend, & for many years your next-door neighbour, may I address you an open letter on a subject that I know you have at heart—an Irish settlement. We have lived long enough to see what seemed a desperate Irish problem solved. In my boyhood in Canada there were two red-letter days—March 17th & July 12th. We were sure of a holiday & a good row between Orange & Green. Time & prosperity have brought a settlement. Where is the Griffin-town that I knew so well in the 70ties in Montreal—filled with the families of the Irish emigrants, many of whom were my earliest patients? Already the intelligence & industry of the children have made comfortable homes for the old people. They have long ago left Griffin-town & are in the best quarters of the city & the suburbs. This is what has happened all over the continent & with it peace—a row anywhere on St. Patrick's Day or on the 12th July is impossible. Time & prosperity which have wiped out the animosities of 200 years in the New World, may be trusted to do the same in Ireland itself. To one basic consideration I wish to urge your earnest attention for no man in the

United States wields the same personal influence as your Eminence. It is this—that the settlement no longer rests with England—nor is it with Ireland, but it is with Hibernia Magna, with the Irish in the United States. They control the situation. It is not so much now that they pay the piper & call the tune, but the moral force is the telling leverage today. The main truth is that the Irish in the United States demand an independent republic. Grt. Britain could no more tolerate a hostile republic at her doors than would the United States tolerate a hostile kingdom in Texas & [illegible] in Canada or in Cuba. It would mean the break up of an empire the strength of which is the most important single ally of the United States in the maintenance of a threatened civilization. . . . Please throw the weight of your strong influence in favour of a direct repudiation by Irishmen of an Irish republic as an essential preliminary to any enduring settlement, etc.

Here the scribble tails off; and in all probability it was never sent; but it shows at least his momentary impulse. Later in the day, from the Victoria Hotel, Sidmouth, he wrote to Malloch:

Your letter was here on our arrival. So sorry to hear that Bill is laid up. I hope it is nothing serious & that he can get a bit of leave. This would be a glorious place for him, beautiful sea & coast. We have been very busy—same rush at the house. Yesterday four men & Ronald Ross for lunch & a nice fellow from St. Louis. I shall be glad of a rest & change. We finished the anaesthesia section as far as possible, last week. I think it will be A.A.1. & give a most interesting picture of the evolution of the whole business. I still lack one or two important items but they will turn up. We intend to keep Revere's books together & my general literature books—the Miltons, Shelleys &c—will go with them. Later I will talk to you & Bill of the plans. [D.] MacAlister has sent me two big bundles of reprints &c, many of which are duplicates & I will keep them for you. He was very much interested in my grouping &c of the library. I have to do a lot of reading for the Presidential Address of the Classical Association! Every other year an outside man is chosen—not a classical scholar, & Morley, Asquith, Balfour, Bryce have been recent ones. I am the first Doctor, so I take it as a compliment, but a bit of a burden. I shall talk on 'The classical Tradition in Science'. I am deep in a Post-graduate scheme—& am chairman of the committee of the London Schools which has the matter in hand. Yours, W. O.

The post-graduate scheme to which he refers had for some months occupied his attention. Whatever might be the outcome of the war, it behoved those of his profession to look forward to better days for medicine and medical teaching in England. Early in the year he had written to J. Y. W. MacAlister:

> Yes, a small Executive to arrange for the representative meeting, with a definite programme. As a matter of policy, should we not ask Fisher to preside? I think we should. The profession must get over this infantile dread of Govt. interference & this scheme must be on an imperial basis. Think over the strong, young men for the Executive.

So at this time he had prepared an elaborate report on Post-graduate Medical Education, and it was suggested that the Dominion authorities co-operate with the American University Union, of which Professor J. W. Cunliffe was the London representative, in establishing a bureau for graduate students coming to England, similar to the information depot which had had much to do with the pre-war position which Vienna had enjoyed as a great medical teaching centre. On April 25th he wrote to Adami:

> No reason why you should not mention it, but do not show the circular as it is not to be made public until after the Schools have reported. The Association will be a Bureau & a home for all p.g. students. Should we fail to get the schools united we can run our own Bureau, & bring the schools to our terms. Cunliffe was with us last Sunday. We have a half promise of active financial aid if the London schools will unite. . . .[1]

While at Sidmouth he became engrossed in W. F. Smith's newly published 'Rabelais in his Writings', and sent off for the *Lancet*[2] a most appreciative review—'we have now the real Rabelais, freed from legend, prejudice, and misrepresentation'. This was a pleasant diversion from which he was aroused by some expressions of pessimism from America which moved him to profanity, as rare in his letters as in his speech. On May 5th he wrote to Dr. George Dock:

> Such a nice letter from Geo. Jr. came in the same mail with yours.

[1] The inaugural meeting of the future Fellowship of Medicine was held July 18, 1918, and was presided over by Lord Eustace Percy.

[2] May 4, 1918, i. 644 (unsigned). It led to an interesting correspondence with the author in an effort to get him to read a paper on Rabelais before the Historical Section of the R. S. M., which later he did.

He seems in the thick of it. I have written urging him to try & come to us for a rest & change, if possible. The strain is very heavy on these young fellows. I am afraid we are in for a long business. Germany is far from defeat & the U. S. will have to give the knockout blow. It is wonderful what she has done already. Tell the damned pessimists to shut up. I am ashamed to meet them—there are a few here who growl that enough has not been done.

I am struggling with a catalogue raisonné & find it interesting but slow. My sec. is away but I have a meticulous vestal who does very well & a Bodley girl comes from 4–7 to help. I have the books all grouped I, Bibl. prima; II, B. secunda; III, B. litteraria; IV, B. historica; V, B. biographica; VI, B. bibliographica; VII, Incunabula; VIII, MSS. The literary section will be the most interesting—poets, novels, plays, works, by Doctors, or in which the profession is portrayed. Do you know of any good novels in which the Doctor of the West or South figures? The N. E. ones are easy to get. . . .[1]

On the same day to H. B. Jacobs:

I cabled you, or will tomorrow—I have bought the Jenner [portrait] for you, if after inspection on the 15th it seems all right. The price seems a bit suspicious—very low for the original. The photo. which I enclose looks attractive. I hope it turns out a find! Have you got the big Huxley bronze—as large as the Virchow? If not, I should like to give you my copy for your collection; you could have it at any time. What are you doing with your Jenner items? I have as you perhaps remember, the minutes, largely in Jenner's hand of the Glou. Med. Soc. 1789–95. I doubt whether it should leave the country, but the R.C.S. and the R.C.P. have been so slack in collecting, that neither deserves it. . . . This is a lovely spot [Sidmouth]—Far from the Kaiser & Rhondda.

Far enough from the Kaiser and the Food Controller to permit him to think of other things, and when on May 9th in the morning paper he came across the figures giving the returns of the last examination for the Fellowship of the Royal College of Surgeons, he promptly wrote this open letter to Sir George Makins, registering a further protest

[1] 'Dr. Thorne in Anthony Trollope's novel of this name [wrote Osler in one of his many annotations at this time] sketches incidentally the transition in the English profession from the apothecary to the general practitioner. Though a graduate physician and entitled to call himself *doctor*, he compounded his own medicines "putting together common powders for rural bowels, or spreading vulgar ointments for agricultural ailments." . . . I love Dr. Thorne for his theory as to the happiness of children for he argued that the principal duty which a parent owed to a child was to make him happy. Wise man!'

against an abominable system he never failed to attack when he reasonably could:

Dear Mr. President,—All who have at heart the interests of medical students must have been gratified to see in this morning's *Times* the continued (increasing?) high percentage of rejections—82! But must we wait for a total rejection before the College realizes the rottenness of the present system? System it must be, dear Makins; for are not the teachers, who fail so ingloriously, among the best of your Fellows (in anatomy at any rate); are not the examiners, who are so successful, picked men of the same class; and the unhappy victims—well, it seems ridiculous to say so—but are they not our very best students? For results, see *The Times*, 27 rejections out of 34!

In your skill and judgement the profession has unusual confidence. Induce the College to relieve an intolerable situation. Abolish a system which is a reproach alike to teachers and examiners, and worst of all a cruel perversion of mental values to the student at the very time of life when such values count. The alternative? Back to John Hunter:

1. Do away with the necessity for Fellowship classes.

2. Make the candidates spend the time (now wasted in cramming) in the laboratories and hospitals.

3. Let them come to the Examiners' Board with proofs of personal study and research in anatomy *or* physiology for the Primary—and, may I add, in pathology *or* surgery for the Final. . . .

A day later the following letter was received, and answered:

To W. O. from J. Y. W. MacAlister. The Royal Society of Medicine, May 8, 1918.

My dear Osler,—Once before you were offered and refused the Presidency of the Royal Society of Medicine—an unprecedented snub to the premier medical body of the Kingdom—and now I ask you unofficially and confidentially once more whether you will accept nomination, and I say to you quite seriously and solemnly that in the present crisis it is your duty to accept it, for from now on there are great things expected of, and to be done by the Society provided a man of light and leading is at its head, and you are the man to do it! It is the more important in view of the position you have taken up with the Post-graduate Scheme. So please let me have a line or a telegram saying you accept. Yours sincerely, J. Y. W. MacAlister. I shall turn my face to the wall if you say 'No' for it is going to be my last lap.

To J. Y. W. MacAlister from W. O. The Victoria Hotel, Sidmouth, 10.v.18.

Dear MacAlister, I am more sorry than I can say; as I hate to refuse you anything; but it is impossible. On the previous occasion the *snub* as you call it, was certainly not meant as such. I regarded the offer as a great honour Sincerely yours, Wm Osler.

Osler preferred lesser rôles in the R. S. M.,[1] such as that of contributor to the programme of the Historical Section, of which Dr. Raymond Crawfurd was now President. And on May 15th on his return from Sidmouth he gave before the section a paper on 'The First Printed Documents Relating to Modern Surgical Anaesthesia':

The story of surgical anaesthesia illustrates how long it takes an idea to become effective. [So his paper began.] The idea of producing insensibility to pain during a cutting operation is of great antiquity—e.g. *vide* Chapter ii, 21, in the Book of Genesis. Nor is the word anaesthesia modern, as is sometimes said, and invented by Oliver Wendell Holmes. It occurs, Withington tells me, first in Plato ('Timaeus'), and is used by Dioscorides in the modern sense. The extraordinary controversy which has raged, and re-raged every few years, on the question to whom the world is indebted for the introduction of anaesthesia, illustrates the absence of true historical perspective, and a failure to realize just what priority means in the case of a great discovery.

From this he proceeded to show that 'in science the credit goes to the man who convinces the world, not to the man to whom the idea first occurs'—'Morton convinced the world; the credit is his.' And he went on to tell in considerable detail how in his own library he had classified in the Bibliotheca Prima the papers relating to anaesthesia; and since he now had duplicates of some of them he closed the address by saying: 'You remember the rings of Lucretius—well, there is a *vis et vincula librorum*, binding together books, a force just as potent as the *vis et vincula lapidis* which supported the rings; and in the literature of anaesthesia this force is derived from the works here presented to the Library [of the Royal Society of Medicine].'

Back in Oxford the next day, he wrote to H. B. Jacobs:

The Shelley Letters have just come—many thanks for remembering my collection. Dear Isaac was so interested in it & had become such a keen student of S. The Everyman's Library copy of the Poems he carried everywhere. He would have loved this book. I hope to

---

[1] As well as in other societies. A few months before he had been urged, curiously enough, to accept the presidency of the old Medical Society of London, the ancient rival of the society which had grown into the R. S. M.

keep all his books together—for a purpose. His last leave was spent arranging them & his accession book is most interesting—the pen-drawing of the title-page is his own design. The catalogue, & the books he would have loved bring his loss home to our hearts every hour.

Plans for a foundation similar to that of the Elizabethan Club at Yale, to include Revere's collection and the non-medical portion of his own, were evidently formulating in his mind, and in letters to his intimates he frequently alludes to this as well as to another project—'We are making this house freehold, and I am arranging to leave it to Christ Church as a permanent home for my successors.' Such things must always be when a man is confronted with the extinction of his line. But before he could really devote himself to the rounding out of Revere's collection there was still much to do in perfecting his own, if it was to be handed on as he would have it. 'I am involved in a terrible job—this catalogue raisonné', he confessed to F. H. Garrison. 'It is not easy to get everything, & harder to know enough. I wish you could be here for a few weeks to have your brain tapped.'[1]

He participated on May 29th in the second of an important series of meetings held at the Royal Society of Medicine to consider 'the future of the Medical Profession under a Ministry of National Health'. His address, which must have been largely impromptu, sounds more like his natural self than any of his public utterances for a good many months—vigorous, telling; and, as quoted,[2] it was lightened by touches of his customary humour. In speaking of 'Research and the State', he said:

Not even the brilliant work in preventive medicine of Sir John Simon and his colleagues and successors has been able to overcome in certain quarters an invincible prejudice against State aid. It is an academic obsession, peculiarly insular and Anglican. There are those present who will remember the virulent outburst at a meeting of the governing body of the Lister Institute, when it was proposed to wed that somewhat sedate vestal to the [Medical] Research Com-

---

[1] Apparently at this time he had outlined the draft of the Introduction to the Catalogue which he hoped he might live to see published. The manuscript drafts are in existence, from the earlier of which some paragraphs have been taken.

[2] *Lancet*, Lond., June 8, 1918, i, 804.

mittee. The unholy proposal was rejected by an enormous majority. There are no grounds whatever for this distrust. . . . Cut out Lister's work, and in the field of infections practically all the first-hand discoveries made in this country have been by men in official harness, such as Griffith Evans, Manson, Ross, Bruce, Leishman and others. The debt of the profession is one-hundred-fold greater to the Local Government Board for its researches in preventive medicine than to all our universities combined. The mouths of all carpers have been closed by the series of splendid monographs issued during the war by the [Medical] Research Committee. It illustrates what can be done by a group of men with a good organization and an effective executive. That in these days of tribulation Sir Walter Fletcher and his colleagues have been able to accomplish so much is a source of genuine pride. What a rich store of merit they have acquired for the fresh fields and pastures new as a department of a Ministry of Health! . . . A strong Ministry of Health backed by a united profession, could initiate important reforms which seem at present hopeless. The reconstruction of our medical schools, the destruction, preliminary to re-arrangement, of the curriculum, the establishment in our hospitals of up-to-date cliniques, a degree for London students, the abolition of the super-tax on British students by unnecessary examinations—some at least of these reforms a strong central organization could force through the blind opposition of vested interests. These are post-bellum problems for the young men, who will meet them with a new knowledge and with courage and confidence. It will be a pleasure for the seniors to stand by and see fair play between them and the public, as represented by the authorities. Metabolism does not necessarily mean progress, and in the body-politic it is not always easy to distinguish *kata* from *ana*. A full and free discussion, such as Major Dill's paper will bring out, should be most helpful, if it does nothing but quiet that large and important group whom the fear of change perplexes and appals.

On June 27th he wrote again to Garrison:

In D. N. B. vol. xxxix, p. 107, is an account of Chas Morrison, a Surgeon of Greenock, who is described as the first projector of the Electric Telegraph. I have just got the Scots Magazine, 1753, with his account which is certainly remarkable. M. is said to have gone to Virginia, where he died. Prosser, who wrote the life in D. N. B. 1894, states that there is nothing about him in the publications of the Historical Soc. of Virginia. Do you happen to have anything about him in the S. G. L.? Ask one of the men to turn up the cards. There is nothing in the Index Cat. Singer is back from Salonika & with his wife has all sorts of schemes on hand—the biggest, the catalogue of all English scientific MSS. They are deep in Anglo-Saxon medicine.

All goes well—and will go better—with time & patience. America has done nobly. We are so proud to see the nice boys who are in evidence now so much—many old friends & students. I was at a splendid camp at Winchester last week. Greetings to McC & all old friends. . . .

And the next day, June 28th, to J. George Adami:

Those etchings are gems, and are safely in Bright's Travels, a presentation copy of which I have, with an autograph letter. I have written to Matthews. Sorry not to have sent the lecture—I have not had a moment to look it over—examiners here all week. Two treasures recently for Bibl. prima—Copernicus De Revol. Orb. celest. 1543, & the Ed. Prin. of Plato—Aldine 1513. P. comes in as the founder of psychology. We marry Phoebe Wright tomorrow (Latin Chapel of the Cathedral) to Reginald Fitz—our old friend's son.

So they did—a military wedding—and there was a gay reception and tea subsequently on the terrace at the 'Open Arms'; and no one would for a moment have surmised that the hosts were anything but the most light-hearted of people. From others was concealed the sorrow that weighed them down. That they should have arranged for this wedding at Christ Church for an American officer and the daughter of an old Canadian friend, both of whom were serving in France, was not only characteristic of the Oslers but it is expressive of the warmth of feeling which England as a whole felt towards America, whose Independence Day was illogically celebrated throughout Britain a few days later as a popular festival.

Thus the Bibliotheca Osleriana did not engage his attention to the exclusion of other things. One illustration may be given to show another and familiar side of his character. The first cases of encephalitis lethargica (subsequently, in common parlance, known as sleeping-sickness) were beginning to be recognized—a malady with such protean features that Osler said there were '57 varieties'—as many as pickles. He was wrong in the first impression of the nature of the disorder, but this is unimportant. A. Salusbury MacNalty of the Ministry of Health supplies this account:

In the early part of 1918, I was engaged in an investigation of this obscure disease and I early sought Sir William's counsel and advice on the subject. He was at first inclined to regard the cases as examples of Heine-Medin disease or as cerebral types of poliomyelitis. He took an indefatigable and keen interest in the progress of the investigation; this was not merely academic or 'arm-chair study' but personal and active, as his letters indicate:

11.vi.18.

Dear MacN. Where in London are most of the polio cases? We have one in the Radcliffe, very remarkable & possibly another. I was in Leicester last week where they have 5 or 6. I shall be up Friday & Monday. Yours, Wm OSLER.

I arranged to take Sir William to the London Hospital where a good many cases of the new disease were domiciled.

14.vi.18.

Dear Mac I will call for you at 12 on Monday. We could have a bite of lunch & then go to the London or anywhere else. I could not get you this a.m. but I hope you had my telephone message. You might like to have my Heine-Medin literature—a fine big bundle—I lecture on the subject Tuesday. Yours, Wm OSLER.

That was a wonderful day for me. Imagine how illuminating for a worker at an apparently unknown disease to have the personal counsel and advice of one of the greatest physicians of all time. Sir William appeared early in the morning in my room at the Local Government Board, laden with a bundle of books and monographs on the Heine-Medin disease. This loan saved me many hours of laborious research in studying the literature of the subject. He then went through all my notes on the cases I had collected, and my manuscript report, constantly helping me with criticisms and observations drawn from his encyclopaedic store of experience and knowledge. We had little time for lunch so we adjourned to an 'A. B. C.' opposite the Local Government Board where we lunched off coffee, poached eggs and rice. It was by no means the first time Sir William had been in a 'bun-shop' of this kind, which caters chiefly to the economical luncher—the clerk and the typist. He enjoyed it, as did the waitress who nearly swooned with astonishment at his 'tip', far in excess of the usual donation. Then we proceeded to the London Hospital where we saw ten or twelve cases all of which Sir William examined thoroughly. Next we went to the laboratory where we discussed the disease from the pathological standpoint with Professor Bulloch and with Dr. McIntosh who had undertaken the pathological and experimental investigation of the disease.

And Dr. MacNalty's account goes on to tell how they went back to Oxford that night and talked encephalitis all the evening, and how the following day Osler, after first demonstrating a most interesting example of the malady at the Radcliffe Infirmary—a case with choreiform movements—gave in the afternoon a lecture on the general subject of the Heine-Medin disease (epidemic poliomyelitis) before an assemblage of medical officers.

It was a great contribution to our knowledge [Dr. MacNalty adds] and I regret he never published this lecture. One instance of his great and open scientific mind I must mention. I had ventured with some temerity on the preceding day to point out that all my investigations so far tended to controvert the view that we were dealing with the cerebral form of poliomyelitis in this outbreak. Although Sir William's lecture had been based upon the opposite point of view he alluded in the lecture to the fact that the fresh evidence was leading him to reconsider the matter, and in the article on Encephalitis Lethargica which he wrote shortly before his death he gives me more than my meed of recognition for work upon the subject. . . .

Were this single theme followed to the end of a succession of letters there would be little space for other things—but this is enough to show how he loaned himself to others, how he inspired them, and how they felt about it in return.

The influenza epidemic at the time was just beginning, and knowing Osler's condition and his susceptibility to pulmonary infections his friends were greatly concerned about him. 'W. O. grows thinner all the time and I can't have him lose another ounce of flesh, his bones will come through', was Lady Osler's comment at this time. But from the following extracts it does not appear that he had spared himself. They fathered and mothered, without end, the young soldier-children of their old American friends. One of them wrote from 13 Norham Gardens a series of enthusiastic letters home, and says: 'Do you remember my saying in my last letter that I thought I was getting the "flu"? Well, I got it all right; had some temperature, and went to bed for three days. Sir William and Lady Osler took awfully good care of me and made me feel very much at home. They gave me Revere's room.' And the same day Osler wrote to Hunter Robb:

Dear Robin, We are so delighted to have Hampton with us. What a splendid boy! We just love to have him here & he came just in time to have a mild dose of *flu*, which is all-prevalent. He is an A.1. fellow & what good work he seems to have done. We have told him to make this house his home & to come back whenever he can. My love to you all—particularly to Philip-ip-ip-ip! [his long-time pet designation for another of Dr. Robb's children]. All well—except for the aching hearts. Yours ever. . . .

And on the 11th to his nephew, W. W. Francis: 'Thanks for the Bd.-greetings. I shall be 69 tomorrow! Whew! how the time flies. Thankful to be so well—& for so many things. Very much going on every day. Nothing in lately except secundas & a few medicated novels.' Simon Flexner had written urging him to plan for a visit to America, to address the Congress of Physicians and Surgeons of which he was President for the ensuing year, and Osler wrote on the 15th: 'How I should love to come, but if matters go on as at present I could not possibly leave. While there is nothing very essential it would make a good deal of difference to a good many people if I went away for three months. And then I dread the over-warm welcome & the many visits which would tax my heart more than my strength.' And from this he launched into a long account of the polio-encephalitis epidemic, on the trail of which he had just put one of Flexner's disciples to work under the direction of Sir Arthur Newsholme.

Rumours of his ill health had got about, which he disclaims in a note to Adami on July 26th, chiefly given over to the matter of printing Richard P. Strong's report on Trench Fever, and of getting Lawrence Rhea's studies on War Injuries of Bones published by No. 3 Canadian General Hospital; and adds: 'Donald Armour was here for a week-end & with Lady Osler insisted that I was doing too much & looking like the devil, to whom I was rapidly going! & they made me promise to slacken work. The first thing I did was to get out of taking charge of the Swiss delegation for the Govt. which I had promised—& I had to give a reason which I did to John Buchan—hence no doubt the rumour. I shall try to take it easy for a time.' But his idea of 'taking it easy' is made clear by a note of July 22nd to General Gorgas, which reached him by way of the embassy bag from Mr. Page's office, and which says:

Dear Gorgas, I got back this eve from a four days trip to the American Hospitals in course of organization in the south of England

& have had a wonderful time. Such a tonic! Winchester is nothing but a camp. As we passed on Friday a.m. we motored alongside of 3000 men marching to the docks. In the eve we saw the Olympic come in with 6000 men. In the Hursley Hospital were 40 (or 39) men with Typhoid all from one company, who apparently got the infection on shipboard. You will have had reports of the outbreak. All were inoculated. There must have been some blunder somewhere. 'Tis a bad infection—typhoid, all so far. Every precaution is being taken & the men—and the work—are in good hands. The Morn Hill Rest Camp & Hospital is well organized & I had the pleasure of having tea with all the officers after a wonderful lecture by Kipling. Saturday we saw Sarsbury Park in course of transformation, & a big Kentucky & Arkansas Unit from the Olympic unpacking in the old mansion. Sunday I officiated at the flag-raising for the Albany Unit at Portsmouth in a splendid building—the Asylum. Everyone is so enthusiastic about the fine appearance of the American boys. Love to you all. . . .

He does not say that at all of these places he addressed the assembled medical officers, told them what he could of the problems that lay before them and how they could be met; of the Royal Society of Medicine and its library which would be open to them; of the arrangements for a series of demonstrations to be given them in the London military hospitals; and doubtless of how glad 13 Norham Gardens would be to welcome them at any and all times.

On the 24th he wrote to Captain Malloch:

Dear Archie, I do hope your leave will not come while I am away. I shall be at Cambridge 6–9, Colchester 9–10—Oxford 10–13—Lyme Regis 13–20—Newton Abbot 21–23. I got one or two small items at the Huth sale—nothing of moment. I missed a couple of good incunabula. Some good Linnaeus items, a new Malpighi & several biographies in to-day. Let me know definitely when you are likely to be over. A week at Lyme Regis with the girls would do you good. My Class. Ass. address is Jan 7th. Shall probably take 'The Class. Tradition in Science' as Subject. Love to Bill & to Martin who writes very enthusiastically about you both. Bring over any material. Yours, W. O. Tell Bill that his old chum Strong is here reading proofs of his Trench fever work. What an experience you have had in pneumonia. We might have a few days in London together.

Nor is there any evidence of slackening work in the following almost illegible note among his papers, written 'in bed 10 p m Aug 1st 1918'. It begins by saying that he had often wished, in reading the letters of such men as Withering or Redi that he had come across the account of a day's work; and that he regretted he had not left some record of a typical day at Montreal, Philadelphia, or Baltimore. The note so far as it can be deciphered reads:

Breakfast with Major Strong of the U. S. Army, who is staying with us while his Trench Fever Report is going through the Oxford Press.

9 a.m., motored to station, stopping on the way to leave Mrs. Brock & Muriel (who had just come to Oxford) some flowers.

At Paddington Dr. M's car met me; first to 44 Mile End Road to see a case of big spleen with remarkable symptoms. Then to see a Mrs. B. with polycythemia & the most extraordinary spleen I have ever encountered (see report of case). I had seen her 24 years before. Then to see a Mrs. D. with Hodgkin's disease—external & internal, & now pressure on the bronchi.

Tube to Piccadilly Circus; called on Evelyn Harty & the children at the Carlton. Went on to the Canadian Club luncheon for Sir Robt. Borden; sat between Gen. Goodwin & Prof. Adami.

3 p.m. to the American Ambassador & discussed his plans.

4 to the tailor's sending on the way a box of cigarettes to one of my specials & a 'cargo' to two other war girls. Then to a meeting of the editors of the Q. J. M.

5.45 American Women's War Hospital to see two cases—obscure dropsy & a pleurisy with effusion, & case of transposition of viscera.

Caught the 6.50. Dinner at 8.30. At 9 saw a remarkable case of Polio-encephalitis in a man just brought from France.

One wishes that he had said something more about the scene at the embassy when he 'discussed Mr. Page's plans'. The two had become devoted and sympathetic friends, and Page might well enough have said: 'They tell me you are not very well yourself, Osler, but I don't see *you* quitting on your job, even though you are six years my senior.' But Osler must have insisted, and that night Page wrote to President Wilson tendering his resignation.

On Tuesday the 6th Lady Osler wrote in a letter to Captain Malloch: 'We had five American officers over Sunday, all Boston men. New England is much to the fore in the organization of hospitals here in Old England, and they seem to have settled on this as Sunday headquarters. It is delightful but rather exhausting. Sir William was polishing off an address for Cambridge and has gone there to-day.' The address to which she refers was one of a series before the University Extension students, of which the United States appears to have been the general subject of discussion, and he had chosen for his topic, 'The Evolution of Scientific Medicine in America.'[1]

While in Cambridge he stayed with Charles Sayle, and there must have been much talk about the Bibliotheca Osleriana, some of the volumes in which show traces of this Cambridge visit; and his difficulties must have been submitted to his host on the purchase of a first edition of Browning's 'Paracelsus', a presentation copy to 'Fred. Geo. Stephens from Dante G. Rossetti', which led Osler to make some comments on the fly-leaf relating to the seven 'Pre-Raphaelite brothers'. But the point to be considered was whether this bibliophilic gem, in spite of its provenance, should go into a library of the History of Medicine (naturally under Paracelsus, in the Prima section), which has very little to do with Rossetti, Madox Brown, Burne-Jones, and the rest.

His book purchases, indeed, as the late Charles Sayle recalled, left him so out of pocket that he had barely enough to buy his ticket home. Another vivid recollection was of Osler quoting from Macbeth during one of their talks when they got on the subject of 'motive':

> The flighty purpose never is o'ertook
> Unless the deed go with it: from this moment
> The very firstlings of my heart shall be
> The firstlings of my hand.

And Osler confessed that this was the directing and guiding principle of his life. Back in Oxford, he writes that he had found 'Allbutt in fine form, 82 and cycling 10 to 15 miles a day'; also that he had gone on to the Heart Hospital at Colchester, where Lewis had some twenty-five Americans in training, with whom he had talked himself hoarse. On the 10th he wrote to MacAlister:

> That is a fine memo & I hope the purse strings of your friend may be unloosed! Shall you be at home the end of the month? I . . . am off to Lyme Regis on Monday a.m. for two weeks. Tomorrow

[1] This address was not published, but received a long editorial comment in the *British Medical Journal* for Aug. 10, 1918.

Prof. Nettleton of Yale comes to discuss the Am. Univ. Union—135 colleges are combining to arrange for P-G. work in Europe. They hope to establish centres of information &c, which he thinks traverse this [the post-graduate programme] at many points & is much interested. We shall have to consider them in the discussion. I go to Hurst on the rounds. To start a new 'spital would be formidable.

And from Lyme Regis, a few days later to Mrs. Brewster:

. . . What splendid work he [E. S. Martin] has done for the country—always so sane and sensible. Send us word in which regiment his boy is, as we are trying to keep in touch with as many of the young fellows as possible. Grace & Sue Chapin have lists of sons of all their friends who have come over. Such thrilling days! A steady stream passes thro' Oxford—Lvpool to Southampton—& we often go on the platform & talk to the men. Grace found the Chicago unit the other day, many in which were old friends of mine. Two weeks ago we visited the Am. Hospitals at Winchester, Hursley, Southampton, Sarsbury Park and Portsmouth. Imagine a Fall River steamer on Southampton water! tied up opposite the house of one of our friends. U. S. will settle the war & I hope dictate the terms to the German people. Great enthusiasm here about the Am. spirit, & the troops are splendid. Sue has just gone to Paris with Mrs. Whitelaw Reid to see the Red + work & to get it co-ordinated with the London branch. She has proved a trump with a fine gift for organization. We have had a steady stream of visitors, more than ever, scarcely a day passes without a call from someone & the week-ends are always full. We get on very well with the rations—no serious shortage, & Grace manages wonderfully. . . . This is a lovely spot on the Dorset coast. A niece from Toronto with two daughters, the Wrights—mother & three girls—the Hartys, with two adorable children—the Ogilvies with two more—a Boston Gardiner girl, war-widow with a 2 year old—all are here, so that we have very happy beach parties. . . . P.S. before you get this a year will have passed since our dear laddie was killed. It has been a bitter experience & has hit me hard. Poor Grace has been splendid through it all. Everything recalls him, which is only natural, but then the sorrow that he is not here in this beautiful world he loved so much! That he is out of the hell of the front, & at rest is I dare say what he would prefer.

And to Mr. Martin himself, who had just suffered a grievous loss, Osler wrote: 'Grief is a hard companion, particularly to an optimist, & to one who has been a stranger to it for so many years. We decided to keep the flag flying & let no outward action demonstrate, if possible, the aching hearts. You have been a great consoler to many, & the love & sympathy of your friends should help in this hour of trial.'

It was easier to deceive children than their parents; before them at least no outward action betrayed the aching heart, and one may be sure that he was the life of the 'happy beach parties'. There began about this time a long-drawn-out episode which brightened for some months the lives of these 'adorable children'. It concerned 'the Popkins Baby'. Osler had chanced to see a note in the papers about the mysterious disappearance of a little girl from Kensington Gardens, and one day, needing a new subject for a story, that of the Popkins baby came into being.

The ridiculous name of course was his own contribution [so the story is told] as was every detail of the tragic narrative. Most of his stories were continued ones, as was this, and for weeks he harrowed the souls of the two little Harty children picturing the bereaved mother's anguish and her unavailing search for her lost darling. One may picture him at the Hartys' house, where the three of them in the late afternoon often had nursery tea together. He and the little girls would then go off into a corner together, the three in one chair, where they would whisper rapturously and go off into shrieks of laughter. Suddenly Sir William would grow very solemn; he would lift a warning finger and, just loud enough for us scorned adults to hear: 'Look out; don't let these grown-ups hear what we are saying.' Then they would all three squirm with the delight of a secret shared, and continue their conversation, or monologue, with bated breaths. . . .

News about the Popkins baby was supposed to be gleaned from the daily papers, and any listener would have supposed that the British Empire was ringing with the thrill and horror of the infant's adventures. The child was nearly traced, over and over again, till the Harty children were almost frantic. One time the abductors had fled with their victim to Canada—a sensational touch, as the Hartys were shortly returning there. There was even correspondence on the subject, on days when he was away. Thus:

Friday

Sakes alive! The Popkins baby has arrived by the Olympic! Ask Mother if she wants it—if not ask Dinah & Wanda & Phoebe. They might like it a month about. If none of them wish it Mrs. Dann is most anxious to take it. She has 9 teeth—no fits now, but has impetigo, a little eczema, & whooping-cough, but her smile is divine! WILLIE.

There must be an end, however, even to a child's story, and as 'Willie's' heart was as tender as his imagination was fertile, he decided that the Popkins family would have to be reunited lest the children become really too concerned. So one day he borrowed a lovely baby out of a passing perambulator, and after explaining to its surprised mother that she was Mrs. Popkins, the two were enthusiastically produced as the jubilant and reunited Popkinses to the joy of the young Hartys, whose peace of mind was restored—and they all lived happily thereafter.

All this is as typical of Osler as that before his return to Oxford, after leaving Lyme Regis, he should pay the visit of which he writes to H. M. Hurd in a long letter of August 24th: 'I have just returned from a holiday in Devon and spent a few days at one of the neurological hospitals [Dr. Hurst's] where they carry out with extraordinary success the simple practice of mental and moral suasion without any hypnotism or psycho-analysis. Perhaps you have seen the cinema films which I had sent out from the National Research Committee.'

On the 24th he wrote to Dr. Pratt of Boston:

Dear Joseph H. So nice to hear from you. I wish you were over here with your T.b. work, to which I referred the other day in an address at Leicester. I keep hard at work, but at so many little bothering things that my day is much broken & I get very little time for writing. My Library grows, and I am working at a catalogue. Did you know that I made a great haul of Withering's letters &c? A man came in one day with a bag & said—are you interested in W? I said '*rather*' & he pulled out a big bundle of letters & papers & his Edin. diploma. I offered him £20, at which he nearly expired, as he had hoped for not more than £5. I should have gone to double at auction. I have them all in chron. order & beautifully bound. He was a great man—& his plan to which you refer is the only one in giving Dig[italis]. I read his book first in the Lib. at Montreal. . . . 'Tis just a year since the dear laddie was killed. It has been a hard blow—he was such a devoted student of all that was best in literature. . . .

It was a hard time for them, this anniversary of Revere's

death, but they ‘ kept the flag flying ’, and fortunately things were looking better in France. There the tide was turning and Foch was delivering that succession of blows, the first of which had driven the enemy back from the Marne to the Vesle ; and now the British in their turn were rapidly recovering the lost ground on the Somme. As it proved, it was the beginning of the end. During these last months before the Armistice, Osler's chief task was in meeting and addressing the Canadian and American Army medical officers at various camps and hospitals, some of which he mentions in the following letter of September 14th to his old Montreal colleague :

Dear Shepherd, How are you all? Well I hope. We have not seen Ernest, to whom I wrote months ago. We are much the same—very busy with people who come & go all the time. So many American friends now. This week I have been two days at the Shorncliffe Camp, where I lectured twice, & then joined Gen. Winter of the U. S. A. & visited four of the American Hospitals, Tottenham, Dartford, Portsmouth & Hursley. Fine body of men. Many wounded now coming over. I gave a little dinner on Thursday to Finley & Meakins, who returns next week. F. has been splendid. Meakins has done such good work—a great credit to McGill. He is a thoroughly scientific worker.

Please do something for me. Last eve Harvey Littlejohn (who is stopping the week end & sends greetings to you) was talking of the Burke & Hare memories. I told him of the last persistence of body-snatching in Montreal, & he said, why not get S. to write up the story. Will you do it? if not for publication, send it to me to put with my Resurrectionist literature. I picked up the 1829 Parliamentary Report on the Anatomy Act & have Sir A Cooper's MS. note of his evidence. Do write it out & I will put it in the Folio report of 1829, which is full of body-snatching details. The library thrives in spite of the war. I wish you could see it. The Eds. princ. of Copernicus & of Plato are my latest treasures. The anaesthesia section is getting complete. Young Morton sent me a number of his father's pamphlets. I send you a reprint of remarks, made at the presentation of some duplicates to the R. S. M. . . . Love to Gardner & Roddick when you see them. . . .

His manuscript notes of some of these lectures have been preserved. One of the Shorncliffe addresses, for example, given at the officers' mess of the C.A.M.C. depot on the evening of September 9th, was entitled ‘ The Future of the Medical Profession in Canada ’, in which there are many autobiographical notes, some of which have been used in earlier pages. He knew full well that neither in medicine nor in other walks would life be the same for those who had gone through the war:

Uppermost in my mind [he said] when I speak to Canadian or American doctors is a realization of the sacrifice they have made in coming over—a sacrifice appreciated at home, and deeply appreciated here. Then comes the question—what is to happen on your return? It is all very well to leave a practice for a few months or even a year, but what will happen at the end of two, three, or four years? We all know the assets representing much hard work, will have vanished. Many of you will have to start life anew, and some will start not so strong in health or pockets. I am not surprised, then, to have been asked to speak on the future of the profession in Canada. I may claim without conceit to have seen a great deal of it during the fifty years that have passed since I entered the old Toronto School of Medicine. It may not have escaped your notice that while I have always expressed a due Hippocratic reverence for my teachers, in equal proportion has been mixed an affection for the general practitioner, very many of whom have been my dearest friends. How I wish for example, we could have in full the professional story of some of our smaller towns—but it is too late! My good friend Canniff did a great work for the history of the profession in Upper Canada; but there is so much that can never be recovered. The trials and triumphs of the men, their failures and foibles, and the personal traits that make or mar—this is the sort of knowledge we want, but it dies with each generation. Let me try in a few words to reconstruct the story of the profession in the little town of Upper Canada in which my boyhood was spent....

And among other interesting passages he gives the following wise admonition to his young hearers:

A doctor who comes to me with broken nerves is always asked two questions—it is unnecessary to ask about drink, as to the practised eye that diagnosis is easy—about Wall Street, and politics. It is astonishing how many doctors have an itch to serve the state in parliament, but for a majority of them it is a poor business which brings no peace to their souls. There is only one way for a doctor in political life—to belong to the remnant, the saving remnant of which Isaiah speaks, that votes for men not for parties, and that sees equal virtues (and evils) in 'Grits' and Conservatives. I have had one political principle (and practice), I always change with the Government. It keeps the mind plastic and free from prejudice. You cannot serve two masters, and political doctors are rarely successful in either career. There are great exceptions, for example Sir Charles Tupper a first-class surgeon in his day and a politician of exceptional merit. Nor do I forget that the great Clemenceau is a graduate in medicine of Paris, and that we have three members of the profession in the Imperial Cabinet, one of them the Professor of Anatomy at McGill. All the same, let the average man who has a family to support and a practice to keep up, shun politics as he would drink and speculation. As a right-living, clear-thinking citizen with all the interests of the community at heart the doctor exercises the best possible sort of social and political influence.

This talk to his Canadian friends is merely a sample of those to the officers at the various camps where he was enthusiastically welcomed, for though he sounds serious on paper, he was a lively and companionable messmate, and few of the American medical officers who reached England in those late days fail to supply some amusing or touching reminiscence relating to him. The life at Oxford meanwhile went on as usual—even to the refugees, who have been nearly forgotten. In a letter to Howard A. Kelly, Lady Osler writes:

We still have several Belgian Professors and their families here—and the widows of those who have died. All need assistance as they are invalids or only able for some reason to partially support themselves. Then we have a school for Serbian refugee boys who came through the Retreat and have lost every trace of their parents. This school and the boys have to be looked after. Anything you could send would be most gratefully received. The demands here are never ending.

Though his recovered letters tend to dwell chiefly on his library, there are occasional notes which show that this delightful avocation can be pursued only in spare moments. On Saturday, September 15th, he writes:

Dear MacAlister, I am sorry not to be able to come on Tuesday but I have to go to London this a.m. to say good bye to Page; tomorrow I have Billings of Chicago, Philip King Brown of 'Frisco and Seymour of Boston; & Taplow (as usual) Monday. *Thus*, with a revision of my text-book on hand, & the printers squealing I must cut out as much as possible. Yours, W. O.

And on October 10th to Major Malloch:

Dear Archie, Delighted with your 'Turned Soldier' (wh. came this a.m.) paper very well written & full of human interest. Shall I send on the Magazine or have you a copy. I should like a separate one to go after F. & B. [Finch and Baines] in the Bib. Lit. We are deep in a heavy epidemic & I am busy prac. med. helping Collier & others with the doctors' families. McDougall's child has been very ill. Endo-peri-pleuritis etc. The Singers are down—now better—& many others. Bill is at Bd. work in town. Finished the Gui Patin cards last eve. Wonderful old rascal. I think the circulation cards would be worth printing separately as a trial.

The epidemic of influenzal pneumonia will be well remembered, for it was world-wide, and the Regius Professor not only had a sharp attack himself of what, in a letter to one of his little friends, he called the 'flugrip', but on his recovery became engaged for one of the few occasions in his life in the actual house-to-house practice of medicine. He had his own ways of doing this, and with children was a veritable Peter Pan. The child of whom he makes mention in the last letter was a little girl whose mother writes:

He visited our little Janet twice every day from the middle of October until her death a month later, and these visits she looked forward to with a pathetic eagerness and joy. There would be a little tap, low down on the door which would be pushed open and a crouching figure playing goblin would come in, and in a high-pitched voice would ask if the fairy godmother was at home and could he have a bit of tea. Instantly the sick-room was turned into a fairyland, and in fairy language he would talk about the flowers, the birds, and the dolls who sat at the foot of the bed who were always greeted with, 'Well, all ye loves.' In the course of this he would manage to find out all he wanted to know about the little patient. . . .

The most exquisite moment came one cold, raw, November morning when the end was near, and he mysteriously brought out from his inside pocket a beautiful red rose carefully wrapped in paper, and told how he had watched this last rose of summer growing in his garden and how the rose had called out to him as he passed by, that she wished to go along with him to see his little lassie. That evening we all had a fairy teaparty, at a tiny table by the bed, Sir William talking to the rose, his 'little lassie', and her mother in a most exquisite way; and presently he slipped out of the room just as mysteriously as he had entered it, all crouched down on his heels; and the little girl understood that neither fairies nor people could always have the colour of a red rose in their cheeks, or stay as long as they wanted to in one place, but that they nevertheless would be very happy in another home and must not let the people they left behind, particularly their parents, feel badly about it; and the little girl understood and was not unhappy.

But one can imagine that, when Sir William straightened up and ceased to be a goblin on leaving the room, he wept if he did not whistle, for he knew it was to be his last visit.

In another note, of October 14th, to Malloch he says:

> Dear Archie, *Dee*-lighted to hear you are to come over. 'Twill be splendid. Get some good lantern slides if possible. It is to be a big discussion [influenzal pneumonia]. Rolleston asked me to open, but I had nothing special & too busy. U.S. troops in the thick of an epidemic here. Bill here and is well. Fine haul from Harvey Littlejohn. Big ether-day dinner of the Boston men on Wednesday. I am to show the original papers. Final meeting of the Graduate Com. of the Hosp. on Thursday. I have to be in town three days worse luck. . . .

On October 16th the Massachusetts General Hospital holds annually in Boston an 'Ether Day' festival, and it was like Osler to remember this and to gather together for dinner at the American Officers' Club at 9 Chesterfield Gardens a group of the graduates of that hospital—a memorable occasion, and one may be sure that he told the story of anaesthesia, displayed his more important historical pamphlets, and sent messages of greeting to the M. G. H. and to his old friends in Boston who, like John Collins Warren, felt deeply the historical significance of these Ether Day ceremonies.

Mention has been made, in occasional letters which have been quoted, of the fact that for some weeks Major R. P. Strong had been at 13 Norham Gardens seeing his elaborate 'Trench Fever' report through the press. Strong was a Hopkins graduate, a member of the famous first graduating class, who soon after America's entry into the war had been appointed by the Medical Research Committee of the American Red Cross to undertake a study of trench fever and its possible relation to the louse. These experiments had been successfully carried out on volunteers from the newly arrived American contingents during the autumn and winter of 1917–18. It was one of the few really important contributions to our knowledge of certain hitherto unknown infectious diseases which came out of the war. The knowledge gained was quickly disseminated, and led promptly to more active measures for the delousing of troops, but inasmuch as the American Expeditionary Force had no possible means of getting the elaborate Report printed, Strong naturally turned for help to his one-time teacher. And so it came about that the Oxford University Press issued the Report, which was ready for distribution at this time, and of which Osler wrote a long and appreciative review,[1] with the following side-remarks:

> One of the shocks of the great war has been that lousiness and the itch have had such an innings. We had become clean enough, at least in this country and America, to forget the enormous capabilities of the louse. The fate of armies has been decided through the devastations of diseases transmitted through it. The truth is that the 'sparrow hawks of Montagu College', as Rabelais called lice, have always been terrible pests. In a MS. note-book of John Locke is a memorandum of the placards on the walls of streets of Paris giving directions against the prevailing lousiness. Many persons have a curious tolerance of their presence. An Austrian soldier under my care at the Johns Hopkins Hospital assured us that he was never in the best of health unless he was verminous. There is a famous seventeenth-century tractate, *Laus pediculi* (addressed Ad Conscriptos Mendicorum Patres). . . . The idea of harmlessness was widespread, and is expressed in the Beggar's Song in Izaak Walton's 'Compleat Angler':
>
> A hundred herds of black and white
> Upon our gowns securely feed,
> And yet if any dare us bite,
> He dies therefore as sure as creed.
>
> Burns puts a truer feeling in his famous poem 'To a Louse':
>
> Ye ugly, creepin, blastit wonner,
> Detested, shunn'd by saunt an' sinner.
>
> The reports of the English and American commissions should help enforce effective regulations—not in warfare always easy to carry out—against the 'crowlin ferlies' that have done so much damage.

Events in France and Belgium were making it clear that the war was at last drawing to a close. Ludendorff had thrown and lost; and now with Turkey and Bulgaria prostrate and Austria sueing for peace on any terms, Germany was at the end of her resistance. But despite the elation of the Allies over these events, it was a time of poignant sorrow for those bereaved parents whose soldier

[1] Published in the *Lancet* October 12, 1918, ii. 496–9.

boys were not to return with the others—doubly so for those on whom the blow fell during those last hopeful weeks. Among them was his old Montreal colleague, F. J. Shepherd, whose son, an officer of the 42nd Canadian Highlanders, fell near Burlon Wood, and to whom Osler wrote affectionately and sympathetically on the 11th, saying: 'It is particularly hard to have these tragedies happen to us towards the end of our lives when Fortune in other respects has been so kind.'

The terms of the Edward Revere Osler Memorial Fund, 'in grateful recognition of the happy years we spent in Baltimore', had finally been decided upon by the boy's parents, and under the date of October 30th were forwarded to the President of the Johns Hopkins University. 'To encourage the study of English literature of the Tudor and Stuart periods', it was proposed that a club be established with Revere's collection as the nucleus; and that the fund be expended 'for the purchase of further books relating to these periods, and in the promotion of good fellowship and a love of literature among the members.' He wrote to Dr. Hurd:

> Welch will perhaps have told you about our plan for a memorial library in English literature to Revere. He had begun a very interesting collection to which I will add my special non-medical books, the Shelleys, Fullers, Keats, &c. I would like it managed by the students of the English literature department, but the President & Welch with the Professors may make any arrangements they think best.

All this perhaps explains why there is so little in Osler's letters to indicate any jubilation over the events of November 11th. Demonstrations such as occurred in London and Paris were for and by the young. For their elders: 'C'est bien. Mais mon fils ne reviendra pas.' There indeed is only one reference, a note written three days later in the back of Madan's 'Records of The Club':

> 14. xi. 18. The Club dined with the Warden of New College (Dr. Spooner). All present, eleven. After dinner the Warden spoke in touching terms of the great event of the week, the Armistice, & said that the only reference to a public event in our annals was to the Trafalgar Victory more than one hundred years ago. The Club

then proceeded to an election, having first—as is the custom—drunk the three toasts—the health of the Founder, John Banks; our Lady Patroness whose name is not known; and to a successful election. . . . W. O.[1]

Demobilization was not without its responsibilities, in which people as well as governments necessarily shared. No. 13 Norham Gardens was more than ever flooded with guests during the next few months, and it would appear that the medical corps of the Canadian and American Expeditionary Forces felt that this was an official part of the process of demobilization. But those days of rejoicing were no time to loll back idly: constructive thinking was needed then if ever, even if people were inclined to leave all this to those who were sitting in Paris. It was perhaps quixotic for the Presidents of the Colleges of Physicians and Surgeons of England, Scotland, and Ireland, together with the Regius Professors of Medicine of Oxford and Cambridge, to urge upon those entrusted with the drawing up of peace conditions the abolition for the future of all forms of gas warfare. Their letter to *The Times*[2] begins by saying: 'The cessation of hostilities brings with it the great problem of safeguards for the future.' And there was another problem, more urgent, that of the danger to the public health from the possible spread of venereal disease when the army was demobilized, a subject which *The Times*, not without considerable pressure, was prevailed upon to ventilate in its columns.[3]

He wrote to Sir Humphry Rolleston on December 4th:

(1) The Surg. Gen. in France would send Major [George] Walker over. He has been one of the outstanding figures in the A.E.F. & everyone is loud in praise of his work.

(2) Med Section R.S.M. Why should it not be rejuvenated? Let us make a personal appeal to all the Assistant Phy's at the Lond.

[1] For the method of conducting an election, which the note proceeds to describe, see above, p. 313.

[2] November 29, 1918.

[3] November 25, 1918. On December 28th was also published an open letter signed by Osler and many others. Many meetings were held, and the returning officers who had had under their direction in France the prevention of the spread of these diseases were given an opportunity of describing the effective measures they had there instituted.

Gen. Hospitals for the special ones to make it their *first* duty; & help put it in the position of the Société des Hôpitaux.

(3) Talk over the Meeting of the Ass. of Brit. Phy. with Hale-White. Would it not be better to meet in London?

Thus, now that Peace had come, hardly a day passed without some new matter that gained his support and encouragement; and from the post-graduate scheme, the Welsh Commission and much else, it is a relief to return to his library—and to that of others, as in the following note to Miss Charlton of the Toronto Academy of Medicine:

Yes, the Natural Theology of Dr. Bovell came, & I thanked you, & paid, I think, Britnell's bill. I want all the other smaller works of Dr. Bovell. Will you ask B. to look out for them. I hope your library grows. I have some duplicates to send you when opportunity offers. It has been too risky. I have had several losses on the Atlantic & a whole package from Egypt. Are you trying to collect all details about the local profession? Find out who is alive of the Widmer family & of the Canniffs, & of Beaumont? I will write to Miss Hodder & ask if she has any of the doctor's letters & papers & perhaps Miss Barwick has some papers & even books of Dr. Bovell. All such things should go to the Library, & as years pass are of increasing interest & value. Mr. I. H. Cameron may have Dr. H. H. Wright's papers, & one of the Drs. Aikins, Dr. W. H. Aikins' papers, &c. . . . You should start a special section of the library, if you have not done so already, dealing with Ontario Medical History—pictures, books, pamphlets, letters, diplomas, &c. I enclose you $100 to be spent by the Library Committee in this work. There may be many medical papers in the reliques of the late Dr. Scadding, the Historian. . . . Greetings to the Library Committee. . . .

Rumours had been circulated that Osler was to be raised to the peerage, but he sent a card to General Bradshaw, who had ventured to speak of the matter, saying, 'No *second* house for me. This is the spot I like, with my books.' On December 17th he wrote to Dr. George Dock:

Dear G. D. Yours of 26th ult. here this eve when I got in from a very interesting W. O. [War Office] discussion about gas & gassing. 'Tis a problem of the future. I do hope George will be able to visit England before he goes back. The Am. Hosps. here are rapidly closing. We have 25 of the Denver Unit (Tottenham) for lunch tomorrow, and the same no. from Dartford (Brooklyn) Hospital. They have had splendid Hospitals and the Portsmouth one (Albany) is a model. So many nice fellows among them. I have seen a good deal of George Norris & Gibbon of Phila. who have been the consultants over here. They sailed last Saturday. My Library grows—& I am gradually getting it in order. I must print my circulation cards as a sort of example & to see how the general catalogue will look. We have been hard hit with the 'flu', so many young have died. What a virulent type of disease! . . .

And the following day he wrote to J. G. Adami to congratulate him on the early publication of his official account of the Canadian Medical Corps:

You must have put in a lot of heavy work to get the necessary calories for that book. I am delighted that you have done it so promptly & the profession in Canada will appreciate your labour of love. . . . Do give us a week-end after the New Year. There are many things I want to talk over with you. Norman Gwyn is here on leave—laid up for a few days with a mild arthritic purpura. Billy Francis is so much better—he comes for week-ends. I saw Allbutt yesterday at a W. O. meeting. So alert & well.

But War Office meetings and paying pleasant though time-consuming tributes to departing American medical units does not interfere with his lifelong habit of holding out a hand of encouragement to physicians, even though personally unknown to him. Thus on December 18th, to Dr. H. G. Good of Bluffton College, Ohio:

Dear Colleague, A friend has sent me your book on Benjamin Rush. Hearty thanks & congratulations! You have done tardy justice to the memory of a great educator & to a public spirited citizen. I have collected a number of his works & read many of them. Years ago I made notes for a lecture which I gave on his life & work, but it was never published. Your bibliography will be most useful. Should you ever come across collections of his pamphlets & minor works please remember my library as I should be glad to buy them. . . .

And not only does he trouble to send this much-prized note, but he forwards to the *Lancet* an appreciative editorial on the volume which might otherwise have passed unnoticed by the English journals. So these sorrowing days were occupied; and very shortly he wrote to Dr. E. Libman of New York to congratulate him on some papers dealing with endocarditis; adding:

The American troops are getting ready to leave England & the hospitals are closing. . . . It has been a wonderful demonstration of the power of America. I hope now she will consent to act the big brother to the small nations. I am keeping well—very busy with my library. I wish you could see it. So sorry to hear, only yesterday, that Dr. Jacobi had a fire in his house. I will write to him at once. We are having a very busy Xmas—2 Boston, 2 Montreal, 1 New Yorker, 2 B. C. and a Brooklyn man stopping with us. Greetings to all old friends.

For a week before Christmas he had been laid up with another of his pulmonary infections, but pulled himself together and faced what was necessarily a sad Christmas for them both. He confesses to this in a letter on the 25th to Mrs. Brewster, whose husband was one of the household:

Robert came last eve & we are having a very busy Xmas—the house full. My bro. Frank & his wife, Sue Chapin, & Sue Revere a niece who has just come over, Jason Mixter from Boston, in charge of the Hursley Park Amer. Hospital; Major Francis & Col. Gwyn two nephews from France. How I wish you were here with the darlings. . . . All here are so enthusiastic about the U. S. & Mr. Wilson. What a wonderful change in a few months. There may be at last a great peace. Poor dear Isaac! Would that he could have been spared to see it. How he loathed war & all its associations! Kiss the darlings & best wishes to you all.

CHAPTER XXXIX

1919

THE END

Apart from their duration, their stage and scale, history reveals no great difference in wars nor in their aftermath. In writing of those of Henry VIII, Frederick Seebohm says: 'The long continuance of war is almost sure to bring up to the surface social evils which in happier times smoulder on unmolested.' So among the many things which kept Osler busily engaged during the early part of the year was an active revival of the movement which had already enlisted his support—the national campaign against venereal disease. This, like the tuberculosis crusade, was largely a question of educating the public—a difficult matter in the present instance, as the subject was one ordinarily treated by silence, concealment, and taboo; and the proposals for registration and prophylaxis by the signers of the December letter to *The Times* had met with strong opposition by the more conservative elements of the profession and government.

One other time-consuming matter which had long engaged his attention was the scheme for post-graduate medical instruction which had now been temporarily side-tracked by a correlated plan to launch what was first known as the Inter-allied Fellowship of Medicine for the immediate benefit of the overseas medical officers from the Dominions and the United States. Some one who could pilot the organization through uncharted waters was needed, and Osler was the natural choice, but on the 8th he writes to J. Y. W. MacAlister:

> I cannot take the Presidency of the Fellowship. I am tied up now with more things than I can attend to and I *must* finish the revision of my book this year. It seems hopeless with so many distractions that go on in the house to get anything done. I am awfully sorry.

His Text-book revision, three years overdue, was on his conscience, as was also his promised Classical Association address; but this post-graduate scheme was urgent, and in spite of his first emphatic refusal he attended the meeting of organization on January 9th, and was prevailed upon to take the helm. In regard to this *The Times* of January 14th stated:

The choice of Sir William Osler as President [of the Fellowship of Medicine] is one which the whole profession in America as well as the whole profession in Britain will welcome. An international figure, he has been so closely identified with all that is best in American and Canadian medicine that our friends on the other side of the Atlantic claim him with as much pride as we do. His influence on medical thought during the last two decades has, indeed, been almost boundless, while his 'Principles and Practice of Medicine' has enjoyed a vogue rarely attained by any professional work. Sir William Osler, too, has done more than any man of his time to secure a true perspective in health affairs; his outlook has always been of the broadest nature; his instinct for first causes as opposed to end-results has been singularly sure. Those who have enjoyed the honour and privilege of association with him in any capacity have invariably found their view-point enlarged and their imagination stirred. For Sir William is not only a great doctor, he is a great student and a great man. This has been illustrated especially in his dealings with the younger generation of doctors. Many a young man owes his success and the success of his ideas to a discernment which saw the gold among the dross at a time when other eyes missed it, and to a friendliness and warmth of heart which have never been stinted. No man is so capable as Sir William Osler of drawing together British and American medicine. No man has laboured with so single a purpose to this end through so many years. . . .

The position entailed added obligations, but, as indicated in a letter to Sir Edward Kemp, Osler set out with the primary idea of providing opportunities of post-graduate instruction for medical officers who during their years in the army overseas had lost touch with the details of civil medicine and surgery. 'It seems only just', he said, 'to give these men a chance to add to their brain capital.'[1]

[1] A *Bulletin of the Fellowship of Medicine* was issued and courses were established which were at first largely patronized by American medical officers. On October 24, 1919, 'the Fellowship' and the Post-graduate Association were amalgamated. The *Weekly Bulletin of the Fellowship of Medicine and Post-graduate Medical Association* continues to be published and to be of great value as a source of information to medical men visiting

Meanwhile the ‘ Open Arms ’ were being outstretched as usual. He sent on January 10th to an overseas American an invitation typical of many, with its three reactions: hospitality, Revere, and the library.

. . . We have been looking for you—hard. Do get a month here. We could do so much together. I hope they will send you home soon—it is high time & you have done your share. Hugh Cabot & George Shattuck came this week-end. We have had such an interesting group of visitors—a steady stream. We are very well—You will have had the memorandum about the E.R.O. [Revere's] library at the J.H.U. I sent it about six weeks ago. You will be interested & I am sure the dear laddie would have loved to have it so. Something new in every day—3 nice original Pasteur papers from Strong this week. . . .

The next day he telegraphed to MacAlister: ‘ HARVARD UNIT CABOT IN CHARGE ON WAY HOME AFTER THREE YEARS' SERVICE WITH BRITISH OPPORTUNITY FAVOURABLE FOR RECEPTION OR DINNER THOUGH MAY BE TOO LATE AS THEY SAIL WEDNESDAY.’ Not at all too late; it was an opportunity for the ‘ new Fellowship ’ to get into action, and a few days later: ‘ Hearty congratulations on the success of the dinner. Let me know of any deficit which should be my perquisite and privilege. You are a trump ! ’ Small wonder that he sends belated letters of New Year's greetings, in which he says: ‘ These are strenuous days in which I get very little time to myself. The outside claims are many & as the men are flitting west the steady stream of visitors keeps me pretty busy.’ One of these visitors supplies a diary from which a few notes may be transcribed. Thus, under January 9th :

Sunday dinner at ‘ the House ’, the first time in three years they have dined in Hall—about a hundred undergraduates all told. We were at the high table of course with the Dons—I alone in uniform except one or two of the waiters. The war is surely over. It was very fine, Wolsey's great hall by candle-light. Beside me was the Professor of Moral Philosophy—J. A. Stewart, a Greek scholar and Platonist, a fine old gentleman who for all the world looked like

England. The issue of Jan. 3rd, 1920 contains a most touching and appreciative obituary notice. Osler was succeeded by Sir H. D. Rolleston and he by Sir W. Arbuthnot Lane, while Sir John MacAlister continues to obey Osler's last injunction to him to ‘ keep on poking the fire ’.

Newman, whom he said he had heard preach in the Catholic Church in Oxford the first time he had been back since his conversion 25 years before. In due course to the Common Room for fruit, nuts and port—excellent and seductive I may add. Here the Students, i.e. Fellows, rule, and the Dean comes by sufferance. Mr. Hassall sat at one end of the table where the mathematical Dodgson of 'Alice's Adventures' used to sit, invariably entertaining. It was all very pleasant, and after the port and snuff, and with the onset of coffee they began to smoke before going to the smoking-room proper! a break in tradition which they lay at Osler's door—or to the war possibly, for the Students have dined in this room the past three years.

We went into the smoking-room later and there was interesting converse—all the way from Pope's skull, said to be in a strong-box in London and for sale! The story was told. It goes back to a purchase by Spurzheim for his collection; and many subsequent vicissitudes. Then Thomas Browne's skull at Norwich—Ben Jonson's also—and we pass on to a pomander produced by one of the Dons—and we get on to the Member for Oxford, for there is a vacancy and both parties have begged Osler to stand as a fusion candidate, but he has refused and is backing Asquith for whom he is trying to get unanimous support. Asquith a poor boy from Yorkshire, through Oxford to the Premiership, all on his brains. But Sir William will have a hard time in putting it through and as usual he is probably standing up for the under dog. All this is a far cry from prophylaxis against venereal disease but somehow it came up, on the heels of the 'bone dry' legislation of the U.S.A., and Osler told how *The Times* had protested against the letter of warning which he and several others signed and which only after a personal appeal they finally published.

So promptly at 9.30 home and to bed with a hot-water bottle supplied by Lady Osler, and Walt Whitman's 'Memoranda during the Civil War' supplied by Sir William. They have a very modern sound—these memoranda. 'The marrow of the tragedy', he says, 'is concentrated in the hospitals . . . unnamed, unknown, remained and still remain, the bravest soldiers.' And he goes on:

> 'Such was the war. It was not a quadrille in a ball-room. Its interior history will not only never be written, its practicality, minutiæ of deeds and passions, will never be even suggested. The active soldier of 1862–'65, North and South, with all his ways, his incredible dauntlessness, habits, practices, tastes, language, his appetite, rankness, his superb strength and animality, lawless gait and a hundred unnamed lights and shades of camp—I say, will never be written—perhaps must not be and should not be.'

And the same diary gives an account of a dinner of 'The

Club' on the 24th at Merton College as Sir Walter Raleigh's guest, which indicates that Osler, despite his emaciated body, was in good spirits; as does also this note of the next evening from the same diary:

Sir William says it 's a cold day when he does not add something to the library. Today he's been simply cavorting over an Assyrian medical tablet with cuneiform text, baked in clay. Lady O. said: 'Humph, it looks like a piece of Scotch short-cake', and it really does; but we took it over to S. H. Langdon, one-time Reader in Assyriology, more recently private in His Majesty's Army, who fairly ate it up, which sounds a little as though he too held Lady O.'s view. It comes from the temple library of Sennacherib and is of the period of Sardanapalus—one of the few medical tablets, apparently, to have been found at Assur—'the place where the widows howled' as W. O. recalls. It has an interesting provenance and much has happened in the world between the capture by Sennacherib of Jerusalem in 701 B.C. and by Allenby in A.D. 1918. On the outbreak of the war the Germans were excavating at Assur. A German with this tablet in his pocket was taken prisoner by the Arabs in whose possession the tablet was subsequently found at Mosul. It was sent from Assyria to Prof. Scheil of the Académie des Inscriptions by his brother; thence to W. O.

At the annual meeting of the Bibliographical Society that month, he had for the sixth time been re-elected President; and the Secretary, Mr. Pollard, supplies this brief account of the resumed meeting of another dinner-club:

Many of us will remember Sir William most vividly as the president of the Colophon Club, composed of London members of the Bibliographical Society who dine together two or three times in a session and entertain readers of papers, especially any who come from a distance. The Club takes its name from the Colophon or final paragraph in early books, giving details as to their authorship, printer, place and date. The Greek word taken over to denote this means a crowning stroke, and under Osler's chairmanship the Colophon dinners formed an extraordinarily pleasant climax to the Society's meetings. He was always in high spirits, always ready with some graceful compliment to the readers of papers, and full of friendliness and good stories. No dinners were held during the war but he called for one in January 1919 and outdid himself in his efforts to make it a success, incidentally insisting on providing champagne on the patently false pretext that it was the Secretary's birthday! Many of those at this dinner never saw him again, but they could hardly have a brighter memory of him.

Evidently he was making a great effort to pick up the threads of his former life as though the world were the same, but Lady Osler in a letter confessed that 'he is too pathetic, and it is surprising that this everlasting "keeping up" does not kill him'. But there were other and more serious things than club dinners and sojourning Americans to attend to; fortunately he had once more acquired a secretary, though he was no more discursive through this agency than when scribbling his usual post-card. On January 21st he wrote to the Librarian of the National Library of Wales:

Dear Ballinger, Has the Celtic Studies Board done anything about the Summer School of Celtic Studies at Aberystwyth this year? Even if they began in a small way with only a few outside lectures to make a start, it would stir the pool. What about a Professor of Irish? 'Tis a *live* subject. Do you know Flower, who read us a few months ago a remarkable paper on Brian Boru at the Bibliographical Society? He would be an ideal man—young, well-trained, enthusiastic and a good speaker. Tell your boy to come and see us often.

The sort of thing which customarily went on at 13 Norham Gardens may be gathered from a sojourner's letter of the time, describing a Sunday afternoon when—

. . . there was the usual inpouring of visitors. A young South African back from the war—a Rhodes Scholar—very much at home—was abused for not bringing his brother who was said to be too shy to come. 'Just the place for him here', said W. O.; 'this is a School for Shyness.' Countless young men in and out of uniform—V.A.D.'s from Canada and New Zealand—Sir Almroth Wright, Dreyer, the Sherringtons and the Somervilles—Miss Smart the new secretary, greatly impressed and excited about her position—Robert Johnson and other local American M.O.'s—young Capt. Ferris just off the American troop-ship *Narragansett* which went aground Saturday in a snowstorm off the Isle of Wight with 2,500 aboard (Lady O. had spent most of the morning trying to get in communication with his mother)—Marion Emmons, the 'two Sues', Willie Francis and many more. . . .

Probably few of these many visitors realized that he had spent a busy Sunday morning at the Radcliffe Infirmary making his usual ward visit there with a group of graduate physicians; but chance has it that a record of this particular January 26th has been left in one of the very last of his clinical papers, which happens to deal with a subject vitally concerning his own story.[1] A series of letters written on the 31st deals with the usual variety of subjects. Thus to Sir Bertrand (now Lord) Dawson:

So glad you are back and well. Delighted with your letter in *The Times* to-day, & your suggestions are most practical. I am anxious that the overseas people should be given a chance to put all their venereal cards on the table. . . . We should get the Canadian, N. Z. and Amer. experiences. Did you meet George Walker in France? He has succeeded Young, and perhaps of all men living, there is no one who has studied the social and scientific sides more intelligently. He did an extraordinary piece of work in Baltimore, & they tell me an equally good bit in France.

And, pursuing the same topic, to Frederick E. Bradshaw:

I have forgotten exactly what I said but I dare say it is all right. The word 'disinfection' is perhaps better than prophylaxis. We had a great conference yesterday at the National Council of Public Morals at which they badgered me for two hours. We can never do anything until it is made a Public Health matter. . . . Do you not think we should have a meeting this summer of the Association of British Physicians? We shall forget what we all look like! Your myelopathic albumosuria would do for a report. Sorry the Quarterly Journal is so late, but we are to have a double number with a fine article by Bradford.

And on the same day in answer to an appeal from Ernest Barker of New College:

Heavens! What a list of organizations! Why did not Plato succeed in his scheme of a Republic? All the same, so long as this is not another *society* & you say it's all right, I will join & subscribe, particularly as children are the only people in life worth talking to except an occasional College Fellow!

And to Mrs. Harry Marshall:

Dear Mon.[ica] Angelica, You are a saintess—but no wonder with such a mother! Still I have known awful daughters with beatific mothers! I wish I were with you in the sunshine, tho to-day, Mentone could not have been brighter than Norham

[1] A man desperately ill with influenzal pneumonia was brought into the Infirmary that morning, when Osler dictated a long clinical note on his condition. He survived only twenty-four hours, and the Regius Professor in Dr. Gibson's absence conducted the post-mortem examination. It was the last time he officiated in such a capacity. The case was reported in the *Lancet*, Mar. 29, 1919.

Gardens. Hurry home, you have been away a very long time. It is nice to hear that *Ma* is really better. Give her my love & say 'Absence only makes, &c.' She will remember the quotation from Burns! Barbara is better—still limps a bit but not much. Your old man has neglected us lately. Grace is very much better in her wrists—& still far too good for the 'likes o' me'. Love to you both. Affectionately yours, EGERTON YORRICK DAVIS.

An episode of this time serves to show how 'the firstlings of his heart were the firstlings of his hand'. It may be recalled that the blockade was still on and that a British military commission had been dispatched to Austria, rumours of whose desperate plight had reached England. On February 5th Osler sent the following letter to Professor Wenckebach, who shortly before the outbreak of war had been called from Holland to take the premier Chair of Medicine in the Vienna School:

Dear Wenckebach, Lord Parmoor's Committee is anxious to have first-hand evidence with reference to the food conditions in Vienna, particularly among the poor. Could you let me have as soon as possible your impressions. The people in this country are most anxious to do everything possible to relieve the suffering in Vienna which they feel must be very severe. I hope all goes well with you. Lewis has had a big Heart Hospital, first at Hampstead & later at Colchester, to which Allbutt, Mackenzie & I have been attached. Let me know should you ever get back to your native country. I should like so much to visit Holland in the spring. . . .

It took a full month for a letter from Oxford to reach Vienna, and fully another for the answer, which did not come till April 6th. Meanwhile much water had run under the bridge and he had other people to think of, not forgetting his adored children—'the only people in life worth talking to except an occasional College Fellow'—among them Rosalie's 'mother', who must not be neglected, though she is growing up:

Dear Susan, You have been on my desk for several months, looking perfectly angelic. I just love the picture & your face is so little changed. I have the other lovely one on my mantelpiece & I often say 'good morning' to you. 'Big Sue' & 'Little Sue' are here—both so busy. They sail before long. We keep well—though with aching hearts for our dear laddie. Love to your father & mother & it must be nice to have the boys home from the war. Yours affectionately, [&c].

He had an amusing proclivity for giving children nicknames, and was never at a loss. There was a 'Tony' Draper who had come with his war-widowed mother to live in Postmaster's Hall, opposite Merton Gate, and in whose nursery Osler was a frequent late-afternoon visitor. On his second birthday this child received a handsomely bound book he may some day come to read—the 'Athenae Oxonienses' of Anthony à Wood, for the appropriate reason that the author had once resided in Postmaster's Hall; and 'Tony' the child remains. Then, too, he tried to force a name upon the offspring of a young couple from Baltimore who had been engaged in war work in Oxford during the past two years, and were much at home, meanwhile, at the 'Open Arms'. This baby, born in Merton House, was greeted on its arrival with the following note:

Feb. 15/19.

Dearest Walter, I am so glad you have come to such nice people as Robt. & Rose, both old friends of mine in the old days in the Elysian Fields. I am so glad you are to be called after me, as this will give me the right to watch over your intellectual development, & perhaps in 1937 I may have the pleasure of welcoming you to my College as a Rhodes Scholar from Maryland. Affectionately yours,

WALTER DE MERTON.

As already stated, welcome as were Osler's brief notes, they often called for a deal of effort before they could be answered. Thus a card to Edward Withington merely says: 'Has the poem of Ariphron on Health—Athenaeus xv, 63, 702a ever been translated? Rabelais refers to it—introduction to bk. IV. If not translated why not do it—probably short—for the Annals? Love to daughter. W. O.' If Dr. Withington does not, some one else does, and so the translation duly appears in the *Annals of Medical History*. Likewise the account of Nicholas de Cusa, written a year or so later by Dr. Henry Viets, who at this time was on service with the U. S. Army of Occupation, is explained by the following note of February 21st—one of many on the same subject:

Dear H. V., Please occupy your, I hope, abundant leisure in making a study of Nicholas de Cusa, 1401–1463. The town is near Trèves, & he is stated to have founded there a hospital for 33 poor men in the church of which is his heart, to which pay my salutations,

& in the hospital are a number of his MSS.—Heller, *Geschichte der Physik*, p. 210, & in the libraries you will find several works upon him. Though chiefly remembered as a precursor of Copernicus, he really was a great experimental philosopher. I have just got his original ed. princ. to my great delight, & the conclusion of his wonderful *De docta ignorantia* is appropriate—si me amas esto diligens : vale.

Thus the library was a constant under-current in his thoughts. He wrote to Garrison on March 18th that he had the books divided and the catalogue made, but that 'it will take five years at least to furnish the notes, so that it's a race between the Catalogue and Pallida Mors'. Easily five years, with no interruptions ; and these were innumerable. There are letters, for example, to Sir George Newman of the Board of Education regarding the establishment of children's clinics, and he says : 'Paediatrics should be taken up as a specialty & not left as at present in the hands of men almost half ashamed to be regarded as specialists. London could well afford to have five or six cliniques as good or better than those of Howland at the Johns Hopkins.' Then, too, there was much about resuming the publication of Roger Bacon's writings which had been interrupted by the war—a long task, of which Charles Singer writes : 'Steele thinks he can finish off the whole of Bacon in about six years if he gave full time to it.' From Roger Bacon it is a far cry to the Central Control Board of the Liquor Traffic, on which at Lord D'Abernon's insistence he at first agreed to serve. But when at this juncture pressure was brought to bear by H. P. Davison and others to get him to attend the International Red Cross Conference at Cannes, it proved a straw too much. In a letter to A. S. MacNalty dealing primarily with some further details concerning the epidemic of encephalitis, he adds : 'I have had a pleo-polymorphic-cocco-bacterio-bacillary-upper-respiratory-passage infection lately. I have had all I can do to keep it from reaching my gray cortex through the cribriform plate.' Though he could jest, there is little wonder that Lady Osler thought it time to rebel, and on March 6th she wrote to Col. R. P. Strong :

Sir William asks me to write, even before his letter goes, and tell you how much he regrets that he cannot go into this new Red Cross scheme. I honestly tell you it would be most unwise, for he is already too deeply involved. He has not made any visible progress with the Text-book—Tom McCrae writes and cables; Appleton writes and cables. Added to this there is an address for the Classical Association meeting here in May, and it is now only half finished. You can't imagine what this winter has been with people—all the American hospital staffs breaking up in or near London have poured down here; and Canadians as well. It has been the greatest pleasure but it has been impossible to get steadily at any work, and not another thing must be undertaken until these things in hand are finished. Perhaps you will understand. I am very anxious that Sir William should not be over-tired; the strain of the four years and the tragic end and sorrow have told upon him. I am confident that with caution he should live to a good old age and I want to spare him all unnecessary effort, for the good of mankind. It would be wonderful to go to Cannes, but he must stick here and pray for sunshine, which by the way has come to-day. . . .

So under this domestic pressure he withdrew likewise from Lord D'Abernon's Board with one hand, and accepted further engagements with the other—even ones far ahead, as in this note of March 7th to Dr. T. N. Kelynack which looks forward to the June tuberculosis conference:

You see what a broken reed I am! I have not even got that note ready for you about chronic Tb. What a forgiving soul to ask me to preside at the Conference! It's a bad week for me as the Examiners are here, but as they finish on Friday evening I could preside on Saturday the 28th.

Thus there were duties in town as well as in Oxford, where on the following day after a meeting of the Bodleian Curators he made this note in his Macray's 'Annals':

Madan said good-bye to-day, 8.iii.19, after a three years' extension of his term. He spoke of his work in the Library since he joined in 1880, succeeding Ingram Bywater as Sub-librarian. Nicholson served for 30 years, & his earliest work was the occupation of the old schools & then he made the Catalogue rules. Until his day there were none—only tradition! New reading-room, the underground storage also his work. Madan said his chief work has been the Summary Catalogue, Western MSS. & the Curators have put a ring-fence about him for this purpose. . . . He spoke of the difficulties they had had during the war. . . . He spoke feelingly of the wonderful character of the place, of the buildings & of the spell it cast over all who worked in it—of its associations & marvellous contents. The most notable thing in his administration has been the shifting of the centre of gravity from the Librarian to the Curators in the new statute. . . .

Early in March Osler had received formal notification from the Bishop of Southwark, 'in accordance with the formula prescribed from the first by Gibbon', of his election to 'The Club'—sometimes known as 'Dr. Johnson's Club'—the most famous of the dining clubs of the world. It had grown from its membership of nine in the days of Johnson and Reynolds to one of about thirty, its meetings being held fortnightly at Prince's Hotel, Jermyn Street, during the session of Parliament. Shortly after this he wrote:

Thrilled this week by my election to the Johnson Club. As I told you I missed it last year by one vote. I forget who it was who had the largest number, but I did not know that I was to be up again this year. There have been only six doctors in the club since its foundation—Paget the last—Goldsmith, Nugent & Fordyce were the early ones—Banks, Vaughan, Holland the others. I will let you know of our dinners. There is a fascinating book, published the year of the war. I hope you are keeping well. How nice to hear of you all. 200 Am. boys here to-day to arrange Oxford courses. I picked up six & brought them home for tea. Such nice chaps.

And on the back of his menu card of the dinner held on April 1st, is this note:

My first dinner at The Club. The Archbishop of York was to have been in the chair. There were present Sir Henry Newbolt, Kipling, John Buchan, Pember, Bailey, Oman, Kenyon & Fisher. All but Newbolt & Bailey I had known. N. was in the Chair & I sat between him & Fisher, the Minister of Education. Very good evening. The room is a special one in which the Club has dined for 20 years. Oil paintings of the Founders & lithographs of many old members on the walls. Rarely more than 10 or twelve members dine so a round table is prepared for that number. Kipling was in very good form & told many good war stories. He said he would not be surprised if in a few years the monastic life was revived—as men were seeking relief from the burdens of a hard world & turning more & more to spiritual matters. . . .

These were pleasant interludes for a man, who, beset on all sides, was merely paying the penalty of his position—

and his disposition. He wrote to Lord Knutsford on March 21st in reply to a query about the London Hospital:

About the Professor of Pathology a medical school rotates. We never could have gone far at the Johns Hopkins without Welch & his splendidly organized laboratory. I wish indeed I could find you a Rockefeller or a Johns Hopkins, but just think what you have done without one!

And to another who sought advice, he says: 'That's a nice nut in morals you have sent me to crack! I do not believe a conference of Regius Professors could settle it. . . . Why not go & have a frank talk with the man? He is not so much older than you—if he hear you, you have gained a brother.'

An address before the Tuberculosis Society on March 24th, letters regarding the terms under which his library should go to McGill in order that its high standard should be kept up, pressure on the Government 'to get the Medical School of Egypt into first-class order', hints to the people at Amen Corner about promising publications, plans for the Summer Science School, and other things innumerable occupy his time. Some of them are indicated in a few of his letters of March 31st:

To Mr. Humphrey Milford: 'There is (will be) much money to the publisher of proper Motor Itineraries of this country, combining the delightful features of the old road maps (with the hotels and country houses named and marked) & such modern aspects as gradients, repair-shops, &c. A really satisfactory motor road-book does not exist—not one to be put in comparison with that of my friend Theodore de Mayerne, who when a medical student of 18, issued one of the first & the best in Europe (1591).'[1]

To Dr. Charles Singer: 'So glad to see by his reprint that you are joining Sarton on the *Isis*. If it appears in England, I suppose it will save the multiplication of a journal. Get both your energetic minds on the question of a summer school here next year—two weeks of lectures & demonstrations & an additional four for the research students. I would see that Bodley gave every encouragement & we could use my rooms at the Museum for overflow work and demonstrations. Possibly Garrison would come over & help & Streeter. . . . Gunther proposes to have a great show next month of all the

[1] Concerning this exceedingly rare book and the precocity of its author his biographers are silent; cf. 'Bibliotheca Osleriana' (in press).

scientific apparatus in Oxford. I hope he will have it in time for the Classical Association. . . .'

To Dr. Francis R. Packard: 'I hear you are back & at work. Congratulations on Vol. I of the "Annals [of Medical History]". I have sent Dana a brief editorial note on the Currie [1] & will send another on the early botanical work of de Cusa. I enclose a review of Parkes Weber's book [2] which is a very remarkable study. A few months ago Lee, the physiologist, was looking over the cards of my works on the circulation which I have arranged in my Bibliotheca Prima in an interesting way, all under the 1628 "de Motu Cordis" as the fundamental contribution. He suggests that this might be useful as a sort of model for collectors if printed in the "Annals". What do you think? It would take eight or ten pages at least.'

To the Rt. Hon. H. A. L. Fisher: 'About our P.-g. [Post-graduate] programme, last Thursday we had our final meeting of all the representatives of the London medical Schools, the P.-g. colleges, & the special hospitals, & passed finally the scheme which we wish to launch properly on the 29th April, R. S. Med. I was commissioned to ask you to take the Chair. We hope to have the American Ambassador, the representatives of the overseas Dominions & of certain other public bodies interested & a selected group of laymen. I do hope you will be able to come & give us your blessing by taking the Chair. I will make a few introductory remarks, then we shall ask [Sir George] Newman to speak, the American Ambassador & one or two others. It has been a long job to get united action, but the schools are now very enthusiastic & the scheme is one that should have far-reaching benefits for the numerous American & overseas P.-g. students. . . .'

To G. E. MacLean, of the American University Union in Europe: 'Yes, do cable the trustees of how much importance I think this scheme is for the overseas students. Some such words as the following: "Most important to have Union, & home in London for American & Dominion students", with which I hope may be included our medical P.-g. Association. You will receive a notice to attend a meeting on April 29th of our Post-graduate Medical Association at which I hope you will be able to say a few words. It would be much better to have one big Union with separate departments

[1] The 'Journal' of Dr. James Currie, editor of the collected works of Burns, purchased in 1918 by the Public Library, Liverpool. Cf. *Annals of Medical History*, N.Y., vol. ii, p. 81: 'Weir Mitchell who had great admiration for Currie called my attention to his works, which he regarded as among the most valuable in English medical literature.'

[2] 'Aspects of Death and Correlated Aspects of Life in Art, Epigram and Poetry' (third edition)—a volume with a scholarly dedication, 'Gulielmo Osler, medico peritissimo, etc.'

& it would do the medical men good to have fellowship with the other students.' [1]

In a letter of Sunday evening, April 6th, Lady Osler wrote to Dr. Malloch: 'What do you think has happened this eve? Sir William and I are having supper alone!!!' and she goes on to say that calls are never ending; that he would be in town for three days of that week to attend the B. M. A. Meeting for the Colonials and Americans; that she has been 'endeavouring to drag him off to Cornwall for a week, but he wont go'. Also that he 'has just had a letter from Professor Wenckebach which says that they are nearly starving in Vienna: nothing but tough mutton and hard bread for the past ten days'. So an answer had finally come to Osler's inquiry of February 5th; and the same night Osler not only cabled, but wrote:

Oxford, Sunday [April 6th]

Dear Wenckebach, Yours of the 4th of March came to-day & I have sent it on at once to the Foreign Office. I telephoned at once to one of the Secretaries to ask what the action had been & he said food was being hurried through. I am trying to arrange with friends in Schweiz to forward some supplies directly to you. I shall try too to get a telegram through to you if possible. I have asked the Foreign Office if they would like to have a special interview with you in Schweiz. It has made us very sad to hear of all your sufferings. I will give your messages to Allbutt & Mackenzie & Lewis. Thanks for your papers. We lost our dear boy, killed in Flanders. . . .

As Professor Wenckebach says, this for the Viennese was the historical letter which brought them their first gleam of hope, for 'under Osler's personal initiative the con-

[1] Osler presided at the meeting of organization of the Post-graduate Medical Association, held on April 29th at the Royal Society of Medicine. Hardly any other man than he could have secured the cohesion of so many divergent elements as were represented by the many schools and hospitals concerned. In his address he gave an outline of what had gone before, and of what the association proposed to do, saying that 'the important thing for them all was to pool their interests: energy, patience, and organization would do the rest'. Lord Dawson, Sir George Newman representing the Board of Education, Sir John Goodwin representing the army, Professor MacLean, General Birkett of McGill, all spoke warmly in favour of the project, which, be it said, has since continued in active and successful operation.

ditions existing in Vienna were brought before the public and relief work was soon started'. A few weeks later Osler wrote to say:

We are doing everything possible to hasten the sending of food supplies, & we very soon hope to have a special committee to meet the Minister of Foreign Affairs & ask to have supplies specially sent to Vienna hospitals. The American Red Cross people, through Mr. Davison, are also stirring. I sent your former communications directly to the Foreign Office, & copies were also sent to influential people so that I hope they will have done good. I could not possibly go to Holland this spring, but I dare say that very likely a member of the 'Fight the Famine Council' would be glad to meet you if you go there. Ask your daughter to write from Holland if we could do anything to help her with the [Austrian] children.

He had written to Mr. Balfour as follows:

In view of the extreme seriousness of health conditions in Vienna, (of which I have first-hand information from Professor Wenckebach), and the danger which consequently menaces the public health not merely of German Austria but of the rest of Europe through the spread of epidemics and disease, I am venturing to approach you to ask for Government support for concerted medical action.

In particular, we feel that the hospitals of German Austria, which owing to the depletion of their stores are at present unable to give their patients the treatment necessary to save their lives, should at once be supplied with medical appliances, condensed foods, and the ordinary hospital requirements. I should therefore be very much obliged if you would have the kindness to receive a deputation, including Sir Alfred Pearce Gould, Sir Thomas Barlow and myself, who are anxious to lay before you the desirability of the immediate dispatch of medical help and of hospital supplies, including suitable foods for underfed patients, to Vienna, and the allocation of a Government grant to facilitate this purpose.

He received from the Foreign Office this somewhat discouraging reply:

May 8, 1919.

Dear Sir William, I would with pleasure see you and your friends at any time about the situation in Vienna if I felt that I could be of the slightest use. But in the F. O. here we have nothing at this moment to say or to do with the dispatch of relief in any form to Vienna. This is done exclusively in Paris—by the organization in which our chief representative is Lord Robert Cecil; and all we do here is to act as a Post Office and pass on communications to others.

It is obvious that an Allied undertaking such as this can only be carried out from the spot where the Allied representatives are in constant session. When therefore Mr. Balfour suggests as he not infrequently does, that matters of this sort should be dealt with here, all he means is that he is not doing them himself, which is true. But the man who is doing them is there, not here. Yours, &c.,

CURZON.

It was no easy task, and ere long Osler went so far as to organize a town meeting in Oxford to solicit local contributions, a procedure which in spite of his popularity met with no little criticism, for, with many, Austria was still 'the enemy'. Indeed it was not until after Osler's death that a number of British relief committees got actively to work in Vienna, though individuals like Miss Jebb of the 'Fight the Famine Fund', Sir Hector Munro, and others had been already on the ground; but the Austrians as a whole continue to ascribe their relief to the prompt and energetic action taken by Osler in response to Professor Wenckebach's letter, and to the publicity which he gave to the movement. Was there any other course to pursue when children were starving, with the governments slow to act, and the people at Versailles haggling over peace terms? As late as September 2nd, Lord Robert Cecil wrote to Osler among others:

I have been so deeply impressed by the accounts which have been received of the mortality and suffering among the children of Germany due to their totally inadequate milk supply, that I view with dismay the prospect of the immediate cession by Germany, in accordance with a provision contained in the Peace Treaty, of a number of their cows and goats. In this connection it has been suggested to me that something might be gained by laying before the Reparations Committee in Paris the enclosed memorial on the subject. As the prospect of its success must obviously depend upon the position and influence of the signatories I most earnestly hope that you may be willing to sign it.

The three-day special meeting of the British Medical Association, which Lady Osler despairingly mentioned in her letter, was held in London, April 10–12, under the presidency of his brother-Regius of Cambridge, for which reason Osler would have attended if for no other. It was arranged purposely for the medical officers of the Dominions and the U.S.A. who were in England and still in khaki, and they made an enthusiastic gathering. There were special sessions on a number of questions which the war had brought to the fore: on influenza, presided over by Colonel Haven Emerson, U.S.A.; on public health measures relating to venereal disease, presided over by Osler; on cardio-vascular affections, presided over by James Mackenzie; on malaria, with Ronald Ross in the chair; and so on. And there were demonstrations of many sorts, such as of the Air Force tests and of the reconstruction work at the military hospitals like that at Shepherd's Bush. At this meeting, also, a protest was made against the ‘Dogs' Bill’ which the antivivisectionists, now that the war was over, had reintroduced into Parliament, and Osler had some cogent remarks to make on the subject, in effect that he yielded to no one in his love for the dog, but he had a still greater love for his fellow man; that there should be a monument in every city to the ideal dog for the work which his kind has done in saving life by becoming the subject of experiment.

At the association dinner, where were gathered most of those who had been leaders in the R.A.M.C. during the war, Osler was chosen to propose the toast of ‘The Medical Services of the Navy, the Army, and the Air Force’. And in his remarks he paid tribute to certain people he thought deserving of special honour: first of all to Lord Haldane for his far-sighted organization of the Territorial Force and its hospital services; to Sir Alfred Keogh (who luckily had come out of his job alive!); to Sir John Goodwin (who to the coat-of-arms of the War Office had added a pair of scissors with which forever to cut red tape!); and above all to the nurses, adding that a procession of the Guards in Piccadilly would not particularly appeal to him, but he would like to see the nurses who had served in the casualty clearing stations marching in columns of four through that thoroughfare. His ideas regarding service tributes were not those of the ordinary run of people, and on his return to Oxford he wrote to the Mayor: ‘Sorry I cannot be at the meeting about a War Memorial. Put every halfpenny you get into decent houses for the poor.’

With the post-graduate scheme in hand, April was a busy month, yet he found time for those acts which are by now so familiar. He wrote on April 15th to Sir Robert Falconer of the University of Toronto: 'Graham's appointment has been very well received over here, and I am asking all the Professors of Medicine in the United Kingdom to meet him next week at dinner at the Athenaeum.' And as a sample of the invitation to his many guests, he wrote to Sir George Newman:

I hope you will be able to come on Wednesday & see the subject of this cruel Whole-time Professor experiment. I think this is the first man to be appointed in a British School, so that I am asking the teachers of Medicine from the U. K. & Ireland to meet him. . . . Do come & give the young man your official blessing.

So this much appreciated tribute was paid to Professor Duncan Graham, though Osler, alas, was again laid low with another cold and must needs hand over the office of presiding to his friend H. D. Rolleston. As usual, under the circumstance of being housed, he had time to write somewhat more lengthy letters to his friends. Thus on April 24th to Mrs. Robert Brewster:

It just made me homesick to have your Island letter. When the flying night-mails are running à la Kipling I shall land there & spend a month with you & the darlings. Perhaps next year! And we have had a wretched winter—so cloudy & cold but the weather makes no difference in this house. Tell Robert the 'Open Arms' as the boys call it are wide open. We never have had so many—and such interesting fellows. Poor Grace! she has managed wonderfully, considering the food conditions. Sue Chapin goes back this week with 'little Sue' [Revere] as we call her. She has been here 2½ years & has really been a trump—such splendid work. She has promised to call on you at Avalon, & takes out for you three of my special books, as I should like to feel they are with you, & then to go to Sylvia, & when she is a very very old woman she can deposit them some day in Revere's library. I have written the directions in each volume. I bought them in London 1881, had them bound & they have been in my bedside library all these years. They are—a Shelley, In Memoriam, & Shakespeare's Sonnets. Sylvia will be amused.

We take about 200 American students into residence tomorrow. We are looking forward to a busy term & shall have very lively Sundays. Do you realize that I shall be 70 in July? I am already beginning to get congratulatory telegrams from medical societies. I really do not deserve to have lasted so long. I am struggling with an address which I hope you will like—as President of the Classical Association—a body composed of all the professors & teachers of Greek & Latin. Every other year they have an ordinary citizen—that is how I came in; but as Bryce, Morley, Balfour & Asquith are my predecessors I am a bit nervous. I have a good subject, *The Old Humanism & the New Science*. Did you ever hear of *The Club*, founded by Reynolds & Johnson in 1764, a dining club? It has been going on all these years, & the other day I had the delightful surprise of my election as a member. Members chiefly political and literary. I knew nothing of it & I suppose as Rosebery proposed me I went through.

Things are settling well here—the Peace Congress is a bit worrying. I think Wilson will work out all right. I am backing Uncle Ned on him! . . . Such a late spring—the garden is only just beginning to look alive. I am writing in bed—a slight cold. Grace sends love.

And the next day he writes to his old Montreal colleague whom he had prevailed upon to write his reminiscences of the old days at McGill:

Dear Shepherd, I am delighted with your account of the old school & our old teachers. It is well that someone who had intimate knowledge should have put down their main features. Why not print it privately? 'Twould be worth while. The pictures of Fraser & Billy Wright are so good—poor dear 'Old Communicate' [William Fraser]! what a rare old bird he was! Your description of Fenwick is excellent. What an old darling he was! I wonder where that Quebec Med. Jr. is which he 'appropriated' from me, & which I borrowed from Judge Tessier of Quebec. All so glad about [Sir Auckland] Geddes, who has really been one of the great successes as a Minister. Fisher the Minister of Education was here for the week-end lately & says they are all so distressed at the loss & not a little chagrined, that he should turn down so distinguished a political career. I think he is wise. It looks as if Whitnall would go from here as Anatomist—a keen bright fellow & a good investigator. He has an extraordinary sense of humour. Mrs. W. is charming. I have not seen Tait the man who will probably go as Physiologist. Schafer speaks very highly of him. Wyatt Johnston has been with us for 3 weeks. We will lick him into shape. I have given him my rooms at Ch. Church. He has brains & I hope may develop as his father did. Love to Cecil & Dorothy. I wish I could spend a week with you at Como. The Library thrives—something new or old every day. Ever yours, Wm OSLER. [And on the envelope:] Best of all I think is the sketch of Dawson. What a rare man he was!

His indisposition was doubtless providential and forced upon him the realization that if he was to get his Classical Association address completed he must postpone other things, among them a lecture he had promised to give for Sir Walter Raleigh's course in English Literature. On May the 13th Lady Osler wrote in a letter to her sister:

W. O. finished the address last evening and it is in the hands of the Press reader to-day. The meeting will be Friday and Saturday, and the guests stay Sunday when Sir Arthur Evans gives an afternoon party at Boar's Hill. The tea guests have grown to 200, so I have had to put the whole business into the hands of Weeks and hope all will go well. Two years ago to-day since Revere caught his famous fish—what a glorious day it was! Miss Cuming is now working on Revere's books in the evenings, cataloguing them. They will go out in the autumn when the shipping is better and the library ready. I had an hour in St. John's [garden] this morning with Mr. Bidder. *Never* have I seen it so wonderful. The blue poppies will be out in a week. I sent several Americans in to look at it. . . .

The presidency of the Classical Association was not a position to fill lightly, but Osler had a special purpose in the subject on which he had chosen to speak, and he had finally settled upon 'The Old Humanities and the New Science' as his title.[1] Probably no other living man would have ventured to deal with this topic in Oxford of all places, and before a national body of classical scholars—nor could many other men have succeeded in steering an equally safe course through the narrows of his subject. He knew the rocks well, and had been in the same channel many times before. But there had been other things to attend to besides the mere composition of his address. Drawing upon the Bibliotheca Prima section of his library he had selected for exhibition twenty examples to illustrate what were practically the milestones in the evolution of science and medicine: first editions of the contributors, from Hippocrates to Newton. Also, in conjunction with R. T. Gunther, Science Tutor at Magdalen, he had arranged for an exhibition of the early scientific apparatus, much of it of great historical interest, long stored away in obscure

[1] *British Medical Journal*, July 5, 1919; *Classical Association Proceedings*, 1919; London, John Murray, 1919; reprinted by Houghton, Mifflin Co., Boston, 1920, &c.

corners of the Oxford colleges. These objects were lent temporarily to the Bodleian, where they were displayed in the Picture Gallery; and a catalogue of the ancient instruments used or invented by Oxford chemists, astronomers, physicists, and mathematicians of days gone by was prepared and printed for distribution.

Nothing could have served better than this exhibition to recall to the mind of classical Oxford that she had had a glorious and almost forgotten past in experimental science.[1] As Mr. Gunther writes: 'Osler entered into this with his customary enthusiasm and energy; and to have been brought thereby into daily contact with his magnetic and charming personality was a privilege even greater than the invaluable assistance he gave in getting the collection together, for it was a joy to have to do with him!' Of the address itself Sir Frederic Kenyon has this to say:

> Its delivery was a notable occasion. As can be seen by those who read it, it was full of learning, of humour, of feeling, of eloquence, and it contained suggestions of real weight with regard to the interconnection of science and the humanities. But it gained much in delivery from the personality of the speaker. No one could hear it without being impressed with his width of outlook, by his easy mastery of great tracts of literature and learning, by his all-embracing humanity in the widest sense of the term. I hope it made many students of science anxious to extend their knowledge of classical literature; I know it made one student of the classics wish that he had a wider knowledge of natural science. Osler himself was a well-nigh perfect example of the union of science and the humanities, which to some of us is the ideal of educational progress; and his address embodied the whole spirit of his ideal.

Oxford on an early morning in May is likely to be at her best, and Lady Osler wrote:

> I can hardly endure your not being here. Never has Oxford been more wonderful—never. The birds are making such a racket I had to get up; partly that, and partly—one of our guests is a classical chap who takes an hour in the bathroom and I had to get in ahead

[1] The Oxford University Press has since printed [1923] the first two volumes of a work entitled 'Early Science in Oxford', by R. T. Gunther, which provide an elaborate, illustrated catalogue raisonné (1) of the chemical, (2) of the mathematical, and (3) of the astronomical instruments which have been unearthed and which illustrate the history of the early scientific studies made at the University.

of him. Everything has come out at once,—apples, pears, lilacs and all else, so that the streets and parks, to say nothing of the town and river, look as though Nature had gone quite mad. You should see the High, and Cornmarket—Benning simply has to creep by. The congestion is quite the same in the 'Open Arms'. I hardly know how Willie got the address done, he was so beset the early part of the week. . . . In the meantime the Classicals sent word they would like to come Thursday on account of the early meetings on Friday, so they all arrived at 6 p.m. . . .

There were, in addition, other unexpected guests, among them his former colleague, W. H. Welch, who on his return from the Cannes Red Cross Conference had reached Oxford unaware of the Classical Association meeting. In a continuation of her letter, Lady Osler goes on to describe the gathering at the Divinity School, 'with the sun filtering through the Exeter trees and those ancient windows; Willie standing in that black-oak pulpit and, in his scarlet gown and velvet cap, looking mediaeval and wonderful.' And Professor Welch, who had turned to Lady Osler when the address was over, to say: 'That was Osler at his very best', has given this recollection of the occasion:

There have been physicians, especially in England, well known for their attainments as classical scholars, but I am not aware that since Linacre there has come to a member of the medical profession distinction in this field comparable to Osler's election to the presidency of the British Classical Association. It was in recognition not merely of his sympathetic interest in classical studies and intimate association with classical scholars, but also of his mastery of certain phases of the subject, especially the bibliographical and historical sides, and the relation of the work and thought of classical antiquity to the development of medicine, science and culture.

Osler told me that he had never given so much time and thought to the preparation of an address as he did to this one. The occasion and the whole setting were to me most interesting and impressive. At noon the audience of distinguished scholars and guests assembled in the Divinity School. At one end of the hall the Vice-Chancellor of the University presided, and half-way down one of the sides was the high seat of the orator. The distinguished company, the brightly coloured academic gowns and hoods, the traditional ceremonies for such an occasion in Oxford, the figure of Osler himself, the charm and interest of the address and its cordial appreciation and reception by the audience, all combined to make a scene of brilliancy and delight which I shall always carry in my memory. . . .

I shall never forget the hour which I spent with Osler just before the address, in inspecting the wonderful collection of scientific instruments of historical interest assembled from the various colleges at Oxford, especially from Merton, the old home of science. With what delight he showed me and told me the histories and associations of the astrolabes, armillary spheres, orreries, telescopes, lenses, microscopes, books, etc., which he had caused to be gathered together. You will recognize a characteristic touch and thought of his in arranging for such an original exhibit to interest a meeting of scholars. When not long after I said good-bye I little thought that it was to be our final parting, but I rejoice to have been with him then and to remember him as I saw him last on that triumphal day.

It was not the first time by any means that Welch had heard Osler deliver one of his addresses, but this, before an audience less accustomed to hearing him speak, reached a wider public, causing no little stir. And as his 'old and affectionate friend', J. Beattie Crozier, the author of 'The History of Intellectual Development', wrote to him shortly after: 'You have knocked me, the professional philosopher, out of the running altogether, and while holding tight to your own sceptre as a physician, have snatched away mine as well. Bad man!' About all that could be got out of Osler in reply to such eulogies was that 'the Classical people seemed pleased to be scolded, & I had to poke a little fun at the Science men'. But this was only the beginning of a three-day session, and the association promptly devoted itself to a prolonged discussion of Greek in the school curricula until it was time for tea at 13 Norham Gardens, of which the person chiefly concerned wrote:

I was told to expect 200, so I employed Weeks the caterer to do it, and everything was very nice indeed except the waitresses who were dressed in bright green! and no caps! But it was a glorious afternoon and everyone outside. Marion was daughter of the house and did her duty nobly. I asked the American officers who were doing classics and they seemed to enjoy themselves. Thank goodness that 's done. And now for the Text-book. I had arranged a nice trip starting Monday in the car for Lyndhurst and on to Lulworth the next morning, for the week. Willie seemed much pleased, but has just announced he can't go—must be in London two days. I am in despair, and can make no more plans to go away. . . .

And of events later on, she adds:

I forgot to tell you that Willie and the Vice-Chancellor had an 'At Home' for the Classicals at the Ashmolean, Friday evening. I had to go, but escaped from the crowd and got into a quiet corner by myself, unseen, for nearly half an hour. Everyone was congratulating me on 'Sir William's remarkable knowledge'. I thought it was a pity that so wise a doctor-man had shown so little wisdom in selecting so big a jackass for a wife. However, perhaps with his hospitable inclinations his house might not have been as comfortably arranged for guests had he selected an intelligent, artistic, *sloppy* wife; that 's my one consolation.

If having a home that attracted people was a consolation, she had it as a continuous performance just now, with 200 Americans in residence in Oxford, and on the Monday after the Association meeting Osler wrote:

Strenuous days here—so many Americans & we are trying to see as much of them as possible. I wish you could have come on to the terrace yesterday afternoon—25 splendid fellows, from all parts. It is such a pleasure to see them. Wonderful weather at last & Oxford is in its glory, but the fine days bring sadness as thoughts come thick about the laddie & his love of the outdoor life.

No Lyndhurst or Lulworth with this sort of thing going on, and though undergraduates and Rhodes scholars might be side-stepped, a glimpse at his crowded engagement-book and a knowledge of his methods show him as usual to be otherwise deeply involved. In the very midst of the Classical Association meeting he had written to Adami, saying: 'Wednesday next at the Historical Section, W. F. Smith reads his paper on Rabelais—I hope you will be able to come. Do you know of any special Rabelais students who should be included?' In fact with almost every meeting of this sort he was apt to engage himself to such an extent by inviting others, that he was in duty bound to attend, when otherwise he might well enough have spared himself the effort. For meetings such as this, as well as for other occasions, there were dinners to be arranged for—one in Falconer Madan's honour, for example—and as Osler seemed to be the one most likely to originate the idea of these tributes, the duty of making the arrangements, gladly accepted, usually devolved upon him. It consequently gives a feeling of relief to find him at a gathering which demanded no preparation on his part, namely of the Roxburghe Club on June 3rd, of which he has left this memorandum :

> This was the first dinner since the war. Rosebery could not come —ill. Lord Aldenham was in the Chair, & in order round the table Lord Ilchester, John Murray, Churchill, Cockerell, Osler, Kenyon, Hagberg Wright, Hornby & Yates Thompson. The toast of the club & its founders was drunk & we toasted Yates Thompson on the success of his sale held to-day, 30 items, £52,000 ! . . .

He had been drawn into a project to erect what was to be known as 'the American Hospital in Great Britain', a quasi-memorial to the services rendered by the American medical officers attached to the British Army, and he wrote at length to Lord Reading, who had accepted the chairmanship, giving in detail what he thought should be the policies of such an institution.

Another position which he had accepted is mentioned in a note to D'Arcy Power, which says : 'Singer tells me that you have a paper on the Oxford Physic Garden. Could you not give it to us at the Ashmolean of which I happen this year to be President ?' This note recalls that at the beginning of his scientific life the first society to which he was elected was the Montreal Natural History Society, and that the first academic position he had been offered was the Professorship of Botany at McGill. And so, near the end of his life, even though botany and its allied subjects had no claim upon him except through his interest in their historical aspects, he was chosen President of the Ashmolean Natural History Society in Oxfordshire. His successor in this position, Mr. G. Claridge Druce, at the same time Secretary of the British Botanical Society, writes that Osler had chosen as the subject of his presidential address, to be given in January 1920, 'Notes on the Life and Correspondence of William Withering' :

> It had seemed to him a good opportunity to draw attention to one who was not only a great botanist but a great doctor ; for the use of digitalis in medicine we owe to him, and though curiously enough he did not seem to be acquainted with its action on the heart, yet it was in anasarca, often one of the results of heart disease, that he made many cures, and brought foxglove into repute. Withering's

'Arrangement of British Plants', 1776, was the chief British botanical text-book for many years. It was through Osler's intuitive knowledge that a copy of Sibthorp's 'Flora Oxoniensis' was secured, which was full of notes of Ewelme plants. These were found to be by Randolph, Bishop of Oxford, 1798, and they have been recently published in our Annual Report. Though we cannot claim Osler as a botanist, he had a liking for it, especially on the historic side, and shortly before his death he was making inquiries in regard to the earliest evidence of a dried plant other than those in the Egyptian offerings.

May and June also saw the usual succession of meetings: of the Oxford and Reading Branch of the B. M. A., over which he had presided for the past six years; of the Editorial Board of the Medical History of the War at Adastral House, when he was appointed with Sir Wilmot Herringham and Col. T. R. Elliott to form a sub-committee to deal with 'Medicine' (cf. p. 465); meetings in regard to the restoration of the Louvain Library; the 'Commemoratio annua F. Rogeri Bacon' on June 11th; a meeting in the Oxford Town Hall on the 13th to raise funds for starving Europe, at which he presided, and said that 'as human beings they were face to face with a humanitarian problem, and now that the war was over should prove their Christianity and empty their purses to save their starving fellows'. There was also a meeting of the Council of the B. M. A. at which a Liquor Reform Memorial was unanimously passed and submitted to the Government to this effect:

> In view of the great advantages to the efficiency and well-being of the nations, and to public health and order, which have followed the restrictions placed on the sale of intoxicating liquor during the war, the undersigned earnestly request his Majesty's Government to maintain these restrictions until a permanent measure of reform has been enacted by Parliament.

Osler, however, was not a teetotaller, as is evident from a letter to *The Times* of July 18th, in which, after admitting that the majority of the people of the United States have learned that the work of life is as well or better done without the use of alcohol in any form, he went on to say: 'Many wise men doubt the wisdom of total prohibition. There are virtues not worth having, and among them is that "fugitive and cloistered virtue, unexercised and unbreathed" upon which Milton pours his scorn.' These among many other incidents of the next few weeks, not forgetting the spring examinations, may be recorded. Sundays alone on his crowded engagement-block were kept blank, with what result has been seen. So to the Professor of Arabic in Cambridge:

Dear Browne, Yes, I shall be at home on Sunday [28th]. Saturday I have to preside at a meeting in London [Tuberculosis Congress] in the morning, & attend one here in the afternoon & dine with the Electro-therapeutics in the evening. Please lunch with us on Sunday & dine with me at Ch. Ch. in the eve. Can I get out anything for you at Bodley?

On June 24th he wrote to Mrs. Chapin:

Dearest Sister Sue, How I wish you could have been here to-day—such a glorious Encaenia. How you would have enjoyed it. And to see Sister G. sitting in the seat of honour at the All Souls luncheon between Gen. Haig & Admiral Beatty & looking just the part—'twas splendid. Poor dear Isaac! When these things come it adds to the burden of the sorrow to think how he would have appreciated it. Do have a good rest, & take care of yourself. . . . G. will write full details of the Am. Invasion of No 13 to-day. Such a nice group of men.

[And 'G.' writes in turn:] I am sending the papers. We were in an uncertainty about the Hoovers as no message came about Mrs. H—but his wires said *we*, so we supposed it was Mrs., but she is in California and did not come. I was glad to think I needn't go, and asked Nancy Astor to take my place, but the Vice-Chancellor sent another ticket and asked me to be there. So I went of course. Pershing with General Biddle and three aides arrived at 10.45, also Colonel Lloyd Griscom with an aide, also Mr. Hoover with a Captain Somebody: three big U. S. Army cars. Also an orderly to polish up the General—you would have laughed to see the blue room and your bathroom. Twice during the day General Pershing was brushed and polished. It was a very cold morning and I had a nice wood fire in the drawing-room over which they all clung gratefully. There were sandwiches, coffee and drinks in the dining-room and they had a good meal as they had left town at eight o'clock. Nancy arrived in the midst of it, and kissed the General affectionately and said: 'Do let's dance; you are the best dancer in the American Army.' We dressed the degree people up in scarlet gowns and velvet hats, and all went down in cars; Wanda had a seat with me. It was really a wonderful sight. Lord Curzon was gorgeous. The Prince did not come, but the degree was given in absentia. Pershing had a splendid reception, as did Mr. Hoover; but Haig was the hero, I never heard such a racket. Joffre looks old and sad; worn out, I fancy.

As the big doors were opened at the Sheldonian, 'God Save the King' was played, and as Joffre, the first to enter, stepped in he saluted. And one could see all the others in procession behind him; it was a gorgeous mass of scarlet and black, with touches of blue from French uniforms, and M. A. hoods. After the ceremony the All Souls guests walked across the street into the big Quad. At the gate the plan of the table was handed you, and you can fancy my surprise when I saw Sir Douglas Haig was to take me in, and Sir David Beatty on my right. I said I felt I must be Great Britain, I was so protected—Army and Navy on either side and France and America in front. I got on very well with my friends. General Haig said everything that was charming about Bob Bacon. He said he had just had a letter from Billie H. telling him everything, and appreciated so much his writing. Then I had such a delightful time—the best of the day. Wright, our All Souls friend, stood just behind us, looking after the wine. I told Sir Douglas that there had not been a better warrior in the army's forces, so when we got up Sir Douglas spoke to him; shook hands and thanked him. Wright *nearly* cried, and I *did*—I could see him carrying those poor things down the hospital steps. It is an awful thing to say, but I was much happier when the war was on and I was really helping. Now everything is upset, and fuss on all sides: strikes and fights, and daily horrors in Europe. Mr. Hoover was most depressing about the winter outlook, and had to leave directly after luncheon as he was called back—Huns holding up food for Poland. After luncheon General Pershing dashed over to Blenheim to see the palace, etc., then back to the university garden-party at Wadham, then for a walk, and back here. He said he would like a nap, so I tucked him up on the blue-room sofa; an aide on the bed; and Griscom on your bed. At 7.30, having been dusted and polished again they all went to dine at Christ Church and left by motor for London at 10. And back to France at dawn. So that 's all; such a business!

Osler must have got wind of the fact that he was to be victimized by his friends in some way on the occasion of his seventieth birthday. These things can hardly be kept secret, but he at least gave no intimation that he had any knowledge of what was going on. However, in one of her letters his wife wrote: 'The seventieth-birthday business is *out*; no longer a secret; and Willie laughs though I thought he would be furious.' He had in fact by then been formally approached on the subject by the Oxford representative of the committee, and wrote to Adami: 'Singer suggests that Friday [July 11th] after the meeting [Royal Society of Medicine] is a good time. Rolleston of course should be asked officially for permission. It's wonderfully kind of all you men to have taken so much trouble in all this time of sorrow and anxiety.' And with this quite out of mind, to Dr. Charles Singer himself a few days later:

Dear Rabanus Maurus, So glad you have sciatica—'twill do you good. Let me commend the writings of Brother Herpe to you—just suited to ease a bodily affliction. You may remember how the 'Divine cloude of Unknowinge' comforted Andreas Perforatus [i. e. Boorde] in the Fleet Prison. I have been in bed since Sunday fighting a cold—so far with success.

Thank Mrs. Singer for Levy's address. I must write him about Avicenna. In '14 we had almost completed arrangements for the repair of the Prince's tomb at Hamadan. We must take it up again. I have written Neligan, Phy. to the Embassy, to find out just how far he had proceeded, i.e. whether he really had the Shah's consent. Do you not think it should be done under the auspices of the Hist. Sec. R. S. M.?—possibly too the French Soc. He was a great man & the intellectual father of your friend Albertus Magnus. Yours, W. O. I have a sure cure for sciatica but I hesitate to mention it at this early stage of the disease.

It was his turn to submit to the sort of thing he was accustomed to engineer for others, and at that very time he with James Bryce, John Morley, Frederic Harrison, and others was planning to pay a tribute to John Beattie Crozier on his seventieth birthday, nearly coinciding with his own. But in Osler's case there was a presentation to be made, so his attendance must be assured, and he casually writes: 'They are birthdaying me this week in London.'

Such an outburst of expressions of affection as Osler's seventieth birthday called forth has rarely if ever been exceeded. The medical journals in the United States, in Great Britain and her dominions, issued special 'Osler numbers', and from near and far people vied with one another in paying him loving tributes. Only once or twice before had 13 Norham Gardens been so nearly swamped by letters and telegrams and cables from old and young, from within and without the profession. As Abraham

Jacobi wrote: 'Seventy years, or any age, is no period for you. You are eminently the one, the indispensable man in Medicine—the indispensable man! Everybody feels that, knows that. The world is crowded with nonentities, but even they realize your superiority and feel grateful for your existence. So do I. Keep on.' To most of these messages, as usual, he attempted to do justice, longhand, but so beset was he that finally recourse was had to a formula: 'Your birthday greetings warmed my septuagenarian heart—many thanks.' Even before the day arrived, editorials began to appear in the papers, and on the 5th the *Lancet* said:

It is only fifteen years ago that Sir William Osler was appointed Regius Professor of Medicine at Oxford. If his friends on both sides of the Atlantic—and no man has more, or more attached friends, most of whom feel that he is their own private crony—had not united at this moment to give him certain anniversary volumes as an expression of their affection, and by so doing revealed his birthday, no one would have credited him with three-score years and ten. True, he has long been before the medical public and is steeped in the wisdom of the ages; more than twenty years ago a distinguished foreigner, meeting a Johns Hopkins physician, inquired: 'And how is your Osler? He must be centuries old.' But he is always sympathetically of the same age as the person with whom he is talking; indeed he often remarks when anyone's age is discussed: 'Oh, he is our age.' Many a true word is spoken in jest, and as a practical joker of no mean ability the Regius Professor is well able to hold his own with even the youngest of us—but that is another story. . . . [And after enumerating his many services, the editorial continues:] But in spite of all these multifarious activities no one can think of the man without recalling his love for books and their authors. As President of the Bibliographical Society, as an active curator of Bodley's Library, and as a judicious collector of incunabula and other considered treasures, he has enough work to fill up the spare time of most young men. Of his favourite authors, Sir Thomas Browne, Montaigne, Oliver Wendell Holmes, and the Egerton Yorrick Davises, father, son and grandson (a family whom it is hardly an exaggeration to say he has rescued from oblivion) he probably most closely resembles the Knight of Norwich. There are few if any medical men who can give such charming addresses, full of kindly advice and graceful humour. To read his 'Aequanimitas' is a never-failing remedy for bad temper. Of his infinite variety there is much more to say, but this we hope to be here to do on the 100th birthday which is his by hereditary right; and in the meantime we may recall Oliver Wendell Holmes's prophetic dictum: 'To be seventy years young is sometimes far more cheerful and hopeful than to be forty years old.'

A year before, while the war was still in progress, a committee had been organized, with William H. Welch as Chairman and Casey A. Wood as Secretary, with the object of issuing a memorial volume in honour of this birthday. To this many of his old friends and pupils to the number of 150 had found themselves able to contribute, and hundreds more in other times and circumstances would have been glad to. As it was, the proposed volume under the editorship of C. L. Dana of New York had grown into two volumes, and the publisher, beset by printers' strikes and the uncertainty of the times, had been unable to complete his task, with the result that partly printed dummy volumes necessarily had to be presented when the day arrived.[1] It was a very brief and touching ceremony, before a small and devoted gathering. Sir Clifford Allbutt presided, saying:

> To me as one of your oldest friends in time, and perhaps the oldest in age, has fallen the honour of announcing our celebration of your seventieth birthday—one anniversary of many years of supreme service in two kindred nations and for the world. The last lustrum of your three-score and ten, if now merged in victory, has been a time of war and desolation, of broken peoples, and stricken homes; yet through this clamour and destruction your voice, among the voices in the serener air of faith and truth, has not failed, nor your labour for the sufferings of others grown weary. . . .

And Osler, in his reply, made it seem almost as though they had gathered to do Allbutt honour rather than himself. Fearing that his emotion would be too great to let him speak impromptu, he read the following reply; even so, his voice breaking two or three times to such an extent that it seemed he might not recover himself. But he managed somehow to get through with it:

> . . . There is no sound more pleasing than one's own praises, but surely an added pleasure is given to an occasion which graces the honourer as much as the honoured. To you, Sir Clifford, in fuller

[1] The actual presentation volumes did not reach Oxford till December 27th, when Osler was too ill to see them.

measure than to any in our generation has been given a rare privilege: to you, when young, the old listened as eagerly as do now, when old, the young. Like Hai ben Yagzan of Avicenna's allegory, you have wrought deliverance to all with whom you have come in contact. To have enshrined your gracious wishes in two goodly volumes appeals strongly to one the love of whose life has been given equally to books and to men. A glance at the long list of contributors, so scattered over the world, recalls my vagrant career—Toronto, Montreal, London, Berlin and Vienna as a student; Montreal, Philadelphia, Baltimore and Oxford as a teacher. Many cities, many men. Truly with Ulysses I may say, 'I am a part of all that I have met'.

Uppermost in my mind are feelings of gratitude that my lot has been cast in such pleasant places and in such glorious days, so full of achievement and so full of promise for the future. Paraphrasing my lifelong mentor—of course I refer to Sir Thomas Browne—among multiplied acknowledgement I can lift up one hand to heaven that I was born of honest parents, that modesty, humility, patience and veracity lay in the same egg, and came into the world with me. To have had a happy home in which unselfishness reigned, parents whose self-sacrifice remains a blessed memory, brothers and sisters helpful far beyond the usual measure—all these make a picture delightful to look back upon. Then to have had the benediction of friendship follow one like a shadow, to have always had the sense of comradeship in work, without the petty pin-pricks of jealousies and controversies, to be able to rehearse in the sessions of sweet, silent thought the experiences of long years without a single bitter memory—to have and to do all this fills the heart with gratitude. That three transplantations have been borne successfully is a witness to the brotherly care with which you have tended me. Loving our profession, and believing ardently in its future, I have been content to live in and for it. A moving ambition to become a good teacher and a sound clinician was fostered by opportunities of an exceptional character, and any success I may have attained must be attributed in large part to the unceasing kindness of colleagues and to a long series of devoted pupils whose success in life is my special pride.

To a larger circle of men with whom my contact has been through the written word—to the general practitioners of the English-speaking world—I should like to say how deeply their loyal support has been appreciated. Nothing in my career has moved me more, pleased me more, than to have received letters from men at a distance—men I have never seen in the flesh—who have written to me as a friend. And if in this great struggle through which we have passed sorrow came where she had not been before, the blow was softened by the loving sympathies of many dear friends. And may I add the thanks of one who has loved and worked for our profession, and the sweet influences of whose home have been felt by successive generations of students? . . .

Perhaps Lady Osler alone appreciated the added strain he was under, for he was not at all well. Indeed, as an entry in his account-book tells: 'At the College Club dinner sat in a thro draft and got chilled & all week felt as if a cold had come on. Tues & Wed felt seedy & stayed in bed. Friday to town to the Assoc. of Br. Phy. & to the presentation of the birthday volumes. At the meeting in the afternoon I began to cough & by 8 had a high fever.' So from a sick-bed he wrote on July 15th to Sir Humphry Rolleston:

Thanks for all you did in connection with the Anniversary only we did miss you. Friday night my Pneumococcus struck in & I had a high fever & have been in bed ever since. No local signs no pain, but a great deal of irritative cough. Better to-day No fever. I cannot of course be at the Fellowship Meeting. I do not see how the Fellowship can do all we wish & aim at in our P-G. scheme, which is or should be a big educational & social combine. We should have to go to the schools again to ask for reorganization. It is a complicated business. Could we defer? Re. Am. Hospital—I have written Lord Reading. Money is everything No good starting without one million at least. Love to Lady Rolleston & tell her a kind friend sent the 1859 Fitzgerald Omar as a birthday present. I am crazy of course. Yours, W. O.

So there were other gifts besides the anniversary volumes; and propped up in bed he wrote his usual succession of letters, as the following to F. H. Garrison:

Delighted with your anthology idea, particularly as it falls in with an old wish of mine. I will look over the MSS with great interest & I am sure the Press will take it. The sale would be limited in England but in the U. S. there should be a fair demand. I shall be much excited to look over the list & will cut out—if any need! So interested in what you say about Landor, to whom my poor laddie was devoted. An original ed. of the Pericles & Aspasia he brought back with him from the Somme trenches. I must look up the volumes as I should like you to have them, with his book-plate. The Presentation was made by Allbutt, who looked & spoke as only my brother Regius can. He is unique. The volumes look very handsome. . . . Best of all have been the loving greetings from dear friends in the profession whose devotion has made my life so full & so happy.

And to A. W. Pollard:

Dear Brother Colophonist, You will be interested to know how your President survived his admission into the ranks of the 'last lappers'. From our standpoint the birthday was a great success. The anniversary volumes with articles from 150 contributors are themselves a direct encouragement to bibliography. As for the *Regimen contra pestilentiam*, which you & others so kindly sent, please accept my hearty thanks for such a gem—both author & printer have already stimulated my interest, which is the test of the value of any incunabula. An untouched 1859 Omar inscribed to Prof. Max Müller with the compliments of the translator was a pleasant surprise on the breakfast table. A present of the snuff-box of our lamented friend Bannister, whose Vatican mixture had stimulated the pineal gland of all the chief continental bibliographers, has induced your President to take up a habit of such undoubted progeric value.

That a well-ordered 70th birthday may have all the advantages of the final exitus is shown by the July number of the Johns Hopkins Hospital Bulletin, which leaves nothing to be said. The end of the number brought the thrill of the day, when I saw revealed the utter shamelessness of my life—and the true reason of our Secretary's attachment to me! A bibliography of my writings extending to 730 articles! An illuminated address from the staff at Bodley (not to have worshipped at whose shrine I count the day lost), the promise of a medico-literary anthology in my honour, with greetings from scores of dear friends helped to complete a very happy day. . . .

The issue of the *Johns Hopkins Hospital Bulletin* to which he referred contained a series of twenty papers [1] written in a most admiring, friendly, and sometimes amusing spirit, ending with the Herculean effort of Miss M. W. Blogg, Librarian of the hospital, to assemble his bibliography, which he handed on to Dr. Cowley, Bodley's Librarian, saying: 'Here is a tragic record I should like to have buried in the Bodleian.' And one day, pointing to the journal which lay beside him, he jokingly remarked: 'It would have been

[1] Among them was the sonnet beginning: 'William the Fowler, Guillaume l'Oiseleur', written by Basil Gildersleeve in his eighty-eighth year, and of which Professor C. R. Lanman writes: 'As I am greatly interested in the lore of surnames I had often wondered what "Osler" might mean, and now it appears to be a name that I have been familiar with since I began the study of Sanscrit under Whitney at Yale in 1871, for the "Laws of Man" was edited by a French scholar, Loiseleur Deslongchamps, in 1830: that is, by "Fowler Longfields". So here you are.' But the more prosaic derivation, from 'hosteler', is not unsuitable to mine host of the 'Open Arms.'

so much better if my pneumococcus had carried me off—and what a relief to all those good fellows who have written my obituary notices—they would have been saved so much trouble.' Unquestionably it was an embarrassment. But this was not all, for countless similar tributes appeared in journals other than the Bulletin—lay and professional—to which he set himself to make due acknowledgement:

I just loved your reminiscences in the surprise number of the J. H. B. [he wrote to H. M. Thomas], only I wish you had said something of your father & all the good work he did. We do not half realize (& I know it has never been sufficiently acknowledged)—what spade work he did in those early days. I am glad you have put on record those early experiences with Counce [W. T. Councilman] & others. It was a great group. And what a mercy from heaven that such a man as Welch started the ball. It might have been so different. Think how he won over all the local people. We have had a great birthday, & but for the sorrow in our hearts such a joy. I am really surprised to have lasted on in this way, for I must have driven the machine hard in those early days.

Osler's personal memoranda of his illness show that he had a very sharp attack, like his old ones, of bronchial pneumonia, which left him very shaky for some weeks. On the 20th he wrote to MacAlister: 'Dear J. Y. W. I have been laid up ever since the 12th—an anaphylactic birthday bronchial shock! but am all right again—up to-day for the first time. For heavens sake "reck your own rede" & get away. What the D. would the R. S. M. do without you.' This was advice he was now prepared to follow himself, as indicated in a letter of the same date to Thomas McCrae:

Dear Mac, Three things: First, forgiveness for my shocking, inexcusable, unpardonable neglect, but just ask that dear Amy to intercede—though your dear kind letter & that generous article in the July Bulletin show me that your mind is still unhardened. Grace will have told you what a racket & a mess I have been in, but no excuses—it has been just a miserable shifting procrastination of which I am very much ashamed, particularly after all you have done.

Secondly, I hope to get my share of the Text-book finished this fall. We go to Jersey on the 28th & I shall have six weeks free for the Nervous System & some tags that are left over. . . .

Fully conscious of his procrastination, he nevertheless found it difficult to put his mind on the revision even after they reached Jersey. It was not entirely a matter of his illness, but rather that other things interested him more, and as years went on he had found it increasingly difficult, with the resources of the Baltimore clinic no longer ready at hand. He could not detach himself from his old associations. Dr. John Ruhräh, at this time President of the Maryland Faculty, had casually mentioned in the course of his presidential address that ten years had passed since the erection of the new building, and that it was time a renewed effort should be made to clear the Faculty of its debt. Though many had heard the address when delivered, and more had probably read it, it was characteristic that Osler, 3,000 miles away, should have been the first to act upon the suggestion; and out of a clear sky came a cheque for $1,000 with a note saying: 'It is not a very good time to raise money—but it is really a worse time to *save* it.' A good slogan surely with which to start the campaign for subscriptions. The episode recalls his favourite adage—'The flighty purpose never is o'ertook unless the deed go with it.' For he had first written to Ruhräh, promising to make the payment in October, but the same mail contained another letter of like date, saying: 'On second thoughts I am sending a cheque at once.' But there were other things less impulsive and requiring more thought—things which had to do with the progressive movement in medical education not only in England but elsewhere. As a member of the University Grants Committee, he wrote on the 24th to Sir George Newman:

> I had hoped to be able to come up tomorrow, but I am so hoarse that I think it would be safer not to. I have written to [Sir William] M'Cormick urging that the Committee approve of the immediate formation of clinical units at Bart's, London, University College & St. Thomas's. The Royal Free people should also be encouraged to proceed at once. They will need complete reorganization within the next year to meet the heavy clinical demands of the big classes that are coming on.

From this programme affecting the London schools he turns to his own alma mater and sends his former friends and colleagues some very plain talk, enclosing to each of them an open letter written to the Dean regarding the organization of up-to-date hospital university clinics at McGill. 'The matter', he said, 'is urgent if the school is to keep in the van. Do give it your careful consideration, as the matter is vital to the interests of all concerned. It will need whole-hearted & wise management.' And in the 'open letter' he urged a reorganization on modern lines; more sympathetic co-operation between the university and the hospitals—a self-denying ordinance 'on the part of the men at present in charge'; and a public appeal for funds, saying that 'it is a citizens' affair'. But nevertheless on his own responsibility he wrote a personal note to Mr. Rockefeller to lay the situation before him and to urge that the General Education Board take the matter under consideration.

Meanwhile, little was escaping him that had any bearing upon his library and its catalogue, for in one of the volumes, a novel entitled 'The Modern Sphinx', which recalls his Montreal days, he has written: 'I was interested in Barry, as our old Dean, Dr. G. W. Campbell, used to tell us about her when she was stationed in Canada. She lived in the house at the corner of Durocher & Sherbrooke Sts—the one with pillars. Dr. C. said she was very popular, but a martinet & lived a secluded life. He knew her well & attended her professionally but had no suspicion that she was a woman.' And so on the 26th he wrote to Sir Edward Worthington:

> You may have seen that a play—'Dr. James Barry' was produced at a matinee at the St. James Theatre. She was a very remarkable character, & I have been interested in her as we used to hear such remarkable tales about her in Montreal. She died in 1865, & the statement is that the report of the autopsy is in the War Office records, Victoria Street—at least, so Colonel Rogers says in a preface to the book 'The Modern Sphinx'. Keogh thinks the report would be in the Central Registry of the War Office. I should like very much indeed a copy if it is possible to get it.

On August 1st they left for a six weeks' sojourn at St. Brelade's Bay, Jersey, and that evening he wrote to Archibald Malloch: 'Mrs. Your Aunt—the kind lady met us. The pink cottage is very nice & we shall be very happy—if no one calls. The sea & sands & rocks are just right.'

And Lady Osler, writing the same evening, said : 'We have two writing-tables prepared, one for the Nervous System and one for Walt Whitman, ready for hard work.' There is no doubt as to which of the two tables proved the more alluring, for he had not only promised Sir Walter Raleigh to give a lecture on Whitman before his class in English Literature, but had also agreed to speak at the City Temple on November 6th on the same subject. All this led him into a long correspondence with many people—those who knew the poet, and those who knew Horace Traubel, of whose book Weir Mitchell had remarked that 'it was less a biography than an autobiography of the biographer'.

It was a peaceful spot they had found, 'with no telephone, *no troops* arriving; a glorious coast, bathing chez nous at any tide'. And, perhaps more important than all else, 'not a soul to speak to'. In a few days he wrote to F. C. Shattuck that he was 'sweating out a new edition' of his Text-book long over-due, and had 'knocked the Nervous System to pieces, & written in some new sections'. But the other work-table, without doubt, helped to keep McCrae and the publishers of the Text-book uneasy, and the Walt Whitman lecture, never to be delivered, was written out so far as it could be without books of reference, before the Text-book revision had its just dues. It began with this unfinished paragraph :

Chapter [ ] of (George Eliot's) [ ] has as its motto 'Surely whoever speaks to me in the right voice him or her I shall follow as the waters follow the moon, silently, with fluid steps, anywhere around the globe'. Those were the happy days when the novels of the great Englishwoman came out in parts, and those were days when men were really young & impressionable. Beneath the lines were 'Leaves of Grass : Walt Whitman'. The lines stuck like a burr ; the name of the book & the author vanished completely. . . .[1]

His early letters from St. Brelade's confess that the last few years had been a heavy strain—'not only the heart-breaking loss of Revere but a multiplicity of cares & anxieties associated with the war.' They were near enough to France to see after sundown the many flashlights along the French coast, and though their loss was brought home to them

[1] A portion of this uncompleted essay has been quoted on p. 264 of Vol. I.

with increased poignancy, they had chosen to fight it out in seclusion. After all, rest was what he needed to put him once more on his feet. The day's work he had planned was interrupted only by an occasional frolic with 'Cissie Le Bas', a black-and-white spaniel he spoiled by over-feeding; also by visits from a little girl, the daughter of a neighbouring plumber at St. Helier's, who could sing a plaintive French ballad and who would accompany him on his walks. Their evenings were given over to reading aloud, and he wrote: 'Have you seen the Cambridge "History of American Literature" of which Vols. I & II are out? We have been so interested & have got thro both vols in the evenings. Also the "Story of the Sat. Eve. Club" by Emerson is A.1. Such good descriptions of the old Boston worthies.'

So in this out-of-the-way but restful place far from a troubled world, no longer bedevilled by countless calls upon his time and sympathies, he began to regain his appetite and spirits: 'Stout, twice a day! and the lobsters —to say nothing of 10 piglets & 7 puppies to play with, & 28000 tomato-plants within sight!' And by the time the vacation is over he writes to his 'Dearest Sister Sue': 'This place has been a great success. You should see Grace gawalloping in the sea! We have scarcely missed a day. Only 3 bad ones in the 5 weeks. I have got back, I am sure, the 21 pounds I had lost, and no longer see my ribs. Make John read that History of American Literature about which I wrote. We have been so interested. The text-book is booming—so Sister is happy. I am a new man—& my handsprings in the sea are much admired.'

During all this quiet time he had been catching up with the correspondence which had grown out of his having been somewhat 'over-bebirthdayed', as he expressed it. But there were many letters on other subjects: to his McGill friends in which he continued to urge the university authorities to take action on the hospital problems in Montreal; to Wenckebach, through whom supplies and funds were being sent to relieve the starving Austrian children; to Dr. F. G. Crookshank regarding the winter's programme of the Historical Section of the R. S. M., for which he promised a paper on the Centenary of Laennec's 'Traité'; to others urging them to attend the B. M. A. meeting at Cambridge in 1920, for since Allbutt was President they must make it a great occasion; to Mr. John Ballinger, who says of Osler that 'he was the kind of man who could put his hand on the elbow of any other without offence and lead him where he would', asking:

What about the Celtic summer school next year: (1) a group of the best teachers from all over the world, six at least as strong cards; (2) attractive courses of popular lectures in Celtic literature; (3) intensive technical courses 4–6 weeks duration. Get the Celtic Committee to arrange the programme & select the men & form a budget. I think the Subs. & the Treasury Ed. Committee will provide funds—or should! Return to Oxford tomorrow. How is the Med. Student? Tell him to call at once when he comes up.

So even during his vacation he kept in active touch with many projects to occupy the next twelve months, and his correspondents learning that he was romping like a schoolboy on the Jersey sands looked forward to many more years of his friendship and counsel. Alas! *Dis aliter visum.*

September 12th found them once more in Oxford, for the few weeks' quiet they so greatly enjoyed there before the distractions of term time. A note in his account-book tells how this was interrupted: 'Left here the night of Sept. 22nd to see Mrs. M. in Glasgow with Drs. Ness, Cameron & Armstrong. Went on to Edinburgh, stayed with Lovell Gulland. Saw Harvey Littlejohn & others.' And here the story may be taken up by his Edinburgh host:

He stayed with me during his last visit to Edinburgh. I don't think I had seen him since the war began, and I was surprised to find how little the war and his son's death had changed him outwardly. He was as cheerful and jolly as ever, and as enthusiastic. He was full of plans about his own work; talked with me about the edition of his Text-book, about cataloguing his library; insisted on knowing all that we were doing in Edinburgh. There was a great deal to tell him about that, and he cordially approved of all our plans and arrangements. He was on the Treasury Committee for University Grants, and a good deal of his time while he was with me was spent in seeing different professors and hearing about our needs. But he really seemed to be more interested in my grandson (aged four) than in all the rest of us put together; got hold of him whenever he could, and the boy, who called him 'Willie Mosler' loved him, and was quite happy with him. One afternoon my wife found them in the nursery playing bears, with Osler easily the more active and infantile of the two! I was very unwilling to let him travel on the night of the railway strike, but he was very anxious to get home, and insisted on going.

Lady Osler's letter to her sister on the 29th, the day after Sir William's return, will recall to mind those trying days:

. . . Our beloved old Smith the inspector at the station won't 'go out'; he is helping the volunteer workers in every way and says the strikers are quite mad. Even the Northcliffe papers that have been down on the Government say they are in the wrong, and trains are already being run by volunteers, although only one a day from here. Aeroplanes are in full swing, bringing newspapers; and huge lorries with every kind of provision. Hyde Park is the base for the milk supply of London, and the papers to-day—brought by aeroplane—show gentlemen helping to load and unload the huge cans. Willie left Edinburgh Friday night at 10 p.m. and when he awoke at 7 Saturday morning was in Newcastle. The crowd was terrific and as he could get no motor he went to see a doctor friend who borrowed one for him, which he took, leaving Newcastle at 11 a.m. Saturday and reaching here Sunday at 3. He slept in an old inn somewhere, and arrived with an awful cold and is now in bed trying to stop it. The motor was old and slow but got him home, thank Heaven; and he telephoned en route so that I didn't worry, or pretended not to. I had my passport and everything ready for Flanders and was going this week, but of course cannot do so now. . . . The Government has swooped down on all petrol from garages. We had some but must turn it in, and I had to give the man 17 gallons to get back to Newcastle, 282 miles. What a world! Where is peace? Poor Lloyd George had a toothache Friday during the conference with the strikers and I felt so sorry for him. Mr. Wilson pegged out too!! We are rationed closer than ever: 1 lb. of meat a week—at least it says 1s. 8d.-worth—and beef and mutton are 1s. 8d. per lb. 1 oz. butter, 2 of margarine, 2 of sugar, and very little bread this time; but no one is grumbling yet. We all know how to meet it now.

Osler, meanwhile, in bed with his cold, put his mind on the Text-book, and wrote on the 30th to Archibald Malloch, who was doing some special work on pneumonia in one of the London hospitals:

Dear 'Pfeiffer' Please see enclosed [reference to Comby's paper on Acute Encephalitis in Children, *Archives de Médecine des Enfants*,

Oct. 1907, p. 557] as to (1) is it the disease which starts with fever, convulsion & coma, & the child wakes hemiplegic; (2) what is the lesion described? (3) How many p.m.'s? Yours, W. O.

This is but a sample of the notes bravely written the first days of October. It was no new thing for him to be laid up after an exposure such as he had had. He prepared to enjoy himself during the enforced confinement, in his usual fashion, reading and writing in bed, with books and papers and magazines accumulating on coverlet and table until they overflowed to the floor. Though he had always said in a half-joking fashion that the pneumococcus he had harboured so many years would some day carry him off, he had no premonition as yet that his time had come, and wrote on the 2nd to Thomas W. Salmon: 'Please order for me Quixote Psychiatry by Victor Robinson, the review of which is in the July No. of Mental Hygiene. I knew Clevenger & should like very much to have the story of his life. Tell the press to send the bill.' And a few days later to Mrs. Chapin:

> In bed, waiting for Sunday Bkfast with a cold, & no stylo—downstairs—but you will not mind a lead pencil. We have enjoyed your letters so much & hearing all about the family. . . . Grace is in fine form. Jersey did her more good than Harrogate would have done. I am worrying her now with a cold—& *cof* caught on my way from Scotland—she will have told you no doubt. We are all so unhappy about Wilson—poor man no wonder he has broken down. Think of the strain of these years. And the pity of it all is that had he come over as President of the U. S. & not as head of the Dem. Party, & had Root & Lodge with him, all this delay & trouble would have been saved. *Damn Politics and Parties.* We are having a little strike of our own which seems to demonstrate how well the country can get along without the R. R. union. . . . If you see Fred Shattuck or George my love to them. What F. S.[1] & Billy Thayer[2] wrote about me was the bestest.

Aware by that time that he was in for something more serious than usual, he began to call off his engagements, which were many, in Wales and elsewhere, and to with-

[1] 'A Vigorous Medical Septuagenarian.' *Boston Medical and Surgical Journal*, July 10, 1919, p. 46, by F. C. Shattuck.

[2] 'Osler the Teacher.' *Johns Hopkins Hospital Bulletin*, July 1919, xxx. 198–200.

draw from a number of his official positions, as from the University Grants Committee, in whose interests he had just been to Glasgow and Edinburgh. So on the 6th he wrote to Sir George Newman: 'Here I am in bed again with a recurrence of that bronchitis which will prevent my being at the meeting on the 9th. It would be very much better if you and M'Cormick will allow me quietly to drop out of this business. You need a younger man as representative of Medicine & I have written to that effect.'

He had begun to have a good deal of fever by this time, with a most distressing cough, and his colleagues of the Radcliffe Infirmary, A. G. Gibson and William Collier, brought in to see him, found him by no means an amenable patient. No easy task for younger men to attend their Chief, threatened with a malady of which he knew much more than they, and whose fever was likely to make him even more frolicsome than usual. He would greet them by saying: 'I had a good night, and smell the rose above the mould this morning.' And on being asked to explain, replied that Thomas Hood's 'Stanzas' was a good poem for doctors, and all should know it. And so things dragged on, with increasing fever and cough, till one day between his paroxysms he announced that 'pneumonia at seventy is fatal; here is a list of people to give my love and good-bye to'. But in spite of his premonition, the irrepressible spirit and sense of humour were usually uppermost, and it was rare for the mould to get the upper hand. So, on the 19th, to Mrs. Chapin (but omitting the *irrepressible!*):

Help! help! Sister Sue! & several times over you must have heard my *cri du cœur* (though that was not really the place) sent across the waters. . . . Altogether I have had a —— of a time, yet with it all no pain, no headache, distress only when the heavy paroxysm of coughing grips me in a convulsion. There is nothing I do not know of the varieties & vagaries of coughs & coughing—the outcome is far away. Shunt the whole pharmacopoeia, except opium. It alone in some form does the job. What a comfort it has been! Poor Sister! worried to death of course. For two days I felt very ill & exhausted by the paroxysms. We often talked of you & wished you could have been with us. Archie has been here on & off—We expect Bill home on Tuesday or Wed Yours W.

P.S.'s—1. Ask at Goodspeeds some day if Parkman's—the Historians—Essay on *Democracy* is to be had in separate form. It is not in the Ed. I have of his works.

2. The Revision of the Text-book is booming

3. 16 Curzon St. Mayfair will be free in May 1920. Let me know by Cable.[1]

4. The car comes on Wednesday.

5. Mrs Benning [the chauffeur's wife] is in the Radcliffe with swollen legs &c &c &c &c but should do well.

This is no less characteristic of Osler than the detached way in which he would jot down clinical notes of the progress of his illness and send them with messages of greeting to his professional friends—much as though he were the physician in attendance on some patient in whose welfare he knew they would be interested. These reports were almost always hopeful ones, and invariably had some amusing twist of expression. He seemed better by the first of November, and in a cheery bulletin sent to some of his Baltimore friends he reported: 'No fever since the 16th but the cough persists & an occasional paroxysm—bouts as bad as senile whooping-cough. One night they nearly blew my candle out! No. 3 pneumococcus & M. catarrhalis—the organisms. Practically no physical signs—a little impairment of resonance at bases but no râles or tubular breathing. I am mending now & should be up within a week.' On November 5th he wrote:

Dear Pollard, I have had a bad 'knock out'. Two days of last week I felt at the limit, but have gradually improved & am now without fever & with very little cough. It has been one of these low broncho-pneumonias so common after influenza. Lady Osler had instructions to ask you to come, as I should not have considered it proper to go without your blessing, & without a personal message to my friends in the Society. The experience has been encouraging—discomfort of course, but no actual pain & except for the worry about leaving dear ones, singularly free from mental distress. . . .

His illness had naturally become noised abroad, and letters of inquiry and sympathy poured in. 'Better, thank you! though the cough persists & also the trained nurse', he wrote to Mrs. Chapin early in November. 'I

[1] This refers to a long-standing joke with Mrs. Chapin that he and she should set up a rival establishment to 13 Norham Gardens.

have been more than a month in bed—never before for so long. Poor Grace! she has had a tough time, but the nurse has been a comfort. Such a nice woman & she scrubs me like a kid.' The 'nice woman', Sister Edwards, has many touching recollections of these last months, and writes:

When every night between the hours of 2 and 4 a.m. those dreadful attacks of coughing were at their worst, he never complained, and though utterly exhausted with the effort his face would suddenly light up and his eyes flash as he made some humorous remark. He disliked mixtures very much and would, as he put it, only take something 'plain', such as strychnine or digitalis. 'Why spoil a wonderful drug like opium by mixing it with inferior things?' he would say; and I always had the greatest difficulty in persuading him to take some of the mixtures prescribed for him. He was very fond of lemons and always had a plate with small pieces by his bedside, and when he was lying apparently too ill to move he would quietly reach out his emaciated hand for a piece, which would alight with unerring aim on Lady Osler's or my head. I think one of the most lovable things about him were these sudden flashes of fun. I am quite sure that he knew from the first that his illness would prove fatal. He knew every stage so well; and once after the consultants had left him, with a cheery word about his recovery to which he had as cheerily responded, he looked up at me and said: 'Ah, Sister, we know, don't we?' He loved to tease Dr. Gibson of whom he was very fond, and I remember one day his saying: 'There really is nothing the matter with me, Gibson, except this bed-sore of mine.' And when we got outside the room Dr. Gibson looked at me with great consternation and said: 'His back *is* all right, isn't it?' How Sir William chuckled when I returned and told him about it!

He had his own little formulas to which he adhered. The last thing at night, after the hypodermic necessary to give him any rest, he would recite:

And I rest so composedly
    Now, in my bed,
That any beholder
    Might fancy me dead,
Might start at beholding me
    Thinking me dead.

And he always spoke of the toddy which was prescribed for him, as his 'Edgar Allan'. Then every morning, while waiting for his breakfast, he would call for 'the little darling'—a miniature of little Muriel Howard to whom he was devoted, and would hold it on his knee and talk endearments to her. Lady Osler's devotion to him and their devotion to each other was very beautiful, and sometimes in the early morning when he had been coughing for nearly an hour, he would say: 'Poor soul, I'm sure she's awake. Just go in and say that I'm all right, and see whether she would like a cup of tea.' And to me, his nurse, he was always most thoughtful and kind, and would always tell me where I was to go for my walk and what I was to notice; and he would always say: 'Be sure and take big deep breaths, Sister.' . . .

Things looked better for a time at the end of the month. He was up for a short period each day and had begun to read again. On the 5th, in a note to Sir Humphry Rolleston, he says: 'Paroxysms at longer intervals, but yesterday a.m. one nearly blew the lid off. I get up for 3 or 4 hours, but exertion & talking bring on the cough. Meanwhile I am most comfortable and have just finished Vol. VII of Lucas' Lamb. How I should have liked to get drunk with Charles Lamb!' And from Lucas's volumes he filled a page or two of his much worn 'Where Is It?' book with notes not only of things which he wished to remember but of passages which would have interested Revere: '*Vol. I, p.* 76—the beautiful obliquities of the Religio Medici.' '*p.* 249—the purchase of the Beaumont and Fletcher folios. Delicious bit which Revere loved.' '*Vol. VI, p.* 212—Lamb's letter about Izaak Walton, not in Lucas' edition.' '*p.* 526—Refers to a Sonnet of Wordsworth on Iz. W.'

There was talk at this time of his being taken to the Riviera, for English houses were none too warm and comfortable in those days of enforced postbellum economy, but he replied that he preferred to be translated to Heaven from his own bed. Whatever attitude he held before others he was fully aware of the gravity of his malady and made no concealment to his wife and the nurse of his own prognosis. 'I am booked for Golders Green', he would say after one of his bad bouts of coughing; and when Pfeiffer's bacillus was finally identified he was greatly interested, but said: 'There is never but one ending to these protracted influenza cases in old age.' There soon came a turn for the worse, and in a letter to Miss Humpton, his one-time secretary in Baltimore who had helped him with the early editions of his Text-book, he wrote on November 9th:

I have been having a devil of a time—in bed six weeks!—a paroxysmal bronchitis, not in either of your books! Fever for a week, temperature to 102.5; practically no physical signs; cough constant, short couples & then bouts, as bad as whooping-cough. . . . Then the other night, eleven o'clock acute pleurisy. A stab & then fireworks, pain on coughing & deep breath, but 12 hours later a bout arrived which ripped all pleural attachments to smithereens, & with it the pain, not a twinge since! but a dry rub which I can feel now as I breathe & hear like a rhonchus. Very strange attack. I am very comfortable except in my paroxysms. All bronchial therapy is futile—there is nothing my good doctors have not made me try, but the only things of any service whatever in checking the cough have been opiates—a good drink out of the paregoric bottle or a hypodermic of morphin. I have a splendid nurse.

He expressed a desire to see Sir William Hale-White, who came on the 10th and found a sick man, as stoical as Marius. No mould above the rose here. There was evidently a pleurisy but no signs of fluid, and Osler very soon wrote to say: 'Your visit was a great comfort. Lady Osler had become worried at the length of time &c. Report is'—and he jotted down his personal observations. 'The pleurisy continues—dry friction a bit more extensive.' In a letter to Mrs. Chapin on November 11th he says: 'We thought of you & wished you were here in our touching two-minute silence. I have been worrying your sister not a little lately but there is no fever & the outlook is good. Call up Fred Shattuck & say I am better. I dare say there are rumours. Indeed there must be as I have been getting cables.'

Two weeks passed with no great change. His friends, who judged by his brief notes, were sanguine of his recovery; but others knew better. Sir Charles Sherrington tells of the old servant at the laboratory who said: 'No sir, I don't think Sir William will get well. You see, sir, it 's like this: you know how Sir William mostly on his way down to the Infirmary of a morning would drop in for a few moments to see you and the rest. Well, in the old days, coming in, and likewise going out, he had always a good word for me. You know his style sir, like giving a man a cheery dig in the ribs. But now these last months I've noticed him greeting you quite merry-like; but in betweenwhiles his face has been grave as though he had something heavy on his mind and he has walked in and out without once noticing me. It 's Mr. Revere, sir, and Sir William won't get better.' So the old servant had long seen what others missed: that the hair which had been raven black was now thus late in life showing gray, and the Osler with the buoyant step and ready banter carried a grief he could not throw off.

He was still able to write his many postcards, and an occasional longer letter. To H. D. Rolleston on Nov. 13th: 'Still growing stronger—I mean the cough! Appetite good & am enjoying myself! In the recent life of Samuel Butler Vol. I there is a notice of your N.Z. uncle. Love to Lady Rolleston.' And the next day to Allbutt: 'Better—less cough & paroxysms less severe—no fever. General condition good & very comfortable & happy. Love to Lady Allbutt.' Also to J. Y. W. (by now Sir John) MacAlister: 'Send a card for the library & meetings R. S. M. to Dr. Edward Jenner Wood (Hotel Arundel, Strand) of Wilmington N. C.—one of the very best & a dear friend of mine. I make pleasant excursions from one side of the bed to the other & am enjoying life immensely. It is not likely that I shall ever get up again!'

So also, when the examination-time came round again, it was equally characteristic for him to insist that the examiners should stay at the 'Open Arms' as usual. Among them was A. S. MacNalty, who at Osler's suggestion had been appointed Examiner in Public Health, and he writes: 'I saw Sir William twice and my heart forbode me as I saw his face though he hailed me with the same cheery greeting. The influenza bacillus had just been isolated from his sputum and he was pleased about this. "I knew", said he, "there was a nigger in the woodpile." He was reviewing "Sir Victor Horsley's Life" by Stephen Paget for the *Oxford Magazine*. We had some talk on this, but I did not stay long beside his bed for I feared to weary him. And at our parting hand-clasp I think we both realized that we had parted in life for the last time.'

A charming and sympathetic review of Stephen Paget's 'Life of Horsley', written in pencil, 'pad on knee' as of old, was his last bit of writing for publication.[1] It ended:

Such was Victor Horsley, as many of us knew him, and as we love to think of him. Mr. Stephen Paget has performed a very difficult task with rare ability. As Lady Horsley says in a prefatory note, it would be hard to find two men more widely separated in their mental attitude—differing in religious convictions, in politics, in social ideas; and it was both courageous and gracious on her part not to attempt to suppress or to soften in any way the critical attitude of the author. The peace which would have been denied him at home he finds in a soldier's grave in Mesopotamia—and perhaps better so:

He has outsoared the shadow of our night;
Envy and calumny and hate and pain,
And that unrest which men miscall delight
Can touch him not and torture not again;
From the contagion of the world's slow stain
He is secure, and now can never mourn
A heart grown cold, a head grown gray in vain.

The 'Anthology' which F. H. Garrison and Casey Wood had gathered to commemorate his birthday called for a long answer, and he managed to write on the 15th:

Dear Garrison, Yours of Oct. 29th here to-day. Nothing yet from Milford—I suppose the MS is in process of purification! There are still many things in it I wish to see. The Press will follow your wishes as to format. I am sure the Volume will be most attractive. I think I have sent a line since my illness—Still in bed. End of the 5th [7th] week, but better—only an occasional paroxysm of coughing. It has been a slow business but not unpleasant. I love bed, & am very happy with four pillows & my legs drawn up. . . . Do you mean to tell me—through Halsted's article on Goitre—that the S. G. L. has not vol. one of the Detroit Clinic with McGraw's case of goitre—the one which became Myxoedematous! I knew of it, having made the diagnosis of Cach[exia] strum[ipriva] for McG. who was an old friend. Horsley's Life just out & well done of course by Paget—but what a tragedy! Why could he not have collected umbrella handles instead of going into politics. Love to Wood & Noble. No chance of U. S. next year. Yours ever, W. O.

P.S. Since writing—indeed since it was closed—yours of the 28th Sept came up from 'below'. I have not been having my letters until recently & only get at pen & ink by stealth.

---

[1] Published in the *Oxford Magazine*, Jan. 23, 1920.

1. Shall be delighted with the Fletcher which has come, but has not yet reached my bed—Dear old man! How Chas. Lamb would have loved him!

2. I will see to the changes you wish. I have not yet had a proper 'go' at the MS.

3. 'Twas Lamb who started Revere in the old Elizabethans, about whom he picked up an extraordinary amount of information. He had some favourite quotations from Dekker's 'Shoemaker's Holiday'.

4. Mayow. So glad that O. H. H., as I call him, has found an association with Lavoisier but it is curious that Beddoes makes no mention of the fact when he criticizes L. for his neglect of M. (p. xxxiv, 'Chemical experiments and opinions extracted from a work published in the last century', Oxford, 1790). Beddoes was a great man—born out of due time. I collect his books.

5. Love to Streeter—so glad you have him at Historical work again—few do it so well. There is a fine touch in all his writings.

He had also been reading or having read aloud H. F. Jones's 'Life of Samuel Butler', which aroused his ire, and on Nov. 25th he wrote to Dr. Parkes Weber, saying:

Thanks for your letter & papers both most interesting. I have just finished S. B. Life—good but not pleasant reading. He was a selfish pig & his treatment of that poor woman Miss Savage was, as he came to feel himself, shameful. . . . You are wrong P. W. in thinking 'contrast' is necessary. Life of course must be glukupicric—but then I am not a good judge—except in one particular I have had nothing but butter & honey. By the way that Butler poem on Immortality is A.1. & you used it very properly. Yours, W. O. Reynolds' face was a bit Bardolphian but I did not connect it with B.

So in those last few November days before he was too ill to write, he sent brief notes to many people, in Canada, in the States, in England. One of his colleagues at the Bodleian, in reference to Osler's last note to him, which said: 'Abed, coughing, comfortable, hopeful! Appetite good & plenty of books—which are the essentials of life. Greetings to the Selden End', adds: 'He was indeed one of the Saints of God—how beloved of men! We never think or talk of him without feeling the thrill of encouragement that he spread around him.' Nor did he forget his many adored children:

Dear Evelyn & Nadine & Betty Harty, Will you please take the enclosed slip of paper to the bank & get silver & copper for it & go to some shops & N. & B. buy a *little* Xmas present for E., & E. & N.

buy a *little* one for B., & B. & E. buy a *little* one for N. with the dear love of Grace & Willie for Xmas, & while the presents are to be *little* they must smell good, taste good & look good—and you will be sorry to hear that I am still in bed but they say I do look so sweet done up in a pink shawl, & one of my special comforts is what we call *Evelyn* the lavender bag which you gave me I hug her all the time, & we miss you terribly & a very happy Xmas to you all Your loving WILLIE.

Puzzled at times, just as were those in attendance, by the atypical progress of his malady, he admits in a letter to C. P. Howard that he is having a curious attack, but adds: 'I am always suspicious of the pleura with these hard recurrent bouts of cough after an acute pulmonary trouble.' After describing one of the fearful paroxysms of coughing which came in the early morning hours and left him utterly exhausted, Lady Osler wrote on the 27th in her daily bulletin sent to Dr. Malloch: 'Do you know Tennyson's "Tithonus"? Sir William was reciting it as he had his hot milk—I have always expected this.' And among his last notes was a touching letter to Mrs. Brewster, saying:

Yours of the 14th just here—so nice to have it. Very comfortable you must think of me—no pain, except for a few hours when I had a pleurisy. The paroxysms of coughing are distressing, more to poor Grace than to me. No fever & pulse good; but the confounded thing drags on in an unpleasant way—and in one's 71st year the harbour is not far off. And such a happy voyage! & such dear companions all the way! And the future does not worry. It would be nice to find Isaac there, with his friend Izaak Walton & others, but who knows. He may, forty years hence 'choose for you' again as that day in the nursery when he first saw you; your picture & the chicks look at me by the fire light which just catches the proper angle. Love to Robt. & the darlings & your dear self, & dear Uncle Ned. Grace would of course cable should I be worse.

But even his last, or nearly the last, scarcely legible missive, written to Mrs. Chapin, November 28th, shows his irrepressible spirit cropping out: 'Same old cough going on here! We are both very tired of it. My friend Hale-White of London gave a good report yesterday, so that the outlook is favourable. And on most days "I smell the rose above the mould". We are just waiting with real excitement to hear the results of Nancy Astor's election contest at Plymouth. I think it pretty certain. Love to all. Yours Affy E. Y. D.'

By December it was clear that the slow infection was progressing. A second nurse was added. Dr. Malloch joined the household, and from his daily notes and from the letters he sent off at Osler's request, the malady can be followed in detail to the end: the aspiration of his pleurisy; an empyema; the identification of the influenza bacillus; an operation; a pulmonary abscess; another operation with its sudden tragic issue. On December 5th, the day after his chest was first tapped, Malloch's notes read:

> Later in the day he spoke of the flushed feeling about his head and I tried to explain it but he said: 'Archie, you lunatic! I've been watching this case for two months and I'm sorry I shall not see the post-mortem. At any rate the books are there; do you know about Michael Angelo and his tomb? So pathetic! Well, it's Michael Angelo and his tomb, and Osler and his Library!' He had me write to several people and tell about him, and also call on some others. After dinner he got me to fetch Sir Thomas Browne's 'Religio Medici', 'the 1868 edition', but he meant the 1862 one and I got it. He looked for something in it. . . .

What he looked for is apparent; for in this, the Ticknor and Fields edition, his 'constant companion' for fifty-two years, remarkably free from annotations of any kind, considering that it had been so long in the possession of a man who read pencil in hand, he has written this marginal note on page 345 of the 'Urn Burial': 'Wonderful page—always impressed me as one of the great ones in B. 6.xii.19. W. O.':

> But the iniquity of oblivion blindly scattereth her poppy, and deals with the memory of men without distinction to merit of perpetuity. Who can but pity the founder of the pyramids? Erostratus lives that burnt the Temple of Diana; he is almost lost that built it. Time hath spared the epitaph of Adrian's horse, confounded that of himself. In vain we compute our felicities by the advantage of our good names, since bad have equal durations; and Thersites is like to live as long as Agamemnon. Who knows whether the best of men be known, or whether there be not more remarkable persons forgot than any that stand remembered in the known account of time? Without the favour of the everlasting

register, the first man had been as unknown as the last, and Methuselah's long life had been his only chronicle.

Oblivion is not to be hired. The greater part must be content to be as though they had not been, to be found in the register of God, not in the record of man. Twenty-seven names make up the first story, and the recorded names ever since contain not one living century. The number of the dead long exceedeth all that shall live. The night of time far surpasseth the day; and who knows when was the equinox? Every hour adds unto that current arithmetic, which scarce stands one moment.

On the fly-leaf of the volume beneath an earlier entry, written in a vigorous hand: 'This copy goes to E. R. Osler —not to McGill.[1] W. Osler, Sept. 21, 1914', there is found in a shaky script in pencil: 'I doubt if any man can more truly say of this book "Comes viae vitaeque" W. O. 6.xii.19.' He must have remembered a note in his 'Where Is It?' book, made long before, which reads: 'Sir William Browne left in his will: "On my coffin when in the grave I desire may be deposited in its leather case or coffin my pocket Elzevir's Horace, 'Comes Viae Vitaeque dulcis et utilis,' worn out with and by me."'

As talking was likely to bring on a paroxysm of coughing, he was apt to jot down observations on his condition, for his attendants. So when Sir Thomas Horder was called in, he had written out for him:

10.xii.19. 1. The infection is still strongly intrenched, & the irritative cough seems only to be kept in check by the morphia. 2. The heart has done well, but in such bouts could only have one ending. 3. Whether or not the fluid has increased is doubtful—the flat note seems to me higher. 4. Very comfortable until about 7 p.m. when the flushed feelings begin & sense of discomfort & great heat without rise in temperature. Sometimes with this a feeling of nausea & retching. W. O.

He kept on his bedside table under his pad, which he would let no one touch, many scraps of writing which he somehow managed during these last weeks to compose. It was usually done by stealth when Lady Osler or the nurse

[1] In the Introduction to his 'Bibliotheca Osleriana' Osler has written of this volume—the father of his Browne collection: 'In it is a touching association, as in this volume only of this section of the library is found the book-plate of my boy, his own design and etching. He claimed it for his lifetime, promising that it should join the collection at his death.'

had been driven out to get some exercise. One of these slips concerned the destination of certain special books:

1) To British Museum, in appreciation of much valuable help & of my friendship with many members of the Staff, particularly the Keeper, my dear friend Alfred W. Pollard :—

The 1476 unique copy of Rhazes.—Should it have come in they may take the [*unfinished*]

2) To Bodley.

1 The illustrated 1240 Arabic Dioscorides—which will comfort the heart of Dr Cowley—one of, I believe, the three illustrated MSS of this author in arabic

2 The Sir John Haringtons own MS. of the School of Salerno—his well-known translation.

3 Andrew Boo[r]de—whom I love & to whom full justice has never been done in the profession—his MS of the Peregrination of England.

3) To the Library of the Royal College of Physicians

1 The Rules, Regulations, Minutes &c of the Gloucestershire Medical Society 1785–93 [' Regulations and Transactions ', 1788–96], in the handwriting chiefly of Edward Jenner

2 The Theodore de Mayerne case book, which will rejoice the President (Sir Norman's) heart.[1]

These are really the only important items in my library which should not go out of the country.

4) [To the] Faculté de Medecine de Paris

Paré's Anatomie Universelle, 1553 [1561] of which no copy exists in the B. M. or in their library, and only two or three other copies [are] known.

5) [To the] Royal Society of Medicine

Withering's letters, papers & diploma 1762–1793 [1764–99]. And I hope that some member of the Historical section with [*sic*] edit them carefully

6) [To] The University of Leyden

Boerhaave's quadrant presented him with the tables of latitude & longitude when he moved into his country house at Oud-Poelgeest. With a gentle reminder that perhaps they scarcely deserve to have back the treasure which I bought for [ ] gulden in Leyden.

7) [To the] Bibliotheca Lancisiana, Rome

The MS. letter book of Baglivi, the distinguished Roman clinician

---

[1] Mayerne's library which he left to the College was burned in the great fire of 1666. Several other manuscript case books of his are in the British Museum.

with 126 letters from his scientific friends, among them Malpighi, Redi &c & drafts of his replies. No hurry about the return of this which I bought in Rome, at auction for 500 lire. Before it returns some one should work up the letters

8) [To] The Surgeon General's Library, Washington

So difficult to give anything to a collection so rich ; but I thought that perhaps the MS of my farewell address, the Fixed Period, which caused a little excitement would find its best resting-place in a library to which I owe so much & some of whose members—Billings, Fletcher, & Garrison have been my intimate friends. It is the typewritten copy as I read it & I have put a note,[1] the printing of which might be deferred a few years.

9) [To the] College of Physicians Phila—that Montpellier MS. [Bernard de Gordon] Text-book 1373. W.O.

N.B. All these items should appear in my catalogue and the statement where they now are.[2]

He forgot no details—the disposition of his Text-book ; of his manuscript writings ; the completion of the Catalogue ; the promise of his brain to the Wistar Institute ; the post-mortem examination and by whom it should be conducted, even mentioning that Edwin, his 'boy' at the Museum, should be present ; the cremation and the disposal of his ashes. Directions for all these things were found with other scarcely legible notes, one of the last of which read : 'Nothing to worry about but leaving Grace & no Isaac to comfort her, & my inability to write letters to my dear friends & to the dear little darlings in Canada & to Marjorie's children—Muriel's—and Campbell's. W. O.' He had become too ill for letter-writing, but would instruct Dr. Malloch to write in his stead to those who would be expecting some message from him—old friends like Milburn, Ogden, and Shepherd. And after his operation he asked to have a cable sent to the *Journal of the American Medical Association* with a Christmas greeting to the American profession. It was a sort of broadcasting of his farewell blessing.

His fever and the morphia necessary to control the

[1] The note is not in the volume, nor has it been found elsewhere.

[2] The destination of two other books—copies with local associations—had already been ear-marked in his catalogue : for Bodley the annotated copy of Macray's 'Annals', 1868 ; and for the Botanic Garden, Oxford, John Randolph's copy of 'Flora Oxoniensis' (cf. p. 654).

paroxysms gave him much of the time what he called 'a fuzzy-wuzzy feeling', so that during the last two or three weeks he could read little to himself. However, he enjoyed being read to, and had decided views as to what he would like to hear—from Walter Pater's 'Marius'; the Peach Blossom and Wine chapter in Gaston de Latour; from Andrew Lang; from his beloved Plato; Matthew Arnold's 'On Translating Homer'; Sir Thomas Browne, of course; and from Bridges's anthology, 'The Spirit of Man', the things which Revere particularly liked. One night he asked for something from the 'Jungle Books', and after Malloch had read 'The King's Ankus' and had sat quiet in the darkened room thinking his listener was asleep, came a whispered voice saying: 'He was a fine boy.'

On recovering from the anaesthetic on the day of his first operation, he said to Malloch: 'Well, it 's good to have gone so long with so little wrong with me. But I feel with Franklin that "I have been too far across the river to go back and have it all over again". Did you ever read Franklin's Life?—a wonderful book.' When about this time there arrived a package forwarded from Boston by C. E. Goodspeed, containing the numbers of the Boston journal giving the early accounts of ether administrations which he had been wanting so long for the Bibliotheca Prima, he asked Malloch to write in the 1846 volume: 'All things come to him who waits, but it was a pretty close shave this time.'

Mrs. Chapin had arrived, also his nephew, W. W. Francis; and on Christmas Eve he asked to have Milton's 'Nativity' read—wanted it read from his precious first edition, indeed; but after a few stanzas he could bear no more. He had been accustomed to read it himself to Revere on Christmas Eve.

'The days of our age are threescore years and ten . . . so soon passeth it away, and we are gone.' The end came at 4.30 on the afternoon of December 29th, after a haemorrhage from his wound, just as the end had come to many soldiers after wounds in the war—quietly and without pain. Dr. Francis writes: 'The night before, I read to him for quite a long time, things he asked for out of the "Spirit of Man", and we finished with the last

WREN'S TOWER
FROM THE CATHEDRAL DOOR

BURTON'S EFFIGY
AND ST. FRIDESWIDE'S WATCHING-CHAMBER

verses of "The Ancient Mariner". I thought at the time how well it fitted him, and afterwards, what an appropriate valedictory for this lover of men and books:

He prayeth best who loveth best
All things, both great and small. . . .

'When I took leave of him, he said to me, as though I were still a child: "Nighty-night, a-darling!"'

Christ Church has inherited for the daily worship of its members a chapel whose hallowed associations antedate the most venerable of Oxford colleges. They reach back into the obscurities of Saxon times when St. Frideswide erected her priory and last resting-place on the gravel bank above the meadows intersected by the streams of the Isis. Of the many historic services this ancient cathedral has heard, few could have been more simple or more moving than that of the afternoon of January 1st, 1920, over the body of one of the most greatly beloved physicians of all time.

Under Wren's tower and through Wolsey's quadrangle came the mourners, who filled the church to the doors. Two hymns were sung: 'O God, our Help in Ages Past', and Peter Abelard's 'O Quanta Qualia', of which both he and Revere were fond. The Dean had pronounced his brief benediction, and from the dim light of the cathedral into that of a low winter's sun they filed out—the University Marshall, the choir, the chaplains, canons, the Dean, the Vice-Chancellor and Proctors; the representatives of the Government and of the City, the Mayor and members of the Corporation, bearing the crêpe-wreathed city mace; the representatives of learned societies, of scientific bodies, of institutions from all parts of Britain; the members of the university; then those of less renown, whom he loved no less and through whose minds there ran:

He advanced the science of medicine, he enriched literature and the humanities; yet individually he had a greater power. He became the friend of all he met—he knew the workings of the human heart metaphorically as well as physically. He joyed with the joys and wept with the sorrows of the humblest of those who were proud to be his pupils. He stooped to lift them up to the place of his royal friendship, and the magic touchstone of his generous personality helped many a desponder in the rugged paths of life. He achieved many honours and many dignities, but the proudest of all was his unwritten title, 'the Young Man's Friend'.

So they—the living—left him overnight; alone in the Lady Chapel beside the famous 'watching-chamber' which overlooks the shrine of the Saint, and with the quaint effigy of his beloved Robert Burton near by—lying in the scarlet gown of Oxford, his bier covered with a plain velvet pall on which lay a single sheaf of lilies and his favourite copy of the 'Religio', *comes viae vitaeque.*

And perhaps that New Year night saw, led by Revere, another procession pass by the 'watching-chamber'—the spirits of many, old and young—of former and modern times—of Linacre, Harvey, and Sydenham; of John Locke, Gesner, and Louis; of Bartlett, Beaumont, and Bassett; of Johnson, Bovell, and Howard; of Mitchell, Leidy, and Stillé; of Gilman, Billings, and Trudeau; of Hutchinson, Horsley, and Payne; of the younger men his pupils who had gone before—Jack Hewetson, MacCallum, and McCrae; and in still greater number those youths bearing scars of wounds who more recently had known and felt the affection and warmth of the 'Open Arms'—doubly dead in that they died so young.

THE END

INDEX

[Associations and societies, Clubs, Hospitals, and Libraries, will, in general, be found arranged alphabetically under those four headings and *not* under their own *titles*.]

D

E

F

G

H

I

J

K

L

M

Q

R

S

T

Printed in England at the Oxford University Press